See the **Wider** picture

The eccentric Cadillac Ranch, Amarillo, Texas, USA

Three artists built Cadillac Ranch in 1974 beside the famous Route 66. They created the installation by half-burying 10 old Cadillacs nose down in the ground. The cars are placed at the same angle as the face of the Great Pyramid of Giza in Egypt. You can add your own graffiti, but make sure you take a photo because it will soon be painted over by someone else.

What would you paint?

CONTENTS

INTRODUCTION — 3
Wat is WIDER WORLD NL? 3
Hoe werkt WIDER WORLD NL? 3

OVERVIEW OF THE COMPONENTS — 4–5

A UNIT OF THE STUDENTS' BOOK — 6–9

NL PAGES — 10

KEY CONCEPTS BEHIND *WIDER WORLD* — 11–12
The Global Scale of English 11
Assessment for Learning 11
RTTI 11
WIDER WORLD videos 12
21st century skills 12

HOW TO GET THE BEST OUT OF *WIDER WORLD* — 13

STUDENTS' BOOK CONTENTS — 14–15

TEACHER'S NOTES — 16–246

AUDIO SCRIPTS — 247–257
Students' Book audio scripts 247
Workbook audio scripts 254

WORKBOOK ANSWER KEY — 258–272

NL NOTES AND ANSWER KEY — 273–287

INTRODUCTION

WAT IS *WIDER WORLD NL*?

Wider World is wereldwijd een zeer succesvolle lesmethode. Wider World NL is de Nederlandse versie van deze methode en biedt extra oefeningen en uitleg voor de specifieke aandachtspunten van Nederlandstalige leerlingen.

Voor het maken van Wider World is uitgebreid onderzoek gedaan naar wat leerlingen nodig hebben en wat hen aanspreekt. Bij het ontwikkelen van Wider World NL zijn ook Nederlandse docenten geraadpleegd. Er zijn focusgroepen georganiseerd, docenten hebben een vragenlijst ingevuld en Wider World is op een aantal scholen uitgebreid uitgeprobeerd en geëvalueerd.

Uit al dit onderzoek kwamen drie algemene punten naar voren die zowel docenten, leerlingen als ouders belangrijk vonden:

1. Succes op school: leerlingen moeten kwalitatief goed Engels onderwijs krijgen en zich goed voorbereiden op hun eindexamens.
2. Motivatie: leerlingen hebben authentiek en stimulerend lesmateriaal nodig dat voldoende uitdaging biedt, vooral wat betreft de lees- en luistervaardigheid.
3. Vertrouwen: leerlingen ontwikkelen 21e-eeuwse vaardigheden en verbeteren hun cognitieve vaardigheden naast de taalvaardigheid.

Daarnaast kwamen de volgende criteria voor een goede lesmethode naar voren: RTTI-toetsmaterialen en -lesmaterialen, differentiatiemogelijkheden, aandacht voor grammaticale pijnpunten, Cito-voorbereiding en goede woordenlijsten.

HOE WERKT *WIDER WORLD* NL?

In Wider World NL wordt het principe *doeltaal-voertaal* (Monolingual Approach) gehanteerd, wat wil zeggen dat (bijna) alle input en instructies in het Engels is. Nederlands wordt alleen gebruikt ter ondersteuning bij de grammatica, de examenvoorbereiding en de vertaalde woordenlijsten. Wij geloven dat alle leerlingen in alle segmenten de doeltaal-voertaalaanpak aankunnen en op deze manier een dieper cognitief begrip van de taal zullen ontwikkelen.

Een tweede belangrijk uitgangspunt van de methode is de communicatieve aanpak (Communicative Language Teaching), die taal als communicatiemiddel stimuleert. In iedere les wordt het actief gebruiken van de taal gestimuleerd, zodat de stap van passieve naar actieve taalbeheersing wordt gemaakt. Dit sluit ook nauw aan bij het motto 'use-it-or-lose-it', waarin we ervan uitgaan dat taal sterker verankerd wordt wanneer we deze ook echt moeten gebruiken.

Ook de grammatica-aanpak in Wider World NL sluit hier op aan. Grammatica is niet het einddoel, maar een middel om communicatie te bereiken. U vindt in de methode dan ook weinig expliciete grammatica-uitleg. Leerlingen krijgen de grammatica in context aangeboden en verwerven deze door er mee te oefenen.

Wat betekent dit allemaal in de praktijk? Het Students' Book van Wider World NL bevat niet alleen alle bronnen en uitleg, maar ook een aantal, veelal communicatieve, oefeningen, zodat leerlingen direct aan de slag kunnen gaan met de stof. Tijdens de les zullen leerlingen veel aan het woord zijn, vaak in groepjes of duo's, en als docent bent u vooral degene die de les in goede banen leidt en natuurlijk leerlingen helpt daar waar dat nodig is. Pas aan het einde van de les gebruikt u (eventueel) het Workbook of MyEnglishLab. Leerlingen hoeven dus niet beide boeken naast elkaar op tafel te hebben. Deze oefeningen kunnen leerlingen zelfstandig maken, dus u kunt ze ook als huiswerk opgeven.

Het Students' Book Wider World NL heeft 10 units met steeds 7 genummerde inputlessen, waarin nieuwe stof en bronnen worden aangeboden. Doorgaans geldt het principe: one page - one lesson - one skill. In iedere les ligt de focus dus op één van de vaardigheden, grammatica of vocabulaire (of een combinatie van twee). De Integrated-skills aanpak maakt dat ook de andere onderdelen tussendoor aan bod komen.

Na de inputlessen volgen in elke unit nog een aantal extra lessen: *Vocabulary in action, BBC Culture, Revision, Extra Practice, Step It Up* en *Exam Time NL* (alleen achter unit 3, 5, 7 en 9). Achter in het boek zitten nog extra onderdelen: *Grammar Time*-lessen, *Grammar Time NL*-lessen, een *Formal Writing*-les, een *Irregular verbs list*, *Student activities*, *Exam Time*-lessen, *CLIL*-lessen en *Culture*-lessen.

Aanvullend op dit Teacher's Book is er ook IWB software beschikbaar, genaamd ActiveTeach, op USB-stick. Hierop vindt u o.a. een aangepast toetspakket (de originele toetsen staan online in het MyEnglishLab/Extra Online Homework-platform) waarbij alle toetsoefeningen een RTTI-label hebben gekregen. Zo'n label vindt u ook bij de oefeningen uit de *Extra Practice* en *Step It Up*-lessen. RTTI laat goed zien in hoeverre leerlingen de behandelde stof kunnen toepassen en op welk (cognitief) niveau zij zich bevinden. Het biedt de mogelijkheid om gerichte feedback te geven en daar waar nodig bij te sturen. Hierdoor krijgen leerlingen ook inzicht in hun eigen leerproces. Alle gegevens kunnen uiteindelijk gebruikt worden om zorgvuldig te determineren.

OVERVIEW OF THE COMPONENTS

STUDENTS' BOOK

- Ten units with 80–120 hours of teaching material
- Video (drama, BBC Vox Pops and BBC Culture clips) with every unit
- Clear lesson objectives ('I can …') taken from the Global Scale of English (GSE)
- Wordlist with exercises activating key vocabulary, and Revision for every unit
- Grammar Time: grammar reference and practice activities for every Grammar lesson
- Exam Time: the Listening and Speaking parts of the Cambridge English Key for Schools, Preliminary for Schools and Pearson Test of English General Level 2 exams
- 5 extra CLIL lessons
- 2 extra Culture lessons about the English speaking world
- Extra Practice and Step it Up pages for every unit, Exam Time NL every two units. Grammar Time NL and extra Writing Skills lesson (Formal letters) at back of book.

STUDENTS' ETEXT

- The full Students' Book in digital format
- All audio and video embedded into the exercises
- Students' eText is also available with access code to MyEnglishLab and Extra Online Practice (see relevant sections below)

WORKBOOK WITH EXTRA ONLINE HOMEWORK

Workbook

- Additional grammar, vocabulary and skills practice to reinforce material in the Students' Book
- One lesson per unit dedicated to BBC Culture, plus full video scripts
- Exam Time: the Reading and Writing parts of the Cambridge English Key for Schools, Preliminary for Schools and Pearson Test of English General Level 2 exams

Extra Online Homework

- Extra homework activities, based on the BBC Vox Pops, with embedded videos
- All Students' Book videos
- Downloadable Workbook audio
- Review and End of Year tests assigned and released by the teacher
- Downloadable resources for teachers (Tests package, Exam Practice audio and answer key, Teacher's Resource Book)

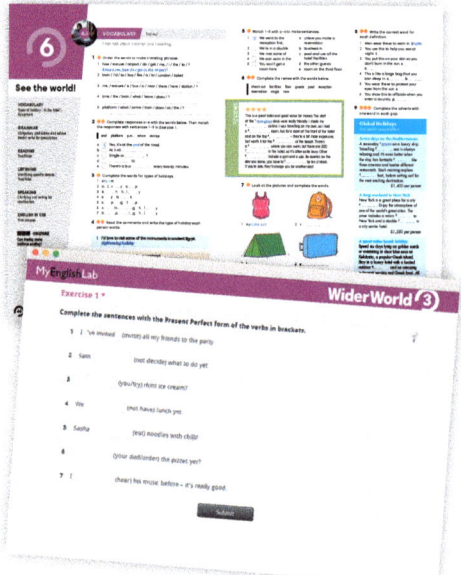

MYENGLISHLAB

- Interactive Workbook with instant feedback; tips and remediation activities with grammar exercises
- Extra homework activities, based on the BBC Vox Pops
- All Students' Book videos
- Downloadable Workbook audio and Self-assessment pages
- Review and End of Year tests assigned and released by the teacher
- Downloadable resources for teachers (Tests package, Exam Practice audio and answer key, Teacher's Resource Book)

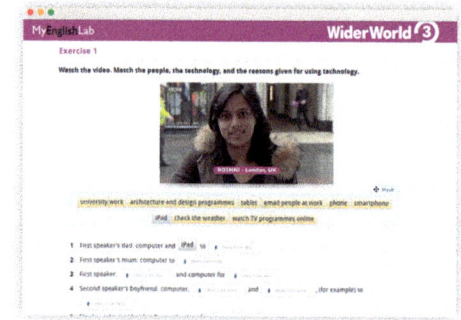

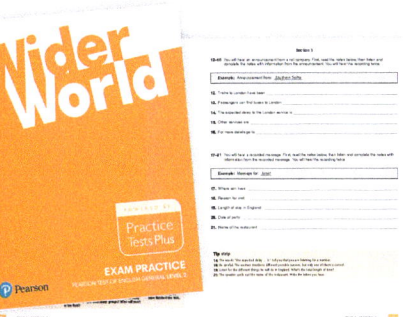

EXAM PRACTICE BOOKS

A series of books which provide additional, intensive practice and support for important international exams. These books work alongside the Level 3 Students' Book:
- Cambridge English Key for Schools and Preliminary for Schools
- Pearson Test of English General Level 2. The audio and answer key are available on MyEnglishLab.

TEACHER'S BOOK

- Unit-by-unit teaching notes with audio scripts and answer keys
- Interleaved with Students' Book pages
- Workbook audio scripts
- Workbook answer key
- Teacher's notes and Answer keys for NL sections

CLASS AUDIO CDS

Audio material for use in class

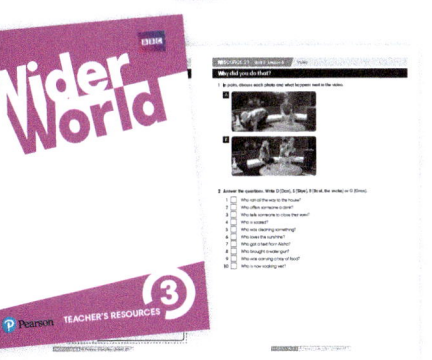

TEACHER'S RESOURCE BOOK

- 120 pages of photocopiable resources
- One page for every lesson
- One extra page for every drama video
- One extra page of Vocabulary, Grammar and Culture activities with every unit
- Available as a printed book or downloadable from the ActiveTeach MEL with instructions and answer keys

ACTIVETEACH USB

- Students' Book pages with embedded audio and video; interactive activities and 'Show answers' functionality
- Workbook pages with embedded audio; 'Show answers' functionality
- Teacher's Resource Book, including instructions and answer key
- Audio resources: audio with audio scripts
- Video resources: all Students' Book videos with subtitles
- Phonetics chart
- Toolbox: Stopwatch and Scoreboard
- Extensive tests package, downloadable A, B and SLD (dyslexic) versions
- RTTI adapted tests package, downloadable A and B versions
- Extended Wordlist in downloadable format
- Student Book and Workbook answer keys

A UNIT OF THE STUDENTS' BOOK

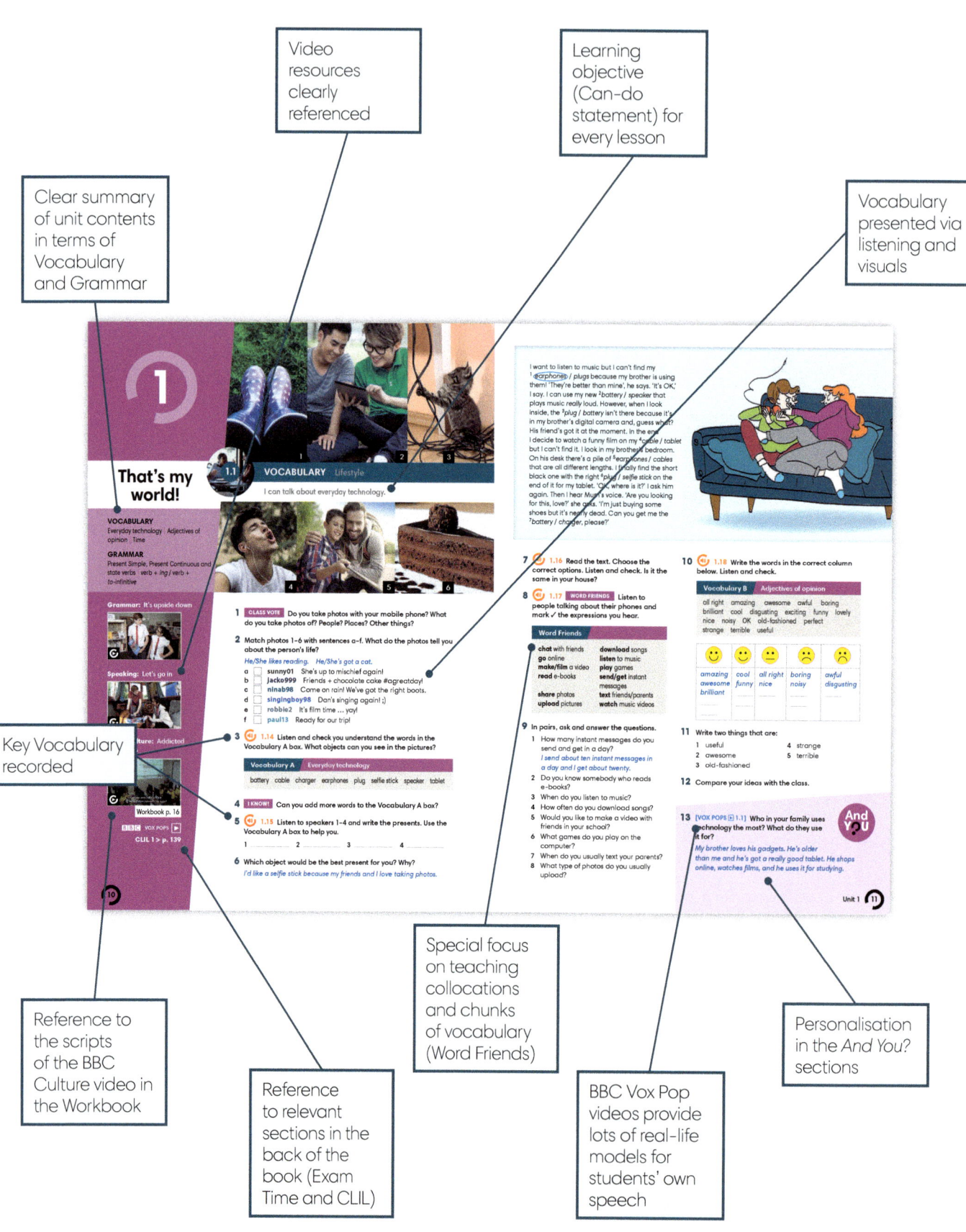

- Video resources clearly referenced
- Learning objective (Can-do statement) for every lesson
- Vocabulary presented via listening and visuals
- Clear summary of unit contents in terms of Vocabulary and Grammar
- Key Vocabulary recorded
- Reference to the scripts of the BBC Culture video in the Workbook
- Reference to relevant sections in the back of the book (Exam Time and CLIL)
- Special focus on teaching collocations and chunks of vocabulary (Word Friends)
- BBC Vox Pop videos provide lots of real-life models for students' own speech
- Personalisation in the And You? sections

One lesson per page or opening

Reading texts in a variety of genres

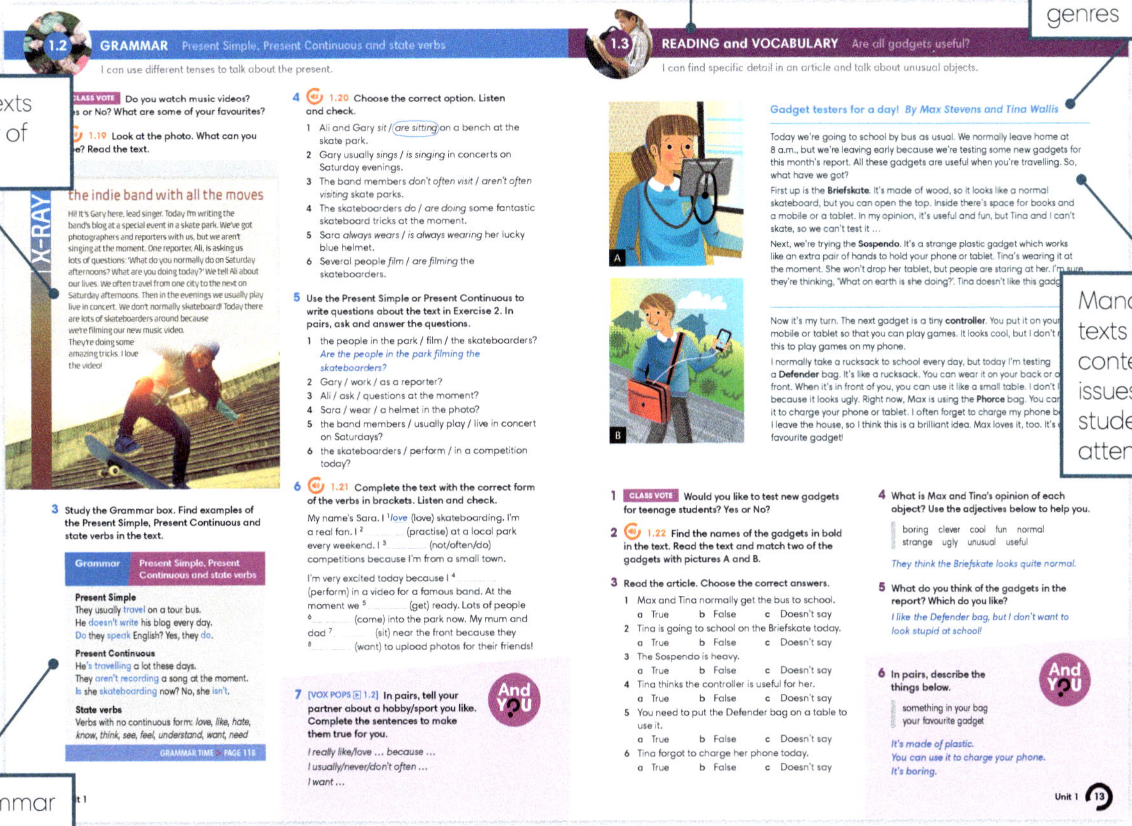

Manageable texts about contemporary issues to engage students' attention

Clear grammar tables

21st century skill of critical thinking

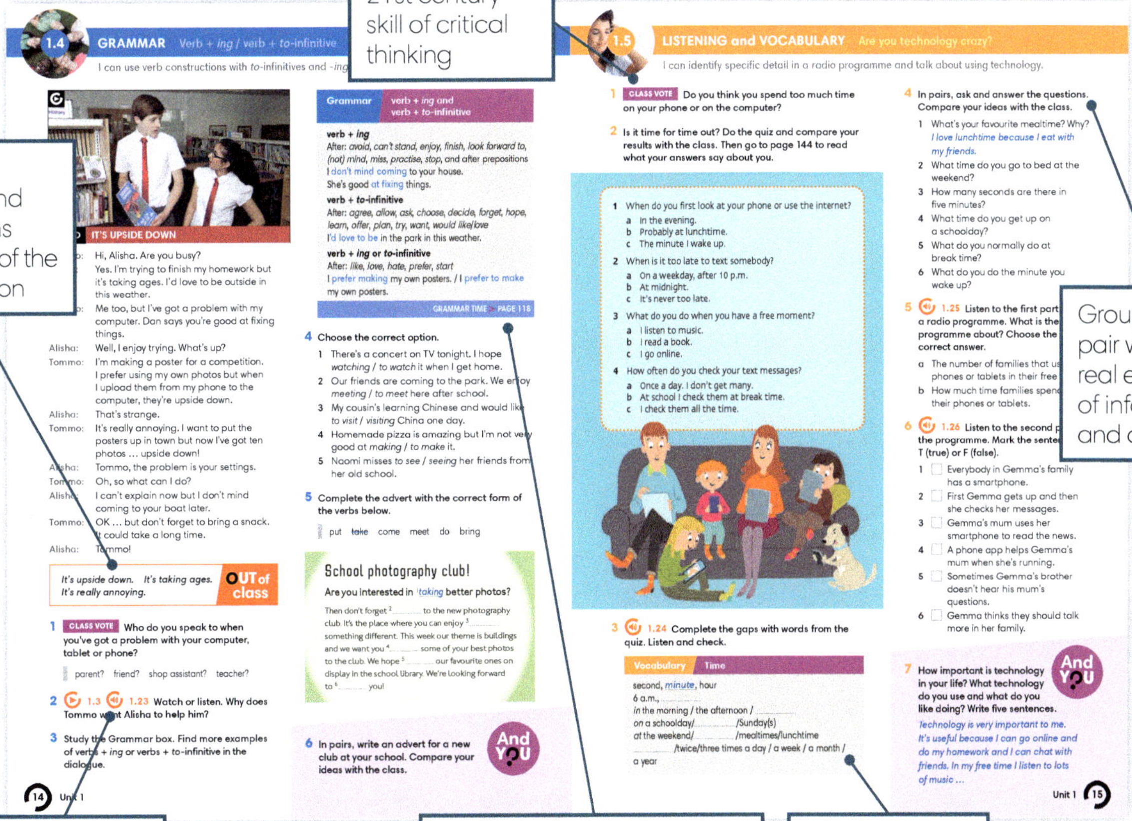

Everyday phrases and expressions pulled out of the presentation

Group and pair work for real exchange of information and opinions

Grammar presented through video

Reference to Grammar Time: full grammar tables and further grammar practice in the back of the book

Vocabulary set pulled out from reading text

A UNIT OF THE STUDENTS' BOOK

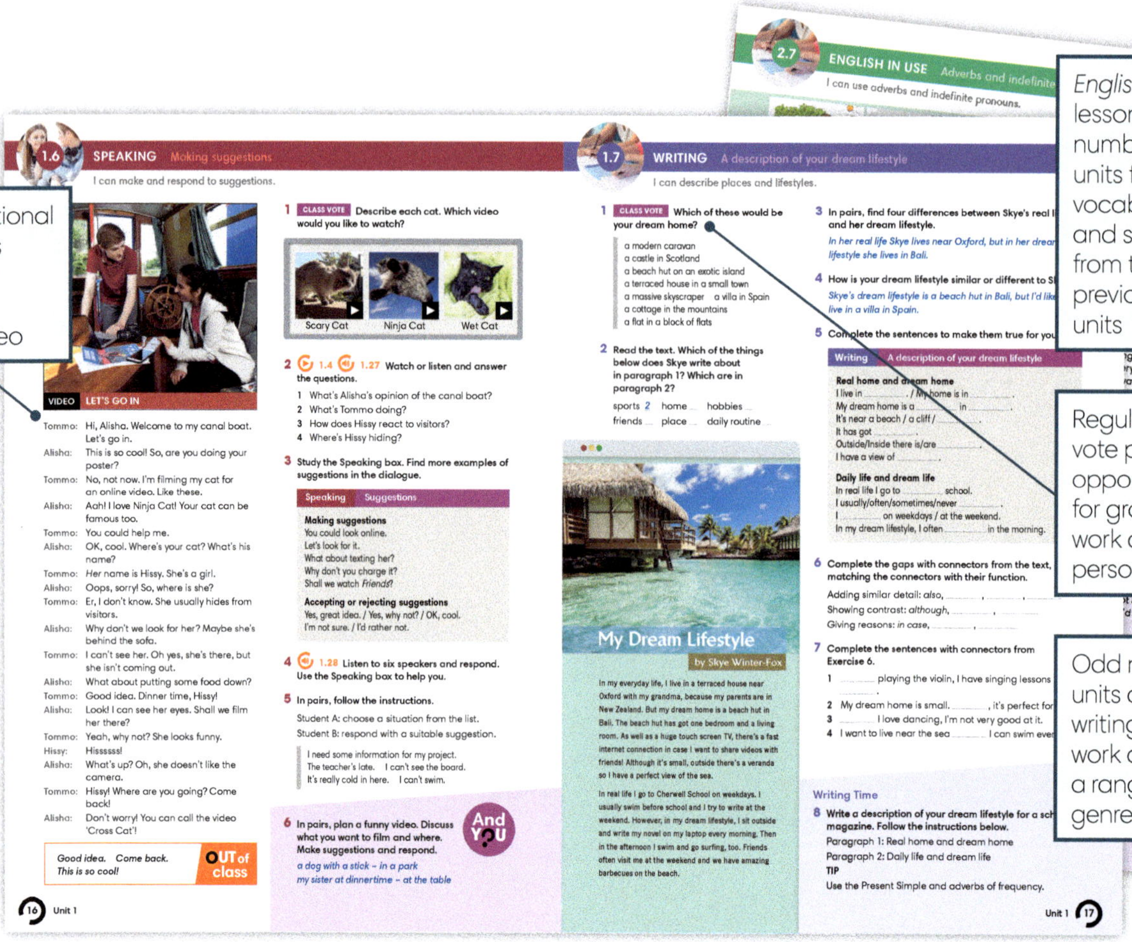

Every functional dialogue is presented through a drama video

Pronunciation activities work with vocabulary from the unit

English in use lessons in even numbered units focus on vocabulary and structures from the previous two units

Regular class vote provides opportunities for group work and personalisation

Odd numbered units contain writing skills work covering a range of genres

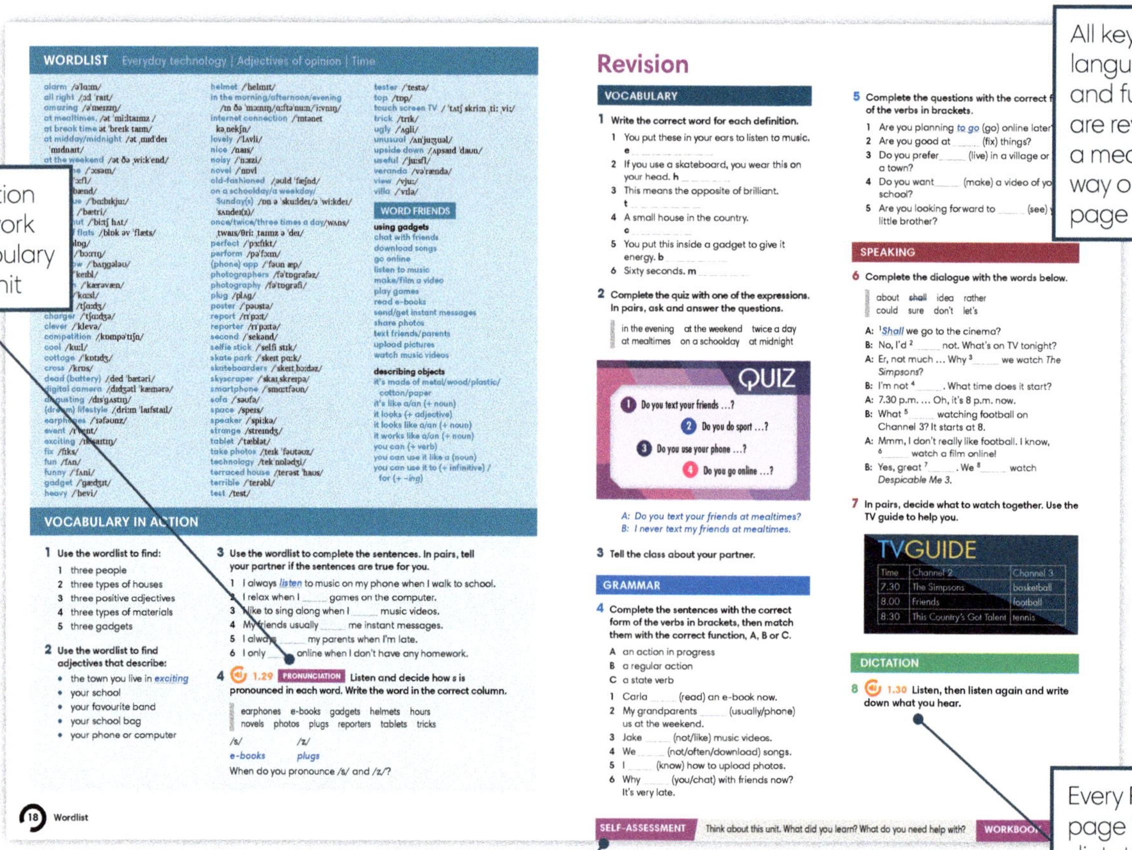

All key language and functions are reviewed in a measureable way on this page

Every Revision page has a dictation on the class audio

Self-assessment backed up by full checklist and activities in the Workbook

8

These lessons develop the 21st century skill of cultural awareness

An intriguing question and photo as a warm-up

A culture topic linked to the unit theme is presented through a reading text, with comprehension exercises

BBC Culture videos provide fascinating real world information, and the opportunity to explore the topic further

Using the language, knowledge and models from the lesson, students create a project about their own country or experience

Glossary for the most difficult words in the text

Grammar Time

Exam Time

CLIL

Culture

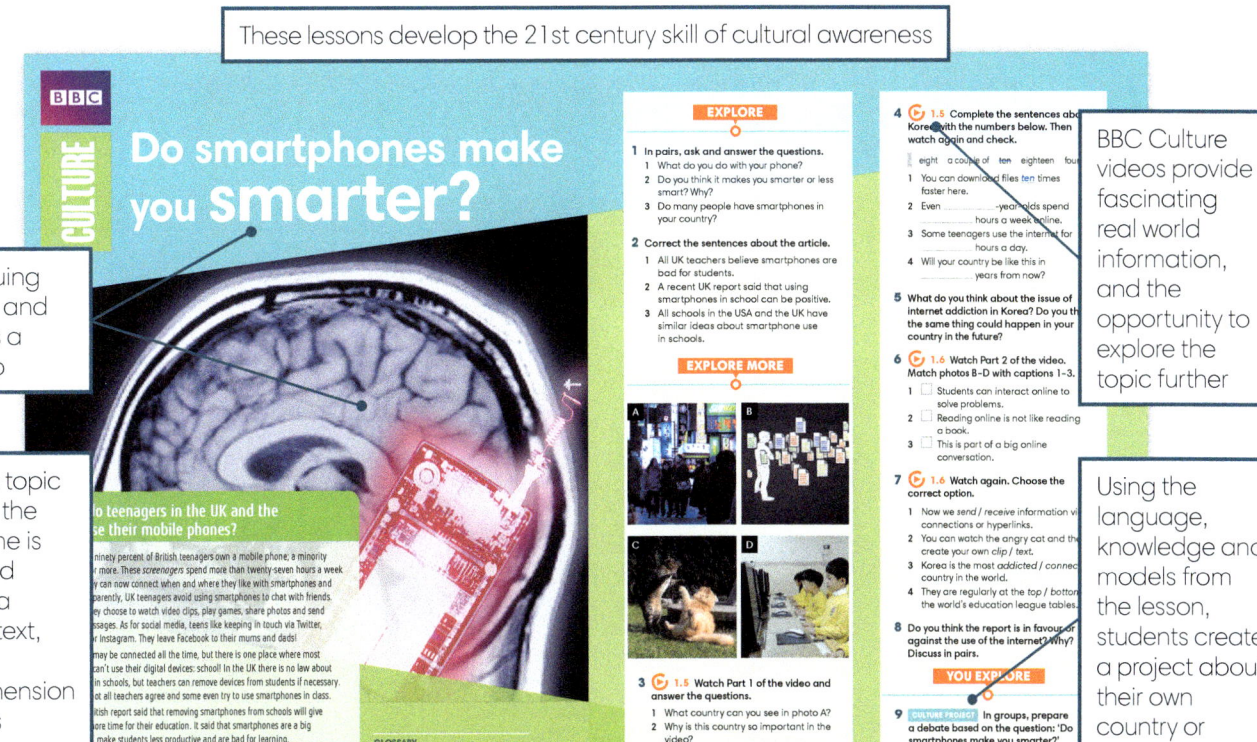

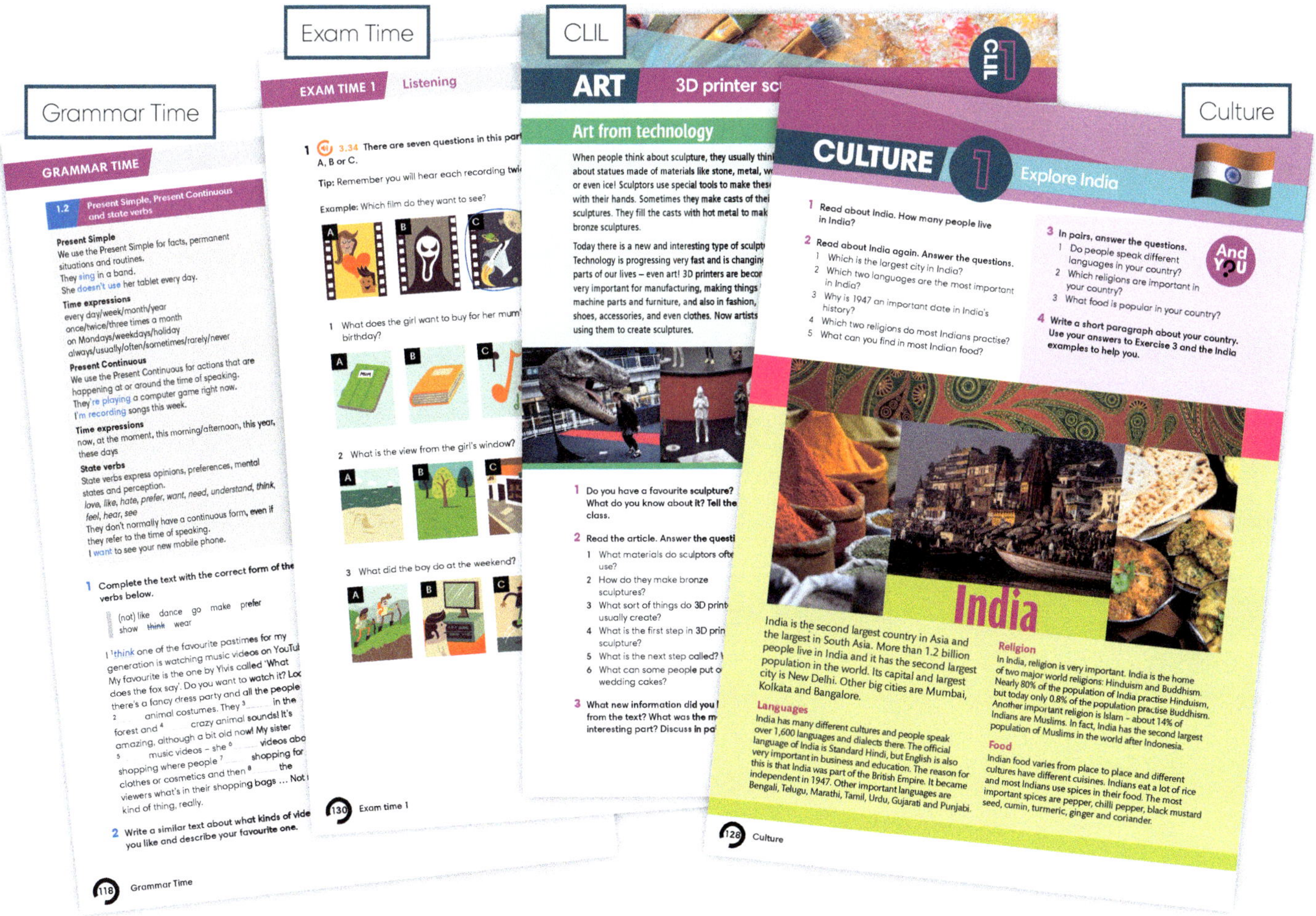

NL PAGES

Extra Practice / Step it Up

Activities adapted to all RTTI classifications for students requiring extra practice at the same level, with the specific purpose of helping students master the different subjects

Differentiation pages provide extra practice and stretch activities

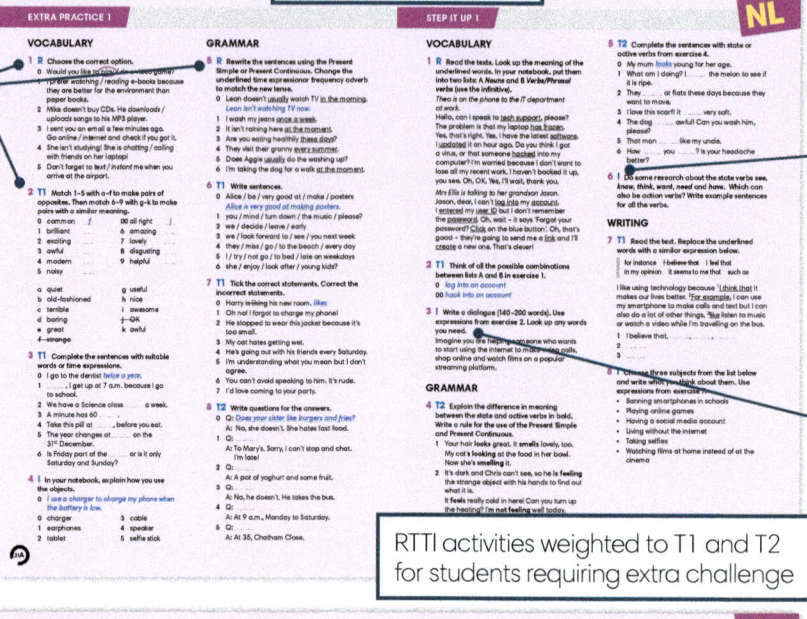

Activities adapted to all RTTI classifications, providing additional challenges both cognitively and linguistically, at a higher level than the coursebook

Expands the vocabulary as new words are introduced

RTTI activities weighted to T1 and T2 for students requiring extra challenge

Exam Time NL

Explanation of key reading strategies needed for the CITO exam

Interesting semi-authentic extracts for reading strategies

Some questions in Dutch, as per the CITO exam

Grammar Time NL

Intensive practice on grammar pitfalls, moving from simple to more challenging

Common grammar pitfalls are highlighted and explained

Personalisation: putting into practice what has been learnt

KEY CONCEPTS BEHIND *WIDER WORLD*

THE GLOBAL SCALE OF ENGLISH

The Global Scale of English (GSE) is a standardised, granular scale that measures English language proficiency. Using the Global Scale of English, students and teachers can now answer three questions accurately: *Exactly how good is my English? What progress have I made towards my learning goal? What do I need to do next if I want to improve?*

Unlike some other frameworks that measure English proficiency in broad bands, the Global Scale of English identifies what a learner can do at each point on a scale from 10 to 90, across each of the four skills (listening, reading, speaking and writing) as well as the enabling skills of grammar and vocabulary. This allows learners and teachers to understand a learner's exact level of proficiency, what progress they have made and what they need to learn next.

The Global Scale of English is designed to motivate learners by making it easier to demonstrate granular progress in their language ability. Teachers can use their knowledge of their students' GSE levels to choose course materials that are precisely matched to their ability and learning goals. The GSE serves as a standard against which English language courses and assessments worldwide can be benchmarked, offering a truly global and shared understanding of language proficiency levels.

Visit www.english.com/gse for more information about the Global Scale of English.

Visit www.english.com/blog/download-gse-young-learners to download the GSE syllabus and descriptors.

ASSESSMENT FOR LEARNING

With the GSE as the solid framework for syllabus design and assessment, *Wider World* offers a uniquely sound and comprehensive Assessment for Learning package.

Any test can be used either as an assessment *of* learning or an assessment *for* learning. Assessment of learning usually takes place after the learning has happened, and provides information about what the student is achieving by giving a mark or a grade. You can also use tests as assessment for learning, by providing specific feedback on students' strengths and weaknesses and suggestions for improvement as part of the continual learning process. It is the combination of both types of assessment which can provide a powerful tool for helping your students' progress.

RTTI

RTTI is a tool to help identify to what extent students can apply what they have learnt and at what cognitive level they are operating. It offers teachers the opportunity to give direct feedback and guidance to students where necessary. In addition, RTTI allows students to gain insight into their own learning process. This input can be used to carefully determine students' levels and progress.

Certain tests (see *) in the Test Package are RTTI labelled (these NL tests can be found on the ActiveTeach USB), as are the exercises in the *Extra Practice* and *Step It Up* lessons in the Student's Book.

In the Students' Book

Every lesson begins with a clear Can-do statement so that students and teachers know exactly what they are doing and why. Every unit has a Revision page which includes a Self-assessment check, followed up in more detail in the Workbook.

The goal of the exam practice section, entitled Exam Time/Exam Time NL at the back of the book, is to provide further examples of and practice in the specific tasks students are likely to face in the high-stakes tests. They focus on the relevant Cambridge English for Schools, Pearson Test of English General and CITO exams.

In the Workbook

Every unit contains a Self-assessment page where students assess how well they did in that unit. This is followed by a Self-check page where students check their knowledge of vocabulary, grammar and functional language from the unit. The key to these exercises is at the end of the Workbook. The Exam Time section at the back of the book provides further exam-type practice in reading and writing and is suitable for individual use at home.

In the in-course Test Package

There are downloadable tests in A and B versions, as well as versions for dyslexic students (SLD).
- Placement test (A/B)
- Grammar lesson checks (A/B/SLD)
- Vocabulary lesson checks (A/B/SLD)
- Unit tests*
  - Language tests: Vocabulary, Grammar, English for speaking and English in use/English for writing (A/B/SLD)
  - Skills tests: Dictation, Listening and Reading (A/B/SLD)
- Review tests*
  - Vocabulary, Grammar and English in use (A/B/SLD)
  - Writing and Speaking (A/B/Teacher's notes)
- End-of-year test*
  - Listening, Reading and English in use (A/B/SLD)
  - Writing and Speaking (A/B/Teacher's notes)

* With NL versions correlated to RTTI (A and B only) - available on Active Teach USB

In MyEnglishLab

The gradebook function in the digital workbook collects all the students' results so that teachers can diagnose and adjust their teaching according to each individual or to class performance.

These tests are provided (teacher view only) on MyEnglishLab and are graded automatically. They are assignable by the teacher for completion for homework.

- Review tests after every second unit (covering Units 1–2, 1–4, 1–6 and 1–8): Vocabulary, Grammar and English in use
- End of Year test: Listening, Reading and English in use

Tests taken on MyEnglishLab offer students feedback on both correct and incorrect answers.

The full assessment package is provided in the Teacher Resources section of MyEnglishLab and Extra Online Homework. They are designed to be downloaded and printed by the teacher and completed by students in class.

KEY CONCEPTS BEHIND *WIDER WORLD*

WIDER WORLD VIDEOS

There are three types of video in *Wider World*.

1 *WOODLEY BRIDGE* DRAMA SERIES

A specially shot, entertaining soap opera-type drama about a group of teenagers, their families and friends. Each video presents the key language of the lesson for one of the Grammar lessons in each unit and all of the Speaking lessons.

All the video episodes are available in audio-only format on the Class audio for those classrooms where video is not readily available.

Detailed teaching notes for each video are provided in the lesson notes.

2 BBC VOX POPS

These are short clips of people filmed by the BBC on the streets of London, answering questions about their lives and opinions, following the topics and themes of the lesson.

3 BBC CULTURE VIDEOS

An intriguing, wider world view of topic-related culture (e.g. art, festivals, sports, food, travel) which recycles the topics and language of the unit. Extracts of high-quality BBC documentary and news footage are re-voiced at an appropriate level for the learner.

By the end of the lesson, students will be able to answer the intriguing question in the lesson heading and to explore the topic further if they wish.

21ST CENTURY SKILLS

Today's learners require materials that will expose them to ideas and 'wider perspectives' – materials that create cultural awareness, materials that will inspire. *Wider World* provides students not only with English language skills, grammar and vocabulary, but also with the confidence they will need to become fully-rounded citizens of the 21st century global community.

The key 21st-century skills in *Wider World* are: *Communication*, *Collaboration*, *Creativity*, *Cultural Awareness and Critical Thinking*, *Digital literacy*, *Assessment for Learning* and *Autonomy*. These are listed in the unit contents boxes in the teaching notes, with examples of where they occur in the lessons.

As in any good language teaching methodology, the skills of **communication**, **collaboration** and **creativity** are central guiding principles and inform all the activities in *Wider World*.

Cultural awareness: in an increasingly globalised world, it is important that students gain an understanding of different cultures. This is done in two ways: firstly in the BBC Culture pages, which give a wider perspective of cultural aspects linked to the unit topics, and secondly via the English Speaking World (ESW) culture pages at the back of the Students' Book. These enable students to compare aspects of ESW culture with their own. In addition, the BBC Vox Pop videos feature people interviewed on the streets of London and expose students to a wide variety of native and foreign accents.

Critical thinking: problem solving and reasoning skills are developed throughout the course, especially via the reading and listening activities.

Autonomy and personal initiative: students are encouraged to *Explore* and then *Explore More* via the intriguing content of the BBC Culture pages. In the *You Explore* sections they are given opportunities to choose and create their own projects so that they connect personally with the topic, often using the internet with their own mobile devices. A similar strategy is applied in the mini projects on the CLIL pages at the back of the Students' Book. Students are prompted to reflect on and take responsibility for their own progress through the regular Self-assessment sections in the Students' Book and Workbook.

Assessment for Learning: see section above on page 11.

Digital literacy: both the content and the format of *Wider World* are rooted in today's digital environment and reflect the way today's teenagers already manage their lives: the topics cover up-to-date technology and media, while the projects suggested on the BBC Culture and CLIL pages encourage the use of digital tools to complete their own projects whether presentations, reports or reviews, or even mini videos.

HOW TO GET THE BEST OUT OF *WIDER WORLD*

We know that there are many different ways to teach English, which will be influenced by your specific teaching context and preferred teaching style, the number of students in your class and their level and background, and many other factors. *Wider World* was designed to be easily customised for each unique teaching situation. Plus, it is designed to make it easy and rewarding to integrate digital tools into your teaching – in a gradual, step-by-step way.

Here are a few possible ways to access the comprehensive set of materials that is *Wider World*:

1 CLASSIC

For the student	For the teacher
Students' Book	Teacher's Book
Workbook	Teacher's Resource Book
Extra Online Homework (Student view)	Extra Online Homework (Teacher view)
	Class audio CDs
	ActiveTeach USB card

This is the classic print option, but with one simple additional digital element for the student: Extra Online Homework. The Interactive Whiteboard software of ActiveTeach, supplied on a handy USB card, allows teachers to present the Students' Book pages on a large screen, and to play the video and audio with one click from the page on screen.

This is the solution for those classrooms which are not connected to the internet, but where students would like a digital form of language practice for homework.

2 BLENDED

For the student	For the teacher
Students' Book	Teacher's Book
MyEnglishLab with Extra Online Homework (Student view)	MyEnglishLab with Extra Online Homework (Teacher view)
	Teacher's Resource Book
	Class audio CDs
	ActiveTeach USB card

Notice that with this combination, the student's print Workbook is replaced by the online digital workbook: MyEnglishLab. The student also has the digital Extra Online Homework (EOH) plus all the Vox Pops on which the EOH is based.

The teacher may not require the print version of the Teacher's Resource Book because all the photocopiable resources are also on MyEnglishLab and the ActiveTeach USB card for download.

3 DIGITAL

For the student	For the teacher
Students' eText	ActiveTeach USB card
MyEnglishLab with Extra Online Homework (Student view)	MyEnglishLab with Extra Online Homework (Teacher view)

If you have a fully digital classroom and students have their own tablets, you can also use *Wider World* in its fully digital configuration. In this case, the student has a Students' eText for use on his/her tablet and the teacher has all resources contained in the ActiveTeach or teacher's area of MyEnglishLab, where he/she can also maintain and view records of student progress via the LMS gradebook.

STUDENTS' BOOK CONTENTS

CONTENTS

	STARTER UNIT Welcome to Woodley Bridge	0.1 INTRODUCING TOMMO Activities and interests; Likes and dislikes; Home and furniture; There is/are with some/any; Possessive adjectives and possessive 's pp. 4–5		0.2 INTRODUCING SKYE Jobs; Present Simple with adverbs of frequency p. 6	
	VOCABULARY	**GRAMMAR**	**READING and VOCABULARY**	**GRAMMAR**	**LISTENING and VOCABULARY**
UNIT 1 That's my world	Talk about everyday technology VOX POPS ▶ pp. 10–11	Use different tenses to talk about the present • Present Simple • Present Continuous • State verbs p. 12 VOX POPS ▶	Find specific detail in an article and talk about gadgets p. 13	Use verb constructions with to-infinitives and -ing forms • verb + -ing • verb + to-infinitive VIDEO Woodley Bridge p. 14	Understand the main point and find specific details in a radio programme, and talk about using technology p. 15
UNIT 2 Wild nature	Talk about the weather and natural disasters pp. 22–23	Use regular and irregular verbs to talk about the past • Past Simple p. 24	Find specific detail in an article and talk about culture p. 25	Talk about an event in the past and what was happening around it • Past Simple and Past Continuous VIDEO Woodley Bridge p. 26 VOX POPS ▶	Identify specific detail in a conversation and talk about being in the wild p. 27
UNIT 3 The taste test	Talk about food and drink pp. 34–35	Use the Present Perfect with ever, never, just, already and yet VIDEO Woodley Bridge p. 36 VOX POPS ▶	Find specific detail in an article and use make and do accurately p. 37	Talk about duration of time, and be general and specific about experiences • Present Perfect with for and since • Present Perfect and Past Simple p. 38	Identify specific detail in speech and describe food p. 39 VOX POPS ▶
UNIT 4 Curtain up!	Talk about films and television VOX POPS ▶ pp. 46–47	Compare different things • Comparatives and superlatives p. 48 VOX POPS ▶	Understand the main points of an article and talk about entertainment p. 49	Talk about quantities of countable and uncountable nouns • Quantifiers VIDEO Woodley Bridge p. 50	Identify specific detail in an interview and talk about festivals p. 51
UNIT 5 The big match!	Talk about sports and sports events pp. 58–59	Talk about plans, predictions, arrangements and timetables • The future: will / going to / Present Continuous VIDEO Woodley Bridge p. 60	Identify specific detail in an article and talk about volunteering at a sports event p. 61 VOX POPS ▶	Talk about possible future situations • First Conditional + if/ unless p. 62 VOX POPS ▶	Identify specific detail in a conversation and talk about sports training p. 63
UNIT 6 See the world!	Talk about holidays and travelling VOX POPS ▶ pp. 70–71	Talk about obligation, prohibition and advice • Modal verbs: must, have to, ought to, should VIDEO Woodley Bridge p. 72 VOX POPS ▶	Find specific detail in an article and talk about travelling p. 73	Speculate about the present • Modal verbs: must, could, might, may, can't p. 74	Identify specific detail in a conversation and talk about trips and excursions p. 75
UNIT 7 Getting to know you	Talk about relationships with family and friends pp. 82–83	Talk about imaginary situations • Second Conditional VIDEO Woodley Bridge p. 84 VOX POPS ▶	Find specific detail in an article and talk about friends p. 85	Be specific about people, things and places • Defining and non-defining relative clauses p. 86	Identify specific information in a monologue and talk about pets p. 87 VOX POPS ▶
UNIT 8 No time for crime	Talk about crime and criminals pp. 94–95	Use verbs in the Passive • Present Simple Passive and Past Simple Passive p. 96	Find specific detail in an article and talk about solving crimes p. 97	Use the construction have/ get something done VIDEO Woodley Bridge p. 98	Identify the main points of a monologue and talk about discovering a crime p. 99 VOX POPS ▶
UNIT 9 Think outside the box	Talk about school life pp. 106–107	Make questions with the correct word order VIDEO Woodley Bridge p. 108	Find specific detail in an article and talk about intelligence p. 109	Use a variety of tenses p. 110 VOX POPS ▶	Identify specific information in a dialogue and talk about awkward moments p. 111 VOX POPS ▶

IRREGULAR VERBS p. 127   WRITING SKILLS p. 127I & 127J   CULTURE 1: Explore India p. 128   2: Explore New Zealand p. 129

Contents

0.3 INTRODUCING DAN Clothes and accessories; Present Continuous; Talking about feelings p.7	0.4 INTRODUCING ALISHA Countries and languages; *was/were*, *there was/were*; Past Simple: regular verbs p. 8		CHARACTER QUIZ p. 9	
SPEAKING	**WRITING** / **ENGLISH IN USE**		**BBC CULTURE** **NL**	
Make and respond to suggestions VIDEO Woodley Bridge p. 16	Write a description of places and lifestyles p. 17	WORDLIST p. 18 REVISION p. 19 GRAMMAR TIME 1 p. 118	Do smartphones make you smarter? VIDEO Addicted to screens pp. 20–21	Extra Practice p. 21A Step it Up p. 21B
Criticise and explain when things go wrong VIDEO Woodley Bridge p. 28	Use adverbs and indefinite pronouns VOX POPS p. 29	WORDLIST p. 30 REVISION p. 31 GRAMMAR TIME 2 p. 119	Nice day, innit? VIDEO Severe weather pp. 32–33	Extra Practice p. 33A Step it Up p. 33B GRAMMAR TIME NL 2a p. 127A & 2b p. 127B
Order food in a café or restaurant VIDEO Woodley Bridge p. 40	Write an email to a friend p. 41	WORDLIST p. 42 REVISION p. 43 GRAMMAR TIME 3 p. 120 EXAM TIME 1 pp. 130–132	What do the British really eat? VIDEO Indian food Liverpool style pp. 44–45	Extra Practice p. 45A Step it Up p. 45B EXAM TIME NL 1 p. 45C - 45D GRAMMAR TIME NL 3 p. 127B
Ask about, express and explain preferences VIDEO Woodley Bridge p. 52	Describe how people do things • Adverbs of manner p. 53	WORDLIST p. 54 REVISION p. 55 GRAMMAR TIME 4 p. 121	How do you like to celebrate? VIDEO London celebrates pp. 56–57	Extra Practice p. 57A Step it Up p. 57B GRAMMAR TIME NL 4 p. 127C
Can ask and talk about plans VIDEO Woodley Bridge p. 64	Write notes and make requests p. 65	WORDLIST p. 66 REVISION p. 67 GRAMMAR TIME 5 p. 122	Where do they toss the caber? VIDEO The Highland Games pp. 68–69	Extra Practice p. 69A Step it Up p. 69B EXAM TIME NL 2 pp. 69C - 69D GRAMMAR TIME NL 5a p. 127D & 5b p. 127E
Clarify what I have said and ask for clarification VIDEO Woodley Bridge p. 76	Use time clauses p. 77	WORDLIST p. 78 REVISION p. 79 GRAMMAR TIME 6 p. 123 EXAM TIME 2 pp. 133–135	Can ironing make holidays exciting? VIDEO Adventures of a lifetime pp. 80–81	Extra Practice p. 81A Step it Up p. 81B
Explain who I am talking about VIDEO Woodley Bridge p. 88	Write a short story p. 89	WORDLIST p. 90 REVISION p. 91 GRAMMAR TIME 7 p. 124	Is moving house good for you? VIDEO On the move pp. 92–93	Extra Practice p. 93A Step it Up p. 93B EXAM TIME NL 3 pp. 93C - 93D GRAMMAR TIME NL 7a p. 127F & 7b p. 127G
Persuade and reassure someone VIDEO Woodley Bridge p. 100	Form and use negative adjectives VOX POPS p. 101	WORDLIST p. 102 REVISION p. 103 GRAMMAR TIME 8 p. 125	Is chewing gum a crime? VIDEO A famous robbery pp. 104–105	Extra Practice p. 105A Step it Up p. 105B GRAMMAR TIME NL 8 p. 127H
Have a casual conversation VIDEO Woodley Bridge p. 112	Write a letter giving information p. 113	WORDLIST p. 114 REVISION p. 115 GRAMMAR TIME 9 p. 126 EXAM TIME 3 pp. 136–138	Can school be fun? VIDEO Two very different schools pp. 116–117	Extra Practice p. 117A Step it Up p. 117B EXAM TIME NL 4 pp. 117C - 117D GRAMMAR TIME NL 9 p. 127H

CLIL ART: 3D printer sculpture p. 139   SCIENCE: Cooking p. 140   DRAMA: Zigger Zagger p. 141
GEOGRAPHY: International Date Line p. 142   SCIENCE: Forensics p. 143   STUDENT ACTIVITIES p. 144

Contents 3

0.1 Introducing Tommo

Extra activity
Follow up Exercise 4 by asking pairs to mime one of their ideas for the class to guess. Elicit all their ideas and write them on the board for other students to copy down.

Further practice
Workbook page 2

0

Welcome to Woodley Bridge

VOCABULARY
Activities and interests | Home and furniture | Jobs | Clothes and accessories | Countries and languages

GRAMMAR
There is/are with *some/any* | Possessive adjectives and possessive *'s* | Present Simple with adverbs of frequency | Present Continuous | *was/were, there was/were* | Past Simple: regular verbs

SPEAKING
Likes and dislikes | Talking about feelings

0.1 INTRODUCING TOMMO

Activities and interests; Likes and dislikes; Home and furniture; *There is/are* with *some/any*; Possessive adjectives and possessive *'s*

1 🔊 **1.02** Read the text. Name the person and objects in the photo.

My name's Alexi Thomas, but my nickname is Tommo. I'm fifteen and I'm from Woodley Bridge, a small town in the UK. My mum is a nurse at the local hospital and my dad is a carpenter. We've got a very unusual home, a canal boat called *Ocean Princess*. It's small, but I haven't got any brothers or sisters, so there's enough space for the three of us. I've got a cat called Hissy. She's a wild cat and she isn't very friendly!

Life on a boat is fun and it's a great place for my favourite hobby, kayaking. I've got my own kayak and I like going out on the canal before school. I'm interested in nature, and I love drawing and painting wildlife, too, so this is the perfect home for me.

Exercise 1
1 canal boat
2 Tommo
3 kayak

2 Work in pairs. Mark the sentences T (true) or F (false). Correct the false sentences.
1 ☐ Tommo's real name is Alexi.
2 ☐ Tommo's parents are doctors.
3 ☐ His home isn't very big.
4 ☐ Tommo's got a younger brother.
5 ☐ He hasn't got any pets.
6 ☐ Tommo often goes kayaking before school.

Exercise 2
1 T
2 F (Tommo's mum is a nurse and his dad is a carpenter.)
3 T
4 F (He hasn't got any brothers or sisters.)
5 F (He's got a cat.)
6 T

3 Read the text again. What are Tommo's hobbies and interests?

Exercise 3
Hobbies: kayaking
Interests: nature, drawing and painting wildlife

4 🔊 **1.03** **I KNOW!** Work in pairs. How many activities and interests can you add to the Vocabulary A box in three minutes?

Vocabulary A	Activities and interests
doing nothing going to the cinema listening to music playing computer games reading books or magazines taking photos	

Exercise 4
Possible answers: collecting things, cycling, playing sports, shopping, writing a blog

16

0.1 Introducing Tommo

Exercise 6

garage, roof, garden, bath, bathroom, shower, cupboard

Exercise 7

Possible answers: armchair, attic, basement, carpet, chair, chimney, cooker, dishwasher, fridge, hall, sofa, study, table, wardrobe

Exercise 8

2 There aren't
3 There's (There is)
4 There are
5 There isn't

Exercise 9

Possible answers:
There's a desk between the window and the stairs.
There are some cupboards in the boat.
There's some grass near the boat.
There's a bag next to the cushion.
There are some pens on the notebook.
There's a window opposite the other window.
There's a tie under a pair of trousers.

Exercise 10

2 's, her
3 's, his, 's
4 your, 's

---

5 Use the Speaking box to tell your partner about your favourite activities and interests.

Speaking	Likes and dislikes

I love … / I like … / He loves …
I don't mind … / She doesn't mind …
I can't stand … / He can't stand …

I love taking photos.

6 🔊 **1.04** Check that you understand the words in the Vocabulary B box. Listen and tick the words that you hear.

Vocabulary B	Home and furniture

bath   bathroom   bed   bedroom   ceiling
cupboard   dining room   floor   garage   garden
kitchen   mirror   roof   shower   wall   window

Skye: Can you teach me to kayak some time?
Tommo: Sure, but not today. My kayak's in the garage.
Skye: But you haven't got a garage.
Tommo: No, we haven't, but my dad's friend has got a garage. My kayak's in there at the moment. Dad makes his furniture there, too. It's like a workshop for him.
Skye: What's that noise? Is it something on the roof?
Tommo: That? Oh, it's probably Hissy in the garden.
Skye: What garden?
Tommo: Well, it's not *really* a garden. Mum's got some flowers in plant pots up on the roof. She calls it a garden. You know, that's her idea of a joke. Come and see. Oh no! Hissy!
Skye: What a mess! Hissy's really dirty! Can we put her in the bath?
Tommo: Well, we haven't got a bath because the bathroom's too small.
Skye: Oh yes! But we can wash her in the shower. Come on, Hissy. There's a good girl.
Tommo: Have you got her? Right. There are some towels in the cupboard there. Oh dear! She can't stand showers.

7 **I KNOW!** Work in pairs. How many items can you add to the Vocabulary B box in three minutes?

8 Study the Grammar A box. Look at the photo and complete the sentences with *there is/are* or *there isn't/aren't*.

Grammar A	There is/are with some/any

	Singular	Plural
+	There's (there is) a bed.	There are **some** clothes.
–	There isn't a desk.	There aren't **any** shops.
?	Is there a chair?	Are there **any** books?

1 *There's* a red rug on the floor.
2 _____ any pictures on the wall.
3 _____ a bed next to the window.
4 _____ curtains.
5 _____ a TV.

9 In pairs, make more sentences about the photo, using *There is/are* and the prepositions below.

between   in   near   next to
on   opposite   under

10 Study the Grammar B box. Complete the sentences with possessive adjectives or possessive *'s*.

Grammar B	Possessive adjectives and possessive *'s*

's = singular   the cat's toys
s' = plural   my parents' boat
adjectives   my/your/his/her/its/our/their bedroom

1 Whose book is it?
   It's Tommo's mum's book.
2 Is it Hissy____ ball?
   Yes, it's ____ ball.
3 Is that Tommo____ room?
   No, it's ____ mum and dad____ room.
4 Is this ____ cat?
   No, it's my friend____ cat.

11 Write three sentences about your home.

There's a big mirror in my parents' room.

 Starter Unit 5

0.2 Introducing Skye

> **Alternative activity**
>
> As an alternative to Exercise 2, put students into groups of four and give each group a different category of job to think about, e.g. outdoor jobs, indoor jobs, jobs with uniforms, part-time jobs for teenagers or students. Elicit each group's ideas for jobs and write them on the board for students to make a written record.

> **Further practice**
>
> Workbook page 3

0.2 INTRODUCING SKYE

Jobs; Present Simple with adverbs of frequency

1 🔊 1.05 Read the text. Find:
1 a surname *Winter-Fox*
2 three jobs _____
3 two things to eat _____
4 an animal _____
5 two sports _____
6 two places _____

> **Exercise 1**
>
> 2 scientist, (yoga) teacher, cook
> 3 (cheese) sandwiches, chilli
> 4 snake
> 5 yoga, running
> 6 (two from) New Zealand, school, café, canal

Hi! I'm Skye Winter-Fox and I'm 15. I live with my Gran because my parents are scientists and they often work abroad. They are in New Zealand at the moment. Gran's really sporty. She's a yoga teacher and she swims every morning. I sometimes go with her but I don't like getting up early!

We usually have breakfast together, then I feed my pet snake. Yes! I've got a beautiful snake called Basil. I have lunch at school, but it's always boring because I have cheese sandwiches every day. After school, I see my friends Tommo, Dan and Alisha. Dan and I like running together. Sometimes we all meet at the café on the canal.

In the evenings, I do my homework and Gran makes dinner. Does she cook every day? Yes, she does. She's the best cook in the world, and she makes a brilliant chilli!

> **Exercise 2**
>
> Possible answers: accountant, architect, dentist, doctor, driver, engineer, journalist, lawyer, receptionist, secretary, teacher

2 🔊 1.06 Study the Vocabulary box. Can you add more words?

Vocabulary	Jobs	
cook/chef	farmer	hairdresser
mechanic	nurse	scientist

 Starter Unit

3 In pairs, describe a job from the Vocabulary box. Your partner has to guess which job it is.

This person can make you better when you are ill. A nurse.
This person likes working with animals …

4 Study the Grammar box. Find more examples of the Present Simple in the text.

Grammar	Present Simple with adverbs of frequency
Affirmative	**Negative**
I live with my Gran.	I don't swim every day.
My parents travel a lot.	They don't live in this country.
Questions	**Short answers**
Do you live near the school?	Yes, I do. / No, I don't.
Does she cook everyday?	Yes, she does. / No, she doesn't.

Always, usually, often, sometimes, never go before most verbs, but after the verb *to be*. **Watch OUT!**

5 Complete the sentences with the correct form of the verbs in brackets.
1 We *don't go* (not go) to school on Saturdays.
2 She _____ (often/be) with her friends in the park café.
3 Mum and Dad _____ (never/sleep) after 8 a.m.
4 _____ (you/live) in a big house?
5 Emma _____ (not eat) lunch at school.
6 Jake _____ (always/cook) for my birthday.

> **Exercise 5**
>
> 2 is often
> 3 never sleep
> 4 Do you live
> 5 doesn't eat
> 6 always cooks

6 **WORD FRIENDS** Study the phrases and underline those that are in the text. Can you add more everyday actions?

> do homework   get dressed   get home   get up early/late
> go to school / go out   have a shower
> have breakfast/lunch/dinner   see friends

7 In pairs, describe a school day.
I always wake up at six o'clock.
I never get dressed before breakfast.

8 In pairs, describe the people in your house. What do they do? What's their routine?

I live with my mum and my dog. Mum gets up early every day. She's a dentist.

And YOU

> **Exercise 6**
>
> Phrases in the text: do homework, get up early, have breakfast, have lunch, see friends
> Possible answers: brush your hair, clean your teeth, do the shopping, feed a pet, get ready for school, go to bed, make your bed, meet friends, stay up late, tidy your bedroom

0.3 Introducing Dan

Extra activity

When students have finished Exercise 7, put them into pairs. Each student chooses an adjective from the Speaking box and mimes it to their partner. Their partner must guess the adjective/feeling. More confident students can choose other adjectives which are not in the Speaking box.

Further practice

Workbook page 4

Exercise 1
They are family.

Exercise 2
2 F
3 F
4 T
5 F

Exercise 3
baseball cap, hoodie, T-shirt

Exercise 4
Possible answers: belt, bracelet, dress, glasses, hat, jeans, necklace, shirt, shoes, skirt, socks, sunglasses, trousers

Exercise 7
Possible answers: angry, happy, surprised

Exercise 8
Possible answers:
1 He's got a lot of homework for Monday.
2 He feels worried because he doesn't know many people.
See page 247 for audio script.

Exercise 6
2 Are you wearing an earring? Yes, I am. / No, I'm not.
3 Are the students talking? Yes, they are. / No, they aren't.
4 Is your friend doing this exercise? Yes, he/she is. / No, he/she isn't.
5 Are you looking at your phone? Yes, I am. / No, I'm not

0.3 INTRODUCING DAN

Clothes and accessories; Present Continuous; Talking about feelings

1 CLASS VOTE Look at the photo. Do you think the boys are family or friends?

2 🔊 1.07 Read the text. Mark the sentences T (true) or F (false).

Hi, I'm Dan. This is a photo of my older brother, Ed, and me. In the photo, we're both wearing sports clothes. I'm wearing my favourite football T-shirt, and Ed's wearing his baseball cap and his favourite hoodie. We're smiling in the photo because Ed's telling a stupid joke! Ed and I were born in the USA. My dad's family is originally from Mexico and we both speak Spanish. I'm in England now because Mum's working at a school here. Ed's at university in New York and he's having a great time. Mum and I are making plans to visit him this summer, and we're really excited. I'm enjoying my new school in England but I don't like the school uniform! I'm glad I've got friends like Tommo, Skye and Alisha. I'm shy, but they're always around when I'm worried about something.

1 [F] Dan is older than Ed.
2 [ ] Dan and Ed were born in Mexico.
3 [ ] Dan and Ed don't speak Spanish.
4 [ ] Ed's in New York at the moment.
5 [ ] Dan likes the school uniform in England.

3 🔊 1.08 Study the Vocabulary box. Which clothes and accessories can you see in the photo?

Vocabulary	Clothes and accessories

baseball cap   earrings   hoodie   jacket
school uniform   T-shirt   watch

4 I KNOW! Work in pairs. How many words can you add to the Vocabulary box in two minutes?

5 Study the Grammar box. Find more examples of the Present Continuous in the text.

Grammar	Present Continuous

Affirmative
I'm wearing my favourite shirt.
He's wearing a hat.
They're wearing hats.

Negative
I'm not wearing my favourite shirt.
He isn't wearing a hat.
They aren't wearing hats.

Questions
Are you wearing a tie?
Is she wearing a tie?

Short answers
Yes, I am. / No, I'm not.
Yes, she is. / No, she isn't.

6 Order the words to make questions. Answer the questions to make them true for you.
1 you / are / going out / ?
   Are you going out? No, I'm not.
2 are / wearing / an earring / ? / you
3 the students / are / talking / ?
4 doing / this exercise / your friend / is / ?
5 you / looking at / are / your phone / ?

7 Study the Speaking box. Can you add more words to describe feelings?

Speaking	Talking about feelings

I'm ... annoyed / bored / excited / frightened / irritated / nervous / relaxed / sad / shocked / tired / worried.

8 🔊 1.09 Listen and answer the questions.
1 What is Dan's problem?
2 How does Dan feel about the party?

9 In pairs, describe how you usually feel:
1 before an exam
2 on your birthday
3 after a party
4 on holiday

Starter Unit 7

0.4 Introducing Alisha

> **Extra activity**
>
> When students have finished Exercise 1, look at the first example (*India – Hindi*) and ask students to think of other countries where the name of the language may not be obvious, e.g. *Brazil – Portuguese, Egypt – Arabic, Switzerland – French/German/Italian, Argentina – Spanish.*

> **Further practice**
>
> Workbook page 5

0.4 INTRODUCING ALISHA

Countries and languages; *was/were, there was/were*; Past Simple: regular verbs

1 🔊 1.10 Add the words below to the correct categories in the Vocabulary box.

China   Chinese   France   French   German
Germany   Italian   Italy   Poland   Polish
Portugal   Portuguese   Turkey   Turkish

Vocabulary	Countries and languages
Countries	**Languages**
India	Hindi
Spain	Spanish

2 **I KNOW!** Work in pairs. How many countries can you name for each letter of the alphabet?

A – Argentina, B – Belgium …

3 🔊 1.11 Read the text. Find two countries and two languages.

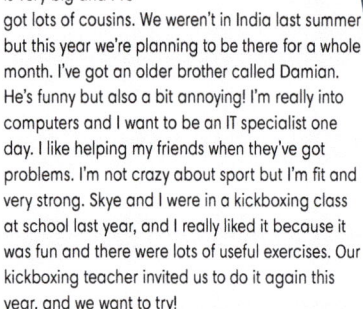

Hi or 'Namaste'! My name's Alisha and I'm half-English and half-Indian. My dad's from India and my mum's from England, so I speak Hindi and English. Dad's family is very big and I've got lots of cousins. We weren't in India last summer but this year we're planning to be there for a whole month. I've got an older brother called Damian. He's funny but also a bit annoying! I'm really into computers and I want to be an IT specialist one day. I like helping my friends when they've got problems. I'm not crazy about sport but I'm fit and very strong. Skye and I were in a kickboxing class at school last year, and I really liked it because it was fun and there were lots of useful exercises. Our kickboxing teacher invited us to do it again this year, and we want to try!

4 Read the text again, and then cover it. Write three things about Alisha.

1 *She's got an older brother.*
2 *She can speak …*

5 Study the Grammar A box. Complete the sentences with *was/were* and *wasn't/weren't*.

Grammar A	*was/were, there was/were*
Affirmative	**Negative**
He was on holiday.	He wasn't on holiday.
We were on holiday.	We weren't on holiday.
There was a party.	There wasn't a party.
There were lots of people.	There weren't lots of people.
Questions	**Short answers**
Was it fun?	Yes, it was. / No, it wasn't.
Were they at home?	Yes, they were. / No, they weren't.
Was there a party?	Yes, there was. / No, there wasn't.
Were there many people?	Yes, there were. / No, there weren't.

1 Naomi and her parents _were_ on holiday in Spain but the weather _____ terrible.
2 _____ you at the cinema last night? No, I _____.
3 The film festival _____ fun and there _____ lots of films to watch.
4 _____ your parents angry when you _____ late home?
5 Liam _____ only 10 years old in 1999.
6 _____ the English test difficult? Yes, it _____. There _____ lots of difficult exercises.

6 🔊 1.12 Study the Grammar B box. Listen and answer the questions.

Grammar B	Past Simple: regular verbs
He lived in California.	
They didn't invite her.	
Did you like the film?	

1 What was Dan like on his first day at school?
2 Who did Dan live with last year?
3 What language does Alisha want to learn?

7 In pairs, tell your partner about five things that were true for you last year, but are NOT true now.

I was in a different class.
I wasn't in the basketball team.

 Starter Unit

Exercise 1

Countries:
China, France, Germany, Italy, Poland, Portugal, Turkey
Languages:
Chinese, French, German, Italian, Polish, Portuguese, Turkish

Exercise 2

Possible answers:
Canada, Denmark, Egypt, Finland, Ghana, Hungary, Iceland, Jamaica, Kenya, Latvia, Mexico, Nigeria, Oman, Pakistan, Qatar, Russia, Sweden, Thailand, Uganda, Vietnam, Wales, Yemen, Zambia (There are no countries beginning with the letter X.)

Exercise 3

Countries: India, England
Languages: Hindi, English

Exercise 4

Possible answers:
Her dad's from India. Her mum's English. She speaks Hindi and English. She's got a lot of cousins. She's planning to go to India this year. She's into computers. She wants to be an IT specialist. She likes helping her friends. She's not crazy about sport. She's fit and very strong. She was in a kickboxing class last year.

Exercise 5

1 were, was
2 Were, wasn't
3 was, were
4 Were, were
5 was
6 Was, was, were

Exercise 6

1 He was shy.
2 He lived with his brother.
3 She wants to learn Spanish.

See page 247 for audio script.

0.5 Character quiz

Extra activity

Put students into groups of three or four. Elicit the words we could start a question with and write these on the board, e.g. *Are, Do, Where, Who, When, What, Is*. Each group thinks of one question starting with each of the words. Tell the groups that they should think of questions that other students can answer. When they have finished, invite groups to ask their questions around the class.

0.5 CHARACTER QUIZ

1 In pairs, describe the photo. Make as many sentences as possible. What do you think life is like in Woodley Bridge?

Exercise 1

Possible answers: Dan is holding a phone. Skye and Alisha are laughing. The friends are standing outside a café. Tommo is between Alisha and Skye. There are some plants. Woodley Bridge looks quiet and safe but maybe a bit boring.

Exercise 2

1 F
2 T
3 F
4 F
5 T
6 F

See page 247 for audio script.

2 🔊 1.13 Listen and mark the sentences T (true) or F (false).

1 ☐ The café is closed.
2 ☐ The café sells lemonade.
3 ☐ Dan hasn't got a mobile phone.
4 ☐ Dan is waiting outside the café.
5 ☐ Dan likes the café.
6 ☐ There are lots of places to hang out in Woodley Bridge.

3 Complete the questions with one word in each gap.

The BIG Character Quiz

1 _____ Dan and his brother from the UK?
2 Where _____ Tommo live?
3 Where _____ Alisha's dad's family from?
4 _____ Skye live with her parents?
5 What _____ Dan's brother's name?
6 _____ lived in America last year?
7 _____ Dan and Alisha speak other languages?
8 _____ Skye and Tommo got pets?
9 Why _____ Dan's mum sad?
10 _____ Skye's parents doctors?
11 _____ Tommo got a kayak?
12 _____ Tommo, Dan, Alisha and Skye often meet in a café?

Exercise 3

1 Are
2 does
3 is/are
4 Does
5 is
6 Who
7 Do/Can
8 Have
9 is
10 Are
11 Has
12 Do

4 In groups, do the quiz about the young people from Woodley Bridge. Use the texts in Lessons 1–4 to help you. How much can you remember?

5 In pairs, write two similar kinds of questions about yourselves. Hand the questions to your teacher and have a class quiz with two teams.

And YU

Exercise 4

1 No (They are from the USA.)
2 Woodley Bridge
3 India
4 No (She lives with her Gran.)
5 Ed
6 Dan
7 Yes (Dan speaks Spanish and Alisha speaks Hindi.)
8 Yes (Skye has a snake and Tommo has a cat.)
9 We don't know.
10 No (They are scientists.)
11 Yes, he has.
12 No (They sometimes meet there.)

1

That's my world!

VOCABULARY
Everyday technology | Adjectives of opinion | Time

GRAMMAR
Present Simple, Present Continuous and state verbs | verb + *ing* / verb + *to*-infinitive

Grammar: It's upside down

Speaking: Let's go in

BBC Culture: Addicted to screens

Workbook p. 16

BBC VOX POPS ▶
CLIL 1 > p. 139

1.1 VOCABULARY Lifestyle

I can talk about everyday technology.

1 CLASS VOTE Do you take photos with your mobile phone? What do you take photos of? People? Places? Other things?

2 Match photos 1–6 with sentences a–f. What do the photos tell you about the person's life?

He/She likes reading.   He/She's got a cat.

a ☐ **sunny01**   She's up to mischief again!
b ☐ **jacko999**   Friends + chocolate cake #agreatday!
c ☐ **ninab98**   Come on rain! We've got the right boots.
d ☐ **singingboy98**   Dan's singing again! ;)
e ☐ **robbie2**   It's film time … yay!
f ☐ **paul13**   Ready for our trip!

3 🔊 **1.14** Listen and check you understand the words in the Vocabulary A box. What objects can you see in the pictures?

Vocabulary A	Everyday technology

battery   cable   charger   earphones   plug   selfie stick   speaker   tablet

4 I KNOW! Can you add more words to the Vocabulary A box?

5 🔊 **1.15** Listen to speakers 1–4 and write the presents. Use the Vocabulary A box to help you.

1 _____   2 _____   3 _____   4 _____

6 Which object would be the best present for you? Why?

I'd like a selfie stick because my friends and I love taking photos.

Unit contents

Vocabulary
- Everyday technology
- Adjectives of opinion
- Time

Grammar
- Present Simple, Present Continuous and state verbs
- Verb + ing / verb + to-infinitive

Communication skills
- Making suggestions

Examples of 21st Century Skills/Competencies
- Critical Thinking: page 11 (Exercise 10), pages 20–21
- Collaboration: page 12 (Exercise 7), page 16 (Exercise 6), page 21 (Exercise 9)
- Assessment for Learning: page 19
- Autonomy and Personal Initiative: page 11 (Exercise 13), page 17 (Exercise 8)

1.1 VOCABULARY Lifestyle

Lesson learning objective
Students can talk about everyday technology.

Lead in: Topic introduction
Write the word TECHNOLOGY vertically on the board. Using the first two letters, make the words *computer* and *internet*.

    compu**T**er
        int**E**rnet

Put students into pairs and give them a time limit to make more words with the other letters of *TECHNOLOGY*. Elicit ideas and write the best ideas on the board.

Exercise 1
Before students open their Students' Books, ask them the questions and encourage a class discussion. Invite students to talk about the last photo they took on their mobile phone and why they took it.

Exercise 2
Invite students to describe what they can see in each of the photos.
Have a class vote about which photo they like best and invite students to give reasons why they like it.
Check that students understand the phrase *be up to mischief*.

Answers: a 3   b 6   c 1   d 4   e 2   f 5

Possible answers:
1 He/She has got new boots.
2 They like watching films/playing computer games.
3 He/She's got a cat.
4 He likes singing.
5 They are on holiday.
6 He/She likes chocolate cake.

Exercise 3 🔊 1.14
When students have finished, ask about details which can't be seen in the photos. For example, *What part of the tablet are the boys looking at?* (the screen) *What is the cable the cat is playing with attached to?* (a plug at one end and a computer, a TV or another electrical appliance at the other end) *What is connected to the boy's earphones?* (an MP3 player or a smartphone) *What is on the end of the selfie stick?* (a smartphone or a camera).

Answers: cable, earphones, selfie stick, tablet

Exercise 4
Tell students to brainstorm ideas in pairs and then to form a group with another pair to compare their ideas. Invite the groups to share their ideas with the class.

Possible answers: headphones, smartphone, USB drive, MP3 player

Exercise 5 🔊 1.15
Tell students to look at the words in the Vocabulary A box and ask which item they think would be the most likely to be given as a present.
When students have listened to the audio, elicit the answers, asking students to explain their answers.

Answers: 1 charger   2 speakers   3 earphones   4 selfie stick

🔊 1.15
1 It's a really cool present from my aunt! It's small and it doesn't have any cables. When I go on school trips, I can use it on the bus … which is great because the battery in my phone doesn't last long.
2 I'm really happy with my birthday present from Dad this year. When friends come to the house, I can use them to play really loud music and the quality is great. They're good for parties too.
3 They're pink and they're very ugly. They're a present from my sister and I think they're cheap ones. You can't hear things well with them. It's a nice idea but … sorry … they're awful!
4 I love it and it's great fun. Sometimes I feel a bit silly when I use it, but if you're with a big group of friends, it's the best way to get a good photo.

Exercise 6
Put students into pairs to discuss their ideas. Before inviting students to share their ideas with the class, tell each pair to imagine that they are going to buy presents for another pair of students. They should discuss which of the objects each student in the other pair would want as a present and then join together with the other pair to say what they chose and to find out if they were correct.

23

Exercise 7 🔊 1.16

Tell students to look at the picture without reading the text and to discuss who the people are and what they think is happening.
Then they should read the text quickly to see how close their guesses were before they do the exercise. (It is a brother and sister arguing about a pair of earphones.)

Answers: 2 speaker   3 battery   4 tablet   5 cables
6 plug   7 charger

Exercise 8 🔊 1.17

Before you play the audio, tell students to read the expressions.
Have a class vote to find out who in the class does each of the activities in the box.

Answers: go online, read e-books, share photos, listen to music, text friends/parents, watch music videos

---

🔊 **1.17**

1 Computers can be slow, but you can go online quickly with a good phone.
2 My new smartphone has a big screen. I can even read e-books on it.
3 The camera is great on this phone and I can share photos with friends.
4 The best thing about mobile phones is … you can listen to music anywhere.
5 I never go out without it. I text friends all the time, especially when we're making plans.
6 It's fun on the school bus because we can watch music videos together.

Exercise 9

When students have finished, invite them to share their answers with the class.
Ask follow-up questions, e.g. *What sort of things do you write about in your messages? Do you always read new messages immediately, whatever you are doing at the time?*

Exercise 10 🔊 1.18

Put students into pairs and tell them to imagine that they have been to the cinema. The pairs take turns to ask *How was the film?* and to answer using one of the adjectives written in the table with an appropriate intonation, e.g. a very enthusiastic intonation if they are saying *amazing* or *awesome*. Invite different students to ask and answer in front of the class to see who can use the most dramatic appropriate intonation.

Answers:

😃 exciting, perfect
🙂 lovely, useful
😐 OK
🙁 old-fashioned, strange
☹️ terrible

Exercise 11

Before students do the exercise, elicit one idea for each adjective and write these on the board. They don't have to have anything to do with technology. Encourage students to use these ideas to help them to think of more ideas for each adjective.

Possible answers:
1 a smartphone, a dictionary
2 a theme park, a film
3 clothes, music
4 a photo, a story
5 an exam, weather

Exercise 12

Invite students to say one of their ideas without mentioning the adjective. The rest of the class should guess which adjective it matches.

Exercise 13

Before students do the exercise, put them into pairs to role play a vox pops interview. The students take turns to play the role of the interviewer and the role of someone in the street. The interviewer asks if they can ask a few questions about technology and, when the other student agrees, the interviewer asks the questions in Exercise 13.
Invite pairs to carry out their interviews in front of the class.
When students write their sentences, they can use the ideas they have heard or any other ideas.

VOX POPS ▶ 1.1

While watching, students should write down one thing said by one of the speakers that is also true for them or for people in their family. After watching, encourage students to share their ideas with the class.

Extra activity

Students work in pairs. They should imagine that one student has just bought a new gadget and the other student is a parent or grandparent who doesn't know much about technology. They should write a conversation where the parent/grandparent asks questions about the gadget and why the student likes it.
When they have finished, invite pairs to act out their conversations in front of the class.

Further practice

- Workbook pages 6–7
- Resource Pack
  Resource 1: Unit 1 Lesson 1 Vocabulary – It's awesome

I want to listen to music but I can't find my
¹ *earphones* / *plugs* because my brother is using them! 'They're better than mine', he says. 'It's OK,' I say. I can use my new ²*battery* / *speaker* that plays music *really* loud. However, when I look inside, the ³*plug* / *battery* isn't there because it's in my brother's digital camera and, guess what? His friend's got it at the moment. In the end I decide to watch a funny film on my ⁴*cable* / *tablet* but I can't find it. I look in my brother's bedroom. On his desk there's a pile of ⁵*earphones* / *cables* that are all different lengths. I finally find the short black one with the right ⁶*plug* / *selfie stick* on the end of it for my tablet. 'OK, where is it?' I ask him again. Then I hear Mum's voice. 'Are you looking for this, love?' she asks. 'I'm just buying some shoes but it's nearly dead. Can you get me the ⁷*battery* / *charger*, please?'

7 🔊 **1.16** Read the text. Choose the correct options. Listen and check. Is it the same in your house?

8 🔊 **1.17** **WORD FRIENDS** Listen to people talking about their phones and mark ✓ the expressions you hear.

Word Friends	
chat with friends	**download** songs
go online	**listen** to music
make/film a video	**play** games
read e-books	**send/get** instant messages
share photos	**text** friends/parents
upload pictures	**watch** music videos

9 In pairs, ask and answer the questions.
1 How many instant messages do you send and get in a day?
   I send about ten instant messages in a day and I get about twenty.
2 Do you know somebody who reads e-books?
3 When do you listen to music?
4 How often do you download songs?
5 Would you like to make a video with friends in your school?
6 What games do you play on the computer?
7 When do you usually text your parents?
8 What type of photos do you usually upload?

10 🔊 **1.18** Write the words in the correct column below. Listen and check.

Vocabulary B	Adjectives of opinion
all right amazing awesome awful boring brilliant cool disgusting exciting funny lovely nice noisy OK old-fashioned perfect strange terrible useful	

😃	🙂	😐	🙁	☹️
amazing	*cool*	*all right*	*boring*	*awful*
awesome	*funny*	*nice*	*noisy*	*disgusting*
brilliant				

11 Write two things that are:
1 useful   4 strange
2 awesome   5 terrible
3 old-fashioned

12 Compare your ideas with the class.

13 [VOX POPS ▶ 1.1] Who in your family uses technology the most? What do they use it for?
My brother loves his gadgets. He's older than me and he's got a really good tablet. He shops online, watches films, and he uses it for studying.

1.2 GRAMMAR   Present Simple, Present Continuous and state verbs

I can use different tenses to talk about the present.

1 **CLASS VOTE** Do you watch music videos? Yes or No? What are some of your favourites?

2 🔊 1.19 Look at the photo. What can you see? Read the text.

X-RAY

the indie band with all the moves

Hi! It's Gary here, lead singer. Today I'm writing the band's blog at a special event in a skate park. We've got photographers and reporters with us, but we aren't singing at the moment. One reporter, Ali, is asking us lots of questions: 'What do you normally do on Saturday afternoons? What are you doing today?' We tell Ali about our lives. We often travel from one city to the next on Saturday afternoons. Then in the evenings we usually play live in concert. We don't normally skateboard! Today there are lots of skateboarders around because we're filming our new music video. They're doing some amazing tricks. I love the video!

3 Study the Grammar box. Find examples of the Present Simple, Present Continuous and state verbs in the text.

Grammar	Present Simple, Present Continuous and state verbs

Present Simple
They usually *travel* on a tour bus.
He *doesn't write* his blog every day.
Do they *speak* English? Yes, they *do*.

Present Continuous
He*'s travelling* a lot these days.
They *aren't recording* a song at the moment.
Is she *skateboarding* now? No, she *isn't*.

State verbs
Verbs with no continuous form: love, like, hate, know, think, see, feel, understand, want, need

GRAMMAR TIME > PAGE 118

4 🔊 1.20 Choose the correct option. Listen and check.
1 Ali and Gary *sit* / (*are sitting*) on a bench at the skate park.
2 Gary usually *sings* / *is singing* in concerts on Saturday evenings.
3 The band members *don't often visit* / *aren't often visiting* skate parks.
4 The skateboarders *do* / *are doing* some fantastic skateboard tricks at the moment.
5 Sara *always wears* / *is always wearing* her lucky blue helmet.
6 Several people *film* / *are filming* the skateboarders.

5 Use the Present Simple or Present Continuous to write questions about the text in Exercise 2. In pairs, ask and answer the questions.
1 the people in the park / film / the skateboarders?
   Are the people in the park filming the skateboarders?
2 Gary / work / as a reporter?
3 Ali / ask / questions at the moment?
4 Sara / wear / a helmet in the photo?
5 the band members / usually play / live in concert on Saturdays?
6 the skateboarders / perform / in a competition today?

6 🔊 1.21 Complete the text with the correct form of the verbs in brackets. Listen and check.

My name's Sara. I ¹*love* (love) skateboarding. I'm a real fan. I ²_____ (practise) at a local park every weekend. I ³_____ (not/often/do) competitions because I'm from a small town.

I'm very excited today because I ⁴_____ (perform) in a video for a famous band. At the moment we ⁵_____ (get) ready. Lots of people ⁶_____ (come) into the park now. My mum and dad ⁷_____ (sit) near the front because they ⁸_____ (want) to upload photos for their friends!

7 [VOX POPS ▶ 1.2] In pairs, tell your partner about a hobby/sport you like. Complete the sentences to make them true for you.

I really like/love … because …
I usually/never/don't often …
I want …

1.2 GRAMMAR   Present Simple, Present Continuous and state verbs

Lesson learning objective
Students can use different tenses to talk about the present.

Lead in: Review of adjectives of opinion from the previous lesson

Invite two students to come to the front of the class. Tell them to sit facing the class and not to turn round. Write the phrase *It's OK.* on the board. The rest of the class, who are facing the board, should ask questions starting: *What do you think of …?* to try to elicit the phrase written on the board. When they have succeeded (or given up), invite two different students to come to the front of the class and write a new phrase on the board, e.g. *It's terrible.* Continue a few times, with different students and different adjectives of opinion.

Culture notes
The original definition of an indie band was one which was signed to an independent record company rather than one of the larger companies such as Sony or EMI. However, the phrase has now become more associated with the genre of music rather than the record company label.
Famous bands which are often referred to as indie bands include *The Killers*, *Arcade Fire*, *Oasis*, *Radiohead*, *The Smiths* and *Imagine Dragons*.

Exercise 1
When the class has discussed their ideas, put them into groups of three or four. Each group should think of a music video that they all know and describe what happens in it. The rest of the class should try to guess which music video it is.

Exercise 2   1.19
After students have read the text, ask more questions. For example, *Who is Gary?* (the lead singer of the band) *Who is Ali?* (a reporter) *Is the person in the photo in the band?* (No, she's a skateboarder who is in the band's video).

Answer: A girl skateboarding in a skate park

Exercise 3
Remind students about when we use the Present Simple (*to state facts and talk about routines*) and when we use the Present Continuous (*to describe things happening now or around now*).

Answers:
Present Simple: It's, We've got, What do you normally do, We tell, We often travel, we usually play, We don't normally skateboard, there are
Present Continuous: I'm writing, we aren't singing, is asking, What are you doing, we're filming, They're doing
State verbs: I love

Exercise 4   1.20
Discuss the example with the class and elicit why the Present Continuous is the correct option (*the sentence is describing what is happening now and sit is not a state verb*). When students have finished the exercise, elicit the answers and explanations.

Answers:
2 sings (*usually* refers to routine)
3 don't often visit (*don't often* refers to routine)
4 are doing (*at the moment* refers to now)
5 always wears (*always* refers to routine)
6 are filming (the sentence describes what is happening now)

Exercise 5
When you elicit the answers, ask students to explain why they have chosen the specific tense.

Answers:
2 Does Gary work as a reporter? (Present Simple – a fact)
3 Is Ali asking questions at the moment? (Present Continuous – *at the moment* refers to now)
4 Is Sara wearing a helmet in the photo? (Present Continuous – asking about what is happening in the photo)
5 Do the band members usually play live in concert on Saturdays? (Present Simple – *usually* refers to routine)
6 Are the skateboarders performing in a competition today? (Present Continuous – *today* refers to now or around now)

Exercise 6   1.21
Elicit the answers and check the spelling of the verbs in items 5 (*getting*), 6 (*coming*) and 7 (*sitting*). Elicit the spelling rules these illustrate (*getting, sitting* – when a one-syllable verb ends with one vowel and one consonant, we double the last consonant; *coming* – when a verb ends in -e, we remove the -e before adding -ing).

Answers: 2 practise   3 don't often do   4 am/'m performing
5 are/'re getting   6 are coming   7 are sitting   8 want

Exercise 7
When students have discussed their ideas, set a time limit to talk to other students in the class about hobbies or sports that they like. Then have a class discussion to find out the most popular hobbies and sport.

VOX POPS   ▶ 1.2
While watching, students should write down the name of one free-time activity mentioned by the speakers. After watching, elicit the activities students wrote down, and ask if students ever do any of them.

Extra activity
Put students into groups of five. In each group, one student plays the role of a reporter and the other four students play the role of members of a band. The group should work together to think of questions that the reporter can ask and the band's answers to these questions. When the groups are ready, invite them to act out their interviews in front of the class. Before each interview, the reporter should introduce the band and explain where they are.

Further practice
- Workbook page 8
- Grammar Time page 118
- Resource Pack
  Resource 2: Unit 1 Lesson 2 Grammar – Find someone who …

1.3 READING and VOCABULARY   Are all gadgets useful?

Lesson learning objective
Students can find specific detail in an article and talk about unusual objects.

Lead in: Review of state verbs

Write these cues on the board.
you / like …?
you / know …?
you / think …?
you / understand why …?
What / you / want / to do …?
Put students into pairs and tell them to make questions from the cues.
When they have finished, join pairs together to form groups of four. Pairs take turns to ask their questions and to answer the other pair's questions.
Invite groups to share some of their questions and answers with the class.

Exercise 1
Tell students not to open their Students' Books yet. Elicit what a gadget tester would have to do and have a class discussion about the question, asking students to give reasons for their answers.

Exercise 2 🔊 1.22
Tell students to open their Students' Books and to look at the two pictures. Discuss what gadget each picture shows and why each gadget might be a good (or bad) idea.

Answers: **A** Sospendo **B** Phorce

Exercise 3
Elicit the answers and the clues in the text for each answer.

Answers:
1 a (*as usual*)
2 b (Tina can't skate)
3 c (the text doesn't mention the weight)
4 b (Tina says that she doesn't need it)
5 b (the Defender bag can be used like a table so it doesn't need one)
6 c (Tina often forgets to charge her phone but the text doesn't mention that she has forgotten today)

Exercise 4
When students have finished, put them into groups of three and ask them to think of one more adjective of their own for each gadget. Elicit ideas and explanations from each group.

Possible answers:
Briefskate: normal, useful, fun
Sospendo: strange
Controller: cool
Defender: ugly
Phorce: clever

Exercise 5
Students should work alone to choose which gadget they like best. Then they should work in pairs and take turns to say which they gadget they chose, giving reasons why. Pairs can rank the gadgets from best to worst.
Elicit ideas and encourage a class discussion to compare students' opinions.

Exercise 6
Check that students understand: *It's made of* + material (*plastic*, *metal*, *paper*, *wood*, etc.).
When the pairs have finished, invite different students to describe one of their objects, to see if the rest of the class can guess what it is.

Extra activity
Students work in groups of four. They brainstorm ideas for a gadget similar to those described in the text and then create an advert for it. The advert should include a picture, some adjectives to describe the gadget and information about what the gadget can do. When the groups are ready, they should present their advert to the class.
When all the groups have presented their adverts, have a class vote for the best gadget. (Tell students that they can't vote for their own gadget.)

Further practice
- Workbook page 9
- Resource Pack
  Resource 3: Unit 1 Lesson 3 Reading and Vocabulary – Match and create

1:3 READING and VOCABULARY   Are all gadgets useful?

I can find specific detail in an article and talk about unusual objects.

Gadget testers for a day! *By Max Stevens and Tina Wallis*

Today we're going to school by bus as usual. We normally leave home at 8 a.m., but we're leaving early because we're testing some new gadgets for this month's report. All these gadgets are useful when you're travelling. So, what have we got?

First up is the **Briefskate**. It's made of wood, so it looks like a normal skateboard, but you can open the top. Inside there's space for books and a mobile or a tablet. In my opinion, it's useful and fun, but Tina and I can't skate, so we can't test it …

Next, we're trying the **Sospendo**. It's a strange plastic gadget which works like an extra pair of hands to hold your phone or tablet. Tina's wearing it at the moment. She won't drop her tablet, but people are staring at her. I'm sure they're thinking, 'What on earth is she doing?'. Tina doesn't like this gadget!

Max

Now it's my turn. The next gadget is a tiny **controller**. You put it on your mobile or tablet so that you can play games. It looks cool, but I don't need this to play games on my phone.

I normally take a rucksack to school every day, but today I'm testing a **Defender** bag. It's like a rucksack. You can wear it on your back or on your front. When it's in front of you, you can use it like a small table. I don't like it because it looks ugly. Right now, Max is using the **Phorce** bag. You can use it to charge your phone or tablet. I often forget to charge my phone before I leave the house, so I think this is a brilliant idea. Max loves it, too. It's our favourite gadget!

Tina

1 **CLASS VOTE** Would you like to test new gadgets for teenage students? Yes or No?

2 🔊 1.22 Find the names of the gadgets in bold in the text. Read the text and match two of the gadgets with pictures A and B.

3 Read the article. Choose the correct answers.
   1 Max and Tina normally get the bus to school.
     a True   b False   c Doesn't say
   2 Tina is going to school on the Briefskate today.
     a True   b False   c Doesn't say
   3 The Sospendo is heavy.
     a True   b False   c Doesn't say
   4 Tina thinks the controller is useful for her.
     a True   b False   c Doesn't say
   5 You need to put the Defender bag on a table to use it.
     a True   b False   c Doesn't say
   6 Tina forgot to charge her phone today.
     a True   b False   c Doesn't say

4 What is Max and Tina's opinion of each object? Use the adjectives below to help you.

   boring   clever   cool   fun   normal
   strange   ugly   unusual   useful

   They think the Briefskate looks quite normal.

5 What do you think of the gadgets in the report? Which do you like?

   I like the Defender bag, but I don't want to look stupid at school!

6 In pairs, describe the things below.

   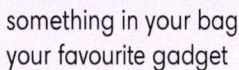

   something in your bag
   your favourite gadget

   It's made of plastic.
   You can use it to charge your phone.
   It's boring.

1.4 GRAMMAR Verb + *ing* / verb + *to*-infinitive

I can use verb constructions with *to*-infinitives and *-ing* forms.

VIDEO   IT'S UPSIDE DOWN

Tommo: Hi, Alisha. Are you busy?

Alisha: Yes. I'm trying to finish my homework but it's taking ages. I'd love to be outside in this weather.

Tommo: Me too, but I've got a problem with my computer. Dan says you're good at fixing things.

Alisha: Well, I enjoy trying. What's up?

Tommo: I'm making a poster for a competition. I prefer using my own photos but when I upload them from my phone to the computer, they're upside down.

Alisha: That's strange.

Tommo: It's really annoying. I want to put the posters up in town but now I've got ten photos … upside down!

Alisha: Tommo, the problem is your settings.

Tommo: Oh, so what can I do?

Alisha: I can't explain now but I don't mind coming to your boat later.

Tommo: OK … but don't forget to bring a snack. It could take a long time.

Alisha: Tommo!

> **OUT of class**
> It's upside down.   It's taking ages.
> It's really annoying.

1 CLASS VOTE Who do you speak to when you've got a problem with your computer, tablet or phone?

   parent?   friend?   shop assistant?   teacher?

2 ▶ 1.3 🔊 1.23 Watch or listen. Why does Tommo want Alisha to help him?

3 Study the Grammar box. Find more examples of verbs + *ing* or verbs + *to*-infinitive in the dialogue.

Grammar | **verb + *ing* and verb + *to*-infinitive**

verb + *ing*
After: *avoid, can't stand, enjoy, finish, look forward to, (not) mind, miss, practise, stop*, and after prepositions
I **don't mind coming** to your house.
She's good **at fixing** things.

verb + *to*-infinitive
After: *agree, allow, ask, choose, decide, forget, hope, learn, offer, plan, try, want, would like/love*
I'd love to be in the park in this weather.

verb + *ing* or *to*-infinitive
After: *like, love, hate, prefer, start*
I **prefer making** my own posters. / I **prefer to make** my own posters.

GRAMMAR TIME > PAGE 118

4 Choose the correct option.
1. There's a concert on TV tonight. I hope *watching / to watch* it when I get home.
2. Our friends are coming to the park. We enjoy *meeting / to meet* here after school.
3. My cousin's learning Chinese and would like *to visit / visiting* China one day.
4. Homemade pizza is amazing but I'm not very good at *making / to make* it.
5. Naomi misses *to see / seeing* her friends from her old school.

5 Complete the advert with the correct form of the verbs below.

   put   ~~take~~   come   meet   do   bring

School photography club!

Are you interested in ¹*taking* better photos? Then don't forget ² _____ to the new photography club. It's the place where you can enjoy ³ _____ something different. This week our theme is buildings and we want you ⁴ _____ some of your best photos to the club. We hope ⁵ _____ our favourite ones on display in the school library. We're looking forward to ⁶ _____ you!

6 In pairs, write an advert for a new club at your school. Compare your ideas with the class.

1.4 GRAMMAR Verb + *ing* / verb + *to*-infinitive

Lesson learning objective
The students can use verb constructions with *to*-infinitives and *-ing* forms.

Lead in: Review of characters
Write the names *Alisha* and *Tommo* on the board and tell students to copy these characters' names into their notebooks as two headings. Explain that you are going to dictate twelve facts about the characters and that they should write each fact under the correct name. There are six facts for each character.
When students have finished, they should compare their answers in pairs and then together as a class.
The twelve facts: half-Indian (Alisha), lives on a boat (Tommo), mother is a nurse (Tommo), has a younger brother (Alisha), speaks Hindi (Alisha), hasn't got any brothers or sisters (Tommo), has a cat (Tommo), is into computers (Alisha), is fit and strong (Alisha), likes kayaking (Tommo), loves drawing (Tommo), likes kickboxing (Alisha)

Exercise 1
Tell students to keep their Students' Books closed. Elicit different things that can go wrong with a computer or a smartphone, e.g. *it's very slow*, *it can't connect to the internet*, *it has a virus*, etc. Ask students which of these things they are able to fix on their own. Then ask the question in the rubric.

Exercise 2 1.3 1.23
Tell students to keep their Students' Books closed. Play the video and then ask the question in the rubric.
After students have given their ideas, tell them to open their Students' Books and to listen to the dialogue once more while they read the text. Ask students if they think this is a difficult problem to solve and encourage them to give their ideas about how to solve it.

Answer:
He's got a problem with his computer and Alisha is good at fixing things.

Exercise 3
Discuss the Grammar box with the class.
Discuss different verbs which can be followed by an *-ing* form or the *to*-infinitive. Remind students that *love*, *like* and *hate* are usually followed by *-ing* and it may be safer for them to use that structure as this is the form expected at this level in exams. Also explain that when *start* is in the continuous form, we don't follow it with *-ing* because it sounds strange to have two *-ing* forms together, e.g. *I am starting to enjoy myself* and not *I am starting enjoying myself*.

Answers:
Verb + *ing*: enjoy trying, prefer using, don't mind coming
Verb + *to*-infinitive: trying to finish, love to be outside, want to put, don't forget to bring

Exercise 4
When students have finished, ask follow-up questions, e.g. *Is there anything you hope to watch on TV tonight? Where do you enjoy meeting your friends? Which country would you like to visit? What food are you good at making? Do you miss seeing your friends from primary school?*

Answers: 1 to watch 2 meeting 3 to visit 4 making
5 seeing

Exercise 5
When students have finished, discuss the idea of after-school clubs and whether or not they are a good idea. Ask if any students go to after-school clubs and encourage them to describe what they do at the club. Invite students to suggest after-school clubs they would like their school to offer.

Answers: 2 to come 3 doing 4 to bring 5 to put
6 meeting

Exercise 6
Put students into pairs and tell them to decide on an after-school club they would both like their school to offer. Explain that in their adverts they should use at least one example each of a verb + *ing* and a verb + *to*-infinitive. When the pairs have finished, invite them to present their adverts to the class.

Extra activity for fast finishers
Write these sentence stems on the board.
1 *Do you like …?*
   It's OK, but I prefer …
2 *What do you want …?*
   Oh, I'd love …
3 *Do you enjoy …?*
   Yes, but I can't stand …
Put students into pairs and ask them to use the sentence stems to make short dialogues.
Invite pairs to perform their dialogues in front of the class.

Further practice
- Workbook page 10
- Grammar Time page 118
- Resource Pack
  Resource 4: Unit 1 Lesson 4 Grammar – I'm the same as you!
  Resource 5: Unit 1 Lesson 4 Video – It's upside down

1.5 LISTENING and VOCABULARY   Are you technology crazy?

Lesson learning objective
Students can identify specific detail in a radio programme and talk about using technology.

Lead in: Review of verb patterns
Tell students to work alone. Dictate some of these sentence stems.
I'm looking forward to …, I don't mind …, I am planning …, Last week I forgot …, I don't want …, I hate …, I would love …
Students should complete the sentences so that they are true for them. They must use a verb with an *-ing* form or a *to*-infinitive and not just a noun, e.g. *I'm looking forward to meeting my friends* not *I'm looking forward to the summer*.
When students have written their sentences, put them into pairs. Students take turns to read aloud one of their endings (without saying the sentence beginning) while their partner guesses the sentence beginning it matches with. Give them a time limit.
Then invite students to share some of their ideas with the rest of the class.

Exercise 1
Tell students to keep their Students' Books closed. Ask the question in the rubric and follow up by asking students how much time they think is too much. Talk about the idea of parents setting time limits and ask students if they think that a time limit is a good or a bad idea.

Exercise 2
Check that students understand the meaning of *break time*. Tell students to complete the quiz on their own. Then do the quiz as a class, saying each question and asking for a show of hands for each answer: a, b or c.

Exercise 3 🔊 1.24
When students have finished, discuss further time expressions that are used with *in*, *on* or *at*. For example:
in + months, seasons, years
on + day, with the time of day (e.g. *Sunday afternoon*), with special days (e.g. *New Year's Eve, my birthday, the first day of the holiday*), dates (e.g. *17 July*)
at + time (e.g. *seven o'clock*), a general holiday period (e.g. *Christmas, Easter*)

Answers: 10 p.m.; (in) the evening; (on) a weekday; (at) midnight; once

Exercise 4
When students have finished, ask them to write their answers in full sentences in their notebooks, e.g. *At the weekend, I go to bed at midnight. There are 300 seconds in five minutes. On schooldays, I get up at seven o'clock.*

Exercise 5 🔊 1.25
Before you play the audio, put students into pairs and tell them to look at the two answers. For each answer, they should think of something the presenter could say, e.g. *75 percent of families use phones or tablets in their free time.* and *Most families spend at least two hours a day on their phone or tablets.* Invite pairs to share their ideas with the class.

Answer: b

🔊 1.25
DJ: And hello from Gold Radio … A report today says that families are spending less time together because they're always on their phones or tablets. In the studio I've got Gemma … Now, you live with your mum and older brother. So, tell me, Gemma, is this true in your house?

Exercise 6 🔊 1.26
Before you play the audio, tell students to imagine that they are being asked the questions. Working in pairs, they should take turns to say if they think the sentences are true or false for them and their family. (They can ignore question 5 if they don't have a brother or answer it about a sister if applicable.)

Answers: 1 T   2 F   3 F   4 T   5 T   6 F

🔊 1.26
See page 247.

Exercise 7
Put students into pairs. Give the pairs four minutes (two minutes each) to take turns to talk about what the people in their families use technology for.
Students use their notes to write their sentences. This can also be done for homework.

Extra activity
Put students into groups of four or five. Each group should think of four or five more questions about using technology, similar to the questions in the quiz in Exercise 2. Each student in the group should write a question and three choices. When they have done this, the students ask each other their question and note the answers the other members of their group give. Then they mingle and ask the same question of as many other students in the class as possible, again noting the answers. When they have finished, they go back to their original groups and calculate the total number of a, b and c answers for each question. Ask the groups to report their results to the class.

Further practice
- Workbook page 11
- Resource Pack
  Resource 6: Unit 1 Lesson 5 Listening and Vocabulary – What do you do?

1.5 LISTENING and VOCABULARY — Are you technology crazy?

I can identify specific detail in a radio programme and talk about using technology.

1 **CLASS VOTE** Do you think you spend too much time on your phone or on the computer?

2 Is it time for time out? Do the quiz and compare your results with the class. Then go to page 144 to read what your answers say about you.

1 When do you first look at your phone or use the internet?
   a In the evening.
   b Probably at lunchtime.
   c The minute I wake up.
2 When is it too late to text somebody?
   a On a weekday, after 10 p.m.
   b At midnight.
   c It's never too late.
3 What do you do when you have a free moment?
   a I listen to music.
   b I read a book.
   c I go online.
4 How often do you check your text messages?
   a Once a day. I don't get many.
   b At school I check them at break time.
   c I check them all the time.

3 🔊 **1.24** Complete the gaps with words from the quiz. Listen and check.

Vocabulary	Time
second, *minute*, hour	
6 a.m., _____	
in the morning / the afternoon / _____	
on a schoolday/ _____ /Sunday(s)	
at the weekend/ _____ /mealtimes/lunchtime	
_____ /twice/three times a day / a week / a month / a year	

4 In pairs, ask and answer the questions. Compare your ideas with the class.
1 What's your favourite mealtime? Why?
   I love lunchtime because I eat with my friends.
2 What time do you go to bed at the weekend?
3 How many seconds are there in five minutes?
4 What time do you get up on a schoolday?
5 What do you normally do at break time?
6 What do you do the minute you wake up?

5 🔊 **1.25** Listen to the first part of a radio programme. What is the programme about? Choose the correct answer.
   a The number of families that use phones or tablets in their free time.
   b How much time families spend on their phones or tablets.

6 🔊 **1.26** Listen to the second part of the programme. Mark the sentences T (true) or F (false).
1 ☐ Everybody in Gemma's family has a smartphone.
2 ☐ First Gemma gets up and then she checks her messages.
3 ☐ Gemma's mum uses her smartphone to read the news.
4 ☐ A phone app helps Gemma's mum when she's running.
5 ☐ Sometimes Gemma's brother doesn't hear his mum's questions.
6 ☐ Gemma thinks they should talk more in her family.

7 **And YOU?** How important is technology in your life? What technology do you use and what do you like doing? Write five sentences.
Technology is very important to me. It's useful because I can go online and do my homework and I can chat with friends. In my free time I listen to lots of music …

Unit 1 15

1.6 SPEAKING Making suggestions

I can make and respond to suggestions.

VIDEO LET'S GO IN

Tommo: Hi, Alisha. Welcome to my canal boat. Let's go in.
Alisha: This is so cool! So, are you doing your poster?
Tommo: No, not now. I'm filming my cat for an online video. Like these.
Alisha: Aah! I love Ninja Cat! Your cat can be famous too.
Tommo: You could help me.
Alisha: OK, cool. Where's your cat? What's his name?
Tommo: *Her* name is Hissy. She's a girl.
Alisha: Oops, sorry! So, where is she?
Tommo: Er, I don't know. She usually hides from visitors.
Alisha: Why don't we look for her? Maybe she's behind the sofa.
Tommo: I can't see her. Oh yes, she's there, but she isn't coming out.
Alisha: What about putting some food down?
Tommo: Good idea. Dinner time, Hissy!
Alisha: Look! I can see her eyes. Shall we film her there?
Tommo: Yeah, why not? She looks funny.
Hissy: Hissssss!
Alisha: What's up? Oh, she doesn't like the camera.
Tommo: Hissy! Where are you going? Come back!
Alisha: Don't worry! You can call the video 'Cross Cat'!

*Good idea.   Come back.
This is so cool!*   **OUT of class**

1 CLASS VOTE Describe each cat. Which video would you like to watch?

Scary Cat   Ninja Cat   Wet Cat

2 1.4 1.27 Watch or listen and answer the questions.

1 What's Alisha's opinion of the canal boat?
2 What's Tommo doing?
3 How does Hissy react to visitors?
4 Where's Hissy hiding?

3 Study the Speaking box. Find more examples of suggestions in the dialogue.

Speaking	Suggestions

Making suggestions
You could look online.
Let's look for it.
What about texting her?
Why don't you charge it?
Shall we watch *Friends*?

Accepting or rejecting suggestions
Yes, great idea. / Yes, why not? / OK, cool.
I'm not sure. / I'd rather not.

4 1.28 Listen to six speakers and respond. Use the Speaking box to help you.

5 In pairs, follow the instructions.

Student A: choose a situation from the list.
Student B: respond with a suitable suggestion.

I need some information for my project.
The teacher's late.   I can't see the board.
It's really cold in here.   I can't swim.

6 In pairs, plan a funny video. Discuss what you want to film and where. Make suggestions and respond.

*a dog with a stick – in a park
my sister at dinnertime – at the table*

1.6 SPEAKING Making suggestions

Lesson learning objective
Students can make and respond to suggestions.

Lead in: Review of prepositions of time
Put students into groups of three. Give each group three pieces of paper. On one piece of paper they write *IN*, on another they write *AT* and on the third they write *ON*. They should write the prepositions so that they are big enough for you to see them at the front of the class. Tell students that you are going to say some time expressions and that they should hold up the correct preposition for each time expression. Explain that the first group to do this will win a point, but that if a group holds up more than one preposition then they will lose a point.

Time expressions: seven fifteen (*at*), the morning (*in*), night (*at*), the weekend (*at*), Sundays (*on*), weekdays (*on*), Sunday evenings (*on*), July (*in*), 1987 (*in*), midnight (*at*), the 17th of July (*on*).

Exercise 1
Before students open their Students' Books, have a class discussion about cat videos that they have watched online. Ask which cat video is their favourite and why.

Exercise 2 1.4 1.27
Review what happened in the last episode of the video. Ask questions to help students remember, e.g. *What problem did Tommo have?* (the photos on his poster were upside down) *Who is going to help him?* (Alisha) *Where are they going to meet?* (on his boat).
Before you play the video, tell students to read the questions and to try and guess the answers.

Answers:
1 She thinks it's cool.
2 He's filming his cat for an online video.
3 She usually hides from visitors.
4 Behind the sofa.

Exercise 3
When students have found examples of suggestions in the dialogue, tell them to look at the Speaking box once more. Elicit which would be a suitable suggestion to give in response to *I want to know what the weather will be like tomorrow* or *Where can I find a good computer shop near here?* (You could look online.)
Put students into pairs and tell them to do the same for the other suggestions in the Speaking box. Invite pairs to share their ideas with the class.

Answers:
Making suggestions:
Let's go in., You could help me., Why don't we look for her?, What about putting some food down?, Shall we film her there?, You can call the video 'Cross Cat'!
Accepting or rejecting suggestions:
OK, cool., Good idea., Yeah, why not?

Exercise 4 1.28
Play the audio once while students listen and think about what would be the best response. Then play the audio again and invite students to give a suggestion in response to each situation. More than one suggestion may be possible for each situation, so elicit alternative ideas.

Possible answers:
1 Why don't you charge it?
2 Let's look for it.
3 Shall we watch *Friends*?
4 You could look online.
5 What about texting her?
6 OK, cool.

1.28
1 My phone isn't working.
2 I can't find my pencil case.
3 What programme do you want to watch?
4 I can't answer this homework question.
5 My mum is late.
6 Let's go for a walk.

Exercise 5
Encourage stronger students to extend the activity by rejecting the first suggestion each time, meaning that the other student has to offer a second suggestion. For example:
A: I need some information for my project.
B: Why don't you look on the internet?
A: I can't. We haven't got wifi at home at the moment. There's something wrong with our connection.
B: You could bring your tablet to my house and use it there.
A: OK, cool. Thanks a lot.
Invite students to share their ideas with the class.

Exercise 6
Discuss the two examples with the students. Build up a possible conversation and write it on the board. For example:
A: Let's make a funny video.
B: OK, cool. Why don't we make a film of a dog with a stick in the park?
A: I'm not sure. We haven't got a dog! What about filming my sister at dinnertime at the table? She says some really funny things.
B: Good idea. Your mum's a great cook. I'd love to come round at dinnertime!
When the pairs have finished planning their videos, invite them to share their ideas with the class. Have a class vote to find out which video idea is the most popular.

Extra activity
Either during the lesson, if students have access to the internet, or at home, students should find a funny video online. Then they work in groups of three or four to tell one another about the video and why they liked it.
Invite the groups to tell the rest of the class about one of the videos they discussed.

Further practice
- Workbook page 12
- Resource Pack
  Resource 7: Unit 1 Lesson 6 Speaking – Why don't we …?
  Resource 8: Unit 1 Lesson 6 Video – Let's go in

1.7 WRITING A description of your dream lifestyle

Lesson learning objective
Students can describe places and lifestyles.

Lead in: Review of making suggestions

Elicit problems that people can have, e.g. *I'm tired, I'm lonely, I'm worried about my exams* and ask students to choose one. Encourage them to take turns telling each other their problem and responding with suggestions. Then invite individual students to say their problem and the best suggestion they received from their classmates.

Exercise 1
Before students open their Students' Books, elicit the names of as many different types of home as possible. Write these on the board and add items from Exercise 1.

Exercise 2
When students have found the answers, elicit examples of the things Skye wrote about, e.g. *sports – swimming, surfing; home – a terraced house, a beach hut*, etc.

Answers: sports 2   home 1   hobbies 2   friends 2   place 1   daily routine 2

Exercise 3
Tell students to use the same structure as in the example for each sentence.

Possible answers:
In her real life Skye lives in a terraced house, but in her dream lifestyle she lives in a beach hut.
In her real life she goes to Cherwell School on weekdays, but in her dream lifestyle she writes her novel on her laptop every morning.
In her real life she swims before school, but in her dream lifestyle she swims and goes surfing in the afternoon.
In her real life she probably doesn't have barbecues very often, but in her dream lifestyle she often has barbecues with her friends at the weekend.

Exercise 4
Tell students to use the same structure as in the example. Invite them to share their ideas with the class.

Exercise 5
Ask students to complete the Writing box.

Exercise 6
Adding similar detail:
- We use *also* either in a separate sentence or joined with *and* or *as well as*, e.g. *There's a huge TV. There is also a fast internet connection. / There's a huge TV and there is also a fast internet connection. / As well as a huge TV, there is also a fast internet connection.*
- We use *as well (as)* at the beginning of a sentence or in the middle of a sentence, e.g. *As well as a huge TV, there's a fast internet connection. / There's a huge TV as well as a fast internet connection.*
- We use *and* in the middle of a sentence, e.g. *I usually swim before school and I try to write at the weekend.*
- We use *too* at the end of the sentence, joined with *and* or *as well as*, e.g. *There's a huge TV and a fast internet connection, too. / As well as a huge TV, there's a fast internet connection, too.*

Showing contrast:
- We use *although* at the beginning of the sentence and separate the two clauses with a comma, e.g. *Although it's small, outside there's a veranda.*
- We use *but* between two contrasting clauses, e.g. *I live in a terraced house, but my dream home is a beach hut in Bali.*
- We use *however* in a new sentence between two sentences, e.g. *In real life I try to write at the weekend. However, in my dream lifestyle, I sit outside and write my novel every morning.*

Giving reasons:
- *In case* means 'because something might happen', e.g. *There's a fast internet connection in case I want to share videos with friends.*
- *So* gives the result of an action or state, whereas *because* gives the reason for an action or state, e.g. *There's a veranda so I have a perfect view of the sea. I have a perfect view of the sea because there's a veranda.*

Answers:
Adding similar detail: as well (as), and, too
Showing contrast: but, however
Giving reasons: so, because

Exercise 7
Tell students that for each sentence they should decide whether they are adding similar detail, showing contrast or giving reasons. Also remind them to look closely at the sentence structure.

Answers: 1 As well as, too   2 However   3 Although   4 so

Exercise 8
Tell students to look once more at Skye's text in Exercise 2. Ask how much of the first sentence they think they could use in a text about their own dream lifestyle. Write on the board: *In my everyday life, I live with my … in a … near (in)… .* Tell students that, when writing their own texts, they should try to use the sentence structures and development of ideas from Skye's text where possible but change the details to make the text true for themselves. Encourage students to look online to find a photo that illustrates their idea of a dream home.

Homework
Ask students to read the text on page 20 of the Students' Book. They should look up any words they don't know and translate them into L1. As an additional task, ask students to write example sentences for these words: *device, distraction, law, minority, remove, productive, resource*.

Further practice
- Workbook page 13
- Resource Pack
  Resource 9: Unit 1 Lesson 7 Writing – My dream

1.7 WRITING A description of your dream lifestyle

I can describe places and lifestyles.

1 CLASS VOTE Which of these would be your dream home?

- a modern caravan
- a castle in Scotland
- a beach hut on an exotic island
- a terraced house in a small town
- a massive skyscraper   a villa in Spain
- a cottage in the mountains
- a flat in a block of flats

2 Read the text. Which of the things below does Skye write about in paragraph 1? Which are in paragraph 2?

sports 2   home ___   hobbies ___
friends ___   place ___   daily routine ___

3 In pairs, find four differences between Skye's real life and her dream lifestyle.

In her real life Skye lives near Oxford, but in her dream lifestyle she lives in Bali.

4 How is your dream lifestyle similar or different to Skye's?

Skye's dream lifestyle is a beach hut in Bali, but I'd like to live in a villa in Spain.

5 Complete the sentences to make them true for you.

Writing A description of your dream lifestyle

Real home and dream home
I live in _____ . / My home is in _____ .
My dream home is a _____ in _____ .
It's near a beach / a cliff / _____ .
It has got _____ .
Outside/Inside there is/are _____ .
I have a view of _____ .

Daily life and dream life
In real life I go to _____ school.
I usually/often/sometimes/never _____ .
I _____ on weekdays / at the weekend.
In my dream lifestyle, I often _____ in the morning.

6 Complete the gaps with connectors from the text, matching the connectors with their function.

Adding similar detail: *also*, _____ , _____ , _____
Showing contrast: *although*, _____ , _____
Giving reasons: *in case*, _____ , _____

7 Complete the sentences with connectors from Exercise 6.

1 _____ playing the violin, I have singing lessons _____ .
2 My dream home is small. _____ , it's perfect for me!
3 _____ I love dancing, I'm not very good at it.
4 I want to live near the sea _____ I can swim every day.

My Dream Lifestyle
by Skye Winter-Fox

In my everyday life, I live in a terraced house near Oxford with my grandma, because my parents are in New Zealand. But my dream home is a beach hut in Bali. The beach hut has got one bedroom and a living room. As well as a huge touch screen TV, there's a fast internet connection in case I want to share videos with friends! Although it's small, outside there's a veranda so I have a perfect view of the sea.

In real life I go to Cherwell School on weekdays. I usually swim before school and I try to write at the weekend. However, in my dream lifestyle, I sit outside and write my novel on my laptop every morning. Then in the afternoon I swim and go surfing, too. Friends often visit me at the weekend and we have amazing barbecues on the beach.

Writing Time

8 Write a description of your dream lifestyle for a school magazine. Follow the instructions below.

Paragraph 1: Real home and dream home
Paragraph 2: Daily life and dream life
TIP
Use the Present Simple and adverbs of frequency.

Unit 1   17

Wordlist and Vocabulary in action

Extra activity

Put students into pairs and tell them to look at the phrases in the second Word friends section (describing objects). Students take turns to think of an object, e.g. a battery charger, and, without saying what it is, describe it using two of the phrases from the wordlist, e.g. *It's made of plastic. It looks like a small box.* Their partner guesses the object, e.g. *Is it your smartphone? No. Is it a battery charger? Yes.*

Further practice

Workbook page 14

WORDLIST Everyday technology | Adjectives of opinion | Time

alarm /əˈlɑːm/
all right /ˌɔːl ˈraɪt/
amazing /əˈmeɪzɪŋ/
at mealtimes, /ət ˈmiːltaɪmz /
at break time ət ˈbreɪk taɪm/
at midday/midnight /ət ˌmɪdˈdeɪ ˈmɪdnaɪt/
at the weekend /ət ðə ˌwiːkˈend/
awesome /ˈɔːsəm/
awful /ˈɔːfl/
band /bænd/
barbecue /ˈbɑːbɪkjuː/
battery /ˈbætri/
beach hut /ˈbiːtʃ hʌt/
block of flats /blɒk əv ˈflæts/
blog /blɒg/
boring /ˈbɔːrɪŋ/
bungalow /ˈbʌŋgələʊ/
cable /ˈkeɪbl/
caravan /ˈkærəvæn/
castle /ˈkɑːsl/
charge /tʃɑːdʒ/
charger /ˈtʃɑːdʒə/
clever /ˈklevə/
competition /ˌkɒmpəˈtɪʃn/
cool /kuːl/
cottage /ˈkɒtɪdʒ/
cross /krɒs/
dead (battery) /ˌded ˈbætəri/
digital camera /ˌdɪdʒətl ˈkæmərə/
disgusting /dɪsˈgʌstɪŋ/
(dream) lifestyle /ˌdriːm ˈlaɪfstaɪl/
earphones /ˈɪəfəʊnz/
event /ɪˈvent/
exciting /ɪkˈsaɪtɪŋ/
fix /fɪks/
fun /fʌn/
funny /ˈfʌni/
gadget /ˈgædʒɪt/
heavy /ˈhevi/

helmet /ˈhelmɪt/
in the morning/afternoon/evening /ɪn ðə ˈmɔːnɪŋ/ɑːftəˈnuːn/ˈiːvnɪŋ/
internet connection /ˈɪntənet kəˌnekʃn/
lovely /ˈlʌvli/
nice /naɪs/
noisy /ˈnɔɪzi/
novel /ˈnɒvl/
old-fashioned /ˌəʊld ˈfæʃnd/
on a schoolday/a weekday/ Sunday(s) /ɒn ə ˈskuːldeɪ/ə ˈwiːkdeɪ/ ˈsʌndeɪ(z)/
once/twice/three times a day/ˌwʌns/ ˌtwaɪs/θriː ˌtaɪmz ə ˈdeɪ/
perfect /ˈpɜːfɪkt/
perform /pəˈfɔːm/
(phone) app /ˈfəʊn æp/
photographers /fəˈtɒgrəfəz/
photography /fəˈtɒgrəfi/
plug /plʌg/
poster /ˈpəʊstə/
report /rɪˈpɔːt/
reporter /rɪˈpɔːtə/
second /ˈsekənd/
selfie stick /ˈselfi stɪk/
skate park /ˈskeɪt pɑːk/
skateboarders /ˈskeɪtˌbɔːdəz/
skyscraper /ˈskaɪˌskreɪpə/
smartphone /ˈsmɑːtfəʊn/
sofa /ˈsəʊfə/
space /speɪs/
speaker /ˈspiːkə/
strange /streɪndʒ/
tablet /ˈtæblət/
take photos /ˌteɪk ˈfəʊtəʊz/
technology /tekˈnɒlədʒi/
terraced house /ˌterəst ˈhaʊs/
terrible /ˈterəbl/
test /test/

tester /ˈtestə/
top /tɒp/
touch screen TV / ˈtʌtʃ skriːn ˌtiː ˌviː/
trick /trɪk/
ugly /ˈʌgli/
unusual /ʌnˈjuːʒuəl/
upside down /ˌʌpsaɪd ˈdaʊn/
useful /ˈjuːsfl/
veranda /vəˈrændə/
view /vjuː/
villa /ˈvɪlə/

WORD FRIENDS

using gadgets
chat with friends
download songs
go online
listen to music
make/film a video
play games
read e-books
send/get instant messages
share photos
text friends/parents
upload pictures
watch music videos

describing objects
it's made of metal/wood/plastic/ cotton/paper
it's like a/an (+ noun)
it looks (+ adjective)
it looks like a/an (+ noun)
it works like a/an (+ noun)
you can (+ verb)
you can use it like a (noun)
you can use it to (+ infinitive) / for (+ –ing)

VOCABULARY IN ACTION

1 Use the wordlist to find:
  1 three people
  2 three types of houses
  3 three positive adjectives
  4 three types of materials
  5 three gadgets

2 Use the wordlist to find adjectives that describe:
  • the town you live in *exciting*
  • your school
  • your favourite band
  • your school bag
  • your phone or computer

3 Use the wordlist to complete the sentences. In pairs, tell your partner if the sentences are true for you.
  1 I always *listen* to music on my phone when I walk to school.
  2 I relax when I ____ games on the computer.
  3 I like to sing along when I ____ music videos.
  4 My friends usually ____ me instant messages.
  5 I always ____ my parents when I'm late.
  6 I only ____ online when I don't have any homework.

4 🔊 **1.29** **PRONUNCIATION** Listen and decide how s is pronounced in each word. Write the word in the correct column.

earphones e-books gadgets helmets hours
novels photos plugs reporters tablets tricks

/s/   /z/
e-books   plugs

When do you pronounce /s/ and /z/?

Exercise 3

2 play
3 watch
4 send
5 text
6 go

Exercise 4

/s/: gadgets, helmets, tablets, tricks
/z/: earphones, hours, novels, photos, plugs, reporters
The plural ending s in nouns is pronounced /z/ if the preceding sound is a vowel, a voiced consonant or an /l/, /m/, /n/, /ŋ/, /r/, /w/ or /j/ sound. The s is pronounced /s/ if the preceding sound is a devoiced consonant.

 Wordlist

Exercise 1
Possible answers:
1 photographers, reporter, skateboarders, friends, parents
2 beach hut, block of flats, bungalow, caravan, castle, cottage, skyscraper, terraced house, villa
3 amazing, awesome, clever, cool, exciting, funny, lovely, nice, perfect, useful
4 metal, wood, plastic, cotton, paper
5 charger, digital camera, earphones, selfie stick, smartphone, speaker, tablet, touch screen TV, e-book

Revision

Extra activity
Extend Exercise 3 by asking students to write sentences about the similarities and differences between them and their partner, e.g. *We both use our phones in the evenings. Sara texts her friends before school but I don't.*

Further practice
- Workbook page 15
- Resource Pack
  Resource 10: Unit 1 Vocabulary – Find the words
  Resource 11: Unit 1 Grammar – How about you?

Revision

VOCABULARY

1 Write the correct word for each definition.
1. You put these in your ears to listen to music. **e**_____
2. If you use a skateboard, you wear this on your head. **h**_____
3. This means the opposite of brilliant. **t**_____
4. A small house in the country. **c**_____
5. You put this inside a gadget to give it energy. **b**_____
6. Sixty seconds. **m**_____

Exercise 1
1. earphones
2. helmet
3. terrible
4. cottage
5. battery
6. minute

2 Complete the quiz with one of the expressions. In pairs, ask and answer the questions.

in the evening   at the weekend   twice a day
at mealtimes   on a schoolday   at midnight

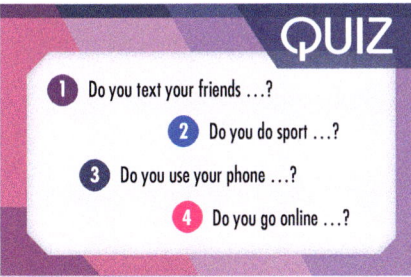

QUIZ
1. Do you text your friends …?
2. Do you do sport …?
3. Do you use your phone …?
4. Do you go online …?

A: *Do you text your friends at mealtimes?*
B: *I never text my friends at mealtimes.*

3 Tell the class about your partner.

GRAMMAR

4 Complete the sentences with the correct form of the verbs in brackets, then match them with the correct function, A, B or C.

A an action in progress
B a regular action
C a state verb

1. Carla _____ (read) an e-book now.
2. My grandparents _____ (usually/phone) us at the weekend.
3. Jake _____ (not/like) music videos.
4. We _____ (not/often/download) songs.
5. I _____ (know) how to upload photos.
6. Why _____ (you/chat) with friends now? It's very late.

Exercise 4
1. is reading, A
2. usually phone, B
3. doesn't like, C
4. don't often download, B
5. know, C
6. are you chatting, A

5 Complete the questions with the correct form of the verbs in brackets.
1. Are you planning *to go* (go) online later?
2. Are you good at _____ (fix) things?
3. Do you prefer _____ (live) in a village or a town?
4. Do you want _____ (make) a video of your school?
5. Are you looking forward to _____ (see) your little brother?

Exercise 5
2. fixing
3. living
4. to make
5. seeing

SPEAKING

6 Complete the dialogue with the words below.

about   shall   idea   rather
could   sure   don't   let's

A: ¹*Shall* we go to the cinema?
B: No, I'd ² _____ not. What's on TV tonight?
A: Er, not much … Why ³ _____ we watch *The Simpsons*?
B: I'm not ⁴ _____ . What time does it start?
A: 7.30 p.m. … Oh, it's 8 p.m. now.
B: What ⁵ _____ watching football on Channel 3? It starts at 8.
A: Mmm, I don't really like football. I know, ⁶ _____ watch a film online!
B: Yes, great ⁷ _____ . We ⁸ _____ watch *Despicable Me 3*.

Exercise 6
2. rather
3. don't
4. sure
5. about
6. let's
7. idea
8. could

7 In pairs, decide what to watch together. Use the TV guide to help you.

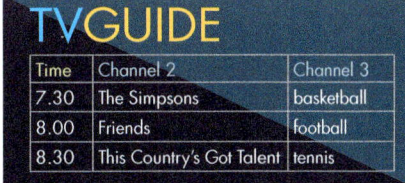

TV GUIDE

Time	Channel 2	Channel 3
7.30	The Simpsons	basketball
8.00	Friends	football
8.30	This Country's Got Talent	tennis

DICTATION

8 🔊 **1.30** Listen, then listen again and write down what you hear.

SELF-ASSESSMENT Think about this unit. What did you learn? What do you need help with?

WORKBOOK p. 14

Exercise 8
We're travelling around Spain in our caravan at the moment. I'm making a video of our trip. We use our caravan every summer. It's old-fashioned and it's got awful plastic chairs, but it's my dream home!

Do smartphones make you smarter?

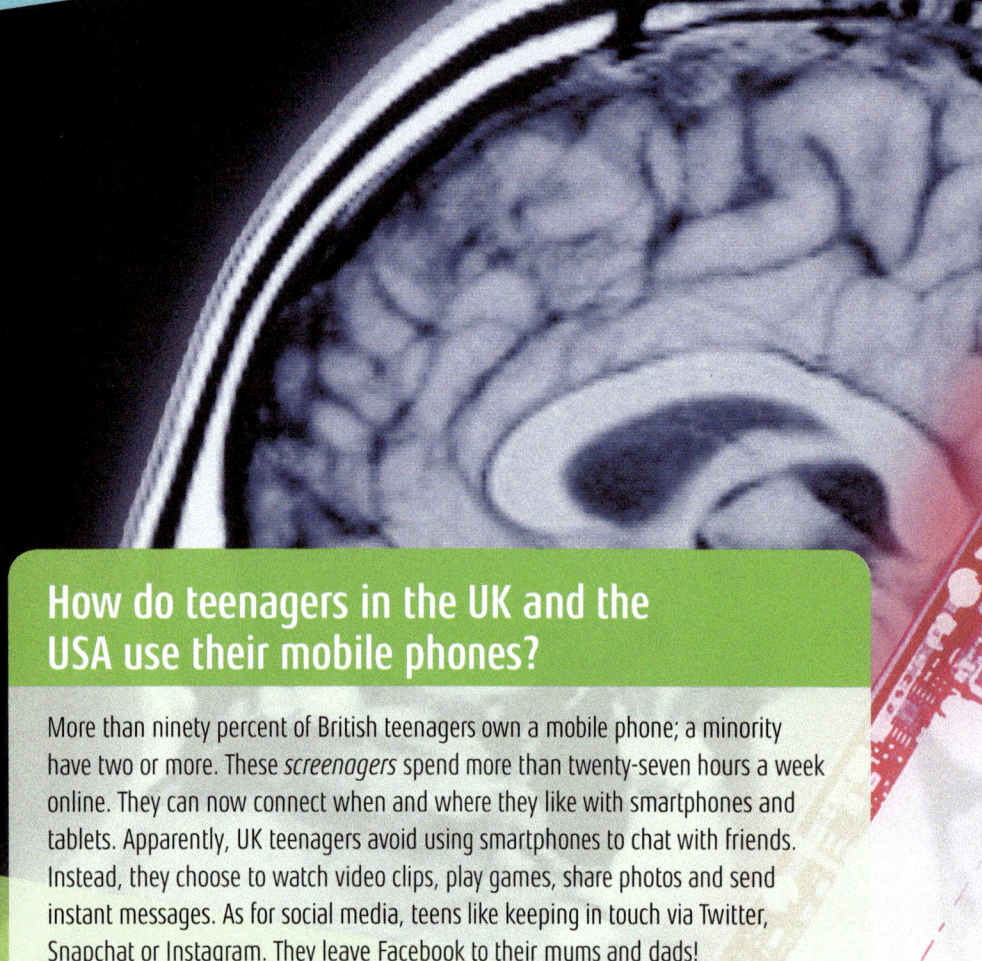

How do teenagers in the UK and the USA use their mobile phones?

More than ninety percent of British teenagers own a mobile phone; a minority have two or more. These *screenagers* spend more than twenty-seven hours a week online. They can now connect when and where they like with smartphones and tablets. Apparently, UK teenagers avoid using smartphones to chat with friends. Instead, they choose to watch video clips, play games, share photos and send instant messages. As for social media, teens like keeping in touch via Twitter, Snapchat or Instagram. They leave Facebook to their mums and dads!

Teenagers may be connected all the time, but there is one place where most teenagers can't use their digital devices: school! In the UK there is no law about phone use in schools, but teachers can remove devices from students if necessary. However, not all teachers agree and some even try to use smartphones in class.

A recent British report said that removing smartphones from schools will give students more time for their education. It said that smartphones are a big distraction, make students less productive and are bad for learning.

However, in the USA some people do not agree. Recently one school in New York decided to allow students to use smartphones at school. They said that smartphones can be an excellent resource for the classroom. We carry a lot of information in our pockets and this information can be really useful. In this New York school, smartphones can definitely make you smarter!

GLOSSARY
device (n) a machine or tool
distraction (n) something that takes your attention away from what you are doing
law (n) a system or rules
minority (n) a small part of a larger group
remove (v) take away

BBC CULTURE Do smartphones make you smarter?

Lead in: Topic introduction

Tell students not to open their Students' Books. Put students into groups of four. If you set the homework suggestion for the unit, ask the groups to discuss any vocabulary they found difficult and their example sentences if you also set the additional task.

If students haven't done the homework, ask them to look at the glossary on page 20. Students should find the words in the text and discuss what they mean in context, e.g. *Two examples of digital **devices** are smartphones and tablets.*

1.5

Addicted to screens

Part 1

How long do you spend online every day? Is this increasing at the moment? And when you're online, what do you do there – chat with friends, listen to music, watch videos, play games, send messages? Can you do them all at the same time? The internet is transforming our society, too. It has a huge impact on culture, politics and business.

Now there are 'screenagers' who live most of their lives in the virtual world. Some people spend more time online than with their families!

And this is the country where people are connected more than anywhere else in the world: South Korea. Here you can access the internet very easily, and it's really fast. You can download files ten times quicker here than in most countries in the world. Even young children of three to five years old use the internet and spend eight hours a week online.

Then there are teenagers using the internet for eighteen hours a day. Experts say that if you take away the internet from these teens, they start to feel anxious and unhappy. So, is Korea creating a nation of screen addicts? And will your country be like this in just two or three years' time?

1.6

Part 2

But is internet addiction a bad thing? Think for a moment about the information that you receive on screens. It's certainly not like reading a book. Now we receive information via connections or hyperlinks. We just click on the link or touch the screen and something new appears.

And what about the videos of pets you watch on YouTube? You think it's funny or superficial, but this is part of a big online conversation. You can watch the angry cat and then create your own clip or meme with a different cat. Sharing these photos and videos is more important than the content itself. It allows us to communicate with people in a more creative way.

So, do smartphones make us smarter or less smart? Let's return to Korea for an answer. There's good news: Korea is the most connected country in the world, but it is also number one for education. It is regularly top of the world's education league tables.

The reason may be that from an early age, Korean children are proficient at working together on the internet to solve problems.

Exercise 1

When students have discussed the questions in the exercise in pairs, have a class discussion and ask students how they think smartphones could make people smarter.

Exercise 2

Get students to work in pairs. They should write the correct sentences in full in their notebooks.

Possible answers:
1 Not all UK teachers believe smartphones are bad for students.
2 A recent UK report said that removing smartphones from schools would give students more time for their education and that phones are bad for learning.
3 One school in New York has different ideas about smart phone use in school.

Exercise 3 1.5

Before students watch Part 1 of the video, tell them to read the questions. Discuss the answer to the first question and then ask students to guess the answer to the second question. After students have watched the video, put them into pairs to discuss the third question and then invite pairs to share their ideas with the class.

Answers:
1 South Korea
2 People in South Korea are connected to the internet more than anywhere else in the world.
3 Students' own answers

Exercise 4 1.5

Students should work in pairs to guess which numbers fit in each sentence. Elicit ideas but don't tell students if their answers are correct or not. Explain that the information shown in the video may be expressed slightly differently to the numbers in the box.

Answers: 2 four, eight   3 eighteen   4 a couple of

Exercise 5

Put students into groups of three to discuss the questions. Then invite the groups to share their ideas with the class.

Extra activity

Put students into pairs. Tell them to imagine that one of them is a reporter and the other is a Korean teenager who uses the internet eighteen hours a day. The pairs should prepare some questions and answers and then role play the interview in front of the class.

Exercise 6 1.6

Before students watch Part 2 of the video, discuss the three photos with the class. Ask students to describe what they can see in the photos and to explain what aspect of the internet they represent. Tell them to guess which sentence matches which picture before they watch the video to check their ideas.

Answers: 1 D   2 B   3 C

Exercise 7 1.6

In pairs, students should read the sentences and discuss the correct answers before they watch the video once more.

Answers: 1 receive   2 clip   3 connected   4 top

Exercise 8

Ask students to decide if the report is in favour or against the use of the internet and to make a list of the arguments given in the video to support this opinion. Encourage pairs to share their ideas with another pair and then invite groups of four to report back to the class.

Answers: in favour

Exercise 9

Explain to students that, when supporting one side of an argument, it is important to anticipate what people with the opposite viewpoint might say. Encourage them to consider one or two reasons against their own opinion and to find ways in which they can show that they don't think these reasons are correct. For example, if they are arguing that smartphones make people smarter, they could say: *Some people claim that smartphones make us lazy and unable to work things out for ourselves. However, there have always been ways of looking up information – in books, with a calculator, on a map. Smartphones just make it easier for us to look things up than in the past.*

Further practice

- Workbook pages 16–17
- Resource Pack
  Resource 12: Unit 1 BBC Culture Lesson – Smartphones at school
  Resource 13: Unit 1 Culture – Two schools

EXPLORE

1 In pairs, ask and answer the questions.
1. What do you do with your phone?
2. Do you think it makes you smarter or less smart? Why?
3. Do many people have smartphones in your country?

2 Correct the sentences about the article.
1. All UK teachers believe smartphones are bad for students.
2. A recent UK report said that using smartphones in school can be positive.
3. All schools in the USA and the UK have similar ideas about smartphone use in schools.

EXPLORE MORE

A

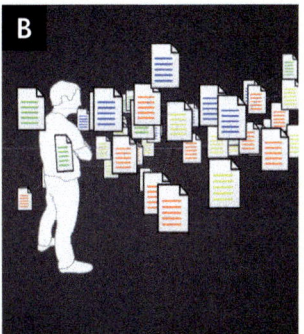
B

C

D

3 ▶ 1.5 Watch Part 1 of the video and answer the questions.
1. What country can you see in photo A?
2. Why is this country so important in the video?
3. How similar is your country to the one in the report?

4 ▶ 1.5 Complete the sentences about Korea with the numbers below. Then watch again and check.

eight   a couple of   ~~ten~~   eighteen   four

1. You can download files *ten* times faster here.
2. Even _____-year-olds spend _____ hours a week online.
3. Some teenagers use the internet for _____ hours a day.
4. Will your country be like this in _____ years from now?

5 What do you think about the issue of internet addiction in Korea? Do you think the same thing could happen in your country in the future?

6 ▶ 1.6 Watch Part 2 of the video. Match photos B–D with captions 1–3.
1. ☐ Students can interact online to solve problems.
2. ☐ Reading online is not like reading a book.
3. ☐ This is part of a big online conversation.

7 ▶ 1.6 Watch again. Choose the correct option.
1. Now we *send* / *receive* information via connections or hyperlinks.
2. You can watch the angry cat and then create your own *clip* / *text*.
3. Korea is the most *addicted* / *connected* country in the world.
4. They are regularly at the *top* / *bottom* of the world's education league tables.

8 Do you think the report is in favour or against the use of the internet? Why? Discuss in pairs.

YOU EXPLORE

9 **CULTURE PROJECT** In groups, prepare a debate based on the question: 'Do smartphones make you smarter?'
1. Prepare a list of points to support your argument.
2. Present your argument to the class.
3. What was the most common point of view among your classmates?

Unit 1 21

2

Wild nature

VOCABULARY
Weather | Temperature |
Natural disasters | In the wild

GRAMMAR
Past Simple: regular and irregular verbs
| Past Simple and Past Continuous |
Adverbs and indefinite pronouns

Grammar: What were you doing while you were away?

Speaking: Why did you do that?

BBC Culture: Severe weather

Workbook p. 28

BBC VOX POPS

2.1 **VOCABULARY**   Weather and natural disasters

I can talk about the weather and natural disasters.

1 **CLASS VOTE** What's your favourite season? Why? Compare your ideas.

I like autumn because the trees are different colours.

2 🔊 **1.31** Fill in the table with the correct words. Listen and check.

Vocabulary A	Weather	
	Noun	Adjective
🌧	rain	rainy
❄		
☀		
🚗💨		
☁		
🌬🌳		
❄❄		
⛈		

snow cloud fog wind ice storm sunny foggy cloudy sun icy stormy windy snowy

Watch OUT!

To describe the weather, we use *It's* + adjective:
It's rainy/foggy/windy.
We can use the Present Continuous:
It's raining/snowing. The sun is shining.
When the weather is beginning to change, we use *get* + adjective:
It's getting sunny/foggy/windy/cloudy.

3 In pairs, describe two photos from the website.

In photo 1 it's very windy and in photo 2 it's cold and there's snow on the ground.

Unit contents

Vocabulary
- Weather
- Temperature
- Natural disasters
- In the wild

Grammar
- Past Simple: regular and irregular verbs
- Past Simple and Past Continuous
- Adverbs and indefinite pronouns

Communication skills
- Criticising

Examples of 21st Century Skills/Competencies
- Critical Thinking: page 22 (Exercise 2), pages 32–33
- Collaboration: page 23 (Exercise 8), page 27 (Exercise 7), page 33 (Exercise 10)
- Digital Literacy: page 33 (Exercise 10)
- Assessment for Learning: page 31
- Autonomy and Personal Initiative: page 25 (Exercise 8)

2.1 VOCABULARY Weather and natural disasters

Lesson learning objective
Students can talk about the weather and natural disasters.

Lead in: Review of vocabulary and grammar from the previous unit

Invite a student to come to the front of the class and give them a piece of paper. Explain that you are going to dictate a sentence with a word or a short phrase missing. The student should write the sentence and choose which word or phrase they want to insert in the gap. Encourage the class to guess the student's word or phrase. When a student guesses correctly, they have a turn to come to the front of the class and the process is repeated with a second sentence.

Suggestions for sentences:
My favourite gadget is my BLANK.
I never eat BLANK. It's disgusting.
I love BLANK. They're brilliant.
I BLANK once a week.
I'm BLANK at the moment.
My BLANK looks cool.
I can't stand BLANK.
I like playing football but I prefer BLANK.
I often BLANK at the weekend.
My dream home is a BLANK.

Background notes

The word *fall* for *autumn* is commonly thought to be American English. In fact, both *autumn* and *fall* originate from England. Chaucer and Shakespeare both used the word *autumn* in their writing and the phrase *'fall of the leaf'* was also popular at that time. When people started to emigrate to America, the word *fall* went with them, while in England the word *fall* became less popular and *autumn* became the more frequently used word for the season.

Exercise 1

Tell students to keep their Students' Books closed. Elicit the names of the four seasons. Ask what Americans call autumn and why (*it is called* fall *because this is the season when the leaves fall from the trees*). Carry out the class vote while students still have their Students' Books closed.

Exercise 2 🔊 1.31

When students have finished, discuss the information in the Watch Out box with the class. Point out that other verbs used in the Present Continuous include *rain/snow is **falling**, the wind is **blowing*** and *it is **clouding*** over (becoming more cloudy).

Answers:

	Noun	Adjective
❄	snow	snowy
☀	sun	sunny
🌫	fog	foggy
☁	cloud	cloudy
🌬	wind	windy
🧊	ice	icy
⛈	storm	stormy

Exercise 3

When the pairs have finished, encourage the class to discuss the photos in more detail, e.g. *Photo 1 looks like a desert. The wind is blowing the sand.*

45

Exercise 4

Look at Fact A with the class. Elicit the correct choices, giving reasons (*sunny – adjective; stormy weather – adjective + noun; snow – noun*) and which photo it is describing (*photo 3 – there is a camel and camels live in the desert but there is also snow*). Students do the same for the rest of the text.

Answers: **4** rain **5** wind **6** sun **7** windy **8** snow **9** cloud **10** ice **11** foggy **12** rainy **13** rain
Photo 1 – C; Photo 2 – D; Photo 3 – A; Photo 4 – E; Photo 5 – H

Exercise 5 🔊 1.32

When students have finished, put them into pairs and tell them to write sentences using three of the words in the exercise. When they have finished, invite pairs to share their sentences with the class, e.g. *We went to Spain last summer and it was **boiling**, so we spent the whole time in the sea. It's quite **chilly** today, so I'm wearing a sweater. Last night the temperature fell to **minus** five and all our plants died.*

Answers: **1** boiling (hot) **2** cool **3** chilly **4** freezing (cold) **5** degrees **6** minus

Exercise 6 🔊 1.33

Put students into pairs. Tell them that for each city, they should listen for the temperature, adjectives to describe the temperature from Exercise 5 and weather vocabulary from Exercise 2.

When you play the audio for the first time, students should listen without writing anything. Then they should try to complete the exercise with their partner.

Play the audio a third time so that the pairs can check their ideas and add any words they missed.

Answers:
New York: cold, −2°, ice/icy
Rio de Janeiro: warm, sunny, 27°, rain
Krakow: cloudy, fog/foggy, 5°, cool

🔊 1.33

And now let's looks at the weather around the world.
In New York it's a very cold day with a temperature of minus 2 degrees. There is some ice on the roads so be careful.
And it's a good time for carnival in Rio de Janeiro, which is very warm and sunny at the moment. The temperature is a comfortable 27 degrees, but there is the possibility of some rain.
And finally, Krakow in Poland is very cloudy today, with some fog that is causing a few problems at the airport. The temperature is around 5 degrees at the moment. This evening it could be cool, so don't forget to keep warm. And that's all from us until …

Exercise 7 🔊 1.34

When they have listened to the audio, go through the meaning of each word and elicit L1 translations if possible. Discuss any examples of natural disasters that students have heard of.

Answers: **1** flood **2** avalanche **3** drought **4** earthquake **5** tsunami **6** hurricane

Exercise 8

Choose one of the words in the Vocabulary C box that doesn't affect the students' own country, e.g. tsunami. Elicit how the phrases in the And You box could refer to a tsunami in some way, e.g. *During a tsunami you shouldn't **stay indoors** if your house is close to the sea. It won't protect you. The waves will break the house's windows and flood the house completely. You need to **go outside** and find higher ground away from the coast. Waves can knock down trees (**trees fall down**) and buildings and flood the coastal area.* When students have finished their discussions, invite pairs to share their ideas with the class.

Extra activity

Students work in pairs. Tell Student A to choose a place in the world and time of year (e.g. Australia, January) and descibe the clothes they are wearing. Student B tries to guess what the weather is like based on what Student A is wearing and then the place and time of the year. Students swap roles.

Further practice

- Workbook pages 18–19
- Resource Pack
  Resource 14: Unit 2 Lesson 1 Vocabulary – What's the weather like in …?

DID YOU KNOW … ?

A It isn't always hot and ¹*sunny / sun* in the desert! In January 2015, because of ²*stormy / stormy weather*, there was enough ³*snow / snowing* to build a snowman.

B Less than 1mm of ⁴*rain / raining* falls every year in Arica, in Chile. It would take 100 years to fill a coffee cup.

C The 'zonda' ⁵*windy / wind* in Argentina is a dry wind that often carries dust over the mountains. When it happens, it makes the ⁶*sunny / sun* look brown.

D When it's very ⁷*wind / windy* in hilly places, ⁸*snowy / snow* can move along the ground and make a snowroller.

E A moustache ⁹*cloud / cloudy* forms when a cloud passes over a column of air. But be quick if you want a photo, it doesn't happen very often!

F It's so cold in the Antarctic that in some places the ¹⁰*icy / ice* is more than 4,000 metres thick.

G The Grand Banks are shallow areas of water on the coast of Newfoundland, Canada. They have more than 200 ¹¹*foggy / fog* days every year.

H It can be very ¹²*rain / rainy* in Kerala, India, but in 2001 the ¹³*rain / raining* was red because it was carrying sand from the desert. Strange, isn't it?

4 Read the text. Choose the correct option. Which facts are shown in the photos?

5 🔊 **1.32** Complete gaps 1–6 with the words below. Listen and check.

> boiling (hot)   cool   chilly   degrees
> freezing (cold)   minus

Vocabulary B	Temperature

1 _____
hot
warm
mild
2 _____
cold
3 _____
4 _____
It's 35 ⁵ _____ .
It's ⁶ _____ 10 today.

We can say: *It's boiling hot* or *It's boiling*,
It's freezing cold or *It's freezing*.

6 🔊 **1.33** Listen to three weather forecasts and complete the gaps below.

New York _____
Rio de Janeiro _____
Krakow _____

7 🔊 **1.34** Match the sentences with the words from the Vocabulary C box. Listen and check.

Vocabulary C	Natural disasters

> avalanche   drought   earthquake   flood
> hurricane   tsunami

1 The water is going into the houses. People are moving upstairs. _____
2 There's a lot of snow and it's coming down the mountain very quickly. _____
3 People are hungry. They can't grow plants because the ground is dry and hard. _____
4 The building is shaking. _____
5 The beach is empty. People are going into the mountains before the wave arrives. _____
6 It's very windy and it's raining. Everybody is inside and the doors and windows are closed. _____

8 In pairs, choose one of the words from the Vocabulary C box. Describe the problems they can cause in your country.

> go outside   grow food   stay indoors
> trees fall down   water leaves a (place)
> windows break

2.2 GRAMMAR Past Simple: regular and irregular verbs

I can use regular and irregular verbs to talk about the past.

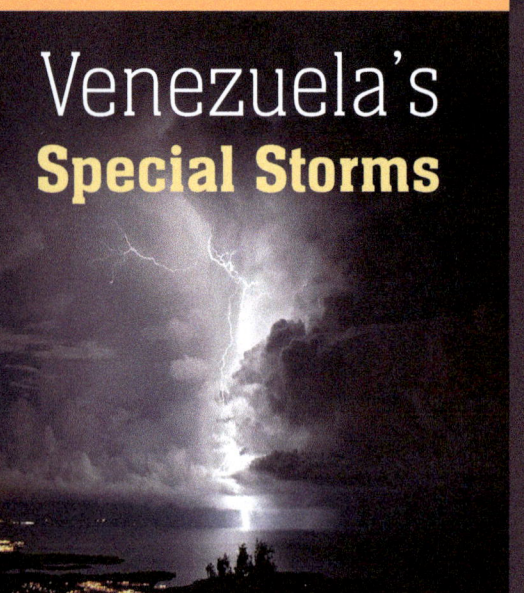

Venezuela's Special Storms

You might find storms fascinating or frightening. But can they be positive? If you live in Venezuela, your answer may be: yes! In 1595 a storm in Venezuela **saved** the country. How **did** that **happen**? Foreign sailors **wanted** to attack but they **saw** strange lightning. It **looked** pinkish-orange, so they **didn't know** what it was. They **felt** scared. In the bright light of the storm, soldiers on land **spotted** the ships.

This **took place** over Lake Maracaibo on the Catatumbo River. It is an area famous for its special storms. Long ago, sailors **used** a storm in the same way as a lighthouse, to help them find their way. The geography of the high mountains by the lake **meant** that storms **didn't move** but **stayed** in the same place. Nowadays Lake Maracaibo holds a Guinness World Record as the place with the most lightning bolts per square kilometre.

1 **CLASS VOTE** Do you enjoy storms? Why? / Why not?

2 🔊 **1.35** Read the text. Find three unusual facts about the colour, place and frequency of the lightning it describes.

3 Study the Grammar box. Find the Past Simple forms of the verbs in the text. Which are regular/irregular? Why do negatives and questions make this difficult to determine?

Grammar | Past Simple

Regular verbs
It **looked** strange.
They **didn't** move.
When **did** that **happen**?

Irregular verbs
We **saw** an unusual storm.
I **didn't know** what to do.
Did you **take** any photos?

We use the Past Simple with time adverbials.
e.g. *yesterday, last week/year; two hours/days/weeks/years ago, in April, in 1595.*

GRAMMAR TIME > PAGE 119

---

4 Change the regular verbs to the affirmative (✓) to make true sentences.
1 The Catatumbo storm didn't happen in Venezuela in 1595.
  The Catatumbo storm happened in Venezuela in 1595.
2 The lightning didn't scare the foreign sailors.
3 The storms didn't help many sailors to find their way.
4 The lightning didn't appear in the same place again and again.

5 Change the irregular verbs to the negative (✗) to make true sentences.
1 The sailors saw green lightning.
  The sailors didn't see green lightning.
2 The sailors felt excited about the storm.
3 Sailors thought the Catatumbo storms were normal.
4 The storms took place over the sea.

6 Complete the sentences with a time adverbial, to make them true for you.
1 I saw snow _____ .
2 We had really bad weather on our school trip _____ .
3 We loved the warm weather on our holiday _____ .
4 I went out in the rain without a coat _____ .

7 Make questions in the Past Simple.
1 who / Marianna / meet?
  Who did Marianna meet?
2 what / the man / study?
3 when / Marianna / go to Lake Maracaibo?
4 how many storms / she / see?
5 where / she / put / the photos?

8 🔊 **1.36** For each question in Exercise 7, write the beginning of the answers, including the verb. Listen and answer the questions.
1 *Marianna met …*

24 Unit 2

2.2 GRAMMAR Past Simple: regular and irregular verbs

Lesson learning objective
Students can use regular and irregular verbs to talk about the past.

Lead in: Review of weather vocabulary

Put students into groups of four. Tell each group to think of a country or city. They should write what the weather is like in each season of the year in that place. Then groups take turns to say what the weather is like during the year. The rest of the class tries to guess the place.

Culture notes
Lake Maracaibo is on the north coast of Venezuela and is a saltwater bay or lagoon which can be reached from the sea. The sailors mentioned in the text, who wanted to attack Venezuela via the lake in 1595, were led by the Englishman Sir Francis Drake and the story of his defeat was written about in the poem *La Dragontea* in 1597 by Lope de Vega. However, Venezuela had already been defeated and colonised by the Spanish after Columbus first discovered the country in 1498, so the lightning wasn't completely able to save the country from invasion!

Exercise 1
Tell students to keep their Students' Books closed. Ask them the question and have a class vote. After the vote, ask if anyone in the class has been caught outside during a storm and encourage them to describe what happened.

Exercise 2 🔊 1.35
Before students open their Students' Books, write *Venezuela* on the board and ask students what they know about the country, e.g. *it's in South America, the capital is Caracas.*

Answers:
Colour: It is pinkish-orange.
Place: It takes place over Lake Maracaibo on the Catatumbo River, which is surrounded by high mountains and means that the storms stay in the same place.
Frequency: Lake Maracaibo has the most lightning bolts per square kilometre.

Exercise 3
When students have finished, put them into pairs. Tell each pair to write down ten verbs and their past forms. When pairs are ready, tell them to join up with a second pair. The pairs should take turns to read out one of their verbs while the other pair gives the Past Simple form.

Answers:
Regular verbs: saved (save), did that happen (happen), wanted (want), looked (look), spotted (spot), used (use), didn't move (move), stayed (stay)
Irregular verbs: saw (see), didn't know (know), felt (feel), took place (take place), meant (mean)
It can be difficult to decide whether verbs in negative sentences and questions are irregular because they use the base form of the verb rather than the past form.

Exercise 4
Elicit the answers. Point out that when a verb ends in one vowel and one consonant, we often double the final consonant, e.g. *drop – dropped*, but with two-syllable verbs, if the stress falls on the first syllable, we don't double the final consonant, e.g. *open – opened*.

Answers:
2 The lightning scared the foreign sailors.
3 The storms helped many sailors to find their way.
4 The lightning appeared in the same place again and again.

Exercise 5
Remind students about how to form negatives in the Past Simple (*did + not (n't) +* the base form of the verb).

Answers:
2 The sailors didn't feel excited about the storm.
3 Sailors didn't think the Catatumbo storms were normal.
4 The storms didn't take place over the sea.

Exercise 6
Look at the first sentence with students and elicit different ways in which the sentence could be finished, e.g. *yesterday, last week, last year, in 2015, in January, five years ago*. Encourage students to use different time expressions for each sentence, e.g. one sentence with *last week/year*, one sentence with *ago*, etc.

Exercise 7
Tell students that they are going to listen to a woman called Marianna talking about a visit she made to see the Catatumbo lightning in Venezuela and that the questions they write in this exercise are about the audio.

Answers:
2 What did the man study?
3 When did Marianna go to Lake Maracaibo?
4 How many storms did she see?
5 Where did she put the photos?

Exercise 8 🔊 1.36
When students have written the beginnings of their answers, elicit what they think Marianna might say, e.g. *1 Marianna met an explorer / a scientist*. When students listen, they should compare their ideas with Marianna's actual answers.

Answers:
1 Marianna met … a scientist / Professor Mendes.
2 The man studied … storms.
3 Marianna went to Lake Maracaibo … two weeks ago.
4 She saw … three storms.
5 She put the photos … on the (radio station's) website.

🔊 1.36

See page 247.

Further practice
- Workbook page 20
- Grammar Time page 119
- Resource Pack
  Resource 15: Unit 2 Lesson 2 Grammar – When did it happen?

2.3 READING and VOCABULARY   Find out about life in a cold country

Lesson learning objective
Students can find specific detail in an article and talk about culture.

Lead in: Review of Past Simple verbs
Tell students that they are going to write a short story about something that happened in the past. Put students into groups of three and elicit a verb from each group. Write all the verbs on the board in their base form. Explain to students that their story must be written in the past and should use all the verbs written on the board as well as any other verbs they wish to include. Give the groups a time limit and, when they have finished, invite each group to read their story to the class.

Exercise 1
Tell students not to open their Students' Books yet. Have a class discussion about the question and encourage students to talk about a time when they felt colder than ever before.

Exercise 2
Before students open their Students' Books, find out if anyone in the class has visited Iceland. If they have, ask what they did and what they saw while they were there. If nobody in the class has visited Iceland, ask students to say if they know anything about the country.

Possible answers:
Title: Land of ice and fire – tells us that the country is cold but also has volcanoes.
Introduction: the writer is happy living in Iceland.
Photo: You can see the Northern Lights there.

Exercise 3 🔊 1.37
When students have answered the questions, ask them to write their surnames in the Icelandic style (i.e. their father's first name + s + *son* (boy) or *dottir* (girl). Invite students to introduce themselves with their Icelandic surnames, e.g. *Hello, my name's Hugo Pedrosson / Sofía Felipesdottir.*

Answers:
1 They drink soup/kakosupa.
2 Because most people haven't got a surname.
3 Lots of small earthquakes take place.
4 He went to an outdoor/natural thermal pool.

Exercise 4
When students have finished, ask them if the text has made them more interested or less interested in visiting Iceland and ask them to give reasons for their answers.

Answers: 1 b   2 e   3 a   4 d   5 c

Extra activity
Put students into pairs and ask them to rank these Icelandic attractions in the order in which they would like to experience them.
Eat cocoa soup
See a volcano erupt
Experience mini earthquakes
Swim in a thermal pool
See the Northern Lights.
Invite pairs to share their order with the class and to give reasons for their choices.

Exercise 5
When students have found the adverbs, elicit more pairs of regular and strong adjectives with similar meanings, e.g. *hot – boiling, difficult – impossible*. Then write a mini-dialogue on the board using a pair of adjectives, for example:
A: Was the test **difficult**?
B: Difficult! It was absolutely **impossible**!
Students work in pairs to write more mini-dialogues of their own. Invite pairs to share their mini-dialogues with the class.

Answers:
adverb + regular adjective: very
adverb + strong adjective: absolutely, totally, completely

Exercise 6
Point out that for item 4, *totally delicious* could also be correct but *really delicious* sounds more natural.
When students have finished, ask them to write similar sentences using the other adverb, e.g. *1 The volcano is **very** impressive.*

Answers: 1 absolutely   2 very   3 completely   4 really

Exercise 7
Put students into pairs and tell them to work together to make sentences. Give them a time limit and then invite pairs to share their sentences with the class, giving more information, e.g. *Our town is really boring. There are no clubs. There is only one cinema and the shops are terrible.*

Extra activity
Put students into groups of four. Each group should decide on a topic they want to discuss, e.g. sports, music, films. Each student in the group should think of a related adverb + adjective phrase, e.g. *absolutely brilliant, quite good*. The rest of the group writes it down in their notebooks. Students should then work alone to think of anything related to their topic for each phrase, e.g. films: *absolutely brilliant – the new Star Wars movie; quite good – Ben Stiller*. Back in their groups, students take turns to share their ideas and to make comments about one another's ideas, e.g. *I think the new Star Wars movie is absolutely brilliant! Really? I thought it was quite boring.*
Invite groups to share some of their ideas with the class.

Exercise 8
Tell students that the introduction to their blog entry should be the same as Ari's: *I love living in … . I hope my diary inspires you to visit my country one day!*
Put students into groups of four so that they can share their ideas before they start writing. The actual writing task can be done as homework.

Further practice
- Workbook page 21
- Resource Pack
  Resource 16: Unit 2 Lesson 3 Reading and Vocabulary – Very good, absolutely wonderful

2.3 READING and VOCABULARY — Find out about life in a cold country

I can find specific detail in an article and talk about culture.

Land of Ice and Fire

I love living in Iceland. I hope my diary inspires you to visit my country one day! *Ari*

Wednesday: It's the end of winter now, but it's absolutely freezing this evening, about −10 degrees C. My sister and I did some knitting. Like all children here, we learned to knit at primary school, but we're not very good at it. Mum makes great jumpers for us, though. I helped my dad make some *kakosupa* – it's cocoa soup, like hot chocolate – lovely, thick and really warm!

Thursday: Our maths teacher, Jakob, gave us a very difficult test this morning. By the way, I'm not completely crazy – it's normal here to use your teacher's first name, because most of us don't have a surname, we take our father's name. So, for example, my dad's name is Jón, so my sister is Eva Jónsdottir (Jón's daughter) and I'm Ari Jónsson (Jón's son).

Friday: This evening the news programmes were full of information about the latest volcanic eruptions here. It was really interesting. There were a lot of small earthquakes before the eruptions. Eva downloaded some pictures from the Internet. They are totally amazing!

Saturday: I spent the whole afternoon with my friend's family at a natural thermal pool. We didn't swim, though. We sat in the open air and talked for hours. It's a normal way to relax in Iceland.

Sunday: I took some great photos of the Northern Lights. You can only see them when the sky is dark. Spring and autumn are good times, sometime between 5 p.m. and 2 a.m. when there are no clouds. I waited for ages, and they started at about 10 p.m. It was a brilliant display, and quite long, too – about fifteen minutes.

1 **CLASS VOTE** What do you do when it's cold outside? Vote for the top three ideas.

2 Look at the title, introduction and photo on the blog. What do they tell you about Ari's country?

3 🔊 1.37 Read the text and answer the questions.
1 What did Ari's family do to feel warm?
2 Why do pupils call their teacher by his/her first name?
3 What happened before the volcanic eruptions?
4 Where did Ari go on Saturday?

4 Match the people with the phrases to make true sentences.
1 ☐ Ari
2 ☐ Ari's mum
3 ☐ Ari's father
4 ☐ Ari's sister
5 ☐ People in Iceland

a is called Jón.
b likes *kakosupa*.
c like relaxing in thermal pools.
d found good photos of volcanoes.
e is good at knitting.

5 **WORD FRIENDS** Look at the highlighted words in the text. Complete the table with the correct adverb.

adverb + regular adjective	adverb + strong adjective
_____ cold	_____ freezing
_____ good	_____ amazing
_____ difficult	_____ crazy

Watch OUT! You can use *really* and *quite* with both adjective types.

6 Choose the correct option.
1 Wow! The volcano is *absolutely* / *very* fantastic!
2 These photos are *totally* / *very* good.
3 Climbing a live volcano is *completely* / *very* ridiculous!
4 *Kakosupa* is *really* / *totally* delicious.

7 Use the Word Friends to make sentences about the things below.

the place where you live   a TV programme
your favourite hobby   a food or drink

8 Write a blog entry about what you did or saw last week that is typical of life in your country.

2.4 GRAMMAR Past Simple and Past Continuous

I can talk about an event in the past and what was happening around it.

VIDEO WHAT WERE YOU DOING WHILE YOU WERE AWAY?

Mom: What's that funny smell? Ugh! Dan! You didn't empty your bag last night.

Dan: Oh, sorry, Mum. Skye called while I was doing it. She wanted to know about the Geography trip. We were chatting for ages and then I forgot about my bag.

Mom: These clothes are wet. What were you doing while you were away?

Dan: Most of the time we were studying rocks, but on the last day we had a walk. We were crossing a river when I fell in. Sorry, Mum. It was funny at the time.

Mom: Mmhh. I'm sure it was. Anyway, take these things to the washing machine. You can put them in now.

Dan: Oh, Mum. I've got to go out. Tommo texted while you were talking to me. Can I do it later? Please …

> *It was an accident.*
> *It was (funny) at the time.*
>
> **OUT of class**

1 CLASS VOTE What's the first thing you do when you arrive home after a school trip?

- eat something   take a shower   unpack my bag
- talk to friends online   fall asleep

2 ▶ 2.1 🔊 1.38 Watch or listen. What did Dan forget to do when he got home last night?

3 Study the Grammar box. Find examples of the Past Simple and the Past Continuous in the dialogue.

Grammar	Past Simple and Past Continuous
Past Continuous It *was raining*. We *weren't studying* Maths. *Were* you *talking*?	**Past Simple and Past Continuous** We *were walking* in the forest *when* I *found* a snake. I *fell while* I *was climbing* the tree.

GRAMMAR TIME > PAGE 119

4 Choose the correct option.
1. We *ate* / (*were eating*) lunch when we *were hearing* / *heard* the avalanche.
2. The rain *was starting* / *started* while we *were swimming* / *swam* in the sea.
3. Emma was walking on the beach *while* / *when* she found the money.
4. I *was taking* / *took* a lot of photos while I *was travelling* / *travel* in Iceland.
5. He was cooking food on the fire *when* / *while* he saw the bear.
6. James *was falling* / *fell* on the ice while he *was skating* / *skated* with friends.

5 Complete the email from Dan's brother with the Past Simple or Past Continuous forms of the verbs in brackets.

Hi Dan,

How was your Geography trip? When I ¹*was doing* (do) Geography at school, we ² _____ (have) a school trip to the Rockies. It was winter and freezing cold.

One day, the weather suddenly ³ _____ (change) while we ⁴ _____ (walk) in the mountains. We soon got lost in the fog! Our teachers had to call for help on their cell phones. While we ⁵ _____ (wait), I ⁶ _____ (hear) a strange noise. It was …

6 What do you think Dan's brother heard?

7 [VOX POPS ▶ 2.2] In pairs, discuss funny things that happened on a school trip or on holiday.

I was skiing down a hill when my phone fell out of my pocket.
We were watching some monkeys when one of them stole my chocolate!

Unit 2

2.4 GRAMMAR Past Simple and Past Continuous

Lesson learning objective
Students can talk about an event in the past and what was happening around it.

Lead in: Review of adverb + adjective combinations

Dictate these adverb + adjective combinations: *absolutely delicious*, *really cold*, *completely impossible*, *totally amazing*, *absolutely brilliant*, *quite interesting*, *very boring*, *absolutely gorgeous*.
Students should write them down in their notebooks. They should think of things they can describe using these adverb + adjective combinations, e.g. *absolutely delicious – a meal I ate at a restaurant in the UK last year. I had … .*
When students have written examples for all the combinations, put them into groups of four to discuss what they have written, explaining their reasons.
Invite groups to tell the class about their most interesting ideas.

Exercise 1
Before students open their Students' Books, have a class discussion about school trips and encourage students to talk about the last school trip they went on.

Exercise 2 ▶ 2.1 ◀» 1.38
When students have watched the video, ask them if they have ever had a similar experience and forgotten to take their wet or dirty clothes out of their bag or if they have left dirty clothes in their bedroom for a long time.

Answer: He forgot to empty his bag of wet clothes.

Exercise 3
Discuss the Grammar box with the class. Ask which tense we use to talk about longer activities in the past (the Past Continuous) and which tense we use to talk about single actions in the past (the Past Simple).
Elicit examples of both and ask how the Past Continuous and the Past Simple can be used together to express two linked ideas, e.g. *I was walking home* (longer activity). *I saw my friend* (single action).
Explain how we can make a stronger link between these two ideas, using *when* or *while*. We use *when* before the single action, i.e. the Past Simple form, e.g. *I was walking home **when** I saw my friend*, and *while* before the longer activity, i.e. the Past Continuous form, e.g. *I saw my friend **while** I was walking home*.

Answers:
Past Simple: didn't empty, called, wanted, forgot, were, had, fell, was, texted
Past Continuous: were chatting, were (you) doing, were studying, were crossing, were talking

Exercise 4
Remind students that they can identify the different tenses by thinking about which is the longer of the two actions. If they aren't sure, tell them to see whether *when* or *while* is used and to follow the rules in the Grammar box and discussed in the previous exercise.

Answers: 1 were eating, heard 2 started, were swimming 3 when 4 took, was travelling 5 when 6 fell, was skating

Background notes
The Rockies are a chain of mountains which stretch 4,800 km from Canada through the USA. The highest peak is Mt Elbert in Colorado, which is about 4,400 m high. The most famous national park in the Rockies is the Yellowstone National Park.

Exercise 5
Ask students what they can remember about Dan's brother (*His name is Ed and he is studying at university in New York*). Elicit what students know about the Rockies.

Answers: 2 had 3 changed 4 were walking 5 were waiting 6 heard

Exercise 6
Put students into groups of four. The groups should work together to write four sentences to tell the story of the strange noise. When they have finished, invite the groups to read out their stories to the class. Have a class vote for the most interesting story.

Exercise 7
Tell students to look at the two examples which both describe a situation as well as something concrete that happened. Ask students to think about something funny that happened to them while they were on a school trip or on holiday. Then put students into pairs to make sentences similar to those in the examples.

VOX POPS ▶ 2.2
Before watching, check that students understand the meaning of these words/phrases: *shave*, *moustache*, *gate (at an airport)*, *sugarcubes*, *paralysed with fear*. After watching, put students into pairs, and tell them to discuss any similar problems they have experienced while on holiday.

Extra activity
Elicit from students different ideas of accidents or problems, e.g. *I broke my tooth. I lost my mobile phone. I hurt my leg.*
Elicit two possible questions we can ask when someone tells us about an accident or problem. For example, to ask about the situation before the accident or problem, we can ask *What were you doing?* To ask about what they did after the accident or problem, we can ask *What did you do?*, e.g. *I broke my tooth yesterday. Really? What were you doing? I was eating some sweets. What did you do? I told my mum and she rang the dentist.*
Students should work in pairs to write one or two similar dialogues. Invite pairs to act out a dialogue in front of the class.

Further practice
- Workbook page 22
- Grammar Time page 119
- Resource Pack
  Resource 17: Unit 2 Lesson 4 Grammar – What were they doing?
  Resource 18: Unit 2 Lesson 4 Video – What were you doing while you were away?

2.5 LISTENING and VOCABULARY   In the wild

Lesson learning objective
Students can identify specific detail in a conversation and talk about being in the wild.

Lead in: Review of the Past Simple and the Past Continuous

Tell students to work alone and give each student two pieces of paper. They should write a sentence using the form: *I was …ing when …*, e.g. *I was having a bath when the phone rang.*

Tell them to write the sentence beginning (*I was …ing when*) on one piece of paper and the sentence ending (subject + Past Simple) on the other piece of paper.

Then put students into groups of four. Tell them to put the four sentence beginnings together face down on one side of the desk and the four sentence endings together face down on the other side of the desk.

Students take turns to pick up a sentence beginning and a sentence ending and, whatever the beginnings and endings say, trying to make a logical link from them, e.g. if they pick up *I was having a shower when … I broke my tooth*, they could say *I was standing in the shower when I suddenly slipped on some soap. I fell and my mouth hit the side of the shower and I broke my tooth.*

Exercise 1
Tell students to keep their Students' Books closed. Ask the question and follow up by asking questions such as, *What activities do you like doing outdoors? Do your parents tell you to go outside at the weekend?*

Exercise 2 🔊 1.39
Discuss the photos with students. Ask what they think the people are doing, where they are and what time of year it is. After students have listened to the audio, elicit the answers and any words or phrases that helped them to decide (1 *our summer camps*; 2 *for 13 to 17-year-olds*; 3 *in the forest, near the beach or at the top of a mountain*).

Answers: 1 T   2 F   3 T

🔊 1.39

Would you like to wake up to the sound of wildlife all around you? Then join us at the *Go Wild* Activity Camp for 13 to 17-year-olds. Our summer camps are all about being outdoors. That's why our camps are all in beautiful places. You can stay in the forest, near the beach or at the top of a mountain – we let you decide. Come and learn how to make a fire and cook a meal outside. Have fun sleeping under the stars and discover plants and animals that live around us. So what're you waiting for? It's time to find your wild side …

Exercise 3 🔊 1.40
Put students into pairs and encourage them to guess the correct choices before they listen to the audio.

Answers: sleep   make   listen to   watch   look for   discover

🔊 1.40

See page 247.

Exercise 4 🔊 1.40
Warn students that events may not be mentioned in chronological order, so they have to listen carefully.

Answers: Monday: make a shelter   Tuesday: make a fire
Wednesday: look for wild animals   Thursday: watch the stars
Friday: discover unusual plants

Exercise 5 🔊 1.40
When students have finished, ask them which activities on the camp they would most and least like to do.

Answers:
1 Because it was cold at night.
2 Because she was asleep / slept so well.
3 It was too cold for them.
4 Possible answer: He's tired of listening to Abigail.

Exercise 6 🔊 1.41
Check that students understand the meaning of *landscape*. When they have finished the activity, discuss the plural of *leaf (leaves)* and elicit what is different about the plural of *path* (*th* is pronounced /θ/ in *path* but /ð/ in *paths*).

Answers:
Elements of landscape: cave, leaf (leaves), path, sky, star, sunset, waterfall
Animals: bat, bear, spider, wildlife

Exercise 7
Put students into groups of four. When the groups have finished, elicit all the new vocabulary, with explanations or translations, and write the new words on the board.

Exercise 8
When students have finished, ask follow-up questions, e.g. *Would you be more scared of a bear or a big spider? Have you ever seen a special sunset?*

Answers: 2 cave   3 bear   4 sunset   5 sky

Exercise 9
Tell students to imagine that a friend has asked them if they want to go on the *Go Wild!* camp with them this summer. Explain that they should make the paragraph a part of an email reply to their friend, explaining why they would or would not like to go.

Extra activity
Put students into pairs. Tell them to imagine that one student has just returned from a *Go Wild!* camp and is telling the other student about it. They should think of some questions and answers about the camp.

Further practice
- Workbook page 23
- Resource Pack
  Resource 19: Unit 2 Lesson 5 Listening and Vocabulary – Categorise and draw

2.5 LISTENING and VOCABULARY — In the wild

I can identify specific detail in a conversation and talk about being in the wild.

1 CLASS VOTE Do you enjoy being outdoors? Why? / Why not? Compare your ideas with the class.

2 🔊 **1.39** Look at the photos from the *Go Wild!* camp. Decide if sentences 1–3 are true (T) or false (F). Listen and check.
1. ☐ The *Go Wild!* camp is a summer camp.
2. ☐ The *Go Wild!* camp is for families.
3. ☐ The *Go Wild!* camps are in different locations.

3 🔊 **1.40** WORD FRIENDS Listen to Abigail telling Max about her experience with *Go Wild*. Choose the correct option.

Word Friends
- (make) / build a fire
- sit / sleep outside
- make / build a shelter
- learn about / listen to the wildlife
- see / watch the stars
- look for / find wild animals
- grow / discover unusual plants

4 🔊 **1.40** Listen again. Match the activities from Exercise 3 with the days of the week in Abigail's diary. There are two extra activities.

Monday ...
Tuesday make a fire
Wednesday ...
Thursday ...
Friday ...

5 🔊 **1.40** Listen again and answer the questions.
1. Why didn't Abigail sleep outside in the end?
2. Why didn't Abigail listen to the wildlife?
3. Why weren't there any spiders in the camp?
4. Why do you think Max has a headache?

6 🔊 **1.41** Study the Vocabulary box, using a dictionary. Write the words in the correct category. Listen and check.

Vocabulary — In the wild
bat   bear   cave   leaf (leaves)   path   sky
spider   star   sunset   waterfall   wildlife

- elements of landscape: _____
- animals: _____

7 I KNOW! Work in groups. Can you add more words to each category in Exercise 6? Each word scores one point. Which group wins?
- elements of landscape: *mountain*, …
- animals: *tiger*, …

8 Choose the correct option.
1. My favorite season is autumn, when the *stars* / (*leaves*) fall off the trees.
2. We walked into the *cave* / *waterfall*, where it was cold and dark.
3. In the distance, there was something big and brown. A *bear* / *spider* was standing and looking at us.
4. At the end of the day, there's an amazing *path* / *sunset* over the lake.
5. The sun was shining and the *sky* / *star* was blue. It was a perfect day to go out on the boat.

9 Choose the correct option to make the sentence true for you. Write a short paragraph.

I'd love/hate to go on a Go Wild! camp because …

Unit 2

2.6 SPEAKING Criticising

I can criticise and explain when things go wrong.

VIDEO WHY DID YOU DO THAT?

Dan: Phew! I ran all the way here. I'm boiling now.
Skye: But it's so hot today! What were you thinking of? Do you want a drink?
Dan: Oh, yes. Cheers. Thanks.
Skye: Can I introduce you to Basil?
Dan: Who's Basil?
Skye: He's my pet. Close your eyes … Surprise!
Dan: Urgh! What did you do that for? I hate snakes!
Skye: Oh, I didn't realise. I didn't mean to scare you. I brought Basil outside because I was cleaning his tank. He loves the sunshine! Snakes like warm places. Twenty-nine degrees centigrade is just right. But they need a shady place to cool down.
Dan: Me too! Can we go to the pool yet?
Skye: Yes. Alisha texted. She and Tommo are nearly here.
Dan: Great. I brought my water gun for a water fight.
Skye: Brilliant. Get them when they come round the corner … ready?
Gran: Oh! I'm soaking wet! Why did you do that?
Skye: Oh, Gran. I'm so sorry. We thought you were Tommo.
Gran: Well, just be more careful next time!

*I'm boiling.   Cheers.
Surprise!   It's just right.*   **OUT of class**

1 CLASS VOTE How do you feel about snakes?

I'm scared of them.   I don't like them.
I'm fine with them.   I think they're great!

2 ▶ 2.3 🔊 1.42 Watch or listen and answer the questions.
1 Why did Dan feel hot?
2 How did Skye scare Dan?
3 Who were Skye and Dan waiting for?
4 What happened to Skye's grandmother?

3 🔊 1.43 Complete the dialogues with the phrases from the Speaking box. Listen and check.

Speaking	Criticising
Criticising	**Explaining**
What did you do that for?	I didn't mean to.
Why did you do that?	I didn't realise.
What were you thinking of?	I really wanted (to) …
Just be more careful next time.	I thought you were / it was …

1 A: Hey, why did you push in to the queue? I was here first.
   B: Oh! I _____ to push in. I _____ you were standing in the queue.
2 A: I was so angry. I just shouted at the teacher.
   B: _____ for?
   A: I didn't see who it was. I _____ another student!
3 A: You did the wrong exercise for homework! What _____ of?
   B: Oh, sorry!
   A: Never mind. Just _____ .

4 In pairs, role play the situations. Follow the instructions.
• I had an argument with a family member.
• I copied my homework from a friend.
• I didn't buy my friend a birthday present.
• I spent a lot of money on a concert/sports ticket.

A: Say what happened and give extra information.
B: Criticise your partner's actions.
A: Explain your reasons.
B: Give your opinion or say if you understand now.

5 [VOX POPS ▶ 2.4] In pairs, tell your partner about a time when you had a problem.

2.6 SPEAKING Criticising

Lesson learning objective
Students can criticise and explain when things go wrong.

Lead in: Review of vocabulary from the previous lesson

Put students into groups of four and give each group eight pieces of paper. The groups should think of four animals and four elements of the landscape and write each word on a separate piece of paper. When they have finished, they swap their pieces of paper with another group, so that each student in a group has one piece of paper with a new animal word and one piece of paper with a new landscape word. Explain to students that they should keep their words secret from the rest of their group.

Students then take turns to draw their animal and their element of the landscape while the rest of the group tries to guess the words. The first student to guess correctly gets the piece of paper with the word written on it. At the end of the activity, the student with the most pieces of paper is the winner.

Exercise 1
Before students open their Students' Books, have a class discussion about any insects or other animals students may be frightened of. Elicit different ideas and then ask students to open their Students' Books and to choose the sentence which describes themselves most accurately.

Exercise 2   2.3   1.42
Discuss what happened in the last episode of the video. Ask *What did Dan forget to do?* (Unpack his wet clothes after a school trip.) *Why did he have to go out?* (Tommo texted him.)

When students have watched the video, ask them if they have ever done something similar (i.e. done or said something to someone, thinking that they were someone else).

Answers:
1 Because he ran all the way to Skye's house on a hot day.
2 She showed him her pet snake.
3 Tommo and Alisha.
4 She was sprayed with water by Skye and Dan.

Exercise 3   1.43
Check that students understand the meaning of *to criticise*. Ask students who most often criticises them – their parents, their friends, their teachers or other people?

When they have listened to the dialogues, ask who they think is talking in each dialogue. (*1 two strangers 2 two friends or a child and a parent   3 a teacher and a student*.)

Answers:
1 didn't mean, didn't realise
2 What did you do that, thought it was
3 were you thinking, be more careful next time

Exercise 4
Encourage students to use different phrases from the Speaking box for each situation. When pairs are ready, invite them to act out one of their dialogues in front of the class.

Exercise 5
Give students a minute to think of ideas. If they can't think of a real problem or if they prefer not to talk about a problem, encourage them to use their imaginations.

VOX POPS ▶ 2.4

After watching, put students into groups of four to discuss what they have heard. Invite groups to tell one of the stories in their own words.

Extra activity

Put students into groups of four. Read out the following situations and ask them to choose one.
You're wearing jeans, a shirt, a jumper and a coat, but the temperature is 25 degrees centigrade.
Your clothes are wet and your socks are different colours.
You're late for school and you have mud on your jeans.
You have an elastoplast on your finger.

Explain that they are going to write an explanation for each situation in four or five sentences. Give an example:
I was travelling from London to Dublin. When I arrived at the airport, I weighed my luggage. It was too heavy so I had to take some things out. I decided to put on all of my clothes.
Encourage students to be as creative as possible and to write funny explanations. When all the groups have read out their explanations, ask the class to vote for the best one.

Further practice
- Workbook page 24
- Resource Pack
  Resource 20: Unit 2 Lesson 6 Speaking – I didn't mean to
  Resource 21: Unit 2 Lesson 6 Video – Why did you do that?

2.7 ENGLISH IN USE   Adverbs and indefinite pronouns

Lesson learning objective
Students can use adverbs and indefinite pronouns.

Lead in: Review of language for criticising

Elicit problems it is possible for students to have at school, e.g. getting told off by a teacher, forgetting their books, having an argument with a friend.

Put students into pairs and tell them to write a short dialogue that takes place between a student and a parent after school. The parent should ask what happened at school and the student should describe the mistake that they made. The parent should criticise the student for their actions and the student should explain their reasons for the mistake. Tell students to make sure they use phrases from the Speaking box on page 28.

When pairs are ready, invite them to act out their dialogues in front of the class.

Exercise 1
When students have read the cartoons, ask them to say what kind of weather the parents, daughter and dog prefer, giving reasons why. Ask students if their school has ever had to close because of bad weather.

Exercise 2
Remind students of the difference between *some* and *any* and elicit when we use each one. (We use *some* in positive statements and *any* in negatives and questions.)

When students have done the matching activity, put them into groups of four. Each group should make sentences with *some-*, *any-*, *no-* and *every-*, using a variety of endings (i.e. *-body*, *-thing* and *-where*). When the groups are ready, invite them to share their ideas with the class.

Answers: A 3   B 4   C 2   D 2

Exercise 3
When students have finished, discuss their opinions about the ideas in the sentences and then tell students that they are going to try to find an idea that everyone in the class likes. Elicit different ideas and, for each idea, ask students to raise their hands if they don't like it. Challenge students to think of an idea that nobody raises their hand for (i.e. that everyone in the class likes).

Answers: 1 nothing   2 everybody   3 anywhere
4 somebody   5 anything

Exercise 4 🔊 1.44
Before students do the activity, ask what they know about the island of Crete. Ask if anyone in the class has been there and if they can say what the island is famous for, e.g. beaches, mountains, gorges, the Minoan civilisation, the palace of Knossos.

Answers: 2 everything   3 nobody   4 everywhere
5 somebody   6 anything

Exercise 5
Discuss the example with the class and make sure they understand the instructions. When pairs have finished their discussions, ask them to think of other similar items they could ask about, e.g. something they'd like to do and something they wouldn't like to do this evening or somewhere they'd like to go with their friends and somewhere they'd like to go with their families.

Extra activity
Put students into pairs. Write these incomplete song titles on the board and ask students to complete them using indefinite pronouns. (Missing words given in brackets.)
… *hurts* (Everybody)
… *has a dream* (Everybody)
… *I need* (Something)
Money for … (nothing)
… *compares to you* (Nothing)
Ask pairs to share their answers with the class before giving the correct answers.

Homework
Tell students to read the text on page 32 of the Students' Book. They should look up any words they don't know the meaning of and translate them into L1. They should also pay attention to the pronunciation of the words in the text.
As an additional task, tell students to look at the photo on page 32 and to write a few sentences about the kind of weather that is shown.

Further practice
- Workbook page 25
- Resource Pack
  Resource 22: Unit 2 Lesson 7 English in Use –
  Tell me anything

2.7 ENGLISH IN USE   Adverbs and indefinite pronouns

I can use adverbs and indefinite pronouns.

Mum: Perfect weather? I love it when it's sunny and warm. We can do something together like have a picnic…
Dad: …or play basketball, go somewhere for a walk. Rufus loves walks.

Perfect weather? I love it when it's snowy and minus twenty! The school is closed, I don't have to go anywhere and I can do nothing!

Perfect weather? I love it when it's rainy! There's mud everywhere and everybody's happy!

1 Read the cartoon. Who do you agree with most?

2 Study the Language box. Match rules 1–4 with sentences below.

Language	Adverbs and indefinite pronouns	
People	**Things**	**Places**
somebody	something	somewhere
nobody	nothing	nowhere
everybody	everything	everywhere
anybody	anything	anywhere, anyplace

1 We use adverbs and indefinite pronouns with *some-* in positive statements.
*I want to go **somewhere**.*
2 We use adverbs and indefinite pronouns with *any-* in negative statements and questions.
*We can't do **anything** because it's raining.*
*Did you go **anywhere** at the weekend?*
3 We use adverbs and indefinite pronouns with *no-* with positive verbs, but the meaning is negative.
*There's **nothing** on TV. = There isn't anything on TV.*
4 Pronouns with *every-* are used in both positive and negative statements, and in questions with singular verbs.
***Everybody** loves sunny weather.*

A ☐ It was cold outside, so nobody was in the park.
B ☐ Wow, everything looks fantastic!
C ☐ Was there anything about snow in the weather forecast?
D ☐ It's raining today. I don't want to go anywhere.

3 Choose the correct option. Are the sentences true for you?
1 I need some time to stay at home and do *nothing / nowhere*.
2 There is nothing that *everything / everybody* likes.
3 I don't want to go *anywhere / everywhere* now. I just want to sit and relax.
4 It's important to have *nobody / somebody* you can talk to.
5 Do you want *nothing / anything* from the supermarket?

4 🔊 1.44 Complete the text with words from the Language box. Listen and check.

Aunt: Hanna, how was your outdoor survival camp on Crete?
Hanna: It was fun! There was ¹*something* different to do every day. We made a shelter in the mountains. We went fishing in a river and cooked fish over a fire … It's a long list, but I think we tried ² _____ last week! It was all exciting, so ³ _____ was bored and we travelled ⁴ _____ on the island. It's an amazing place. People there were very friendly, too. There was always ⁵ _____ to talk to.
Aunt: Was there ⁶ _____ you didn't try?
Hanna: Well, we didn't go swimming in the lake because there was a storm that day, so it was too dangerous!

5 In pairs, follow the instructions and decide if your partner's answers are for the first or second part of the instruction.

1 Name somewhere you'd like to go to on a hot day and somewhere you'd hate to go to on a hot day.
2 Name somebody you'd like to travel with and somebody you'd like to stay at home with.

A: Name somewhere you'd like to go to on a hot day and somewhere you'd hate to go to on a hot day.
B: Er, a desert and the swimming pool.
A: I think on a hot day you'd like to go to the swimming pool and you'd hate to go to the desert.
B: Yes, that's right.

Wordlist and Vocabulary in action

Extra activity

When students have finished Exercise 3, ask them to choose either *today* or *yesterday*. Students use words from the Wordlist to write a short paragraph about today's or yesterday's weather.

Further practice

Workbook page 26

WORDLIST Weather | Temperature | Natural disasters | In the wild

the Antarctic /æn'tɑːktɪk/
area /'eəriə/
avalanche /'ævəlɑːntʃ/
bat /bæt/
beach /biːtʃ/
bear /beə/
boiling /'bɔɪlɪŋ/
camp /kæmp/
Canada /'kænədə/
cave /keɪv/
chilly /'tʃɪli/
cloud /klaʊd/
cloudy /'klaʊdi/
coast /kəʊst/
cold /kəʊld/
column /'kɒləm/
conditions /kən'dɪʃnz/
cool /kuːl/
create /kri'eɪt/
degrees /dɪ'ɡriːz/
desert /'dezət/
drought /draʊt/
dry /draɪ/
dust /dʌst/
earthquake /'ɜːθkweɪk/
erupt /ɪ'rʌpt/
fire /faɪə/
flood /flʌd/
fog /fɒɡ/
foggy /'fɒɡi/
freezing /'friːzɪŋ/
grow /ɡrəʊ/
geography /dʒi'ɒɡrəfi/
ground /ɡraʊnd/
happen /'hæpən/
hilly /'hɪli/
hot /hɒt/

hurricane /'hʌrɪkən/
ice /aɪs/
Iceland /'aɪslənd/
icy /'aɪsi/
India /'ɪndiə/
island /'aɪlənd/
lake /leɪk/
land /lænd/
landscape /'lændskeɪp/
leaf (leaves) /liːf (liːvz)/
light /laɪt/
lighthouse /'laɪthaʊs/
lightning /'laɪtnɪŋ/
lightning bolt /'laɪtnɪŋ bəʊlt/
mild /maɪld/
minus /'maɪnəs/
mountain /'maʊntɪn/
move /muːv/
natural disaster /næt∫rəl dɪ'zɑːstə/
Northern Lights /ˌnɔːðən 'laɪts/
open air /ˌəʊpən 'eə/
outdoor /ˌaʊt'dɔː/
path /pɑːθ/
plants /plɑːnts/
rain /reɪn/
rainy /'reɪni/
river /'rɪvə/
rocks /rɒks/
sailor /'seɪlə/
sand /sænd/
save /seɪv/
season /'siːzn/
shady /'ʃeɪdi/
shallow /'ʃæləʊ/

sky /skaɪ/
snake /sneɪk/
snow /snəʊ/
snowmen /'snəʊmæn/
snowy /'snəʊi/
spider /'spaɪdə/
spot /spɒt/
spring /sprɪŋ/
star /stɑː/
storm /stɔːm/
stormy /'stɔːmi/
summer /'sʌmə/
sun /sʌn/
sunny /'sʌni/
sunset /'sʌnset/
sunshine /'sʌnʃaɪn/
survival /sə'vaɪvl/
temperature /'temprɪtʃə/
thermal pool /'θɜːml 'puːl/
thick /θɪk/
thunder /'θʌndə/
tsunami /tsu'nɑːmi/
Venezuela /ˌvenə'zweɪlə/
volcanic eruption /vɒl'kænɪk ɪˌrʌpʃn/
warm /wɔːm/
waterfall /'wɔːtəfɔːl/
water fight /'wɔːtə faɪt/
wave /weɪv/
wet /wet/
wild /waɪld/
wildlife /'waɪldlaɪf/
wind /wɪnd/
windy /'wɪndi/
winter /'wɪntə/

WORD FRIENDS

absolutely freezing
completely crazy
quite long
really interesting
totally amazing
very difficult
soaking wet
weather forecast
make/build a fire
sit/sleep outside
make/build a shelter
learn about / listen to the birds
see/watch the stars
look for / find wild animals
grow/discover unusual plants

VOCABULARY IN ACTION

1 Use the wordlist to find:
1 five weather words
2 three words to describe temperature
3 four natural disasters
4 three things you can do outdoors
5 three countries

2 In pairs, use the wordlist to discuss two things that are:
1 totally amazing
2 completely crazy
3 very difficult
4 absolutely freezing

3 Compare your ideas with the class.

4 In pairs, make sentences with three words and/or phrases from the wordlist.

Student A: *sleep under the stars / absolutely freezing / spider*
Student B: *Last weekend I slept under the stars but it was absolutely freezing and we had a big spider in the tent.*

5 🔊 1.45 **PRONUNCIATION** Listen and underline the stress in the sentences below. Where does the stress fall when there is just an adjective, and where does it fall when there is an adverb with the adjective?

It was freezing in the park.
It was absolutely freezing in the park.

6 🔊 1.46 Listen and repeat.

That test was really difficult.
You're completely crazy.
What a totally amazing party!
My hair is soaking wet.
I think he's really interesting.

 Wordlist

Exercise 2

Possible answers:
1 seeing the Northern lights, swimming in a thermal pool in winter
2 skiing during an avalanche, chasing after a hurricane
3 driving on a foggy day, skiing in heavy snow
4 winter in the Antarctic, swimming in a lake in Canada in the winter

Exercise 5

It was <u>freezing</u> in the park.
It was <u>absolutely</u> freezing in the park.
When there is no adverb, the stress falls on the adjective. When there is an adverb + adjective combination, the stress falls on the adverb.

Exercise 1

Possible answers:
1 cloud, cloudy, fog, foggy, ice, icy, rain, rainy, snow, snowy, storm, stormy, sun, sunny, wind, windy
2 boiling, chilly, cold, cool, freezing, hot, mild, warm
3 avalanche, drought, earthquake, fire, flood, hurricane, tsunami, volcanic eruption
4 camp, make/build a fire, sit/sleep outside, make/build a shelter, learn about/listen to the birds, see/watch the stars, look for/find wild animals, grow/discover unusual plants
5 Canada, Iceland, India, Venezuela

Revision

Activity for fast finishers
If any students finish Exercise 1 early, ask them to write similar definitions for four more words from the wordlist. Ask them to swap their definitions with another fast finisher and try to guess the words.

Further practice
- Workbook page 27
- Resource Pack
  Resource 23: Unit 2
  Vocabulary – N in everything
  Resource 24: Unit 2
  Grammar – Create a story

Revision

VOCABULARY

1 Write the correct word for each definition.
1. A small creature with eight legs. **s** _____
2. A very cold area around the South Pole. the **A** _____
3. A person who sails on boats or ships, especially as a job. **s** _____
4. A storm with very strong, fast winds. **h** _____
5. Very hot. **b** _____
6. Animals and plants that live in natural conditions. **w** _____

Exercise 1
1. spider
2. Antarctic
3. sailor
4. hurricane
5. boiling
6. wildlife

2 Look at the pictures and write the words.

1   2   3

4   5   6

Exercise 2
1. clouds/cloudy
2. bear
3. lightning/storm/stormy
4. snow/snowy/ice/icy
5. sunset
6. cave

3 Make sentences with as many words as you can from Exercises 1 and 2.
A big bear was looking at us, so we ran away.

GRAMMAR

4 Complete the text with the Past Simple form of the verbs in brackets.

Hi Dan,
Turkey is amazing. Yesterday we ¹*visited* (visit) a thermal pool and ² _____ (sit) in it for ages. In the evening we ³ _____ (watch) the sunset on the beach, and then we ⁴ _____ (make) a fire and ⁵ _____ (eat) sausages, but I ⁶ _____ (not like) them. They ⁷ _____ (be) disgusting! ⁸ _____ (you/enjoy) your trip to London? I ⁹ _____ (not see) your photos online. #hopeitwasok

See you soon,
Anna

Exercise 4
2. sat
3. watched
4. made
5. ate
6. didn't like
7. were
8. Did you enjoy
9. didn't see

5 Complete the sentences with the correct form of the verbs in brackets.
1. It *was snowing* (snow) when I *left* (leave) the house.
2. When I _____ (find) Jack and Emma, they _____ (make) a shelter.
3. We _____ (not see) any bears while we _____ (travel) across Canada.
4. The family _____ (eat) breakfast when the tsunami _____ (happen).
5. When we first _____ (see) the wave, it _____ (not move) very quickly.
6. While we _____ (sleep) outdoors, we _____ (hear) some strange noises.

Exercise 5
2. found, were making
3. didn't see, were travelling
4. was/were eating, happened
5. saw, wasn't moving
6. were sleeping, heard

6 Choose the correct option.
1. We didn't hear *something / anything* before the hurricane started.
2. This drought is very bad. *Nothing / Anything* can grow when there's no water.
3. *Everybody / Somebody* can learn to make a shelter. It's not difficult.
4. We looked *nowhere / everywhere* but we couldn't find the spider.
5. Does *nobody / anybody* know what the temperature is?

Exercise 6
1. anything
2. Nothing
3. Everybody
4. everywhere
5. anybody

SPEAKING

7 Complete the texts with the phrases below.

I thought it was mine.   What did you do that for?
Just be more careful next time.   I didn't mean to.

A: Hey, you've written on my notebook. ¹ _____ .
B: Sorry, ² _____ because it's the same color.
A: You left your new phone at school!
B: ³ _____ But it's OK. Gemma has it.
A: ⁴ _____ .

Exercise 7
1. What did you do that for?
2. I thought it was mine
3. I didn't mean to.
4. Just be more careful next time.

8 In pairs, role play the situations below.
- I borrowed my friend's jacket and now it's dirty.
- I forgot to invite a friend to my party.

DICTATION

9 🔊 1.47 Listen, then listen again and write down what you hear.

Exercise 9
I was with friends when the storm started. The wind was strong and it was raining. We found a cave and ran inside. We were freezing cold and hungry. We made a fire and started to eat. We didn't see the bear in the dark.

SELF-ASSESSMENT Think about this unit. What did you learn? What do you need help with?   **WORKBOOK** p. 26

BBC CULTURE

Nice day, innit?

What's the weather like?

If you don't know what to talk about, there's always the weather. In the UK we do this a lot because although the weather is quite mild, it changes a lot.

But American weather systems are very different – they have great extremes. When it's freezing cold in the Midwest, you can barely go outside. In the South East, tropical storms form in the Atlantic. They can build into tornadoes or hurricanes and bring high winds, torrential rain, floods and devastation. The population is prepared for this and there are even storm chasers. They are people who follow tornadoes at high speed to see the damage they cause and to warn local people of the dangers.

In the UK it seems that people are never prepared! When extreme weather comes, it's always a shock. Last year a freak snowstorm brought chaos to transport in the country. British Rail cancelled trains because of 'the wrong kind of snow'! On the night of 15 October 1987 people were going to bed when a terrible storm suddenly hit the country. Trees fell down and the conditions were chaotic. But the weather forecasters didn't predict it at all.

And can the weather affect our moods or character? Well, there is a saying in the UK: 'I feel a bit under the weather'. It means you don't feel very well. People who live in sunny climates seem happier. Those who live with grey skies and little light in winter can be more melancholic. But that's certainly not the whole story. Economic and social factors are more important to people's well-being than whether the sun is out or not.

GLOSSARY
devastation (n) ruin
freak (adj) very unusual
innit? (col) isn't it?
predict (v) to say that something will happen
torrential rain (n) very heavy rain

BBC CULTURE   Nice day, innit?

Lead in: Topic introduction

Tell students not to open their Students' Books. Put students into groups of four. If you set the homework suggestion for the unit, ask the groups to discuss any vocabulary they found difficult.

If students haven't done the homework, ask them to look at the glossary on page 32. Tell them to find the words in the text and to discuss what the words mean in context, e.g. *Last year an unusual snowstorm brought* **devastation** *to the country.*

Then have a class discussion about what students know or have found out about the weather shown in the photo.

2.5

Severe weather

Part 1

This is the wildest ocean on Earth! It is home to totally amazing marine life: penguins, seals, whales, dolphins and sharks – and people who battle the roughest seas. It stretches 16,000 km from its shallow waters in the sunny tropics to the deep dark waters of the Arctic and Antarctic. It is an ocean of great extremes. It is unpredictable and dangerous, but at the same time absolutely beautiful. This is a strange paradise! Welcome to the Atlantic!

2.6

Part 2

This is Cape Verde, a group of islands off the coast of Africa. Here hot winds from the Sahara Desert have made the sea turn wild. The waves are huge and the conditions are difficult. These men were fishing without any problem in the ocean. But suddenly, they decided to turn back. It was too dangerous to continue.

Winds like this cross the Atlantic quickly. Warm air rises from the sea and creates black clouds. A vortex then forms and the water of the ocean spins around very fast. The storm crosses the ocean very quickly and it grows stronger with every mile. At 120 km per hour, this storm is now a hurricane! It's an unstoppable force of nature and is now moving towards the Caribbean. Dolphins swim to deeper water. They must stay together through the storm. Torrential rain arrives on land and enormous waves and strong winds cause devastation. Paradise is now hell!

2.7

Part 3

This hurricane was particularly strong. Here in the Bahamas it destroyed houses, trees and businesses, but the people were able to escape.

However, in the sea there is no protection for the animals. Hurricanes break up dolphin groups. Somewhere in the ocean this young dolphin was swimming with its group when it was separated from the others in a big wave. Now it's at risk from a shark attack. Here a manatee finds safety in a mangrove forest. In fact, these underwater forests protect this area very well from storms because the vegetation is so thick.

Soon the coral reefs recover and our young dolphin is reunited with the group.

And so life in the tropical Atlantic returns to normal. The stormy conditions will come again, but for now all is calm in paradise.

Exercise 1
Set a time limit for the discussion and ask students to report back their ideas in open class.

Exercise 2
Encourage students to read the statements before they look at the text. Elicit guesses from students for the first statement and encourage them to give reasons for their guess. After students have completed the exercise, elicit the answers and students' explanations for their answers.

Answers:
1 F (The population is prepared for extreme weather.)
2 T (The weather forecasters didn't predict it at all.)
3 F (It means you don't feel very well.)
4 F (The topic is serious but the use of exclamation marks and informal language indicates that it is quite light-hearted.)

Exercise 3
Discuss the first question with the class. Ask them where they can find the information to answer this question (*in the final paragraph*). Then put students into groups of four to talk about the second question.

Possible answer:
1 The writer says it can have an affect, but that other things are more important such as economic and social factors; Students' own answers
2 Students' own answers

> **Background notes**
>
> Manatees are sometimes called sea cows because they are animals that live in the sea, mainly eat plants and are large, slow and gentle. They live in warm water in the Caribbean, the Gulf of Mexico and West Africa and can't survive in water with a temperature lower than 15°C. Manatees can grow to up to four metres in length and weigh up to 590 kg.

Exercise 4 2.5
Tell students to do the matching activity before they watch Part 1 of the video. Have a class discussion to find out what students know about the different animals and where they think they could be found in the wild.

Answers: 2 B 3 E 4 A 5 F 6 D

Exercise 5
Put students into pairs to discuss the three statements. Allow students to watch the video again if necessary and then elicit students' answers and their explanations for their choice. Don't give the correct answer until each pair has had a chance to give their idea.

Possible answers:
A (The narrator states how far it stretches and calls it strange.)
B (The narrator uses the same words to describe it – It is unpredictable and dangerous, but at the same time absolutely beautiful.)
C (The narrator doesn't say that it is the most famous so this is not the best answer.)

Exercise 6 2.6
Check that students understand the meaning of these words: *waves, torrential, enormous, devastation*.
Before they watch Part 2 of the video, they should work in pairs to guess the correct options.
Elicit the answers and ask students to explain why it couldn't be correct to say *giant* in sentence 2. (The adjective *giant* can only be used before a noun, e.g. *a giant wave*. When we want to use the adjective after the noun, it is *gigantic*.)

Answers: 1 hot, wild 2 huge, difficult 3 Warm, black
4 Torrential, enormous, strong

Exercise 7
Put students into groups of three to discuss the questions. Then invite groups to share their ideas with the class.

Extra activity
Students should remain in their groups of three to do this extra activity. Tell them to imagine that they are in the Caribbean and there has recently been a hurricane. One student should play the role of a reporter and the other two students should play the role of either locals or holidaymakers who have been caught in the storm. The group should work together to think of some questions and answers. When the groups are ready, invite them to role play the interview in front of the class.

Exercise 8 2.7
Before students watch Part 3 of the video, elicit different ways in which the four sentences could be completed. Write students' ideas on the board so that they can compare their ideas with what the narrator says in the video. After students have watched the video, elicit the answers and ask where the hurricane took place (*in the Bahamas*) and what students think was lucky (*that people escaped*).

Answers: 1 houses, trees and businesses
2 it is alone / sharks might attack it
3 protects the area from storms 4 the weather

Exercise 9
Elicit one or two weather problems that the students' country has faced in the past and then put students into groups of four to discuss the questions in more detail. Invite the groups to share their ideas with the class.
Ask students if they have ever experienced extreme weather, either in their own country or abroad.

Exercise 10
Help students develop their ideas for the content of their presentation, e.g. an extreme weather event, a weather forecast, photos taken in different parts of the country at different times of the year, climate charts showing average sunshine, rainfall or temperatures.
As students take turns to give their presentations, encourage the other students to note down any new facts that they have learned from one another's presentations.

Further practice
- Workbook pages 28–29
- Resource Pack
  Resource 25: Unit 2 BBC Culture Lesson – Hurricanes
  Resource 26: Unit 2 Culture – Oceans of the world

EXPLORE

1 Do you think the weather can affect you? How? Disuss in pairs.

2 Read the article. Mark the sentences T (true) or F (false). Correct the false sentences.
   1 ☐ Americans are less prepared for bad weather than the British.
   2 ☐ The great storm of 1987 in the UK was a surprise.
   3 ☐ To be *under the weather* means 'to be depressed'.
   4 ☐ The tone of the article is quite serious.

3 Read the article again. Answer the questions.
   1 Does the writer think that the weather can affect mood or character greatly? Do you agree with this opinion?
   2 Think about people from different parts of your country. Are their characters very different depending on the weather where they live?

EXPLORE MORE

4 ▶ 2.5 Watch Part 1 of the video. Match animals 1–6 from the video with photos A–F. Which of these animals live in your country?
   1 [C] whale   4 ☐ seal
   2 ☐ penguin   5 ☐ dolphin
   3 ☐ shark   6 ☐ manatee

A

B

C

D

E

F

5 What does the narrator say about the Atlantic Ocean? Choose the best summary.
   A It's very large and mysterious.
   B It's dangerous and beautiful at the same time.
   C It's the most famous ocean in the world.

6 ▶ 2.6 Watch Part 2 of the video. Choose the correct option.
   1 Here *warm / hot* winds from the Sahara Desert have made the sea turn *wild / crazy*.
   2 The waves are *huge / giant* and the conditions are *terrible / difficult*.
   3 *Warm / Cool* air rises from the sea and creates *thick / black* clouds.
   4 *Torrential / Light* rain arrives on land and *frightening / enormous* waves and *heavy / strong* winds cause devastation.

7 What images do you remember of the storm? What most surprised you about it? Discuss in groups.

8 ▶ 2.7 Watch Part 3 of the video. Complete the sentences.
   1 The strong hurricane destroyed …
   2 The young dolphin is in danger because …
   3 The thick vegetation in the mangrove forests is good because it …
   4 The Atlantic can be a heaven or a hell, depending on …

9 Do you have examples of extreme or changeable weather in your country? Where? What kind of weather can you get there?

YOU EXPLORE

10 **CULTURE PROJECT** In groups, prepare a presentation about the weather in your country.
   1 Use the internet or other sources to research different types of weather in your country.
   2 Write a short script and think about images or videos to use in your presentation.
   3 Give your presentation to the class.
   4 Report back: what did you learn from the other presentations?

Unit 2 33

3

The taste test

3.1 VOCABULARY Food and drink

I can talk about food and drink.

VOCABULARY
Food and drink | Flavours
Describing food

GRAMMAR
Present Perfect with *ever, never, just, already, yet, for* and *since*
Present Perfect and Past Simple

Grammar: I've heard it's funny

Speaking: What can I get you?

BBC Culture: Indian food Liverpool style

Workbook p. 40

BBC VOX POPS ▶
EXAM TIME 1 > p. 130
CLIL 2 > p. 140

1 **CLASS VOTE** Which is your favourite meal of the day? Why?

   breakfast   lunch   dinner   supper   snack

2 🔊 1.48 Study the Vocabulary A box. Listen and see if you can find the items you hear in the picture.

Vocabulary A	Food and drink
beef bread rolls cheese chewing gum chilli cream crisps cucumber flour fruit juice garlic grapes honey ice cream lemonade lettuce nuts peach pear pineapple smoothie tuna yoghurt	

3 🔊 1.49 Match the sentences with the people in the picture. Complete the sentences with words from the Vocabulary A box then listen and check.

1 ___ This person has got a shopping list. She is looking for chilli, cream and some ___.
2 ___ These people want to buy ___, honey, yoghurt and ___.
3 ___ The shop assistant is near the ___, grapes and ___.
4 ___ The grandmother wants lettuce, ___ and some ___.
5 ___ The child is looking at the fruit juice and ___.
6 ___ The man is buying ___, beef and ___.

4 Match the words from the Vocabulary A box with the correct sign.

FRUIT
peach, ___, ___, ___,

VEGETABLES, SALAD AND HERBS
lettuce, ___, ___, ___,

MEAT AND FISH
beef, ___,

DAIRY
cheese, ___, ___,

CEREALS
bread rolls, ___,

SWEETS AND SNACKS
ice cream, *chewing gum*, ___, ___,

DRINKS
fruit juice, ___, ___

34

Unit contents

Vocabulary
- Food and drink
- Flavours
- Describing food

Grammar
- Present Perfect with *ever, never, just, already, yet, for* and *since*
- Present Perfect and Past Simple

Communication skills
- Ordering food

Examples of 21st Century Skills/Competencies
- Critical Thinking: page 34 (Exercise 4), pages 44–45
- Collaboration: page 35 (Exercise 5), page 37 (Exercise 4), page 40 (Exercise 5), page 45 (Exercise 10)
- Assessment for Learning: page 43
- Autonomy and Personal Initiative: page 36 (Exercise 6), page 41 (Exercise 7)

3.1 VOCABULARY Food and drink

Lesson learning objective
Students can talk about food and drink.

Lead in: Review of vocabulary from the previous unit

Tell students that you are going to say a word from the previous unit backwards. They should guess what the word is and tell you what it means.
Say *tab* and elicit *bat* (a flying animal).
Put students into groups of four. Tell the groups that this time, as soon as they have guessed the word, they should put their hands up. Whichever group puts their hands up first has a chance to guess the word.
Say *tresed* and elicit *desert*.
Tell the groups to each choose two more words from the wordlist on page 30 of the Students' Book. Tell them to write the words backwards and to practise saying them. When they are ready, the groups should take turns to say their words backwards while the other groups guess what the words are.

Exercise 1
Check that students understand the words for the different meals, what the meals usually consist of and when the meals are eaten, although be aware that there are regional variations in the names used for meals. Point out that in England the main meal of the day can be either in the middle of the day or in the evening and that most people won't eat a main meal at both. The difference between the meals is that lunch is always eaten in the middle of the day whereas dinner may be eaten in the early evening.

Exercise 2 1.48
Discuss the picture with students before they look at the Vocabulary A box. Elicit what the picture shows (*a supermarket*) and what students can see in the picture. After students have listened to the audio, go through the vocabulary with the class to make sure they understand the meaning of each word.

Exercise 3 1.49
Look at the first sentence with the class. Elicit which person in the picture is holding a shopping list (C) and what she is thinking about (in the thought bubble above her head we can see a chilli pepper, a carton of cream and a fish).
Put students into pairs and ask them to look at the other sentences before you play the audio.

Answers: 1 C tuna   2 D bread rolls, cheese
3 F pineapples, peaches   4 A cucumber, pears
5 E lemonade   6 B flour, garlic

> **Background notes**
>
> Sometimes food can be difficult to categorise. For example, tomatoes are, botanically, a fruit but are considered a vegetable by most people. Eggs are often categorised as a dairy product but really dairy products come from milk. Some people consider eggs to be a meat product.

Exercise 4
When students have finished, discuss the different categories in the exercise. You might like to elicit or point out some of these points. Fruit contains seeds and grows from a flower on the plant. Vegetables are any other part of a plant which can be eaten. Nuts could be classified as fruit, but they are different in that they are one seed rather than something containing a seed. Salad vegetables are vegetables that we usually eat raw in a salad. Herbs are plants which we use to give flavour to food. Dairy products are made from milk. Cereals are grains used for food. These include corn (maize), rice, wheat and oats and the products made from them such as bread and pasta.

Answers:
FRUIT: grapes, pear, pineapple
VEGETABLES, SALAD AND HERBS: chilli, cucumber, garlic
MEAT AND FISH: tuna
DAIRY: cream, yoghurt
CEREALS: flour
SWEETS AND SNACKS: crisps, honey, nuts
DRINKS: lemonade, smoothie

Exercise 5 🔊 1.50
Divide the class into seven groups. After the one-minute time limit, allocate a category to each group and invite them to read out their words for that category. Encourage the other groups to add any more words they had thought of.

Extra activity
Put students into groups of three. Each group should choose one mealtime from Exercise 1 and decide what kind of food they would like to prepare for their perfect meal. When the groups have decided, they should present their meal to the class. If more than one group has chosen the same meal, have a class vote for the best idea.

Exercise 6 🔊 1.50
Ask students if they like ice cream and to say where the best place in their town is for buying an ice cream. When students have discussed the flavours in the Vocabulary B box, ask if they can name any other ice cream flavours. Discuss the difference between creamy ice cream and sorbet-type ice cream and ask students which kind they prefer.

Exercise 7 🔊 1.51
Discuss the photo with the class, asking students if they can name what kind of food it is and where it comes from. (*It is chilli con carne from Mexico.*) When students have finished the exercise, have a class discussion about why people in hot countries often eat spicy food, when it can make them feel even hotter. (Three possible reasons are: spicy food makes people sweat and sweating is a way of cooling the body; spicy food makes people drink more, which is a good thing to do when the weather is hot; and spices can keep meat fresh longer, which is important in hot weather.)

Answers: **2** coffee **3** mint **4** drink **5** taste **6** dishes **7** beef **8** Chilli

Exercise 8 🔊 1.52
For each question, when the speaker says *What is it?*, pause the audio, elicit ideas from students and then continue the audio so they can listen to the answer. Ask students if they ever use garlic when they have a cold, if they ever use honey instead of sugar (e.g. in tea) and if they ever eat fresh pineapple.

Answers: **1** garlic **2** honey **3** pineapple

🔊 1.52
Now it's time for this week's mini quiz. Our topic this week is food. Listen to the clues and guess the food. Here's question one.
It's small, white and has a very strong taste. It's very good for you because it has a lot of vitamin B and C and it helps you to fight the flu or cold. Your mouth smells after you eat it, but you can eat lemon to make the smell go away. It's from the same family of plants as an onion. What is it? … It's garlic!
Did you guess right? Now for question two.
This food never goes bad. You can eat it after thousands of years! You can put this food on a cut or a scratch to make it better. It comes from flowers. It's very sweet, like sugar. Bees make it. What is it? … It's honey!
And, finally, question three.
This food doesn't grow on trees. It grows on a small plant near the ground. It often looks green when it's growing, but it's not a vegetable. Only one fruit grows on each plant. Each fruit takes two or three years to grow. It's yellow inside and very sweet. What is it? … It's a pineapple!

Exercise 9
Tell the class some strange food facts about one kind of food and ask them to guess the kind of food. For example:
This fruit contains potassium and so it is slightly radioactive.
This fruit is actually a berry, although you probably wouldn't think so.
This fruit contains chemicals which can cheer you up.
The official name for a bunch of this fruit is 'a hand'. One fruit on its own is called 'a finger'.
(The kind of food is bananas.)
At the end of the exercise, invite each group of four to share some of their food facts with the class.

Extra activity
Write on the board two quotes about food. For example:
When a man's stomach is full, it makes no difference whether he is rich or poor. (Euripides)
If you want to eat well in England, eat three breakfasts. (William Somerset Maugham)
Put students into pairs and tell them to decide what the quotes mean and to discuss whether or not they agree with the quotes. Then tell them to search online to find another quote about food that they think is interesting.
When the pairs are ready, invite them to share their quotes with the class and to explain why they like their quote.
Have a class vote for the quote they like best. (Tell them they can't vote for their own quote.)

Further practice
- Workbook pages 30–31
- Resource Pack
  Resource 27: Unit 3 Lesson 1 Vocabulary – Food choices

5 **I KNOW!** Work in groups. How many words can you add to each category in Exercise 4, in one minute? Compare your ideas with the class.

6 🔊 1.50 In pairs, use the words from the Vocabulary B box to discuss the ice cream flavours. Which is your favourite flavour?

Vocabulary B	Flavours

chocolate   coconut   coffee   lemon
melon   mint   strawberry   vanilla

These words can be used as adjectives or nouns.
I like strawberries. [noun]
I like strawberry ice cream. [adjective]

I think the white ice cream is vanilla.
Yes, or maybe it's …

7 🔊 1.51 Complete the text with the words below. Listen and check. Can you think of other kinds of food that makes your mouth feel hot or cold when you eat them?

beef   chilli   coffee   dishes   drink   ~~ice cream~~   mint   taste

Taste and Temperature

People usually enjoy ¹*ice cream* in the summer because it is cold, in the same way they enjoy hot tea or ² _____ in the winter. But did you notice that some food is not really hot or cold but makes you feel like that? For example, in some hot countries ³ _____ lemonade is very popular. It's a cool, refreshing ⁴ _____. But does this herb really make your mouth cold?

When you ⁵ _____ mint flavours, your mouth sends a message to your brain: 'Hey, that feels cold!' In fact, it's a 'trick' because the temperature in your mouth doesn't change. Spicy ⁶ _____ do the opposite, they make you feel hot. Take chilli con carne, for example — a famous Mexican dish with meat — usually ⁷ _____ and beans, served with rice. ⁸ _____ doesn't really make you hot. But it makes you FEEL hot.

8 🔊 1.52 Listen to three questions from a food quiz. Did you guess the answers?

9 In pairs, follow the instructions.
- Choose a food that you like.
- Find or think of 2–4 facts about this food.
- Write your facts but DON'T write the answer.
- Swap clues with another pair and guess the food.

3.2 GRAMMAR Present Perfect with *ever*, *never*, *just*, *already* and *yet*

I can use the Present Perfect with *ever*, *never*, *just*, *already* and *yet*.

VIDEO I'VE HEARD IT'S FUNNY

Tommo: I've never seen so much food. Ah, smell that pizza!
Alisha: Yes, I've already had some! This market is great for Chinese food, too. Have you ever eaten noodles?
Tommo: Yes, I have. Dad's cooked them at home.
Alisha: Tommo, look! That's Oliver Jenkins, the famous TV chef. Have you seen his programme?
Tommo: No, but I've heard it's funny.
Alisha: Perhaps he's brought some nice food?
Tommo: Well, he's just opened an ice cream shop. Let's go and see. Perhaps we can try some.
Alisha: Look. There's cheeseburger flavour or chilli or pea-and-mint. He's used weird flavours!
Tommo: You bet!
Alisha: I hate peas, but cheeseburger flavour sounds OK. What about you?
Tommo: I haven't decided yet … What's it like?
Alisha: Yuck! That's disgusting. Hang on, let's try another. Mmhh, chilli. Now, that's the best ice cream I've ever eaten!

> You bet!   Yuck!   Hang on.   **OUT of class**

1 **CLASS VOTE** Which strange food would you like to try?

   cheeseburger ice cream   pizza with bananas
   cucumber and garlic smoothie

2  3.1   1.53 Watch or listen and answer the questions.
   1 Where are Tommo and Alisha?
   2 Who is Oliver Jenkins?
   3 What type of shop does Oliver Jenkins have?
   4 What flavour ice cream does Alisha try first?

3 Study the Grammar box. Find more examples of the Present Perfect in the dialogue.

Grammar	Present Perfect
Have you **ever tried** pizza with banana? I've **never eaten** so much food. He's **just made** a new TV programme. I've **already tried** it. I **haven't finished yet**. **Have** you **done** it **yet**?	

GRAMMAR TIME > PAGE 120

4 Complete the sentences and questions with the correct form of the words in brackets.
   1 Alisha *has already eaten* (already/eat) some pizza.
   2 _____ Tommo _____ (ever/cook) noodles at home?
   3 Alisha and Tommo _____ (just/see) Oliver Jenkins.
   4 Tommo _____ (never/watch) Oliver Jenkins on TV.
   5 Tommo _____ (not have) pea-and-mint ice cream yet.
   6 _____ Alisha and Tommo _____ (try) all the ice cream yet?

5 1.54 Complete the text with the Present Perfect form of the verb in brackets. Listen and check.

Hi Ed,
Sorry I [1]_____ (not call) you. I [2]_____ (have) a bad cold and I [3]_____ (not speak) to anyone. [4]_____ (you/decide) about the summer yet? I hope I can come and see you. A new pizza restaurant [5]_____ (just/open) in town. My friends [6]_____ (already/try) it. The speciality is pizza with banana on it! I [7]_____ (never/have) that before but I'd like to try it.
Speak soon,
Dan

6 [VOX POPS ▶ 3.2] Write about a place where you like to eat with friends.

   1 What's it called?
   2 Who have you been there with?
   3 What food have you tried?

It's called Marco's and I've been there with …

Unit 3

3.2 GRAMMAR Present Perfect with *ever, never, just, already* and *yet*

Lesson learning objective
Students can use the Present Perfect with *ever, never, just, already* and *yet*.

Lead in: Review of food vocabulary
Write all the letters of the alphabet on the board, except for the letters *q*, *x* and *z*. Say: *I went to the supermarket and bought an apple.* Tell students that they are going to repeat what you have said and then add an item beginning with the next letter in the alphabet (*b*). Invite a student to try this. Continue the process with the other letters and encourage students to help one another if they forget any of the items that have been said before or if they have difficulty thinking of an item with the next letter in the alphabet. Try to keep the activity going until students reach the letter *y*.

Exercise 1
Tell students not to open their Students' Books yet. Ask the class if they have ever eaten any kind of strange food, either something they thought was tasty or something they thought wasn't tasty. Elicit ideas.

Exercise 2 ▶ 3.1 🔊 1.53
Tell students to close their Students' Books. Play the video with the sound switched off. Put students into pairs and tell them to discuss what they saw in the video and what they think the characters were saying. Invite pairs to share their ideas with the class.
Then tell them to open their Students' Books and to see if they can answer the questions before you play the video again, this time with the sound switched on.

Answers: 1 at a market   2 a famous TV chef
3 an ice cream shop   4 cheeseburger flavour

Exercise 3
When students have found the examples, explain that we use the Present Perfect to talk about things happening in the past during an unfinished time (e.g. *in my life*, *this morning*, *today*) or during a time that is not stated. Explain that we also use the Present Perfect with:
- *ever* in questions to mean *at any time in my life*.
- *never* to mean *at no time in my life*.
- *just* to say that something happened a very short time ago.
- *already* to emphasise that something has happened and can be used to contradict what someone else has said.
- *yet* in questions and negatives to mean that although it hasn't happened we think it is going to happen in the future.

Explain how we form Present Perfect statements: subject + *have/has* + past participle; and Present Perfect questions: *have/has* + subject + past participle.

Answers:
I've never seen so much food; I've already had some!;
Have you ever eaten noodles?; Yes, I have. Dad's cooked them;
Have you seen his programme?; I've heard it's funny;
Perhaps he's brought some nice food;
he's just opened an ice cream shop; He's used weird flavours!;
I haven't decided yet; that's the best ice cream I've ever eaten!

Exercise 4
When students have finished the exercise, look at the example sentence with the class and ask for situations where we might use: *I've already eaten …* . For example:
at the cinema: *The film hasn't started yet and I've already eaten my popcorn!*
at school: *It's only 10 a.m. and John has already eaten his lunch!*
Students should work in groups of three to think of other ideas. Invite groups to share their ideas with the class and make sure they are using *already* appropriately.

Answers:
2 has (Tommo) ever cooked
3 have just seen
4 has never watched
5 hasn't had
6 Have (Alisha and Tommo) tried

Exercise 5 🔊 1.54
Tell students to look at the first three gaps in the exercise and elicit why we would use the Present Perfect in this situation (*because the time is unstated*). Ask students which tense they would use for the three verbs if at the end of the first sentence the writer wrote *last week* (*Past Simple, because a time in the past would be stated*).

Answers: 1 haven't called   2 've/have had
3 haven't spoken   4 Have you decided   5 has just opened
6 have already tried   7 've/have never had

Exercise 6
Remind students to use the Present Perfect and not to mention a specific time when they have been to the café or restaurant. Elicit more questions that students could ask someone about the café or restaurant, e.g. *How many times have you been there? Have you ever had something you didn't like there?*
When students are ready, put them into pairs and tell them to take turns to ask questions using the Present Perfect or other tenses, e.g. *How often do you go there?*

VOX POPS ▶ 3.2
Before watching, check that students understand the meaning of these words/phrases: *a baguette, bangers and mash, shepherd's pie*. While watching, students should write down the names of any cuisines they hear. Elicit what students know about each cuisine, which ones they have already tried and which ones they would like to try.

Further practice
- Workbook page 32
- Grammar Time page 120
- Resource Pack
  Resource 28: Unit 3 Lesson 2 Grammar – Have you had an exciting life?
  Resource 29: Unit 3 Lesson 2 Video – I've heard it's funny

3.3 READING and VOCABULARY A cookery TV show

Lesson learning objective
Students can find specific detail in an article and use *make* and *do* accurately.

Lead in: Review of the Present Perfect
Write these phrases on the board. Students write true sentences about themselves.
*I have just …   I have never …   I haven't … yet.
I have already …*
Tell students to write their names on their papers and to give them to you. Look through the papers to find interesting sentences and read them aloud to the class to see if students can guess who wrote the sentences. If the sentences contain errors in verb form or sentence order, encourage the class to correct the errors (without saying who wrote the sentences).

Exercise 1
Tell students not to open their Students' Books yet. Discuss the question with the class and, after having a class vote, discuss students' favourite TV chefs and why they like them. Ask students if they have ever tried cooking a recipe that they have seen on TV or on the internet and, if they have, whether or not the recipe worked.

> **Culture notes**
>
> *The Great British Bake Off* is a reality cooking show on British television. The show starts off with twelve contestants and each week there are three different challenges. One contestant is eliminated by the judges each week. The three challenges are to bake something that the contestants often cook, to follow a recipe that is not very detailed to find out about the contestants' knowledge of baking and to bake something that looks and tastes perfect. In the final episode of the series, when there are only three contestants left, the contestants battle against one another to determine who will be the winner.

Exercise 2
When students have answered the question, ask what the TV show is called (*The Great British Bake Off*), what Martha has already made for the programme (*cakes*) and what she is going to make for next week's programme (*cupcakes*).

Answers: b

Exercise 3 🔊 1.55
Elicit the answers and ask students for explanations for their answers and for reasons why they think the other choices are incorrect.

Answers: 1 c   2 c   3 d   4 b
Reasons for the answers:
1 c *she hasn't finished yet* – Martha wants to spend more time baking
2 c *I've never understood the science behind it* – understanding the science of food will help her to discover what happens when you cook food
3 d *she set her oven gloves on fire*
4 b *it's important that they keep her calm*
Reasons why the other choices are incorrect:
1 a *She's done her homework*
  b *Martha has posted messages and photos on Twitter*
  d *there's no time for 17-year-old Martha to relax with friends tonight*

2 a The text doesn't say that Food Technology will help Martha to avoid disasters in the kitchen.
  b The text doesn't say that she loves all kinds of science.
  d While Martha is going to study Maths and Chemistry as well, the text doesn't say that the subjects go well together.
3 a *She was very happy*
  b The disaster was with her oven gloves, not her cake.
  c The text doesn't say that the other students left.
4 a *Her parents have watched her on TV every week.*
  c The text doesn't say that they tell her when she's making mistakes.
  d The text doesn't say that they help her with her schoolwork.

Exercise 4
When students have completed the exercise, elicit the answers. Check the word stress for each word and point out to students when the word stress is different between the verb and the noun, e.g. com*pete* – compe*ti*tion).

Answers: 1 contestant   2 competition   3 appearance
4 building   5 winner   6 weight

Exercise 5
When students have found the phrases in the text, ask them to write three true sentences about themselves, using any three of the phrases, e.g. *I know how to make cakes. I often make a mess when I am cooking. I always do my homework.* Students then join together in groups of three to share their sentences.

Answers: make   do

Exercise 6
When students have finished, ask them to change the questions so that they can ask about their partner, using *Have you …?* and *Did you …?*, e.g. *Have you done your Maths homework yet? Have you made any cakes this week? Did you make a mess when you were a child? Have you made any important decisions this week? Have you ever found it difficult to make time for your homework?*
Put students into pairs and tell them to take turns to ask and answer the questions.

Answers: 1 yes   2 cupcakes   3 in the kitchen
4 study Food Technology   5 her school work

Extra activity
Keep students in pairs. Tell them to search online or to use a dictionary to find five more collocations with the verbs *make* or *do*. When pairs are ready, draw on the board a table with the headings *make* and *do*. Invite pairs to write their ideas in the table.

Further practice
- Workbook page 33
- Resource Pack
  Resource 30: Unit 3 Lesson 3 Reading and Vocabulary – Make and do

3.3 READING and VOCABULARY   A cookery TV show

I can find specific detail in an article and use *make* and *do* accurately.

1 **CLASS VOTE** Do you watch cookery programmes? Where do you watch them: on TV or online?

2 Read the title and the first paragraph of the article. What does the title refer to?
  a Martha's cookery class at school.
  b Martha's experience on a TV show.

3 🔊 1.55 Read the article. Choose the correct answers.
  1 Why can't Martha go out with her friends tonight?
    a She wants to study at home.
    b She wants to upload some photos on Twitter.
    c She wants to bake more cupcakes.
    d She wants to relax at home.
  2 Why has Martha chosen to study Food Technology?
    a Because she wants to avoid disasters in the kitchen.
    b Because she loves all kinds of science.
    c Because she wants to discover what happens when you cook food.
    d Because it goes well with Maths and Chemistry.
  3 What happened during the school cookery competition?
    a Martha got angry with the other students.
    b Martha had a disaster with her cake.
    c The other students left and went home.
    d Martha's oven gloves caught fire.
  4 Why are the people in Martha's family so important?
    a They go and watch every show.
    b They can help Martha to stay calm.
    c They tell her when she's making mistakes.
    d They help her with her schoolwork.

'I have loved every minute of it!'

She's done her homework but there's no time for 17-year-old Martha to relax with friends tonight. Martha is the youngest contestant in a national cooking competition, *The Great British Bake Off*, and she's got to practise for the next show. Every week she has to impress the judges with different recipes. Next week it's cupcakes. She's already made 24 cakes today, but she hasn't finished yet. Since her first appearance on the show, Martha has posted messages and photos on Twitter. Her profile says: 'I only have friends because I make good cake. Seriously.' So when did this passion begin?

Martha started baking when she was about seven years old. She often made a mess in the kitchen and the results weren't always good. At school she made a decision to study Maths, Chemistry and Food Technology because she says, 'I've always loved food but I've never understood the science behind it.' It hasn't always been easy. Martha has had a few disasters, and once she set her oven gloves on fire during a school cooking competition and the whole building was evacuated. But the judges announced that Martha was one of the winners. She was very happy!

What about Martha's family? Her parents have watched her on TV every week. They know that the competition is getting tough and that Martha is tired. Martha wants to do her best and hates making mistakes so it's important that they keep her calm. Her granddad, James, is incredibly proud that she has made time for both her schoolwork and the TV show. They're all enjoying the competition although, as Martha says with a smile, 'We have all put on a bit of weight!'

4 **WORD BUILDING** Find nouns from the verbs below in the text. In pairs, make sentences with each noun.
  1 contest _____
  2 compete _____
  3 appear _____
  4 build _____
  5 win _____
  6 weigh _____

5 **WORD FRIENDS** Find the phrases in the text. Write *make* or *do* in the correct place in the box.

Word Friends	*make* and *do*
_____ :	a cake (cakes) a decision time a mess mistakes
_____ :	(my/your/his/her) homework my/you/his/her best

6 Read the text again. Answer the questions.
  1 Has Martha done her homework?
  2 What type of cakes has Martha made today?
  3 Where did Martha make a mess when she was a child?
  4 What did Martha make a decision to do at school?
  5 What has Martha made time for during the competition?

Unit 3

3.4 GRAMMAR Present Perfect with *for* and *since*; Present Perfect and Past Simple

I can talk about duration of time, and be general and specific about experiences.

1 **CLASS VOTE** What's your favourite flavour for a fruit juice or smoothie?

2 🔊 1.56 Read the text. In pairs, answer the questions.

The best drink ever!

We've been in Rio since yesterday afternoon. I'm so excited! My parents are from Brazil but we haven't visited the country many times. The plane tickets are very expensive! We didn't want to go sightseeing yesterday, but we went to the beach. My favourite thing in Rio is the juice bars on every street corner. I've never seen so much fruit!

The owner of one juice bar, Rodrigo, has lived in Rio for many years. His father opened Rio's first juice bar in 1958. Many other juice bars have opened since then. I found out that there are 146 different types of fruit in Brazil! Some of them are very unusual. Have you ever heard of cashew apple? It looks like a red apple, but the cashew nut grows at the top of the fruit. I've just tried it. It's amazing.

Amanda

1 What surprises Amanda about Rio?
2 How many types of fruit are there in Brazil?
3 What drink did Amanda try?

3 Study the Grammar box. Which set of words and phrases do we use with *for*? Which do we use with *since*?

A: two o'clock   yesterday   Monday
   last weekend   1958

B: five minutes   a few hours   a long time
   two weeks   three years

Grammar	Present Perfect and Past Simple

Present Perfect with *for* and *since*
I've lived in Rio **for** many years. (a period of time)
They've had this bar **since** 1970. (a point in time)

Present Perfect and Past Simple
We**'ve been** to Sao Paolo.
We **went** to Sao Paolo in 2012.
Have you **ever drunk** a mango smoothie?
Did you **like** it?

GRAMMAR TIME > PAGE 120

4 Make sentences in the Present Perfect using *for* or *since*.

1 I / not / have / a chocolate bar / a month.
  I haven't had a chocolate bar for a month.
2 My family / own / this café / 2010.
3 We / not eat / any food / breakfast time.
4 This cookery programme / be / on TV / a few months.
5 Have / you / see / the cookery teacher / last lesson?
6 They / be / at the juice bar / half an hour.

5 Find more examples in the text of the Present Perfect and Past Simple.

6 🔊 1.57 Complete the dialogue with the Present Perfect and Past Simple forms. Listen and check.

Mia: ¹*Have* you had any fruit juice yet today?
Miguel: No, I ²_____ had any yet, but I'd like some now.
Mia: ³_____ you ever tried sugar apple juice?
Miguel: Yes, I ⁴_____ some yesterday. Sugar apples look like pears! They're very good for you.
Mia: ⁵_____ you like it?
Miguel: Yes, I ⁶_____. Why don't you try some?
Mia: Yeah. I'd love to try it. Where ⁷_____ you buy it?
Miguel: At the juice bar on the beach.

7 Write questions in the Present Perfect and Past Simple. In pairs, ask and answer the questions.

Start with a general question with *ever* (Present Perfect):

- Have you ever eaten … ?
- Have you ever drunk … ?

Then ask about details (Past Simple):

- When did you try it?
- Did you like it?
- What was it like?

3.4 GRAMMAR Present Perfect with *for* and *since*; Present Perfect and Past Simple

Lesson learning objective
Students can talk about duration of time and be general and specific about experiences.

Lead in: Review of *make* and *do*
Write a short dialogue on the board:
A: *Hi, Sam. Do you want to meet later?*
B: *I can't. I've got three pages of History to finish.*
Ask students to say what Sam is doing, using a phrase with *make* or *do*. Elicit: *Sam is doing his homework.*
Then put students into pairs. Each pair should think of a phrase with *make* or *do* and write a two-line dialogue to illustrate their phrase. Invite pairs to act out their dialogues while the class guess what the phrase is.

Exercise 1
Tell students to keep their Students' Books closed. Check that students understand the difference between *a fruit juice* and *a smoothie* (*a fruit juice is just the juice, whereas a smoothie is the whole fruit blended into a liquid*). Ask students to name their favourite flavours and ask if they make them at home or, if not, how often they buy them.

Culture notes
The area where Rio de Janeiro now exists was discovered by the Portuguese on 1 January 1502 and this is why the area was given its name (translated from Portuguese, the name means 'January River'). The city is now the second largest city in Brazil, with a population of about six million people. Rio was the capital of Brazil until 1960, when the city of Brasilia was built specially to be the new capital. Rio is famous for its carnival, for Copacabana beach and for Sugarloaf mountain.

Exercise 2 🔊 1.56
Before students answer the questions, ask them to find the exclamation marks in the text. Ask students why the writer uses them (*to show emotion or something interesting or strange*). Ask which exclamation marks indicate something surprising (*I've never seen so much fruit!, there are 146 different types of fruit in Brazil!*).

Answers:
1 that there are so many juice bars and that there are so many different types of fruit
2 146
3 cashew apple

Exercise 3
Tell students to write in their notebooks the headings *for* and *since*. They should search the text to find time expressions including these prepositions and then write them under the correct heading. Elicit the answers (*since yesterday afternoon, for many years, since then*). Ask students what they think the rules could be for using each of the prepositions. Then tell them to check their ideas by reading the first part of the Grammar box.
Check that students understand the difference between *I have lived in London for five years* (and I am still in London) and *I lived in London for five years* (but I now live somewhere else).

Answers: A since   B for

Extra activity
Write these gapped sentences on the board.
This lesson started ... minutes ago.
This lesson started at ... .
We have been in this lesson for ... .
We have been in this lesson since ... .
Elicit the correct missing information. Ask students to write four sentences about this school year, covering when the year started and how long they have been in this school year, e.g. *The school year started two months ago.* Encourage students to write the time expressions from this activity under the headings they wrote in their notebooks.

Exercise 4
Students again add time expressions to the lists in their notebooks.

Answers:
2 My family has/have owned this café since 2010.
3 We haven't eaten any food since breakfast time.
4 This cookery programme has been on TV for a few months.
5 Have you seen the cookery teacher since last lesson?
6 They've been at the juice bar for half an hour.

Exercise 5
Tell students to look at the second part of the Grammar box. Ask why the first two sentences use two different tenses (*the first sentence refers to sometime in their life so far, the second sentence uses the finished time expression in 2012*). Then tell students to look at the third and fourth sentences. Explain that we ask *Have you ever ...?* (Present Perfect) questions to find out about 'anytime in your life' experiences and that if the response is in the affirmative, our follow-up questions will use the Past Simple because we will be asking about a specific past time. For example, *Have you ever tried a smoothie? Yes, I have. Did you like it? Yes, I did.* Then elicit the examples from the text and the reasons why each tense has been used.

Answers:
Present Perfect: 've been, haven't visited, 've never seen, has lived, have opened, Have you ever heard of, 've just tried
Past Simple: didn't want, went, opened, found out

Exercise 6 🔊 1.57
Elicit the correct answers, asking students to explain their choices.

Answers: 2 haven't 3 Have 4 had 5 Did 6 did 7 did

Exercise 7
When the pairs have finished, give students a time limit to mingle and ask one another their questions.

Further practice
- Workbook page 34
- Grammar Time page 120
- Resource Pack
  Resource 31: Unit 3 Lesson 4 Grammar – Have you? Did you?

3.5 LISTENING and VOCABULARY A dream cake

Lesson learning objective
Students can identify specific detail in speech and describe food.

Lead in: Review of *for* and *since*

Dictate these sentences to students.
I got my mobile phone in …
I met my best friend … ago
I started listening to … in …
Tell students to complete the sentences so that they are true for them. Then put students into groups of four. They should tell one another the information in their three sentences, using the Present Perfect + *for/since*.

Exercise 1
Tell students to keep their Students' Books closed. Ask the question and then ask if students' parents usually make their birthday cake or if they usually buy their cake in a shop.

Exercise 2   🔊 1.58
When students have finished, go through the words in the Vocabulary box with the class to make sure that they have a good understanding of the meaning of each word. Then put them into pairs and tell them to try to make sentences using the words not used in the exercise (i.e. *bitter, dry, fresh, sweet, tasty*). Invite pairs to share their ideas with the class.

Answers: 1 spicy   2 bland   3 delicious   4 rich   5 sour
6 stale

Exercise 3   🔊 1.59
Play the audio twice, the first time so that students can find the answers and the second time to note down the specific phrases that helped them find the answers.

Answers:
1 T (*we went to an amazing show in New York*)
2 F (*He and his team worked for four days to make the cake*)
3 T (*there wasn't enough space in the shop and they made it outside*)
4 F (*it weighed about 700 kilos*)
5 F (*It was really tasty and sweet, but it wasn't very fresh* – meaning that Gianni liked the flavour, even though the cake wasn't perfect)

🔊 1.59

My dad often takes me to car shows. We've been to places like Boston and Washington, and a few years ago we went to an amazing show in New York. When we went in, there was a massive cake in the shape of a car – a yellow Chevrolet Camaro. The top of the cake was like a Transformer robot from the movie. The baker from the cake shop was there and he told people about his baking. He and his team worked for four days to make the cake! It was really big, about three metres high, so there wasn't enough space in the shop and they made it outside! I was there when they cut the cake. There was plenty for everyone because it weighed about 700 kilos! I tried a piece. It was really tasty and sweet, but it wasn't very fresh. It had been there for a few days, so it was a little bit stale.

Exercise 4
Elicit the kind of information that is missing and ask students to guess what it could be, e.g. benny@bennysbakery.com, benny@dreamcakes.com, etc.

Possible answers:
1 words (an email address)
2 a number (a price)
3 words (a flavour)
4 a word (something people need to send)
5 a number (a date)
6 words (a prize e.g. free cakes)

Exercise 5   🔊 1.60
When students have finished, have a class discussion about competitions. Ask if anyone in the class has ever won a prize in a competition and, if they have, what the prize was.

Answers: 1 amazing cakes   2 50   3 coffee   4 birthday
5 31   6 cupcakes

🔊 1.60

Today's competition is very special: you can win a cake from Benny's Bakery for your birthday. In fact, you can design the cake yourself then, if you are chosen as the winner, they will make your ideal cake! Anyone can enter the competition. You need to draw a picture of your perfect cake. Then send an email of your drawing to this address: benny@amazingcakes.com … That's 'amazing cakes' – all one word, no spaces!
The team at Benny's Bakery are very clever. They can make any cake you can think of! And, remember, their birthday cakes usually sell for fifty dollars, so this is an amazing prize!
So, what next? You've designed your cake and you've attached your picture to an email. There are two more things you need to do …
First, choose a flavour. You can choose: chocolate, coffee or vanilla. The chocolate one has fresh cream in the middle, the coffee one has a tasty butter icing, and the vanilla one has a delicious strawberry jam filling.
After that, there's one more important piece of information – tell them your birthday! Don't forget!
Finally, the closing date of the competition for all you cake-lovers. Send your entry by the end of this month. That's Friday January 31.
One more thing: there's a special runners-up prize for five people – twelve fantastic cupcakes in your favourite flavour! So start drawing now!

Exercise 6
When the pairs are finished, join pairs together into groups of four and ask each group to make a decision about which of their cakes sounds the best.

VOX POPS ▶ 3.3
Before watching, check that students understand the meaning of these words/phrases: *crumble, crust, whipped cream, icing, moist*. While watching, students should decide which cake sounds the best and why. Invite students to share their ideas with the class.

Further practice
- Workbook page 35
- Resource Pack
  Resource 32: Unit 3 Lesson 5 Listening and Vocabulary – Food adjectives

◀ 76

3.5 LISTENING and VOCABULARY — A dream cake

I can identify specific detail in speech and describe food.

1 **CLASS VOTE** Is it important to have a special cake on your birthday? Compare your ideas with the class. Vote *Yes* or *No*.

2 🔊 1.58 Study the Vocabulary box, using a dictionary. Choose the correct option. Listen and check.

Vocabulary	Describing food

bitter   bland   delicious   dry   fresh   rich
sour   spicy   stale   sweet   tasty

1 I like chilli popcorn because it's so *spicy / stale*.
2 These cupcakes aren't very tasty, they're quite *sweet / bland*.
3 I love this fruit juice, it's really *dry / delicious*.
4 This cake has icing and a filling with butter, so it's very *rich / bitter*.
5 This milk has been in the sun too long, it tastes *sour / fresh*.
6 This bread is old, I think it's *stale / bitter*.

3 🔊 1.59 Listen to Gianni talking about a very special cake. Mark the sentences T (true) or F (false).

1 ☐ Gianni saw the cake in New York.
2 ☐ The cake took a week to make.
3 ☐ The baker didn't make the cake in his shop.
4 ☐ The cake weighed around 70 kilos.
5 ☐ Gianni didn't like the cake at all.

4 Look at the text. In pairs, decide what kind of information is missing from gaps 1–6: words or numbers?

Is it a car? Is it a robot? No … it's a cake!

5 🔊 1.60 Listen to information about how to enter the competition. Complete the text in Exercise 4.

6 [VOX POPS ▶ 3.3] In pairs, describe the best cake you've ever had. Ask and answer the questions:
- What did it look like?
- What did it taste like?
- What flavour was it?
- Who made it?

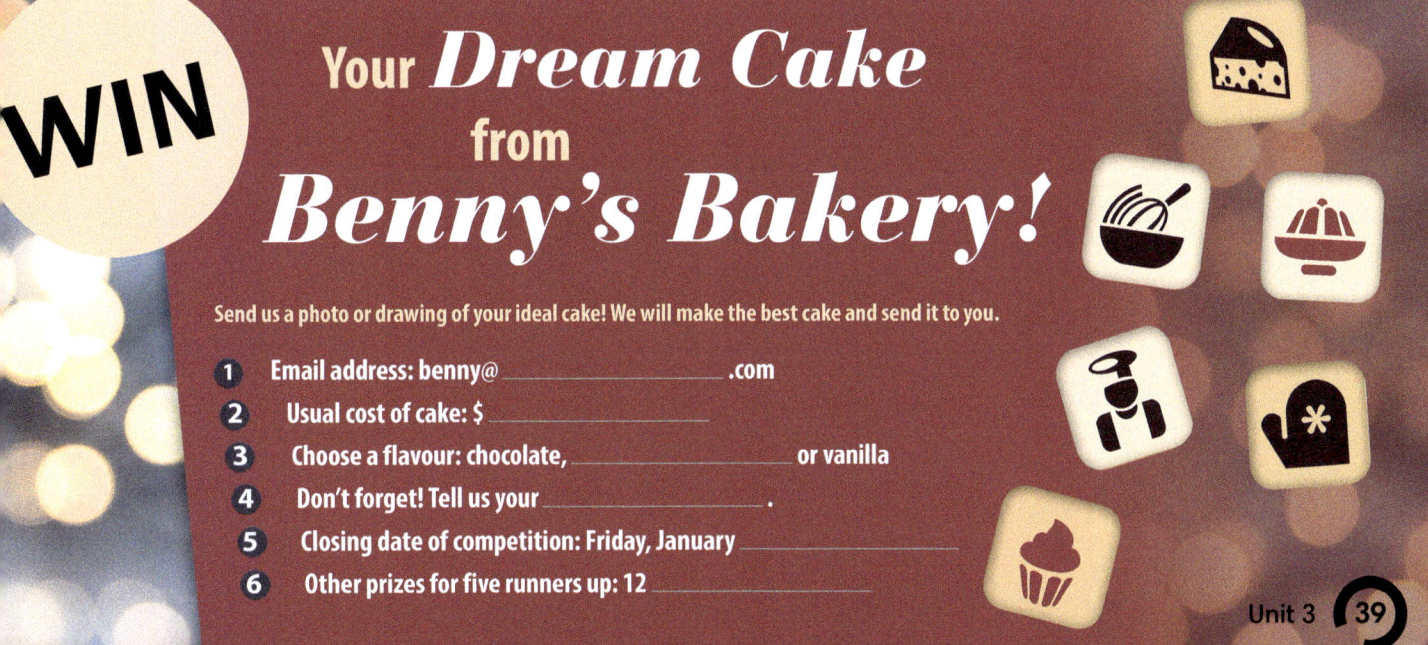

WIN Your *Dream Cake* from *Benny's Bakery!*

Send us a photo or drawing of your ideal cake! We will make the best cake and send it to you.

1 Email address: benny@_____.com
2 Usual cost of cake: $_____
3 Choose a flavour: chocolate, _____ or vanilla
4 Don't forget! Tell us your _____.
5 Closing date of competition: Friday, January _____
6 Other prizes for five runners up: 12 _____

Unit 3   39

3.6 SPEAKING Ordering food

I can order food in a café or restaurant.

Annie's Café

eat in or take away!

Homemade tomato soup and roll
Toasted cheese sandwich
Salad with tuna or cheese
Chocolate cupcakes
A selection of biscuits

Today's speciality: green cake!
ALSO Why not try a smoothie?
Melon-and-mango or
banana-and-strawberry
OR our homemade lemonade!

1 CLASS VOTE What would you like from the menu?

2 ▶ 3.4 🔊 1.61 In pairs, discuss what you think green cake is. Watch or listen and check.

3 🔊 1.61 Read and listen to the dialogue. What do Dan, Alisha, Tommo and Skye order?

VIDEO WHAT CAN I GET YOU?

Annie:	Hi! Take a seat and I'll get you the menus. Here you are. Now what can I get you to drink?
Alisha:	I'll have an apple juice, please.
Dan:	Just water for me, thanks.
Tommo:	Could I have a melon-and-mango smoothie, please?
Annie:	Of course. Are you ready to order?
Alisha:	Nearly. That green cake looks interesting. What's in it?
Annie:	Green tea and yoghurt. It's quite sweet.
Tommo:	Mmmh. I'd like that, please.
Alisha:	Me too.
Dan:	Um, I don't fancy cake today. I'll have a toasted cheese sandwich, please.
Annie:	So that's one toasted sandwich and two slices of cake.
Tommo, Dan and Alisha:	Thanks.
Skye:	Hi, guys. Sorry I'm late.
Tommo:	We've just ordered. What do you want?
Skye:	It's OK. I'll get it. Excuse me. Can I have a hot chocolate, please?
Annie:	Of course. Would you like anything to eat?
Skye:	Not for me, thanks.

OUT of class

Hi, guys. I'll get it!
I don't fancy (cake today).

4 Study the Speaking box. Match questions 1–5 with answers a–e.

Speaking Ordering food

Customer
I'll have … / I'd like a … / a slice of …
Excuse me, can/could I have …
Just … for me, please.
Not for me, thanks.

Waiter
Take a seat and I'll get you the menu.
What would you like to drink?
Are you ready to order?
Would you like anything to eat?
Can I get you something?
Here you are.

1 ☐ Are you ready to order?
2 ☐ What's in it?
3 ☐ What soup do you have?
4 ☐ What can I get you to drink?
5 ☐ Would you like anything to eat?

a Homemade tomato.
b I'll have a cola, please.
c Nearly.
d Not for me, thanks.
e It's just fruit and yoghurt.

5 In pairs or small groups, use the Speaking box to order food from the menu in Exercise 1.

3.6 SPEAKING Ordering food

Lesson learning objective
Students can order food in a café or restaurant.

Lead in: Review of food adjectives

Write on the board the names of four kinds of food, e.g. *chilli con carne, Madras curry, spaghetti bolognese, Hungarian goulash.*

Ask students if they can guess the odd one out of the four kinds of food. Elicit ideas. Elicit or explain that spaghetti bolognese is the odd one out because the other kinds of food are all spicy.

Put students into pairs and tell them to do the same but with a different adjective from the Vocabulary box on page 39 of the Students' Book.

When pairs are ready, invite them to take turns to read out their lists so that the class can guess the odd one out. If students disagree with a pair's ideas, ask them to explain why they disagree and encourage other students to give their opinions.

Exercise 1

Before students open their Students' Books, ask them to think about the last time they ate at a restaurant or café. Students should work in groups of four to tell one another where the restaurant or café was, what kind of choices there were on the menu and what they chose to eat and drink.

Invite students to share their ideas with the class. Then ask them to open their Students' Books and choose from the menu.

Exercise 2 3.4 1.61

Elicit ideas about what green cake might be. Ask what students would do in a restaurant if there was something strange on the menu. Would they choose it, would they reject it or would they ask the waiter to explain what it is?

Answers: A cake made with green tea (and yoghurt).

Exercise 3 1.61

Before you play the audio, encourage pairs to discuss what they can remember from watching the video.

Answers:
Dan: water and a toasted cheese sandwich
Alisha: apple juice and green cake
Tommo: melon-and-mango smoothie and green cake
Skye: hot chocolate

Exercise 4

Elicit who asks the five questions (*the waiter asks 1, 4 and 5; the customer asks 2 and 3*).

After you have elicited the answers, put students into pairs to practise saying the questions and answers. One student should play the role of the waiter and one student should play the role of the customer. Invite pairs to perform the mini dialogues in front of the class.

Answers: 1 c 2 e 3 a 4 b 5 d

Extra activity

Ask students to think of meals that are traditionally eaten in their country. Write on the board the names of four of these meals. Put students into pairs. Each pair discusses how they could explain each meal – what it contains, what it tastes like, why people like it, etc.

Have a class discussion about each meal and a class vote for which meal students prefer.

Exercise 5

Put students into groups of three, so that they can play the roles of two customers and one waiter. When the groups have practised their dialogues, invite them to perform in front of the class. Arrange a desk and two chairs so that students can role play coming into a restaurant, being greeted and being shown to the table.

Further practice

- Workbook page 36
- Resource Pack
  Resource 33: Unit 3 Lesson 6 Speaking – What's in it?
  Resource 34: Unit 3 Lesson 6 Video – What can I get you?

3.7 WRITING   An email to a friend

Lesson learning objective
Students can write an email to a friend.

Lead in: Review of menu items
Write the following on the board:
… soup
Toasted … sandwich
Salad with … or …
Chocolate …
A selection of …
Today's speciality: …
Why not try a … and … smoothie or our homemade …?
Tell students to look at the menu on page 40 and to complete the sentences with their own ideas for food items (i.e. different from the menu).
Then put students into pairs. One student says one of their food items and their partner has to guess which menu item it matches, e.g. A: cheese; B: salad with cheese? A: No. A selection of cheese. Invite pairs to share some of their food items with the class.

Exercise 1
Before students open their Students' Books, ask if they have ever organised a party for friends at their home and, if so, whether they offered their friends food. When organising the class vote, invite students to choose three food items and see which food item is the most popular.

Exercise 2   🔊 1.62
Check that students understand the difference between the words in the Vocabulary box, e.g. when we *slice* we get thin pieces which are the same size as the original item – we slice bread, cucumber, ham, etc. – and when we *chop*, the pieces can be smaller than the original item; we *boil* in water and *fry* in oil).

Answers: A boil   B fry   C slice   D mix   E chop

Exercise 3
Encourage students to think of food items that aren't in the photos or the example. Elicit ideas and check that students are using the vocabulary correctly, as often the same food can be cooked in different ways, e.g. we can fry or boil potatoes and we can chop or slice onions.

Possible answers:
You can boil eggs and vegetables.
You can chop tomatoes and herbs.
You can fry chicken and potatoes.
You can mix mayonnaise with lemon juice.
You can slice eggs and tomatoes.

Exercise 4
When students have finished reading Alisha's email, put them into groups of four. Ask each group to think of a different kind of simple salad and how to make it. Invite groups to share their ideas with the class.

Exercise 5
Elicit the answers and ask students for more details. For example, *What news does Alisha comment about?* (her friend's school trip) *What does Alisha say about her life now?* (she's just finished her exams and is having a party)

What does Alisha invite her friend to do? (come to her party)
How does Alisha ask her friend to reply? (Alisha asks her friend to let her know).

Answers: a 2   b 3   c 1   d 4

Exercise 6
Ask students if they ever write emails to English-speaking friends. If anyone says yes, ask them if they have ever used any of the phrases in the Writing box. If not, ask for examples of how they start or finish their emails.

Answers:
Starting the email: Thanks for getting in touch.
Responding to news: It was great to hear about your school trip.
Giving your news: Tommo and I have just finished our exams; we've decided to have a party
Explain why you're writing: Anyway, I was wondering if you'd like to come.
Ending your email: Let me know if you can make it.

Exercise 7
Tell students to imagine that their friend has sent different news (i.e. not about a school trip). Elicit ideas about what their friend's news might be. Then elicit ideas of other kinds of food that students could make for a party. Finally, ask students to think of different ideas for something they could ask their friend to bring. This brainstorming should help students develop their ideas for their email.
Then look at the first part of Alisha's email. Elicit how else she could have started her email, e.g. *Hi, Great to hear from you! Your school trip sounded great and I loved the photos. They were brilliant. How are things now you're back home?*
Encourage students to use different phrases from Alisha's email, where possible. The email can be written in class or for homework.

Extra activity for fast finishers
If students do the writing activity in the class, tell students who finish early to swap emails with a partner. They should read each other's emails and correct any mistakes they find and suggest possible improvements to their partner's writing.

Homework
Tell students to read the text on page 44 of the Students' Book. They should look up any words they don't know the meaning of and translate them into L1. They should also pay attention to the pronunciation of the words in the text.
As an additional task, tell students to find the origin of the words *chopsticks, cuisine, gourmet* and *bazaar*. Also ask them to list words on the topic of food which their language has taken from other languages.

Further practice
- Workbook page 37
- Resource Pack
  Resource 35: Unit 3 Lesson 7 Writing – Hi!

3.7 WRITING An email to a friend

I can write an email to a friend.

1 **CLASS VOTE** What food would you have at a party with friends?

2 🔊 1.62 Study the Vocabulary box, using a dictionary. Match the words with the pictures.

Vocabulary | Cooking verbs
boil   chop   fry   mix   slice

3 Use the words in the Vocabulary box to make sentences about two types of food.

You can boil potatoes and peas.

4 Read Alisha's email. Does it mention your ideas from Exercise 1?

PARTY TIME

Hi,

Thanks for getting in touch. It was great to hear about your school trip. The photos were awesome.

Tommo and I have just finished our exams and we've decided to have a party tomorrow on his boat! He's bought lots of yummy food, including sausages and cheese. I'm making my famous chicken salad. It's really easy. First, I fry the chicken and boil some eggs. Then I slice them. After that, I chop tomatoes into small pieces and mix everything together with some mayonnaise. I can't tell you how good it is!

Anyway, I was wondering if you'd like to come. We're asking everybody to bring some fruit or some juice because we want to make smoothies of different flavours.

Let me know if you can make it.

Alisha

5 Read the text again. Order the information as it appears in the text.
a ☐ Alisha talks about what's happening in her life now.
b ☐ Alisha invites her friend and asks her friend to do something.
c ☐ 1 Alisha thanks her friend and comments on her friend's news.
d ☐ Alisha asks her friend to reply to the invitation.

6 Look at the Writing box. Underline the sentences that are in the text in Exercise 4.

Writing | Email to a friend

Starting your email
How are things?
Great to hear from you.
Thanks for getting in touch.

Responding to news
It was great to hear about your school trip.
I can't wait to hear more about it.

Giving your news
Tommo and I have just finished our exams.
We've decided to have a party.
I'm making a cake for the party.

Explain why you're writing
Anyway / By the way, I was wondering if you'd like to come.
I'm writing to ask if you'd like to come to the party.

Ending your email
Let me know if you can make it.
See you soon.
Bye for now.

Writing Time

7 Write an email to a friend. Follow the instructions below:
1 thank your friend for his/her email and comment on his/her news
2 explain that you're having a party and describe what food you're making
3 invite your friend and suggest something he/she can make for it

TIPS
• It's important to use the correct style when you write to a friend.
• Use different tenses and don't forget contractions. They make your email sound friendly and informal.

Wordlist and Vocabulary in action

Extra activity

Allocate one column of the Wordlist to each group and ask each group to choose five words with difficult spellings.

Ask one group to dictate their words. One student from each of the other two groups must write the words correctly on the board. A point is awarded for each correct spelling and the group with the most points wins.

Further practice

Workbook page 38

Exercise 1

Possible answers:
1. coffee, lemonade, smoothie, tea
2. dinner, lunch, snack, supper
3. bland, delicious, dry, fresh, refreshing, rich, sour, spicy, stale, sweet, tasty
4. chop, fry, mix, slice
5. baker, chef, cookery teacher, waiter, winner

Exercise 2

2. winner
3. sour
4. bland
5. stale

WORDLIST Food and drink | Flavours | *make* and *do* | Describing food

appearance /əˈpɪərəns/
baker /ˈbeɪkə/
beef /biːf/
bitter /ˈbɪtə/
bland /blænd/
boil /bɔɪl/
bread roll /ˈbred rəʊl/
breakfast /ˈbrekfəst/
building /ˈbɪldɪŋ/
cheese /tʃiːz/
chef /ʃef/
chewing gum /ˈtʃuːɪŋ gʌm/
chicken /ˈtʃɪkɪn/
chilli /ˈtʃɪli/
chocolate /ˈtʃɒklɪt/
chop /tʃɒp/
coconut /ˈkəʊkənʌt/
coffee /ˈkɒfi/
competition /ˌkɒmpəˈtɪʃn/
contestant /kənˈtestənt/
cook /kʊk/
cookery class /ˈkʊkəri klɑːs/
cookery teacher /ˈkʊkəri ˌtiːtʃə/
cream /kriːm/
crisps /krɪsps/
cucumber /ˈkjuːkʌmbə/
cupcake /ˈkʌpkeɪk/
dairy /ˈdeəri/
delicious /dɪˈlɪʃəs/
dinner /ˈdɪnə/
dish /dɪʃ/
dry /draɪ/
egg /eg/
enter /ˈentə/
filling /ˈfɪlɪŋ/
fish /fɪʃ/
flavour /ˈfleɪvə/

flour /flaʊə/
Food Technology /ˈfuːd tekˌnɒlədʒi/
fresh /freʃ/
fruit /fruːt/
fruit juice /ˈfruːt dʒuːs/
fry /fraɪ/
garlic /ˈgɑːlɪk/
grapes /greɪps/
herbs /hɜːbz/
homemade /ˌhəʊmˈmeɪd/
honey /ˈhʌni/
ice cream /ˌaɪs ˈkriːm/
icing /ˈaɪsɪŋ/
lemon /ˈlemən/
lemonade /ˌleməˈneɪd/
lettuce /ˈletɪs/
lunch /lʌntʃ/
mango /ˈmæŋgəʊ/
mayonnaise /ˌmeɪəˈneɪz/
meal /miːl/
meat /miːt/
melon /ˈmelən/
mint /mɪnt/
mix /mɪks/
noodles /ˈnuːdlz/
nuts /nʌts/
order /ˈɔːdə/
oven gloves /ˈʌvən glʌvz/
pea /piː/
peach /piːtʃ/
pear /peə/
pineapple /ˈpaɪnæpl/
popcorn /ˈpɒpkɔːn/
recipe /ˈresəpi/
refreshing /rɪˈfreʃɪŋ/
rice /raɪs/
rich /rɪtʃ/

salad /ˈsæləd/
sausage /ˈsɒsɪdʒ/
serve /sɜːv/
shopping list /ˈʃɒpɪŋ lɪst/
slice /slaɪs/
smoothie /ˈsmuːði/
snack /snæk/
soup /suːp/
sour /saʊə/
speciality /ˌspeʃiˈæləti/
spicy /ˈspaɪsi/
stale /steɪl/
strawberry /ˈstrɔːbəri/
supper /ˈsʌpə/
sweet /swiːt/
sweets /swiːts/
taste /teɪst/
tasty /ˈteɪsti/
tea /tiː/
try /traɪ/
tuna /ˈtjuːnə/
vanilla /vəˈnɪlə/
vegetables /ˈvedʒtəblz/
waiter /ˈweɪtə/
weight /weɪt/
winner /ˈwɪnə/
yoghurt /ˈjɒgət/

WORD FRIENDS

make a cake (cakes)
make a decision
make a mess
make mistakes
make time
do my/your/his/her homework
do my/your/his/her best
put on weight

VOCABULARY IN ACTION

1 Use the wordlist to find:
1. four drinks: *fruit juice*, …
2. four types of main meal or small meal: *breakfast*, …
3. ten adjectives to describe food: *bitter*, …
4. four actions you do when you're cooking: *boil*, …
5. four people: *contestant*, …

2 Use the wordlist to find the opposites of the words below.
1. disgusting *delicious*
2. loser _____
3. sweet _____
4. spicy _____
5. fresh _____

3 In pairs, ask your partner about the spelling of one word in each category in Exercise 1 or 2.

How do you spell tasty?   It's T-A-S-T-Y.

4 🔊 1.63 **PRONUNCIATION** Listen to the underlined vowels in each word and repeat.

/ə/
van<u>i</u>lla   cuc<u>u</u>mber   br<u>ea</u>kfast   may<u>o</u>nnaise
flav<u>ou</u>r   comp<u>e</u>tition

5 In pairs, find more words in the wordlist with the /ə/ sound.

42 Wordlist

Revision

Extra activity

When students have finished Exercises 5 and 6, write on the board *Have*, *Has* and *Did*. Tell students that the whole class is going to work together to make questions. Invite a student to choose one of the three words, e.g. *Has*. That student then chooses a second student, who gives the next word in the question, e.g. *your*. They then nominate a third student to give the next word, e.g. *brother*, and so on, until a question has been completed.

Further practice

- Workbook page 39
- Resource Pack
  Resource 36: Units 1–3
  Vocabulary – Compounds and collocations
  Resource 37: Units 1–3
  Grammar – Questions and tasks

Revision

VOCABULARY

1 Write the correct word for each definition.
1. This person takes part in a competition. **c** o n t e s t a n t
2. This is a type of meat. **b** ___
3. This is a synonym for tasty. **d** ___
4. These are small, round fruit and can be green, red, or black. **g** ___
5. You do this to cook food in very hot water. **b** ___

Exercise 1
2 beef
3 delicious
4 grapes
5 boil

2 In pairs, complete the questions. Then ask and answer the questions in pairs. Make your own food quiz.

Exercise 2
2 sandwich
3 smoothie
4 sweet
5 salad

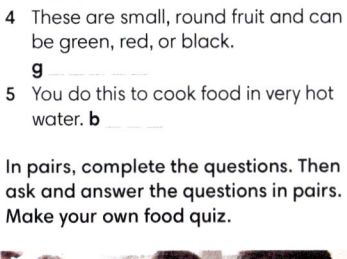

QUIZ Favourite foods beginning with 's'

1. Some people like garlic and chilli with everything! Do you like s**picy** food?
2. You have two slices of bread and butter and you want to make a s____. What filling do you like?
3. You're buying a s____ in a juice bar. What flavour do you choose?
4. You'd love something s____ to eat, like cake. What do you want?
5. Your family is having a nice, healthy, green s____ for dinner. What do you put in it?

3 Complete the sentences with *make* or *do*.
1. I often *make* cakes for my friends.
2. I never ____ mistakes in English lessons.
3. I listen to music when I ____ my homework.
4. I always tidy up when I ____ a mess.
5. I ____ my best to eat healthy food.

Exercise 3
2 make
3 do
4 make
5 do

GRAMMAR

4 Complete the dialogue with the words below.

already yet just for since

Ana: Hi, Mum! Have you made my birthday cake ¹*yet*?
Mum: Yes, I've ² ____ taken it out of the oven. It's still warm.
Ana: Brilliant! We haven't had cake ³ ____ ages! It looks amazing. What about the rest of the food? Is there any pizza?
Mum: Yes, everything's ready for the party. Go and look.
Ana: Oh, you've ⁴ ____ put all the food on the table. Thanks, Mum.
Mum: I'm glad you like it. I've been in the kitchen ⁵ ____ midday!

Exercise 4
2 just
3 for
4 already
5 since

5 Write five questions using one word or phrase from each column.

	your mum/dad	ever been in a competition?
	you	go to the supermarket last weekend?
Have/Has Did	your brother/sister	ever made a cake?
	your friends	cook dinner yesterday?
	your teacher	ever had a picnic or a barbecue outside?
	your parents	take the family to a restaurant last year?
	your grandparents	ever eaten too much at a party?

Did you cook dinner yesterday?

6 In pairs, ask and answer your questions from Exercise 5.

Did you cook dinner yesterday?
No, I didn't cook yesterday, but I've cooked dinner a few times.

SPEAKING

7 In pairs, role play the situation. Follow the instructions.

Student A, you are a waiter. Ask the customer
- to take a seat, and offer to get the menu.
- if he/she is ready to order food.
- what he/she would like to drink.

Student B, you are a customer. Make your order from the menu on page 144.

DICTATION

8 🔊 1.64 Listen, then listen again and write down what you hear.

SELF-ASSESSMENT Think about this unit. What did you learn? What do you need help with?   **WORKBOOK** p. 38

Exercise 8

Adam's wanted to be a chef since he was five, so he's entered a cooking competition. Yesterday he made delicious bread rolls. Today the contestants have been in the kitchen for hours, but Adam hasn't done well. His cake isn't very tasty.

CULTURE

What do the British really eat?

Popular food in the UK

Most people think that food in Britain is all about fish and chips, chip butties or afternoon tea, but that's not the whole story. There are so many different cultures in the UK that you have a huge choice of flavours and cuisines to choose from.

1. Indian food has been the country's favourite for years. Every town has at least one Indian restaurant. People even say that the national dish is now *chicken tikka masala*, a spicy curry usually served with rice or Indian bread called naan. It's delicious!

2. American food is everywhere. There's not only McDonald's now, but new gourmet burger restaurants like Five Guys. American food is popular because the recipes are very familiar to British people – hot dogs, fried chicken, pepperoni pizza, nachos and BBQ ribs are all big favourites.

3. People have a passion for fresh and healthy food these days and that's why Japanese food is popular. It's also easy to eat as a takeaway meal. Young people now prefer to eat sushi at lunchtime to the traditional British sandwich, although some still have problems with chopsticks!

Do you want to try more international food? Then check out the amazing Zaza Bazaar in Bristol! It opened in 2011 and has become one of the most popular places to eat in the city. It's also the biggest restaurant; they can serve over 1,000 people and have food from everywhere – Vietnam, Italy, China, Thailand, as well as Britain's three favourites, of course!

GLOSSARY
chopstick (n) a pair of thin sticks used for eating in China and Japan
cuisine (n) style of cooking typical of a country or region
gourmet (adj) (of food) high quality

BBC CULTURE   What do the British really eat?

Lead in: Topic introduction

Tell students not to open their Students' Books. Put students into groups of four. If you set the homework suggestion for the unit, ask the groups to discuss any vocabulary they found difficult. If you also set the additional task, ask them also to discuss the words on the topic of food which their language has taken from other countries.

If students haven't done the homework, ask them to look at the glossary on page 44. Students should find the words in the text and discuss what their own country's cuisine would include and how a gourmet burger would differ from a normal burger.

Students then discuss as a class their favourite cuisine and why they like it, e.g. *I love Italian cuisine because I like pasta and cheese.*

 3.5

Indian food Liverpool style

Part 1

This is Anjum Anand. She's a food writer and a chef born in London, but of Indian origin. In this series she travels to different cities in the UK to find a wide range of Indian food and flavours. She also teaches inexperienced cooks how to make great Indian food.

In this programme she's in Liverpool, where there's a large community from the Southern Indian state of Kerala. She meets Lynn Mitchell, who works for a hospital in the city. The plan is to take part in a local farmers' market to raise money for charity. Lynn wants to sell Indian food at the market. The problem is that Lynn has never cooked Indian food, so it's going to be a real challenge.

Kerala is in the south-west of India and is a popular holiday destination for British people. A lot of Keralan people have come to Liverpool in the last ten years to look for work. There are now over one thousand families there. Anjum is going to teach Lynn three traditional Keralan dishes – coconut chicken with ginger, which has a lovely sweet flavour, delicious salmon wraps with curry leaves and finally, rice noodles. Keralan specialities include a lot of fruit and fish. The cuisine is very light and healthy compared to other Indian food.

In Liverpool it's easy to find the ingredients for these dishes – Anjum can find all the fruit, vegetables and spices that she needs in special Keralan shops.

 3.6

Part 2

N = Narrator   A = Anjum   L = Lynn
B, C, D = Farmers' market customers

N: First, Lynn chops and fries up all the ingredients. When the dishes are ready, Anjum tries them. They are really tasty! Lynn hasn't made any mistakes yet.
A: Mmm, that's amazing!
L: Oh good, oh good!
A: That's perfect!
L: Oh, fantastic!
N: Now they're both ready to take the food to the market with Lynn's daughter. More than 5,000 people visit Liverpool's monthly farmers' market. Indian food is very popular but the question is, will the local people like these Keralan specialities?
At first, things are not easy – people are not sure. It's the first time Lynn has ever cooked outside and she's very nervous. But then things change – people seem to love the food and soon all of it has gone!
B: Beautiful!
C: Mmm, tastes lovely!
D: That is excellent – but very hot!
N: Since she began this project, Lynn has learnt a lot about cooking Indian food and they have raised lots of money for charity. Lynn's really, really happy! So, what do the British really eat? Keralan food – at least in Liverpool they do!

Exercise 1

Tell students that, for the first two questions, they should talk not only about national dishes but also about any popular foreign food. Invite pairs to share their ideas with the class.

Exercise 2

Discuss the glossary with students. Ask if anyone in the class has ever tried using chopsticks and if they found them easy or difficult to use. Elicit or explain how to pronounce *cuisine* and *gourmet* and ask students which language they think these words come from (*French*). Elicit the answers to Exercise 2 and ask students to give reasons from the text.

Answers:
1. T (they think of traditional food whereas nowadays there is food from all over the world)
2. T (*Every town has at least one Indian restaurant*)
3. F (examples include burgers, hot dogs, fried chicken, pepperoni pizza, nachos and BBQ ribs)
4. F (young people eat it at lunchtime)
5. F (*as well as Britain's three favourites* – these were identified as being Indian, American and Japanese food)

Exercise 3

When students have finished, put them into groups of four. Tell each group to add more adjectives to describe the three cuisines. They should then think of two more cuisines and write adjectives to describe them, e.g. *French cuisine – rich, creamy, tasty*. Tell students they can use both positive and negative adjectives. Invite groups to share their ideas with the class.

Answers: 1 c 2 a 3 b

Exercise 4 ▶ 3.5

Play Part 1 of the video with the sound switched off. Pause at these points and elicit what is being shown: 5s (*tomatoes*), 11s (*garlic – sliced*), 26s (*a herb – parsley or coriander – chopped*), 41s (*potatoes – sliced*), 59s (*onions – fried*). Then play Part 1 of the video again, this time with the sound switched on and tell students to answer the questions in Exercise 4.

Answers:
1. Anjum – a food writer and chef; Lynn – a cook in a hospital
2. Indian food

Exercise 5 ▶ 3.5

Put students into pairs. Before you play Part 1 of the video again, tell them to read the sentences and to discuss what they remember.

Answers: 1 southern 2 raise money for charity 3 light and healthy 4 easy

Exercise 6

Ask them to look at the choices in the exercise and to try to remember what the narrator said in the video.

Answers: 2, 3 and 5

Exercise 7

Put students into groups of three. Tell them to discuss the questions and then invite groups to share their ideas with the class.

Exercise 8 ▶ 3.6

Before you play Part 2 of the video, encourage students to read the questions and to discuss their ideas in pairs. Ask students if they have ever watched a cooking demonstration, with food being given to people to taste or with food being sold.
When students have watched Part 2 of the video, ask if they would buy the food if they were at the market at that time and, if they wouldn't, to give reasons why not.

Answers: 1 Yes (she says it is *amazing* and *perfect*) 2 5,000 3 No (at first they aren't sure) 4 Yes (*soon, all of it has gone*)

Exercise 9

Elicit ideas about when students may have cooked for a lot of people, e.g. on a scout camp, at home, for a party.
Put students into groups of four to discuss the questions. When they are ready, invite groups to tell the class about their experiences.

Extra activity

Keep students in their groups of four. Tell them to imagine they are at the Liverpool farmers' market and will be cooking some dishes from their own country to raise money for charity. The food should be easy to cook and attractive for people who don't know this kind of food. When each group has decided which dishes they will cook, two students play the role of the cooks and two students play the role of English customers. The English customers ask the cooks what the dishes are called and what kind of food they contain, they buy the dishes, try them and then comment on the dishes. When they are ready, invite each group to act out their role play in front of the class.

Exercise 10

Discuss questionnaires with the class. Elicit what kinds of questions could be asked in a questionnaire and which tenses could be used, e.g. Present Simple – *Do you like …?* / *How often do you …?*; Past Simple – *When did you last …?*; Present Perfect – *Have you ever …?*
Discuss why questionnaires often have *yes/no* or multiple-choice answers (*because they make it easier to work out the results*). Point out, though, that it could be interesting to include at least one open question, e.g. *What's your favourite …?*
Put students into groups of four and, when they have prepared their questionnaire, make sure that each student in the group has a copy of the same questionnaire, so that everyone in the group is asking the same questions to their friends and family. Give them a time limit for collecting their results. Allocate a time in a future lesson for the groups to present their results to the class.

Further practice

- Workbook pages 40–41
- Resource Pack
  Resource 38: Unit 3 BBC Culture Lesson – English food
  Resource 39: Unit 3 Culture – Cuisines

EXPLORE

1 In pairs, ask and answer the questions.
1. What do people like eating in your country?
2. What are your favourite dishes?
3. What do you think British people really eat?

2 Read the article. Mark the sentences T (true) or F (false). Then check your answers to question 3 in Exercise 1.
1. ☐ People have the wrong idea about food in the UK.
2. ☐ It's easy to find an Indian restaurant in the UK.
3. ☐ American food is not very varied.
4. ☐ A lot of people eat sushi for their evening meal.
5. ☐ Zaza Bazaar doesn't serve Indian food.

3 According to the article, why is each food particularly popular? Match types of food 1–3 with adjectives a–c.
1. American   a. practical
2. Japanese   b. tasty
3. Indian   c. familiar

EXPLORE MORE

4 ▶ 3.5 Watch Part 1 of the video and answer the questions.
1. Who are Anjum and Lynn?
2. What type of food are they cooking?

5 ▶ 3.5 Watch again. Choose the correct option.
1. Kerala is in *northern / southern* India.
2. Anjum and Lynn go to the market to *raise money for charity / help the community*.
3. Keralan food is *heavy and spicy / light and healthy*.
4. It's *easy / difficult* to find the ingredients for Keralan dishes in Liverpool.

6 Tick the three dishes that Anjum and Lynn are going to make.
1. ☐ coconut curry with pepper
2. ☐ coconut chicken with ginger
3. ☐ spicy salmon wraps
4. ☐ rice and salmon wraps
5. ☐ rice noodles
6. ☐ vegetable noodles

7 Which of the three dishes would you like to try? Why?

I'd like to try the first dish because I love coconut.

8 ▶ 3.6 Watch Part 2 of the video. Answer the questions.
1. Does Anjum like Lynn's cooking?
2. How many people visit Liverpool's farmers' market?
3. Do the people at the market buy Lynn's food immediately?
4. Do they sell all the food?

9 Have you ever cooked for a lot of people? Or have you ever helped out in the kitchen? What did you do?

I once helped my mum cook dinner for six.

YOU EXPLORE

10 **CULTURE PROJECT** In groups, prepare a survey based on the question: 'What do people really eat in your town?'
1. Prepare a questionnaire. Include local and international dishes (e.g. pizza, burgers).
2. Give the questionnaire to friends and family. Then collect the results.
3. Report your results to the class.

Unit 3 45

Curtain up!

VOCABULARY
Types of films | Film and TV | Compound nouns

GRAMMAR
Comparatives and superlatives | Quantifiers | Adverbs of manner

Grammar: How many bangles are you wearing?

Speaking: Do you want to try it?

BBC **Culture:** London celebrates

Workbook p. 52

BBC VOX POPS

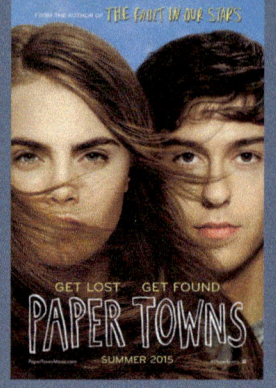

4.1 VOCABULARY Film and TV

I can talk about films and television.

1 🔊 **2.01** Study the Vocabulary A box. Use the words to describe the films in the posters. Sometimes more than one word is possible.

Vocabulary A	Types of films
action film cartoon comedy documentary fairy tale fantasy romantic film sci-fi thriller	

I think Arctic Tale *is a documentary.*

2 **I KNOW!** Can you add more film types to the Vocabulary A box?

3 🔊 **2.02** Match speakers 1–6 to films in the Vocabulary A box.

1 documentary   3 _____   5 _____
2 _____   4 _____   6 _____

4 In pairs, talk about your favourite film or TV programme.

A: *My favourite film is* Minions. *It's a cartoon.*
B: *What's it about?*
A: *It's about some minions. They're small, yellow creatures.*
B: *What's it like?*
A: *It's very funny.*

Speaking	Talking about a film or TV programme
My favourite film is … It's a (*comedy, an action film etc*). What's it about? It's about (*a group of friends*). Who's in it? … is/are the main actor(s). What's it like? It's + adjective (*exciting/scary/strange/dramatic*).	

Unit contents

Vocabulary
- Types of films
- Film and TV
- Compound nouns

Grammar
- Comparatives and superlatives
- Quantifiers
- Adverbs of manner

Communication skills
- Talking about preferences

Examples of 21st Century Skills/Competencies
- Critical Thinking: page 46 (Exercise 1), pages 56–57
- Collaboration: page 47 (Exercise 8), page 51 (Exercise 6), page 57 (Exercise 10)
- Assessment for Learning: page 55
- Autonomy and Personal Initiative: page 48 (Exercise 6)

4.1 VOCABULARY   Film and TV

Lesson learning objective
Students can talk about films and television.

> **Lead in: Review of vocabulary and grammar from the previous unit**

Put students into pairs. Explain that you are going to give them clues or definitions of words and that they should write the word. When they have finished, tell the pairs to swap their answers with another pair. Go through the answers and see which pairs have the most correct answers.
Possible clues and definitions:
Cook in water (boil)
A person whose job is to cook in a restaurant (chef)
A very hot spice (chilli)
Food such as milk, cream, butter and cheese (dairy)
An adjective to describe food that is old and not fresh (stale)
You wear these to stop your hands getting burnt when you take something out of the oven (oven gloves)
Instructions to show you how to cook something (recipe)
An adjective to describe things like lemon juice; it is the opposite of sweet (sour)
An adjective to describe food which is very tasty and good (delicious)
A person who brings you food in a restaurant (waiter)

> **Background notes**
>
> *The Avengers* is a series of popular action films starring several super heroes. In the film *Age of Ultron*, a program (Ultron) that has been created to protect the world starts to go wrong and threatens the planet. The superheroes work together to stop Ultron.
> *Paper Towns* is a mystery romance about two teenagers. A girl who loves mysteries takes her neighbour on a night-time tour of their town and then suddenly disappears, leaving clues for her friend about how to find her.
> *Ghost Protocol* is the fourth film in the *Mission Impossible* action series starring Tom Cruise. In this film, he has to fight terrorists who want to use nuclear bombs against the USA.
> *Mirror Mirror* is a comedy adventure film starring Julia Roberts. It is based on the famous fairy story *Snow White*. A princess, with the help of seven dwarves, tries to save her land from an evil queen and, at the same time, win back the prince who she once loved.
> *Arctic Tale* is a documentary film looking at both a walrus mother and her calf and a polar bear mother and her cubs. It shows how difficult and dangerous life in the Arctic can be.

Exercise 1   2.01

When students have finished, ask the class which of the films they have seen and what they thought about them. If students haven't seen the films, ask if any of the posters would make them want to see the films.

Possible answers:
The Avengers: action film, fantasy, thriller
Paper Towns: romantic film (officially also *drama* and *mystery*)
Ghost Protocol: action film, thriller
Mirror Mirror: comedy, fairy tale, fantasy
Arctic Tale: documentary

Exercise 2

Put students into pairs. Give a time limit of two minutes. Students should think of an example for every genre of film.

Possible answers: crime film (e.g. *Sherlock Holmes*), drama (e.g. *Romeo and Juliet*), horror (e.g. *The Ring*), musical (e.g. *Les Miserables*), mystery (e.g. *Veronica Mars*), romcom (e.g. *Bridget Jones' Diary*), war film (e.g. *Saving Private Ryan*), western (e.g. *The Lone Ranger*)

Exercise 3   2.02

When students have finished, put them into pairs and ask them to write a similar one- or two-sentence example of something that might be said in other types of films. When they are ready, invite pairs to read out their sentences, to see if the other students can guess the type of film.

Answers: 2 romantic film   3 thriller   4 fairy tale   5 sci-fi   6 action film

2.02

See page 247.

Exercise 4

Go through the example dialogue and the Speaking box. When the pairs have finished, invite them to perform their dialogue in front of the class, replacing the title of the film with the word *blank*, e.g. *My favourite film is blank*. When the other students have listened to the whole dialogue, they should guess the title of the film.

Exercise 5

Point out that the words in the third column are also nouns, but that these nouns refer to people rather than things. If students have difficulties with the second, fifth and sixth gaps, give them these clues: *you don't **perform** special effects*, so **perform** can't be the correct answer; the film *Bears* is presumably a documentary about bears, so the bears themselves are the **performers** and it must be the **producers** who had to learn about them; *musical **production*** could also be correct in this sentence.

Answers: **2** produce **3** act **4** entertainment **5** producer(s) **6** performance

Exercise 6

Give a strict time limit for this exercise, to encourage students to practise their scanning skills and not try to complete the gaps during their first read-through.

Answers: **1** an old **2** time machine

Exercise 7   2.03

When students have completed the text, ask questions to check their understanding of the vocabulary.
What do we call the creation of images in a film using computer graphics, models or other methods? (special effects)
What do we call a person in a story, for example, James Bond or Jason Bourne? (a character)
What do we call the people who watch a film, TV show or play? (an audience)
What do we call articles in newspapers, magazines or websites which give the writer's opinion of a film, a TV show or a play? (reviews)
What do we call a TV show with several parts which are shown each week? (a series)
What do we call each individual part of a series? (an episode)
What do we call a film, a song, a book, etc., which is very popular? (a hit)

Answers: **2** series **3** hit **4** reviews **5** audience **6** special effects **7** episode **8** character

Exercise 8

Before students start their discussions, elicit one or two examples of each topic. When students have finished, invite pairs to share their ideas with the class.

Exercise 9   2.04

Answers:

	Emma	Max
Favourite TV series	Star Trek	The Simpsons
Type of programme	sci-fi	cartoon/comedy
What's it like?	dramatic/cool	funny/sad
Best special effect/scene	a spaceship destroys a city	Bart Simpson fails an exam

2.04

E = Emma   M = Max

E: Did you see *Star Trek* on TV last night, Max? It was so good.
M: No, I can't stand it. I'm not really into sci-fi or action programmes.
E: But it was really dramatic and the special effects are so cool.
M: Oh, yes, I know. My brother was watching it. I saw the spaceship destroy the city … yes, that was good. But then I carried on watching *The Simpsons*.
E: Ugh, I hate cartoons.
M: I know you do, but I love them. And … although it's a comedy, there's a mixture of funny and sad scenes. Last night, for example, Bart Simpson failed an exam … by one point! … He was really sad … I nearly cried.
E: Oh, perhaps I should watch that episode. It sounds good.

Background notes

Star Trek is an American sci-fi series about the *Starship Enterprise* and its exploration of the universe. The original TV series ran from 1966–1969. Each episode started by saying the mission was *to boldly go where no man has gone before*. In 1987 a new TV series started, called *Star Trek: The Next Generation*. There have also been many *Star Trek* films (thirteen films between 1979 and 2016).

The Simpsons is an animated TV series which started in 1989. In 2009 it became the longest-running American TV series and there have now been over 600 episodes. The main characters are Homer and Marge Simpson and their three children, Bart, Lisa and Maggie.

Exercise 10

When the pairs have discussed their favourite TV series, ask them to tell the rest of the class about their partner.

VOX POPS ▶ 4.1

After watching, elicit the titles of the programmes mentioned by the speakers, and what students learned from the speakers about these programmes. Ask students if they have ever heard of or watched any of the programmes and, if they have, elicit their opinions.

Extra activity

Put students into groups of three. Tell each group to think of a film or TV series and a particular line which is said by one of the characters, e.g. *My name's Bond, James Bond*. Two of the students should role play being directors and tell the third student, the 'actor', their line. They explain how the actor should say the words in the line and how he/she should act and give advice and criticism until they are happy with the actor's performance. When the groups are ready, each actor performs his/her line in front of the class.

Further practice

- Workbook pages 42–43
- Resource Pack
  Resource 40: Unit 4 Lesson 1 Vocabulary – That's entertainment

MINIONS!

5 **WORD BUILDING** Study the table. Complete the sentences.

Verb	Noun	Person
act	action	actor
entertain	entertainment	entertainer
produce	production	producer
perform	performance	performer

TEENLINK:
film and TV news by you for you!

- I'm not sure about the new *Mission Impossible*. Tom Cruise is a good ¹a*ctor* but I didn't like the story.

- I'd love to know how they ²p_____ the special effects in *The Avengers*. They're really cool.

- The costumes and the make-up were brilliant in the film. I don't know how they can ³a_____ with all that stuff on their faces.

- Yes, we all watched *Minions* in our house. My dad said it was great family ⁴e_____.

- Before making the film *Bears*, the ⁵p_____ had to learn a lot about them.

- I liked the *Mamma Mia* film much better than the musical ⁶p_____ it was based on!

★★★★★

6 Read the website. Choose the correct option.

Dr Who

1 *Dr Who* is *a new / an old* TV programme.
2 The Tardis is a *type of car / time machine*.

7 🔊 **2.03** Study the Vocabulary B box, using a dictionary. Complete the text with the words. Listen and check.

Vocabulary B	Film and TV

audience   character   episode   hit
reviews   ~~screen(s)~~   series   special effects

He's 900 years old and we love him!

The first *Doctor Who* appeared on our TV ¹*screens* in 1963. The producers wanted a family adventure ²_____ for Saturday evenings. It was an instant ³_____ and received great ⁴_____ from people of all ages. Although it was in black and white, the TV ⁵_____ liked the ⁶_____ which were difficult to produce in those days. In the first ⁷_____, two school teachers follow one of their pupils home. They discover that she lives with her grandfather, and that's when we meet the amazing ⁸_____ of the Doctor! He owns the Tardis, a time machine that can transport people through time. When the teachers enter the Tardis, they go back in time …

8 In pairs, discuss the topics below.
- a popular TV series at the moment
- your favourite character from a film or from TV
- an example of a special effect
- a song that was a big hit last year
- a film that had bad reviews

9 🔊 **2.04** Listen to the dialogue. Complete the table.

	Emma	Max	You
Favourite TV series			
Type of programme			
What's it like?			
Best special effect/scene			

10 [VOX POPS ▶ 4.1] Think about a TV series you like, and complete the table to make it true for you. In pairs, discuss your ideas.

4.2 GRAMMAR   Comparatives and superlatives

I can compare different things.

Curtain Up! ★★★★★

Your seat moves, you feel water on your face and you can smell something. It's the latest 4D cinema experience. The screens are bigger and the seats are in the most comfortable position for your eyes and neck. But, is it fun? 'It's more exciting than 3D,' said 15-year-old Adam, 'because it's brighter and louder.' His friend Jessica agrees. 'The most exciting scene was in the car. I felt like I was driving but I wasn't going fast enough.' For others, the experience isn't as good as 3D, and you can feel dizzy. 'The moving seats were worse than the sound,' said Alice. 'I was too uncomfortable. Some special effects are also scarier in 4D. Of course, the tickets are also more expensive, but it seems some people are happy to pay for "the best feeling" in the world!'

1 **CLASS VOTE** Do you prefer watching films at home or at the cinema?

2 🔊 **2.05** Read the text quickly. Choose the correct option.
1. Adam has just watched a film in *3D / 4D*.
2. They watched the film *in a theatre / at the cinema*.

3 Study the Grammar box. Find more examples of comparatives and superlatives in the text.

Grammar	Comparatives and superlatives

Comparative
The new screens are *brighter*.
It's *more interesting than* the theatre.

Superlative
It's *the latest* sci-fi film.
The most exciting part was at the end.
It's *the best* cinema in the town.

too / (not) enough
I was *too* hot.
I felt like I was walking but I was*n't* going fast *enough*.

(not) as … as
However, others say the film is*n't as* good *as* the book.

GRAMMAR TIME ▶ PAGE 121

4 Complete the sentences with the correct form of the words in brackets.
1. *Doctor Who* is the *best* (good) series ever!
2. It's _____ (cheap) to watch films at home than at the cinema and it's _____ (relaxing).
3. *Top Gear* is the _____ (funny) programme on TV.
4. The book is _____ (interesting) than the film.
5. The _____ (expensive) cinema ticket is £20.
6. The _____ (bad) thing is when people keep talking in the cinema.

5 Complete the second sentence so that it means the same as the first one.
1. In the film, the adults aren't as good as the children.
   In the film, the children are *better than* the adults.
2. Our town isn't big enough to have a good theatre.
   Our town is _____ to have a good theatre.
3. The film is funnier than the book.
   The book isn't _____ the film.
4. The main character in the fairy tale is too old.
   The main character in the fairy tale isn't _____.
5. The French thriller isn't as scary as the Danish thriller.
   The Danish thriller is _____ the French thriller.

6 [VOX POPS ▶ 4.2] What's your opinion? Write two sentences for each comparison.
1. the theatre / the cinema
   The cinema is cheaper than the theatre.
   The theatre isn't as exciting as the cinema.
2. comedies / documentaries
3. films / books
4. sci-fi films / fairy tales

4.2 GRAMMAR Comparatives and superlatives

Lesson learning objective
Students can compare different things.

Lead in: Review of vocabulary for types of film

Put students into groups of three. Tell students that you are going to dictate some headings and that they should write the heading and think of examples to write under it. Dictate: *TV series, science-fiction film, action film, fantasy, romantic film, cartoon.*
When students are finished, elicit their examples and write them on the board.

Exercise 1
Tell students to keep their Students' Books closed and ask the question. After you have held the class vote, ask students to work in pairs and to write a list of the advantages and disadvantages of each choice. Invite pairs to share their ideas with the class.

Exercise 2 🔊 2.05
Students should keep their Students' Books closed. Ask students if they can say what the difference is between 2D and 3D films. Ask which they prefer to watch and to name the best 3D film they have seen. Then discuss 4D films and ask students if they can say what the difference is between 3D and 4D films (*4D films have an additional non-visual aspect, e.g. vibrating seats, wind/rain effects, smoke, smell*). Then tell students to open their books and to read the text while they listen to the audio.

Answers: 1 4D   2 at the cinema

Exercise 3
Explain when we use the different forms.
Comparatives – we use these to compare two things, e.g. *Daniel Craig is a **better** James Bond than Pierce Brosnan.*
Superlatives – we use these to compare three or more things, e.g. *Sean Connery is **the best** James Bond.*
too/(not) enough – we use these to show that there is a problem, e.g. *I don't want to go out. I'm **too** tired. / I can't go to see this film. I'm **not** old **enough**.*
(not) as … as – we use this as an alternative (or more polite) way to compare two things, e.g. *Tom is **not as** intelligent **as** Claire* sounds more polite than *Tom is stupider than Claire.*

Answers:
Comparatives: bigger, more exciting, brighter, louder, isn't as good as, worse, scarier, more expensive
Superlatives: the most comfortable, the most exciting, the best

Exercise 4
Discuss the example with the class. Ask why it uses a superlative (*it is comparing all TV series ever, not just two TV series*).
When students have finished, elicit the answers and the reasons why in each case either the comparative or the superlative is correct.

Answers: 2 cheaper, more relaxing   3 funniest
4 more interesting   5 most expensive   6 worst

Exercise 5
Before students do the exercise, put them into pairs and tell them to write three comparative sentences about any topics they like. They should use a mixture of short adjectives which take the *-er* form and long adjectives which take the *more* + adjective form. Elicit a few examples, to make sure the pairs are writing them correctly. Tell fast finishers to rewrite their sentences using (*not*) *as … as*.

Answers: 2 too small   3 as funny as   4 young enough
5 scarier than

Exercise 6
Tell students that for each topic they should use a comparative form and a (*not*) *as … as* form.
When students have finished, put them into groups of four so that they can compare their opinions. Invite groups to share some of their sentences with the class.

VOX POPS ▶ 4.2
While watching, tell students to find out which topics from Exercise 6 are **not** discussed in the video (i.e. *science fiction, fairy tales*), and for which topics the speakers have different opinions (i.e. *documentaries, comedies*). After watching, invite students to give their opinions about what the speakers said.

Extra activity
Put students into groups of three. Tell each group to think of a film or TV series, e.g. *The Avengers*. Explain that they should write a sentence about their film or TV series using each of the structures in the Grammar box (i.e. a comparative, a superlative, an example of *too* or (*not*) *enough* and an example of (*not*) *as … as*. For example:
*The Avengers is **the best** superheroes series.*
*Robert Downey Jr is a **better** actor than Chris Evans.*
*The third Avengers film is**n't as good as** the first.*
*Sometimes the situations in the films are **too** unbelievable.*
When the groups have finished, invite them to read out their sentences to the class.

Further practice
- Workbook page 44
- Grammar Time page 121
- Resource Pack
  Resource 41: Unit 4 Lesson 2 Grammar – Bourne is better than Bond

4.3 READING and VOCABULARY   A theatre evening

Lesson learning objective
Students can understand the main points of an article and talk about entertainment.

Lead in: Review of comparatives and superlatives

Discuss the Oscars with the class and ask them what they can remember about any Oscar winners. Tell students that they are going to hold their own Oscar awards. Write on the board the headings: *Best Actor*, *Best Actress*, *Best Film*. Then elicit the names of five actors, five actresses and five films and write these on the board.

Put students into groups of four. Tell them to imagine that they are the judges at the Oscars. For each category, they should discuss the five names on the board and decide which one they think is the best, giving reasons why. If there is any disagreement, students should give their opinions and try to persuade the rest of the group to agree with their opinion. When the groups are ready, invite them to present their Oscar winners, giving their reasons, e.g. *We chose … as the best film. It's got better special effects than … . Also, the dialogues are more interesting and the story is more believable.*

Exercise 1
Tell students to keep their Students' Books closed. Discuss the question with the class and encourage students to give reasons for their opinions. If students have been on a school trip to the theatre, ask what show they saw and whether or not they enjoyed it.

Exercise 2
Explain to students that they may not see the actual objects in the pictures, but that they should try to use the words given somehow in their descriptions.

Exercise 3 🔊 2.06
Elicit the answer. Then ask how many friends Nathan can take with him (*three*) and why it is difficult for him to make a decision (*because he thinks that all the shows look good*).

Answer: His mother is getting him theatre tickets for his birthday.

Exercise 4 🔊 2.07
Before students read and listen, ask them which show they would choose to go to, just by looking at the pictures and without knowing anything about the four shows. Elicit ideas and encourage students to give reasons for their choices.
When students have done the exercise, elicit the reasons for each answer, e.g. *Katie – musical, fun, finishes before 9 p.m.*; *Elena – things in her life (friendship, family and love), good actors (brilliant performance)*; *Luke – drama, classical plays, fresh interpretation*).

Answers: Katie C   Elena D   Luke A

Exercise 5
Ask students if they have changed their minds about which show they would choose, now that they have learnt more about them. Invite students to share their ideas with the class.

Extra activity
Put students into pairs and tell them to role play Nathan and one of his parents. Now that they have had these three responses from Nathan's friends, they aren't sure which show to choose. They want to choose one that all the friends will enjoy and be able to go to. The pairs should discuss and decide on one show, giving reasons why. When they are ready, invite pairs to tell the class their ideas.

Exercise 6 🔊 2.08
Discuss the highlighted vocabulary with students. Elicit the meanings of the different phrases. For example:
hands-on workshop: a workshop in which you take part in activities and don't just listen to a speaker
go on stage: have a chance to stand where the performers have stood and to experience what this feels like
starred in the film: played a leading role in a film version of the story (i.e. Johnny Depp is not appearing in this musical)
When students have done the exercise, elicit the answers and make sure that students use the correct verb forms:
2 Present Simple, third person singular form (for a fact)
3 gerund (after *enjoy*)
4 Present Continuous (for something happening now)
5 Present Simple third person singular form (for a fact)
6 Present Continuous (for something happening now).

Answers: 2 gets   3 watching   4 doing   5 tells   6 starring

Further practice
- Workbook page 45
- Resource Pack
  Resource 42: Unit 4 Lesson 3 Reading and Vocabulary – What's on?

4.3 READING and VOCABULARY A theatre evening

I can understand the main points of an article and talk about entertainment.

1 **CLASS VOTE** Does your school have enough trips to the theatre?

2 Study the words below, using a dictionary. Use the words to describe the pictures in the *High Five Entertainment Guide*.

> circus   costume   lights   make-up   mime
> puppet   stage

3 🔊 2.06 Read the text. Why is Nathan going to the theatre?

> Hi Kate, Elena and Luke,
> Mum's getting some theatre tickets for my birthday and I can take three friends. I don't know which show to choose because they all look good. Send me a text telling me what you like most.
> Nathan

4 🔊 2.07 Read the texts and *The High Five Entertainment Guide*. Match each person with the best show for them. There is one extra option.

> **Katie** ☐
> Brilliant idea! You know I love anything with music, and I prefer funny stories. I want to have fun! By the way, I have to be home before 9 p.m.
>
> **Elena** ☐
> I'm not keen on funny plays. I like stories that make me think about the world and things in my life. I also love watching good actors perform, so the cast is very important for me!
>
> **Luke** ☐
> Hi, Nathan, thanks. I'm not really into comedies or musicals. They're too childish. I prefer dramas and classical plays. I like new and fresh interpretations of classical plays, as well.

5 Which show would you choose? Why?

6 🔊 2.08 Look at the highlighted phrases in the text and complete the sentences. Listen and check.

1. He's been an actor for a long time but he's always nervous when he *goes* on stage.
2. The producer is very happy when the show _____ good reviews.
3. There was a lot of noise during the show, and I didn't enjoy _____ the performance.
4. Jake wants to learn robotic dancing so he's _____ a workshop.
5. The film _____ the sad story of a boy who loses his dog.
6. She's always wanted to be famous, and now she's _____ in a film in Hollywood.

The High Five Entertainment Guide

FIND OUT WHAT'S ON NEAR YOU

A LOOK, NO STRINGS!
Puppets aren't just for kids! Join the Look, No Strings puppet show for a weekend of serious Shakespeare. Our youth theatre makes its own puppets and writes the stories. This weekend it's Macbeth. Come and be surprised, and stay for a class on puppet making (Saturday only).

B NO WORDS, LOTS OF FUN!
Words can't describe how much fun we have on stage. That's why we don't use them! Don't miss the excitement and drama of our new mime show. It combines a fantastic mix of movement and music. If you would like to learn more, do our hands-on workshop after the show at 9.30 p.m.

C ENJOY INDIAN ENERGY!
Welcome to Dance Bollywood, for one day only. This happy musical experience brings Indian energy and fun to the stage. It's getting good reviews, so come and enjoy great dancing and amazing costumes! You can also go on stage after the show for your first Bollywood dance class. The class ends at 8 p.m.

D THE SAD STORY OF EDWARD
Johnny Depp starred in the film and now the musical is here! Meet Edward Scissorhands, and watch a brilliant performance as he tries to find friendship, family and love. There are no spoken words, but music, dance and songs tell this sad story. Tickets are selling fast, so hurry!

4.4 GRAMMAR Quantifiers: *some, any, much, many, (a) few, (a) little, a lot of, lots of*

I can talk about quantities of countable and uncountable nouns.

VIDEO HOW MANY BANGLES ARE YOU WEARING?

Tommo: Cool music. You look great! Thanks for letting me take a few photos for the school magazine.

Alisha: No problem. Come in.

Tommo: Let's stand near the window. So, when do you wear these clothes?

Alisha: Mostly at weddings and *Diwali*, the festival of light. I've got lots of cousins, and we dance too … Like this.

Tommo: Cool, but stand still. This is awesome material. Is it from India?

Alisha: No, we get some material at the market here. There aren't many shops, and there's very little choice, so we mostly buy online.

Tommo: Don't move your hands. Wow, how many bangles are you wearing?

Alisha: Lots! We always wear a lot of jewellery. I've got some anklets too …

Tommo: This is perfect. How much time does it take to paint your hands?

Alisha: Ages! My gran does them, but she doesn't have much patience!

Tommo: Awesome! But stand still, please. I haven't got any photos of the whole outfit.

OUT of class *Like this. Lots! Ages!*

1 **CLASS VOTE** Do you sometimes wear a traditional costume? Why? / Why not?

2  4.3 2.09 Look at the photo. Why do you think Alisha is wearing her traditional costume? Watch or listen and check.

3 Study the Grammar box. Find more examples of quantifiers in the dialogue.

Grammar	Quantifiers
Countable nouns	**Uncountable nouns**
We learn **a lot of** / **lots of** songs. How **many** bracelets are you wearing? There aren't **many** markets near here.	I've got **a lot of** / **lots of** money. How **much** luggage has she got? We haven't got **much** furniture.
We've got **some** DVDs. I haven't got **any** bracelets. Have you got **any** pictures?	I've got **some** orange juice. I haven't got **any** water. Have you got **any** sugar?
Thanks for letting us take **a few** magazines. There are very **few** people.	I've got **a little** money. There's very **little** information.

GRAMMAR TIME > PAGE 121

4 Find four countable nouns and four uncountable nouns in the dialogue.

5 Choose the correct option.

teenfestblog

In ¹*a lot of* / *much* countries, there aren't ²*many* / *much* days when you can wear a traditional costume. However, for ³*some* / *any* lucky teenagers in Seville in Spain there are ⁴*a few* / *any* days in April, during the April Fair, when they can put on costumes, dance and enjoy ⁵*much* / *some* hot chocolate with *churros*.

6 Complete the sentences with one word in each gap.

1 I'd like to buy *some* new shoes today.
2 How _____ material do you need?
3 I've got a _____ of cousins.
4 We haven't got _____ time to make a costume. It isn't possible in ten minutes!
5 She's got a _____ text messages from him.

7 In pairs, ask and answer questions. Use *How much … ? / How many … ?* and the words below.

jewellery / wear   hours / study at night
music / buy   sport / do   classes / do

Unit 4

4.4 GRAMMAR   Quantifiers: *some, any, much, many, (a) few, (a) little, a lot of, lots of*

Lesson learning objective
Students can talk about quantities of countable and uncountable nouns.

Lead in: Review of countable and uncountable nouns

Tell students that you are going to write some words in two columns. Students have to guess what the headings are for each column. Write *bananas* in the first column and *yoghurt* in the second column. Elicit ideas for the headings, e.g. *fruit, dairy*, but don't tell students if they are correct or not. Keep adding more words to both columns. For example:
Column 1: *grapes, eggs, onions, tomatoes, sausages*
Column 2: *beef, fruit juice, coffee, cheese, chocolate*
Then dictate one word at a time and ask students which column you should write it in, e.g. *meat, chips, hamburgers, money, time, days*. If students still haven't guessed the headings for the two columns, write the letter *C* above the first column and the letter *U* above the second column and try to elicit the headings *Countable* and *Uncountable*.

Exercise 1
Tell students to keep their Students' Books closed. Write *traditional costume* on the board and elicit what this means. Ask students if they know any traditional costumes from their own country or from other countries. Then ask the questions from the Students' Book.

Culture notes
Diwali, or 'the festival of light', is a Hindu festival which takes place in October or November each year. People dress up in their best outfits and light lamps and candles inside and outside their homes. There are fireworks, people eat a big meal and give one another presents. *Diwali* celebrates the victory of light over darkness, knowledge over ignorance, good over evil and hope over despair.

Exercise 2 4.3 2.09
Ask students to describe what Alisha is wearing and what country her traditional costume is from (*India*).
After students have watched the video, ask questions to check that students have understood specific information. For example: *What is Diwali?* (The festival of light, a Hindu festival) *Where did Alisha get the material from?* (some from the market but mostly online) *Where is she wearing jewellery?* (on her arms and ankles) *Who paints Alisha's hands?* (her grandmother).

Answers: So Tommo can take photos for the school magazine.

Exercise 3
Go through the Grammar box with the class. Ask students if there is any difference between *a lot of* and *lots of* (*there isn't any difference*). Ask about the difference between *few* and *a few* and *little* and *a little* (*few* and *little* mean 'a very small number' but *a few* and *a little* mean 'some'). Compare *I've got a little money* (this has a fairly positive meaning – i.e. *I've got some money*) and *I've got little money* (this has a negative meaning – i.e. *I'm poor*).

Answers: a few (photos), lots of (cousins), some (material), (are)n't many (shops), very little (choice), (how) many (bangles), a lot of (jewellery), some (anklets), (How) much (time), (does)n't (have) much (patience), (have)n't (got) any (photos)

Exercise 4
Point out that *clothes* is an example of a plural noun which can take a plural verb form. Similar plural nouns are *trousers* and *shorts*. We can't say *two clothes, three trousers*, etc. and there is no singular form of the noun.

Possible answers:
Countable nouns: photos, magazine, window, weddings, festival, cousins, market, shops, hands, bangles, anklets, outfit
Uncountable nouns: music, material, choice, jewellery, time, patience

Background notes
Churros are similar to doughnuts. They are made of pastry which is deep fried and sprinkled with sugar. *Churros* are sometimes eaten for breakfast and, in some places in Spain, you can buy them as a snack from sellers in the street.

Exercise 5
Tell students to read the text quickly, to find out where and when the festival takes place and what people eat and drink at the festival.

Answers: **1** a lot of **2** many **3** some **4** a few **5** some

Exercise 6
Remind students that there is only one word missing from each sentence and also that they should only use words from the Grammar box, so they can't use *a lot of* in sentence 5 or *enough* in sentence 4.

Answers: **2** much **3** lot **4** much **5** few

Exercise 7
When the pairs have finished, elicit their questions and answers. Encourage students to ask each other follow-up questions such as *What kind of jewellery do you wear? How many rings are you wearing at the moment?*

Extra activity
Write these sentence beginnings on the board:
There are few …   There is little …   There are a lot of …
There is a lot of …   There aren't many …
There isn't much …

and ask students to work in pairs to complete the sentences. When they are ready, ask one or two pairs to read their sentences to the class.

Further practice
- Workbook page 46
- Grammar Time page 121
- Resource Pack
  Resource 43: Unit 4 Lesson 4 Grammar – Similarities and differences
  Resource 44: Unit 4 Lesson 4 Video – How many bangles are you wearing?

4.5 LISTENING and VOCABULARY The Junino festival

Lesson learning objective
Students can identify specific detail in an interview and talk about festivals.

Lead in: Review of quantifiers

Put students into groups of four. They should work together to make true sentences, using these sentence beginnings: *We've got a lot of …*; *We haven't got much …*; *We haven't got many …*; *We haven't got any …* .
Tell them to write their ideas for each sentence beginning in their notebooks and give them a time limit. Invite groups to take turns to read out their ideas, e.g. *books* and encourage the other groups to guess the complete sentence, e.g. *They've got a lot of books.*

Exercise 1

Remind students about the festivals mentioned in the previous lesson (*Diwali* and the *April Fair*) and elicit examples of festivals in the students' own country.

Exercise 2   2.10

Ask students to say what they know about the three different countries, e.g. languages spoken, major cities. Elicit the answer and ask students to explain how they decided on the answer, e.g. *Santiago's parents come from Brazil. He speaks Portuguese, but he was born in the United States and goes to school there.*

Answer: A

2.10

See page 248.

Exercise 3   2.11

Before you play the audio, tell students to read the questions and the choices. Ask whether they think the festival Santiago is talking about takes place in the USA or in Brazil. When they have done the exercise, elicit the answers and encourage students to give reasons why they think the other two choices are incorrect.

Answers: 1 c   2 a   3 b   4 b   5 c

2.11

P = Radio presenter   S = Santiago

P: So, the Junino festival takes place every year … in June, of course.
S: Yes, it's a huge family party for me. The festival is at the end of winter in Brazil, but it's summer vacation for me so I visit the family. It's the perfect chance for a huge family party. We enjoy doing things together.
P: What costumes do you wear?
S: Well, they're country clothes … what people wore when they worked on the land. The boys have jeans and checked shirts, with straw hats that protect your head in the sun. In the past, the girls wore party dresses, but now they're also beginning to wear jeans with a shirt … and they paint freckles on their faces.
P: Now, I heard that there are a lot of games.
S: Yes, in one of the traditional games, you send a message to somebody, but you don't say who you are … it's fun … And last year there was a game with toilet paper … you wrap a person in toilet paper so that you can't see them at all. People were running around with lots of toilet paper on them!
P: What about the music? Is it like a carnival with dancing in the streets?
S: Not at all. It's traditional music that celebrates life in the country. We do a traditional square dance with partners. Old and young people do it and it's lots of fun.
P: And the food?
S: … and the food is … brilliant! Corn was the food people had at the beginning of winter so there are a lot of corn dishes. There's popcorn, of course, a corn cake, which is nice and sweet, and a type of corn pudding … I think that's the dish I like most.
P: Well, thanks for that, Santiago. Now it's …

Exercise 4   2.12

When the groups have discussed their ideas, invite them to share their ideas with the class and elicit the meaning of each compound noun. Then ask students if they can think of any more ideas for each noun in the list, e.g. *family photograph*, *summer holidays*, etc.

Answers:
summer: clothes, dress, hat, party, vacation
country: clothes, dance, music
straw: hat
party: clothes, dance, dress, hat, music
carnival: clothes, dance, dress, music
square: cake, dance, hat

Exercise 5

Tell students to see if they can remember one of the games that is played at the festival and what is needed to play it (*toilet paper*) and also if they can remember what they eat at the festival (*corn cakes, corn pudding*).

Possible answers: toilet paper, corn dishes, corn cake, corn pudding

Exercise 6

When the pairs compare their answers with the class, elicit reasons for why students think certain things are or are not important. Ask if they can think of any more things that a good festival needs, e.g. market stalls, a parade.

Extra activity

Put students into groups of four. Tell them that they are going to create their own festival. They should choose a day of the year, a name for the festival, a reason for holding the festival and what will happen at the festival. Invite groups to present their ideas to the class and have a class vote to decide on the best idea. (Tell them they can't vote for their own idea.)

Further practice

- Workbook page 47
- Resource Pack
  Resource 45: Unit 4 Lesson 5 Listening and Vocabulary – What's the word?

4.5 LISTENING and VOCABULARY   The Junino festival

I can identify specific detail in an interview and talk about festivals.

1 **CLASS VOTE** What's your favourite festival?

2 🔊 2.10 Listen to the first part of an interview with Santiago. Where does he live?

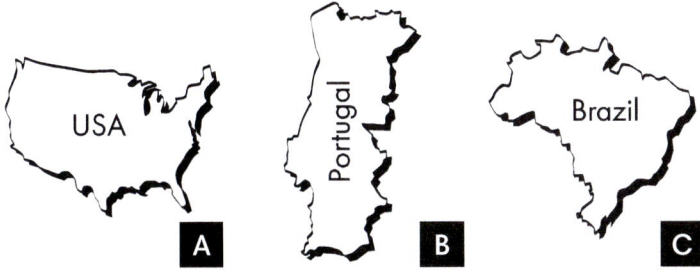

3 🔊 2.11 Listen to the second part of the interview. Choose the correct answers.

1 Why is the festival special for Santiago?
   a He doesn't have to go to school.
   b He enjoys the winter in Brazil.
   c He likes being with his family.
2 How are the costumes different now?
   a The girls wear the same type of clothes as the boys.
   b The boys don't wear checked shirts any more.
   c They don't paint their faces now.
3 What happens in the toilet paper game?
   a People run with the paper in their hand.
   b One person wraps another person in toilet paper.
   c People write secret messages on the paper.
4 What does the music celebrate?
   a Old and young people.
   b Country life.
   c Carnival tradition.
5 What is Santiago's favourite food at the festival?
   a Corn cake.
   b Popcorn.
   c Corn pudding.

4 🔊 2.12 In groups, complete the compound nouns in the Vocabulary box with the words below. Compare your ideas with the class. Which group has the most compound nouns? Listen and check.

cake   clothes   dance   dress   hat
music   party   vacation

Vocabulary	Compound nouns
Noun +	**noun**
family	*party, vacation*
summer	
country	
straw	
party	
carnival	
square	

5 How many more compound nouns can you remember from Exercise 3?

6 In pairs, discuss what you think makes a good festival. Compare your ideas with the class.

✗ (not important) ✓ (quite important)
✓✓ (important) ✓✓✓ (very important)

good entertainment   tasty food
friendly people   sunny weather
cheap tickets   fun games
carnival music

We think fun games for all the family are very important.
We don't think sunny weather is important.

Unit 4 51

4.6 SPEAKING Talking about preferences

I can ask about, express and explain preferences.

VIDEO DO YOU WANT TO TRY IT?

Dan: How was the African dance class, Skye?
Skye: Good, but it was hot. Do you want to try it?
Dan: No, thanks, I'm not mad about dancing. I'd prefer to watch something.
Skye: Well, there are two activities this afternoon. There's the outdoor cinema that's showing a comedy, or a puppet show. What would you prefer to see?
Dan: Definitely the comedy. It sounds very funny. Let's go together.
Skye: OK. We should take some food with us. I'd rather eat outside in this weather.
Dan: Great! How about a pizza?
Skye: Mmhh. I'd prefer to get something different. After all, it is an international festival.
Dan: OK. What would you rather have?
Skye: I think I'd prefer a Mexican dish. Maybe the chilli with rice.
Dan: OK. Cool! Let's see what we can find.

> *I'm not mad about (dancing).*
> *It sounds (very funny).*

OUT of class

1 CLASS VOTE **What do you like doing with your friends?**

- do music/dance classes   eat out
- go to music events   play instrument(s)
- watch films or shows

2  4.4 2.13 Study the Speaking box. Watch or listen. Find examples of talking about preferences in the text.

Speaking	Talking about preferences

Asking about and expressing preferences
(What) would you rather + *verb*?
(What) would you prefer to + *verb*?

I'd rather + *verb*   I'd prefer to + *verb*

Giving reasons
It sounds very funny/great/boring …
It looks good.   It's healthier.

3 Make questions with the words below. Ask and answer them. Use the ideas in brackets to help you.

1. you / rather / do / tonight? (stay in / go out)
   What would you rather do tonight?
   I'd rather stay in.
2. you / prefer / to watch / at the cinema? (a horror / spy film)
3. you / rather / have for dinner? (Chinese food / Indian food)
4. you rather / learn? (the drums / the electric guitar)
5. you / prefer / dance to? (salsa / hip hop)

4 Study the poster. In pairs, discuss which activities you'd prefer to do.

Would you rather listen to … or … ?
I'd rather … because …

'Don't miss the fun!… comedy shows, outdoor cinema, live music, puppet shows, dance and drama classes, games, tasty food… and more!'

Unit 4

4.6 SPEAKING Talking about preferences

Lesson learning objective
Students can ask about, express and explain preferences.

Lead in: Review of compound nouns

Put students into pairs. Dictate five words that students know, e.g. *school, head, car, book, home*. Then ask students to add words to these, to make five compound nouns.

Join two pairs of students together to make groups of four. The pairs take turns to say one of their words while the other pair guesses which of the dictated words it forms a compound noun with.

Invite groups to share some of their compound nouns with the class.

Exercise 1
Tell students to keep their Students' Books closed. Have a class discussion about different free-time activities that they enjoy. Elicit various ideas, then tell students to open their Students' Books and to choose the free-time activity they like best.

Exercise 2 4.4 2.13
Play the video and tell students to close their Students' Books.

Ask these questions to check students' understanding of specific detail in the video: *What activity was Skye doing before she met Dan?* (she was at an African dance class) *What are Skye and Dan going to watch this afternoon?* (they are going to watch a comedy film) *What are they going to do before they watch the film?* (they are going to get something to eat).

Then tell students to open their Students' Books and go through the Speaking box with the class before you play the video again.

Point out that when we talk about general likes, we use *prefer* without *would* and follow it with *-ing*, e.g. *Do you like walking? Yes, but I prefer cycling.* When we talk about something we want to do now, we add *would* before *prefer*, e.g. *I usually prefer cycling but I would prefer to walk today because it is too windy to cycle.*

Answers:
Asking about and expressing preferences:
I'd prefer to watch something; What would you prefer to see?; I'd rather eat outside; I'd prefer to get something different; What would you rather have?; I'd prefer a Mexican dish
Giving reasons: It sounds very funny; I'm not mad about dancing.

Exercise 3
Tell students that they should use the same word in their answer as in the question (i.e. *rather* or *prefer*). Elicit reasons for students' answers, e.g. *I'd rather stay in because I feel tired.*

Answers:
2 What would you prefer to watch at the cinema? I'd prefer to watch …
3 What would you rather have for dinner? I'd rather have …
4 What would you rather learn? I'd rather learn …
5 What would you prefer to dance to? I'd prefer to dance to …

Exercise 4
Elicit possible alternative choices, e.g. *watch a comedy show, watch a film at the outdoor cinema, go to a dance class, go to a drama class, eat Indian food, eat Mexican food.*

Extra activity

Tell students to think of any two alternative activities, e.g. *do a test or write an essay*. Explain that they are going to do a class survey to find out which of their two activities students would rather do. Remind them that they can use either *rather* or *prefer* when they are asking about students' preferences. Give students a time limit and encourage them to mingle and to make a note of all the responses they receive.

When they have finished, invite students to report back to the class about what they found during their survey.

Further practice

- Workbook page 48
- Resource Pack
  Resource 46: Unit 4 Lesson 6 Speaking – I'd rather not
  Resource 47: Unit 4 Lesson 6 Video – Do you want to try it?

4.7 ENGLISH IN USE Adverbs of manner

Lesson learning objective
Students can describe how people do things.

Lead in: Review of talking about preferences

Elicit the names of different jobs and, as students say them, write the names in pairs on the board, e.g. *teacher / doctor*, *police officer / nurse*.

When there are five pairs of jobs written on the board, put students into pairs. Tell the pairs to take turns to say, for each pair of jobs, which one they would rather do / prefer to do, giving reasons why, e.g. *I'd rather be a teacher than a doctor because I hate seeing blood!* Tell them also to take turns to use *prefer* and *rather*, so that they can practise both ways of talking about preferences.

When pairs have discussed all five pairs of jobs, invite them to share their ideas with the class.

Exercise 1

Check that students understand the meaning of the words *escape artist*. Ask students if they have ever seen an escape artist or been to any other type of magic show. If they haven't, ask whether or not they think they would enjoy it.

Possible answer: He's afraid he won't be able to escape from the water tank.

Exercise 2

Elicit the examples of adverbs in the cartoon. Then discuss the Language box with the class. Point out that for all adverbs ending in *-ly*, the comparative and superlative are formed with *more/most* + adverb, e.g. *He talked **more loudly** than the other students.* Explain that when an adverb has the same form as an adjective, the comparative and superlative form is the same as for the adjective, e.g. *She worked **harder** than the other students.* Also, that the comparative forms of *well* and *badly* are *better* and *worse*, e.g. *He behaved **better** this term than last term.*

Answers:
Add *-ly*: listen carefully, breathe deeply, think positively, waiting patiently
Change *-y* to *-ily*: do it easily
No change: running late

Exercise 3

Discuss the example with the class. Ask students to explain why we don't put the adverb after the object (*because on TV last night is an indirect object and not a direct object, we put the adverb directly after the verb*).

Answers:
2 She won the competition easily.
3 They were sitting quietly during the mime show.
4 Everyone clapped loudly at the end.
5 Please text him quickly.
6 The performer worked hard to perfect her act.

Exercise 4

Before students do the exercise, ask if they know the story of *War Horse* and have either seen the film or read the book. Explain that for each gap in the exercise, they should decide whether it requires a normal adverb or a comparative or a superlative adverb and they should also think about the correct form.

Answers: 1 d 2 c 3 c 4 a

Culture notes

War Horse, originally a novel written by Michael Morpurgo, was made into a film by Steven Spielberg in 2011. In the story, a horse is sold to the army at the start of the First World War. We see how the horse survives the war, sometimes working for the British army, sometimes working for the Germans and sometimes working for local people in Belgium and northern France. At the end of the war, the horse is reunited with his original owner and is taken back to his farm.

Extra activity

Tell students that you are going to make some changes to your behaviour in the next few months, e.g. *I'm going to shout more loudly when you behave badly. I'm going to watch you more carefully during exams.*

Put students into pairs and tell them to think of three ways in which they can change their behaviour in the next few months. When they are ready, join two pairs together to make groups of four so that they can compare their ideas. Invite groups to share some of their ideas with the class.

Homework

Tell students to read the text on page 56 of the Students' Book. They should look up any words they don't know the meaning of and translate them into L1. They should also pay attention to the pronunciation of the words in the text.

As an additional task, ask students to write an example sentence illustrating the meaning of each of these words: *highlight* (verb), *head for* (phrasal verb), *parade* (noun) *annual* (adjective), *varied* (adjective). Tell them that the sentences must, in some way, be connected to festivals and celebrations.

Further practice

- Workbook page 49
- Resource Pack
  Resource 48: Unit 4 Lesson 7 English in Use – How well do they do it?

4.7 ENGLISH IN USE Adverbs of manner

I can describe how people do things.

1 Read the cartoon. Why is Bendy Benny scared?

2 Find examples of adverbs in the cartoon. Match them with the correct rule below.

Language	Adverbs of manner

To form adverbs from adjectives, add **-ly**.
bad – bad**ly**   beautiful – beautifu**lly**

For adjectives that end in -y, change -y to **-ily**.
angry – angr**ily**   happy – happ**ily**

Some adjectives are irregular: **good** – **well**

Some adjectives don't change: **early**, **hard**, **straight**

We use adverbs to describe how we do something. They *usually* come after the direct object OR (if there is no object) after the verb.

He arrived **late**.
She ate the cake **slowly**.

Comparatives and superlatives of adverbs of manner are formed like adjectives.
fast – **faster** – **the fastest**
slowly – **more slowly** – **the most slowly**

3 Rewrite the sentences with the correct form of the words in brackets.

1 Anna performed on TV last night. (brilliant)
Anna performed brilliantly on TV last night.
2 The other singers weren't very good. She won the competition. (easy)
3 They were sitting during the mime show. (quiet)
4 Everyone clapped at the end. (loud)
5 Please text him. (quick)
6 The performer worked to perfect her act. (hard)

4 Read the text. Choose the correct answers.

Star review ...

I've just seen the play *War Horse*. It's about a young man, Albert, who [1]_____ on his dad's farm. Albert has a horse called Joey that he loves, but his dad sells him. He decides to go and look for Joey. In the play, the horse changes the lives of everyone he meets. The stage model of the horse was amazing. The actors moved it [2]_____ across the stage. Although the film [3]_____ when Albert finds Joey, a few people in the audience were crying [4]_____ because the story was so moving.

1 a works harder
   b works hardest
   c hardly works
   d works hard

2 a beautiful
   b more beautifully
   c beautifully
   d most beautiful

3 a ends happy
   b ends happier
   c ends happily
   d happily ends

4 a quietly
   b quiet
   c quieter
   d more quietly

Unit 4 53

Wordlist and Vocabulary in action

Extra activity
When students have finished Exercise 3, join pairs into groups of four. Explain that they should make sentences using superlative adjectives, for example about the tastiest type of cuisine you can eat in a restaurant in the students' own town, about the easiest instrument to learn to play, etc. Encourage them to think of a different superlative adjective for each sentence.

Further practice
Workbook page 50

WORDLIST — Types of films | Film and TV | Compound nouns

act /ækt/
action /'ækʃn/
actor /'æktə/
angrily /'æŋgrəli/
anklets /'æŋkləts/
artist /'ɑːtɪst/
audience /'ɔːdiəns/
badly /'bædli/
bangles /'bæŋglz/
beautifully /'bjuːtəfli/
black and white film /ˌblæk ənd ˌwaɪt 'fɪlm/
brilliantly /'brɪljəntli/
carefully /'keəfli/
carelessly /'keələsli/
carnival /'kɑːnɪvl/
carnival clothes/dress/music/dance /ˌkɑːnɪvl 'kləʊðz/'dres/'mjuːzɪk/'dɑːns/
cartoon /kɑːˈtuːn/
cast /kɑːst/
character /'kærəktə/
checked /tʃekt/
childish /'tʃaɪldɪʃ/
circus /'sɜːkəs/
clap /klæp/
classical /'klæsɪkl/
clearly /'klɪəli/
comedy /'kɒmədi/
corn cake/pudding /'kɔːn keɪk/ˌpʊdɪŋ/
costume /'kɒstjuːm/
country clothes/music/dance /ˌkʌntri 'kləʊðz/'mjuːzɪk/'dɑːns/
dancing /'dɑːnsɪŋ/
deeply /'diːpli/
dizzy /'dɪzi/
documentary /ˌdɒkjuˈmentəri/
dramatic /drəˈmætɪk/
early /'ɜːli/
easily /'iːzɪli/
entertain /ˌentəˈteɪn/
entertainer /ˌentəˈteɪnə/

entertainment /ˌentəˈteɪnmənt/
episode /'epɪsəʊd/
escape /ɪˈskeɪp/
excitement /ɪkˈsaɪtmənt/
exciting /ɪkˈsaɪtɪŋ/
experience /ɪkˈspɪəriəns/
fairy tale /'feəri teɪl/
family party/vacation /ˌfæmli 'pɑːti/vəˈkeɪʃn/
fantasy /'fæntəsi/
fast /fɑːst/
festival /'festɪvl/
freckles /'freklz/
hands-on /ˌhændz 'ɒn/
happily /'hæpɪli/
hard /hɑːd/
hip-hop /'hɪp hɒp/
hit /hɪt/
international /ˌɪntəˈnæʃnl/
interpretation /ɪnˌtɜːprɪˈteɪʃn/
jewellery /'dʒuːəlri/
late /leɪt/
lights /laɪts/
loudly /'laʊdli/
make-up /'meɪk ʌp/
material /məˈtɪəriəl/
mime /maɪm/
movement /'muːvmənt/
musical /'mjuːzɪkl/
outdoor /ˌaʊtˈdɔː/
party clothes/hat/dress/music /ˌpɑːti 'kləʊðz/'hæt/'dres/'mjuːzɪk/
patiently /'peɪʃntli/
perform /pəˈfɔːm/
performance /pəˈfɔːməns/
performer /pəˈfɔːmə/
play (n) /pleɪ/
politely /pəˈlaɪtli/
positively /'pɒzətɪvli/
poster /'pəʊstə/
produce /prəˈdjuːs/
producer /prəˈdjuːsə/

production /prəˈdʌkʃn/
puppet /'pʌpɪt/
quickly /'kwɪkli/
quietly /'kwaɪətli/
review /rɪˈvjuː/
romantic /rəʊˈmæntɪk/
safely /'seɪfli/
salsa /'sælsə/
scary /'skeəri/
scene /siːn/
sci-fi /ˌsaɪ faɪ/
screen(s) /skriːn(z)/
series /'sɪəriːz/
serious /'sɪəriəs/
show /ʃəʊ/
special effects /ˌspeʃl əˈfekts/
square hat/dance/cake /ˌskweə 'hæt/ˌskweə dɑːns/ˌskweə 'keɪk/
stage /steɪdʒ/
star /stɑː/
straight /streɪt/
strange /streɪndʒ/
straw hat /ˌstrɔː 'hæt/
theatre /'θɪətə/
thriller /'θrɪlə/
toilet paper /'tɔɪlət ˌpeɪpə/
traditional /trəˈdɪʃnəl/
well /wel/
workshop /'wɜːkʃɒp/

WORD FRIENDS
do a/the workshop
do music/dance classes
eat out
get good reviews
go on stage
go to music events
play instrument(s)
star in a/the film
tell a (sad/happy) story
watch a/the performance
watch films or shows

VOCABULARY IN ACTION

1 Use the wordlist to find:
1 four people who work in the theatre or in films
2 three adverbs that are the same as the adjective
3 four types of music and dance
4 five types of film
5 two items of jewellery
6 four adjectives that describe a film/play

2 Use the wordlist to complete the sentences.
1 I don't like cooking at home. I prefer to _____ out.
2 I'd like to learn to _____ an instrument but I'm not very patient.
3 I enjoy _____ workshops where I can learn with other people.
4 If a film _____ a bad review, I don't go and watch it.
5 I'd like to _____ in a film or a TV show one day.
6 When somebody _____ me a sad story, I often cry.

3 In pairs, tell your partner if the sentences in Exercise 2 are true for you.
I like cooking at home. It's fun.

4 🔊 **2.14 PRONUNCIATION**
Listen to the words and decide if the stress is on the first or the last syllable.

actor artist cartoon
costume escape outdoor
patient perform produce
puppet review

First syllable	Last syllable
actor	

 Wordlist

Exercise 2
1 eat
2 play
3 doing
4 gets
5 star
6 tells

Exercise 4
First syllable: artist, costume, patient, puppet
Last syllable: cartoon, escape, outdoor, perform, produce, review

Exercise 1
Possible answers:
1 actor, entertainer, performer, producer
2 early, fast, hard, late, straight
3 carnival music/dance, classical, hip-hop, salsa, traditional
4 action, black and white film, cartoon, comedy, documentary, fairy tale, fantasy, musical, romantic, sci-fi, thriller
5 anklets, bangles
6 childish, dramatic, exciting, scary, serious, strange

Revision

Extra activity

Write these structures on the board.

I can + verb + adjective + noun   *I'm good at* + verb + *-ing*
I + verb (+ object) + adverb

Give an example of each structure, e.g.

I can speak good English.   *I'm good at speaking English.*   *I speak English well.*

Tell students to write each of their sentences from Exercise 5 in two different ways.

Further practice

- Workbook page 51
- Resource Pack
  Resource 49: Unit 4
  Vocabulary – Cross out the letters
  Resource 50: Unit 4
  Grammar – Make a sentence

Revision

VOCABULARY

1 Write the correct word for each definition.
1. The place in a theatre where people perform. s_____
2. A meeting where people learn something new. w_____
3. A performance with movement but no words. m_____
4. A film with characters that an artist has drawn. c_____
5. One of the parts of a TV or radio story. e_____
6. A person who makes a film. p_____
7. The clothes that an actor wears in a play or film. c_____
8. An exciting film, programme or book about a crime. t_____

Exercise 1
1. stage
2. workshop
3. mime
4. cartoon
5. episode
6. producer
7. costume
8. thriller

2 Complete the text with the words below.

comedy   country music   music events
outdoor cinema   performance   reviews
~~summer vacation~~

Harry,
Hope you're OK. I've just come back from ¹summer vacation in Turkey. My dad is really into music and he loves going to ²_____. On our last night we watched a ³_____ by local belly dancers. Mum and I tried it but we were awful … How was the festival in your village? Did you listen to ⁴_____, or was it more carnival music? I love dancing in the street. Maybe we can go to the ⁵_____ in the park on Saturday. It's good weather for it. There's a ⁶_____ on with Steve Martin in it. It's got great ⁷_____ and everybody says it's funny.
Speak soon,
Elli

Exercise 2
2. music events
3. performance
4. country music
5. outdoor cinema
6. comedy
7. reviews

GRAMMAR

3 Order the words to make sentences.
1. are / for / festival tickets / students / most / expensive / too
2. isn't / good / the old one / the new TV series / as / as
3. singing / the performance / the worst part / the / was / of
4. find / at the market / you / cheapest / the / costumes / can
5. concerts / relaxing / than / music festivals / more / are / pop

Exercise 3
1. Festival tickets are too expensive for most students.
2. The new TV series isn't as good as the old one.
3. The worst part of the performance was the singing.
4. You can find the cheapest costumes at the market.
5. Music festivals are more relaxing than pop concerts.

4 Choose the correct option.

How ¹*many* / (*much*) free time have you got this weekend? If you've got ²*a few* / *some* extra hours, come to one of our weekend workshops. We offer ³*any* / *lots of* activities. In our workshops you can make basic puppets with ⁴*some* / *much* wood, help paint the stage (we've got ⁵*a lot of* / *a few* black paint!), or learn how to make costumes with ⁶*any* / *some* old material.

We don't think there are ⁷*many* / *much* theatres that offer this range of activities and you don't need ⁸*some* / *any* experience … so what are you waiting for?

Exercise 4
2. a few
3. lots of
4. some
5. a lot of
6. some
7. many
8. any

5 In pairs, tell your partner about two things you can do:
- fast   *I can get dressed fast in the morning.*
- brilliantly
- patiently

SPEAKING

6 Complete the dialogues.

Would you prefer   Would you rather
I'd prefer   I'd rather

A _____ do dance classes or play an instrument?
B _____ learn to play an instrument because I want to be in a band.
A _____ to have a summer vacation in your country or somewhere else?
B _____ to stay here because it's beautiful.

Exercise 6
A Would you rather
B I'd rather
A Would you prefer
B I'd prefer

7 Work in pairs. Use the prompts to ask about, express and explain preferences.

Student A
wear a traditional costume to school / wear your own clothes?
go to the theatre / go to the circus?

Student B
watch a documentary about lions / watch a sci-fi film?
perform on stage / help behind the stage?

DICTATION

8 🔊 2.15 Listen, then listen again and write down what you hear.

Exercise 8

Oliver loves acting and performs around the world. He gets up early and works very hard. Some actors get scared before going on stage. They don't want to forget their lines. Oliver never has that problem. He's a mime artist!

SELF-ASSESSMENT   Think about this unit. What did you learn? What do you need help with?   **WORKBOOK**   p. 50

CULTURE

How do you like to celebrate?

Multicultural festivals in London

The eighteenth-century writer Samuel Johnson said, 'If you're tired of London, you're tired of life.' Looking at the city's annual calendar of cultural events, it's easy to agree with him!

There is such a mixture! There are traditional festivities that have existed for generations and new events which highlight the city's varied population. If you're looking for tradition, why not head for **Trooping the Colour** in June? It's a summer military parade which celebrates the Queen's official birthday.

For something more international, a big favourite is the five-day Hindu Festival of Lights, called **Diwali**. It is held in the autumn and celebrates the victory of good over evil. Head for Trafalgar Square to see the best contemporary Asian music and dance, and the most beautiful costumes. You also have the chance to taste delicious Indian food.

Don't forget the **Chinese New Year**, usually held in February. There's a parade in Chinatown, which changes each year to celebrate a different animal – the horse, the monkey, the cow, the dragon, etc. There's also a great atmosphere in the streets and restaurants nearby.

Finally, if it's Caribbean culture you're after, go to Europe's biggest summer street festival – the **Notting Hill Carnival**. You'll find live reggae, calypso and soul sounds, costume parades and the most amazing party atmosphere in the streets!

GLOSSARY
highlight (v) if you highlight something, you say it is very important
head for (phr) go towards
parade (n) an event in which people walk through the streets and play music

BBC CULTURE — How do you like to celebrate?

Lead in: Topic introduction

Tell students not to open their Students' Books. Put students into groups of four. If you set the homework suggestion for the unit, ask the groups to discuss any vocabulary they found difficult and their example sentences if you also set the additional task.

If students haven't done the homework, ask them to look at the glossary on page 56. Students should find the words in the text and discuss what they mean in context, e.g. A **parade** *is a lot of people, maybe in costumes or uniforms, all walking or marching together, perhaps to celebrate a national day.*

4.5

London celebrates

Part 1

N = Narrator   M = Man   W = Woman   G = Group

N: A melting pot of cultures – London is quite unique. Now it's February, the usual time to celebrate Chinese New Year. This year is the Year of the Horse. The entertainment certainly is impressive, so it's a great tourist attraction.
M: I'm from China – Shanghai. We are visitors here and we happen to be here. It's a quite exciting place.
W: It's getting better and better, and it has got a Western touch which makes it very unique.
N: This is the largest Chinese New Year Celebration that London has ever seen. It's also the largest celebration outside China with tens of thousands of people here in Central London. It's a great opportunity for Chinese businesses to make some money. With Chinatown just next door to the celebrations in London's Trafalgar Square, you can enjoy a complete Chinese experience. There is lots of singing and dancing here, as well as the delicious food in Soho. As the Chinese say:
G: *Happy New Year* [in Chinese]
N: 'Happy New Year'.

4.6

Part 2

N = Narrator   W = Woman   M = Man   G = Group

N: For a louder experience, come to the capital at the end of August to see Londoners celebrating the Notting Hill Carnival. So, why is it so special?
W1: The food, the music, the vibes … the rain can't stop us. Let's face it.
W2: It's just the atmosphere – it's so friendly. Everybody's having such a fantastic time.
M: It's part of the culture. We're here to celebrate that culture. We're here to celebrate our people.
N: For fifty years, people have celebrated UK Caribbean culture with all of the features that make Carnival so unique. There are colourful costumes, great live music performances and lots of partying in the streets. Even the typical British summer weather – light rain and a few clouds – can't stop these people having a good time! It's now the biggest street festival in Europe, with more than a million people coming to the party over the festive weekend – both tourists and locals.
G: Welcome to the final day of the Notting Hill Carnival!
N: These are steel pan instruments from the West Indies. But you can expect modern dance music and a great diversity in the crowd too. In fact, there are people of all ages here, coming together to forget their troubles and have a great time!
To make sure everyone is safe, there are 7,000 police officers here to patrol the event. But today the festival is much safer than it was. It's a shame that it's only two days long. When the party is over on Sunday night, the big clean-up begins!

Exercise 1

When the pairs have discussed the question, have a class discussion about the most popular celebration in the students' own country and the festival they like best.

Exercise 2

Give students a time limit to find the answers. Check in open class.

Answers: 2 traditional 3 parade 4 animal

Exercise 3

Elicit the answers and the words in the text which provide the relevant information.

Answers:
1 b (the festival celebrates the Queen's official birthday and birthdays are always on the same day of the year)
2 a (It's a five-day festival)
3 d (the festival changes each year to celebrate a different animal)
4 c (reggae, calypso and soul sounds)

Exercise 4

Put students into four groups and allocate a different festival to each group. Tell the groups to find information about their festival that will help them persuade the rest of the class that it will be an interesting and enjoyable festival to attend. They should use the information from the text as a starting point and should try to find out more information by searching online. When all the groups have presented their festival, have a class vote for the festival students would most like to attend.

Extra activity

Put students into groups of four. Tell them to think about a festival in their country. They should discuss what happens at the festival, why it happens and why it is worth seeing. When they are ready, tell them to write a short text about the festival, using quantifiers (e.g. *a lot of*, *many*, *much*, *a few*) and comparatives and superlatives (e.g. *better than*, *the most exciting*, *not as crowded as*) to make their festival sound as appealing as possible. Invite each group to present their ideas to the class.

Exercise 5 4.5

Before you play Part 1 of the video, tell students to read the questions and to try to guess the answers. Elicit their ideas and write them on the board. Then play the video and encourage students to compare their guesses to the actual answers.

Answers:
1 Shanghai
2 'It has got the western touch which makes it very unique' – It has a mixture of traditional Chinese and western influences so is different from other Chinese New Year celebrations.
3 It's the largest Chinese New Year Celebration outside China with tens of thousands of people – i.e. more than ten thousand but probably less than a hundred thousand (or it would say *hundreds of thousands*).

Exercise 6 4.5

Before you play Part 1 of the video again, put students into pairs and ask them to try to do the exercise based on what they can remember.

Elicit the answers. Then write these compound nouns and collocations on the board and ask students what they think they mean.

a melting pot: a society where different nationalities mix together – e.g. *London is a **melting pot** of people from different cultures.*

a tourist attraction: an event or place which is popular with tourists – e.g. *The London Eye is a popular **tourist attraction**.*

Answers: 1 February 2 money 3 near to

Exercise 7 4.6

Ask students to read the exercise items and to guess which of the festivals from the text is going to be shown in Part 2 of the video. Elicit students' ideas and their reasons, e.g. *Notting Hill Carnival: it takes place during the summer, so there is sunny weather and people will be wearing T-shirts; there are costume parades, so there may be face make-up, and music, so there may be steel pan drums; it is a street festival, so there will be lots of people in the street, dancing and celebrating.* Point out to students that there are some items in the list that won't be shown in the video.

Answers: These items should be ticked: 2 (one man playing the steel drums had a blue T-shirt), 3 and 5

Exercise 8 4.6

Before you play Part 2 of the video again, put students into pairs and tell them to try to complete the text. When they are ready, play the video so that they can check their answers. Then ask if they would like to attend the Notting Hill Carnival and to give reasons why or why not.

Answers: 2 Caribbean 3 costumes 4 biggest 5 million 6 ages 7 police 8 weather

Exercise 9

Tell students to work on their own to think about a festival they have been to. Tell them to think about the following points in relation to their festival and to consider how similar or different it was to the festivals shown in the video: multicultural, street parade, tourist attraction, food, costumes, music, performers, good atmosphere.

Then put students into groups and tell them to take turns to describe their festival. When everyone has had a chance to talk, invite groups to tell the class about the most interesting festival that they talked about.

Exercise 10

Elicit different questions that could appear on a questionnaire about festivities, e.g. *Are there any festivals that you go to every year? Do you prefer street parades or entertainment on a stage?*

Put students into groups of four. When the groups have prepared their questionnaire, make sure that each student in the group has a copy of the same questionnaire, so that everyone in the group will ask their friends and family the same questions. Give the groups a time limit for collecting their results and allocate a time in a future lesson for the groups to present their results to the class.

Further practice

- Workbook pages 52–53
- Resource Pack
  Resource 51: Unit 4 BBC Culture Lesson – A new festival
  Resource 52: Unit 4 Culture – Celebrating carnival

EXPLORE

1 What events do you celebrate in your country?

2 Read the text. Complete the sentences with the words below.

> ~~multicultural~~   parade   animal   traditional

1. A lot of London's new festivals are *multicultural*.
2. One of the most _____ festivals is linked to the Royal Family.
3. Many of the festivals in the text have a _____.
4. The Chinese New Year features a different _____ each year.

3 Match festivals 1–4 with descriptions a–d.

1. [b] Trooping the Colour
2. [ ] Diwali
3. [ ] Chinese New Year
4. [ ] Notting Hill Carnival

a. It lasts for a few days.
b. It happens on the same day every year.
c. There are lots of types of music.
d. It's a little different every year.

4 Which of the festivals from the text would you most like to go to? Why?

EXPLORE MORE

5 ▶ 4.5 Watch Part 1 of the video and answer the questions.
1. Where is the Chinese man from?
2. What does the woman like about Chinese New Year in London?
3. How many people attend the celebrations?

6 ▶ 4.5 Watch again. Choose the correct option.
1. The Chinese New Year is usually celebrated in *December / February*.
2. It's a great opportunity for Chinese businesses to make *contacts / money*.
3. Chinatown is *near to / far from* the celebrations in Trafalgar Square.

7 ▶ 4.6 Watch Part 2 of the video. Tick the things you see.
1. [ ] sunny weather
2. [ ] a man with a blue T-shirt
3. [ ] a lot of people in the street
4. [ ] man with green face make-up
5. [ ] people playing steel pan drums
6. [ ] people celebrating on a train

8 ▶ 4.6 Watch again. Complete the text with the words below. There are four extra words.

> police   costumes   parties   weather
> million   Caribbean   ages   happiest
> ~~fifty~~   much   biggest   British

The Notting Hill Carnival is ¹*fifty* years old. It celebrates ² _____ culture. It's famous for its colourful ³ _____ and great live music and performances. It's now the ⁴ _____ street festival in Europe, with more than a ⁵ _____ people coming to the party! There are people of all ⁶ _____ here – both young and old. 7,000 ⁷ _____ officers are at the Carnival to help keep everybody safe. The only problem is the London ⁸ _____!

9 Have you ever been to a festival like the ones in the video? What were the differences and similarities?

YOU EXPLORE

10 **CULTURE PROJECT** In groups, prepare a survey based on the question: 'How do you like to celebrate?'

1. Prepare a questionnaire about festivities. Ask about favourite forms of entertainment and types of festivals.
2. Give the questionnaire to friends and family. Collect the results.
3. Report your results to the class. Are there differences or similarities? What are the most popular festivals? Why?

5

The big match!

VOCABULARY
Sports | Sporting events
Phrasal verbs with *up*

GRAMMAR
The future: *will* / *going to* / Present Continuous | First Conditional + *if/unless*

Grammar: We're having a competition

Speaking: What are you up to?

BBC Culture: The Highland Games

Workbook p. 64

BBC VOX POPS ▶
CLIL 3 > p. 141

MAYFIELD SUMMER SPORTS CAMPS
Click on an icon to find out more.

5.1 VOCABULARY — Sports and sporting events

I can talk about sports and sports events.

1 **CLASS VOTE** In groups, suggest the names of three sportswomen and three sportsmen for 'sports person of the year' in your country. Compare your ideas with the class, and vote for top sportswoman and top sportsman.

2 🔊 **2.16** Study the Vocabulary A box. Listen and match the pictures with the names of sports.

Vocabulary A	Sports		
badminton ☐	basketball ☐	climbing ☐	diving ☐
gymnastics ☐	handball ☐	horse-riding ☐	ice hockey ☐
ice-skating ☐	kayaking ☐	skateboarding ☐	snowboarding ☐
surfing ☐	table tennis ☐	volleyball ☐	yoga ☐

3 🔊 **2.17** Listen to people taking part in the Mayfield sports camp. Complete the gaps with the names of sports.

1. Katia _____
2. Max and Heather _____
3. The red and blue teams _____
4. The green team _____
5. Alexia _____
6. Leo _____

4 **I KNOW!** Work in pairs. How many words can you add to the Vocabulary A box, in two minutes? Use the notes to give yourselves a score.

Score:
- *one point for each item*
- *two points if you are the only team to think of that sport!*

5 Use the Vocabulary A box and the words from Exercise 4 to give three examples of each type of sport.

- indoor sports
- outdoor sports
- team sports
- individual sports
- water sports
- winter sports

Unit contents

Vocabulary
- Sports
- Sporting events
- Phrasal verbs with *up*

Grammar
- The future: *will* / *going to* / Present Continuous
- First Conditional + *if/unless*

Communication skills
- Talking about plans

Examples of 21st Century Skills/Competencies
- Critical Thinking: page 63 (Exercise 5), pages 68–69
- Collaboration: page 64 (Exercise 4), page 69 (Exercise 9)
- Digital Literacy: page 69 (Exercise 9)
- Assessment for Learning: page 67
- Autonomy and Personal Initiative: page 60 (Exercise 6), page 65 (Exercise 7)

5.1 VOCABULARY Sports and sporting events

Lesson learning objective
Students can talk about sports and sports events.

Lead in: Review of vocabulary from the previous unit
Divide the class into four groups and tell them to keep their Students' Books and notebooks closed. Explain that you are going to write some words on the board and you will be writing them one letter at a time. As you write each letter, give each group a chance to try to guess the word. Give groups one guess only for each letter you write. Proceed until one of the groups guesses the word correctly and give them a point. For example, *A* (elicit guesses), *AU* (elicit guesses), *AUD* (group guesses *audience*). If the group can correctly define or translate the word, give them a second point but, if they can't, give the other groups a chance to do this so that they can earn the point. The winning group is the group with the most points at the end of the activity. Suggested words: *bangles*, *character*, *costume*, *dramatic*, *episode*, *festival*, *movement*, *performance*, *production*, *review*, *scene*, *stage*

Exercise 1
Tell students to keep their Students' Books closed. Have a class discussion about sporting heroes in different countries, including the students' own country. Tell students to think of one sportsman and one sportswoman from their country who they would like to nominate for 'sportsperson of the year'.
Put students into groups of four and explain that they need to choose the top three sportswomen and sportsmen. When the groups are ready, invite them to share their ideas with the class, giving reasons for their choices.

Exercise 2 2.16
When students have done the matching exercise, have a class discussion about the different sports. Find out who in the class has done any of the sports, which sports they can do at school, which sports students would like to try in the future and which sports students say they would never like to try.

Answers: 1 climbing 2 horse-riding 3 diving 4 handball
5 kayaking 6 badminton 7 surfing 8 table tennis
9 volleyball 10 ice hockey 11 ice-skating 12 basketball
13 snowboarding 14 yoga 15 gymnastics
16 skateboarding

Exercise 3 2.17
After students have listened to the audio, elicit the answers. Then play the audio again and ask students to note down the key word(s) for each item. Elicit the key words and how these key words give clues to the answers.

Answers:
1 diving (*board*, *enter the water*)
2 kayaking (*lake*)
3 handball (*score*, *20–22*, *ball*, *goalkeeper*)
4 ice hockey (*ice*, *scored*)
5 table tennis (*ball*, *table*)
6 gymnastics (*move*)

 2.17

See page 248.

Exercise 4
This exercise could be done by asking for a sport for each letter of the alphabet. Tell students to put their hands up if they can think of a sport beginning with *A*. Elicit ideas and award points as appropriate. Repeat the process with *B*, *C*, *D*, etc.

Exercise 5
Put students into pairs. Point out that some sports can be categorised in many ways, e.g. tennis can be played indoors or outdoors and individually or in pairs.
When they are ready, invite a pair to share their ideas for one of the categories and ask the other pairs if they have any different examples. Then invite a different pair to share their ideas for another of the categories. Repeat the process until all the categories have been discussed.

Possible answers:
indoor sports: basketball, table tennis, yoga
outdoor sports: climbing, horse-riding, kayaking
team sports: basketball, ice hockey, volleyball
individual sports: gymnastics, skateboarding, surfing
water sports: diving, kayaking, surfing
winter sports: ice-skating, skiing, snowboarding

Exercise 6 2.18

When students have finished, discuss the rules for using *do*, *go* and *play* and elicit more examples of sporting activities used with each word.

Answers:
2 karate, yoga, gymnastics
3 ball games or competitive games
4 swimming, walking, climbing, skiing
5 a sport
6 a sport

Exercise 7

Put students into groups of four to discuss the questions. When they have finished, elicit their answers and ask for more details, e.g. *Do you like all the sports you do in PE? Do you play for a team outside school or do you just practise for fun?*

Exercise 8 2.19

Go through Vocabulary box B with the class and ask questions to check their understanding, e.g. *What kit does your local football team wear? Can you describe a mascot you have seen at a sporting event? Can you name a famous football stadium?*

Answers: *stadium, changing rooms, kit, mascot* and *seats* can be seen in the photos in Exercise 8; *fans, kit, pitch* and *team* can be seen in the photo in Exercise 9

> **Culture notes**
>
> The original Wembley Stadium opened in 1923. It was designed to hold 100,000 people, but for the first big match at the stadium, the 1923 FA Cup Final, it held 200,000–300,000 people. The original stadium building was demolished in 2002 and the new stadium, shown in the photo on page 59, opened in 2007. It is designed to hold 90,000 people and is used for football, rugby and boxing events, as well as non-sporting events such as concerts.

Exercise 9 2.20

Discuss the photo with students. Ask students how they would have felt at that age if they had been chosen to be a mascot at a major football match.

Answers: 2 Stadium 3 changing rooms 4 kit 5 pitch
6 fans 7 seats 8 scoreboard

Exercise 10

Tell students to work alone to think of ideas. When they are ready, put students into groups of four and tell them to discuss their ideas. Invite groups to share the most interesting answer with the class.

Extra activity

Tell students to imagine that the BBC are having a contest to find the Best Young Commentator of the Year. Explain that the contestants can commentate on any sport and the winner is the commentator who gives interesting and accurate information as fluently as possible. Put students into pairs. Tell them to work together to decide on a sport and to think about what information TV viewers will want to hear. One partner plays the role of the commentator, who says what is happening in the sporting action and the other partner plays the role of the co-commentator, who only makes factual comments, e.g. *That's the third goal he's scored in his last three matches* or gives opinions, e.g. *That was a beautiful move and the trainer is delighted*.

Tell students to write down what they are going to say and to practise saying it together. When the pairs are ready, invite them to say their commentary to the class. Have a class vote for the best piece of commentary. (Tell students they can't vote for their own commentary.)

Further practice

- Workbook pages 54–55
- Resource Pack
  Resource 53: Unit 5 Lesson 1 Vocabulary – Sports

6 🔊 **2.18** `WORD FRIENDS` Complete the gaps with the words below. Listen and check.

> a sport (x2)   ball games or competitive games
> ~~football lessons~~   karate, yoga, gymnastics
> swimming, walking, climbing, skiing

1 have *football lessons*
2 do _____
3 play _____
4 go _____
5 practise _____
6 take up _____

7 Which sports from the Vocabulary A box (or your own list) …
- do you play or do in your PE classes?
- do you practise outside school?
- do you watch on TV?
- would you like to take up in the future?

8 🔊 **2.19** Study the Vocabulary B box. Listen and match as many words as you can to the pictures.

Vocabulary B	Sporting events
changing rooms fans goal kit mascot match pitch score scoreboard seats stadium team	

Stadium tour

Meet our team mascot!

9 🔊 **2.20** Complete the text with words from the Vocabulary B box. Listen and check.

Mascot for the day!

Yesterday afternoon I was a team mascot for the English football ¹*team*. There were twelve of us mascots, boys and girls, and we had a tour of the famous Wembley ² _____ in London in the morning. Before the match, we went to get ready in the ³ _____ . I was very excited because they gave each of us a present, a new white-and-red ⁴ _____ to wear!

Finally, we walked along the tunnel in pairs, with each mascot next to a player. Then we came into the stadium, and we stood on the beautiful green ⁵ _____ . The crowd made a lot of noise because there were thousands of ⁶ _____ . When the match started, we sat in special ⁷ _____ at the front. By the end of the match, the score on the big ⁸ _____ was 2–1. Our team won!

10 Would you like to be a team mascot? Why? / Why not? What sport and what team would you choose?

I'd like to be a team mascot because I'm a big sports fan. I'd be a football mascot for my favourite team, FC Barcelona.

Unit 5   59

5.2 GRAMMAR   The future: *will / going to /* Present Continuous

I can talk about plans, predictions, arrangements and timetables.

Skye: Oh, you got weights. Cool!

Tommo: Yeah, we're having a competition at the kayak club next month. I'll be one of the youngest, so I'm going to train well for it.

Skye: They aren't very heavy!

Tommo: They don't have to be heavy. The important thing is to use them every day.

Skye: You won't have much free time then.

Tommo: Yes, I will. It doesn't take long. Look, I'll show you. You lift your arms like this, and repeat about ten times.

Skye: Here, let me have a quick go. Hey, my swimming training starts next week. These exercises will help.

Tommo: Why don't you stay and do some more?

Skye: Sorry, Tommo, I can't. Oh, I'm going to be late and I'm meeting Dan for a run.

Tommo: Oh, OK, but don't forget. You have to use them every day.

Skye: I know.

VIDEO   WE'RE HAVING A COMPETITION

OUT of class

The (important) thing is (to use them every day).
It doesn't take long.   Let me have a (quick) go.

---

1 CLASS VOTE   Do you regularly go to a gym or do exercise at home?

2 5.1 2.21   Watch or listen. What sports do Tommo and Skye mention?

3 Study the Grammar box. Find more examples of talking about the future in the dialogue.

> **Grammar   The future**
>
> **Predictions or decisions made at the moment of speaking**
> You**'ll be** one of the fittest.
>
> **Plans and predictions based on what we know now**
> She**'s going to** train for it.
>
> **Arrangements**
> We**'re having** a sports day at school on Tuesday.
>
> **Timetables**
> The judo classes for beginners **start** next month.
>
> GRAMMAR TIME > PAGE 122

4 Complete the sentences with the future form of the verbs in brackets.

1 Next year, the football club *is going to have* (have) new changing rooms. GOING TO
2 The fans _____ (not be) happy with the result. WILL
3 The basketball match _____ (start) in ten minutes. PRESENT SIMPLE
4 We _____ (go) to Nick's house after the match. PRESENT CONTINOUS
5 _____ (you/buy) your tickets for the match online? GOING TO

5  2.22   Complete the text with the words below. Listen and check.

> are offering   ~~are you doing~~
> begins   is going to help
> will be   will need   won't have

What ¹*are you doing* this summer?

If you don't have any plans, join us at your local park. *Fitness in the Park* is a new idea that ²_____ you to get fit and make friends. The fun ³_____ on June 22 with a special yoga class for beginners. All you ⁴_____ is a good pair of trainers and a bottle of water. Each day for four weeks we ⁵_____ a different activity for you to try. We think it ⁶_____ the best summer ever so don't miss out. Call us now to register. But hurry! We ⁷_____ enough places for everyone.

6 Complete the sentences to make them true for you.

1 This evening I'm going to …
2 Tomorrow the weather will be …
3 On my birthday I'm not going to …
4 In two years everybody in this class will …
5 In 2050 I will …
6 When I'm 50, I won't …

5.2 GRAMMAR   The future: *will* / *going to* / Present Continuous

Lesson learning objective
Students can talk about plans, predictions, arrangements and timetables.

Lead in: Review of sports vocabulary
Write the names of four sports on the board: *football, karate, tennis, volleyball*.
Ask students which sport is the 'odd one out' and why (*karate, because it doesn't use a ball*).
Then put students into pairs and tell them to make three more sets of words that include an odd one out. When the pairs are ready, join two sets of pairs together to make groups of four. The pairs should take turns to say their sets of words to test if the other pair can identify the odd one out. When they have finished, tell each group to say one set of words to test the class.

Exercise 1
Tell students to keep their Students' Books closed. Have a class discussion about the question and divide the class into two groups, one group who regularly go to a gym or do exercise at home or elsewhere and one group who don't do exercise regularly. The first group should try to convince the second group that doing exercise regularly is a good idea. Then the second group should give reasons why they don't go to a gym or do exercise regularly. When both groups have put forward their arguments, have a class vote to see which group is the winner.

Exercise 2   5.1   2.21
Tell students to keep their Students' Books closed while they watch the video. Elicit the names of the sports.

Answers: weights (weightlifting), kayaking, swimming, running

Exercise 3
Ask students to say when the competition at the kayak club is going to take place (*next month*) and when swimming training is going to start (*next week*). Play the video again, if necessary, and elicit the answers.
Ask students if these events are in the past, the present or the future. Then tell students to open their Students' Books and to look at the Grammar box.
Discuss the difference between a plan and an arrangement (*an arrangement is a plan involving someone else*) and explain that we use the Present Simple for timetables.
For each example from the dialogue, elicit why the speaker is using that particular structure.

Answers: we're having (the competition is an arrangement between the organisers and the contestants), I'll be (this is not in the Grammar box – we often use *will be* for future facts – e.g. *I'll be fifteen years old next month*), I'm going to train (this is a personal plan), you won't have (a prediction Skye makes at the moment of speaking), Yes, I will (a prediction Tommo makes at the moment of speaking), I'll show you (a decision Tommo makes at the moment of speaking), starts (this is a timetabled event), will help (a prediction Skye makes at the moment of speaking), I'm going to be late (a prediction Skye makes based on what she knows now), I'm meeting (an arrangement between Skye and Dan)

Exercise 4
After students have done the exercise, put them into pairs. Tell them to match each sentence with one of the rules in the Grammar box, so that they can justify their choice of future form.

Answers:
1 *is going to have* (a plan)
2 *won't be* (a prediction made at the moment of speaking)
3 *starts* (a fact / timetabled event)
4 *'re/are going* (an arrangement)
5 *Are you going to buy* (asking about a plan)

Exercise 5   2.22
After students have done the exercise, elicit explanations for the choice of each future form and discuss possible alternative forms. For example: 2 *will help* is also possible, but *going to* is used to show that there is evidence for the advert's prediction; 5 *going to* is also possible – the use of Present Continuous gives the idea of an arrangement already made, but it could also be seen as a plan; 6 *going to* is also possible here as a prediction with evidence.

Answers: 2 is going to help   3 begins   4 will need
5 are offering   6 will be   7 won't have

Exercise 6
When students have worked on their own to think of ideas, elicit the question we would ask to get the answer in 1 (*What are you going to do this evening?*). Then put students into pairs and tell them to take turns to ask and answer about the six sentences in the exercise. When they have finished, invite pairs to share their most interesting ideas with the class.

Extra activity
Tell students to write one question about the future that they could ask their classmates. When they are ready, give a time limit and encourage students to mingle and ask their question. Then invite students to tell the class what their question was and some of the most interesting responses they received.

Further practice
- Workbook page 56
- Grammar time page 122
- Resource Pack
  Resource 54: Unit 5 Lesson 2 Grammar – Future chat
  Resource 55: Unit 5 Lesson 2 Video – We're having a competition

5.3 READING and VOCABULARY — Why don't you volunteer at *Force4Sport* festival?

Lesson learning objective
Students can identify specific detail in an article and talk about volunteering at a sports event.

Lead in: Review of future forms
Put students into pairs and tell them to write four sentences: a decision made at the moment of speaking (e.g. *I'll do it*), a plan (e.g. *I'm going to* listen to my new CD), an arrangement (e.g. *I'm meeting* Max) and a timetabled fact (e.g. The Maths lesson *starts* at 1.30).
When the pairs are ready, join two pairs to make a group of four. The pairs take turns to say one of their sentences and to say something that could precede that sentence, e.g. *I'll do it – I need someone to wash up.*
When the groups have finished, invite them to share one of their mini-dialogues with the class.

Exercise 1
Tell students to keep their Students' Books closed. Discuss the questions with the class and have a class vote. Then discuss the advantages and disadvantages of watching sports live instead of on TV or online.

Exercise 2   2.23
Elicit the answer and ask students what sort of voluntary work they would choose to do at a sports event.

Answer: In the summer

Exercise 3   2.24
Before students read the text, elicit ideas about the missing information in the volunteer's pass. For example: 1 a sport or activity (e.g. *volleyball, archery, swimming*); 2 a date (e.g. *8 June*); 3 an amount of time (e.g. *two hours, three days*); 4 a number (e.g. *three*); 5 a task (e.g. *show people to their seats*); 6 other voluntary work the person has done (e.g. *none, first aid at a festival*). Write ideas on the board so that after students have read the text they can see how close their guesses were to the actual answers.

Answers:
1 (international) gymnastics competition
2 17 July
3 two weeks
4 5/five
5 take photographs
6 won photography competitions

Exercise 4
Go through the phrasal verbs with the class. Discuss their meanings or encourage students to check their meanings in a dictionary.
Elicit the answers and then ask students for alternative ways to complete the gaps without using phrasal verbs, e.g. 1 *start*, 2 *stop*, 3 *lose the game in the end* or just *lose the game*, 4 *start doing*, 5 *collect*, 6 *tidy*).

Answers: 2 give up   3 end up   4 take up   5 pick up
6 tidy up

Extra activity
Dictate a few sentence beginnings and tell students to complete the sentences in any way they choose.
For example:
John wanted to be a doctor but he ended up …
I had to give up football because …
Can you pick up my …?
My friends and I have set up a …
Next year, I'm going to take up …
Our teacher told us to tidy up the …
When they are ready, put students into groups of four and tell them to read out their sentences. Invite groups to share their most interesting sentences with the class.

Exercise 5
Put students into pairs and tell them to decide which of the experiences can be positive (*watching/learning about different sports*, *getting free tickets*, *taking great photos*) and which of the experiences can be negative (*crowds, not earning anything*). Encourage them to try to think of more positive and negative experiences too. Then tell students to work on their own to write their true sentences. Invite students to read out one of their sentences to the class.

VOX POPS ▶ 5.2
Before watching, check that students understand the meaning of: *CV (curriculum vitae)*. While watching, students should decide which speaker's ideas are the closest to their own. After watching, invite students to share their ideas with the class, giving reasons why they agree with a particular speaker.

Further practice
- Workbook page 57
- Resource Pack
  Resource 56: Unit 5 Lesson 3 Reading and Vocabulary – Up

5.3 READING and VOCABULARY — Why don't you volunteer at *Force4Sport* festival?

I can identify specific detail in an article and talk about volunteering at a sports event.

Force4Sport

You're not into sport but you like watching it. Why not take up a new hobby as a volunteer at the Force4Sport summer sports festival? You decide how many hours you want to volunteer and what kind of job you'd like to do. Our volunteers do lots of different things, from helping competitors to tidying up the stadium. Click on our case studies now, and find out more about our volunteers.

1 CLASS VOTE Do you regularly go to sports events? What is the most popular event?

2 🔊 2.23 Read the website. When is the Force4Sport festival?

3 🔊 2.24 Read the text. Complete gaps 1–6 below.

Hi, my name's Danielle Marley and I'm 16 years old. My cousins volunteered two years ago, and talked non-stop about it. I ended up applying to volunteer this year, and I'm really excited. I'm going to help at an international gymnastics competition at our local sports stadium. I did gymnastics when I was younger, but gave up a couple of years ago because I didn't have enough time. The event starts on 17 July and it lasts for two weeks. I'm only doing the first week, from Monday to Friday. I can't do the weekend. On the first day I'm going to help set up the spectators' area. After that I'm going to take photographs for the local newspaper and for the website. They've offered me a digital camera to take action shots and some team photos. I'm picking it up this afternoon so that I can practise with it. I've already won photography competitions, so I think I'll do a good job. In the future I'd like to study photography, so this could be very useful. I'm excited about volunteering because I enjoy watching sport. I don't think there'll be much chance to do that though, because I'll be too busy!

4 PHRASAL VERBS Use the phrasal verbs to complete the sentences.

Vocabulary	Phrasal verbs with *up*
end up give up pick up	
~~set up~~ take up tidy up	

1. Let's *set up* a gym in the garage and we can train there.
2. I don't want to _____ horse-riding but it is very expensive.
3. The team isn't doing well. They could _____ losing the game.
4. Emma loves trying new sports. She's just decided to _____ karate.
5. I've got to _____ the tickets. I paid online and they're at the ticket office.
6. There are clothes all over the floor. I want everybody to _____ the changing room.

Volunteer's PASS

Name: Danielle Marley
Age: 16
Type of event: 1 _____
Start date for the event: 2 _____
Length of competition: 3 _____
No. of days as volunteer: 4 _____
Volunteer role: set up spectators' area and 5 _____
Previous experience: 6 _____

5 [VOX POPS ▶ 5.2] Would you like to be a volunteer at a sports event? Use the ideas below to make true sentences.

I would/wouldn't like to be a volunteer because …

watch/learn about different sports …
get free tickets …
take great photos …
crowds at the stadium …
not earn anything for hard work …

Unit 5

5.4 GRAMMAR First Conditional

I can talk about possible future situations.

1 Look at the photo. Describe what the girl is doing.

> walk   fall   balance   rope

2 **CLASS VOTE** Do you think you can do this activity? Yes or No?

3 🔊 2.25 Read the poster. What is a slackline?

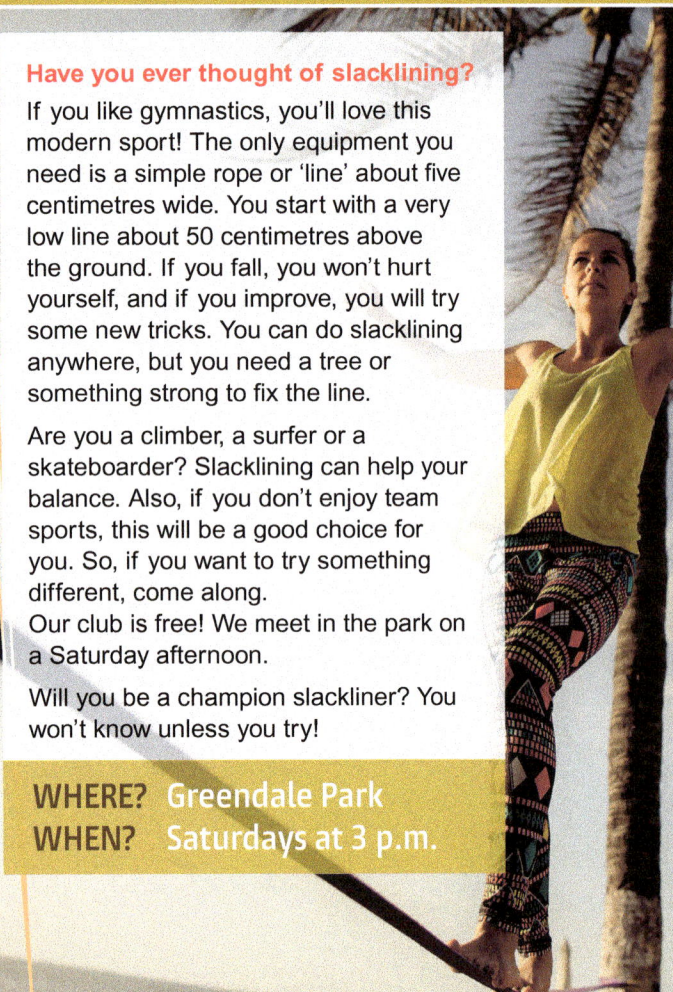

SLACKLINING CLUB

Have you ever thought of slacklining?

If you like gymnastics, you'll love this modern sport! The only equipment you need is a simple rope or 'line' about five centimetres wide. You start with a very low line about 50 centimetres above the ground. If you fall, you won't hurt yourself, and if you improve, you will try some new tricks. You can do slacklining anywhere, but you need a tree or something strong to fix the line.

Are you a climber, a surfer or a skateboarder? Slacklining can help your balance. Also, if you don't enjoy team sports, this will be a good choice for you. So, if you want to try something different, come along.
Our club is free! We meet in the park on a Saturday afternoon.

Will you be a champion slackliner? You won't know unless you try!

WHERE? Greendale Park
WHEN? Saturdays at 3 p.m.

4 Study the Grammar box. Find more examples of the First Conditional in the poster.

Grammar	First Conditional + *if* / *unless*

You **won't know if** you **don't try**!
You **won't know unless** you **try**!

Time clauses with *when* are constructed similarly.
When I'm back home, **I'll watch** some slacklining videos.

GRAMMAR TIME > PAGE 122

5 Match phrases 1-4 with phrases a-d to make sentences.
1 ☐ If you do slacklining, …
2 ☐ You won't do any special tricks …
3 ☐ I won't go to the slacklining club …
4 ☐ You'll see people slacklining …

a unless you're very good.
b if you go to the park on Saturday.
c you will improve your balance.
d unless a friend comes too.

6 🔊 2.26 Read and complete the sentences with the correct form of the verbs in brackets. Listen and check.

Goodbye to the Sports Centre!

The old Riverside Sports Centre will close next week. The new sports centre, with a large pool, tennis courts and a modern gym, won't be ready until next year.

1 If they *close* (close) the sports centre, we *won't play* (not play) handball for ages!
2 I _____ (not stop) playing badminton if they close it.
3 We _____ (not have) karate lessons unless the teacher _____ (find) a new classroom.
4 I _____ (go) swimming every week if they _____ (build) a pool at the new centre.
5 If there _____ (be) tennis courts, I _____ (take up) tennis.
6 We _____ (join) the new gym if it _____ (not be) too expensive.

7 [VOX POPS ▶ 5.3] Finish the sentences to make them true for you. In pairs, discuss your ideas.

What will you do if there's a new sports centre in town?

I'll take up tennis.

1 If there's a new sports centre in town, …
2 If my friends are free this evening, …
3 If I get some money for my birthday, …
4 If the weather's nice at the weekend, …

5.4 GRAMMAR First Conditional

Lesson learning objective
Students can talk about possible future situations.

Lead in: Review of phrasal verbs with *up*

Write on the board: *Last year I _____ up going to Spanish lessons because I wanted to spend more time doing gymnastics.* Ask students to identify the missing word (*gave*). Then ask groups of three to write sentences using the phrasal verbs *end up*, *give up*, *pick up*, *set up*, *take up* and *tidy up*, leaving a gap in the place of the verb. When they finish, groups swap their sentences and try to complete them. Groups then return the sentences to the original groups who check to see if they have been completed correctly.

Exercise 1
Put students into pairs and tell them to try to use all four words as they describe what the girl in the photo is doing.

Possible answer: The girl is trying to walk on a rope. She has to balance carefully so that she doesn't fall off.

Exercise 2
Ask students if they have ever tried this. After the vote, have a class discussion about whether students would like to do the activity and how they think they would feel if they watched someone walking high above the ground.

Exercise 3 🔊 2.25
When students have answered the question, write on the board the numbers 5 and 50. Ask students what these numbers refer to (*the rope is 5 cm wide*; *when you first try slacklining, the rope is about 50 cm above the ground*).

Answer: It's a rope, about 5 cm wide.

Exercise 4
When students have found the examples in the text, give them some more practice with the form. Write on the board:
_____ *school finishes today, I will go shopping.*
_____ *I see something I want to buy, I will take a photo of it and check prices online.*
Elicit that we use *when* in the first sentence because we are talking about what I am going to do after a future event, whereas we use *if* in the second sentence because I might not see something I want to buy.
Then look at the difference between *if* and *unless*. Write:
You won't pass your exams _____ you work hard.
You won't pass your exams _____ you don't work hard.
Elicit that *unless* has the meaning *if not*, so we use *unless* in the first sentence and *if* in the second sentence.
Point out that we can't always substitute *unless* for *if*. For example:
If you like gymnastics, you'll like this modern sport.
Unless you like gymnastics, you won't like this modern sport.
The first sentence means that everyone who likes gymnastics will also like this modern sport. Using the word *unless* changes the meaning to **Only** people who like gymnastics will like this modern sport.
We can never replace *if* with *unless* when the meaning is *even if*.

Answers:
If you like gymnastics, you'll love this modern sport!
If you fall, you won't hurt yourself
if you improve, you will try some new tricks.
if you don't enjoy team sports, this will be a good choice for you.
if you want to try something different, come along.

Exercise 5
Elicit the answers. Then ask students to rewrite the *if* sentences as *unless* sentences and vice versa.
1 You won't improve your balance unless you do slacklining. (This is not necessarily true – you could improve your balance in different ways.)
2 You won't do any special tricks if you aren't very good. (Note that the negative has been added to the second clause and that this sentence has the same meaning as the sentence with *unless*.)
3 I won't go to the slacklining club if a friend doesn't come too. (Again, note that the negative has been added to the second clause and that this sentence has the same meaning as the sentence with *unless*.)
4 You won't see people slacklining unless you go to the park on Saturday. (This is not necessarily true – you may see slacklining somewhere else.)

Answers: 1 c   2 a   3 d   4 b

Exercise 6 🔊 2.26
Tell students that we use *when* for situations which will definitely happen and *if* for situations which are likely to happen. Point out that in sentences 4 and 5 *if* is better than *when*, because something may stop the centre being built, e.g. lack of money.

Answers: 2 won't stop   3 won't/will not have, finds
4 'll/will go, build   5 are, 'll/will take up
6 'll/will join, isn't/'s not/is not

Exercise 7
After students have discussed their ideas in pairs, ask them to think of a new question using *What will you do if …?* Set a time limit for students to mingle and ask their question. Then invite students to tell the class their question and any interesting answers they received.

VOX POPS ▶ 5.3
Before watching, ask pairs to predict one thing the speakers might say for each situation (e.g. *new sports centre – I'll go to it*). While watching, pairs will find out how many of their ideas were mentioned. After watching, invite pairs to say which of their ideas were and weren't mentioned by the speakers.

Further practice
- Workbook page 58
- Grammar Time page 122
- Resource Pack
  Resource 57: Unit 5 Lesson 4 Grammar – What if …?

5.5 LISTENING and VOCABULARY A Norwegian footballer

Lesson learning objective
Students can identify specific detail in a conversation and talk about sports training.

Lead in: Review of the First Conditional

Divide the class into three groups and give each group a piece of paper. Ask each group to write two First Conditional questions that they would like to ask their classmates, e.g. *If it is sunny on Saturday, what will you do?* Collect in the pieces of paper with questions and then invite one student from each group to come to the front of the class with a pen and a piece of paper. Say one of the questions and tell the three students to write their answers to that question. Give each group an opportunity to guess the three students' answers and then ask them to read out their answers. Continue the process until all six questions have been answered.

Exercise 1
Tell students to keep their Students' Books closed and put them into groups of four. Ask the questions and tell the groups to think of and write reasons to support each view.

Exercise 2 2.27
Play the audio and elicit the answers.

Answers: **1** B **2** A

2.27
… and the exciting news from the world of football today is that Champions League winners Real Madrid have just signed up Martin Ødegaard from Norway. Ødegaard was born in 1998 and, at just sixteen years and thirty-six days, is the youngest in the team. It's less than a year since he first appeared in his number seventy-six shirt playing for Norway. In fact, Ødegaard only played in a few games for his mother country but he managed to score five times. What type of player is he? Does he like to run with the ball or head it? Ødegaard says he likes to have the ball and 'kick it'. What an exciting future he's going to have …

Background notes
Martin Ødegaard was born on 17 December 1998. When he played for Strømsgodset Toppfotball on 13 April 2014, he was the youngest player ever to play in the Norwegian League and on 16 May 2014 he became the youngest player ever to score in the league. On 23 May 2015, when Martin came on as a substitute against Getafe, he became the youngest player ever to represent Real Madrid. Martin's first international game was against the United Arab Emirates on 27 August 2014, when he was only 15 years and 253 days old and he was the youngest player ever to play an international game for Norway. When he played for Norway against Bulgaria, Martin became the youngest player ever to play for any country in a European Championship qualifying game.

Exercise 3 2.28
Before you play the audio, ask students to read the sentences. Tell them to imagine they have been chosen to pay for Real Madrid or any other famous team outside their own country. Elicit what they think the answers could be for questions 1–4 and 6.

Answers:
1 T
2 F (Avril thinks Martin Ødegaard will learn Spanish quickly because he'll be with Spanish people all day.)
3 F (Martin Ødegaard won't have lots of free time because he'll be very busy with football practice.)
4 T
5 F (Martin Ødegaard's dad is going to be his coach.)
6 T

2.28
See page 248.

Exercise 4
When the pairs have discussed what they can remember, invite each pair to tell the class one fact.

Exercise 5
Elicit the answers and check that students know how to use *score* as a noun, e.g. *What was the score at the end of the match?*

Answers: **1** noun (action) **2** verb **3** noun (action) **4** verb **5** noun (person) **6** verb

Exercise 6
Before students complete the gaps, elicit what kind of word is needed in each gap and how we know this (*2 is a noun because there is an article (a) and an adjective (fantastic) which describes a noun; 3 is a noun because it is followed by a verb (will be); 4 is a verb, because will is followed by a verb (an infinitive without to); 5 is a noun because there is an adjective (extra) which describes a noun*).

Answers: **2** score **3** practice **4** coach **5** training

Exercise 7
When pairs have finished their discussions, invite them to share their ideas with the class.

Extra activity
Keep students in pairs. Tell them to role play a young sports person thinking about going to practise a sport in a different country and a worried parent. They should write a short dialogue, with the parent asking questions and the player trying to reassure them. Encourage students to practise the First Conditional, e.g. *What will you do if you feel homesick? What will you do if you can't understand anyone?* When they are ready, invite pairs to act out their dialogues in front of the class.

Further practice
- Workbook page 59
- Resource Pack
  Resource 58: Unit 5 Lesson 5 Listening and Vocabulary – Complete the gaps

5.5 LISTENING and VOCABULARY — A Norwegian footballer

I can identify specific detail in a conversation and talk about sports training.

1 **CLASS VOTE** Should a 16-year-old play sport professionally or wait until he or she is older? Why?

2 🔊 **2.27** Listen to the sports news. Choose the correct answers.

1 What number football shirt did Martin first play football in?

A   B   C

2 What does Ødegaard like to do in football?

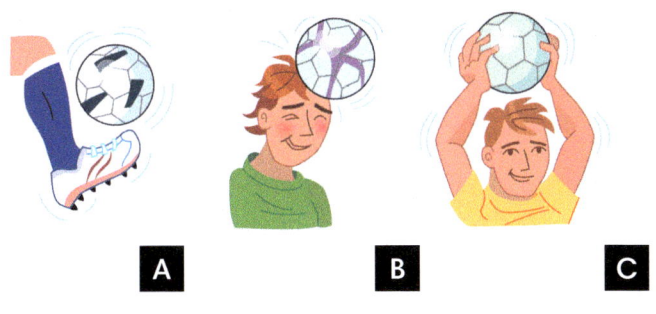

A   B   C

3 🔊 **2.28** Listen to a dialogue. Mark the sentences T (true) or F (false). Correct the false sentences.

1 ☐ Ben would be afraid to live in a different country.
2 ☐ Avril thinks Martin will learn Spanish quickly because he'll do a language course.
3 ☐ Martin will have lots of free time when he finishes training.
4 ☐ Ben thinks it will be difficult for Martin to be without his family.
5 ☐ Martin Ødegaard's uncle is going to be his coach.
6 ☐ Ben says Martin will be rich if he plays well.

4 In pairs, tell your partner what you can remember about Martin Ødegaard. Use Exercises 2 and 3 to help you.

Martin joined Real Madrid. He's only 16.

5 **WORD BUILDING** Study the table. Decide if the word underlined is a verb, noun (action) or noun (person).

1 Jack was too tired to finish the <u>race</u>.
2 Four nil! Do you know who <u>scored</u> the goals?
3 There's no football <u>practice</u> today.
4 The team are <u>training</u> very hard.
5 Their <u>coach</u> doesn't look very happy.
6 He's useless! He can't <u>kick</u> the ball at all.

Verb	Noun (action)	Noun (person)
train	training	trainer
run	running	runner
play	–	player
practise	practice	–
coach	–	coach
race	race	–
score	score	–
kick	kick	–

6 Complete the text with one word in each gap. Use Word Building to help you.

Interschool Handball Victory 28–33

Well done to all handball ¹p<u>layers</u> who joined us on Saturday! It was a great match and a fantastic ²s_____. Handball ³p_____ will be on Tuesday next week. As you know, Ms Ennis will ⁴c_____ the team from now on. She would also like to offer extra ⁵t_____ on Saturdays for anybody who is interested.

7 **And YOU?** Would you like to train for your favourite sport in a different country? Discuss in pairs. Use the ideas below to help you.

family and friends
earn money
the weather
meet other teams/players
learn another language

I wouldn't want to …
It would be nice to …

Unit 5

5.6 SPEAKING Talking about plans

I can ask and talk about plans.

VIDEO   WHAT ARE YOU UP TO?

Alisha: So, is this the Wild Run course you organised?
Dan: Yep. Well, a lot of people helped, of course.
Alisha: Well done! But why is it called a Wild Run? I hope there aren't any wild animals?
Dan: Don't be daft! It's just a fun run! What are you up to before it starts?
Alisha: Nothing much.
Dan: Well, if you come with me, I'll explain it all. Over two hundred people are running here later, so I need to check everything. First, they're going under a net.
Alisha: Seriously? It's very muddy!
Dan: Yeah. Try it! Yeah, that's it.
Alisha: Well, if they don't like dirt, they won't enjoy this run!
Dan: Come on. Then they're crossing a stream and running up a hill.
Alisha: Oh no! It's fun, but I'm tired already! Have you got any plans for after the run?
Dan: Yes. When you all finish, we'll give you a medal. Then we're going to have a barbecue.
Alisha: Great. I'll need a medal. Wish me luck!

Don't be daft!   *Seriously?* 
Wish me luck.

1 In pairs, look at the photo. What do you think is happening?

2 5.4   2.29 Watch or listen and check your answer to Exercise 1. Mark the sentences T (true) or F (false).
1 ☐ Dan is going to run.
2 ☐ The event isn't a competition.
3 ☐ There will be two hundred volunteers.

3 2.30 Study the Speaking box. Order the sentences. Listen and check.

Speaking   Talking about plans

Asking
What are you up to today / at the weekend?
Have you got any plans for this evening / after the run?
What are you doing on Sunday / next Monday?

Answering and following up
I'm visiting my grandma / going to the cinema.
First (of all) I'm going to / I'm seeing …
Then … / After that … / Later …
I don't have any plans. / I don't know yet.
What about you? / And you? / What are your plans?

a ☐ Sam: Yes, OK. I'll probably see you on Sunday, then.
b ☐1☐ Sam: What are you up to this weekend?
c ☐ Tara: We'll get home late, so I'm definitely going to have a lie-in on Sunday … Then I'll probably do some homework. We could go to the cinema after that, if you like?
d ☐ Tara: Well, first I'm visiting my grandparents on Saturday morning. Then we're going to go to a basketball match together. It starts at 4 p.m.
e ☐ Sam: That's nice. Have you got any plans after that?

4 In pairs, ask and answer about your plans for the weekend. Use the ideas below to help you.

sports and activities   shopping
family and friends   relaxation
homework   entertainment
trips   special events

5 Tell the class about some of your partner's plans.

Linda is going to see her grandparents on Saturday afternoon. Then they're going to the cinema in the evening.

5.6 SPEAKING Talking about plans

Lesson learning objective
Students can ask and talk about plans.

Lead in: Review of verbs and nouns

Write *dinner* on the board. Ask students to say what kind of word it is (*a noun*) and then ask them to define it, e.g. *it's a meal that you eat in the afternoon or evening*. Then write *win*. Again, ask students to say what kind of word it is (*a verb or a noun*) and ask them to define it, e.g. *it means to come first in a competition and is the opposite of the verb lose or it means a victory and is the opposite of the nouns defeat and loss*.

Put students into pairs and tell them to do the same with any four words of their choice. When the pairs are ready, join two pairs together into a group of four. For each of their words, tell them to take turns to say what kind of word it is and to define it. When they are finished, invite groups to share some of their words and definitions with the class.

Exercise 1
Invite pairs to describe what they can see in the photo and what they think is happening.

Exercise 2 5.4 2.29
After students have watched the video, ask if they think non-competitive sports are a good idea or if they prefer sports where there can be a winner. Encourage students to give reasons for their opinions.

Answers: 1 F 2 T 3 F

Extra activity

Put students into groups of three. Elicit what runners have to do in the fun run shown in the video (*go under a net, cross a stream, run up a hill*). Tell the groups to think of some more ideas for a fun wild run. When they are ready, invite each group to tell their ideas to the class. Have a class vote for the best idea.

Exercise 3 2.30
When students have ordered the dialogue, give them more practice of the different ways of talking about plans. Divide the class into three groups. One group should think of a question to ask using *What are you up to (tonight / tomorrow / at the weekend / etc.)?* The second group should think of a question using *Have you got any plans for …?* The third group should think of a question using *What are you doing on …?*

Encourage the different groups to mingle and to ask and answer the questions. Give them a time limit. Then elicit any interesting answers that were given.

Answers: a 5 b 1 c 4 d 2 e 3

Exercise 4
Discuss with the class some possible answers they could give using each of the ideas in the exercise, e.g. *I'm playing tennis with …* (sports and activities); *We're visiting my aunt …* (family and friends). Encourage students to use sequencers, (*first, then, next*, etc.) to show the order of their plans for the weekend.

Exercise 5
Make sure students use the Present Continuous when talking about arrangements and *going to* when talking about plans. Tell the class that they should listen to find out if any of the plans they hear about are the same as their own plans for the weekend. After everyone in the class has had a chance to talk about their partner's plans, invite students to compare with their own plans, e.g. *I'm going to visit my grandparents too, but I'm visiting them on Sunday, not Saturday*.

Further practice

- Workbook page 60
- Resource Pack
  Resource 59: Unit 5 Lesson 6 Speaking – Tell me your plans
  Resource 60: Unit 5 Lesson 6 Video – What are you up to?

5.7 WRITING Notes, making a request

Lesson learning objective
Students can write notes and make requests.

Lead in: Review of talking about plans
Put students into groups of four. Tell students to ask one another about their plans for the weekend and to write their four answers on a piece of paper. Groups should swap their papers with another group, who should try to guess which student gave each answer. The groups should then join together into a group of eight and ask one another about their plans, to check if their guesses were correct. Invite groups to tell the class how well or badly they guessed one another's plans.

Exercise 1
Before students open their Students' Books, elicit different ways that they send messages to their friends. Then tell them to open their books and to see if all the ideas they discussed have been mentioned. Have a class vote to find out the most popular way of sending messages and the usual speed of their replies.

Exercise 2
Elicit from students how they determined the types of messages they are. For example, the first message has examples of text speak – *Thkq* (Thank you), *4* (for), *gr8* (great), *u* (you). Elicit any other text speak students know and/or use quite often. The second message is to a group. Ask students if they are members of any groups on a social media site and, if they are, to explain when and why they send group messages.

Answers: A text message and a message on social media

Exercise 3
Ask students how they would answer each message. Tell them to imagine they are Dan replying to Skye, e.g. *Of course, no problem. Glad you enjoyed the race. Hope you can come to the next one* and to imagine they are replying to Dan's message, e.g. *Thanks very much. I'd love a photo and I'll definitely come to the race next month.*

Answers:
1 Dan wants the runners to email him if they want a photo of themselves with their medal.
2 Skye asks Dan to keep her trainers at his house.

Exercise 4
Elicit the order and ask for more information, e.g. *What does Skye thank Dan for? How does she introduce the topic of the race? What does she ask Dan to do?*

Answers:
1 Skye thanks Dan.
2 Skye introduces the topic of the race.
3 Skye asks Dan to do something.

Exercise 5
When students have found all the phrases in the texts, ask if they ever write messages in English. If students say they do, ask them which form of greeting and ending they usually use. Then tell them to rewrite one of the two messages, using a different way of greeting, thanking, introducing the topic, making a request and ending the message, e.g. *Hiya, Just a quick note to thank you for your help on Saturday. The race was very enjoyable and … .*

Answers:
Hey
Thkq 4 your help …
I had a gr8 time at the race, …
Would u mind …?
If it's OK with u, …
Hi
Just a quick note to thank you for …
If you'd like …, could you please …?
All the best

Exercise 6
When students have finished, discuss the different kinds of sentence structure for making requests:
If you would like to …, please …?
Would you mind -ing?
If it's OK with you, + can/could I/we …?
Would it be possible + to …? / for you to …?
Put students into pairs and ask them to use these sentence structures to make different requests, e.g. *Would you mind helping me with my homework?*

Answers: 1 e 2 d 3 a 4 c 5 b

Exercise 7
Discuss the writing task with the class and explain that they should write their note on a piece of paper. Elicit a few ideas for what the runner might ask Dan to do, so that there are some ideas for students to choose from. When students have finished writing, tell them to swap their note with a partner. They should check that their partner has followed the exercise instructions and has used the correct form for making a request.

Homework
Tell students to read the text on page 68 of the Students' Book. They should look up any words they don't know the meaning of and translate them into L1.
As an additional task, ask students to write an example sentence illustrating the meaning of each these words: *bounce* (verb), *goalpost*, *league*, *oval*, *tackle*. Tell them that the sentences must, in some way, be connected to sport.

Further practice
- Workbook page 61
- Resource Pack
  Resource 61: Unit 5 Lesson 7 Writing – Would you mind …?

5.7 WRITING — Notes, making a request

I can write notes and make requests.

1 **CLASS VOTE** How do you and your friends usually send messages to each other? How long does it usually take you to reply?

- a text message an email a postcard
- an instant message a message on paper
- a message on Facebook or social media

2 Read the messages. What types of messages are they?

> Hey Thkq 4 your help on Saturday. I had a gr8 time at the race but it was fast! Glad I trained 4 it. Left my trainers in the changing rooms :(Would u mind keeping them at your house? If it's OK with u, I'll pick them up at the weekend. Skye

GROUP CHAT

Hi,

Just a quick note to thank you all for competing on Saturday. More than 200 runners entered the race and we think everybody enjoyed themselves. We're now planning another race, which will take place in Northfield Park next month. Details will be on our website soon.

I've also got some great photos of the event. If you'd like a photo of you with your medal, could you please email me before June 30?

All the best,

Dan

2 mins ...

3 Read the messages again and answer the questions. Underline where in the messages you found your answers.
1. What does Dan want the runners to do?
2. What does Skye want Dan to do?

4 Order the information in Skye's message.
- [ ] Skye asks Dan to do something.
- [ ] Skye introduces the topic of the race.
- [ ] Skye thanks Dan.

5 Study the Writing box. Find the phrases from the Writing box in the texts in Exercise 2.

Writing | Notes, making a request

Greeting
Hi ... / Hi, there / Hiya / Hey ...

Thank the other person
Thanks for your note/message/present ...
Thanks for inviting me/writing/sending/coming ...
Just a quick note to thank you for ...

Introduce the topic
I had a great time at the race, although ...
I really enjoyed meeting the ...

Making a request
If you'd like ..., could you please ... ?
Would you mind ... ?
If it's OK with you, could we ... ?
Would it be possible to ... ?
Let me know if that's OK.

Ending
Bye! / Cheers! / All the best. / See you later.

6 Match phrases 1–5 with phrases a–e to make requests.
1. [ ] If you'd like to join the kayak club,
2. [ ] Would you mind
3. [ ] If it's OK with you,
4. [ ] Would it be possible
5. [ ] I could start at 8 p.m.

a could we meet at the tennis club at 7 p.m.?
b Let me know if that's OK.
c to train on Friday instead of Tuesday?
d helping with the sports day?
e please email us with your name and address.

7 You were a runner at the Wild Run. Write a note to Dan. Follow the instructions below:
1. thank him for his message
2. describe what you did at the race
3. ask Dan to do something for you

Unit 5 65

Wordlist and Vocabulary in action

Extra activities

After students have completed Exercise 5, write the following on the board:
/əʊ/ coach, goal   /eɪ/ trainer, weight   /iː/ seat, team
Put students into pairs and ask them to add more words to each sound group. Explain that their words must include two vowels together. For example:
/əʊ/ road ✓, rode ✗   /eɪ/ main ✓, made ✗   /iː/ eat ✓, be ✗
Invite pairs to say their words for each sound group and drill the words.

Further practice

Workbook page 62

WORDLIST — Sports | Sporting events | Phrasal verbs with *up*

badminton /ˈbædmɪntən/
balance /ˈbæləns/
basketball /ˈbɑːskɪtbɔːl/
changing rooms /ˈtʃeɪndʒɪŋ ruːmz/
climber /ˈklaɪmə/
climbing /ˈklaɪmɪŋ/
coach (v) /kəʊtʃ/
compete /kəmˈpiːt/
competition /ˌkɒmpəˈtɪʃn/
competitor /kəmˈpetɪtə/
crowd /kraʊd/
diving /ˈdaɪvɪŋ/
end up /ˌend ˈʌp/
equipment /ɪˈkwɪpmənt/
event /ɪˈvent/
exercises /ˈeksəsaɪzɪz/
fall /fɔːl/
fan /fæn/
fitness /ˈfɪtnəs/
football shirt /ˈfʊtbɔːl ʃɜːt/
footballer /ˈfʊtbɔːlə/
game /ɡeɪm/
get fit /ˌget ˈfɪt/
give up /ˌɡɪv ˈʌp/
goal /ɡəʊl/
gym /dʒɪm/
gymnastics /dʒɪmˈnæstɪks/
handball /ˈhændbɔːl/
head a ball /ˌhed ə ˈbɔːl/
horse-riding /ˈhɔːs ˌraɪdɪŋ/
ice hockey /ˌaɪs ˈhɒki/
ice-skating /ˈaɪs ˌskeɪtɪŋ/
improve /ɪmˈpruːv/
individual sports /ˌɪndəˈvɪdʒuəl spɔːts/
indoor sports /ˈɪndɔː spɔːts/
judo /ˈdʒuːdəʊ/
karate /kəˈrɑːti/
kayaking /ˈkaɪækɪŋ/
kick (v/n) /kɪk/

kit /kɪt/
lead (in the lead) /liːd (ˌɪn ðə ˈliːd)/
lift (v) /lɪft/
lose /luːz/
mascot /ˈmæskət/
match /mætʃ/
medal /ˈmedl/
net /net/
outdoor sports /ˌaʊtˈdɔː spɔːts/
PE /ˌpiː ˈiː/
pick up /ˌpɪk ˈʌp/
pitch /pɪtʃ/
play /pleɪ/
player /ˈpleɪə/
pool /puːl/
practice (n) /ˈpræktəs/
practise (v) /ˈpræktəs/
race (v/n) /reɪs/
register /ˈredʒɪstə/
rope /rəʊp/
run (v/n) /rʌn/
runner /ˈrʌnə/
running /ˈrʌnɪŋ/
score (v/n) /skɔː/
scoreboard /ˈskɔːbɔːd/
screen /skriːn/
seat /siːt/
set up /ˌset ˈʌp/
skateboarder /ˈskeɪtbɔːdə/
skateboarding /ˈskeɪtbɔːdɪŋ/
skiing /ˈskiːɪŋ/
slackline /ˈslæklaɪn/
slackliner /ˈslæklaɪnə/
snowboarding /ˈsnəʊbɔːdɪŋ/
spectator /spekˈteɪtə/
sports camp /ˈspɔːts kæmp/
sports centre /ˈspɔːts ˌsentə/
sports festival /ˈspɔːts ˌfestəvl/

sportsperson / sportsman
sportswoman / sportspeople
/ˈspɔːts.pɜːsn/ˈspɔːtsmən/
ˈspɔːts.wʊmən/ˈspɔːts.piːpl/
stadium /ˈsteɪdiəm/
surfer /ˈsɜːfə/
surfing /ˈsɜːfɪŋ/
swimming /ˈswɪmɪŋ/
table tennis /ˈteɪbl ˌtenəs/
take up /ˌteɪk ˈʌp/
team /tiːm/
team sports /ˈtiːm spɔːts/
tennis court /ˈtenəs kɔːt/
ticket /ˈtɪkɪt/
tidy up /ˌtaɪdi ˈʌp/
train /treɪn/
trainer /ˈtreɪnə/
trainers /ˈtreɪnəz/
training /ˈtreɪnɪŋ/
tricks /trɪks/
volleyball /ˈvɒlibɔːl/
volunteer /ˌvɒlənˈtɪə/
walking /ˈwɔːkɪŋ/
water sports /ˈwɔːtə spɔːts/
weights /weɪts/
whistle /ˈwɪsl/
win /wɪn/
winter sports /ˈwɪntə spɔːts/
yoga /ˈjəʊɡə/

WORD FRIENDS

do karate, yoga, gymnastics
go swimming, walking, climbing, skiing
have (a sport) lessons
play ball games or competitive games
practise (a sport)
take up (a sport)

VOCABULARY IN ACTION

1 Use the wordlist to find:
1 five places where you can do sport
2 six different people
3 three sports for which you need a ball
4 two pieces of sports equipment
5 two things you wear to do sports
6 three types of sports
7 three verbs that are the same as nouns

2 In pairs, ask your partner about the spelling of one word in each category in Exercise 1.

   How do you spell 'weights'?

   It's W-E-I-G-H-T-S.

3 Choose the correct option. Use the wordlist to check your answers. In pairs, say if the sentences are true for you.
1 I often (go) / play swimming.
2 I never *take up* / *have* any new sports.
3 I sometimes *go* / *play* basketball at school.
4 I'd like to *do* / *have* karate.
5 I *go* / *have* PE lessons twice a week.

4 🔊 2.31 **PRONUNCIATION** Look at the underlined vowels in each word. Do you think we say them as one syllable or two? Listen and check.

   c**oa**ch   g**oa**l   tr**ai**ner   w**ei**ght   s**ea**t   t**ea**m

5 🔊 2.32 In pairs, say these words. Listen and check.

Exercise 1

Possible answers:
1 gym, pitch, pool, sports camp, sports centre, stadium, tennis court
2 climber, coach, competitor, fan, footballer, mascot, player, runner, skateboarder, slackliner, spectator, sportsperson, sportsman, sportswoman, sportspeople, surfer, trainer, volunteer
3 basketball, football, handball, table tennis, tennis, volleyball
4 net, rope, slackline, weights
5 football shirt, kit, trainers
6 individual sports, indoor sports, outdoor sports, team sports, water sports, winter sports, ball games, competitive games
7 balance, coach, crowd, fall, head, kick, lead, race, run, score, win

Exercise 3

2 take up
3 play
4 do
5 have

Exercise 4

one syllable

Revision

Extra activity

When students have completed Exercise 1, write *football shirt/kit* on the board. Ask students to say what the difference is between the two words, e.g. *a football shirt is part of a football kit, which should also include shorts, socks and boots.*
Put students into pairs. Tell them to study the wordlist to identify two words with fairly similar meanings. Invite pairs to say their two words and invite the class to explain the difference between the words.

Further practice

- Workbook page 63
- Resource Pack
  Resource 62: Unit 5
  Vocabulary – Collect the words
  Resource 63: Unit 5
  Grammar – The party

Exercise 1
1 volunteer
2 seat
3 practise
4 scoreboard
5 medal

Exercise 2
1 score: the other words are all people
2 karate: you don't use a ball in karate
3 give up tennis: 'give up' is about not doing sport
4 horse-riding: it is the only one that is not a water sport
5 race: it is not a piece of sports equipment

Exercise 3
1 won't get, c
2 is going to play, a
3 finishes, e
4 Are you coming, d
5 'll/will get, b

Exercise 4
1 go
2 finishes
3 have
4 gives

Revision

VOCABULARY

1 Write the correct word for each definition.
1 This person helps at events but isn't paid any money. v_____
2 You can sit on this in a stadium, cinema or theatre. s_____
3 If you want to be good at a sport, you must do this: p_____
4 This is the object which shows spectators how each person or team is doing. s_____
5 If you win a race, you might get this. m_____

2 Read the word groups. Choose the odd one out. Give a reason for your decision. In pairs, make your own quiz questions.

1	player	competitor	coach	score
2	karate	tennis	volleyball	football
3	do karate	practise judo	play volleyball	give up tennis
4	kayaking	horse-riding	diving	swimming
5	net	race	kit	ball

GRAMMAR

3 Complete the sentences with the future form of the verbs in brackets. Match the sentences with their function below.
1 ☐ I *won't get* (not get) a medal, but I hope to do well. (WILL)
2 ☐ My favourite team _____ (play) at the stadium on Saturday. (GOING TO)
3 ☐ The karate class _____ (finish) at 8 p.m. (PRESENT SIMPLE)
4 ☐ _____ (come) to the cup final next week? (PRESENT CONTINUOUS)
5 ☐ Thank you! I'll be happy to come. I _____ (get) the tickets for us all, then. (WILL)

a plan
b decision at the moment of speaking
c prediction
d arrangement
e timetable

4 Complete the questions with the correct forms of the verbs in brackets.
1 What new sport will you try if you _____ (go) to summer sports camp?
2 Will you meet me when school _____ (finish)?
3 If you _____ (have) some free time in winter, where will you go?
4 What will you do if someone _____ (give) you some money for your birthday?

5 Choose the correct option.
A: What are you doing for Sports Day tomorrow?
B: ¹(First)/ *Then* I'm watching the races. ²*Then / Later* I'm taking part in football. After that I'm going to try karate, I think. What about you?
A: ³*Then / First* I'm taking part in the street dance display. ⁴*First / After that* I'm not sure. I'll probably watch the volleyball competition ⁵*later / then*.
B: What are your plans for the evening?
A: I'm definitely going to take part in the sports quiz. And you?
B: I'm playing live music with one of the bands. ⁶*First / Then* I'll probably go to the barbecue, too.

6 In pairs, make your own dialogue. Use the sports day programme.

School sports day

Time	Events	Display
3 p.m.	football competition	skateboard display
4 p.m.	volleyball competition	gymnastics display
5 p.m.	try-it-yourself sessions: karate slacklining yoga skateboarding	
Evening 6 p.m. – 8 p.m.	live music with school bands barbecue sports quiz (teams of four–six people)	

Exercise 5
2 Then
3 First
4 After that
5 later
6 Then

DICTATION

7 🔊 2.33 Listen, then listen again and write down what you hear.

SELF-ASSESSMENT Think about this unit. What did you learn? What do you need help with?

WORKBOOK p. 62

Exercise 7
A: What are we doing this evening?
B: We're going to watch an ice hockey match. It's very popular here. Some famous players will be there.
A: Great! But if I don't arrive on time, will you wait?
B: Of course!

127

CULTURE
Where do they toss the caber?

Aussie Rules

If you think the most popular sport in Australia is rugby or cricket, think again. It's a sport that you have probably never heard of, called Australian Rules Football. Commonly known as 'Aussie Rules', big matches attract huge crowds, especially in the large stadiums of Sydney or Melbourne.

So what is Aussie Rules? Well, it's very different from the football that you and I know. The game is played between two teams of eighteen players and the field is oval-shaped. Though called football, it is more similar to rugby. For example, the ball is oval and you score points by kicking it between two goalposts, just like in rugby.

However, players can be anywhere on the field and they can use any part of their bodies to move the ball. Running with the ball is fine, but you have to bounce it or touch it on the ground at the same time. Throwing the ball is not allowed. Aussie Rules includes a lot of physical contact and can be dangerous. Players can tackle each other using their hands or even their whole body!

The sport was invented in the 1850s in Melbourne, but amazingly, a national competition didn't take place until the 1980s. It is equally popular among men and women, although there isn't a women's league yet. Because it is purely Australian, it is rich in cultural history and references. Australians identify with it greatly. They are very proud to have a sport that they can call their own.

It is only really played in Australia, but it has fans worldwide. Who knows? Perhaps one day it will become very popular in the UK too!

GLOSSARY
bounce (v) (of a ball) hit the ground and go up
goalpost (n) one of the two posts of a goal in games such as football
league (n) a group of sports teams or players who compete against each other
oval (adj) shaped like an egg
tackle (v) to try to take the ball from another player

BBC CULTURE Where do they toss the caber?

Lead in: Topic introduction

Tell students not to open their Students' Books. Put students into groups of four. If you set the homework suggestion for the unit, ask the groups to discuss any vocabulary they found difficult and their example sentences if you also set the additional task.

If students haven't done the homework, ask them to look at the glossary on page 68. Students should find the words in the text and discuss what they mean in context, e.g. *The ball used in Aussie Rules is **oval** and shaped like an egg.*

5.5

The Highland Games

Part 1

The Highland Games are a very old tradition. They were set up as way of bringing together Scotland's historical families. They capture the cultural life and sports of this magical nation. They include the colours and symbols of a culture that almost disappeared, but is now stronger than ever.

The Highland Games are a meeting place of strength, speed and celebration. Today on sports grounds, farmers' fields and city parks across this country, they are Scotland's very own Olympics!

This is the village of Ceres. It is home to Scotland's oldest Highland Games. For centuries the whole village has gathered for this annual summer celebration. For the people of Ceres, it's a day as important as Hogmanay – New Year's Eve in Scotland – or Christmas.

5.6

Part 2

The Highland Games are a mixture of fact and fantasy. They are a unique blend of sport and culture.

There is highland dancing, bagpipes and drums and there is a series of sports, too. There is usually athletics, sometimes cycling and wrestling, but always the 'heavy events'. These include the stone shot, the hammer throw and tossing the caber.

At most games the caber is people's favourite sport. It's the final event and a symbol of the Highland Games. The caber is about six metres long and weighs about fifty-five kilograms. Competitors have to throw it, then flip it over and the caber has to land flat. If it lands absolutely straight, it's a perfect throw.

The Highland Games are now also celebrated outside Scotland – in the USA, Canada, Australia and the Far East. These games are organised by families who emigrated from Scotland. The biggest Highland Games in the world take place here, in the Blue Ridge Mountains in North Carolina. They last over four days and 22,000 people come every year to enjoy this traditional Scottish event of their ancestors.

The Highland Games are the most visible display of Scottish identity that you can imagine. They are about competing, of course, but they are also about community, keeping tradition alive and making time for old friends. If you come, you won't regret it!

Exercise 1

Tell students to keep their Students' Books closed. Explain that they are going to read about a sport which is similar to rugby or American football and is popular in Australia. Ask students to think of sports which are often associated with a particular country, e.g. *Sumo wrestling – Japan*, *boules – France*. Then ask students to open their books and to answer the questions, in pairs.

Exercise 2

Drill the word *Aussie* with a /z/ sound (i.e. /ˈɒzi/ sounds like *Ozzie*) and explain that this is a short form of the word *Australian*. Put students into pairs to discuss the questions. Invite pairs to share their ideas with the class.

When students have read the article and completed the exercise, ask if they think the sport sounds interesting or not and encourage them to give reasons for their answers.

Possible answers:
1 it is rich in cultural history and references, Australians identify with it, they are proud to have a sport they can call their own
2 e.g. American football

Exercise 3 ▶ 5.5

Explain to students that the video may show some of the actions in the background but that they should wait until it focuses on each specific action, e.g. for item *b* they should wait until the video shows spectators only and for item *d* they should wait until they see both the pipe players and the drummers together at the same time.

Answers: c 1   g 2   f 3   e 4   a 5   b 6   d 7

Exercise 4 ▶ 5.5

Before you play Part 1 of the video again, put students into pairs and tell them to try to complete the sentences. Elicit students' answers and play the video so that they can check if their answers were correct.

Answers: 2 disappeared   3 celebration   4 parks
5 Olympics

Exercise 5 ▶ 5.5

Before you play Part 1 of the video again, ask the pairs to read the sentences and discuss what they can remember.

Answers:
1 the cultural life and sports of Scotland
2 they are the oldest in Scotland
3 summer
4 Hogmanay (New Year's Eve) and Christmas

Exercise 6 ▶ 5.6

Go through the list of sports with students and elicit what is done in these sports: tossing the caber, hammer throw, stone shot.

Answers: cycling, tossing the caber, running, wrestling, hammer throw, stone shot

Exercise 7 ▶ 5.6

Before you play Part 2 of the video again, ask the pairs to read the sentences and discuss what they can remember.

Answers: 1 culture   2 always   3 fifty-five   4 outside
5 friends

Exercise 8

When students have discussed the questions, have a class discussion about whether they thought the Highland Games looked interesting and whether their own country has anything similar. Encourage students to think of sports that could be included in an event celebrating their own national games.

Extra activity

Put students into pairs. Tell them to imagine that one of them is a visitor to Scotland and the other one is a friend who lives in Scotland and is Scottish. Explain that the visitor is going to attend the Highland Games and wants to know what happens during the Games and why they are important to Scotland. Tell the pairs to develop and practise their dialogues. When they are ready, invite them to perform their dialogues in front of the class.

Exercise 9

Put students into groups of three and invite the groups to choose a country to write about. When they have chosen a country, they should put up their hands and say the name of their country. Once a country has been chosen by a group, it can't be chosen by another group.

Discuss some ideas for the content of students' presentations, e.g. the rules of the sport, special events, the history of the sport, its popularity outside the country.

Give them a time limit for creating their presentations. Allocate a time in a future lesson for the groups to present these to the class.

Further practice

- Workbook pages 64–65
- Resource Pack
  Resource 64: Unit 5 BBC Culture Lesson – An unusual sport
  Resource 65: Unit 5 Culture – Alternative games

EXPLORE

1 In pairs, ask and answer the questions.
1. What sports do you practise? Who do you play with? Why do you play them?
2. What is the national sport in your country?
3. What role do sports have in your country?

2 Read the article and answer the questions.
1. In what ways is Aussie Rules culturally important for Australia?
2. Do you think many sports have this cultural role? Why? / Why not?

EXPLORE MORE

3 ▶ 5.5 Watch Part 1 of the video with no sound. Order the actions as they appear in the video.
- a ☐ men running a race
- b ☐ spectators watching the sports
- c [1] a man throwing a large piece of wood (the 'caber')
- d ☐ men playing bagpipes and drums
- e ☐ a man throwing a hammer
- f ☐ two men wrestling
- g ☐ two girls dancing

4 ▶ 5.5 Watch Part 1 of the video with sound. Complete the sentences with the words below.

> Olympics   parks   ~~tradition~~
> celebration   disappeared

1. The Highland Games are a very old *tradition*.
2. They include the colours and symbols of a culture that almost _____.
3. The Highland Games are a meeting place of strength, speed and _____.
4. Today the Games are played on sports grounds, farmers' fields and city _____.
5. For Scottish people, the Highland Games are Scotland's _____.

5 ▶ 5.5 Watch again. Answer the questions.
1. What do the Games capture?
2. Why are the Games in the village of Ceres important?
3. At what time of the year do they hold the Highland Games?
4. For many Scots, the Highland Games are as important as which other events?

6 ▶ 5.6 Watch Part 2 of the video. Tick (✓) six sports you hear or see.
1. ☐ cycling
2. ☐ horse-riding
3. ☐ climbing
4. ☐ tossing the caber
5. ☐ running
6. ☐ wrestling
7. ☐ hammer throw
8. ☐ handball
9. ☐ stone shot
10. ☐ hockey

7 ▶ 5.6 Watch again. Choose the correct option.
1. The Highland Games are a unique blend of sport and *fantasy / culture*.
2. The Games usually include athletics and *sometimes / always* heavy events.
3. The caber is six metres long and weighs *fifteen / fifty-five* kilos.
4. There are more Highland Games celebrated *in / outside* Scotland.
5. The Games are about competing and also making time for old *traditions / friends*.

8 In pairs or groups, ask and answer the questions.
1. Would you like to attend the Highland Games? Why? / Why not?
2. Which part of the Highland Games would you enjoy the most: the music and dancing or the sports? Why?

YOU EXPLORE

9 CULTURE PROJECT In pairs or groups, prepare a presentation about a national sport in other countries.
1. Research national sports of other countries.
2. Write a short script and think about images or videos to use in your presentation.
3. Give your presentation to the class.

6 See the world!

VOCABULARY
Types of holidays | At the hotel | Equipment | Travel: confusing words

GRAMMAR
Obligation and prohibition | Modal verbs for speculation | Time clauses

Grammar: You mustn't do that!

Speaking: I didn't catch that

BBC Culture: Adventures of a lifetime

Workbook p. 76

BBC VOX POPS
EXAM TIME 2 > p. 133

My Trips

6.1 VOCABULARY Travel

I can talk about holidays and travelling.

1 **I KNOW!** How do you prefer to travel? Look at the pictures below. How many types of transport can you name for each?

by sea   by road   by rail   by air

> We say *by sea/road/rail/air* and *by boat/car/bus/train/plane* but *on foot*.   **Watch OUT!**

2 Match questions 1–5 with responses a–e. In pairs, ask and answer the questions with your books closed.

Speaking	Travelling phrases
1 ☐	Excuse me, is the bus/train station near here?
2 ☐	What time does the bus/train arrive/leave?
3 ☐	What platform does the train arrive at / leave from?
4 ☐	Excuse me, how do I get to the airport?
5 ☐	I'd like a bus/train ticket to Paris, please.

a Single or return?
b At 9.15 a.m.
c There's a bus service every half hour.
d Platform 6.
e Yes, it's at the end of the road.

3 Do you ever write a diary when you're on holiday? Why? / Why not? What sort of information can you include?

4  2.34 Study the Vocabulary A box. Match the words with photos 1–7.

Vocabulary A	Types of holidays
☐ activity camp	☐ backpacking holiday	☐ beach holiday
☐ camping trip	☐ city break	☐ cruise	☐ sightseeing holiday

Unit contents

Vocabulary
- Types of holidays
- At the hotel
- Equipment
- Travel: confusing words

Grammar
- Obligation and prohibition
- Modal verbs for speculation
- Time clauses

Communication skills
- Understanding a conversation

Examples of 21st Century Skills/Competencies
- Critical Thinking: page 71 (Exercise 6), pages 80–81
- Collaboration: page 75 (Exercise 8), page 76 (Exercise 5), page 81 (Exercise 8)
- Digital Literacy: page 81 (Exercise 8)
- Assessment for Learning: page 79
- Autonomy and Personal Initiative: page 73 (Exercise 7), page 74 (Exercise 6)

6.1 VOCABULARY Travel

Lesson learning objective
Students can talk about holidays and travelling.

Lead in: Review of vocabulary from the previous unit

Put students into two groups. Explain that you are going to think of a word from the previous unit and write on the board gaps for each letter. The groups should take turns to try to guess the letters. Each time a group guesses a letter correctly, they win a point. If a group wants to guess the whole word, they should say what they think it is and, if they are correct, they win a point for each missing letter. For example:
Think of a word (*football*) and write gaps for each letter:

_ _ _ _ _ _ _ _
Group 1 guesses *a*, so write the letter and award 1 point:
_ _ _ _ _ a _ _
Group 2 guesses *o*, so write the letter (x2) and award 2 points: _ o o _ _ a _ _
Group 1 guesses *e*, so they get no points.
Group 2 guesses *football*, so award them 5 more points, so they now have seven points altogether.
After the word has been guessed, elicit the meaning of the word.
Ideas for words to use: *climbing, crowd, equipment, gymnastics, improve, kick, pitch, stadium, ticket, whistle*

Exercise 1
Put students into pairs to discuss their ideas. When they have finished, ask about the type of transport they think they would use for different kinds of journeys, to find out their preferred form of travel for each. For example, from their home to the centre of town, to a town not far from the student's school, to an area of their country a long way away and to a different country bordering theirs.

Possible answers:
by sea: cruise ship, ferry, ocean liner, yacht
by road: bike, bus, car, coach, motorbike
by rail: train, tram, underground
by air: balloon, helicopter, plane

Exercise 2
After students have done the matching and before they ask and answer in pairs, discuss the vocabulary: *arrive (at), leave (from), platform, single/return (ticket)*. Also make sure students understand the difference between *arrive at a station / an airport / someone's house* and *arrive in a town / a country*.

Answers: 1 e 2 b 3 d 4 c 5 a

Exercise 3
Discuss the questions with the class. Also ask about holiday blogs or updates on social media, to see if students write those instead of writing a diary.

Exercise 4 2.34
Put students into pairs and tell them to discuss what they can see in the photos. Then do the matching as a whole-class activity. Discuss what each type of holiday actually involves. For example: *an activity camp is a holiday where a group of people, often young people, stay in one place and, during the day, do activities such as sports; a backpacking holiday is one where people carry everything in a backpack and they may carry a tent and a sleeping bag for camping or they may stay in hostels or hotels.*

Answers: 1 backpacking holiday 2 cruise 3 city break
4 camping trip 5 activity camp 6 beach holiday
7 sightseeing holiday

Exercise 5 🔊 2.35

Before you play the audio, put students into seven groups and allocate one type of holiday to each group. Tell the groups to imagine what it would be like to be on this type of holiday. They should write a short conversation between two people on that type of holiday, without mentioning the type. When the groups are ready, invite each group to act out their conversation, while the rest of the class tries to guess the type of holiday.

Then discuss key words and phrases which students may hear in the audio referring to each type of holiday, e.g. *cruise – ship, sea, get off and look round the town, see land in the distance*.

When students have listened to the audio, elicit which words and phrases helped them to identify the type of holiday. If students say that item 2 could be a sightseeing holiday, elicit why city break is a better answer (*because the dialogue refers to a short trip and because the speakers mention tall buildings but they don't talk about specific interesting sights, guidebooks or taking photos*).

Answers: **1** backpacking holiday **2** city break **3** beach holiday **4** activity camp **5** cruise

---

🔊 **2.35**

1
- A: At last, I thought we would never find the train station. I'm hot, this backpack is really heavy and my legs are tired.
- B: I know, but come on. Let's get on the train and then we can rest. In four hours we'll be in Spain.

2
- A: Look at the view from the window, Anna. It's beautiful at night, especially the tall buildings on the other side of the bridge.
- B: Wow, that's amazing! Two days isn't enough time to do everything.
- A: You're right. I think we should come back next year and have a longer holiday here.

3
- A: Come on, Jack! The sea's really warm.
- B: No, thanks, Emma. I don't fancy going in the water at the moment. I think I'll go and get an ice cream at the shop.

4
- A: That was the best thing I have ever done! I didn't know zip-wiring was so cool.
- B: Hah! You looked very scared.

5
- A: Look at this postcard from Grandma and Grandpa, Mum … It's a photo of their ship and it's got *two* swimming pools … It says they're sailing from Portugal to Spain and then Italy … Cool!
- B: Yes, I think they're having a very relaxing holiday.

Exercise 6

When the pairs have finished, invite them to share their ideas with the class. Then hold a class vote for the most interesting type of activities to do at an activity camp; the best area to go cruising, e.g. the Caribbean, the Mediterranean, the Fjords; the best place to visit for sightseeing; the biggest advantage of going on a backpacking holiday and the best city to visit for a city break.

Exercise 7 🔊 2.36

Discuss hotels that students have stayed in and what they liked and didn't like about them. Then go through the words in the Vocabulary box and ask students which hotel facilities would be the most important for them.

Answers: **2** check in **3** reservation **4** double rooms **5** single rooms **6** floor **7** view **8** facilities **9** pool **10** guests

Exercise 8

Elicit more questions that the pairs could ask each other, e.g. *Who did you go with? What was the room like?* When they have finished, invite pairs to share their travel experiences with the class.

Exercise 9 🔊 2.37

When the pairs have finished, elicit students' definitions. Ask questions using the vocabulary, e.g. *Do you or your parents take a guidebook with you when you go on holiday? Have you ever slept in a sleeping bag / tent? Do you prefer to take a suitcase or a rucksack?*

Exercise 10

Ask students if, when they go on holiday, they make a list of things to take with them so that they don't forget anything. Before students start their discussions, elicit one item students would take for each type of holiday. When the pairs are ready, invite them to share one of their lists. The class should guess which holiday it corresponds to.

VOX POPS ▶ 6.1

Before watching, check that students understand the meaning of these words/phrases: *compass, suntan lotion, the brim of a hat*. While watching, tell students to decide for each holiday which of the items mentioned they think is the most important. After watching, elicit students' ideas and their reasons.

Extra activity

Put students into groups of three. Tell each group to think of a type of holiday that they would like to advertise. The group should work together to create a poster showing what the holiday offers and giving reasons why people might want to choose that type of holiday. When the groups have created their posters, invite them to present their holiday to the class. Have a class vote for the best holiday. (Tell students they can't vote for their own holiday.)

Further practice

- Workbook pages 66–67
- Resource Pack
  Resource 66: Unit 6 Lesson 1 Vocabulary – Words and definitions

5 🔊 **2.35** Listen and match dialogues 1-5 with the types of holidays in the Vocabulary A box.

1 ____ 2 ____ 3 ____
4 ____ 5 ____

6 In pairs, describe:
1 three things to do at an activity camp.
2 four countries to visit on a cruise.
3 three things to see on a sightseeing holiday.
4 three things to do on a backpacking holiday.
5 two places to stay during a city break.

7 🔊 **2.36** Study the Vocabulary B box. Use the words to complete the text. Listen and check.

Vocabulary B	At the hotel
check in/out double room(s) facilities floor guests pool ~~reception~~ reservation single room(s) view

Diary

We arrived late last night at the hotel. Nobody was working in ¹*reception* so we couldn't ² ____ to our rooms. In the end, Mum phoned the hotel from her mobile! The manager arrived, but there was a problem with our ³ ____ . We needed two ⁴ ____ because there are four of us, but the hotel only had two ⁵ ____ .

In the end, the manager found us another hotel and here we are, in a better hotel! We're on the top ⁶ ____ and there's a brilliant ⁷ ____ of the city. It's got great ⁸ ____ and I can't wait to use the ⁹ ____ and the gym. There are lots of ¹⁰ ____ and they're all speaking different languages … I'm very excited to be here!

8 In pairs, discuss the last time you travelled. Use the questions below to help you.
• Where did you go?
• Where did you stay?
• What facilities were there?

I went to Austria with the school and we stayed in a big hotel. We had a view of the mountains but we didn't have a pool.

9 🔊 **2.37** Study the Vocabulary C box, using a dictionary. In pairs, describe the words.

Vocabulary C	Equipment
guidebook map passport rucksack/backpack sleeping bag suitcase sun cream sunglasses tent torch trunks/swimsuit

A: This has your personal information and a photograph, and you must bring it when you travel to another country …
B: It's a passport!

10 [VOX POPS ▶ 6.1] Choose a holiday from the list below. In pairs, make a list of things you should take with you. Compare your ideas with the class.
• a backpacking holiday with friends
• a city break in Ireland
• a cruise around the Mediterranean
• an activity camp in the mountains

Unit 6 71

6.2 GRAMMAR — Modal verbs for obligation, prohibition and advice: *must, have to, ought to, should*

I can talk about obligation, prohibition and advice.

Gran: Skye, can you come down? Your mum's calling soon about our visit. We ought to have a quick chat first … Oh, you look lovely, dear.

Skye: Thanks. It's my party outfit. Have you got the tickets yet?

Gran: No, I'll get them soon, but I must know the exact date you finish school.

Skye: Our exams finish on June 16th, but I have to be here for Sue's birthday party on July 29th.

Gran: Yes. You mustn't miss that! Should we go the first week of July, then?

Skye: Perfect. Do Mum and Dad have to work in July?

Gran: They don't have to work every day. It rains quite a lot in July, so they ought to have some free time to be with us.

Skye: Hang on. What do you mean, it rains? I wanted a beach holiday.

Gran: Sorry, Skye. In July it's winter in New Zealand.

Skye: In that case, Mum and Dad should come here.

Gran: Then I think you have to ask them, Skye.

VIDEO: YOU MUSTN'T MISS THAT!

> **OUT of class**
> *What do you mean, (it rains)?*
> *In that case, (they should come here).*

1 CLASS VOTE How important is good weather on holiday?

2  6.2 2.38 Watch or listen. Why is Skye disappointed?

3 Study the Grammar box. Find more examples in the dialogue of obligation and prohibition.

Grammar — Obligation and prohibition

obligation and prohibition
You **must** visit us in Paris.
You'll **have to** take warm clothes.
You **mustn't** be late for the flight.

advice
We **ought to** ask them about their plans.
You **shouldn't** take too much luggage.

lack of obligation
They **don't have to** go by car.

GRAMMAR TIME > PAGE 123

4 Choose the correct option.

1 I'm going to China soon. I *must / don't have to* buy a guidebook.
2 You can never find your passport. You *should / shouldn't* put it in a safe place.
3 *Do we have to / Should we* get a visa for the USA?
4 The plane leaves at 9 a.m., but we *mustn't / don't have to* be there until 7 a.m.
5 I *shouldn't / ought to* pack my bags. We leave in an hour.
6 It's going to be very hot at the beach. We *must / mustn't* forget the sun cream.

5 2.39 Complete the text with the words below. Listen and check.

> don't have to   have to   must
> mustn't   ~~ought~~   should

Mountain fun

Are you looking for adventure this summer? Then you ¹*ought* to try our mountain activity camp. You ²_____ bring any special equipment because we provide everything. You ³_____ be between 13 and 17 years old and have your parents' permission. All you ⁴_____ bring are enough clothes for a week of camping, hiking and climbing and, of course, you ⁵_____ forget a warm coat for evenings around the camp fire. Reserve a place now and you ⁶_____ hear from us before the end of the month.

6 [VOX POPS ▶ 6.3] Finish the sentences to make them true for you. Compare your ideas with the class.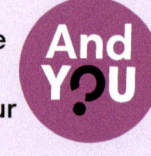

1 When you're on a beach holiday, you should …
When you're on a beach holiday, you should use sun cream.
2 In a plane, people mustn't …
3 When I'm on holiday with my parents, I don't have to …
4 On an activity camp, you have to …

6.2 GRAMMAR   Modal verbs for obligation, prohibition and advice: *must*, *have to*, *ought to*, *should*

Lesson learning objective
Students can talk about obligation, prohibition and advice.

Lead in: Review of holiday vocabulary

Put students into seven groups. Give each group a piece of paper with a holiday type written on it: activity camp, backpacking holiday, beach holiday, camping trip, city break, cruise, sightseeing holiday. Tell the groups to discuss how they can mime their type of holiday. Then invite the groups to perform their mimes, while the rest of the class guesses the type of holiday and the activities they are doing in their mime.

Exercise 1
Tell students to keep their Students' Books closed and ask the question. After the class vote, ask students to think of ways in which they can enjoy a holiday even if the weather isn't good.

Exercise 2   6.2   2.38
Ask students to look at the photo and say how Skye is feeling. What is she holding in her hands (*sunglasses*, *swimsuit*)? Play the video.

> **Answer:** Skye is disappointed because she wanted a beach holiday and it is winter in New Zealand and it rains a lot in July when she will be visiting.

Exercise 3
Check that students understand the meanings of the words *obligation* and *prohibition*. Remind students that in this exercise they should only look for examples of obligation and prohibition and they shouldn't look for examples of advice or lack of obligation.

When students have found the examples, discuss the second part of the Grammar box and elicit the difference between advice (i.e. it's a good idea) and obligation (i.e. you don't have a choice). Also discuss the difference between *don't have to* (i.e. you have a choice) and *mustn't* (i.e. prohibition) and tell students to find examples of these in the text. Point out that we can use *must/mustn't* for very strong advice, e.g. *you mustn't miss that*). Explain that this is different from prohibition in that it indicates that the speaker strongly recommends that you do something.

> **Answers:**
> **Obligation:** I must know the exact date, I have to be here, Do Mum and Dad have to work in July?, you have to ask them
> **Strong advice (see above):** You mustn't miss that!
> **Advice:** We ought to have a quick chat, Should we go the first week in July, they ought to have some free time, Mum and Dad should come here
> **Lack of obligation:** They don't have to work every day.

Exercise 4
When students have finished, ask follow-up questions, e.g. *Do you keep your passport in a safe place? Have you ever been somewhere where you needed a visa? Do you pack your bags a long time before your holiday or right at the last minute?*

> **Answers:** 1 must   2 should   3 Do we have to
> 4 don't have to   5 ought to   6 mustn't

Exercise 5   2.39
Tell students to look at the heading of the text and the first two sentences. Elicit what sorts of activities students think the camp might offer. Ask if anyone in the class has been on an activity camp in the mountains and if they enjoyed it. When students have finished completing the text, elicit the answers and discuss the last gap. Ask how this gap is different from the others (*it isn't giving advice, instead it is using* should *instead of* will *to show that what they are saying is expected but isn't definite*). Give similar examples, e.g. *I should pass my exams because
I have done a lot of work – but I can't guarantee it. The concert should be good because the bands playing at it are all good – but I can't guarantee it*).

> **Answers:** 2 don't have to   3 must   4 have to   5 mustn't
> 6 should

Exercise 6
Put students into four groups. Discuss the example sentence and invite each group to give a piece of advice for a beach holiday. Keep eliciting ideas until the groups can't give any more relevant pieces of advice. Then tell students to work alone to complete sentences 2, 3 and 4.

VOX POPS   ▶ 6.3
Before watching, check that students understand the meaning of the phrase: *to show up on time*. Put students into pairs, and tell them to write in their notebooks the modals *should*, *don't have to*, *have to*, *mustn't*. While watching, students should identify which three of the modals are mentioned and they should write down the verb which comes immediately afterwards (e.g. in the example in Exercise 6, students would just write the verb *use*). After watching, elicit the verbs (i.e. *should - remember, look at*; *don't have to – see, worry*; *have to – be, make*). Tell students to think of other ways of using these words in sentences (e.g. *You should remember to take sun cream / a good book / a hat*).

Extra activity
Tell students to work on their own. Ask them to imagine a holiday they would like to go on, e.g. *a sightseeing trip to Paris*. When everyone has chosen a holiday, encourage students to mingle with their classmates. They should take turns to tell their classmate their holiday plan and to give a piece of advice about their classmate's holiday plan. Set a time limit of five minutes. When they have finished, invite students to say their holiday plan and the best (and worst) piece of advice they received.

Further practice
- Workbook page 68
- Grammar Time page 123
- Resource Pack
  Resource 67: Unit 6 Lesson 2 Grammar – Holiday advice
  Resource 68: Unit 6 Lesson 2 Video – You mustn't miss that!

6.3 READING and VOCABULARY   Live life outside

Lesson learning objective
Students can find specific detail in an article and talk about travelling.

Lead in: Review of modals

Write a 'problem' on the board: e.g. *I have got important exams soon.* Elicit any advice, prohibition or obligation that students could say in response to this 'problem', e.g. *You should go to bed early. You must start studying. You mustn't cheat. You shouldn't worry too much.*

Invite two students to sit at the front of the class facing the other students. Tell them not to look at the board. Write *I'm always tired* on the board. Students facing the board should give advice or orders to the two students at the front of the class, who should try to guess what the 'problem' is. When one of them guesses, or if they give up, invite two different students to come to the front of the class, to guess a different 'problem'.

Suggested 'problems':
My sister annoys me.
I feel sick.
I've lost my phone.
I'm not very good at English.
I can't see the teacher's writing on the board.

Exercise 1
Tell students to keep their Students' Books closed. Discuss the question with the class and ask them to give reasons for their opinions. After the class vote, put students into pairs and ask them to write a list of what they think are the top five most important things about travel. Invite students to share their lists with the class.

Exercise 2
When the pairs have discussed the main photo, invite them to describe what they can see to the class and to try to guess what the text might be about.

Possible answer: There are some boys in a small building. One of the boys is holding a surfboard.

Exercise 3   🔊 2.40
Before students read the text, elicit what they can see in each of the four small photos (*A a notebook; B a video camera; C an iPod; D a hammock*).

When students have completed the exercise, ask how the four objects in the photos relate to the text (*A Booker always takes a notebook with him on his trip, perhaps it has his list of where he wants to go or perhaps it is to make notes about what he sees and does; B He's made videos of his trips since he was young; C He always listens to a different song on his iPod; D His favourite place to sleep is a hammock*).

Answers: 1 D   2 B   3 A   4 C

Exercise 4
Tell students to write the answers in their notebooks, using full sentences, e.g. *Skateboarding language has helped Booker to … .*
Elicit the answers and where each answer can be found in the text.

Answers:
1 It's helped him to explore different places around the world and meet local people in different countries.
2 Because he has parents who have always travelled with him.
3 He enjoys the feeling of adventure that goes with travelling.
4 His skateboard or surfboard, a video camera and a notebook.
5 He rides his skateboard to school.

Exercise 5
Put students into pairs and tell them to try to complete the sentences without checking in the text. After they have tried to complete all the sentences, allow them to check in the text for any sentences they weren't sure about.

Answers: 2 luggage   3 sleep   4 plan   5 route   6 fascinating

Extra activity
Keep students in pairs. Tell them to imagine that Booker has just returned from holiday and is being interviewed by a reporter. The pairs should think of the reporter's questions and Booker's answers. Give them a time limit to practise the interview. Then invite a student to come to the front of the class, to play the role of Booker. The rest of the class should play the role of the reporter and ask Booker questions about his holiday. It is likely that some of the class's questions will be different from the questions that the student practised in pairs, so explain that he/she needs to think of new answers. Allow the class to ask Booker three questions and then invite a different student to play the role of Booker.

Exercise 6
When students have found the word *friends* in the text, put them into groups of three. Tell the groups to think of more phrases which collocate with the verbs they found, e.g. *learn how to swim, learn about different cultures, learn to tie your shoelaces.* Invite groups to share their ideas with the class.

Answers: explore different places, meet local people, share an experience, plan a trip, go on holiday/sightseeing

Exercise 7
Have a class discussion about the amount of luggage we can take on different kinds of holidays or transport, e.g. *If we go on holiday by car, we can take quite a lot of things because we can put things in the boot of our car. If we go backpacking, we shouldn't take very much luggage because it is difficult to carry a heavy rucksack on your back.*
Then put students into pairs and tell them to talk about their own experiences. Invite pairs to share their experiences with the class.

Further practice
- Workbook page 69
- Resource Pack
  Resource 69: Unit 6 Lesson 3 Reading and Vocabulary – Make friends

6.3 READING and VOCABULARY
Live life outside

I can find specific detail in an article and talk about travelling.

1 **CLASS VOTE** Do you agree that travel is important? Why? / Why not?

2 In pairs, describe the main photo.

3 🔊 2.40 Read the text quickly. Order photos A–D as you find them in the article.

1 ☐ 2 ☐ 3 ☐ 4 ☐

Live life outside

Most travellers know that learning a new language can make a holiday more fun. But what about *frontside*, *lipslide*, *kickflip*? What sort of language is this?

It's the international language of the skateboarding world, and a language that teens like Booker Mitchell from New York know well. It has helped him to explore different places around the world and meet local people in different countries. Booker knows he's lucky to have parents who have always travelled with him. He's made videos of his trips since he was young. With the help of his mum, who's a film-maker, Booker has made videos that share an experience of skateboarding and surfing with the rest of the world.

Booker loves travelling and enjoys the feeling of adventure that goes with it. He doesn't think you should travel with a lot of luggage, and says the most important thing is to feel comfortable wherever you are. His favourite place to sleep is in a hammock, even if he's at home in New York! Of course, like the rest of us, there are some things Booker has to travel with. In his case, it's a skateboard or surfboard, a video camera and a notebook.

Does Booker sometimes go on holiday at the last minute? No way! Planning a trip is really important. Before every trip, he makes a list of where he wants to go sightseeing and why. He learns about the culture, food, music and scenery. He thinks that's the best way to enjoy somewhere.

Back at home, Booker rides his skateboard to school. He never takes the same route, and always listens to a different song on his iPod. He likes to see the different things that are happening around him. 'Life is fascinating, no matter where you live', he says. 'You just have to look at it the right way.'

4 Read the text again. Answer the questions.
1 What has skateboarding language helped Booker to do?
2 Why does Booker think he's lucky?
3 What does Booker like about travelling?
4 What does Booker always travel with?
5 How does Booker get to school?

5 Complete the sentences with one word in each gap.
1 Booker's *mother* has helped him with his skateboarding and surfing videos.
2 Booker doesn't think it's right to take much _____ when you travel.
3 When he's travelling, or at home, Booker prefers to _____ in a hammock.
4 It's important for Booker to _____ where he wants to go on a trip.
5 At home, Booker always uses a different _____ to get to school.
6 Booker thinks that if you look at life in the right way, it's _____.

6 **WORD FRIENDS** Find the words in the text and complete the Word Friends. Use the words in the correct form.

Word Friends	Travel phrases
learn a new language	
_____ different places	
_____ local people	
_____ an experience	
_____ a trip	
_____ on holiday / sightseeing	

7 Booker doesn't think people should travel with a lot of luggage. What about you?

I take a huge suitcase. I always pack too many clothes.
I don't take much, and I often forget things. Last year I forgot my swimsuit!

6.4 GRAMMAR Modal verbs for speculation: *must, could, might/may, can't*

I can speculate about the present.

1 CLASS VOTE Look at the photo. Is this a fun place to sleep? Why? / Why not?

2 🔊 2.41 Read the text. What are the advantages and disadvantages of hanging tents?

My camping blog

TENTS

Hi Guys,
Welcome to my camping blog, the best place for all the latest camping news. This month I've discovered these amazing tree tents. It might be difficult to find them in the shops at the moment, but I think they're going to be popular. They're warm and comfortable, and great fun. I slept in one last weekend, in the middle of a forest, and it was awesome! Have a look and let me know what you think.

JO123 6.30 p.m.	They don't look very big. It can't be easy to stand up in them if you're tall.
TENTFAN 7.10 p.m.	It might be fun to sleep up in the air, but it must be difficult to go to the loo in the middle of the night!
TIMABC 8.00 p.m.	They are cool! But they must be expensive because I haven't seen many of them.
CAMPER 8.30 p.m.	They may look cool, but I think they could be really uncomfortable because they move around with the wind.

3 Study the Grammar box. Find more examples of speculating in the text.

Grammar	Modal verbs for speculation

must + infinitive
It **must be** cold outside. People are in jackets.

could/might/may + infinitive
It **might be** difficult to travel with the suitcase because it's very big.

can't + infinitive
That **can't be** our tent. It's the wrong colour.

GRAMMAR TIME > PAGE 123

4 Choose the correct option.
A: That's a strange tent? It looks like a balloon.
B: Oh, that ¹(must)/ can't be the new tree tent. I've seen them on the internet.
A: I'd love to get one. Are they expensive?
B: They ²can't / could be expensive because my uncle's got one, and he hasn't got much money.
A: Is there a campsite near here?
B: I'm not sure. There ³might / must be one near the lake. I've seen people there in summer. Why?
A: I'd love to try a tree tent. Can we ask your uncle if we can borrow it?
B: OK, but today ⁴could / can't be a bad time. He's going on holiday with it!

5 Rewrite the sentences, using the verbs from the Grammar box. Sometimes more than one answer is possible.
1 I'm sure this is Ellie's tent. That's her rucksack.
   This **must** be Ellie's tent. That's her rucksack.
2 They're very quiet. Perhaps they're sleeping.
   They _____ be sleeping.
3 I'm sure this isn't the same campsite.
   This _____ be the same campsite.
4 Dad thinks this is your ticket, but your ticket is in your hand.
   This _____ be your ticket because your ticket is in your hand.
5 I'm sure the map is on the table. I put it there.
   The map _____ be on the table. I put it there.
6 Here's a guidebook, but perhaps it's the wrong one.
   Here's a guidebook, but it _____ be the wrong one.

6 What do you think of these ideas for unusual holiday accommodation? Use the Grammar box to help you.
- a canal boat in Holland
- a tree house in a forest
- an ice hotel in Sweden
- a castle on an island

It could be noisy in a tree house in a forest because of all the animals.

74 Unit 6

6.4 GRAMMAR Modal verbs for speculation: *must, could, might/may, can't*

Lesson learning objective
Students can speculate about the present.

Lead in: Spectulating

Draw a table on the board with four columns headed *Photo*, *Definitely true*, *I think* and *Definitely not*. Write the numbers 1 to 7 under the heading Photo.

Put students into groups of four and tell them to look at the seven photos in the Students' Book on pages 70 and 71. For each photo, the groups should work together to find something to say for each heading in the table, e.g. *1 Definitely true – It is summer; I think – They are in England; Definitely not – They aren't in Egypt*. They should write these sentences in the table in their notebooks. When they have finished, invite groups to share their ideas for each photo, giving reasons for each one, e.g. *It is definitely summer because they are wearing light clothes and carrying camping equipment.*

Exercise 1
Ask students to describe what they can see in the photo. Then put them into pairs and ask them to discuss what they think could be the advantages and disadvantages of staying in the structure shown in the photo. Invite pairs to share their ideas, then hold the class vote.

Exercise 2 🔊 2.41
Elicit the answers from the text and compare them with students' own ideas from Exercise 1. Ask students if they would like to change their vote, now that they have learnt more about the structure in the photo.

Answers:
Advantages: warm, comfortable and fun
Disadvantages: not very big, difficult to get out of them at night, expensive, they move around with the wind

Exercise 3
Go through the Grammar box with the class. Check that they understand the meaning of *speculation* and *to speculate*. Then discuss these important points about modal verbs for speculation.
- Students should recognise the modal verbs we use for speculation, but they will have seen them used for different functions, e.g. *must* for obligation. Write on the board:
  *I'm tired. I **must** go to bed.*
  *He's gone to bed. He **must** be tired.*
  Explain that in the first sentence *must* is used for obligation and in the second sentence *must* is used for speculation. Then do the same with the modal *can't*:
  *Mum says I **can't** go to the cinema today.* (prohibition)
  *It's two a.m., so he **can't** still be at the cinema.* (speculation)
- Although we use *must/can't* when we **think** that something is true or untrue, we don't use them when we **actually know** that something is true or untrue. For example, we wouldn't say *I must be in my English lesson now*, because we know that this is true.
- *May*, *might* and *could* can all be used when we **aren't sure** if something is true or untrue. Because these modals are interchangeable, it's good to vary their usage, e.g. *The hanging tent **could** be comfortable, but it **might** be cold.*

- Although we use *could* and *can't* for speculation, we don't use *couldn't* or *can*. Write these two examples for students to copy, with the incorrect words crossed out:
  Where's Paul? He ~~can~~ could/may/might be in the garden.
  Paul ~~couldn't~~ can't be in the garden. It's raining.

When students have found the examples in the text, point out that most of the modals of speculation are in the forum comments and that the writer of the text only uses one modal of speculation (about finding the tents in the shops). Elicit that the writer doesn't need to speculate about the tent because he/she knows what it is like, but the people in the forum do need to speculate because they don't know what it is like.

Answers: It might be difficult, It can't be easy, It might be fun, it must be difficult, they must be expensive, They may look cool, they could be really uncomfortable

Exercise 4
Discuss the example with the class. We know the correct option is *must* because if the speaker had used *can't*, he/she would have had to give a reason why it could not be the case, e.g. *It can't be the new tree tent. I've seen them on the internet and they look totally different.*

Answers: 2 can't 3 might 4 could

Exercise 5
Discuss the example with the class and what this means about the speaker's knowledge of Ellie's rucksack and tent (*the speaker recognises the rucksack, and therefore concludes that the tent is hers too*).

Answers: 2 could/might/may 3 can't 4 can't 5 must 6 could/might/may

Exercise 6
Put students into groups of four. Tell them to discuss what they think could be the advantages and disadvantages for each kind of accommodation. When the groups are ready, put students into new groups according to their lists (i.e. all lists for canal boats together, all lists for tree houses together, etc.). Tell the new groups to compare their lists and to use the information in the lists to write sentences using modals of speculation, e.g. *It could be exciting in a … because …*, *It might be uncomfortable in a … because …; It must be cold in a … because … .*

Extra activity

Put students into pairs. Tell them to look once more at the photos on pages 70–71 of their Students' Books and to speculate about each one, e.g. *1 They must be a couple. They could be looking at a beautiful waterfall. Their backpacks must be heavy. They can't be lost – they look too happy.*

Further practice

- Workbook page 70
- Grammar Time page 123
- Resource Pack
  Resource 70: Unit 6 Lesson 4 Grammar – He must be …

6.5 LISTENING and VOCABULARY Jess lives the dream!

Lesson learning objective
Students can identify specific detail in a conversation and talk about trips and excursions.

Lead in: Review of modals of speculation
Tell students you are going to draw a picture on the board and that they should use modals of speculation to say what they think it could be, what they think it can't be and, finally, what they think it must be. Keep eliciting students' speculations as you draw a horizontal line, then draw a vertical line on one end of the horizontal line, then make this into a square and then draw a roof. Try to elicit *It must be a house* from the class. Complete drawing the house, adding windows and a door.

Invite students to come to the board to draw a picture and repeat the process.

Exercise 1
Discuss the two example sentences and why the first sentence doesn't use a modal of speculation (*because we can see that it is true*) and why the second sentence does (*because we don't know if it is true*).

Exercise 2 2.42
When students have listened to the audio, elicit the word *blind* and its meaning.

Answers: Nick organises holidays for blind teenagers / teenagers who need help because they can't see.

2.42
See page 248.

Exercise 3 2.43
Before you play the audio, tell students to read the first sentence and to say whether they think it is true or false (*it is false*). Ask them to speculate about what information in the sentence is false, e.g. *the place could be false, Nick might have met a boy and not a girl*. Then put students into pairs and tell them to do the same for the other sentences.

Answers:
1 F (Nick was *on holiday* in South America.)
2 T
3 T
4 F (Nick says the journey is *as* important as the holiday.)
5 T
6 F (The summer activity camps are the most popular.)

2.43
See page 248.

Exercise 4 2.43
Before you play the audio again, tell the groups to discuss what they can remember from the first listening.

Answers:
activities: swimming, sailing, hiking, cycling
holidays: city breaks, beach holidays, activity camps
problems: can't read a menu, eating can be frustrating, can't read the number on their key or on the door to their hotel room

Exercise 5 2.44
Elicit the answers and check that students understand the meaning of *mast*. Ask students when Jess became blind (*when she was born*).

Answers: 1 16, New Zealand 2 sailing holiday
3 something different (she climbed the mast)

2.44
See page 248.

Exercise 6
Before pairs start their discussions, point out that Jess said two things at the end of the audio. Give students the gapped sentence *You're going to … and you're going to …* and elicit what Jess said (*You're going to have a good time and you're going to get lots of help*).

Exercise 7 2.45
Elicit the specific meaning of each of the words. (*An excursion is an organised day trip to go to see something, e.g. an excursion from the hotel to go to see a Roman palace. A journey is the act of getting from one place to another. Travel (noun) is a general word often used to talk about different forms of transport, e.g. train travel is very relaxing. Travel (verb) means to go somewhere different. A trip is usually a holiday or a short visit somewhere. A voyage is a long journey. It implies a journey of exploration and is commonly used to talk about journeys made by early explorers. It is also used to talk about space exploration and the American programme to explore the outer reaches of the solar system is called the Voyager programme, with the two spacecraft used being Voyager 1 and Voyager 2.*)

Answers: 1 journey 2 voyage 3 travel (noun) 4 trip
5 excursion 6 travel (verb)

Extra activity
Put students into groups of three and tell them to discuss a school trip, a journey and an excursion that they have been on. Give them a time limit and then invite groups to share some of their experiences with the class.

Exercise 8
Look at the examples with the class. In the first example, both *excursion* and *trip* could be used. In the second example, *journey* is the only word possible because it is referring specifically to the time it would take to get from A to B, whereas words such as *trip* or *excursion* refer to the total time away.

Further practice
- Workbook page 71
- Resource Pack
  Resource 71: Unit 6 Lesson 5 Listening and Vocabulary – Complete the gaps

6.5 LISTENING and VOCABULARY — Jess lives the dream!

I can identify specific detail in a conversation and talk about trips and excursions.

1 In pairs, describe the photo. What do you think is happening?

They're on a boat.
It might be a sailing holiday.

2 🔊 **2.42** Listen to the first part of the interview. What does Nick do?

3 🔊 **2.43** Listen to the second part of the interview. Mark the sentences T (true) or F (false).

1. ☐ Nick was working in South America when he met a girl who couldn't see.
2. ☐ The girl was on holiday with her family.
3. ☐ Special bikes are popular with kids who don't usually cycle.
4. ☐ Nick thinks the journey is more important than the holiday.
5. ☐ Hotel staff don't always realise how difficult it is for blind guests.
6. ☐ The winter holidays are the most popular.

4 🔊 **2.43** Work in groups of three. Listen again. Write down:
- four activities mentioned in the interview
- three kinds of holidays
- three problems that blind people might have

5 🔊 **2.44** Listen to Jess's story. Answer the questions.

1. How old is Jess and where does she come from?
2. What type of holiday did she go on?
3. What did Jess want to do during the trip?

6 In pairs, discuss why this sort of holiday is important for people like Jess. Compare your ideas with the class.

It's an adventure.
It might help them to meet people.

7 🔊 **2.45** Use a dictionary to check the words in the Vocabulary box and choose the correct option. Listen and check.

Vocabulary	Travel: confusing words

excursion   journey   travel (noun)
travel (verb)   trip   voyage

1. It was a three-hour car *journey* / *excursion* to the beach.
2. The *trip* / *voyage* across the Atlantic took two months and the cabins were comfortable.
3. Air *travel* / *journey* is very expensive at the moment.
4. The school is organising a two-day *travel* / *trip* to London.
5. Let's get tickets for the afternoon *journey* / *excursion* to the castle.
6. I'd love to *travel* / *voyage* to the North Pole one day.

8 **And YOU** Imagine your school has invited some students from another country. In pairs, discuss the best trips and excursions in your area. Compare your ideas with the class.

They could go on an excursion to the waterpark.
They could visit the capital city, but it's a long journey.

Unit 6

6.6 SPEAKING Understanding a conversation

I can clarify what I have said and ask for clarification.

VIDEO I DIDN'T CATCH THAT

Dan: Tickets, yes. Passport, yes … Hi, Ed. I'm just in the middle of packing for New York, but I can't see you. The camera's not working.
Ed: It doesn't matter. I can see you. What time …?
Dan: Sorry, I didn't catch that. You're breaking up.
Ed: What I said was, what time does your plane leave?
Dan: At seven, but I've got to be at the airport for four in the morning. Now, what should I pack?
Ed: You just need lots of sports clothes and …
Dan: Hang on, this is really annoying. Mum, I'm trying to talk to Ed. I didn't get the last part, Ed. What did you say?
Ed: I was just saying that you should bring things for the beach.
Dan: OK. How about these?
Ed: You must be joking. Dan, promise me …
Dan: Sorry, can you say that again?
Ed: Don't bring those smelly sneakers.
Dan: What was that?
Ed: Forget it, Dan. Thanks. See you tomorrow …

OUT of class
*Forget it. You're breaking up.
This is really annoying.*

1  **CLASS VOTE** Do you like packing when you go on holiday? Do you prefer somebody else to do it for you? Why? / Why not?

I like doing it because I know I'll pack the right things.

2 Look at the photo. Would you take these things on holiday?

3 6.4 2.46 Watch or listen and answer the questions.
1 What's Dan packing for?
2 What time does Dan have to be at the airport?
3 What type of clothes should Dan take?
4 What doesn't Ed want Dan to take?

Speaking	Understanding a conversation

Asking for clarification
Sorry, I didn't catch that.
Sorry, can you say that again?
What was that?
Sorry, I didn't get the first/last part.
Could you speak louder / more slowly?

Clarifying
What I said/asked was …
I said that …
I was just saying …
I just wanted to ask you about …

4 Complete the dialogues with the phrases from the Speaking box. In pairs, say the dialogues.
1 A: Hi, Maria! There's a school trip to Venice this year.
   B: _____ ?
   A: _____ there's a trip to Venice this year.
2 A: I think we need a visa for our holiday.
   A: _____ ?
   B: _____ we need a visa for our holiday.

5 In pairs, role play the situations. Follow the instructions.

A You're at the train station and your train is late. Call your friend and explain what's happening.

B Your friend calls from the station but it's noisy. You want to know what time she is arriving.

A: Hi, it's me. I'm at …

Unit 6

6.6 SPEAKING Understanding a conversation

Lesson learning objective
Students can clarify what they have said and ask for clarification.

Lead in: Review of travel words

Put students into six groups. Give each group a piece of paper that has a word from the previous lesson written on it: *excursion*, *journey*, *travel* (noun), *travel* (verb), *trip*, *voyage*. Tell each group to write a sentence or short paragraph which includes their word. When the groups are ready, ask them to read out their sentence or paragraph, saying *blank* instead of the word. The other groups should guess the missing word. Whichever group guesses first wins a point.

Exercise 1
Tell students to keep their Students' Books closed. Have a class discussion about packing for holidays and find out how many students pack for themselves when they go on holiday.

Exercise 2
Ask students to give reasons for their decisions and to choose one other item which they would not want to travel without.

Extra activity

Tell students to imagine that they are going on holiday. They should work on their own to decide where they are going, what time of year it is and what they are going to pack for the holiday. When students are ready, put them into groups of three. They should take turns to say what they are going to pack, while their group guesses where they are going and what time of year it is. Give them a time limit and then invite groups to share some of their ideas with the class.

Exercise 3 6.4 2.46
When students have watched the video, check that they understand the word *sneakers* (it's an American word for trainers). Ask students why they think that video links or phone calls sometimes break up and whether they have ever experienced this.

Answers:
1 a trip to New York
2 four in the morning
3 lots of sports clothes
4 his smelly sneakers

Exercise 4
Discuss the Speaking box and ask students to think of when they might use these phrases apart from when a phone call or video link breaks up, e.g. *if I'm chatting somewhere noisy like a disco or on a windy day*. Point out that we can make these expressions more polite by adding *please* to the end of the sentence, e.g. *Sorry, can you say that again, please?* and we can use *Excuse me* instead of *Sorry* to make the expressions more formal. Encourage students to use different phrases in the two conversations.

Possible answers:
1 B: Sorry, can you say that again
   A: I said that
2 B: What was that
   A: I was just saying that

Exercise 5
Set a time limit for pairs to write down their dialogue and practise it. Tell them that they should include three pieces of information that Student B isn't able to hear properly. When the pairs are ready, invite them to perform their dialogue in front of the class.

Further practice
- Workbook page 72
- Resource Pack
  Resource 72: Unit 6 Lesson 6 Speaking – Sorry, what did you say?
  Resource 73: Unit 6 Lesson 6 Video – I didn't catch that

6.7 ENGLISH IN USE   Time clauses

Lesson learning objective
Students can use time clauses.

Lead in: Review of clarifying
Tell students to imagine that they are on holiday in another country and that they are going to phone or video call a friend who is also on holiday, in a different country. They should think of three things they want to ask their friend. When students are ready, put them into pairs. Tell them to stand back-to-back and explain that they shouldn't turn around while they are doing the activity. The pairs should take turns to ask each other their questions. Because their classmates will also be asking and answering questions, they may have difficulty hearing each other and so they should ask for clarification when necessary. When the pairs have asked, answered and understood all three questions, tell them to find another partner and repeat the process. Make sure that noise levels don't rise too much during this activity.

Exercise 1
Tell students to keep their Students' Books closed. Check that students understand the meaning of these words: *starving*, *tent pegs*. Ask them if their parents have ever got lost during a journey on holiday. If so, elicit what happened. Then ask students to open their Students' Books and to answer the two questions.

Answers: 1 a camping holiday   2 they are feeling hungry

Exercise 2
When students have found all the time clauses in the cartoon, discuss the specific meaning of each time clause in the Language box. Check the meaning of *when*, *while*, *after* and *before* by asking these questions.
*What do you do **when** you are in the classroom?*
*What do you do **while** you are travelling to school?*
*What do you do **after** school finishes?*
*What do you do **before** you leave for school?*
Check the meaning of *until* by giving these example sentences.
*You can leave the classroom when I tell you = You can't leave the classroom **until** I tell you.*
*I will eat when I'm hungry = I won't eat **until** I'm hungry.*
Check the difference between *as soon as* (immediately) and *when* by giving this example sentence.
***When** I get home, I'm going to check my emails.* (at some point after I arrive home)
***As soon as** I get home, I'm going to make a cup of tea.* (immediately after I arrive home)
Discuss the use of the Present Simple in the examples above and in the Language box. Ask students to think about which other word they have studied in a previous unit that is used to talk about a future situation but is followed by the Present Simple (*if*).

Answers: as soon as, when, while

Exercise 3
Remind students which tense we use after time expressions (*the Present Simple*).
When students have finished, elicit the answers. Then ask students to think of different verbs which could be used after the time expression in each sentence, e.g. *We'll wait until she finishes/phones/arrives; Jack will drive us to the party as soon as you get here / he finishes work.*

Answers: 1 comes   2 are   3 go   4 have   5 sunbathe

Exercise 4
Before students do the exercise, ask if they have ever heard about Interrail train passes. Explain what the passes are and ask students for their opinions about travelling by train, and for their reasons.
When students have finished the exercise, elicit the answers. Then ask students to identify the piece of advice that they think is the most useful, giving reasons why.

Answers: 1 as   2 leave   3 until   4 get   5 while

Culture notes
Interrail offers different rail passes that make it cheaper to travel around Europe by rail. The passes are available for young people, adults and families who live in Europe. Residents of other countries can use a similar Eurail pass. You can either buy a One Country Pass, for free train travel in one country, or you can buy a Global Pass, for free train travel in thirty countries. In addition to train travel, the pass provides discounts on the cost of ferry journeys and hotel accommodation and on some entrance fees for museums and galleries. About 300,000 people use Interrail passes each year.

Extra activity
Put students into a total of up to seven groups. Allocate each group a type of holiday (i.e. activity camp, backpacking holiday, beach holiday, camping trip, city break, cruise or sightseeing holiday) and tell them to think of a related question to ask in a travelling forum, like in the text for Exercise 4. They should write their question on a piece of paper and, when all the groups are ready, pass their paper to the group on their left. The groups should read the question they have received and then work together to write a response comment to the forum. Invite the groups to say their question and the best piece of advice or most interesting comment that they received.

Homework
Tell students to read the text on page 80 of the Student's Book. They should look up any words they don't know the meaning of and translate them into L1.
As an additional task, ask students to write an example sentence illustrating the meaning of each these words: *abroad*, *budget*, *combine*, *destination*, *guaranteed*, *lazy*, *occupation*, *unpredictable*. Tell them that the sentences must, in some way, be connected with holidays or travel.

Further practice
- Workbook page 73
- Resource Pack
  Resource 74: Unit 6 Lesson 7 English in Use – Future time

6.7 ENGLISH IN USE — Time clauses

I can use time clauses.

Boy: Are we nearly there? I'm starving!
Mum: Not long now. We'll eat as soon as we arrive.

Mum: I think we're lost.
Dad: You're right. It'll be dark when we get there.

Dad: Oh no! I've forgotten the tent pegs.
Mum: Look, I've got an idea. I'll find a hotel while you get some food.
Boy and Girl: Yay! We always wanted to stay in a hotel!

1 Read the cartoon and answer the questions.
1. What type of holiday is the family planning to have?
2. How are the teenagers feeling in the car?

2 Find examples of time clauses in the cartoon.

Language — Time clauses

When I'm at the station, I'll buy the tickets.

What are you going to do **while** you're waiting for the bus?

I will have a party **after** I finish my exams.

Before we go hiking, we'll look at the map.

We'll wait here **until** the ticket office opens.

I'll call you **as soon as** I arrive.

We use the Present Simple in future time clauses with *when, while, before, until, as soon as*.

Put a comma after the time clause if it comes first in a sentence.

3 Complete the sentences with the correct form of the verbs in brackets.
1. We'll wait until she _____. (come)
2. Jack will drive us to the party as soon as you _____ ready. (be)
3. Write to me when you _____ on holiday? (go)
4. Alice and Ben will leave after they _____ breakfast. (have)
5. Before you _____ (sunbathe), put on some sun cream.

4 Choose the correct answers.

Interrail

I love the idea of travelling by train, but it could be a disaster. Has anybody got any advice or ideas?

tedyy 10:52 Just enjoy it! Interrail is simply the best choice! I'm sure you'll agree as soon ¹*after/when/so/as* your journey begins.

Ella 11:06 The interrail company will help you plan your journey before you ²*leave/leaves/left/will leave*. It's really easy.

Mark 12:41 It was easy to buy the tickets online. I'm waiting for them to arrive, but I won't relax ³*after/as soon as/until/while* I get them.

Tom12 12:53 Go for it! As soon as you ⁴*'ll get/get/gets/'re getting* on the train, you'll meet lots of people.

Mike 12:55 You'll travel through amazing scenery ⁵*while/after/before/until* you're on the train, and the trains are comfortable.

Wordlist and Vocabulary in action

Extra activity

Before students look at Exercise 4, write this sentence on the board:
I went to the cinema with David on Friday evening.
Underline *cinema* and drill the sentence with this word stressed. Ask what question might have led to this answer (*Where did you go with David on Friday evening?*).
Then ask students which word(s) will be stressed in answer to these questions.
Who did you go to the cinema with on Friday evening? (*David* will be stressed.)
When did you go to the cinema with David? (*Friday evening* will be stressed.)

Further practice

Workbook page 74

WORDLIST — Types of holidays | At the hotel | Equipment | Travel: confusing words

accommodation /əˌkɒməˈdeɪʃn/
activity camp /ækˈtɪvəti kæmp/
adventure /ədˈventʃə/
airport /ˈeəpɔːt/
annoying /əˈnɔɪɪŋ/
arrive at /əˈraɪv ət/
the Atlantic /ðɪ ətˈlæntɪk/
backpack /ˈbækpæk/
backpacking holiday /ˈbækˌpækɪŋ ˌhɒlədeɪ/
balloon /bəˈluːn/
beach holiday /ˈbiːtʃ ˌhɒlədeɪ/
blind /blaɪnd/
break up /ˌbreɪk ˈʌp/
bus service /ˈbʌs ˌsɜːvəs/
bus station /ˈbʌs ˌsteɪʃn/
cabin /ˈkæbɪn/
camera /ˈkæmərə/
camping /ˈkæmpɪŋ/
camping trip /ˈkæmpɪŋ trɪp/
campsite /ˈkæmpsaɪt/
castle /ˈkɑːsl/
check in /ˌtʃek ˈɪn/
check out /ˌtʃek ˈaʊt/
city /ˈsɪti/
city break /ˈsɪti breɪk/
climbing /ˈklaɪmɪŋ/
country /ˈkʌntri/
cruise /kruːz/
culture /ˈkʌltʃə/

diary /ˈdaɪəri/
double room /ˌdʌbl ˈruːm/
excursion /ɪkˈskɜːʃn/
facilities /fəˈsɪlətiz/
fascinating /ˈfæsɪneɪtɪŋ/
film-maker /ˈfɪlmmeɪkə/
floor /flɔː/
forest /ˈfɒrɪst/
guest /gest/
guidebook /ˈgaɪdbʊk/
hammock /ˈhæmək/
hanging tent /ˌhænɪŋ ˈtent/
hiking /ˈhaɪkɪŋ/
hotel /həʊˈtel/
ice hotel /ˈaɪs həʊˌtel/
island /ˈaɪlənd/
journey /ˈdʒɜːni/
key /kiː/
leave from /ˈliːv frəm/
loo /luː/
luggage /ˈlʌgɪdʒ/
manager /ˈmænɪdʒə/
map /mæp/
mast /mɑːst/
the Mediterranean /ðə ˌmedɪtəˈreɪniən/
noisy /ˈnɔɪzi/
the North Pole /ðə ˌnɔːθ ˈpəʊl/
notebook /ˈnəʊtbʊk/
organisation /ˌɔːgənaɪˈzeɪʃn/
pack /pæk/
passport /ˈpɑːspɔːt/

platform /ˈplætfɔːm/
pool /puːl/
popular /ˈpɒpjʊlə/
provide /prəˈvaɪd/
reception /rɪˈsepʃn/
reservation /ˌrezəˈveɪʃn/
reserve /rɪˈzɜːv/
return ticket /rɪˈtɜːn ˌtɪkɪt/
Rome /rəʊm/
route /ruːt/
rucksack /ˈrʌksæk/
safe (n) /seɪf/
sailing holiday /ˈseɪlɪŋ ˌhɒlədeɪ/
scenery /ˈsiːnəri/
school trip /ˈskuːl trɪp/
ship /ʃɪp/
sightseeing holiday /ˈsaɪtˌsiːɪŋ ˌhɒlədeɪ/
single ticket /ˌsɪŋgl ˈtɪkɪt/
single room /ˌsɪŋgl ˈruːm/
sleeping bag /ˈsliːpɪŋ bæg/
smelly /ˈsmeli/
suitcase /ˈsuːtkeɪs/
summer holidays /ˌsʌmə ˈhɒlədeɪz/
sun cream /ˈsʌn kriːm/
sunglasses /ˈsʌnˌglɑːsɪz/
swimsuit /ˈswɪmsuːt/
tent /tent/
tent peg /ˈtent peg/
ticket /ˈtɪkɪt/
ticket office /ˈtɪkɪt ˌɒfəs/

top /tɒp/
torch /tɔːtʃ/
train station /ˈtreɪn ˌsteɪʃn/
transport /ˈtrænspɔːt/
travel (n,v) /ˈtrævl/
traveller /ˈtrævlə/
tree house /ˈtriː haʊs/
tree tent /ˈtriː tent/
trip /trɪp/
trunks /trʌŋks/
view /vjuː/
visa /ˈviːzə/
visit /ˈvɪzɪt/
voyage /ˈvɔɪɪdʒ/
winter holidays /ˌwɪntə ˈhɒlədeɪz/

WORD FRIENDS

learn a new language
explore different places
meet local people
share an experience
plan a trip
go on holiday
go sightseeing
on foot
by sea/road/rail/air
by boat/car/plane/train/bus

Exercise 1

Possible answers:
1 by boat/car/plane/train/bus
2 backpack, camera, diary, guidebook, luggage, map, notebook, passport, rucksack, sleeping bag, suitcase, sun cream, sunglasses, swimsuit, tent, torch, trunks
3 learn a new language, explore different places, meet local people, share an experience, go sightseeing
4 double room, pool, reception, safe (n), single room

VOCABULARY IN ACTION

1 Use the wordlist to find:
1 five different means of transport
2 five things that you would take on holiday
3 three things that you could do on holiday
4 two facilities you might have at a hotel

2 In pairs, discuss the differences between the words below.
1 a voyage / a cruise
2 a visa / a passport
3 a sightseeing holiday / a city break
4 a camping holiday / a backpacking holiday
5 a single ticket / a return ticket

3 Use the wordlist to complete the sentences. Use the words in the correct form. In pairs, say if the sentences are true for you.
1 You don't have to _____ a trip but it can be exciting.
2 You need a lot of money to _____ sightseeing.
3 It's best to _____ different places by bus.
4 An activity camp is a good place to _____ an experience.
5 It's easy to _____ a new language when you have to use it every day.

4 🔊 2.47 **PRONUNCIATION** Sentence stress falls on the important information in a sentence. Underline the important words in the sentences. Listen, check and repeat.
1 The children enjoyed the activity camp, but the weather was terrible.
2 I'd love to sail across the Atlantic in the future.
3 We stayed on a campsite near the river.
4 They were waiting at the bus station for two hours.
5 We can leave the luggage in the hotel reception.
6 Don't forget to take the map and the guidebook with you.

Exercise 3

1 plan
2 go
3 explore
4 share
5 learn

Exercise 4

1 The children <u>enjoyed</u> the <u>activity</u> camp, but the <u>weather</u> was <u>terrible</u>.
2 I'd <u>love</u> to <u>sail</u> across the <u>Atlantic</u> in the <u>future</u>.
3 We <u>stayed</u> on a <u>campsite</u> near the <u>river</u>.
4 They were <u>waiting</u> at the <u>bus station</u> for <u>two hours</u>.
5 We can <u>leave</u> the <u>luggage</u> in the <u>hotel</u> <u>reception</u>.
6 <u>Don't forget</u> to take the <u>map</u> and the <u>guidebook</u> with you.

Revision

Activity for fast finishers

If any students finish Exercise 3 early, ask them to stay in their pairs and to think of more questions using the verbs in the box in Exercise 2, e.g. *Do you **pack** a long time before your holiday or at the last minute? When in the year do you start **planning** your summer holiday?* When the rest of the class has finished Exercise 3, tell the fast finishers to ask them their questions.

Further practice

- Workbook page 75
- Resource Pack
  Resource 75: Units 4–6
  Vocabulary – Half a crossword
  Resource 76: Units 4–6
  Grammar – Talk about it

Revision

VOCABULARY

1 Write the correct word for each definition.
1. The area you see from a place. **v** _____
2. This helps you to see things in the dark. **t** _____
3. A big bag you put things in for your holiday. **s** _____
4. The place where you wait to get on a train. **p** _____
5. Put things in bags ready for a journey. **p** _____
6. A place where you stay on holiday, e.g. a hotel. **a** _____

Exercise 1
1. view
2. torch
3. suitcase
4. platform
5. pack
6. accommodation

2 Complete the text with the words below.

travel   learn   meet   go   pack   plan

HOW MUCH OF A TRAVELLER ARE YOU?
Do you like exploring new places or would you rather stay closer to home?

1. What's the first thing you _____ in your bag when you're getting ready to travel?
2. Would you try to _____ a new language before visiting a different country?
3. What's the best way to _____ local people when you're on holiday?
4. When you _____ sightseeing, do you always take photos?
5. What type of trip would you like to _____ for this summer?
6. Who would you rather _____ to another country with, family or friends? Why?

Exercise 2
1. pack
2. learn
3. meet
4. go
5. plan
6. travel

3 In pairs, ask and answer the questions. Tell the class about your partner.
The first thing Anna packs is her make-up!

GRAMMAR

4 Choose the correct option.
1. When you're on holiday, you *must / ought* to buy food in local shops.
2. On a hot sunny day, you *don't have to / must* put on lots of sun cream.
3. When you visit a new country, you *should / mustn't* try to learn the language.
4. You *don't have to / have to* go to a travel agency. You can buy your tickets online.
5. It's a long train journey. We *must / mustn't* forget to take lots of food and water.

Exercise 4
1. ought to
2. must
3. should
4. don't have to
5. mustn't

5 Match sentences 1–6 with sentences a–f.
1. ☐ I've just had a postcard from Julia.
2. ☐ That can't be my rucksack.
3. ☐ It's a bit cloudy to go to the beach.
4. ☐ The maps might be in reception.
5. ☐ It's a very long journey for the children.
6. ☐ Let's have a camping holiday.

a. It's the wrong colour.
b. Hotels often put them there.
c. It could be too cold to swim.
d. They must be very bored.
e. It could be fun in a tent.
f. She's on holiday.

Exercise 5
1. f
2. a
3. c
4. b
5. d
6. e

6 In pairs, speculate about the situations below.
1. Your friends have arrived at the airport but can't find a taxi.
2. You're going on holiday tomorrow but you can't find your tickets.
3. You arrive at your hotel but there aren't any rooms.

SPEAKING

7 In pairs, role play the situations. You and your partner meet in a noisy café at a train station. Follow the instructions.

A
- Say hello and ask why your friend is at the station.
- Explain that you couldn't understand what he/she said. Ask him to say it again.
- Tell your friend that you didn't hear the first or the last part.
- Tell your friend to have a good trip.

B
- Explain where you're travelling to and why.
- Repeat what you said.
- Repeat the part that your friend didn't hear.

DICTATION

8 🔊 **2.48** Listen, then listen again and write down what you hear.

Exercise 8
Last summer, I did an activity camp. We stayed on a campsite near the beach. One night I went for a walk. I was tired when I got back. I soon found my tent and climbed in. But it was the wrong tent!

SELF-ASSESSMENT Think about this unit. What did you learn? What do you need help with?   **WORKBOOK** p. 74

149

CULTURE
Can ironing make holidays exciting?

The Brits on holiday

It could be because their weather is so unpredictable, but British people – the Brits – love to go abroad. They even invented the concept of budget airlines. In fact, these cheap airlines have allowed more people to travel to more destinations for less money. So, what kind of holiday do they prefer and what activities do they like most?

Unsurprisingly, even though extreme ironing was invented in 1997 in the UK, it is not the most popular sport among the British. Not many people fancy ironing and even fewer doing it in remote locations. Beach holidays are still their preferred option and sunbathing their favourite occupation. After the beach, sightseeing remains very popular and city breaks are the way many Brits like to sightsee. Some wonderful destinations are just a short flight away, so people go there for a long weekend. Some lazy Brits love a cruise holiday, while more dynamic travellers choose activity holidays which involve outdoor sports, trekking or camping.

So, what city could combine all of these holiday types? It's easy: Barcelona in Spain! It's unique because it combines the beach and sightseeing. And as an important port, Barcelona also attracts cruises, especially in summer. You can even have an adventure holiday in the Pyrenees mountains nearby. Its football team, Barça, is also a great attraction.

But it's not just Barcelona. Spain has been the Brits' clear favourite since 1994. More than twelve million Brits visit every year. Obviously, the weather is a key factor. Sun is guaranteed most of the year round in most places. There are large ex-pat communities along the coast, so speaking English is not a problem. Spanish people also have a friendly reputation and the food is popular, especially the tapas. It's a surprise that the Brits haven't taken over completely!

GLOSSARY
abroad (adv) to a different country
budget (adj) here: cheap
lazy (adj) a lazy person doesn't like to work
occupation (n) a way of spending your time
unpredictable (adj) changing a lot so it is impossible to know what will happen

BBC CULTURE — Can ironing make holidays exciting?

Lead in: Topic introduction

Tell students not to open their Students' Books. Put students into groups of four. If you set the homework suggestion for the unit, ask the groups to discuss any vocabulary they found difficult and their example sentences if you also set the additional task.

If students haven't done the homework, ask them to look at the glossary on page 80. Students should find the words in the text and discuss what they mean in context, e.g. *The weather in England is so **unpredictable** that it is difficult to know what it will be like from one day to the next.*

Background notes

The photo shows two people doing extreme ironing. It's a sport in which people take an ironing board and iron to remote locations, such as mountain peaks, or do the ironing while doing an extreme sport e.g. paragliding, diving or jetskiing.

6.5

Adventures of a lifetime

Part 1

These are the Maldives, a beautiful series of islands located in the Indian Ocean, where the sun is always shining. It's popular with travellers looking for a luxury option. In fact, most tourists here have their own private island for total relaxation! But further out to sea, there are more energetic options.

Meet our hosts, Kirstie and Phil. Here in the Indian Ocean the sea temperature is a wonderful twenty-seven degrees Celsius – just perfect for swimming, snorkelling, scuba diving, fishing, windsurfing and the sport we're going to see now: jet skiing!

Kirstie is nervous at first, but she soon gets the idea. This is the most popular and comfortable model because you can sit down in it. You can go up to eighty kilometres per hour, so it's better to hold on tight! Jet skiing is great fun, but expensive. Other tourists might also get annoyed by the noise, so it's best to do it for short lengths of time.

6.6

Part 2

Kirstie and Phil are now off to a much colder place. In fact, the temperature has dropped to minus twenty degrees Celsius. They have come to Iceland to try their next adventure sport: snowmobiling!

Here glaciers cover eleven percent of the country, but they are not easy to get to. Kirstie and Phil have to travel in a specially prepared 4x4 vehicle. It's a long and a bit of a rough ride! The landscape looks like the surface of the Moon. In fact, astronauts came here to practise for their expeditions.

Obviously, to ride one of these vehicles, you need to wear special protective clothing. The good news is that the accelerator and handle bars are heated! The snowmobile's top speed is ninety-five kilometres per hour, but the terrain here is tough, so Kirstie and Phil are taking it easy.

With snowmobiling, you should always follow your guide's advice. It's best to do it when snow has just fallen. If not, you might fall through the snow when the ice melts. It can be very dangerous. Again, it's not a cheap option, but the landscapes are unique, especially as night falls over the glacier.

6.7

Part 3

Kirstie and Phil's final adventure holiday is a much more relaxing option: hot-air ballooning! They are now in Morocco, between the city of Marrakech and the Atlas Mountains. There's only one drawback: to do this sport, you have to get up really early. Balloons fly in the early morning before the wind starts to blow. It's six o'clock in the morning now. The sun is rising over the Atlas, the sky is blue, but the stars are still out. It's a beautiful moment as the dawn breaks.

Compared to the other sports we've seen, the wonderful thing about flying in a hot-air balloon is the slowness and the total silence. You feel like you're floating and the views are stunning. You see everything from such a different perspective. Yes, it's the perfect place to get away from it all, but it's also the most expensive of all the trips. If you want to do it more cheaply, you can share a balloon with other travellers. Enjoy the ride!

Exercise 1
When the pairs have discussed the questions, invite them to share their ideas with the class.

Exercise 2
Encourage students to read the questions before they read the text. Ask students to speculate about the answers to question 5.

Possible answers:
1 Because the weather in Britain is unpredictable.
2 There are lots of cheap, budget airlines.
3 There are many destinations close enough for a weekend break.
4 Because activity holidays are active and cruises are relaxing and lazy.
5 It's got a beach, a port for cruise ships, mountains nearby and attractions such as the football club. In addition, being in Spain, the weather is good, lots of people speak English, the people are friendly and the food is popular.

Extra activity

Put students into groups of four. Explain that lots of foreign people are keen to visit their country for a sightseeing holiday or city break. The groups should discuss and decide on their recommendations for the best places to visit in their country, what people can see and do there and what food to eat. When the groups are ready, invite them to present their ideas to the class.

Exercise 3 6.5
Tell students to read the sentences and to guess whether sentences 1 and 3 are true or false.
When students have watched Part 1 of the video, ask them what else they have learned about the ocean and the sports in the Maldives (e.g. *in the Maldives, the temperature of the sea is twenty-seven degrees Celsius; different sports that people do there are swimming, fishing, scuba diving, snorkelling, windsurfing and jet skiing; jet skis can travel at speeds up to eighty kilometres per hour*).

Answers: 1 T 2 F (She's nervous at first) 3 F (It's expensive.)

Exercise 4 6.6
Before you play Part 2 of the video, check that students understand the meaning of *glaciers* and *4x4 vehicle*. Then tell students to read through the sentences and to choose what they think will be the correct option.
After you have played the video, ask students to say the temperature that was mentioned (*minus twenty*) and also the speed of the snowmobile (*up to ninety-five kilometres per hour*).

Answers: 1 clothing 2 dangerous 3 the Moon

Exercise 5 6.7
Play Part 3 of the video with the sound switched off. Ask students to say where the ballooning takes place and what they think of this activity. Then play the video again, this time with the sound switched on.

Answers: 1 relaxing 2 silence 3 perspective

Exercise 6 6.5–6.7
Put students into groups of three. Tell them to read the sentences and to do the matching activity. When they have finished, play the three parts of the video once more. Then elicit the answers and references from the videos.

Answers:
1 a (swimming, fishing, scuba diving, snorkelling and wind surfing are all mentioned in the video)
2 b (*the accelerator and handle bars are heated*)
3 b (*The landscape looks like the surface of the Moon* and *the landscapes are unique, especially as night falls over the glacier*)
4 c (*you can share a balloon with other travellers*)
5 a (*Other tourists might also get annoyed by the noise*)
6 c (*to do this sport, you have to get up really early*)
7 a (*it's better to hold on tight*)
8 c (*the views are stunning*)
9 c (*a much more relaxing option* and *Compared to the other sports we've seen, the wonderful thing about flying in a hot-air balloon is the slowness and total silence*)

Exercise 7
Give a time limit for students to discuss their ideas in pairs. When they have finished, join two pairs together to make groups of four, so that they can compare their ideas. Tell the groups to choose one of the activities and to create a poster, explaining the rules and regulations, the equipment needed, advice for a newcomer to the sport and some imaginary positive comments from people who have tried the activity.

Exercise 8
Discuss different adventure sports with the class. Write these words in three columns on the board.
Column 1: *air, land, sea*
Column 2: *winter, summer, indoor, outdoor, group, individual*
Column 3: *fast, dangerous, relaxing, cheap, expensive*
Elicit adventure sports that can be done in the students' own country and write them in a fourth column.
Ask students which word(s) in the first three columns describe the adventure sports. They can add more words if they wish, e.g. *windsurfing – sea, summer, outdoor, individual, fast, (exciting, difficult)*.
Then put students into groups of four and tell each group to choose one adventure sport. Make sure that each group chooses a different sport. Tell them to divide their presentation into four sections so that each person can present an equal part, e.g. rules, reasons for doing it, where to do it, equipment needed.
Give them a time limit for creating their presentations. Allocate a time in a future lesson for the groups to present these to the class.

Further practice

- Workbook pages 76–77
- Resource Pack
  Resource 77: Unit 6 BBC Culture Lesson – Popular destinations
  Resource 78: Unit 6 Culture – Adventures around the world

EXPLORE

1 In pairs, ask and answer the questions.
1. What type of holiday do you prefer? Do you like to:
   - relax?
   - try something new?
   - do lots of activities?
2. Where is your favourite holiday destination?
3. Would you like to go on an adventure holiday? Why? / Why not?
4. Would you like to try extreme ironing?

2 Read the article. Answer the questions.
1. Why do the British love to go abroad?
2. Why can more people travel by plane now than in the past?
3. Why is it easy for the Brits to sightsee abroad?
4. Why are cruises and activity holidays opposites?
5. Why is Barcelona such a popular city with tourists?

EXPLORE MORE

3 ▶ 6.5 Watch Part 1 of the video. Mark the sentences T (true) or F (false). Correct the false sentences.
1. ☐ The Maldives is a luxury holiday destination.
2. ☐ Kirstie really wants to do jet skiing from the beginning.
3. ☐ Doing jet skiing is quite cheap.

4 ▶ 6.6 Watch Part 2 of the video. Choose the correct option.
1. To do snowmobiling in Iceland, you need special protective *clothing* / *vehicles*.
2. You should follow your guide's advice because the sport can be *difficult* / *dangerous*.
3. Icelandic landscapes look like the surface of *Mars* / *the Moon*.

5 ▶ 6.7 Watch Part 3 of the video. Complete the sentences with one word in each gap.
1. The hot-air ballooning option is a much more _____ choice.
2. The great thing about this sport is the total _____ when you're up there.
3. You see the landscapes below from such a different _____.

6 ▶ 6.5–6.7 Watch the three parts of the video again. Match sports a–c with sentences 1–9 used to describe them.
a. jet skiing (the Maldives)
b. snowmobiling (Iceland)
c. hot-air ballooning (Morocco)
1. You can also do other less energetic sports there.
2. The vehicle is specially prepared.
3. The landscapes are unique there.
4. You can do the sport with many others.
5. Some people get annoyed by this sport.
6. You can only do this at a certain time of day.
7. You have to hold on tight when you do this sport.
8. The views are particularly special.
9. It's the best possible way to relax.

7 Which of these three sports would you most like to do? What rules and regulations do you have to follow to do each one? How would you imagine doing each sport? Discuss in pairs.

YOU EXPLORE

8 CULTURE PROJECT In groups, prepare a presentation about an adventure sport.
1. Use the internet or other sources to research an adventure sport.
2. Write a short script and think about images or videos to use in your presentation.
3. Give your presentation to the class.

7
Getting to know you

VOCABULARY
Phrasal verbs | Talking about friends

GRAMMAR
Second Conditional | Defining and non-defining relative clauses

Grammar: I'd come if I was free

Speaking: Who's the guy at the back?

BBC Culture: On the move

Workbook p. 88

BBC VOX POPS ▶
CLIL 4 > p. 142

'Miss Baker, I've got something to tell you about my project. My dad helped me a bit. Any mistakes are his.'

A

7.1   **VOCABULARY**   Family and friends

I can talk about relationships with family and friends.

1 **CLASS VOTE** Who would you like to spend a day with?

grandfather   grandmother   teacher   neighbour   aunt   uncle   cousin

2 **WORD BUILDING** Read the texts. Use the words in bold to complete the definitions (1–3).

> My **great**-grandmother, Julia, is ninety and she's my **grand**mother's mother. Julia was adopted.

> I've got a little **half**-brother. He's my father's son from his second marriage.

> I really like my **step**sister. Some people say we are similar, although we aren't really related by blood.

1 The prefix _____ describes a family relative who is two generations away from you. Add an extra _____ for each extra generation.
2 The prefix _____ describes a brother, sister or parent who is related to you by marriage but not by blood.
3 The prefix _____ describes a brother or sister who is related to you through one shared parent.

3 🔊 2.49 Look at the cartoons. Guess the relationships between the people. Give reasons. Listen and check.

parent, stepparent and neighbour
parent, child and teacher
great-grandparent and great-grandchild

82

Unit contents

Vocabulary
- Phrasal verbs
- Talk about friends

Grammar
- Second Conditional
- Defining and non-defining relative clauses

Communication skills
- Identifying people

Examples of 21st Century Skills/Competencies
- Critical Thinking: page 83 (Exercise 4), pages 92–93
- Collaboration: page 83 (Exercise 7), page 88 (Exercise 5), page 93 (Exercise 10)
- Digital Literacy: page 93 (Exercise 10)
- Assessment for Learning: page 91
- Autonomy and Personal Initiative: page 84 (Exercise 5), page 89 (Exercise 5)

7.1 VOCABULARY   Family and friends

Lesson learning objective
Students can talk about relationships with family and friends.

Lead in: Review of vocabulary from the previous unit

Divide the class into four groups and tell them to keep their Students' Books and notebooks closed. Explain that you are going to write on the board individual letters that spell a word from the previous unit backwards. As you write each letter, give each group one guess to say what they think the word could be. Continue the process until one group guesses correctly. Give the group a point and give them a second point if they can define or translate the word correctly. If they can't, give the other groups a chance to define or translate the word so that they can earn the point. For example: *T* (elicit guesses) *RT* (elicit guesses) *ORT* (elicit guesses) *PORT* (group guesses *airport*).

Suggested words: *accommodation*, *camera*, *country*, *cruise*, *guest*, *luggage*, *route*, *suitcase*, *swimsuit*, *torch*, *view*, *voyage*.

Exercise 1
After the class vote, invite students to describe the person they chose and the sorts of activities they would like to do if they spent the day with them.

Exercise 2
When students have completed the exercise, point out that we can use the suffix *great-* with other relatives too, e.g. a *great-aunt* or *great-uncle* is the sister or brother of one of your grandparents and a *great-grandson* or *great-granddaughter* is the son or daughter of one of your grandchildren.
Ask students if they have any relatives with these prefixes.

Answers: 1 great-, great-   2 step-   3 half-

Exercise 3   2.49
When students have answered the question, check that they understand the meaning of *niece* (and *nephew*). To follow up, put students into groups of three and tell them to think of another situation that involves three people who are related in some way. The groups should develop and practise a short dialogue. When they are ready, invite groups to perform their dialogue and encourage the class to try to identify the relationship between the three people.

Answers:
A parent, child and teacher
B parent, stepparent and neighbour
C great-grandparent and great-grandchild

Exercise 4 2.50
Put students into pairs and tell them to discuss what they think the meanings are for each of the phrasal verbs in the Vocabulary box. After you have played the audio, elicit meanings and example sentences, e.g. *My friend can't **deal with** having a lot of work at one time. I **fell out with** my friend because of an argument about our favourite football teams!*

Exercise 5
Check that students understand the meaning of the phrase *have a lot / things in common*.

When students tell the class about their similarities to and differences from their partner, encourage the class to ask follow-up questions to find out more information, e.g. if a student doesn't like being on their own, another student might ask: *What do you do when there is no one else to talk to?*

Extra activity
Put students into pairs. Tell them to choose four of the phrasal verbs from the Vocabulary box and to write four more questions for a personality test, with each question using a different phrasal verb, e.g. *Do you **get on with** your brother or sister?* a) *Yes, always* b) *Most of the time* c) *No, we're always arguing*. When the pairs are ready, they should join up with a second pair and take turns to ask and answer one another's questions. Invite the groups to share their questions and answers with the class.

Exercise 6 2.51
Elicit things that are important for young people, e.g. hobbies, favourite types of music, favourite sports teams, character. When students have given some suggestions, encourage them to compare themselves and their best friends and to think about which things they have in common and which things they have different opinions about. Invite students to share their ideas with the class.

After students have looked at the texts, tell them to make a written record in their notebooks of the useful phrases and to check the meaning of each of the phrases (*share interests, have the same sense of humour, spend time together, get on someone's nerves, have arguments, enjoy each other's company, get to know someone, come from different backgrounds, spend time on your own, see each other*).

Answers: 1 share 2 have 3 spend 4 get 5 have
6 enjoy 7 get 8 come 9 spend 10 see

Exercise 7
When the pairs have discussed the question, tell the class that they are going to represent their opinion by standing somewhere in the classroom. Tell them that the left side of the classroom represents the opinion *Yes, friends should definitely share interests* and the right side of the classroom represents the opinion *No, it doesn't matter at all whether friends share interests or not*. Explain that they can show their strength of opinion by where they stand on the left or on the right and if they have no particular opinion either way then they can stand in the middle of the classroom. When all students have chosen where they want to stand, put students with similar opinions into pairs. The pairs should sit together and write a short paragraph similar to those in Exercise 6, indicating their opinion and their reasons for it. Give them a time limit and then invite pairs to share their ideas with the class.

Further practice
- Workbook pages 78–79
- Resource Pack
  Resource 79: Unit 7 Lesson 1 Vocabulary – Complete and answer

Oh, they're not all our children! These are my nieces, Clara and Sara. This is David's son, Max, and these are Max's friends, Tom and Tara.

When I was your age, things were very different. We only had ONE screen, and the whole family gathered around to spend a lovely evening all together!

4 **2.50** Listen and check you understand the words in the Vocabulary box. Complete the personality test.

Vocabulary	Phrasal verbs
deal with (a problem)	go out
fall out with	hang out with
get on with	put up with
go ahead	laugh at

5 In pairs, discuss your answers. What have you got in common? Tell the class about your partner.

Both of us like/dislike …
I think I'm quite similar to/different from …

6 **2.51** **WORD FRIENDS** Choose the correct option. Listen and check. Who do you agree with? Jessica or Mark?

Should friends have a lot in common?

JESSICA: Yes! My friend Sarah and I ¹share/get loads of interests. We both like horse-riding and cinema. We ²have/get the same sense of humour, too. We ³share/spend a lot of time together and we're like sisters. My singing can ⁴share/get on her nerves sometimes, but we never ⁵see/have arguments.

MARK: I disagree. I'm completely different from my friend Mike, but we ⁶enjoy/see each other's company. When I ⁷enjoy/get to know people, I find them more interesting if they ⁸come/have from different backgrounds. Mike loves to ⁹spend/see time on his own, so we don't ¹⁰have/see each other often, but when we meet, we have fun.

PERSONALITY TEST

1 Can you put up with being on your own?
a Yes
b No
c It's OK

2 Do you like to go out and meet new people?
a I find it difficult
b I love it
c I like it

3 Do you ever fall out with other people?
a Never
b Sometimes
c Not often

4 Do you get on well with big groups of people?
a I find it difficult
b I love it
c I like it

5 Are you good at dealing with friendship problems?
a No
b Yes
c Not always

6 Do you like to hang out with just a small group of friends?
a Yes
b No
c It's OK

7 Are you the first one in your group to go ahead and try new things?
a Never
b Yes, I hate things to be boring!
c Sometimes

8 Is it important for you and your friends to laugh at the same things?
a Yes, I like my friends to be similar to me
b No, but they must be fun to be with
c No, I get on with everyone

Go to page 144 to read about your answers.

7 Should friends share interests? In pairs, discuss your opinions.

7.2 GRAMMAR Second Conditional

I can talk about imaginary situations.

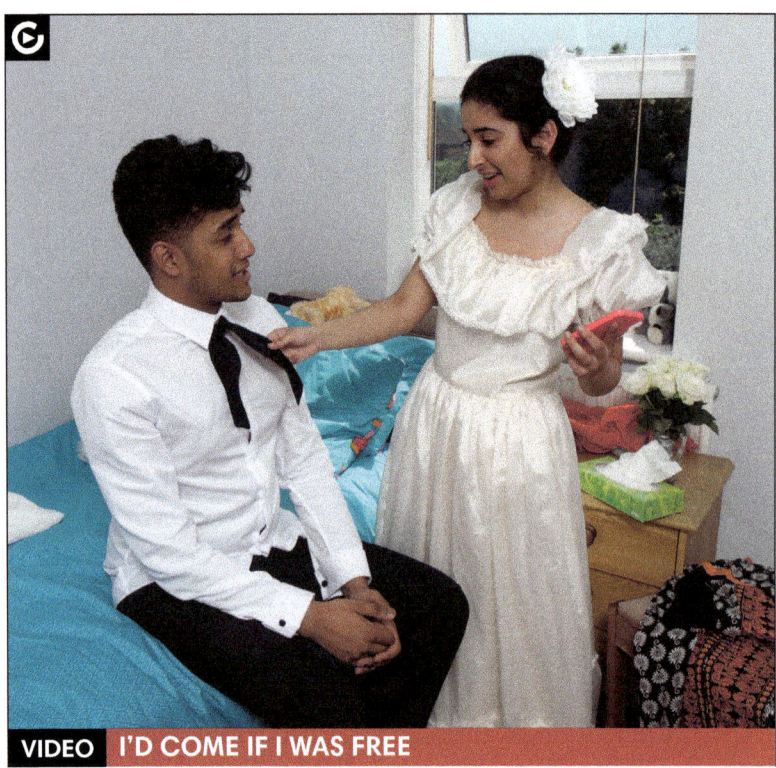

VIDEO I'D COME IF I WAS FREE

Damian: Alisha? I can't tie this bow tie. If mum wasn't busy, she'd help, but …

Alisha: I can do it. There you go. The bow tie's smart, but you look like a waiter! And your hair's a mess. It would look much better if you had some gel in it. Here.

Damian: Get off! Stop bothering me. Anyway, you look like a giant cream cake.

Alisha: *(mobile rings)* Skye! Swimming? Oh! I'd come if I was free, but we've got a family wedding. My auntie's getting married and I'm her bridesmaid. I can't talk now, I'm getting ready. Sorry. Bye!

Mum: Damian! Alisha! Hurry up. We're going in five minutes.

Alisha: Nooo! I'm not ready yet! *(sneezes)* Hold this a sec.

Damian: What's up? Your eyes are really red.

Alisha: I know! I'm allergic to these flowers. *(sneezes)* I keep sneezing!

Damian: If I were you, I'd take some tissues. Loads of tissues!

Alisha: Agh! What a nightmare.

There you go.   Stop bothering me.   **OUT of class**
Get off!   Hold this a sec.

1 CLASS VOTE Which of these family events do you prefer? What do you like/dislike about them?

   a meal   a wedding   a short visit / holiday

2 7.1 2.52 Watch or listen. Why does Alisha need to take tissues?

3 Study the Grammar box. Find more examples of the Second Conditional in the dialogue.

Grammar	Second Conditional

I'd come if I was free. (but I'm not free)
What would you do if you were me?

GRAMMAR TIME > PAGE 124

4 2.53 Complete the sentences with the Second Conditional form of the verbs in brackets. Listen and check.

1 If she _____ (have) enough time, she _____ (help) him.
   If she had enough time, she would help him.
2 If you _____ (listen) carefully, you _____ (understand) the lesson.
3 _____ (you/go) to the beach if _____ (you/be) free today?
4 He _____ (not be) here if he _____ (not want) to.
5 What _____ (you/do) if _____ (you/win) a lot of money?
6 I _____ (phone) your mum if I _____ (be) you.

5 [VOX POPS ▶ 7.2] In pairs, finish the sentences to make them true for you.

1 If my friend phoned when I was busy, …
2 If I didn't like my clothes, …
3 If there was a big wedding in our family, …
4 If I was late for a family meal, my parents …
5 I'd be very worried if …
6 It would be a nightmare for me if …

If my friend phoned when I was busy, I'd probably talk to her. What about you?

7.2 GRAMMAR Second Conditional

Lesson learning objective
Students can talk about imaginary situations.

Lead in: Review of the First Conditional

Remind students about when we use the First Conditional and what we use it for (*to talk about the result of a likely or possible future situation*). Put students into pairs and tell them to think of a First Conditional sentence. When they are ready, invite a pair to say the *if* clause of their sentence and encourage the class to guess the result clause of that sentence. After the class has guessed, the pair should give their actual result clause. Repeat the process with other pairs and their sentences. Then write on the board:
First Conditional: *If* + Present Simple, + *will* + infinitive.
Leave this on the board so that you can refer to it later.

Exercise 1
Tell students to keep their Students' Books closed. Write on the board the choices from the exercise. After students have voted, ask questions about the last family meal students went to, about family weddings that students have attended and about the last family holiday that students went on.

Exercise 2 ▶ 7.1 🔊 2.52
Check that students understand the meaning of *tissue*. Tell students to keep their Students' Books closed while they watch the video. When the video has finished, ask the question in the rubric. Then tell students to open their books and read the dialogue.
Play the video again and then check that students understand the meaning of *bow tie*, *hair gel*, *bridesmaid*, *allergic to* and *nightmare*. Ask whether anyone in the class has ever worn a bow tie, used hair gel or is allergic to something.

Answers: Because she keeps sneezing because she is allergic to the flowers.

Exercise 3
Discuss the Grammar box with the class. Elicit the form and write it on the board underneath the form of the First Conditional:
Second Conditional: *If* + Past Simple, + *would* + infinitive
Point out that when using the Second Conditional, it is more formal to use *were* instead of *was*, e.g. *If it were (was) warmer, I would go swimming.* Explain, though, that in informal speech it is fine to use *was*. Tell students that it's only possible to use *were* in the phrase *If I were you.*
After students have found the examples in the dialogue, discuss the difference in use between the First Conditional and the Second Conditional (*the First Conditional is used when the situation is likely and the Second Conditional is used when the situation is unlikely, impossible or imaginary*). Use an example to show the difference between the two, e.g. an Icelandic student in December might say *If it snows tomorrow, I will go skiing* but an Egyptian student in June would say *If it snowed tomorrow, I would build a snowman.* Elicit or explain the reasons why we use the First Conditional in the first sentence and the Second Conditional in the second sentence (*snow in Iceland in December is very likely, whereas snow in Egypt in June is very unlikely or impossible*). Then discuss why the Second Conditional is used in the examples from the dialogue (*they describe imaginary situations, because Mum is actually busy, Damian hasn't actually got any gel, Alisha isn't actually free and Damian isn't actually Alisha*). Point out that to give advice we often use the structure *If I were you, I would …*, e.g. *You should wear a jacket. If I were you, I'd wear a jacket.*

Answers: If Mum wasn't busy, she'd help; It would look much better if you had some gel in it; I'd come if I was free; If I were you, I'd take some tissues.

Exercise 4 🔊 2.53
Discuss the example with the class. Remind students that it is possible to reverse the order of the two clauses, but that when the *if*-clause comes at the beginning, it is followed by a comma, e.g. *If I were older, I would go to a night club.* = *I would go to a nightclub if I were older.*

Answers: **2** listened, would understand
3 Would you go, you were   **4** wouldn't be, didn't want
5 would you do, you won   **6** would phone, were

Exercise 5
Look at the first sentence beginning with the class and elicit reasons why they may be busy, e.g. *doing homework, eating dinner, watching TV*. Ask how their sentence endings may be different in each situation, e.g. *If my friend phoned while I was doing my homework, I'd have a break and a chat. If my friend phoned while I was eating dinner, my mum would tell me not to answer it!*
Encourage students to think of different situations for the other sentences, so that they can finish the sentences in more than one way. When the pairs have finished, tell them to join together to make groups of four and share their idea.

VOX POPS ▶ 7.2

Before watching, check that students understand the meanings of these phrases: *to drop everything* (not literally to drop something on the floor, but to ignore whatever you are doing and to do something else), *a date* (a person, not an event), *to make something up* (to lie or create an imaginary story), *to screw up* (very informal, to do something completely wrong). After watching, ask students which of the speakers' answers they think are not likely to be true (*I would run around naked, my parents would kill me*).

Further practice
- Workbook page 80
- Grammar Time page 124
- Resource Pack
  Resource 80: Unit 7 Lesson 2 Grammar – Tell your group why
  Resource 81: Unit 7 Lesson 2 Video – I'd come if I was free

7.3 READING and VOCABULARY Friendship day

Lesson learning objective
Students can find specific detail in an article and talk about friends.

Lead in: Review of the Second Conditional

Ask students if they have ever seen a film about a real person. If they have, ask who the person was and which actor played them in the film. Ask students whether or not they think it is important that the actor looks and sounds like the real person. Give some examples, e.g. Ashton Kutcher – Steve Jobs, Daniel Day Lewis – Abraham Lincoln, Anthony Hopkins – Richard Nixon, Will Smith – Mohammed Ali.

Then give each student a piece of paper and tell them to work on their own. Ask students to write this question and then to answer it: *If Hollywood made a film about your* (the student's) *life, who would play you and your family? Why?* Explain that their answer should be a full sentence, i.e. *If Hollywood made a film about my life, … would play me because …* .

When students have finished, collect all the pieces of paper. Read out students' answers one by one and encourage the class to try to guess who wrote each answer.

Exercise 1
Tell students to keep their Students' Books closed. Introduce the topic of friendship and what friendship means to students. Discuss the fact that there are special days to celebrate our parents (i.e. Mother's Day, Father's Day), our children (some countries celebrate Children's Day and Santa Claus Day) and our romantic partners (i.e. Valentine's Day), but we don't have special days to celebrate our friendships. Then ask the question in the rubric and encourage students to give their opinions.

Exercise 2 🔊 2.54
Tell students to keep their Students' Books closed. Explain that they are going to listen to a recording about Friendship Day. Ask them to listen carefully for the names of different countries and for the specific years and dates that are mentioned.

After you have played the audio, invite students to recount any years and dates that they can remember connected to the USA (*1930 – Joyce Hall planned a Friendship Day, 2 August – the date of the first Friendship Day in the USA*), South America / Paraguay (*1958 – the date since which Friendship day has been celebrated in some South American countries, 30 July – the date of the celebration of friendship and understanding*) and worldwide (*2011 – the UN agreed to support International Friendship Day*).

Then tell students to open their books, to read the sentences in Exercise 2 and to read the text to find the answers. When students are ready, elicit the answers and ask students to justify their answers with extracts from the text.

Answers:
1 F (She was an American woman.)
2 T (Many Americans sent cards.)
3 T (It began with a group of friends in Puerto Pinasco, Paraguay.)
4 F (People in India and China also took up the idea.)
5 T (They set up activities for children and teenagers.)
6 F (Everybody takes one card with a name and buys a small present for that person.)

Exercise 3 🔊 2.55
When students have found the vocabulary in the text, discuss the exact meanings. For example: *buddies* and *mates* both mean close friends; *schoolmates* and *workmates* are people you know from school or work and some may be close friends who you spend a lot of time with outside of school or work, while others may not be close friends; a *stranger* is someone who you don't know; an *enemy* is someone who you don't like.

Answers:
Synonyms: schoolmates, workmates, buddies
Antonyms: stranger
Phrases: make (new) friends

Exercise 4
When students have completed the sentences, put them into pairs. Ask the pairs to write three more sentences using words or phrases from the Vocabulary box that relate to their own lives, e.g. *There are some people in my class I don't talk to very much, but I haven't got any enemies.*

Answers: 2 best friend 3 make (new) friends 4 workmate(s)
5 classmates/schoolmates

Exercise 5
Tell students to work alone to think of an idea for Friendship Day. When they are ready, tell one half of the class to stay seated and the other half of the class to stand up and mingle with the students who are seated. Explain that students who are standing should interview as many seated students as possible, to ask them about their ideas. Give a time limit and then tell students to swap roles, so that students who were standing now sit and students who were seated now stand and interview them.

When they have finished, invite students to tell the class which idea they heard for Friendship Day that they thought was the best and why they liked it.

Extra activity

Put students into groups of four and tell them to plan a Friendship Day at their school that includes several events to promote friendship between people. They can use some of the ideas that were generated during Exercise 5. When the groups have decided on their events, tell them to create a poster that includes details of the events that will take place on Friendship Day. Display the posters and, when students have looked at all the posters, have a class vote for the best poster. (Tell students they can't vote for their own poster.)

Further practice

- Workbook page 81
- Resource Pack
  Resource 82: Unit 7 Lesson 3 Reading and Vocabulary – Friends

7.3 READING and VOCABULARY Friendship day

I can find specific detail in an article and talk about friends.

Friendship Day

The idea of a special friendship day has several origins. An American woman, Joyce Hall, owned a greetings card company. In 1930 she planned a Friendship Day to create more business. She thought, 'If people had a new celebration, they would buy more cards.' The first Friendship Day in the USA was on 2 August. Many Americans sent cards, but then this tradition died out after a few years.

However, a different idea of Friendship Day has been celebrated in some South American countries since 1958. It began with a group of friends in Puerto Pinasco, Paraguay. They decided to celebrate friendship and understanding on 30 July every year. One man in the group, Ramon Artemio Bracho, wanted to do more. He wanted to turn strangers into friends. He worked hard to start celebrations in other countries. Thanks to Ramon's work, people in India and China also took up the idea. Friendship Day was growing.

Finally, in 2011, the celebration became International Friendship Day when the United Nations agreed to support it. They saw it as a good way to encourage peace by getting different cultures to communicate more. They set up activities for children and teenagers of mixed nationalities, such as fun runs or friendly games. The hope is that these kinds of events help people to respect one another's culture and to make new friends.

In some countries, people have a meal, phone friends or use social media to send messages. In Paraguay, the 'Invisible Friend' game is played one week before the special day. All names of schoolmates or workmates are written on pieces of paper and put in a box. Then everybody takes one card with a name and buys a small present for that person, wraps it and writes the name on it. When you get your gift on Friendship Day, you don't know who bought it! However, if I wanted to do something for my buddies, I would give them friendship bands because they are so popular.

Jyoti Singh, age 15, India

---

1 **CLASS VOTE** Is it important to have a special day to celebrate friendship? Why? / Why not?

2 🔊 2.54 Read the text. Mark the sentences T (true) or F (false).

1. ☐ Joyce Hall owned a company in the UK.
2. ☐ In the USA in 1930s, people celebrated by giving cards.
3. ☐ The decision to spread the celebration to more countries was made in Paraguay.
4. ☐ Asian countries are not keen on Friendship Day.
5. ☐ The United Nations encourage younger people to take part.
6. ☐ The 'Invisible Friend' game involves writing a message to your friends.

3 🔊 2.55 Study the Vocabulary box. Find more examples in the text.

Vocabulary	Talking about friends

synonyms for *friends*
mates   classmates   best friends
_____ _____ _____

antonyms for *friends*
enemy   _____

phrases with *friends*
have a friend   be friends   _____

4 Complete the sentences with the words from the Vocabulary box.

1. At first I felt like a *stranger* here. Nobody knew me.
2. Of all my friends, Ezra is my _____ because he understands me.
3. She was nervous about the new school but it was easy to _____.
4. My dad sometimes plays tennis with his _____ from the office.
5. He started secondary school early, so his _____ are older than him.

5 What would you like to do with your friends to celebrate Friendship Day?

Unit 7

7.4 GRAMMAR Defining and non-defining relative clauses

I can be specific about people, things and places.

PARK STREET PUZZLE
Who lives in these houses?

1 Lucy lives in one of the flats above the café.
2 One of Lucy's friends lives in a house which has a big tree in the garden.
3 In front of another friend's house, there is a small space where he leaves his bike.
4 Mr and Mrs Morris, who are Lucy's grandparents, live next door to her.
5 Mrs Morris loves colourful flowers, which she grows in window boxes.
6 Paddy lives in a house which is next to the bus stop.
7 Lucy doesn't know the man who has just moved to the house with a pink roof.
8 The man's cat loves the balcony, where it can watch the birds.

☐ Lucy ☐ Molly ☐ Paddy ☐ Frank Jones ☐ Mr and Mrs Morris

1 🔊 **2.56** Who lives in each house? Read the puzzle and write the house numbers next to each name. Which is the house where nobody lives?

2 Study the Grammar box. Find examples of defining and non-defining relative clauses in the puzzle.

> **Grammar** | **Defining and non-defining relative clauses**
>
> **Defining relative clauses**
> The man **who** (that) moved to Park Street is Frank.
> Molly lives in a house **which** (that) is a hundred years old.
> That's the cafe **where** the children often buy ice cream.
>
> **Non-defining relative clauses = extra information**
> Frank, **who** moved to Park Street, has a cat.
> Molly's house, **which** has a tree in the garden, is very old.
> There's a café in the street, **where** we buy ice cream.
>
> **Be careful!**
> The woman that/who grows flowers is Mrs Morris.
> Mrs Morris, ~~that~~/who grows flowers, is Lucy's grandma.
>
> GRAMMAR TIME ▶ PAGE 124

3 Choose the correct option. Which pronouns can be replaced with *that*?

1 The children *who / which* are in the park live nearby.
2 Here's the office *where / which* my mum works.
3 I live in a flat *which / who* is in the town centre.
4 Frank Jones's cat, *which / who* is five years old, loves hunting.

4 Combine the sentences with relative pronouns.

1 Lucy has a good friend. **She** lives near Park Street.
   Lucy has a good friend who lives near Park Street.
2 In Molly's garden there's a tree. **It**'s 100 years old.
3 That's the café. Lucy sometimes meets her friends **there**.
4 There's a park. The children play **in it**.

5 Rewrite the sentences, using non-defining relative clauses.

1 Mrs Morris is sixty-seven. (who/be/ Lucy's grandmother)
   Mrs Morris, who is Lucy's grandmother, is sixty-seven.
2 Paddy uses his bike every day. (which/ be/new)
3 Number 24 is a beautiful house. (where/ Molly/live)
4 Frank has a cat. (who/used to work/at the hospital)

6 Make one true and one false sentence about your house, street or town. In pairs, say if your partner's sentences are true or false.

7.4 GRAMMAR Defining and non-defining relative clauses

Lesson learning objective
Students can be specific about people, things and places.

Lead in: Review of vocabulary related to friends

Put students into groups of four. Tell them to imagine that they are summer camp organisers and that everybody has arrived at the camp but nobody knows anybody else. Each group should think of a short, simple activity which will help people get to know one another and make friends. Give the groups a time limit to think of an activity and then invite each group to demonstrate their activity.

Exercise 1 🔊 2.56

Point out that there are six houses, but only five sets of people, so there will be one house where nobody lives. When students are finished, elicit the answers and the key words which helped to identify them, e.g. *one of the flats above the café*, *window boxes*, *pink roof*, *balcony*.

Answers: Lucy: 32   Molly: 24   Paddy: 28   Frank Jones: 26
Mr and Mrs Morris: 34   Nobody: 30

Exercise 2

Go through the Grammar box with students.

Defining relative clauses
- **Use:** Defining relative clauses give us information that is necessary to make sense of a sentence. If this clause were omitted, we wouldn't be able to determine which person, place or thing was being talked about. For example: *The car which we saw this morning is my teacher's*. Without the clause we have: *The car is my teacher's*, but we have no information about which car is being talked about.
- **Form:** We use *which* or *that* for things, *who* or *that* for people and *where* for places. There are no commas separating the clause from the rest of the sentence.

Non-defining relative clauses
- **Use:** Non-defining relative clauses give us extra information that is not necessary to make sense of the sentence. If this clause were omitted, we would still be able to determine which thing, person or place was being talked about. For example: *I saw our teacher's car, which is red, this morning*. Without the clause we have: *I saw our teacher's car this morning*.
- **Form:** We don't use *that* as a non-defining relative pronoun. We use commas to separate the clause from the rest of the sentence.

Answers:
Defining relative clauses: a house which has a big tree; a small space where he leaves his bike; a house which is next to the bus stop; the man who has just moved
Non-defining relative clauses: Mr and Mrs Morris, who are Lucy's grandparents; colourful flowers, which she grows; the balcony, where it can watch

Exercise 3

Before they do the exercise, students should read out the sentences without the relative clauses to see if they make sense.

Answers: 1 who (that)   2 where   3 which (that)   4 which

Exercise 4

Before students do the exercise, write on the board: *I've got a friend*. Elicit sentences about the friend, e.g. *He lives in London. He likes cats.*

Next, write on the board: *I've got a phone*. Elicit sentences about it, e.g. *It is silver. It cost £100.*

Then write *I've got a friend who lives in London.* and *I've got a phone which is silver.* on the board to show how the sentences can be linked by replacing the pronoun *he*, *she* or *it* with a relative pronoun.

Explain to students that they are going to write similar sentences. When they have finished, invite them to read out their sentences.

Answers:
2 In Molly's garden there's a tree which is 100 years old.
3 That's the café where Lucy sometimes meets her friends.
4 There's a park where the children play.

Exercise 5

Before students do the exercise, write on the board:
My mum   Age: 65   Lives: Liverpool   Likes: cats
Discuss alternative ways of writing non-defining relative clauses about this information. For example:
My mum, who lives in Liverpool, is 65 years old.
My mum, who likes cats, lives in Liverpool.
My mum, who is 65 years old, likes cats.
Ask students to do the same. They should write three facts about someone and then write three different non-defining relative clauses.

Answers:
2 Paddy uses his bike, which is new, every day.
3 Number 24, where Molly lives, is a beautiful house.
4 Frank, who used to work at the hospital, has a cat.

Exercise 6

Tell students that they should use one defining relative clause and one non-defining relative clause for their two sentences, e.g. *My house, which is 230 years old, is haunted. The street where I live is the most dangerous street in our town.*

Extra activity

In groups of three, students write five simple sentences about famous people and famous places, e.g. *George Clooney is an actor. The Eiffel Tower is in Paris.* Ask them to swap sentences with another group. They should then create non-defining relative clauses to add information to their new sentences, e.g. *George Clooney, who is married to a Lebanese lawyer, is an actor. The Eiffel Tower, which is France's most famous tourist attraction, is in Paris.*

Further practice

- Workbook page 82
- Grammar Time page 124
- Resource Pack
  Resource 83: Unit 7 Lesson 4 Grammar – The student who …

163

7.5 LISTENING and VOCABULARY A friend in need ...

Lesson learning objective
Students can identify specific information in a monologue and talk about pets.

Lead in: Review of relative clauses

Give each student a piece of paper and tell them to draw three squares on it. Explain that these should represent photos of things that are important to them in their lives – one is a photo of people, one is a photo of a possession and one is a photo of a place.

In groups of three, students should take turns to describe their pictures, using relative clauses.

When the groups have discussed their pictures, invite students to come to the board, draw a picture and describe it to the class.

Exercise 1
Tell students to keep their Students' Books closed. Put students into groups of four, ask the question and tell the groups to list reasons for and against.

Exercise 2
Have a class discussion about the questions and check that students understand the meaning of *wheelchair*. Discuss ideas such as dogs which help blind people, dogs used to search for people in the snow after avalanches, guard dogs and dogs which help sufferers of depression.

Exercise 3
Before students do the exercise, elicit ideas about how a dog could help someone like Grace with her morning routine. Then put students into pairs to discuss the questions and guess the answers.

Exercise 4   2.57
When students have listened to the audio, elicit the answers and encourage students to see if they can remember which words in the audio helped them to find the answers (*1 take a long time; 2 when she was nine; 3 tickling her feet; 4 intelligent, understands, knows how to help*).

Answers: 1 c   2 b   3 a   4 c

2.57
See page 248.

Exercise 5
Discuss with students the types of information in the box and elicit examples. For example: opinions: *In my opinion, rock music is more exciting than rap.*
When students have finished the exercise, elicit the answers, with reasons.

Answers:
1 detailed meaning of a word or phrase (of the phrase *puppy trainer*)
2 feelings (we're discussing Ash's feelings)
3 specific information (about who did the training)
4 general topic (we're discussing the general topic of assistance dogs)

Exercise 6   2.58
Elicit the answers and explanations for them.

Answers:
1 b (a is wrong, because the dogs are young (puppies), c is wrong because the dogs are not unwanted)
2 a (a is correct because Ash sometimes cried)
3 c (c is correct because the audio says *I trained him – with a bit of help from my stepmum*)
4 c (c is correct because the audio says people *who are disabled in some way* and so the dogs can help with different disabilities.)

2.58
See page 249.

Exercise 7   2.59
When students have completed the matching exercise, elicit more examples for each meaning of the verb *get*, e.g. *buy – get a new computer; find – get a girlfriend; arrive/reach – get to the airport; receive – get a present; bring/fetch – get something from your room; become – get sick*).

Answers: 2 find   3 arrive/reach   4 receive   5 bring/fetch   6 become

Exercise 8
When students have finished, put them into pairs. Ask them to change the ending of the sentences to make them true for themselves.

Answers: 2 a text   3 a glass of water   4 home

Exercise 9
When students have discussed their ideas in pairs, encourage them to mingle with their classmates and talk about their situations.

VOX POPS ▶ 7.3

Before watching, tell students to listen out for the following information: the name of the dog, the cost of the vet bills, and what the celebrating people drank in the pub (i.e. *Jet, £2000, shots*). After watching, explain that the Latin phrase the speaker uses is *magna cum laude*, which means 'with great honours'. (Although the speaker says this means she graduated top of her class, there is a higher grade called *summa cum laude*, which means 'with highest honours'.)

Homework
Ask students to bring a photo to the next lesson which contains several people. Explain that they are going to ask and answer questions about the people in the photo.

Further practice
- Workbook page 83
- Resource Pack
  Resource 84: Unit 7 Lesson 5 Listening and Vocabulary – Get

7.5 LISTENING and VOCABULARY — A friend in need ...

I can identify specific information in a monologue and talk about pets.

1 **CLASS VOTE** Can animals be your friend or part of your family? Why? / Why not?

2 Look at the photos. Which person do you think might have a disability, and how do you think the dog is helping? What else do you think dogs can do to help people?

Snoopy and Grace **1**

Scooby and Ash **2**

3 Look at questions 1–4 below. What do you think Grace's sister will talk about?
1 What does Grace think of her morning routine?
   a It was boring.   b It was sad.   c It was slow.
2 How old was Grace when she got Snoopy?
   a a baby   b a child   c a teenager
3 What does Snoopy do to help with Grace's everyday routine?
   a tickles her   b washes her feet
   c puts her socks on
4 Based on Grace's sister's account, which adjective best describes Snoopy?
   a busy   b funny   c clever

4 🔊 **2.57** Listen and answer the questions in Exercise 3.

5 Look at the answers for questions 1–4 below. Match the answers to the types of information below.

> opinions?   feelings?   detailed meaning of a word or phrase?
> specific information?   general topic?

1 What does a puppy trainer do?
   a looks after old dogs
   b teaches young dogs special skills
   c finds new homes for unwanted dogs
2 When the dogs left, Ash felt
   a sad.   b bored.   c happy for them.
3 Scooby's training was done
   a by Ash on his own.
   b by Ash's stepmum.
   c by Ash and his stepmum together.
4 What is the main thing we learn from Ash's explanation of assistance dogs?
   a They often go to different owners.
   b They take a long time to learn things.
   c They can help with a wide range of needs.

6 🔊 **2.58** Listen and answer the questions in Exercise 5.

7 🔊 **2.59** **WORD FRIENDS** Match the meaning of *get* (1–6) to the correct words below. Listen and check.

> arrive/reach   become   bring/fetch
> buy   find   receive

> **Word Friends**
>
> *Get* can have several meanings:
> 1 Get a pet = *buy*
> 2 Get a job = _____
> 3 Get home = _____
> 4 Get a letter/phone call / an email = _____
> 5 Get someone's socks/book / a drink (for someone) = _____
> 6 Get better/worse   get dressed
>   get married   get old(er)   get ready
>   get upset/angry/scared/stressed/
>   bored/excited = _____

8 Choose the correct option.
1 My brother wants to get (a job) / ready in the police force.
2 I've just got *dressed / a text* from my gran!
3 Shall I get *a glass of water / married* for you?
4 The train was late, so we didn't get *home / a pet* until midnight.

9 [VOX POPS ▶ 7.3] In pairs, tell your partner about one of the situations below. Describe how you felt and the reasons why you felt that way.
• a time you got a pet
• a time you got bored, scared, angry or stressed
• a time you got an important letter / email / phone call

Unit 7

7.6 SPEAKING Identifying people

I can explain who I am talking about.

VIDEO   WHO'S THE GUY AT THE BACK?

Tommo:	Boo! What are you two up to?
Alisha:	I'm just showing Skye the photos from the wedding.
Tommo:	Oh, yeah. This one's really funny. You were stressed because you had a bridesmaid's dress that looked like a cream cake!
Alisha:	Hey! Give it back.
Skye:	Come on, guys. Let's see the other photos.
Tommo:	Yeah, it'll be a laugh!
Alisha:	Huh! Right, that's my Auntie Lara and my new Uncle Andy in the middle, of course. Then there's my little cousin.
Tommo:	Which one?
Alisha:	The cute one who's wearing the smart white shirt. He got really bored. He was pulling faces all the time.
Skye:	Aww! Who's this guy at the back?
Alisha:	Where? Oh, that's, um, Adam. He's the bridegroom's stepbrother.
Skye:	Right … He looks nice. Very good looking too.
Tommo:	Who? Let's see. Pass it here. Oops!
Alisha:	Tommo! Now look what you've done!

> Boo!   It'll be a laugh.   What are you (two) up to?   Pass it here.

OUT of class

1 🔊 **2.60** Listen and check you understand the words in the Vocabulary box.

Vocabulary	People at a wedding
bride bridegroom bridesmaid guests pageboy	

2  **7.4** 🔊 **2.61** Listen or watch. What four people are mentioned in the dialogue?

3 Answer the questions.
1 What does Tommo think about the photos?
2 How does Alisha feel when Tommo says 'It'll be a laugh!'?
3 What is the bridegroom's name?
4 How did Alisha's little cousin behave during the wedding?
5 Who is Adam and what does he look like?

4 Work in pairs. Choose a photo from page 132 or 138 and describe a person in it. Follow the instructions.

Speaking	Identifying people

Talking about people in a photo
She's/He's standing/sitting/talking to … / playing with …
She's/He's wearing …
She's/He's in front of/behind/next to/on the left/on the right/near/in the middle/ at the front/at the back.

Asking
Who's this/that boy/girl on the left who is wearing …
Which one/girl/boy/man/woman/guy?

Explaining
The one who is …
The cute/tall one.
Which one do you mean?

- Choose a person to describe.
- Other people ask you questions.
- Answer the questions with one piece of information at a time.

A: *Who are you thinking of?*
B: *A person who is wearing / looks …*
A: *Where is this person?*
B: *She's/He's in front of / behind …*

5 Work in pairs. Show your partner a photo where there are people he/she doesn't know. Ask and answer questions.

Unit 7

7.6 SPEAKING Identifying people

Lesson learning objective
Students can explain who they are talking about.

Lead in: Review of the meanings of *get*

Put students into pairs. Explain that they are going to write three sentences and each sentence should include two different uses of the verb *get*. Write an example on the board: *I got excited when I got a tablet for my birthday.* Explain that their three sentences should include all six uses of *get* (i.e. *arrive/reach*, *become*, *bring/fetch*, *buy*, *find*, *receive* – refer students to the Word Friends box on page 87 of the Students' Book).
When the pairs have finished, put students into groups of four. The pairs should swap sentences and check that the other pair has included all the uses of the verb. Invite pairs to read to the class the sentence written by the other pair that they think is the most interesting.

Exercise 1   2.60
Elicit the meanings of the words in the Vocabulary box.

Exercise 2   7.4   2.61
Before you play the video, put students into pairs. Explain that the three friends, Alisha, Skye and Tommo, are looking at some photos. Tell the pairs that they should read the final two lines of the dialogue and try to guess what happened when Tommo tried to look at the photo.
After you have played the video, discuss the Out of class box with the class. Elicit another use of *Boo!* (*it can also be used to show displeasure, e.g. at a sports event*).

Answers: Auntie Lara, Uncle Andy, cousin, the bridegroom's stepbrother Adam

Exercise 3
Keep students in pairs and tell them to cover the dialogue in their books with a piece of paper. They should try to answer the questions in their own words. When they are finished, elicit students' answers. Then tell them to look at the dialogue and, for each question and answer, find the related section in the text.

Answers:
1 He thinks they are funny.
2 She feels cross.
3 His name is Andy/Uncle Andy.
4 He pulled faces.
5 He's the bridegroom's stepbrother and is very good looking.

Exercise 4
Discuss the Speaking box with students. Remind students that, to identify someone, they can describe what the person is doing, what they are wearing, where they are, what they look like and how they look, e.g. *bored, happy*.
After students have done the exercise, choose someone in one of the photos and ask students questions about what he/she is doing, what he/she is wearing, where he/she is, how he/she looks and what he/she looks like.

Exercise 5
If students have done the homework from Lesson 5, they will have brought a photo with them to this lesson. If they haven't, tell them to describe an imaginary photo. Put students into pairs to ask and answer questions about someone in the photo.

Extra activity
Invite eight students to come to the front of the class. Tell them to imagine that they are in a family photo and to stand with shorter students in front and taller students behind them. When they are ready, invite two new students to stand next to the group. Explain that the students still sitting are going to ask questions about the people in the family photo, e.g. *Who's the girl wearing a yellow shirt? Who's the tall boy who looks bored?* The two students standing should use their imaginations to answer the questions, e.g. *That's Susie. She's my cousin from California; That's Tom, my sister's boyfriend. He's a film star.*
Repeat the activity with different students in the photo and different students answering questions about them.

Further practice
- Workbook page 84
- Resource Pack
  Resource 85: Unit 7 Lesson 6 Speaking – Identify them
  Resource 86: Unit 7 Lesson 6 Video – Who's the guy at the back?

7.7 WRITING A short story about friendship

Lesson learning objective
Students can write a short story.

Lead in: Review of identifying people
Tell students to look carefully at all their classmates. Give them a time limit of one minute to do this. Then invite two students to stand at the front of the classroom, facing away from the rest of the class. The rest of the class should choose one student to describe and then make sentences about him/her, e.g. *He's wearing a black T-shirt. He's sitting next to Simon. He's tall with blond hair. He looks tired.* The two students at the front should try to guess which student is being described. When one of them guesses correctly, both students should be replaced by two new students at the front of the classroom and the process should be repeated.

Exercise 1
Before students do the exercise, elicit what they can see in each picture, e.g. *1 a science lab, a microscope, test tubes; 2 a corridor, lockers; 3 and 4 a playground, a bench*. Then put students into pairs to discuss what they think is happening in the pictures. Invite pairs to share their ideas with the class.

Exercise 2
When students have found the answers in the text, ask questions about the people in the pictures. For example: *Who is the boy in the green sweater?* (Nick); *Who is the girl in the red top?* (Christina); *Who is the boy sitting on the bench with a book?* (Tom); *Who is the boy standing behind the bench?* (Aris)

Answers:
1 Nick – good at science, doesn't have time to help
2 Christina – a neighbour, doesn't understand the homework
3 Aris – a new classmate, popular, a big-head and bossy
4 Tom – has a lot in common with Aris and the same sense of humour

Exercise 3
When students have finished, discuss the answers. Ask: *How do we start the story?* If students reply: *setting the scene*, ask them to explain what this means in their own words, e.g. *We describe what the story is about – a problem, a journey, a dream*, etc.
Point out that paragraphs make a story easier to read because they separate different events and they make it easier for readers to see where one event finishes and another starts.

Answers: 1 d 2 c 3 a 4 e 5 b

Exercise 4
Point out that in the story each paragraph starts with a word or phrase that shows the order of events: *Last week, Next, Just then, That day*. Explain that this also helps to make it easier for the reader to understand what is happening.

Answers:
1 (Last week) I was feeling stressed about …
2 (Aris) is popular, but …
3 Just then, …
4 That day, …
5 Afterwards, …
6 'I can help,' he offered.
7 I think we'll be good friends from now on.

Extra activity
Put students into pairs. Tell each pair to develop their own story, similar to the one in Exercise 2. They should draw four pictures to show what happens in their story, similar to the pictures in the Students' Book. Give the pairs a time limit and, when the time has finished, tell the pairs to swap their pictures with another pair. The pairs should look at the other pair's pictures to try to work out what their story is about. When they are ready, the two sets of pairs should join up to make a group of four, so that they can share their ideas and tell one another how close their guesses were.

Exercise 5
Before students start writing, elicit a situation for a story, e.g. a party, and how the story could start, e.g. *Last month, I organised a party for my fifteenth birthday.* Write this on the board. Then elicit a different situation and a different opening sentence and write this on the board too.
Elicit and write on the board four or five different situations and opening sentences, so that there are plenty of ideas for students to choose from if they can't think of their own original ideas. Then discuss the tips with students and elicit what the relevant past tenses are (*Past Simple and Past Continuous*).

Homework
Tell students to read the text on page 92 of the Students' Book. They should look up any words they don't know the meaning of and translate them into L1.
As an additional task, ask students to write an example sentence illustrating the meaning of each these words: *discomfort, expert, retired, rootless, trailer park, decade*. Also tell students to find out the meaning of the phrase *broadens your horizons* and to write a sentence about themselves which illustrates the meaning of the phrase.

Further practice
- Workbook page 85
- Resource Pack
  Resource 87: Unit 7 Lesson 7 Writing – Making new friends

7.7 WRITING A short story about friendship

I can write a short story.

1 Look at the pictures and describe what is happening.

2 Read the text and name each person in Exercise 1. What do we find out about each friend?

A friend in need …

Last week I was feeling stressed about my science homework. I asked my friend Nick to help. 'I'd explain it if I was free, but I'm quite busy.' Nick and I get on well, and he's good at science, so I was disappointed.

Next, I went to my neighbour. 'Sorry, Tom. If I understood the homework, I'd help you,' said Christina, 'but it's difficult.'

Just then, a new classmate, Aris, heard us. He is popular, but we don't speak often because he's the kind of person who knows all the answers. He's a big-head. In fact, I fell out with him once because he was so bossy. 'I can help,' he offered.

That day, Aris explained the science homework to me carefully. Afterwards, we sat and chatted. We got to know each other and found we have a lot in common and the same sense of humour. I think we'll be good friends from now on.

3 Read the text again. Match events a–e with descriptions 1–5.

1 ☐ Setting the scene
2 ☐ The first event
3 ☐ The second event
4 ☐ The main event (the climax)
5 ☐ The solution or outcome

a Tom's neighbour can't help him.
b Aris and Tom become friends.
c Tom's friend can't help him.
d Tom has a problem.
e Tom has a surprise offer of help.

4 Study the Writing box. Complete gaps 1–7 with phrases from the text.

Writing   A short story

Starting your story and setting the scene
My birthday was a fantastic day.
Have you ever had a really difficult day?
1 _____

Introducing your characters
Nick and I got on well …
2 _____

Using time words and phrases to show order of events
Last week …
Next …
Afterwards …
3 _____ 4 _____ 5 _____

Using direct speech
'I'd explain it if I was free, but I'm quite busy.'
6 _____

Ending your story
All's well that ends well.
I never want to do that again!
7 _____

Writing Time

5 Write a story for a competition in an English language magazine. Follow the instructions:

1 Use the title: *A friend in need*.
2 Write about 100 words.

TIPS

Set the scene and organise the order of events.

Include some speech and use speech marks.

Use relevant past tenses.

Wordlist and Vocabulary in action

Extra activity

Write these sentences on the board and elicit the answers (*aunt, bow tie, assistant dog*):
The woman who is married to my uncle is my …
The thing which I am wearing around my neck is a …
The animal which helps my disabled grandmother is an …
In pairs, students write five similar sentences using words from the wordlist. Invite them to read out their sentences except for the final word. The rest of the class should guess what the word is.

Further practice

Workbook page 86

WORDLIST Family and friends | Phrasal verb | Talking about friends

adopted /əˈdɒptɪd/
adoption /əˈdɒpʃn/
assistance dog /əˈsɪstəns dɒɡ/
aunt /ɑːnt/
baby /ˈbeɪbi/
be friends /bi ˈfrendz/
behind /bɪˈhaɪnd/
best friends /ˌbest ˈfrendz/
big-head /ˈbɪɡ hed/
bossy /ˈbɒsi/
bow tie /ˌbəʊ ˈtaɪ/
bride /braɪd/
bridegroom /ˈbraɪdɡruːm/
bridesmaid /ˈbraɪdzmeɪd/
buddy/buddies /ˈbʌdi/ˈbʌdiz/
by blood /ˌbaɪ ˈblʌd/
celebrate /ˈseləbreɪt/
celebration /ˌseləˈbreɪʃn/
chat (v) /tʃæt/
classmates /ˈklɑːsmeɪts/
communicate /kəˈmjuːnɪkeɪt/
confident /ˈkɒnfɪdənt/
cousin /ˈkʌzn/
crowd /kraʊd/
deal with (a problem) /ˌdiːl wɪð ə ˈprɒbləm/
disability /ˌdɪsəˈbɪləti/
disappointed /ˌdɪsəˈpɔɪntɪd/
enemy /ˈenəmi/
fall out (with) /ˌfɔːl ˈaʊt wɪð/
friendship /ˈfrendʃɪp/
friendship bands /ˈfrendʃɪp bændz/
generation /ˌdʒenəˈreɪʃn/
get married /ˌɡet ˈmærɪd/
get on with /ˌɡet ˈɒn wɪð/
go ahead /ˌɡəʊ əˈhed/
go out /ˌɡəʊ ˈaʊt/

great-grandfather /ˌɡreɪtˈɡrændˌfɑːðə/
great-grandmother /ˌɡreɪtˈɡrændˌmʌðə/
great-grandparents /ˌɡreɪtˈɡrændˌpeərənts/
greeting card /ˈɡriːtɪŋ kɑːd/
group /ɡruːp/
guest /ɡest/
half-brother /ˈhɑːf ˌbrʌðə/
hang out (with) /ˌhæŋ ˈaʊt wɪð/
have a friend /ˌhæv ə ˈfrend/
in front of /ɪn ˈfrʌnt əv/
international /ˌɪntəˈnæʃnəl/
laugh at (sb/sth) /ˈlɑːf ət (ˌsʌmbədi/ ˌsʌmθɪŋ)/
make friends /ˌmeɪk ˈfrendz/
marriage /ˈmærɪdʒ/
married /ˈmærɪd/
mates /meɪts/
nationality /ˌnæʃəˈnæləti/
near /nɪə/
neighbour /ˈneɪbə/
next to /ˈnekst tə/
on the left /ˌɒn ðə ˈleft/
on the right /ˌɒn ðə ˈraɪt/
origin /ˈɒrɪdʒɪn/
pageboy /ˈpeɪdʒbɔɪ/
parents' evening /ˈpeərənts ˌiːvnɪŋ/
part of the family /ˌpɑːt əv ðə ˈfæmli/
peace /piːs/
pull faces /ˌpʊl ˈfeɪsɪz/
put up with /ˌpʊt ˈʌp wɪð/
related /rɪˈleɪtɪd/
relation /rɪˈleɪʃn/
relative /ˈrelətɪv/
respect (n) /rɪˈspekt/
schoolmates /ˈskuːlmeɪts/

social media /ˌsəʊʃl ˈmiːdiə/
solution /səˈluːʃn/
stepbrother /ˈstepbrʌðə/
stranger /ˈstreɪndʒə/
stressed /strest/
surprise /səˈpraɪz/
uncle /ˈʌŋkl/
wedding /ˈwedɪŋ/
workmates /ˈwɜːkmeɪts/

WORD FRIENDS

come from similar/different backgrounds
enjoy each other's company
get (your/his/her) socks/book / a drink (for someone)
get a job
get a letter / phone call / email
get a pet
get better/worse
get dressed
get home
get married
get on someone's nerves
get old(er)
get to know
get ready
get upset/angry/scared/stressed/ bored/excited
have an argument
have something in common
have the same sense of humour
see each other after school/at weekends, etc.
share an interest in
spend time with / spend time on your own

Exercise 2

1 c
2 b
3 a

VOCABULARY IN ACTION

1 Use the wordlist to find:
1 four types of friends
2 four phrasal verbs
3 six adjectives
4 five nouns that are NOT people

2 Choose the correct answers.
1 Which person is the same generation as you?
  a your grandfather
  b your mother
  c your half-brother
  d your aunt
2 Which phrase can be used about people who feel very good together?
  a fall out (with)
  b get on well (with)
  c have arguments
  d get on someone's nerves

3 Which person is related to you by blood?
  a half-sister
  b stepdad
  c adopted sister
  d schoolmate

3 In pairs, use the wordlist to describe your relationship with a person in your family.

4 🔊 **2.62** **PRONUNCIATION** Listen to the underlined letters and decide how they are pronounced. Listen again and repeat. What is the rule for pronouncing the final *-d* sound?

/d/ /t/ or /ɪd/?
bor<u>ed</u>   crow<u>d</u>   dress<u>ed</u>   marri<u>ed</u>
relat<u>ed</u>   stress<u>ed</u>

5 Use the wordlist to find more words ending in -*d*. How are they pronouced?

Exercise 4

bored /d/
crowd /d/
dressed /t/
married /d/
related /ɪd/
stressed /t/

We pronounce the final -*d* as /ɪd/ in words ending in -*ted*, -*ded*, as /d/ when the preceding sound is a vowel, a voiced consonant or the sound /r/, /n/, /m/, /l/ and as /t/ if the preceding sound is /s/.

Exercise 5

/d/ behind, big-head, bridesmaid, blood, ahead, card, friend, old, scared, spend
/ɪd/ adopted, disappointed, excited

 Wordlist

Exercise 1

Possible answers:
1 best friends, buddy/buddies, classmates, mates, schoolmates, workmates
2 deal with, fall out (with), get on with, go ahead, go out, hang out (with), laugh at (sb/sth), put up with
3 adopted, bossy, confident, disappointed, international, related, stressed
4 adoption, assistance dog, bow tie, celebration, crowd, disability, friendship, friendship bands, generation, greeting card, group, marriage, nationality, origin, parent's evening, peace, respect, social media, solution, surprise, wedding

◀ 170

Revision

Extra activity

Elicit a Second Conditional question relating to an adjective of personality, e.g. *shy*:
If you were at a party, would you …
a) *talk to everyone?* b) *talk to a few friends?* c) *sit by yourself and not talk to anyone?*
Ask groups of four to choose three adjectives of personality. For each adjective, they should think of a situation, think of a Second Conditional question and write three choices. When they are ready, tell them to ask their classmates and tell them what their answer says about their personality.

Further practice

- Workbook page 87
- Resource Pack
  Resource 88: Unit 7
  Vocabulary – Have you got …?
  Resource 89: Unit 7
  Grammar – Make a sentence

Revision

VOCABULARY

1 Complete the words in the sentences.

1 Your father's mother's mother is your
   g_____-g_____.
2 At a wedding, two people will do this:
   g___ m_____
3 If you spend time relaxing with friends, you do this. h_____ _____
4 If you practise speaking English, you
   g___ b_____ quickly.

Exercise 1
1 great-grandmother
2 get married
3 hang out
4 get better

2 Match phrases 1–5 with phrases a–e to make sentences.

1 ☐ My best friend is standing in front
2 ☐ My brother and I laugh
3 ☐ Luckily, we don't often have
4 ☐ I sometimes get
5 ☐ My mum and dad both have

a angry with my baby sister.
b at the same things.
c the same sense of humour.
d of me in the photo.
e big arguments.

Exercise 2
1 d
2 b
3 e
4 a
5 c

GRAMMAR

3 Choose the correct answers to complete the song lyrics.

If you ¹_____ your friends about your problem, they would help you. (but you don't tell them)
If you didn't keep quiet, they ²_____ understand. (but you don't say anything)
Just ask them, 'What would you do if you ³_____ me?' (you'll be surprised)
If you just ⁴_____ up, they would hold your hand.
So, would you listen if your friends ⁵_____ problems? (of course you would)
What would you do if you ⁶_____ them cry? (you'd go and help them)
So, next time you feel worried, you should speak out. Share things with your friends. Give it a try.

1	a tell	b telling	c told
2	a would	b will	c won't
3	a were	b was	c are
4	a open	b opened	c opens
5	a had	b have	c has
6	a seen	b saw	c see

Exercise 3
1 c
2 a
3 a
4 b
5 a
6 b

4 Complete the text with one word in each gap. Then add commas for any of the non-defining relative clauses.

You and your ancestors

For every person on the planet, there are two people ¹_____ are their biological parents, four grandparents and eight great-grandparents. Above is a diagram ²_____ shows one person's ancestors for four generations. The top row ³_____ has 16 people shows your great-great-grandparents. It's interesting to think of all the different places ⁴_____ they lived and the people ⁵_____ they married. If you go back 200 years in time to the 19th century, you'll probably find as many as 128 ancestors! So a stranger ⁶_____ you pass in the street could be your long-lost cousin!

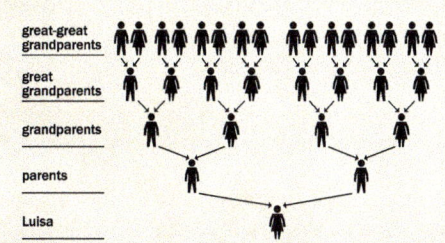

Exercise 4
1 who
2 which/that
3 which (commas: …, which has 16 people, …)
4 where
5 who/that
6 who/that

SPEAKING

5 Complete the dialogue with questions a–c.

A: Where's Will?
B: ¹_____
A: Oh, I've found him. He's holding a book.
B: ²_____
A: He's at the front.
B: ³_____
A: Yes, that's right.

a Is he the one who is wearing glasses?
b I don't know. Which one is Will?
c There are two people holding books. Which one do you mean?

Exercise 5
1 b
2 c
3 a

DICTATION

6 🔊 **2.63 Listen, then listen again and write down what you hear.**

SELF-ASSESSMENT Think about this unit. What did you learn? What do you need help with?

WORKBOOK p. 86

Exercise 6

I'm from Mexico and my best friend is Italian. She's older than me, but we're neighbours, so we often hang out. I love Italian culture. They have big family celebrations with amazing food. It's great to have international friends!

CULTURE: Is moving house good for you?

Mobile homes in the USA

Some people say that moving house is the most stressful thing in the world. That's why Americans only move home once a decade on average. However, some people are on the move the whole time!

In the USA there are 8.5 million mobile homes. In South Carolina almost twenty percent of all homes are mobile and many people live in trailer parks. These parks, which have a bit of an image problem in the country, are often home to poor or rootless people. But that is not always the case.

In states like Florida there are trailer parks full of retired couples. They often have a great community spirit. Mobile housing expert John O'Reilly explains why: 'People in these parks put up with a little discomfort to feel part of a group and have a sense of identity. The atmosphere is great, people hang out with each other and get on really well. They're like one big happy family.'

Some people stay in the same trailer park for years, but others travel around. For Michael Branston, who has just bought a new trailer with his family in Alabama, choosing a mobile home was all about freedom. 'Even if I could, I wouldn't change my mobile home for a fixed one. Trailer parks are usually quiet, clean and safe and there are no parking problems! We would rather buy our own mobile home than rent an apartment in the city. At least you have a place you can call your own and you're free to move when and where you like. Moving house is great because you see many places and it broadens your horizons. Go ahead and try it!'

GLOSSARY
discomfort (n) a feeling of being uncomfortable
expert (n) someone with special knowledge
retired (adj) a retired person doesn't work because they are old
rootless (adj) often moving from place to place
trailer park (n) caravan park; a place where caravans (trailers) are parked and used as people's homes

BBC CULTURE   Is moving house good for you?

Lead in: Topic introduction

Tell students not to open their Students' Books. Put students into groups of four. If you set the homework suggestion for the unit, ask the groups to discuss any vocabulary they found difficult and their example sentences if you also set the additional task.

If students haven't done the homework, ask them to look at the glossary on page 92. Students should find the words in the text and discuss what they mean in context, e.g. *I think I would feel **rootless** if I moved house every couple of years.*

7.5

On the move

It is winter. We are far above the Arctic Circle and this is a typical Dolgan village. It is home to just two extended families. These people, who are originally from central Asia, came here during the eighteenth century to look after reindeer. Here, in the coldest part of the Arctic, life is very hard. The only way to get water for nine months of the year is to melt ice from the frozen rivers.

Outside it is absolutely freezing, with temperatures in the winter as low as −40°C. Survival is only possible because of reindeer fur, which makes very warm clothing. This warm clothing is especially important for the children. But the Dolgan even use reindeer fur to insulate their huts as well.

Community is very important to the Dolgan people. Everybody helps each other. Good relationships are essential here, so they all get on well. Reindeer are so valuable that the people only eat them if they have to. Their favourite food is raw fish from the frozen rivers.

Every week or so, these families get ready to travel once more. They must find new grounds for their herds. If they didn't move, the reindeer would die because of the lack of food. First, they round up their strongest animals with lassos. This is a skill which their ancestors brought with them from central Asia. Then, literally, they move house. There is a lot to carry, but a whole Dolgan village can be taken down and moved in just a few hours. Over a year, these nomadic people travel hundreds of miles like this across the vast frozen tundra.

The first Dolgan people came to the Arctic a long time ago because of the large number of reindeer all over this area. Their ancestors still follow the same lifestyle today. Here man and reindeer live in perfect harmony. Moving is not just good for them – they could not live in any other way.

Exercise 1

Ask students the first question and, if possible, put students into pairs in which at least one student has moved house, so that they can share their experiences. When students have discussed the questions in pairs, ask those who have moved house in their lives to describe what happened, how they felt about leaving their house and what they liked and didn't like about their new house.

Exercise 2

Keep students in pairs. Encourage them to read the sentences before they read the text and to share their ideas in pairs. When the pairs have done the exercise, elicit the answers and the corrected sentences or the specific extracts from the text which show that sentences are true. Ask students if they have ever seen any films or TV shows in which people lived in mobile homes in trailer parks. Ask them to describe what the people were like.

Answers:
1 T (*have a bit of an image problem*)
2 F (*… are often home to poor or rootless people. But that is not always the case.*)
3 F (*Some people like living in mobile homes in Florida because they feel part of a group.*)
4 T (*others travel around*)
5 F (*According to the article, trailer parks are usually quiet, clean and safe.*)

Exercise 3

Tell students to look in the text for references to the advantages and the disadvantages of living in trailer parks or moving house. Tell them to list all of these in their notebooks and to find out whether, overall, the text mentions more positive things or more negative things.

Positive answers:
1 positive – In paragraph 2 the writer mentions some problems but all the information in paragraphs 3 and 4 is positive.
2 The only mention of moving house is in the first paragraph where it states that it is stressful. In the last paragraph, the person talking about moving house is talking about moving with his (mobile) home, not changing one house for another.

Exercise 4 ▶ 7.5

Check that students understand the meaning of *lasso* (n/v), *reindeer*, *sack* and *raw*. Before you play the video, encourage students to read the sentences so that they know which actions they should look out for. If you think students may need help, pause the video after each action and ask what the people are doing.

Answers: h 2   f 3   g 4   b 5   i 6   a 7   c 8   e 9

Exercise 5

When students have discussed the answers in pairs, elicit some of their ideas and write them on the board. Explain that when they watch the video with the sound switched on, they can see which guesses were closest.

Exercise 6

Tell students the name of the tribe, the Dolgan, and where they came from originally, i.e. Central Asia.

Answers:
1 Far above the Arctic Circle (actually in Russia although it isn't stated).
2 Difficult – very cold temperatures, no water (except for ice) for much of the year.
3 To find new food for the reindeer to eat.
4 It takes a few hours to take down the houses and move.

Exercise 7

Where students' guesses were different to the actual facts of what was shown in the video, encourage students to explain why they guessed their ideas.

Exercise 8 ▶ 7.5

Put students into pairs. Before you play the video again, encourage students to read the sentences and discuss with their partner anything they can remember from the video.

Answers: 1 two   2 winter   3 for clothes and their homes
4 raw fish   5 hundreds   6 reindeer

> **Background notes**
>
> The word *nomad* originates from the Greek *nomas*, meaning someone who moves from place to place to search for food. Some nomads are hunter-gatherer nomads, who move as the animals they hunt move or who move when different fruits are in season. Pastoral nomads keep their own animals and move to find food for them at different times of the year. Some famous nomadic people are the Bedouins of the Middle East, the Sami of Finland, the Navajo Native Americans and the Mongols of East Central Asia and the Berbers of North Africa.

Exercise 9

Put students into pairs to discuss the questions. Then invite students to talk about the best and worst things about Dolgan life and what they would miss most about their life now if they went to live with a Dolgan family.

Extra activity

Keep students in pairs. Tell the pairs to imagine that one of them has just come back from staying with a Dolgan family for a month and the other is a TV presenter who is interviewing them. They should work together to develop some questions and answers for their interview. When the pairs are ready, invite them to act out their interview in front of the class.

Exercise 10

Put students into groups of four and write on the board a list of nomadic tribes. Each group should choose a different tribe to research and write about. Discuss some ideas for the content of the presentations, e.g. where their nomadic tribe lives, what they eat, what their homes look like, why they travel, which animals they keep. While the groups give their presentations, tell the rest of the class to make notes, to encourage them to listen more carefully.

Further practice

- Workbook pages 88–89
- Resource Pack
  Resource 90: Unit 7 BBC Culture Lesson – I love my mobile home
  Resource 91: Unit 7 Culture – The Dolgans

EXPLORE

1 How would you feel if you had to move house?

2 Read the article. Mark the sentences T (true) or F (false). Correct the false sentences.
1. ☐ Trailer parks have a negative image in the USA.
2. ☐ Trailer parks are always home to poor people or people without families.
3. ☐ Some people like living in mobile homes in Florida because they want to live alone.
4. ☐ Some people prefer to live in mobile homes because they don't like to stay in one place.
5. ☐ According to the article, trailer parks are often dangerous places to live.

3 Read the article again. Answer the questions. Give reasons for your answers.
1. Does the article present mobile homes in a positive or negative way?
2. Does the article present moving house in the same way?

EXPLORE MORE

4 ▶ 7.5 Watch with no sound. Order the actions as they appear in the video.
- a ☐ a family eating together
- b ☐ a child standing in a big coat
- c ☐ a man throwing a rope over a reindeer
- d ☐ *1* white dogs sitting in the snow
- e ☐ people moving house with reindeer
- f ☐ a man cutting ice with a knife
- g ☐ a man putting frozen fish in a sack
- h ☐ people collecting wood
- i ☐ a man cutting raw fish

5 In pairs, ask and answer the questions.
1. Where do you think these people live?
2. Is it an easy or a difficult life? Why?
3. Why do you think they move house?
4. How long do you think they take to move house?

6 ▶ 7.5 Watch with sound. Check your answers to Exercise 5.

7 Were you surprised by the answers? Discuss in pairs.

8 ▶ 7.5 Watch again. Choose the correct option.
1. The village in the video is home to *two / a few* extended families.
2. Temperatures in the *autumn / winter* are as low as -40ºC.
3. The Dolgan people use reindeer fur *only for clothes / for clothes and their homes*.
4. Their favourite food is *raw fish / reindeer meat*.
5. Over a year, the Dolgan people travel *hundreds / thousands* of miles.
6. The Dolgan people first came to the Arctic because of the *fishing / reindeer*.

9 Would you like to live like the Dolgan people in the Arctic? Why? / Why not? Do you know of any other kinds of nomadic people in the world?

YOU EXPLORE

10 **CULTURE PROJECT** In groups, prepare a presentation about nomadic people.
1. Use the internet or other sources to research nomadic people in the world.
2. Write a short script and think about images or videos to use in your presentation.
3. Give your presentation to the class.
4. Report back: what did you learn from the other presentations?

Unit 7 93

8

No time for crime

VOCABULARY
Criminals | The law
Action verbs | Solving crimes

GRAMMAR
Present Simple Passive and Past Simple Passive | *have/get something done* |
Negative prefixes for adjectives

Grammar: Murder in the dark

Speaking: Dress rehearsal

BBC Culture: A famous robbery

Workbook p. 100

 BBC VOX POPS ▶

8.1 VOCABULARY Crime

I can talk about crime and criminals.

1 🔊 **3.01** Find the criminals in the picture. Use the words in the Vocabulary A box to complete the sentences. Listen and check.

Vocabulary A	Criminals
burglar pickpocket robber shoplifter ~~thief~~ vandal	

1 The *thief* is wearing a black hat.
2 The _____ is holding a necklace.
3 The _____ are wearing earphones.
4 The _____ is very hot.
5 The _____ can't get out of the window.
6 The _____ is chatting on her mobile.

2 **WORD FRIENDS** Complete the sentences with the verbs below.

breaks into ~~commits~~ damages robs steals

1 A criminal is someone who *commits* a crime.
2 A shoplifter is someone who _____ things from a shop.
3 A bank robber is someone who _____ a bank.
4 A burglar is someone who _____ flats or houses.
5 A vandal is someone who _____ buildings or other things in public places.

3 🔊 **3.02** **WORD BUILDING** Use a dictionary to complete the table with the names of the crimes. Listen and check.

Person	Crime
(bank) robber	1 *(bank) robbery*
burglar	2 _____
pickpocket	3 _____
shoplifter	4 _____
thief	5 _____
vandal	6 _____

Unit contents

Vocabulary
- Criminals
- The law
- Action verbs
- Solving crimes

Grammar
- Present Simple Passive and Past Simple Passive
- *have/get something done*
- Negative prefixes for adjectives

Communication skills
- Persuading and reassuring

Examples of 21st Century Skills/Competencies
- Critical Thinking: page 101 (Exercise 2), pages 104–105
- Collaboration: page 95 (Exercise 13), page 98 (Exercise 5), page 99 (Exercise 7), page 100 (Exercise 5), page 101 (Exercise 4), page 105 (Exercise 10)
- Digital Literacy: page 105 (Exercise 10)
- Assessment for Learning: page 103
- Autonomy and Personal Initiative: page 96 (Exercise 7), page 97 (Exercise 6), page 98 (Exercise 5)

8.1 VOCABULARY Crime

Lesson learning objective
Students can talk about crime and criminals.

Lead in: Review of vocabulary from the previous unit

Put students into groups of four. Explain that you are going to say a word from the previous unit backwards and students should try to guess the word. As soon as they think they know the answer, they should raise their hands. If they are correct, give their group a point. If they or any other group can say the correct meaning, give another point. Start off with an example: *regnarts = stranger*. Say the word several times while students try to guess.
Suggested words: *detpoda* (adopted), *edirb* (bride), *puorg* (group), *setam* (mates), *detaler* (related), *evitaler* (relative), *desserts* (stressed).

Exercise 1 🔊 3.01
Before students look at the Vocabulary box, ask them to find the six criminals in the picture and to describe what each criminal is doing (*one is climbing out of a window above the bank, one is running along the street with a sack on his back, one is stealing something from a woman's back pocket, one is kicking a litter bin, one is running away with a woman's handbag, one is in a shop stealing jewellery*).
When students have completed the exercise, discuss the differences between the vocabulary words: a *thief* (someone who openly steals from people); a *burglar* (someone who steals specifically from people's houses); a *robber* (someone who steals from banks, trains, etc.); a *shoplifter* (someone who steals from shops while pretending to be a customer); a *pickpocket* (someone who steals from people's pockets while they aren't looking).

Answers: 2 shoplifter 3 vandals 4 burglar 5 robber 6 pickpocket

Exercise 2
Again, check that students understand the differences in meaning between the words in the box: *break into* focuses on the act of illegally entering somewhere, e.g. a bank or a home, in order to commit a crime; *rob* and *steal* focus on the crime itself. *Rob* collocates with the place in which the crime takes place, e.g. *rob a bank, rob a post office*, and *steal* collocates with the items taken during the crime, e.g. *steal money, steal jewels*. It may also be worth giving students the word friend *break out of* and asking if they can guess where a criminal may break out of (*prison*) and elicit the meaning (*escape from prison*).

Answers: 2 steals 3 robs 4 breaks into 5 damages

Exercise 3 🔊 3.02
When students have completed the table, elicit the corresponding verb for each: i.e.
robber, robbery, to rob
burglar, burglary, to burgle
pickpocket, pickpocketing, to pick someone's pocket. The verb *to pickpocket* is rarely used alone – it can be used with an article or an amount, e.g. *to pick a pocket, to pick several pockets*) or, most often, it can be used with a direct object, e.g. *to pick someone's / people's / shoppers' pockets*.
shoplifter, shoplifting, to shoplift
thief, theft, to steal. There is a verb *to thieve*, but it is less common than *to steal*.
vandal, vandalism, to vandalise
Encourage students to make a written record in their notebooks.

Answers: 2 burglary 3 pickpocketing 4 shoplifting 5 theft 6 vandalism

Exercise 4 🔊 3.03

When students have listened to the audio, elicit the answers and ask questions about specific detail: where the robbery took place (*at the city bank*); what things the vandals damage (*the seats and bins in the local park*); what the shoplifter stole (*jewellery*).

Answers: robbery, robbers, vandals, shoplifter

🔊 **3.03**

I live in a big city and I sometimes hear about crime on the news. Once there was a robbery at the city bank and it was quite dramatic. Helicopters flew over the city and the police caught the robbers quite quickly.

My dad says there are more vandals now and they damage the seats and bins in the local park, but I don't think it really happens that often. My friends and I use the park and it's a nice place to go.

The only criminal I've really seen is a shoplifter. Once I was in a shop in the city centre when a shop assistant chased a girl into the street. She was carrying a bag of jewellery. I don't know what happened to her.

Exercise 5

When the pairs have discussed crimes they have heard or read about, invite them to share their ideas with the class. Have a class discussion about whether or not students think vandalism is a big problem in their town or if there are any areas of town which may be dangerous to go to.

Exercise 6 🔊 3.04

When students have looked up the words in the Vocabulary box and completed the exercise, elicit the meaning of each word. Then put students into pairs and ask them to write their own sentences showing the meaning of each word. Explain that each sentence can contain more than one of the words, e.g. *The **burglar** had to go to court to see what punishment the **judge** would give him.*

Answers: **2** prison   **3** Judge   **4** fine   **5** lawyer

Exercise 7 🔊 3.05

Discuss the meaning of the words in the Vocabulary box with the class. Then tell them to do the matching exercise either on their own or in pairs. Ask students for their ideas of how the words could be used to talk about crimes. For example: *The police **chased** the burglar. The burglar **climbed** into the house through the open bedroom window. The vandals **pushed** the bin over. The criminals **escaped** from prison. The robbers **pulled** the locked drawer until it opened. The burglar **jumped** out of the bedroom window when he heard the police cars arriving. The police caught the thief when he **fell** while he was running away. The woman **tripped** and a pickpocket stole her bag while he helped her get up.*

Answers: **1** chase   **2** escape   **3** pull   **4** trip   **5** climb   **6** jump   **7** fall   **8** push

Exercise 8

Discuss students' ideas about different actions that criminals might do, e.g. *run*, *hit*, *grab*. Then put students into groups of four and tell them to see if they can think of more ideas. Give them a time limit and then invite groups to share their ideas with the class. Write the words on the board and ask students to write the words in their notebooks.

Exercise 9

If students have already used the words in the Vocabulary C box to make sentences about crimes, as suggested in Exercise 7, now ask them to use the words to make different sentences, not related to crimes and similar to the example. When they are ready, invite pairs to share some of their sentences with the class.

Exercise 10 🔊 3.06

Play the first two sentences of the audio (up to … *chasing me*). Elicit which word from the Vocabulary C box students have heard (*chase*) and tell them to put a tick next to that word in the box. Explain that when they have listened to the complete story, all the words in the box should have a tick next to them except for one word.

Answer: *fall* is not in the story

🔊 **3.06**

It was night time and it was dark. I was in a huge house and somebody or something was chasing me. … I couldn't see anything. … I ran to the door, but it was stuck. I pushed it once … and again. … Finally, it opened … and I looked inside. Just a large, dark space. Something was on the floor, but I couldn't see what it was and then I tripped. … I knew I had to escape. Above me, there was a window. I started to climb up to it … but … then … someone or something was behind me.
'Let me go,' I said.
Suddenly something jumped on me, it was pulling my jacket. …

Exercise 11 🔊 3.06

Put students into pairs. Before you play the audio again, tell them to discuss what they can remember about the story. Explain that when they listen to the story once more, they should note down key words, e.g. *night*, *dark*, *huge house*, *chasing*.

After they have listened, they should compare with their partner what they have written down, retelling the story together and imagining what happens next. Then invite pairs to share their ideas with the rest of the class.

Exercise 12

When students have completed the texts, ask if they have read or heard about any other funny crime stories, e.g. *a burglar who fell asleep inside the house he was robbing* or *a robber who wrote a demand for money on the back of an envelope with his address on it*.

Answers: **2** were chasing   **3** tripped   **4** jumped   **5** pushed   **6** to escape   **7** pulled

Exercise 13

The ideas talked about in Exercise 12 should have given students some ideas for their funny crime stories. Give them a time limit for writing and then invite pairs to read their stories to the class, saying if they are true stories or stories they have imagined.

Further practice

- Workbook pages 90–91
- Resource Pack
  Resource 92: Unit 8 Lesson 1 Vocabulary – Mime, define, draw

4 🔊 **3.03** Look at Exercise 3 again and listen to a person talking about crime. Mark the crimes or criminals you hear.

5 In pairs, discuss which crimes you have heard or have read about where you live.

6 🔊 **3.04** Study the Vocabulary B box, using a dictionary. Choose the correct option.

Vocabulary B	The law
court fine judge law lawyer prison/jail punishment reward	

1 £500 *punishment* / *reward* for information on local vandals.
2 Thirty years in *prison* / *court* for diamond thieves.
3 *Judge* / *lawyer* decides young thief should work for the community.
4 Old man falls asleep in car park and gets a *fine* / *reward* of £50.
5 Ex-criminal goes back to school to study and become a *lawyer* / *court*!

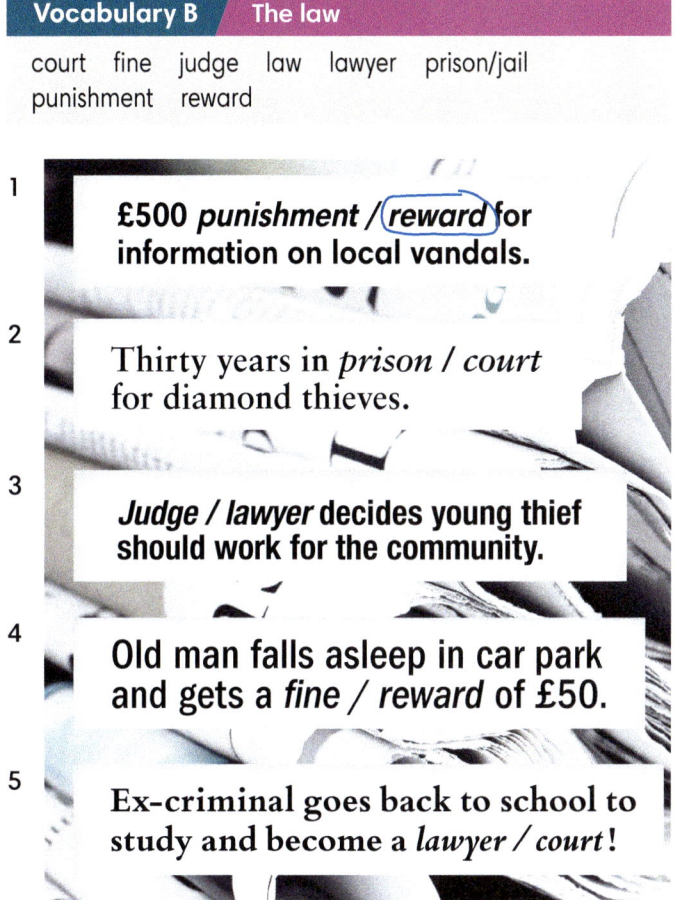

7 🔊 **3.05** Match the pictures with the words from the Vocabulary C box.

Vocabulary C	Action verbs
chase climb push escape pull jump fall trip	

8 **I KNOW!** Add more action verbs to the Vocabulary C box.

9 In pairs, make sentences with the words in the Vocabulary C box.

It's easy to trip when you can't see where you are walking.

10 🔊 **3.06** Listen to the story. Mark the words from the Vocabulary C box that you hear. Which word is NOT in the story?

11 🔊 **3.06** Listen again and make notes. In pairs, retell the story and discuss what you think happened at the end.

12 Complete the text with these words.

> jumped   were chasing   ~~fell~~   tripped
> to escape   pulled   pushed

Crazy crimes!

The thief without a belt
A vandal ¹*fell* and hurt his leg while police officers ² _____ him last night. The vandal told the police he ³ _____ because his new trousers were too big and fell down.

The hungry thief
A woman was walking with a fast-food meal when a thief ⁴ _____ out of a bush. He ⁵ _____ her to the ground and ran off with her burger.

A good phone connection
A shoplifter had a problem when he tried ⁶ _____ with an expensive mobile phone. He ⁷ _____ the mobile off the shelf, but didn't notice it had a security cable that was one metre long. He got to the door, then suddenly realised he couldn't go any further.

13 In pairs, choose three action verbs and write a funny crime story.

8.2 GRAMMAR — Present Simple Passive and Past Simple Passive

I can use verbs in the Passive.

Show what you know … The Sherlock Holmes Quiz

1. The Sherlock Holmes detective stories were written 100 years ago by
   a Arthur Conan Doyle.
   b Agatha Christie.
2. Holmes had a famous assistant. What was he called?
   a Doctor Who.
   b Doctor Watson.
3. The stories were first published
   a in a book.
   b in a magazine.
4. Sherlock's flat is located at number 221B of a famous London street, called
   a Sherlock Street.
   b Baker Street.
5. Which famous Sherlock Holmes quote is never really used by Sherlock Holmes?
   a 'Elementary, my dear Watson.'
   b 'My mind is like a racing engine.'

1 **CLASS VOTE** What do you know about Sherlock Holmes? In pairs, make a list.

2 🔊 3.07 In pairs, ask and answer the quiz questions. Listen and check.

3 Study the Grammar box. Find more examples of Present Simple Passive and Past Simple Passive in the quiz.

Grammar	Passive
Present Simple Passive Those words are not used.	
Past Simple Passive The detective stories were written by a British author.	

GRAMMAR TIME ▸ PAGE 125

4 Write the Past Simple and past participle form of the verbs below. Use the table on page 127 to help you.

> catch make see use watch
> ask hide chase

catch – caught – caught

5 Complete the sentences with the past participle form of the verbs in brackets.
1. CCTV cameras are *used* (use) to find clues about many crimes.
2. The thief was _____ (catch) because she talked about her crime on social media.
3. Yesterday evening two car thieves were _____ (chase) by police in fast cars.
4. Sometimes CCTV films are _____ (watch) by special detectives.
5. Last night the witnesses were _____ (ask) questions by police officers.
6. This camera is _____ (hid) so that the shoplifters don't know about it.

6 Complete the text with the passive form of the verbs in brackets. Add *by* where necessary.

> The Nancy Drew stories are among the most famous detective stories ever. The first stories about Nancy Drew ¹*were published in the 1930s* (publish/in the 1930s). Different series have appeared since that time. The books ² _____ (create/for teenagers). The Nancy Drew detective stories ³ _____ (write/several different authors). The name Carolyn Keene ⁴ _____ (use/all the authors) but Nancy's name ⁵ _____ (change) in some countries. It may be surprising, but this old series ⁶ _____ (read/thousands of young people) even today, and each year lots and lots of copies ⁷ _____ (sell).

7 Tell the class about a detective story/film you know.

8.2 GRAMMAR — Present Simple Passive and Past Simple Passive

Lesson learning objective
Students can use verbs in the Passive.

Lead in: Review of crime vocabulary

Put students into groups of four. Write *Crime in films* on the board. Ask each group to write a short summary of a film, but without giving the name of the characters. Each group reads their summary and other groups try to guess the title.

Exercise 1
Tell students to keep their Students' Books closed and put them into pairs. Write on the board *Sherlock Holmes* and ask them to make a list of anything they can think of that is related to Sherlock Holmes, for example: names (e.g. *Sir Arthur Conan Doyle*, *Benedict Cumberbatch*, *Dr Watson*); places; book titles and general words (e.g. *mystery*, *murder*). When the pairs have made their lists, put students into two groups. Students from each group should take turns to come to the board and write one of their words. If necessary, the other members of their group can help them with ideas, but each turn should allow a different student to have a chance to write on the board. If a student writes a word which doesn't have an obvious connection with Sherlock Holmes, ask them to explain why they have written the word. Continue until neither group can think of any more words to add.

Exercise 2 🔊 3.07
Students may have answered some of these questions already in Exercise 1. When students have listened to the audio, ask how many of the questions each pair got correct.

Answers: 1 a 2 b 3 b 4 b 5 a

Exercise 3
Before students look at the quiz and the Grammar box, write these two sentences on the board.
Somebody stole my watch.
The BBC often shows episodes of Sherlock.
Elicit the tense of each sentence (Past Simple, Present Simple) and rewrite them as:
My watch was stolen.
Episodes of Sherlock are often shown by the BBC.
Explain to students that the passive is formed by using the correct form the the verb *be* + the past participle of the main verb and that the object of the active sentence becomes the subject of the passive sentence.
Active: *He doesn't use these words.*
Passive: *These words are not used.*
Active: *A British author wrote the detective stories.*
Passive: *The detective stories were written by a British author.*
We can use *by* to say who performed an action if this is important.
Then ask students to look in the quiz to find examples of the Passive. Tell them to write the examples in their notebooks under the headings *Present Simple Passive* and *Past Simple Passive*.

Answers:
Present Simple Passive: is located, is never really used
Past Simple Passive: were written, were first published

Exercise 4
Remind students that when the Past Simple form is regular, the past participle is also regular, e.g. *watched*, *played*. Some other verbs are also the same in both forms, e.g. *caught*, *had*.

Answers: make – made – made; see – saw – seen; use – used – used; watch – watched – watched; ask – asked – asked; hide – hid – hidden; chase – chased – chased

Exercise 5
Remind students that the main verb in the passive is always in the past participle form.

Answers: 2 caught 3 chased 4 watched 5 asked 6 hidden

> **Culture notes**
> Nancy Drew is a fictional amateur detective. In the early versions of the series, Nancy is a sixteen-year-old high school student, but in later versions she is eighteen. In all the stories, Nancy lives in the fictional town of River Heights with her father, a lawyer and their housekeeper. Her mother died when Nancy was very young. She has many talents – she has studied psychology, can paint, speak French, dance and drive. She is good at shooting, rowing, cooking, playing tennis and golf, and can ride a horse 'like a cowboy'.

Exercise 6
Ask if anyone in the class has read any Nancy Drew stories or watched a Nancy Drew film. If they haven't, give them some background information. After students have completed the text, ask for students' opinions about keeping the same author's name on a series of books even though they are written by different authors.

Answers:
2 were created for teenagers
3 were written by several different authors
4 was used by all the authors
5 was changed
6 is read by thousands of young people
7 are sold

Exercise 7
Put students into groups of four and tell them to discuss fictional detectives. Invite each group to share their ideas with the class. Then tell students to work on their own. Explain that they should choose a fictional detective that they know something about. They should write notes about what they know, including their opinion about films or books that the detective appears in. When they are ready, invite students to share what they have written with the class.

Further practice
- Workbook page 92
- Grammar Time page 125
- Resource Pack
  Resource 93: Unit 8 Lesson 2 Grammar – Quiz time

8.3 READING and VOCABULARY   Who is Sherlock nowadays?

Lesson learning objective
Students can find specific detail in an article and talk about solving crimes.

Lead in: Review of passives

Write *the thief* on the board. Elicit passive sentences about the thief, e.g. *The thief was caught. The thief was sent to prison. The thief was punished. The thief was chased.* Then tell students to write these words in their notebooks:
the money, the bank, the house, the bus shelter, the person who helped catch the criminal, the driver who drove too fast
Put students into groups of four and tell them to make similar sentences about each of the items they have written in their notebooks.
When they have finished, invite the groups to take turns to say the ending of one of their sentences while the other groups try to guess which of the dictated items complete the sentence, e.g. *was fined – the driver who drove too fast*. The first group to guess correctly each time wins a point.

Exercise 1
Tell students to keep their Students' Books closed. Discuss the question with the class and, if they have watched more than one, e.g. the BBC series with Benedict Cumberbatch and the films with Robert Downey Jr, ask which they preferred and why.

Exercise 2
Tell students to read the introduction to the text in Exercise 3 and to try to guess the correct answer. Elicit students' ideas and their reasons.
After students have read the text, ask if they have changed their minds and, if they have, ask for their reasons. Some students may think the text is an article rather than a review, as it discusses the continuing popularity of the Sherlock Holmes stories and it doesn't give an opinion about how good the series is. Either answer (a TV review or an article) is acceptable as long as students can explain their reasons.

Answer: a TV review or an article

Exercise 3   3.08
When students have found the names of the people, ask what they have learned about each of them from reading the text, e.g. *Martin Freeman plays the part of Dr Watson. The character of Sherlock Holmes was based on Dr Bell. Arthur Conan Doyle went to medical school.*

Answers:
an actor: Benedict Cumberbatch / Martin Freeman
a medical school teacher: Dr Bell
a detective: Sherlock Holmes
a writer: Conan Doyle
a friend: Dr John Watson

Culture notes
Martin Freeman is an English actor who first became famous in the TV series *The Office*. Since then, he has appeared in many films and TV series and is best known for playing the main character, Bilbo Baggins, in the film *The Hobbit* and Lester Nygaard in the American TV series, *Fargo*.

Exercise 4
As students do the exercise, tell them to note down where in the text they found the information, so that they can refer to this when you elicit the answers.

Answers:
1 c (Paragraph 2 – Sherlock can get information online, check CCTV cameras)
2 d (Paragraph 4 – Dr Bell looked at his patients and told them things about their lives, just like Sherlock Homes does)
3 b (Paragraph 3 – playing Sherlock is 'a form of mental and physical gymnastics' and Paragraph 4 – viewers like to try to think as quickly as Sherlock.)
4 a

Exercise 5   3.09
When students have finished the exercise, ask questions about the words in the Vocabulary box, to make sure they understand the words correctly. For example, *Are all suspects criminals?* (No, suspects are people the police think may be criminals, but sometimes the police are wrong.)

Answers: 2 fingerprints   3 case   4 witness

Extra activity
Put students into pairs and give each pair a dictionary. Tell them to look up the words in the Vocabulary box that were not used in Exercise 5 (i.e. *CCTV camera, clue, detective, magnifying glass*). They should use the words in their own sentences to show the meaning of the words. When they have finished, invite pairs to share their sentences with the class.

Exercise 6
Discuss each of the phrases with the class. Ask: *If someone woke up late today, which clues could you spot?* (e.g. they aren't dressed properly, they are hungry because they missed breakfast, they are out of breath from running to school).
Then write on the board: *M T W T F S* and ask students to put their hands up when they have guessed the next letter in the sequence (*S* – these are the first letters of the days of the week).
Ask who in the class is good at noticing small details about things. Invite a few students to leave the classroom (or to cover their eyes) while you change the position of something or someone in the classroom. When the students come back (or uncover their eyes), tell them to guess what has changed. Then ask the pairs to discuss the questions and, when they are ready, invite them to share their ideas with the class.

Further practice
- Workbook page 93
- Resource Pack
  Resource 94: Unit 8 Lesson 3 Reading and Vocabulary – Can you work it out?

8.3 READING and VOCABULARY   Who is Sherlock nowadays?

I can find specific detail in an article and talk about solving crimes.

1 **CLASS VOTE** Have you watched any Sherlock Holmes films?

2 Look at the text. What is it?

   a story?   a TV review?   an article?

3 🔊 3.08 Read the text. Match the words below with the people in the text.

   an actor   a medical school teacher
   a detective   a writer   a friend

Who is Sherlock nowadays?

The BBC series, Sherlock, starring Benedict Cumberbatch, has been a big hit. There have been over 250 films about the famous detective, so what's different about the new series?

Many Sherlock Holmes films, like the original stories, are set in the shadows of Victorian London. In those days, the best technology was a magnifying glass to look for fingerprints. However, the BBC series is set in the 21st century, and this adds a fresh perspective and helps to create some clever twists in the plot of each story.

In this modern version, Sherlock has a mobile and a website. He can get information about suspects and witnesses online. He can even check CCTV cameras to look for extra clues, so his job has become very different. His friend Dr John Watson, who is played by Martin Freeman, still helps him. In fact, Watson writes a blog about each of Sherlock's cases, and you can find these online!

Isn't it strange that Sherlock is over 100 years old but he is still popular? Cumberbatch explains that playing Sherlock is 'a form of mental and physical gymnastics'. His character was based on Conan Doyle's teacher at medical school. The teacher, Dr Bell, was very clever and noticed little things. He often looked at his patients and told them about their activities and their illnesses before they even spoke to him! Similarly, Sherlock Holmes solves crimes with the power of his intelligence. What may explain the popularity of the stories today is that it is a chance to find out if you can think as quickly as Sherlock!

4 Read the text again. Choose the correct answer.

1 What has changed for Sherlock in the 21st century?
   a He can do lots of different jobs.
   b He doesn't use a magnifying glass anymore.
   c He has new ways of solving crimes.
   d He's no longer friends with Dr Watson.
2 How did Dr Bell inspire Conan Doyle?
   a He didn't speak to his patients.
   b He wrote lots of notes about his patients.
   c He talked to his patients kindly.
   d He solved problems by finding clues.
3 Why is Sherlock still popular?
   a Because he's been around a long time.
   b Because his character is fascinating.
   c Because he's famous.
   d Because he looks great on screen.
4 What is the writer's main aim in the text?
   a To explain why Holmes is still popular.
   b To describe the old films about Holmes.
   c To tell readers how Conan Doyle wrote these stories.
   d To describe the personality of a detective.

5 🔊 3.09 Complete the sentences with words from the Vocabulary box. Listen and check.

Vocabulary	Solving crimes

case   CCTV camera   clue   detective
fingerprints   magnifying glass   ~~suspect~~   witness

1 The police caught the *suspect* because he put photos on the internet.
2 The burglar didn't wear gloves, so she left _____ on the window.
3 The detectives are working on a very difficult _____.
4 My mum saw a pickpocket, so police asked her to be a _____.

6 Which of these skills are you good at? Would you like to be a detective? In pairs, discuss the ideas below.

   spotting clues   thinking quickly
   noticing little things   using technology

8.4 GRAMMAR *have/get something done*

I can use the construction *have/get something done*.

VIDEO MURDER IN THE DARK

Alisha: *Murder in the Dark* … that's a great poster for the play, Tommo. Did you design it?

Tommo: Yes, but I want to have some photos taken for it.

Alisha: I've got a good camera. I'll take the photos and you can have the posters printed later.

Tommo: OK, that's sorted!

Alisha: What's happening with the costumes?

Tommo: They're here, look! This is for me … and this is for you …

Alisha: You're joking! I am not wearing this wig. What about Dan?

Tommo: He's going to have a jacket made by his aunt. I gave him my dad's old coat … but he didn't like it. He's so fussy! He wants to have his hair styled today so that he looks like a real detective. He's taking it very seriously. The play should be called *Detective Dan*, not *Murder in the Dark*!

Alisha: Mmhh … What about the furniture?

Tommo: Dad's made these for us. I had them painted this morning.

Alisha: Wow, they're great!

Tommo: Watch out! The paint's still wet!

OK, that's sorted!   Watch out!   **OUT of class**

---

1 Discuss in groups. What plays or dramas are shown in your school? Who organises them?

2  8.1 3.10 Study the Grammar box. Watch or listen. Find more examples of *have/get something done* in the dialogue.

Grammar	*have/get something done*

She wants to **have some photos taken** today.
She **has her hair cut** at Angelo's.
We **had the costumes made** for us.
You can **have the poster printed** in town.
I'm going to **have my face painted** for the play.
In spoken English, *get something done* is more common.

GRAMMAR TIME > PAGE 125

3 Match phrases 1–6 with phrases a–f to make sentences.

1. ☐ I'm not happy with my hair. I …
2. ☐ When I do English exercises. I always …
3. ☐ Your coat's dirty. You must …
4. ☐ I love that photo. I should …
5. ☐ I can't see what's written on the board. I'm going to …
6. ☐ If I buy the present here, I can …

a. have it printed for my room.
b. have my eyes tested.
c. have it cleaned.
d. have it wrapped.
e. had it cut at the weekend.
f. have them checked by the teacher.

4 Complete the sentences with the correct form of *have* and the verbs in brackets.

1. The burglar made a mess in the house, but we're going to <u>have</u> it <u>cleaned</u> (clean).
2. We need to catch the robber. Let's _____ some posters _____ (print) with his photo on.
3. The detective always _____ a coffee _____ (bring) to him when he arrives at work.
4. That girl chased the criminal and then she _____ her photo _____ (take) for the newspaper.
5. I never leave my bike without a lock. I don't want to _____ it _____ (steal).
6. He writes great crime stories. He should _____ them _____ (make) into films.

5 In pairs, say if the sentences are true for you. Correct the false sentences.

1. I have my bedroom cleaned at the weekend.
2. I have my lunch made every day.
3. I never have my hair coloured.
4. I want to have my nose pierced.
5. We sometimes have pizza delivered to our house.

No, I don't have my bedroom cleaned at the weekend. I clean it myself on Saturday!

8.4 GRAMMAR *have/get* something done

Lesson learning objective
Students can use the construction *have/get something done*.

Lead in: Preview of *have/get something done*
Write these phrases on the board.
paint my room, fix my bike, install new programs on my computer, check my teeth, cut my hair, do my homework, make my clothes, cut my nails
Tell students to copy the phrases into their notebooks and then to tick the activities they do themselves and to put a cross next to the activities someone else does for them. Put students into pairs and tell them to compare their responses. Then have a class discussion to find out who does the most and least things themselves.

Exercise 1
Tell students to keep their Students' Books closed. Put students into groups of three. Ask the questions and tell the groups to discuss them. When they have finished, ask if anyone in the class has ever appeared in a school play. If they have, ask them to provide some details about their experience, e.g. to describe the play, the character they played, how they felt when they were on stage.

Exercise 2   8.1   3.10
Ask students to describe what they can see in the photo. After you have played the video, ask students which items Tommo and Alisha have got for the play (*a poster, costumes, furniture*).
Discuss once more students' experiences of school plays and ask them about costumes they wore, the furniture and other props which were used and where and how the play was advertised.
Then tell students to look at the Grammar box. Elicit the form for *have something done*.
- Correct form of *to have* + a thing (or place, person, body part, object) + the past participle.
- Point out that we use *to get* in informal spoken English. Elicit its use (*to organise someone else to do something for you*).
When students have found the examples in the text, ask how these could be rewritten, avoiding the structure *have/get something done*, e.g. *I want to have some photos taken = I want to ask someone to take some photos.*

Answers: have some photos taken, have the posters printed, have a jacket made, have his hair styled, had them painted

Exercise 3
Check that students understand the meaning of the phrase *to wrap a present*.
When students have completed the matching exercise, ask questions to give students the opportunity to relate the ideas in the sentences to their own experiences.
For example: *Have you ever been unhappy after a haircut? Do you always ask your teacher to check your English exercises? Do you ever have presents wrapped in the shop or do you always wrap your presents yourself? Have you ever had your eyes tested?*

Answers: 1 e   2 f   3 c   4 a   5 b   6 d

Exercise 4
Tell students that for each of the sentences they should think carefully about the form of the verb *to have*. When they have finished, ask which sentence has a different usage of *have something done* (sentence 5). Explain that this usage is a less common and informal way of talking about crimes that happened, e.g. *I had my car stolen.* Point out to students that they should be careful about using this, as it may sound as if they have organised the crime, e.g. *I had my house broken into. Why? Were you trying to get money from your insurance company?*

Answers: 2 have, printed   3 has, brought   4 had, taken   5 have, stolen   6 have, made

Extra activity
Tell students to look once more at the sentences they ticked and crossed in the lead in activity. Elicit that if they put a tick next to a phrase, they wouldn't use *have/get something done* when talking about it and if they put a cross next to a phrase, they would use *have/get something done* when talking about it.
Ask students to write a true sentence for each of the eight phrases, e.g. *I do my homework. I have my bedroom painted. I have my eyes tested. I install new programs on my computer.* When they have finished, invite students to tell the class about the things they do and the things they have done.

Exercise 5
Discuss the sentences with the class. Point out that *have something done* usually means that we arrange for someone to do something for us. It would sound strange to use the first two sentences if we were talking about our parents because it would sound as if we were telling them what to do and when to do it. We could say: *I clean my bedroom. My parents clean my bedroom. I have my bedroom cleaned (by a cleaner who comes to our house).*
When the pairs have finished, invite them to tell the class about the sentences which are true for them, saying how they changed the other sentences to make them true.

Further practice
- Workbook page 94
- Grammar Time page 125
- Resource Pack
  Resource 95: Unit 8 Lesson 4 Grammar – She's having her hair cut
  Resource 96: Unit 8 Lesson 4 Video – Murder in the dark

8.5 LISTENING and VOCABULARY A burglary

Lesson learning objective
Students can identify the main points of a monologue and talk about discovering a crime.

Lead in: Review of *have/get something done*

Tell students to think of a problem that someone needs to fix for them, e.g. *I can't see the board very well. My phone won't connect to the internet*. When everyone has thought of a problem, remind them about how to give advice or make suggestions, e.g. *You should …, Why don't you …?, If I were you, I would …* . Then encourage students to mingle with their classmates, to find different partners to speak with. They should take turns to say their problem and to give advice using *have/get something done*, e.g. *I can't see the board very well. – If I were you, I would have your eyes tested*.

Exercise 1
Tell students to keep their Students' Books closed. Ask the question and elicit students' ideas. Give one positive example and one negative example: *1 The police can put details of crimes on Twitter and ask if people can provide any information about them. 2 Members of the public sometimes post wrong or misleading information online and the police might waste time investigating it.*

Exercise 2 🔊 3.11
Put students into pairs and tell them to discuss the two pictures. Elicit some ideas about what students think is happening in the pictures. Then play the audio and elicit what the story is really about. Ask students to guess how social media helped to find the criminals.

Answers: The people in the pictures went out and came back later to find their door open.

🔊 3.11
See page 249.

Exercise 3 🔊 3.12
Before you play the audio, encourage students to read the sentences and to try to guess a logical order for the events.

Answers: A 7 B 2 C 1 D 5 E 4 F 3 G 6

🔊 3.12
See page 249.

Exercise 4 🔊 3.12
After students have completed the exercise, put them into pairs and ask them to answer these two questions in their own words: *1 What happened while Katrina and her mother were out? 2 How did Katrina and her friend use social media to help find the criminals?*

Answers:
1 The family was burgled while Katrina and her mother were out.
2 They used social media to find out if anyone was selling the items that were stolen.

Exercise 5
After students have completed the exercise, discuss the meaning of each phrase and elicit other useful word friends, e.g. *find clues, leave fingerprints*.

Answers: 2 interview a witness 3 arrest a criminal
4 searching the area 5 take fingerprints 6 looking for clues

Extra activity
Dictate these sentences and ask students to rewrite the sentences on a piece of paper in the Past Simple Passive. Students swap their answers to check and award one point for each correct sentence.
1 The police arrested the criminal.
2 The police interviewed the witness.
3 The police found some clues.
4 The police searched the area.
Answers:
1 The criminal was arrested by the police.
2 The witness was interviewed by the police.
3 Some clues were found by the police.
4 The area was searched by the police.

Exercise 6 🔊 3.13
For each item, elicit what kind of information students need to listen out for (*two times of day, what the stolen items are, a phone number, an amount of money*).

Answers: 2 3 p.m., 5 p.m.
3 digital camera (Nikon D61-0) and laptop (HP Omen)
4 07836 198477 5 20/twenty

🔊 3.13
See page 249.

Exercise 7
Before students do the exercise, discuss which structure they will use to ask and answer these questions, giving reasons why (*the Second Conditional, because the situations are unlikely*). Elicit the full question for each of the situations, e.g. *What would you do if you had your mobile phone stolen in town?*, and the full answer, *If I had my mobile phone stolen in town, I would …* .

VOX POPS ▶ 8.2
Before watching, tell students that, for one of the questions, a speaker says they wouldn't do anything at all and, for another question, a speaker describes how they would feel. Ask students to guess which questions they think will provoke these responses. After watching, elicit the correct answers and how the speaker said she would feel (i.e. *upset*).

Further practice
- Workbook page 95
- Resource Pack
  Resource 97: Unit 8 Lesson 5 Listening and Vocabulary – Word friends

8.5 LISTENING and VOCABULARY A burglary

I can identify the main points of a monologue and talk about discovering a crime.

1 **CLASS VOTE** Can social media help the police to find criminals? Why? / Why not?

2 🔊 **3.11** Listen to the first part of the podcast and look at the pictures. What do you think happened?

3 🔊 **3.12** Listen to the second part of Katrina's story. Order the events.

- A ☐ The police went to the burglar's house.
- B ☐ Katrina discovered her laptop was missing.
- C ☐ 1 Katrina and her mum discover the burglary.
- D ☐ A friend told Katrina about a conversation in the park.
- E ☐ Katrina showed the smartwatch box to the police.
- F ☐ The police took fingerprints and photos.
- G ☐ Katrina and her friend started looking on social media.

4 🔊 **3.12** Listen again. Check your answers to Exercises 2 and 3.

5 **WORD FRIENDS** Study the phrases below, using a dictionary. Choose the correct option.

> arrest a criminal   interview a witness   look for clues
> search the area   solve a crime   take fingerprints

1. Detectives can *solve a crime* / *take fingerprints* more quickly when there's a good witness.
2. Police want to *interview a witness* / *arrest a criminal* who saw somebody go into the house.
3. We believe the police are going to *search the area* / *arrest a criminal* this evening, but they won't say who it is.
4. The crime took place near the forest, and police officers are *solving a crime* / *searching the area* now.
5. The police couldn't *take fingerprints* / *interview a witness* because the burglar was wearing gloves.
6. The detective is *arresting a criminal* / *looking for clues* at the crime scene, but she hasn't found anything yet.

6 🔊 **3.13** Listen to the final part of the podcast. Complete the notes with a word or phrase.

> Date of burglary: ¹ 2nd October
> Time of burglary: between
> ² _____ and _____
> Items stolen: ³ _____
> Call: ⁴ _____
> Reward: ⁵ £ _____

7 [VOX POPS ▶ 8.2]  In pairs, tell your partner what you would do in the situations below.

1. You have your mobile phone stolen in town.

   I'd call the phone company, then I would tell all my friends …
2. You see a person who is shoplifting.
3. Some people are vandalising a wall near your school.

Unit 8

8.6 SPEAKING — Persuading and reassuring

I can persuade and reassure someone.

VIDEO — DRESS REHEARSAL

Miss Jones:	Right, this is our first dress rehearsal for *Murder in the Dark*. We'll start with scene two, after the murder.
Alisha:	I'm so nervous. I can't remember my lines!
Miss Jones:	It's all right, Alisha. I know you can do it. Just take a deep breath.
Alisha:	OK, I'll try.
Miss Jones:	Great. Off you go. Skye, could you give me a hand, please?
Tommo:	Come on, Alisha! You'll be fine.
Lady Harrington (Alisha):	Oh, poor Sir Hugo! What happened? Was he killed by the fall?
Butler (Tommo):	Or … was he murdered?
Lady Harrington (Alisha):	Pardon, Jeeves?
Butler (Tommo):	Nothing, Lady Harrington. Don't worry. The police will be here soon …
Miss Jones:	Hello? Can I help you?
Stranger:	Excuse me, I'm here about the crime.
Miss Jones:	Oh dear! A crime? What happened?
Tommo:	Miss Jones, it's Dan!
Miss Jones:	Dan? Oh my goodness! I didn't recognise you!
Dan:	Do you like my costume? I had it made specially for the play!

OUT of class
Oh my goodness!
Can you give me a hand?
Off you go.

1 In pairs, look at the photo. What do you think is happening?

2 ▶ 8.3 🔊 3.14 Watch or listen and check your answer to Exercise 1. Who is at the door?

Speaking — Persuading and reassuring

Persuading
Come on.
Please!
Just try it. /
Why don't you try?

Responding
OK, I'll try.
I don't know.
I suppose I can do it.

Reassuring
Don't worry!   It's all right. / OK.
You'll/It'll be fine.
I know. / I'm sure. / Of course you can do it.
Just … practise a bit more / try again.

3 🔊 3.15 Study the Speaking box. Complete the dialogues with one word in each gap. Listen and check.

1   A: Could you come to a rock concert with me?
    B: I don't *know* … I'm not keen on rock concerts.
    A: Please! *The Wild Monsters* are playing.
    B: I _____ I can come, but I haven't got much money.
    A: Don't _____! I'll pay for your train fare.
2   A: I'm scared of water. I can't go in.
    B: Of _____ you can. I'll be with you.
    A: It's too cold.
    B: It's not cold, I promise. You'll be _____.
3   A: Let's go to the fish restaurant.
    B: I never eat fish.
    A: _____ on. _____ try it. It's really good.
4   A: I can't play this song.
    B: I'm _____ you can do it.
    A: But it's really difficult.
    B: Just _____ a bit more.

4 In pairs, role play one of the situations.
- Reassure a friend who's worried about his/her maths test.
- Persuade a friend to go to a party. (he hates parties)
- Reassure your friend that he can succeed in a kayaking competition.

Student A State your problem.
Student B Persuade your partner to do/try something.
Student A Give a reason why you're worried.
Student B Reassure your partner.

5 In pairs, talk about something you find difficult to do. Persuade each other that you can do it.

I can't write the English essay …

8.6 SPEAKING Persuading and reassuring

Lesson learning objective
Students can persuade and reassure someone.

Lead in: Review of crime vocabulary

Write *draprtnraielosnmtpoy* on the board.
Put students into groups of four. Explain that there is a crime word hidden in the letters and that the letters are in the correct order, but with other letters in between them. Also explain that the word means something that the police do to criminals. Tell students to put up their hands when they think they have guessed the word (*arrest*). The first group to guess the word correctly wins a point.
Do the same for these words.
midrnataefsrtuvaeiolefdnwstp (interview)
sawinbtmsnaloedcsatsep (witness)
dactilwedusaetf (clue)
dasurehkaioprdtcuklher (search)
frasiogtlndwvateyr (solve)
mcaeroniplmwsaet (crime)
afuilhnegetuirlpaeraimdnwdtaksol (fingerprints)

Exercise 1
Remind students about what happened in the last episode of the video (*Alisha and Tommo were talking about the school play and the things that were needed for it*).
After the pairs have discussed the photo, invite them to tell the class their ideas.

Exercise 2 8.3 3.14
Check that students understand the meaning of the following: *to rehearse / a rehearsal*, *to learn/remember lines* (in a play), *a deep breath*. Ask students how they think these words and phrases could relate to what they are going to watch in the video.
After you have played the video, ask students once more about how the words and phrases relate to the video (*It is the first rehearsal of the school play. Alisha can't remember her lines* and *the drama teacher advises Alisha to take a deep breath to make her feel calmer*).

Answer: Dan, dressed as a detective.

Exercise 3 3.15
Make sure that students understand the difference in meaning between *to persuade* and *to reassure*. Ask students to give examples of when they would try to persuade someone to do something and when they would try to reassure someone about something.
Elicit which character reassures Alisha (*Miss Jones*) and which character persuades Alisha to do something (*Tommo persuades her to start acting*).

Answers:
1 *know*, suppose, worry
2 course, fine
3 Come, Just
4 sure, practise

Extra activity
Put students into groups of three. One student should play the role of the drama teacher in the video. The other two students should play the roles of two actors saying the lines that Lady Harrington and the butler say in the video. Tell the students playing the roles of the actors to read the lines a few times and to try to remember them. The groups should then practise acting out their parts. If the actors forget their lines, the drama teacher (who can check the dialogue in the book) should tell them what to say and should reassure them that they can do it. When they are ready, invite groups to act out their role plays in front of the class.

Exercise 4
Discuss the first situation in the exercise with the class. Elicit what people in the situation could say, following the instructions, and write students' ideas on the board.
For example:
A: *I'm worried about my Maths test.*
B: *Why don't you ask Ben for help? He's good at Maths and great at explaining things.*
A: *I don't know. I don't think Ben likes me very much. He never talks to me.*
B: *Don't worry. I'm sure he'll be happy to help. He's just shy.*
Then ask the pairs to role play one of the other two situations and give them a time limit. If any pairs finish quickly, tell them to role play the other situation as well. When the pairs are finished, invite them to act out their role plays in front of the class.

Exercise 5
Discuss the task with the class and elicit ideas about things that they could find difficult to do, e.g. *giving a speech in front of the class, starting a blog, making new friends*. Write them on the board, so that students have some ideas to choose from, as well as their own ideas.
After the pairs have completed their discussions, encourage students to mingle with their classmates and to tell one another about the thing that they find difficult to do. Tell students that they should either try to reassure each other or they should try to persuade each other to give it a go or to try it out, giving advice when necessary.

Further practice
- Workbook page 96
- Resource Pack
  Resource 98: Unit 8 Lesson 6 Speaking – Don't worry!
  Resource 99: Unit 8 Lesson 6 Video – Dress rehearsal

8.7 ENGLISH IN USE Negative prefixes for adjectives

Lesson learning objective
Students can form and use negative adjectives.

Lead in: Review of adjectives

Put students into pairs. Give each pair an adjective written on a piece of paper. Explain that they should think of a short, two-line dialogue that would demonstrate this adjective.
Give an example for *excited*.
A: I've got tickets for the concert tonight.
B: Oh, wow! Brilliant! I can't wait!
Tell the pairs to work together to write a similar short, two-line dialogue.
When they are ready, invite each pair to act out their dialogue and encourage the other students to try to guess which adjective is being demonstrated.
Suggested adjectives: *happy, honest, patient, correct, logical, legal, responsible, comfortable, important, possible, interesting, friendly, polite*.

Exercise 1

When students have read the story, discuss each individual frame and ask what students think is happening.
(*1 The two detectives are following a set of footprints. One of them is complaining about his magnifying glass and his job.
2 The detective finds a clue – a can of spray paint.
3 The other detective says that the can of spray paint isn't a clue, it's just a piece of rubbish. The criminal hides from the detectives by pretending to be part of the graffiti.
4 The detectives walk past the criminal. They give up looking for clues and trying to solve the crime of who did the illegal graffiti.*)

Possible answers: The detectives are useless, not very clever and complain a lot. The criminal is clever.

Exercise 2

Check that students understand the meaning of *prefix*.
When students have completed the table in the exercise, put them into pairs. Tell them to choose from the table three negative adjectives, each with a different negative prefix and to write sentences to illustrate the adjectives, e.g. *The chairs in this classroom are really **uncomfortable**. Why is this sentence **incorrect**? I get **impatient** when I have to wait for friends for more than five minutes.* When they have finished, invite pairs to share their sentences with the class.

Answers:
un-: + fair = unfair; + interesting = uninteresting; + important = unimportant; + comfortable = uncomfortable; + usual = unusual
im-: + possible = impossible
in-: + visible = invisible
il-: + legal = illegal

Exercise 3

Make clear to students that while the rules in the exercise provide general guidelines, there can be exceptions to these rules. Explain that although there are several negative adjectives with *im* + /p/ (e.g. *impossible, impolite*), *ir* + /r/ (e.g. *irregular, irresponsible*) and *il* + /l/ (e.g. *illogical, illegal*), there are also adjectives starting with these sounds which use different prefixes (e.g. *unpopular, unreliable, unlucky*).

Answers: 1 *un-*, unfriendly 2 *im-*, impolite 3 *ir-*, irrelevant 4 *il-*, illegible

Exercise 4

Discuss the first sentence with the class and elicit ways they could finish it, e.g. *If I was invisible, I would watch films at the cinema without buying a ticket.*
When the pairs have discussed all the sentences, invite them to share their ideas with the class.

VOX POPS ▶ 8.4

While watching, tell students to choose the answer they like best for each question. After watching, invite students to share their ideas with the class, giving reasons for their preferences.

Extra activity

Remind students about the activity they did at the start of the lesson, with the short dialogues demonstrating different adjectives.
Write a new short dialogue on the board to illustrate the negative adjective *unexcited*.
A: I've got tickets for the concert tonight.
B: Oh. OK, I guess I'll come with you. They aren't my favourite band, but I haven't got anything else to do.
Tell students to write a new short dialogue that demonstrates the negative form of the adjective they used at the start of the lesson. When they are ready, invite the pairs to act out their short dialogues in front of the class and encourage the other students to try to guess which negative adjective is being demonstrated.

Homework

Tell students to read the text on page 104 of the Students' Book. They should look up any words they don't know the meaning of and translate them into L1.
As an additional task, ask students to write an example sentence illustrating the meaning of each these words: *attitude, busker, income, petty crime, vary*.

Further practice

- Workbook page 97
- Resource Pack
  Resource 100: Unit 8 Lesson 7 English in Use – Dominoes

8.7 ENGLISH IN USE Negative prefixes for adjectives

I can form and use negative adjectives.

1 Look at the cartoons. What do you find out about the character of the detectives and the 'criminal'?

Footprints … more footprints. I hate my magnifying glass. It's so old-fashioned. It's really unfair! The boss gives us all the uninteresting jobs.

We'll never find out who did all this illegal graffiti. Hey! Wait a minute, Dimwit! There's a can of spray paint. Is it a clue?

This is like being invisible.

Don't be stupid, Brains. It's just a piece of rubbish. Put it in the bin. It's obviously unimportant.

2 Study the information about prefixes. Find more examples of negative prefixes in the cartoons. Complete the table.

Phew! That was getting a bit uncomfortable.

Well, it's impossible to find any clues here. There's nothing unusual at all. Let's go home and write a report. Next time, I hope we get an interesting job.

Language — Negative prefixes for adjectives

We can use prefixes before an adjective to change its meaning. Prefixes with adjectives usually give the meaning 'not'.

negative prefix	+ adjective		= adjective with negative meaning	
un-	happy		unhappy	
dis-	honest	pleased	dishonest	displeased
im-	patient		impatient	
in-	correct		incorrect	
il-	logical		illogical	
ir-	responsible	regular	irresponsible	irregular

3 Use the table in Exercise 2 to complete the rules 1–4. Add the correct prefix to the words below and use as examples.

> friendly   legible   polite   relevant

1 The most common negative prefix is *un-*, e.g. _____ .
2 If the adjective begins with the sound /p/, we usually add _____ , e.g. _____ .
3 If the adjective begins with the sound /r/, we usually add _____ , e.g. _____ .
4 If the adjective begins with the sound /l/, we usually add _____ , e.g. _____ .

4 [VOX POPS ▶ 8.4] In pairs, finish the sentences to make them true for you.

1 If I was invisible, I would …
2 The most impossible thing I've ever done was …
3 One unusual place I'd like to see is …
4 If I saw someone doing something illegal, I would …
5 One really uninteresting film I've watched is …

Wordlist and Vocabulary in action

Extra activity

Put students into groups. Tell half the groups to work from the words in the first two columns of the wordlist and the other half to work from the words in the last two columns. They should look for three words which they think their classmates won't remember the meanings of. They should look up the definitions of the words and write down the words and the definitions. When they are ready, join two groups together who have worked from different columns of the wordlist. They should take turns to read out a definition and to try to guess the word.

Further practice

Workbook page 98

WORDLIST   Criminals | The law | Action verbs | Solving crimes

assistant /əˈsɪstənt/
(bank) robbery /ˈbæŋk ˌrɒbəri/
bin /bɪn/
brain /breɪn/
burglar /ˈbɜːɡlə/
burglary /ˈbɜːɡləri/
case /keɪs/
catch /kætʃ/
CCTV camera /ˌsiː siː tiː ˈviː ˌkæmərə/
chase /tʃeɪs/
climb /klaɪm/
clue /kluː/
correct /kəˈrekt/
court /kɔːt/
crime /kraɪm/
crime scene /ˈkraɪm siːn/
criminal /ˈkrɪmɪnl/
detective /dɪˈtektɪv/
diamond /ˈdaɪəmənd/
dishonest /dɪsˈɒnɪst/
displeased /dɪsˈpliːzd/
(dress) rehearsal /(ˈdres) rɪˌhɜːsl/
e-criminal /ˌiː ˈkrɪmɪnl/
escape /ɪˈskeɪp/
expected /ɪkˈspektɪd/
fair /feə/
fall /fɔːl/
fine /faɪn/
fingerprints /ˈfɪŋɡəˌprɪnts/
footprints /ˈfʊtprɪnts/

fussy /ˈfʌsi/
glove /ɡlʌv/
hide /haɪd/
honest /ˈɒnɪst/
illegal /ɪˈliːɡl/
illegible /ɪˈledʒəbl/
illness /ˈɪlnəs/
illogical /ɪˈlɒdʒɪkl/
impatient /ɪmˈpeɪʃənt/
impolite /ˌɪmpəˈlaɪt/
impossible /ɪmˈpɒsəbl/
incorrect /ˌɪnkəˈrekt/
invisible /ɪnˈvɪzəbl/
irregular /ɪˈreɡjʊlə/
irrelevant /ɪˈreləvənt/
irresponsible /ˌɪrɪˈspɒnsəbl/
item /ˈaɪtəm/
jail /dʒeɪl/
judge /dʒʌdʒ/
jump /dʒʌmp/
law /lɔː/
lawyer /ˈlɔːjə/
legal /ˈliːɡl/
legible /ˈledʒəbl/
lock (n) /lɒk/
logical /ˈlɒdʒɪkl/
magnifying glass /ˈmæɡnɪfaɪɪŋ ɡlɑːs/
mess /mes/
missing /ˈmɪsɪŋ/
murder /ˈmɜːdə/
mysterious /mɪˈstɪəriəs/

necklace /ˈnekləs/
old-fashioned /ˌəʊld ˈfæʃnd/
patient /ˈpeɪʃənt/
pickpocket /ˈpɪkˌpɒkɪt/
pickpocketing /ˈpɪkˌpɒkɪtɪŋ/
pleased /pliːzd/
plot /plɒt/
police officer /pəˈliːs ˌɒfəsə/
polite /pəˈlaɪt/
poster /ˈpəʊstə/
prison /ˈprɪzn/
publish /ˈpʌblɪʃ/
pull /pʊl/
punishment /ˈpʌnɪʃmənt/
push /pʊʃ/
recognise /ˈrekəɡnaɪz/
regular /ˈreɡjʊlə/
relevant /ˈreləvənt/
report (n) /rɪˈpɔːt/
responsible /rɪˈspɒnsəbl/
reward /rɪˈwɔːd/
robber /ˈrɒbə/
rubbish /ˈrʌbɪʃ/
security cable /sɪˈkjʊərəti ˌkeɪbl/
shadows /ˈʃædəʊz/
shoplifter /ˈʃɒpˌlɪftə/
shoplifting /ˈʃɒpˌlɪftɪŋ/
spot /spɒt/
spy /spaɪ/
suspect /ˈsʌspekt/

theft /θeft/
thief (thieves) /θiːf (θiːvz)/
trip /trɪp/
twist /twɪst/
uncomfortable /ʌnˈkʌmftəbl/
unexpected /ˌʌnɪkˈspektɪd/
unfair /ʌnˈfeə/
unhappy /ʌnˈhæpi/
unimportant /ˌʌnɪmˈpɔːtənt/
unintelligent /ˌʌnɪnˈtelɪdʒənt/
uninteresting /ʌnˈɪntrəstɪŋ/
unusual /ʌnˈjuːʒuəl/
vandal /ˈvændl/
vandalising /ˈvændəlaɪzɪŋ/
visible /ˈvɪzəbl/
vandalism /ˈvændəlɪzəm/
witness /ˈwɪtnəs/

WORD FRIENDS

arrest a criminal
break into flats or houses
commit a crime
interview a witness
look for clues
rob a bank
search the area
solve a crime
steal things from a shop
take fingerprints
tell the truth

Exercise 1

Possible answers:
1 burglar, pickpocket, robber, shoplifter, thief
2 judge, lawyer
3 climb, pull, push

VOCABULARY IN ACTION

1 Use the wordlist to find:
1 four people who steal things
2 two people who work in a court
3 three verbs that describe actions in which you use your hands

2 In pairs, use the wordlist to describe a situation that is:
1 uncomfortable
   A criminal is hiding from a police officer in a bin, but it's hot and very dirty.
2 illegal
3 unfair
4 dishonest
5 impolite

3 Compare your ideas for Exercise 2 with the class.

4 Use the wordlist to complete the sentences. Use the words in the correct form.
1 The man escaped last night and police are *searching* the area now.
2 He _____ a bank when he was young and spent a few years in prison.
3 It's impossible to _____ these new flats because the locks are very strong.
4 We'd like to _____ a witness who was near here at the time of the crime.
5 The detectives are _____ for clues at the crime scene now.

5 🔊 3.16 **PRONUNCIATION** Listen and repeat the pairs of words. Is the stress the same or different when there is a prefix?

1	correct	incorrect
2	honest	dishonest
3	logical	illogical
4	legal	illegal
5	polite	impolite
6	relevant	irrelevant
7	visible	invisible

Exercise 4

2 robbed
3 break into
4 interview
5 looking

Exercise 5

The stress stays on the adjective. Prefixes aren't generally stressed.

Wordlist

Revision

Extra activity

Elicit the different tenses and structures that students know, e.g. the Present Simple, the Past Simple, the Present Perfect, *must*, *going to*, the First Conditional. Elicit how we would form *have my hair cut* using the different tenses and structures (e.g. *I often have my hair cut, I had my hair cut last week, I have just had my hair cut, I must have my hair cut, I'm going to have my hair cut, If I have time this weekend, I will have my haircut*). Put students into pairs and tell them to make five *have something done* sentences using different structures or tenses.

Further practice

- Workbook page 99
- Resource Pack
  Resource 101: Unit 8
  Vocabulary – Solve the clues
  Resource 102: Unit 8
  Grammar – Who might say this?

Revision

VOCABULARY

1 Write the correct word for each definition.
1. This person steals things from people's pockets or bags. **p** i c k p o c k e t
2. This person tries to discover who has committed a crime. **d** _____
3. This is a crime where a person breaks into a building to steal things. **b** _____
4. This person sees a crime and can say what happened. **w** _____
5. A piece of information that helps to solve a crime. **c** _____
6. A building where criminals go for punishment. **p** _____

Exercise 1
2 detective
3 burglary
4 witness
5 clue
6 prison

2 Complete the text with the words below.

CCTV cameras   fingerprints   ~~murders~~   reward
shoplift   uncomfortable

Exercise 2
2 shoplift
3 fingerprints
4 CCTV cameras
5 reward
6 uncomfortable

Did you know …
1. Most *murders* happen on a Monday.
2. The most popular items that people _____ are electric toothbrushes and smartphones.
3. The best _____ are often found on soap or cheese.
4. There are about 25 million _____ around the world. On average, a person is seen 300 times a day.
5. Police in the USA offered a $5 million _____ for paintings that were stolen from an art gallery. The paintings are still missing.
6. It isn't always _____ in prison. One prison in Norway offers cottages and relaxing activities such as fishing and horse-riding.

3 Read the text again. What surprises you most and why?

GRAMMAR

Exercise 4
2 is hidden
3 are written
4 are caught
5 is used
6 are sold

4 Complete the sentences with the Present Simple passive form of the verbs in brackets.
1. A lot of TV programmes *are made* (make) about crime.
2. The jewellery _____ (hide) in a secret place.
3. Great crime books _____ (write) by ex-detectives.
4. A lot of criminals _____ (catch) abroad.
5. Fingerprint powder _____ (use) to detect fingerprints.
6. A lot of stolen items _____ (sell) on the internet.

5 Make questions in the Past Simple Passive. Read the text and answer them.
1. When/the man/arrest?
   When was the man arrested?
2. Where/the man/find?
3. What/hide/under the man's jacket?
4. Why/the cakes/steal?

Thief caught with cream cakes

Last night, police in Manchester arrested a man who they found in the kitchen of a police station. The man escaped through a window. He was hiding something under his jacket. It was a selection of cream cakes in a box. The man said he was painting the kitchen in the police station when he saw the cakes in the fridge. 'I wanted to take them home for my wife's birthday,' he said.

6 Complete the sentences with the correct form of *have something done* and the words in the brackets.
1. We've designed a 'No Time for Crime' poster. We're going to *have it printed* (it/print) later.
2. There was a burglary at the shop, so I _____ (the locks/change).
3. The vandals wrote on the gym wall, so we want to _____ (it/paint).
4. I _____ (my hair/dye) red when I was in town at the weekend.
5. The thieves stole our car and left it in town. We're going to _____ (it/check) before we use it again.

SPEAKING

7 In pairs, role play the situations on page 144. Take it in turns to listen to your friend's problem. Then try to persuade and reassure them.

DICTATION

8 🔊 3.17 Listen, then listen again and write down what you hear.

Exercise 5
1 *When was the man arrested?* The night before.
2 Where was the man found? In the kitchen of the police station.
3 What was hidden under the man's jacket? A selection of cream cakes in a box.
4 Why were the cakes stolen? The man wanted to take them home for his wife's birthday.

Exercise 6
2 had the locks changed
3 have it painted
4 had my hair dyed
5 have it checked

SELF-ASSESSMENT Think about this unit. What did you learn? What do you need help with?

WORKBOOK p. 98

Exercise 8

Last year some thieves broke into a museum. A beautiful necklace was stolen. The police never found the criminals. Then, last year, my mum was sent a present. It was a necklace from her best friend. But, guess what? It was the missing necklace!

193

Is chewing gum a crime?

Crime facts from around the world

Countries pass different laws because they often have different attitudes to certain crimes. Punishments vary greatly too. Here are a few facts about laws from some of the safest countries in the world:

Did you know that in Singapore it is illegal to chew gum because it damages the city's pavements and gets stuck in subway doors? You can get a fine or even go to prison for a petty crime like that!

Hong Kong has some of the strangest and strictest laws in the world. For example, it is illegal to play music in the streets. If you are a busker, it's certainly not the place for you!

In Finland fines for certain crimes are based on your income. If you are rich, you pay more! A few years ago the director of mobile phone company, Nokia, was caught speeding and got a fine of over €100,000! Do you think that's fair?

In Iceland, thefts and robberies almost never happen. House burglaries are unknown. People leave the front door to their houses open or their bicycles unlocked on the street. The police are largely invisible.

Of course, some street crime exists in Britain, but there are more CCTV cameras per person here than anywhere else in the world. If you have your bag stolen, there is a good chance that the police will catch the criminal. For that reason, British people feel quite protected. Edinburgh in Scotland is considered to be the country's safest city and it's also a beautiful place to visit!

GLOSSARY
attitude (n) what you think and feel about something
busker (n) someone who plays music in the streets to earn money
income (n) the money you earn
petty crime (n) a crime that is not very serious
vary (v) if things vary they are all different from each other

BBC CULTURE Is chewing gum a crime?

Lead in: Topic introduction

Tell students not to open their Students' Books. Put students into groups of four. If you set the homework suggestion for the unit, ask the groups to discuss any vocabulary they found difficult and their example sentences if you also set the additional task.

If students haven't done the homework, ask them to look at the glossary on page 104. Students should find the words in the text and discuss what they mean in context, e.g. *Countries can have different* **attitudes** *about the seriousness of certain crimes.*

8.5

A famous robbery

Part 1

In April 2015, just before the long Easter weekend, London's most famous jewellery vault was robbed in a spectacular operation. It seemed like something from a film. Professional robbers stole millions of pounds worth of diamonds from safe deposit boxes which were kept in the vault.

The vault in central London's well-known jewellery quarter is called the Hatton Garden Safe Deposit Company. It was opened in the 1950s and had an underground vault which was used by local diamond dealers to store their jewels. It was considered one of the safest in the country.

On Thursday 2 April 2015, at 21.19, the operation started. The robbers disconnected all the CCTV cameras except one. At 21.23, one robber appeared with a large black sack, but his face was hidden from the camera.

The first challenge was how to get into the vault, which was located in the basement. The robbers had crucial information about this building and worked out that if they could climb down inside the lift, they could eventually enter the vault. They climbed down the inside of the lift using ropes. Then they forced open this security door from the lift. Now they were just one step away from the security boxes with the jewels inside. On the streets above, no one knew that one of the biggest ever robberies was happening.

It was now twenty past midnight, just three hours after the start of the operation. The next big challenge was to drill through the wall of the vault – it was fifty centimetres thick. We tried it out here with some drilling specialists. It took us just two hours and twenty minutes to drill exactly the same holes as the robbers.

8.6

Part 2

Once inside the vault, they could open the safe deposit boxes. It's easy to do with a simple hammer. Look! You can crack these open in just five minutes!

The police only discovered the robbery two days after the robbers escaped with the jewels, or 'the loot'. Nobody knows how much they escaped with. They were eventually captured by the police six months later. Their downfall was the technology they used. The police were much smarter; they traced their mobile phones, analysed the CCTV images, recorded their conversations and followed their cars. It was the end to an amazing story, to what seemed to be the perfect crime. The police eventually solved the mystery of the largest burglary in English legal history.

Exercise 1
When students have discussed the questions in pairs, discuss them together as a class. Ask students if they worry about burglaries and if their homes have alarms or other forms of protection.

Exercise 2
Encourage students to read the sentences and to guess the answers before they read the text. When they have finished, elicit the answers and the corrected sentences or references from the text that show the sentences are true.

Answers:
1. F (*It is illegal to chew gum in Singapore because it damages the city's pavements and gets stuck in subway doors.*)
2. F (*The writer thinks chewing gum is a petty crime, i.e. a small, unimportant crime.*)
3. T (*some of the strangest … laws in the world*)
4. T (*fines for certain crimes are based on your income*)
5. F (*In Iceland, thefts, robberies and house burglaries almost never happen so the police can't have a lot to do.*)

Exercise 3
Tell students to work on their own to read the text once more and think about the questions. When they are ready, put students into groups of three and tell them to discuss their ideas. Invite groups to share their ideas with the class.

Answers:
1. Different – different activities are considered crimes and there are different forms of punishment for crimes.
2. Students' own answers
3. Students' own answers

Extra activity
Put students into groups of four. Tell them to identify and discuss activities which they think should be illegal and activities which are illegal, but which they believe should not be. Give them a time limit and then invite the groups to try to persuade the rest of the class about their ideas. Have a class vote for one activity which should be illegal and one crime that should be legal.

Exercise 4 8.5
Ask students to read the questions and, after they have watched Part 1 of the video, to discuss their answers in pairs.

Answers:
1. 2 April, 2015
2. London (Hatton Garden)
3. Possible answer: The robbery was similar to those you often see in films where a gang plans a raid and carries it out successfully.

Exercise 5 8.5
Before you play Part 1 of the video again, ask students to discuss the questions in pairs and to try to remember the answers.

Answers:
1. They climbed down inside the lift.
2. The video describes two challenges – getting into the vault and drilling through the wall of the vault – but doesn't say which was bigger.
3. 50/fifty cm
4. two hours and twenty minutes

Exercise 6
When students have matched the words with the photos, check that they understand the meaning of each word. Ask detailed questions about Part 1 of the video: *Where was the vault?* (under the ground); *Where were the security boxes?* (in the vault); *What was in the security boxes?* (diamonds); *What happened to the CCTV cameras?* (the robbers disconnected all of them except one).

Answers: 1 B 2 D 3 A 4 C

Exercise 7
Set a time limit for students to prepare their stories. Ask one or two pairs to present their versions of the story.

Exercise 8 8.6
Play Part 2 of the video with the sound switched off. Ask students to describe what they saw and to say what information they think they will learn from the video.

Play Part 2 of the video again, this time with the sound switched on, so that students can compare their ideas with the information from the video.

Answers:
1. easy (It takes five minutes with a hammer.)
2. two days
3. don't know
4. caught (six months later)
5. more intelligent (They used technology to trace their mobile phones, follow their cars, record conversations, etc.)

Exercise 9
Have a short class discussion about the questions. If any students know about any big robberies, they can share them with the class. Also elicit one or two examples of digital crimes. Ask if they know the following expressions: *phishing* (sending an email supposedly from a bank or other organisation to ask for passwords, PIN numbers, etc.), *identity fraud* (pretending to be someone else after stealing their personal information online). Then put students into groups of four and tell them to discuss the questions in more detail. When the groups have finished, invite them to share their ideas with the class.

Exercise 10
Discuss films about robberies with students, e.g. *Ocean's Eleven*, *Now You See Me*, *The Bank Job*, *Tower Heist*.

Put students into groups of three. Tell them to discuss films about robberies that at least one of them has seen and to choose one film that they would like to present to the class. They should divide their presentation into three sections, so that each student in the group can present an equal part. Explain that they should include the following information in their presentation: the name of the film's director, the year the film was made, the main actors, the plot and whether or not the film was based on a true story.

Further practice
- Workbook pages 100–101
- Resource Pack
  Resource 103: Unit 8 BBC Culture Lesson – Crime and punishment
  Resource 104: Unit 8 Culture – The Great Train Robbery

EXPLORE

1 In pairs, ask and answer the questions.
1. What countries do you think are the safest and the most dangerous in the world?
2. Is there much crime where you live?
3. What kinds of crimes happen, if any? Are they serious or not?
4. Do you think the laws where you live are fair? Why? / Why not?

2 Read the article. Mark the sentences T (true) or F (false). Correct the false sentences.
1. ☐ You cannot chew gum in Singapore because it's bad for you.
2. ☐ The writer thinks that chewing gum is a serious crime.
3. ☐ In Hong Kong there are some unusual laws.
4. ☐ In Finland the punishment varies depending on the money you earn.
5. ☐ The police have a lot to do in Iceland.

EXPLORE MORE

3 Read the article again. Answer the questions.
1. Does the article say that safe countries have similar or different kinds of laws?
2. Do you think CCTV cameras are a good way to make a place safer? Why? / Why not?
3. Which of the countries' laws mentioned in the text do you agree/disagree with? Why?

4 ▶ 8.5 Watch Part 1 of the video. Answer the questions.
1. When did the robbery happen?
2. Where did it take place?
3. Why is it described as a robbery from a film?

5 ▶ 8.5 Watch again. Answer the questions.
1. How did the robbers get from the building to the vault?
2. What was the robbers' biggest challenge?
3. How thick was the concrete wall?
4. How long did it take the specialists to drill the same holes as the robbers?

6 Match words 1–4 with photos A–D.

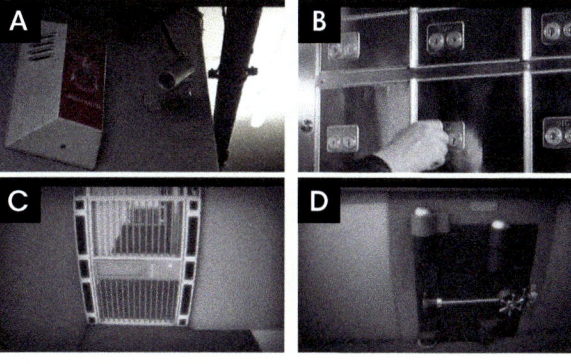

1. ☐ security boxes
2. ☐ vault
3. ☐ CCTV camera
4. ☐ security door

7 In pairs, retell the story of how the robbers got to the diamonds. Use the words from Exercise 6 and the photos to help you.

First, they switched off all the CCTV cameras except one. Then they climbed down the lift …

8 ▶ 8.6 Watch Part 2 of the video. Choose the correct option.
1. According to the video, it's *easy / difficult* to open the boxes.
2. The police only discovered the crime *a day / two days* after the robbery.
3. We *know / don't know* exactly how much loot the robbers escaped with.
4. The police *caught / didn't catch* the robbers in the end.
5. The police were *faster / more intelligent* than the robbers with technology.

9 In pairs or groups, ask and answer the questions.
1. Do you think robberies like this still happen in your country? Why? / Why not?
2. What kinds of crimes are committed digitally?

YOU EXPLORE

10 CULTURE PROJECT In groups, present a famous film about a robbery.
1. Find out about a film you like.
2. Write notes about what happens in the film.
3. Tell the story to the class.

Unit 8 **105**

9
Think outside the box

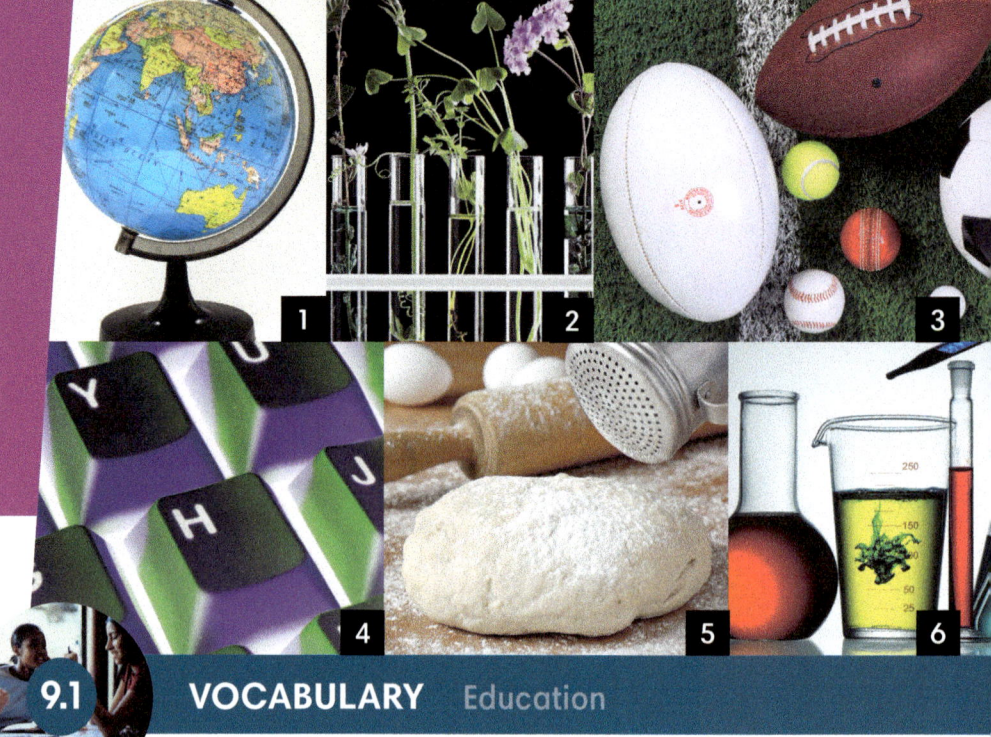

VOCABULARY
School subjects | Learning and assessment | Describing students

GRAMMAR
Word order in questions | Mixed tenses

Grammar: Could you give me a hand?

Speaking: How was your journey?

BBC Culture:
Two very different schools

Workbook p. 112

BBC VOX POPS ▶
EXAM TIME 3 > p. 136
CLIL 5 > p. 143

9.1 VOCABULARY Education

I can talk about school life.

1 **CLASS VOTE** What is your favourite school subject? Why?

2 🔊 **3.18** Match six words in the Vocabulary A box to the pictures. Listen and check.

Vocabulary A	School subjects
Art Biology Chemistry Citizenship Cooking English French Geography Health History ICT Literature Maths Music PE Philosophy Physics Spanish	

3 **CLASS VOTE** Are the subjects below taught in your school? If not, which of them would you add to the school curriculum? Which should be compulsory? Which should be optional or extracurricular?

driving   fashion design   film-making   gardening
karate   photography   yoga

4 **I KNOW!** In pairs, how many words can you add to each category?

Types of schools: *primary school*, _____
People at school: *head teacher*, *form tutor*, _____
Places at school: *library*, *canteen*, _____

5 🔊 **3.19** Study the Vocabulary B box. Then choose the correct options. Listen and check.

Vocabulary B	Learning and assessment
Learning learn memorise revise study	
Types of assessment performance practical exam project speaking exam written exam	

1 (memorise) / *revise* a poem
2 *revise* / *learn* for a speaking exam
3 *learn* / *study* for the whole night
4 *revise* / *learn* about the ancient Romans

Unit contents

Vocabulary
- School subjects
- Learning and assessment
- Describing students

Grammar
- Word order in questions
- Mixed tenses

Communication skills
- Exchanging personal information

Examples of 21st Century Skills/Competencies
- Critical Thinking: page 106 (Exercise 3), pages 116–117
- Collaboration: page 109 (Exercise 6), page 110 (Exercise 7), page 117 (Exercise 8)
- Digital Literacy: page 117 (Exercise 8)
- Assessment for Learning: page 115
- Autonomy and Personal Initiative: page 111 (Exercise 7), page 113 (Exercise 7)

9.1 VOCABULARY Education

Lesson learning objective
Students can talk about school life.

Lead in: Review of vocabulary from the previous unit

Put students into groups of three. Explain that you are going to dictate ten words. For each one, students should write a word from the same root but in a different form e.g. *noun – adjective*; *verb – noun*; *thing – person*; *adjective – negative adjective*.
Give an example. Say *happy – write a noun from happy* and elicit *happiness*.
When they have finished, the groups should swap their answers with another group. Write the answers on the board so that the groups can mark the answers, giving a point for each correct answer. Find out how many points each group got.
Words:
1. *assist* – write the word for a person who assists
2. *burglar* – write the crime burglars carry out
3. *correct* – add a negative prefix
4. *crime* – write the person who commits crimes
5. *honest* – add a negative prefix
6. *legal* – add a negative prefix
7. *mystery* – write the adjective from mystery
8. *polite* – add a negative prefix
9. *thief* – write the crime thieves commit
10. *vandal* – write the crime vandals commit

Answers: 1 assistant 2 burglary 3 incorrect 4 criminal
5 dishonest 6 illegal 7 mysterious 8 impolite 9 theft
10 vandalism

Exercise 1
Tell students to keep their Students' Books closed. Ask the question and have a class vote.
Elicit different factors for a subject to be students' favourite, e.g. *nice teacher, interesting information, easy to learn, will be useful in future life*, and ask students to rank these factors in order of importance.

Exercise 2 3.18
Ask students to describe the objects in the photos and elicit: *globe, plants, balls, keyboard, cake/bread dough, flasks* (the first and fourth items in photo 6), *a beaker* (the second item) and *a cylinder* (the third item).
When students have completed the exercise, discuss what students do or what equipment is used in the other subjects in the Vocabulary A box, e.g. *Art – students draw or paint; they use brushes, easels, charcoal, etc.*

Answers: 1 Geography 2 Biology 3 PE (Physical Education)
4 ICT (Information and Communications Technology)
5 Cooking 6 Chemistry

Exercise 3
Explain that the question is asking if students think any of the activities should be done as lessons in the school timetable or during an after-school club. If students select any of the subjects, ask which age they think would be a good time to start learning the subject.

Exercise 4
When the pairs have completed the exercise, elicit the spelling and the meaning of each word students have thought of.

Possible answers:
Types of school: boarding school, nursery school, private school, secondary school, state school,
People at school: principal, school secretary, teacher
Places at school: gymnasium, science lab

Exercise 5 3.19
Ask students to look at the Vocabulary B box. Discuss the verbs under the heading *Learning* and elicit the difference between the verbs: we *learn* something new; we *memorise* the exact wording of e.g. a part in a play or a poem; we *revise* for a test; *study* is a general word that encompasses the meanings of *learn, memorise* and *revise*.
Do the same with the words under the heading *Types of assessment*: a *performance* is when we act in a play, sing in a concert, recite a poem, etc.; a *practical exam* is where we have to produce a piece of work, e.g. for art (a painting) or for cooking (some food), or perform an experiment; a *project* is often an extended piece of work which we can produce at home and present and talk about for assessment; a *speaking exam* is often used to test our language ability; a *written exam* is a more traditional exam where we are each given a question paper and write the answers at a certain time and in a certain place, with a teacher observing to ensure that no cheating takes place.

Answers: 2 revise 3 study 4 learn

Exercise 6

Tell the pairs that as they do the exercise they should also take turns to describe what they can see in the photos, e.g. *Photo A looks like some sort of dance routine, possibly involving singing too.*

Answers: **A** performance **B** project **C** practical exam **D** speaking exam

Exercise 7 🔊 3.20

Before you play the audio, put students into groups of three. Tell some groups look at photo A, some photo B, some photo C and some photo D. Encourage them to use their imaginations to predict what someone in their photo might say before or after the time the photo was taken, e.g. *Photo A: Wow, that was great! Everyone danced well and nobody made any mistakes. I think we will win this competition!*

Give the groups a time limit to discuss and then invite each group to share their ideas while the rest of the class guesses their photo.

When students have listened to the audio, elicit the answers and ask which key words helped them to match the speakers and the photos.

Answers:
Speaker A: Photo C (*science, practical exam, experiment, equipment*)
Speaker B: Photo B (*group project*)
Speaker C: Photo D (*speaking exam, pairs*)
Speaker D: Photo A (*dance, moves, audience, performance*)

🔊 **3.20**

Speaker A: I'm feeling quite nervous this morning because we've got a science exam. I don't mind written exams, but this is a practical exam. We have to do an experiment on our own, and we get marks for things like safety and setting up the equipment properly.

Speaker B: This term we studied alternative sources of energy. This is our group project – we did everything ourselves and it took ages to make. We're very proud of it, so we're hoping for a good mark.

Speaker C: This afternoon we've got a speaking exam. I've revised lots of vocabulary and memorised some useful phrases. We're working in pairs, so I think it will be OK. Wish me luck!

Speaker D: We're going on stage in a minute to do our dance. We created it ourselves and learned all the moves, but this is the first time we'll have an audience. Our teacher and an examiner will watch us and give us marks for artistic creativity, dance moves, individual performance and group performance.

Exercise 8

After the pairs have completed the exercise, ask students to think of a test they have taken recently. The pairs should take turns to describe what happened, how they felt and whether their test result was better or worse than they anticipated.

Exercise 9 🔊 3.21

Go through the Vocabulary C box with the class. Ask students which adjectives they would use to describe themselves. When they have completed the exercise, ask students for their ideas about how much critical thinking, teamwork and problem solving they use in each of the different subjects in their timetable.

Answers: **2** confident **3** creative **4** critical thinking
5 problem solving **6** teamwork **7** general knowledge
8 hard-working
Not in the text: lazy, talented/gifted

Exercise 10 🔊 3.22

Explain to students that the life skill tested in the first riddle is provided as an adjective in the Vocabulary C box and that they should transform this into a noun (i.e. *creative – creativity*).

When the pairs have discussed the riddles, elicit their ideas and their reasons and then play the audio.

Check the answers and elicit that the first riddle is about creativity because students have to use their imaginations and 'think outside the box' and the second riddle could be either critical thinking or problem solving because these two skills both involve careful systematic thinking.

Answers: **1** creativity **2** critical thinking

🔊 **3.22**

J = Jacob A = Anne

J: What are you doing, Anne?
A: I'm doing riddles in a magazine. Look at this one. I've got to think of as many uses of paper clips as possible.
J: What for? Paper clips are used to hold papers together.
A: Sure, but you can also use them as a bookmark, for example. You can make earrings from them, or a bracelet … This tests your creativity, Jacob.
J: You're right. In fact I often use them to push the emergency restart button on my mobile or to keep headphone wires in place … They're very useful. Anything else?
A: Err … my mum uses them to close bags of rice or cornflakes, and to hang decorations on the Christmas tree.
J: Are there any other riddles?
A: Yes. Listen to this one. Two boys are registering at a new school. When they fill out their forms, the head teacher sees that they have the same parents. He also notices that they share the same birthday. 'Are you twins?' asks the head teacher. 'No,' reply the boys.
Is it possible?
It's difficult, isn't it? It looks impossible …
J: No, it's not! They can have a third brother who was born on the same day – they can be triplets. Or even quadruplets!
A: Wow, amazing. You've always been good at critical thinking Jacob!

Exercise 11

Refer students to the Vocabulary C box and give them a minute to think about which skills they are good at and which skills they could improve. Then put them into pairs and tell them to do the same for their partner's skills. Tell the pairs to take turns to share their views about each other's skills and to see if their own views of themselves are the same as their partner's views. Invite pairs to share what they have found out with the class.

Further practice

- Workbook pages 102–103
- Resource Pack
  Resource 105: Unit 9 Lesson 1 Vocabulary – Hidden words

6 In pairs, match the pictures A–D to the types of assessment in the Vocabulary B box.

7 🔊 **3.20** Listen and match the speakers to the photos.

A

B

C

D

8 In pairs, discuss which types of assessment you might have for different school subjects. Which types do you like? Which do you dislike? Why?

9 🔊 **3.21** Complete the text with words and phrases from the Vocabulary C box. Which words are NOT in the text? Listen and check.

Vocabulary C	Describing students

confident   creative   hard-working   intelligent   lazy
talented/gifted

good at: critical thinking   general knowledge
problem solving   teamwork

Life skills are important, too!

It's easy to think that school life is all about how ¹*intelligent* you are, in other words, your *ability* to understand things. However, good life skills help you more than intelligence, at school and beyond.

One key skill is how ²_____ you are. That is, *you believe that you can do things successfully*. It's important to build this skill because it helps with many areas of life. Once you believe in yourself, you can start being ³_____, *using your imagination*, which is helpful in all subjects, not just arts.

Another life skill, which is a new school subject in some areas, is ⁴_____. This teaches you *how to think clearly and ask questions*. Part of this subject also involves ⁵_____. Students develop *the ability to identify a problem and work out a solution*. Also, students learn *how to work well with others* which is all part of another key skill, ⁶_____.

Of course, traditional skills are important, too, such as ⁷_____, *knowing information about the world around you*. And don't forget about being ⁸_____, which means that *you always put in a lot of effort*, as that's the secret to many people's success.

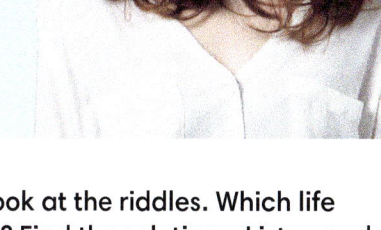

10 🔊 **3.22** Work in pairs. Look at the riddles. Which life skill is each of them testing? Find the solutions. Listen and check.

A You have two minutes to think of as many uses as possible for paper clips.

B Two boys are registering at a new school. When they fill out their forms, the head teacher sees that they have the same parents. He also notices that they share the same birthday. 'Are you twins?' asks the head teacher. 'No,' reply the boys. Is it possible?

11 How would you describe yourself as a student? Which skills could you improve and how?

9.2 GRAMMAR Word order in questions

I can make questions with the correct word order.

VIDEO   COULD YOU GIVE ME A HAND?

Alisha: Hey, Tommo. What are you doing?

Tommo: I'm getting ready for my water safety test tomorrow. I'm just checking the life jacket.

Skye: Cool. Will you get a certificate?

Tommo: Yeah, definitely … if I pass! Have you ever been kayaking?

Skye: No, I haven't tried it. I did windsurfing once, though.

Tommo: Did you enjoy it? Who taught you?

Skye: No, not much. My dad taught me, but it was really hard.

Tommo: Could you guys give me a hand moving this?

Alisha: Sure. Is it heavy?

Tommo: No, it's quite light, but you have to be careful with it.

Alisha: Where do you want it? Here, near the water?

Tommo: Yeah, that's great. OK, thanks. I think I'm ready.

Alisha: Good luck!

Skye: Are you going to become an instructor?

Tommo: I hope so. Maybe one day!

> Good luck!
> Where do you want it?
> I hope so.
>
> **OUT of class**

1 Have you got any certificates? What were they for and when did you get them?

2  9.1   3.23 Look at the photo. What are Tommo, Alisha and Skye doing? Watch or listen and check.

3 Study the Grammar box. Find more examples of questions in the dialogue.

Grammar	Word order in questions

Yes/No questions

Inversion
You are hungry. → **Are** you hungry?
You have finished. → **Have** you finished?
I enjoyed it. → **Did** you enjoy it?
She cycles. → **Does** she cycle?

Wh- questions

Question word + inversion
Why are you hungry?
Why did you enjoy it?

Subject questions
Who taught you? My dad taught me.

Object questions
Who did they see? They saw Tommo.

GRAMMAR TIME > PAGE 126

4 Match the responses with the questions in Grammar box.

1 A: _____
   B: Yes, I have.
2 A: _____
   B: Yes, I am.
3 A: _____
   B: No, I didn't.
4 A: _____
   B: Yes, she does.

5 Write questions for these sentences.

1 Yes, I had pasta for dinner last night.
   Did you have pasta for dinner last night?
2 No, I left home at six-thirty this morning.
3 Yes, we're going to Italy for our holidays.
4 Yes, I saw two films at the cinema last week.
5 No, I'm not going to do anything tonight.

6 Write subject and object questions about the underlined words.

1 A fire started in the science lab yesterday.
   What happened in the science lab?
   Where did the fire start?
2 Class 12D had a maths test this morning.
3 Everyone in my class has read this book!
4 Tom saw me when I was at the burger bar.

7 In pairs, ask and answer the questions in Exercise 5. Some of your answers may be false. Say if your partner's sentences are true or false.

And YOU

108 Unit 9

9.2 GRAMMAR   Word order in questions

Lesson learning objective
Students can make questions with the correct word order.

Lead in: Review of school subjects

Explain that you are going to write and draw on the board and that students should try to guess the school subject. Write: $(x + 3)^2 - (2x - 4) = y$ and students should guess *Maths*.
The first student to guess the subject should come to the board to do the same, e.g. writes *Bonjour!* for the school subject *French*.
Repeat the process for ten school subjects.

Exercise 1
Tell students to keep their Students' Books closed. Write *certificate* on the board and elicit what we can get certificates for, e.g.: good results, achievements in swimming, etc.
Put students into groups of four and tell them to discuss any certificates that they have got, what the certificates are for and when they got them. Invite each group to say how many certificates they have got and what they are for.

Exercise 2   9.1 3.23
When students have watched the video, ask them what they think a water safety test might involve (*being able to escape from a kayak if it overturns, swimming a certain distance while wearing clothes, keeping a kayak upright in a strong sea current, etc.*).

Answers: Tommo is getting ready for his water safety test (checking his life jacket). Alisha and Skye are helping Tommo with his kayak.

Exercise 3
Write these headings on the board, with the sentences below (which are answers to questions).
- Questions with auxiliary *do*
  I went to the cinema.   *I like pizza.*
- Questions with other auxiliary verbs: *be*, *have*, *will*, *may*, *might*, etc.
  He will be here soon.   *They have been to Sweden.*

For each sentence/answer, elicit the related question and how we form it.
Questions with auxiliary *do*: (question word) + auxiliary + subject + main verb – e.g. *Where did you go?*
Questions with other auxiliary verbs: (question word) + auxiliary + subject + main verb – e.g. *When will he be here?*
This should help students see that a question is formed in the same way each time.
Now write *Shakespeare wrote Hamlet* on the board.
Elicit that *Shakespeare* is the subject of the sentence and *Hamlet* is the object. Explain that if we ask a related *What …?* question, we are asking about the object (e.g. *What did Shakespeare write? Hamlet*) and if we ask a related *Who …?* question, we are asking about the subject (e.g. *Who wrote Hamlet? Shakespeare*).
Tell students to look at the questions in the Grammar box. For each question, elicit the auxiliary verb, the subject and the main verb.

Answers:
Yes/No questions: Will you get a certificate?;
Have you ever been kayaking?; Did you enjoy it?;
Could you guys give me a hand moving this?; Is it heavy?;
Here, near the water?; Are you going to become an instructor?
Wh- questions: What are you doing?; Who taught you?;
Where do you want it?

Exercise 4
When students have completed the exercise, elicit that in short responses, we just use: *Yes/No* + the subject + the correct auxiliary verb.

Answers: 1 Have you finished?   2 Are you hungry?
3 Did you enjoy it?   4 Does she cycle?

Exercise 5
Explain to students that, in reality, they would probably answer with a short response (*Yes, I did* or *No, I didn't*), rather than the full sentences shown in the exercise. Also explain that for some answers in the exercise only one question is possible, but for other answers more than one question may be possible.

Possible answers:
2 Did you leave home late / at seven this morning?
3 Are you going on holiday this year? / Are you going to Italy for your holidays?
4 Did you see any films at the cinema last week? / Did you go to the cinema last week?
5 Are you going to do anything tonight? / Are you going to the cinema tonight?

Exercise 6
Before students do the exercise, remind them about the rules for forming subject questions and ask them to identify the subject in each sentence (*A fire*, *Class 12D*, *Everyone*, *Tom*).

Possible answers:
2 Who had a Maths test this morning? What did Class 12D do this morning?
3 Who has read this book? Which book has everyone in your class read?
4 Who saw you when you were at the burger bar? When did Tom see you?

Exercise 7
Encourage students to give more information in each of their answers. For example, if their answer to the first question is *Yes*, they could describe the pasta (e.g. *Yes, I had spaghetti bolognese.*) and if their answer is *No*, they could provide more information (e.g. *No, I didn't. I had fish with potatoes and peas.*).

Further practice
- Workbook page 104
- Grammar Time page 126
- Resource Pack
  Resource 106: Unit 9 Lesson 2 Grammar – Ask and answer
  Resource 107: Unit 9 Lesson 2 Video – Could you give me a hand?

9.3 READING and VOCABULARY Does intelligence change?

Lesson learning objective
Students can find specific detail in an article and talk about intelligence.

Lead in: Review of word order in questions
Give each student a piece of paper and tell them to write a short answer at the top of the paper, e.g. *Yes, I am*; *No, he isn't*; *Yes, they have*. Then tell students to mingle with their classmates. They should take turns to say their own short answer and to think of and say a question which leads to their partner's short answer. Students should write on their piece of paper their partner's question.

Set a time limit. Invite students to share some of their questions and answers.

Background notes
At the start of the twentieth century, the French government asked psychologist Alfred Binet to help decide which students were most likely to experience difficulty in schools. Binet worked with another French psychologist, Theodore Simon, to develop a test involving a number of questions which focused on things not taught in schools, such as attention, memory and problem-solving skills. This first intelligence test became the basis for IQ tests still in use today. However, Binet always said that intelligence is far too complicated to be quantifed with a single number.

Exercise 1
Tell students to keep their Students' Books closed. Have a class discussion about how *intelligence* differs from *knowledge*. Ask students if they think that exams are a good test of intelligence and, if not, encourage them to say how they think intelligence can be tested more effectively.

Exercise 2 🔊 3.24
Tell students to read through the headings and, for each one, to think of what they would like to find out from the corresponding paragraph. For example:
a) The different reasons why tests can be difficult
b) An explanation of how IQs have improved
c) What the report is about
d) A list of reasons for certain situations or activities
e) How tests have changed
f) An explanation and justifications for the sentence.

Tell students that, when they have done the matching, they should have the information they wanted to find out. If they can't find the information for a heading, this means that the heading doesn't match any of the paragraphs.

Elicit the answers and the information found in each paragraph.

Answers:
1 c (The new report is a Scottish one, which says that people are getting more intelligent.)
2 a (The tests are so hard because people's scores keep getting higher.)
3 b (A score of 100 today would have been 118 in 1950 and 130 in 1910.)
4 d (The reasons why IQ scores are improving are diet, health, and also because we live in a fast-paced digital world.)

Exercise 3 🔊 3.24
As students do the exercise, tell them to note the section of text which indicates whether each of the sentences is true or false. Elicit these along with the answers:

Answers:
1 T (*researchers in Scotland … young people are more intelligent than their great-grandparents were*)
2 F (*Steven Pinker has taken a look at IQ test results over many years*)
3 T (*the test writers made changes and the tests became harder*)
4 F (*If … teenagers went back in time, … would be higher …* – nobody went anywhere, this is a Second Conditional hypothetical situation)
5 T (*made improvements in diets and health … this is the main reason*)
6 F (*Answers to vocabulary, Maths or general knowledge questions haven't changed so much*)

Exercise 4
Ask students to look at the first paragraph and elicit possible questions that could be asked about the information. For example, *Where were the researchers from?* (Scotland) *What did the researchers find?* (That today's teenagers are more intelligent than their great-grandparents.) Explain that they should do the same with the other paragraphs.

Exercise 5
Tell students to try to guess the correct Word Friends before they check in the text or a dictionary.

Answers: 2 take 3 make 4 take/make 5 make 6 take 7 make 8 make

Exercise 6
Explain that some of the example ideas in the exercise may be true, some may be false and some may be true but irrelevant. Encourage the pairs to discuss their opinions about all the ideas as well as thinking of some ideas of their own. When they have finished, invite pairs to share their ideas with the class.

Extra activity
Ask students if they know of any logic or intelligence puzzles. Write this puzzle on the board and encourage students to think of the next number in the sequence.
1, 1, 2, 3, 5, 8, 13, … (*21 – the number is always the total of the previous two numbers*)
Then ask students to guess the ending of the following sentences:
A glove to a hand is like a shoe to a … (foot)
Monday is to January like Sunday is to … . (December)
Ask students to work in groups of four to make similar sentences. Then students swap their sentences with another group and try to guess the ending.

Further practice
- Workbook page 105
- Resource Pack
  Resource 108: Unit 9 Lesson 3 Reading and Vocabulary – Make or take?

9.3 READING and VOCABULARY — Does intelligence change?

I can find specific detail in an article and talk about intelligence.

Bright sparks!

1 _____

Is modern education rubbish? Are today's teenagers poor learners who can't think for themselves? Not according to a report from researchers in Scotland. The good news is that young people are more intelligent than their great-grandparents were!

2 _____

Intelligence Quotient (IQ) tests are a way of measuring general intelligence. An average score in a given population is 100 points. Scientist Steven Pinker has taken a look at IQ test results over many years and made notes about what he found. Every few years, people did better in the tests, so the test writers made changes and the tests became harder.

3 _____

If some average modern teenagers went back in time, their IQ score would be higher than the people around them. If your IQ is 100 now, and you travelled back to 1950, you would probably have an IQ of 118. If you went back to 1910, you would have an IQ of 130. That's better than 98 percent of other people in 1910! To look at it another way, an average person from 1910 who visited us today would have an IQ measurement of only 70.

4 _____

Now, why are people getting cleverer? In order to find the reasons, we have to ask 'How have people changed?' We have made improvements in diets and health, and because they influence the brain, this is the main reason. Answers to vocabulary, maths or general knowledge questions haven't changed so much, but we have become better at problem solving. We have made progress with puzzle questions, such as 'GLOVE is to HAND as SHOE is to what?' This is also because we live in a fast-paced digital world where we have to think and react quickly, and we can't be afraid of making mistakes.

---

1 **CLASS VOTE** Do you think intelligence can be measured? Why? / Why not?

2 🔊 3.24 Read the text quickly. Match headings a–f with paragraphs 1–4. There are two extra headings.

  a Why are tests so hard?
  b IQs have improved
  c A new report
  d What are the reasons?
  e Tests have changed
  f Intelligence has no use

3 🔊 3.24 Read the text again. Mark the sentences T (true) or F (false).

  1 ☐ Researchers believe that humans are cleverer now than in the past.
  2 ☐ Steven Pinker based his report on IQ tests which he took himself.
  3 ☐ Test writers had to make the tests more challenging.
  4 ☐ Some teenagers travelled a long way for an experiment.
  5 ☐ A change in lifestyle is responsible for the better test scores.
  6 ☐ Big improvements were made in answers to all types of questions.

4 In pairs, write two *Wh*- questions about the article and ask the class.

5 **WORD FRIENDS** Complete the Word Friends with *make* or *take*. Sometimes more than one answer is possible.

  1 *make* changes
  2 _____ a test/exam
  3 _____ sense
  4 _____ notes
  5 _____ progress
  6 _____ a look
  7 _____ an improvement
  8 _____ a mistake

6 In pairs, discuss other reasons for the test results. What's your opinion? Use the ideas below to help you.

We take more tests.
More people go to college and university.
We learn a lot from TV and magazines.
Schools are better.
Parents talk to their children more.
We read more books.

9.4 GRAMMAR   Mixed tenses

I can use a variety of tenses.

Babar Ali – the youngest head teacher in the world

Babar Ali is probably the youngest head teacher in the world, and right now he is working very hard. He sometimes travels and gives talks about his school in order to raise money. The school has already grown and has hundreds of students, so he is opening other branches.

How did this start? He was walking back from school one day when he saw some children in his neighbourhood who didn't have money for school books, uniforms or transport. Babar decided to help them. When he got home, he started teaching children in his backyard. The school grew, and soon many people were talking about it.

The holidays finish soon. This year, Babar Ali is going to train some more of his pupils to become teachers. In fact, some of his original pupils are starting to work as teachers this term. In this way, they will change the lives of more children.

Imagine you enter a school in India, and you meet the head teacher who is a man in his twenties!

1 **CLASS VOTE** Do you think you would be a good teacher? Why? / Why not?

2 🔊 3.25 Read the article quickly. What was Babar Ali's idea? Was it a good one?

3 Study the Grammar box. Match each paragraph with the time: past, present or future. Find more examples of each tense in the text.

Grammar	Mixed tenses

Talking about the present
Present Simple: She often *walks* to school.
Present Continuous: I *am studying* now.

Talking about the past
Past Simple: I *visited* her yesterday.
Past Continuous: She *was working*.

Talking about the present and the past
Present Perfect: Our school *has grown*.

Talking about the future
will: This school *will change* lives.
going to: I *am going to train* as a teacher.
Present Continuous: She *is starting* work tomorrow.
Present Simple: The autumn term *starts* in September.

GRAMMAR TIME ▶ PAGE 126

4 Choose the correct options.

Hi Nadim,
Thanks for your email. I ¹*have* / (*'m having*) / *'ve had* a great time in India, it's really amazing here. We ²*stay* / *'re staying* / *'ve stayed* with some of my cousins.
We ³*get up* / *'re getting up* / *'ve got up* early most mornings. We usually ⁴*have* / *are having* / *have had* breakfast outside. Then we visit some tourist sites. I ⁵*see* / *'m seeing* / *'ve seen* elephants and monkeys but I ⁶*don't go* / *am not going* / *haven't been* to the famous Babar Ali school yet. I'm looking forward to it!
See you soon,
Leyla x

5 Complete the sentences with the Past Simple or Past Continuous form of the verbs in brackets.

1. What *were you doing* (you/do) in town yesterday?
2. Where _____ (you/go) on holiday last year?
3. We _____ (not come) to visit last weekend.
4. I _____ (watch) TV when I heard the phone.
5. They _____ (not work) when the teacher came in.

6 Use *will* or *going to* to answer the questions.

1. Are you going to study this evening?
2. Will you study at college in a few years?
3. What plans do you have for the weekend?
4. What places will you travel to in the future?

7 [VOX POPS ▶ 9.2] In pairs, tell your partner about your first school and first teacher.

9.4 GRAMMAR Mixed tenses

Lesson learning objective
Students can use a variety of tenses.

Lead in: Review of tenses

Write on the board: *a car* and tell students that this is the object of a sentence. Elicit what the sentence could be and the tense used, for example:
I have never driven a car. (Present Perfect)
I can't drive a car. (*can* for ability)
I'm going to learn to drive a car. (*be going to*)
My parents bought a car last week. (Past Simple)
When I'm twenty, I will buy a car. (*will* for future)
If I were older, I would buy a car. (Second Conditional)
Put students into groups of three and tell them to think of a word that can be an object of a sentence and to write it on a piece of paper. The groups should swap their piece of paper with another group. They should use their new word/object in five sentences, each with a different tense or structure.

Exercise 1
Tell students to keep their Students' Books closed. Ask the question and then have a class vote to find out which student the class thinks would make the best teacher.

Exercise 2 🔊 3.25
Before students read the text, tell them to read the sentence under the photo. Ask students if they think someone in their twenties is too young to be a head teacher and elicit reasons for their opinions.

Answer: His idea was to help children who didn't have money for school uniforms, books or transport to school by opening his own school.

Exercise 3
Students should identify the actual structures used in the text and discuss the differences between the use of the structures, e.g. *the Present Simple is used to talk about facts and routines,* but *the Present Continuous is used to talk about what is happening now or around now.*

Answers:
First paragraph: present
Present Simple: is, travels, gives, raise, has
Present Continuous: is working, is opening
Present Perfect: has already grown
Second paragraph: past
Past Simple: did this start, saw, didn't have, decided, got, started, grew
Past Continuous: was walking, were talking
Third paragraph: future
will: will change
be going to: is going to train
Present Continuous: are starting
Present Simple: finish, become

Exercise 4
Discuss the example with the class and ask why the correct answer is *'m having*. Elicit that the writer is talking about what is happening at the moment.

Answers:
2 're staying (at the moment)
3 get up (routine action)
4 have (routine action)
5 've seen (Present Perfect for a past action in an unfinished, present time period – on this holiday)
6 haven't been (Present Perfect for a past action in an unfinished, present time period – on this holiday)

Exercise 5
Remind students that we use the Past Continuous to talk about a longer activity and the Past Simple to talk about a single action. Sometimes both tenses can be possible, e.g. the example would also be correct as *What did you do in town yesterday?*, but in this exercise only one answer is possible for each of the other questions.

Answers: 2 did you go 3 didn't come 4 was watching
5 weren't working

Exercise 6
Remind students that we use *will* for decisions made at the time of speaking and for predictions for which we have no real evidence (and we often use phrases such as *I think, I'll probably* and *Maybe* to show that we aren't sure). We use *be going to* for plans and intentions and for predictions for which there is real evidence.
When answering questions 1 and 3, students will probably use *be going to* for their answers, but they can use *will* if they don't have any plans.
When answering questions 2 and 4, students will probably use *will* for their answers, but they can use *be going to* if they have already started planning their future.

Exercise 7
Put students into pairs and tell them to think of five questions. Explain that if their partner doesn't tell them these things when he/she is talking, they should ask the questions at the end.

VOX POPS ▶ 9.2
Before watching, check that students understand the meanings of these words/phrases: *to sew, reception class, pebbles*. After watching, students should work in pairs to decide which school sounds the best, giving reasons for their preference. Invite pairs to share their ideas with the class.

Extra activity
Ask students to write sentences, starting with *I/My …* and use present, past and future tenses about one of the students in the group. Set a time limit and then invite them to read out their sentences. The class should try to guess which student in the group the sentences refer to.

Further practice
- Workbook page 106
- Grammar Time page 126
- Resource Pack
  Resource 109: Unit 9 Lesson 4 Grammar – Mixed tenses

9.5 LISTENING and VOCABULARY Awkward moments

Lesson learning objective
Students can identify specific information in a dialogue and talk about awkward moments.

Lead in: Review of mixed tenses

Write *study English* on the board. Elicit the different tenses they could use this phrase in (*I study English, I'm studying English at the moment, I started studying English three years ago, I have studied English for three years*, etc.).

Put students into groups of three and give each group a piece of paper. Tell them to think of a verb phrase and to write it at the top of the piece of paper. They should swap their piece of paper with another group and then, with their new verb phrase, think of and write four true sentences that are in four different tenses. When they are finished, they should return the piece of paper to the original group, who should check the sentences and correct any errors. Invite groups to share their corrected sentences with the class.

Exercise 1

Check that students understand the meaning of *awkward* and *embarrassing*. When the pairs have discussed the situations in the exercise, ask if they have ever been in an awkward or embarrassing situation.

Exercise 2 3.26

Before you play the audio, ask students to describe what they can see in the pictures, to prepare them for what to listen out for.

When they have completed the exercise, elicit the answers and an explanation of each embarrassing situation.
(1 The girl dropped some papers. 2 The boy forgot the class trip. 3 The boy washed his trousers with the form in the pocket. 4 The girls were doing their homework during the lesson.)

Answers:
1 B   2 A   3 A   4 C

3.26
See page 249.

Exercise 3 3.26

Remind students that we use the Second Conditional to talk about hypothetical situations. When students discuss how they would behave in a situation, encourage them to use full Second Conditional sentences, e.g. *If I dropped all the exam papers on the floor, I would pick them up as quickly as possible and ask my friends to help me.*

Exercise 4 3.27

Go through the phrasal verbs in the Vocabulary box and make sure that students understand the meanings.
When students have completed the exercise, put them into pairs. Tell the pairs to identify the phrasal verb that is not used in the exercise (*calm down*) and to write one or two sentences to illustrate the meaning of this phrasal verb.

Answers: 2 get on 3 mess about 4 look over 5 look up
6 fill in

Exercise 5 3.28

Before you play the audio, elicit students' ideas about which choice is correct and ask them to say why they think the other choices are wrong, e.g. *In question 1, a uses the wrong auxiliary verb and c gives an answer that doesn't correspond to the question.*

Answers: 1 b   2 c   3 a   4 a

3.28
See page 249.

Exercise 6 3.28

Put students into pairs and tell them to discuss what they can remember. Then play the audio again so that students can check their ideas.

Answers:
1 The essay was too short
2 A poor test mark
3 Falling off a chair while teachers were watching
4 A student has fallen asleep

Exercise 7

Remind students to set the scene (i.e. to say when and where the 'awkward moment' happened and what else was happening at the time), to give some details about the situation, to say how they felt and to explain what they did afterwards. When they have finished, invite students to read out their paragraphs to the class.

VOX POPS 9.3

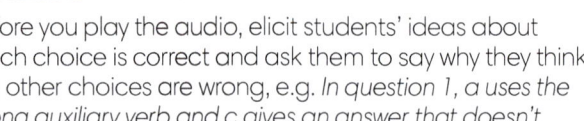

Before watching, check that students understand the meanings of these words/phrases: *prominent, to slate something, to mumble, to skulk off*. After watching: students should work in pairs to decide which situation was the most embarrassing, giving reasons for their opinion. Invite pairs to share their ideas with the class.

Extra activity

Put students into groups of three. Explain that they are going to role play an 'awkward moment' with three people, A, B and C. Tell students the situation: A and B are going to C's party. A knows some people at the party but B doesn't. C answers the door and welcomes A and B to the party. C says hello to A and waits. A wants to introduce B and C to each other, but can't remember C's name.

In their role plays, the groups should try to resolve the situation in a way that overcomes the embarrassment. Give the groups a time limit to practise and then invite them to act out their conversations in front of the class.

Further practice

- Workbook page 107
- Resource Pack
  Resource 110: Unit 9 Lesson 5 Listening and Vocabulary – Calm down!

9.5 LISTENING and VOCABULARY Awkward moments

I can identify specific information in a dialogue and talk about awkward moments.

1 **CLASS VOTE** Have any of these 'awkward moments' ever happened to you? In pairs, discuss what you would say or do in each situation. Which is the most embarrassing?
- you call your teacher 'mum' by accident
- you're playing with your pen when it flies across the classroom
- you realise your T-shirt is dirty

2 🔊 3.26 Listen to four dialogues. Choose the correct answers.

1 What does the teacher want the girl to do before the test?

 A  B  C

2 Where are all the other students now?

 A  B  C

3 What happened to the boy's form?

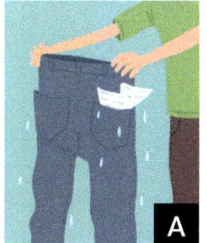 A  B  C

4 What were the students doing?

 A  B  C

3 🔊 3.26 Listen again. Which situation is most embarrassing? How would you behave?

4 🔊 3.27 Study the Vocabulary box. Choose the correct options. Listen and check.

Vocabulary	Phrasal verbs

calm down   fill in (a form)   get on   hand in/out
look over   look up   mess about/around

1 The teacher asked us all to *hand in* / *look up* our homework on time.
2 Pupils who finish early should *get on* / *look up* with some extra reading.
3 Please don't *mess about* / *hand out* in the art lesson.
4 Make sure you *get on* / *look over* all your answers before you finish.
5 You can *look up* / *look over* any words you don't know in a dictionary.
6 We have to *fill in* / *calm down* this form with our name and number.

5 🔊 3.28 Choose the correct answers. Listen and check.

1 Who's ready to hand in their essay?
  a Yes, I will.
  b I've just finished it.
  c No, it wasn't difficult.
2 Are we going to look over the test papers now?
  a Yes, I will.
  b No, it isn't.
  c Yes, we are.
3 Did the teachers see you when you were messing about?
  a No, they didn't.
  b No, I wasn't.
  c Where were they?
4 Could you all calm down, please?
  a Yes, Miss.
  b No, I couldn't.
  c Thank you, Miss.

6 🔊 3.28 Listen again. What was the 'awkward moment' in each dialogue?

7 [VOX POPS ▶ 9.3] Write a short paragraph about an 'awkward moment' that has happened to you.

Unit 9 111

9.6 SPEAKING Exchanging personal information

I can have a casual conversation.

VIDEO HOW WAS YOUR JOURNEY?

Ed: Dan! Great to see you! Sorry I couldn't meet you at the airport.
Dan: That's all right. It was easy by taxi. It's good to be here.
Ed: How was your journey?
Dan: Tiring! I'm feeling shattered.
Ed: Tell me about it! Let's put your bag in my locker, and then we'll get you a drink.
Dan: The college looks amazing. Do you like it here?
Ed: Yeah. I've made some good friends already. What about you? How have you been?
Dan: Everything's fine. The house is quiet without you, though.
Ed: Oh! So, do you miss me?
Dan: Not really. Well … only sometimes!
Ed: Ha! Oh, there's Miguel. Let me introduce you. Hey, Miguel! Come and meet my brother, Dan.
Miguel: Nice to meet you, Dan. Have you been to New York state before?
Dan: No, we lived on the west coast when we were little. I can't wait to look around.
Miguel: So what are you guys doing this evening?
Ed: We're having a drink here, and then I'm going to show Dan around. Would you like to join us?
Miguel: Sure thing. I'd love to.

> Great to see you!   Tell me about it!
> I'm (feeling) shattered.
> Let me introduce you.

OUT of class

1 CLASS VOTE Have you ever changed school? What was it like?

2 ▶ 9.4 🔊 3.29 Watch or listen and answer the questions.
1 How is Dan feeling?
2 Does Ed like his American college?
3 Is this Dan's first time in New York state?
4 What are their plans?

3 🔊 3.30 Use the Speaking box to match the questions with the responses. Listen and check.

Speaking	Exchanging personal information

Past
How have you been?
How was your journey?
Have you been to the USA before?

Present
Do you like it here?

Future
What are you guys doing this evening?
Would you like to join us?

1 A: _____
  B: That would be great. Thanks.
2 A: _____
  B: Fine. What about you?
3 A: _____
  B: Well, it's interesting, but I miss home.
4 A: _____
  B: Yes, I have. We had a holiday in Florida when I was little.
5 A: _____
  B: Well, there's a great pizza restaurant near here. We're going to try it.

4 🔊 3.31 Listen to Miguel, Dan and Ed. Write down the three questions they ask. Which is past, which is present and which is future?

5 Work in groups of three. Role play one of the situations. Students A and B are friends, and they meet Student C, who is a friend of Student A.
1 at a party
2 at the cinema
3 in a sports club

9.6 SPEAKING   Exchanging personal information

Lesson learning objective
Students can have a casual conversation.

Lead in: Review of phrasal verbs

Write seven phrasal verbs, each on a separate piece of paper. Divide the class into seven groups and give each group one of the pieces of paper. Tell them to keep their phrasal verb secret from the other groups. Each group should write a sentence which includes the phrasal verb. When the groups are ready, invite them to read out their sentences, saying *blank* instead of the phrasal verb. The other groups should try to guess the phrasal verb. The first group to guess correctly wins a point.
Suggested verbs: *calm down*, *fill in*, *get on* (with something), *hand in*, *look over*, *look up*, *mess about*

Exercise 1
Tell students to keep their Students' Books closed. If not many students in the class have changed school, ask them to say how they felt when they moved up from primary school to secondary school / middle school.

Exercise 2   9.4   3.29
Before you play the video, remind students about Dan's brother Ed and ask where he lives and what he does (*He lives in New York and is studying at university*). Put students into pairs and tell them to discuss what they can see in the photo.

Answers:
1 very tired
2 yes
3 no
4 They're going to have a drink and then Ed is going to show Dan around.

Exercise 3   3.30
When students have completed the exercise, put them into groups of three. They should take turns for one of the students to stand and the other two students to sit and ask one of the questions from Exercise 3. The student standing can't look in the Students' Book and should think of his/her own answers, e.g. *Would you like to join us? Yes, OK, thanks.*; *How have you been? Not bad, thanks. And you?* Tell the groups to make sure that all the students in the group have an equal chance to ask questions and to answer them.

Answers:
1 Would you like to join us?
2 How have you been?
3 Do you like it here?
4 Have you been to the USA before?
5 What are you guys doing this evening?

Extra activity
Tell students to think of a question that they would like to ask any new person they meet after they have found out their name and where they live. When everyone has thought of a question, encourage students to mingle with their classmates and to ask and answer each other's questions. Set a time limit and then invite students to say their question and the most interesting answer they received.

Exercise 4   3.31
While students are listening to the audio, write on the board the first letters of each word in the questions.
H_____ d_____ y_____ t_____ m_____?
W_____ a_____ y_____ s_____?
W_____ d_____ y_____ w_____ t_____ d_____ i_____ t_____ f_____?
Elicit the questions. Then play the audio again and tell students to listen for the answers.

Answers:
1 How did you two meet? – past
2 What are you studying? – present
3 What do you want to do in the future? – future

3.31

D = Dan   M = Miguel   E = Ed

D: So, Miguel, how did you two meet?
M: We were on the same business course.
E: And we're both in the same basketball team, too.
M: What about you, Dan. What are you studying?
D: Er, I'm still at secondary school, so I'm studying most subjects really.
M: Well, what do you want to do in future?
D: I'd like to do Physics one day, or maybe sports science. That would be cool!

Exercise 5
Explain that Student A should introduce Students B and C to each other. In the role play, most of the questions will be asked and answered by Students B and C, but encourage Student A to join in the conversation as well. The conversations should include at least one question about the past, one question about the present and one question about the future. When they are ready, invite groups to act out their conversations in front of the class.

Further practice
- Workbook page 108
- Resource Pack
  Resource 111: Unit 9 Lesson 6 Speaking – Sort them out
  Resource 112: Unit 9 Lesson 6 Video – How was your journey?

9.7 WRITING A letter giving information

Lesson learning objective
Students can write a letter giving information.

Lead in: Review of exchanging personal information

Put students into groups of four. Explain that one student in each group should role play being a new student at the school and should use their imagination when answering questions during the role play. The rest of the group should role play current students at the school and should answer questions as themselves. Tell the groups that they have five minutes for the current students to get to know the new student and vice versa. When the groups have finished, invite each group to say what the current students found out about the new student and what the new student found out about the current students and the school.

Exercise 1
Tell students to keep their Students' Books closed. Check that they understand the meaning of *school exchange partner*. Ask students if they would like to go to a school in a different country for a few weeks, and for their reasons why or why not. Elicit ideas about the kind of information they would want to be told before they left.

Exercise 2
Tell students to imagine that Nadia was staying with them on her exchange visit. Elicit the questions she asks and how the students would answer her questions about their own school.

Answers: Nadia wants to know information about the school (is it big and if they wear uniforms) and if Kyla is going to meet her at the airport.

Exercise 3
Elicit Kyla's answers to each of Nadia's questions. Then ask students to compare Kyla's school to their own school, e.g. *In our school there are … students. The teachers here are also friendly. We have a basketball club, but they meet on Tuesdays.*

Answer: yes

Exercise 4
Discuss each phrase individually, what it means and when students might use it:

Answers:
I'm looking forward to (meeting you) means that Kyla is excited about meeting Nadia. We often use this phrase at the end of a letter, e.g. *I'm looking forward to hearing more about …, I'm looking forward to seeing you.*
if you like means 'if that's what you want' and we often use this phrase when we are making an offer, e.g. *I can help you if you like.*
you're welcome to come along is an invitation to an event which has already been arranged with someone else, e.g. *I'm going to the cinema with Tom this evening. You're welcome to come along, too.*
We use *just in case* to talk about something we do to prevent problems happening, e.g. *I'm going to take an umbrella just in case it rains. I'm going to save my work on a flash drive just in case something goes wrong with my computer.*
Don't worry about anything means that the other person has organised and thought of everything necessary. We use this phrase to reassure someone who is going to do something new or strange.

Extra activity

Put students into pairs. Tell them to imagine that one student is going to visit the other student for the weekend and is phoning up to find out about transport, what they should bring with them, where they will sleep, etc. The pairs should write the dialogue, making sure that they use all the coloured phrases in Kyla's letter in their questions and answers. When the pairs are ready, invite them to act out their phone calls in front of the class.

Exercise 5
Before students do the exercise, elicit an example of each function from students' own lives, e.g. a past event: *Yesterday, we had a test.*

Answers:
Present Continuous: I'm looking forward (something happening now)
Past Simple: asked (a past event)
Present Simple: are, wear, like, have (regular habits)
Present Simple: here's (a fact), Don't worry (an instruction)
be going to: we're going to meet, going to have fun (plans)
will: I'll be, we'll have (a promise)
can: I can lend (a possibility or an offer)

Exercise 6
When students have completed the exercise, tell them to close their Students' Books. Ask about the different stages of Kyla's letter, e.g. *How did she start her letter? Why was she writing? What useful information did she give? What arrangements did she make? How did she finish the letter?*

Answers: a Thanks for your letter.
b You asked about my school.   **c** I have basketball club …
d you're welcome to come along.

Exercise 7
Ask students to read the letter and then to close their Students' Books. Put students into pairs and tell them to ask and answer questions about the letter. For example: *Who is it from?* (Jack); *Who is it to?* (Bryan); *When is Jack arriving?* (next week); *How is he travelling?* (by train); *What does he need to know?* (what to do when he arrives, what to bring).
Tell students to work on their own to write their reply, which can be done either in class or for homework.

Homework

Tell students to read the text on page 116 of the Students' Book. They should look up any words they don't know the meaning of and translate them into L1.

As an additional task, ask students to write an example sentence illustrating the meaning of each of these words: *achieve, allergy, clay, discourage, in turns, interactive, memorise, potential.*

Further practice

- Workbook page 109
- Resource Pack
  Resource 113: Unit 9 Lesson 7 Writing – Hi, Amelia

9.7 WRITING — A letter giving information

I can write a letter giving information.

1 CLASS VOTE What information would you give a school exchange partner who was coming to your school?

2 Read the letter from an exchange partner. What does she want to know?

Hi Kyla,

As you know, I'm arriving next Monday evening. I'm attaching a recent photo so you can see what I look like! I know it will be term time, so please can you tell me a few things about your school? Like, is it big and do you wear uniforms? Also, are you going to meet me at the airport, or shall I get a taxi?

See you soon,

Nadia

3 Read Kyla's reply. Does she include all the information that Nadia asked for?

Dear Nadia,

Thanks for your letter. I'm *looking forward to meeting you* as well.

You asked about my school. Well, there are about a thousand pupils, and the teachers are friendly. We wear uniforms, but I can lend you a spare one *if you like*. I have basketball club after school on Fridays, so *you're welcome to come along*.

Of course we're going to meet you on Monday! I'll be at the airport with my parents. We'll have a big card with your name on, but here's a photo, too, *just in case*.

Don't worry about anything, we're going to have fun!

Best wishes,

Kyla

4 Look at the phrases in colour. What do they mean? Why does Kyla use them?

5 Underline and name the tenses in Kyla's letter. Match each tense with its function.

a past event   regular habits
something happening now   plans   a promise

6 Study the Writing box. Complete gaps a–d with sentences from Kyla's letter.

Writing — A letter giving information

1 Starting your letter
Dear (name), …
It was good to hear from you.
a _____
It was nice to hear your news.

2 Making it clear why you're writing
You wanted to know about my school. Well, …
You asked for information about the school here.
b _____

3 Giving useful information
There are about a thousand pupils.
I can lend you a uniform / PE kit / bag.
c _____

4 Making arrangements
We'll definitely meet you.
We'll be there at 7.15 p.m.
d _____

5 Before you finish
I'm really looking forward to seeing you (again).
We're going to have a great time.
It will be good to meet you at last.

6 Ending your letter
All the best, / See you soon,

Writing Time

7 Read Jack's letter and then write a reply.

Hi Bryan,

As you know, I'm arriving next week by train. What are the plans for meeting me? Shall I phone you from the station, or take a taxi? Should I bring anything special with me (e.g. warm clothes, sports equipment, hiking boots, etc.)? I'm not sure about the weather, and your plans for the weekend. Please, let me know.

Jack

In your letter, you should
1 thank Jack for his letter and say why you're writing
2 reply to all the questions
3 express your feelings about the visit

Wordlist and Vocabulary in action

Extra activity

Explain that, in Britain, students usually study eight to twelve subjects between the ages of fourteen and sixteen and then three to four subjects between the ages of sixteen and eighteen. Tell students to imagine they are choosing which subjects they want to study. They should choose ten subjects to study between the ages of fourteen and sixteen and four subjects to study between the ages of sixteen and eighteen. Invite students to say which subjects they have chosen and why.

Further practice

Workbook page 110

Exercise 1

Possible answers:
1 performance, practical exam, project, speaking exam, written exam
2 average, confident, creative, gifted, hard-working, intelligent, lazy, talented
3 critical thinking, general knowledge, problem solving, teamwork
4 memorise, revise, study

WORDLIST School subjects | Learning and assessment | Describing students | Phrasal verbs

ability /əˈbɪləti/
Art /ɑːt/
average /ˈævərɪdʒ/
awkward /ˈɔːkwəd/
Biology /baɪˈɒlədʒi/
board /bɔːd/
brain /breɪn/
brainstorm /ˈbreɪnstɔːm/
branch /brɑːntʃ/
calm down /ˌkɑːm ˈdaʊn/
certificate /səˈtɪfɪkət/
cheat /tʃiːt/
Chemistry /ˈkemɪstri/
Citizenship /ˈsɪtɪzənʃɪp/
college /ˈkɒlɪdʒ/
compulsory /kəmˈpʌlsəri/
confident /ˈkɒnfɪdənt/
Cooking /ˈkʊkɪŋ/
copy /ˈkɒpi/
creative /kriˈeɪtɪv/
critical thinking /ˌkrɪtɪkl ˈθɪŋkɪŋ/
curriculum /kəˈrɪkjʊləm/
driving /ˈdraɪvɪŋ/
education /ˌedjʊˈkeɪʃn/
educational research /ˌedjʊˌkeɪʃnəl rɪˈsɜːtʃ/
effort /ˈefət/
essay /ˈeseɪ/
examiner /ɪɡˈzæmɪnə/
experiment /ɪkˈsperɪmənt/
extracurricular /ɪkˈsperɪmənt/
fashion design /ˈfæʃn dɪˌzaɪn/
fill in (a form) /ˌfɪl ɪn ə ˈfɔːm/
film-making /ˈfɪlm ˌmeɪkɪŋ/
gardening /ˈɡɑːdnɪŋ/
general knowledge /ˌdʒenrl ˈnɒlɪdʒ/

Geography /dʒiˈɒɡrəfi/
get on /ˌɡet ˈɒn/
gifted /ˈɡɪftɪd/
hand in/out /ˌhænd ˈɪn/ˈaʊt/
hard-working /ˌhɑːd ˈwɜːkɪŋ/
head teacher /ˌhed ˈtiːtʃə/
Health /helθ/
Humanities /hjuːˈmænətiz/
ICT /ˌaɪ siː ˈtiː/
imagination /ɪˌmædʒɪˈneɪʃn/
improvement /ɪmˈpruːvmənt/
influence /ˈɪnfluəns/
information /ˌɪnfəˈmeɪʃn/
instructor /ɪnˈstrʌktə/
intelligence /ɪnˈtelɪdʒəns/
intelligent /ɪnˈtelɪdʒənt/
IQ /ˌaɪ ˈkjuː/
lazy /ˈleɪzi/
learn /lɜːn/
learner /ˈlɜːnə/
life skill /ˈlaɪf skɪl/
Literature /ˈlɪtərətʃə/
locker /ˈlɒkə/
look over /ˌlʊk ˈəʊvə/
look up /ˌlʊk ˈʌp/
marks /mɑːks/
Maths /mæθs/
measure /ˈmeʒə/
memorise /ˈmeməraɪz/
mess about/around /ˌmes əˈbaʊt/ əˈraʊnd/
miss a lesson /ˌmɪs ə ˈlesn/
Music /ˈmjuːzɪk/
optional /ˈɒpʃənl/
pass /pɑːs/
PE /ˌpiː ˈiː/

performance /pəˈfɔːməns/
Physics /ˈfɪzɪks/
population /ˌpɒpjuˈleɪʃn/
practical exam /ˌpræktɪkl ɪɡˈzæm/
presentation /ˌprezənˈteɪʃn/
problem solving /ˈprɒbləm ˌsɒlvɪŋ/
progress /ˈprəʊɡres/
project /ˈprɒdʒekt/
pupil /ˈpjuːpl/
raise money /ˌreɪz ˈmʌni/
revise /rɪˈvaɪz/
school exchange /ˈskuːl ɪksˌtʃeɪndʒ/
Science /ˈsaɪəns/
score /skɔː/
shattered /ˈʃætəd/
solution /səˈluːʃn/
speaking exam /ˈspiːkɪŋ ɪɡˌzæm/
study /ˈstʌdi/
subject /ˈsʌbdʒɪkt/
talented /ˈtæləntɪd/
teamwork /ˈtiːmwɜːk/
technical /ˈteknɪkl/
term /tɜːm/
train /treɪn/
uniform /ˈjuːnɪfɔːm/
written exam /ˈrɪtn ɪɡˌzæm/

WORD FRIENDS
make changes
take a test/an exam
make sense
take/make notes
make progress
take a look
make an improvement
make a mistake

VOCABULARY IN ACTION

1 Use the wordlist to find:
1 four types of test or assessment
2 five adjectives to describe students
3 three life skills
4 two synonyms of the word 'learn'

2 In pairs, use the wordlist to discuss which subjects:
1 are useful for you
2 are not very useful for you
3 are hard to understand
4 are fun
5 you would like to try in the future

3 Use four words from the wordlist to describe an 'ideal' student. Compare with a partner. Are your ideas the same?

4 Complete the sentences with the words below.

mistake   notes   progress   sense   test

1 My sister's taking her driving _____ today.
2 It doesn't make _____ to me.
3 Listen and take _____ .
4 My marks are improving, so I'm making _____ .
5 I didn't get 100 percent in the exam because I made a _____ in one question.

5 🔊 3.32 **PRONUNCIATION** Listen to the intonation in each question and repeat.

Do you like it here?
What are you doing this evening?
Would you like to join us?
Did you enjoy the film?
Have you been here before?
Are you going to visit your family?

6 Does the intonation rise or fall in questions? In pairs, ask the questions from Exercise 5 with the correct intonation.

Exercise 4
1 test
2 sense
3 notes
4 progress
5 mistake

Exercise 6
Intonation usually rises in questions.

 Wordlist

Revision

Extra activity
After students have done Exercise 2, put them into pairs. They should take turns to talk about themselves, saying why each adjective applies or doesn't apply to them, giving examples, e.g. *I prefer to relax and not work hard, but when I have to work hard, I do. I'm not lazy. I'm quiet when I'm with people I don't know. I'm not very confident.*

Further practice
- Workbook page 111
- Resource Pack
  Resource 114: Units 7–9
  Vocabulary – Crossword
  Resource 115: Units 7–9
  Grammar – Choose and ask

Revision

VOCABULARY

1 Write the correct word for each definition.
1. great poems, novels and other books
   l
2. a piece of paper you get when you pass an exam
   c
3. If you have an exam tomorrow, you should do this. r
4. a person who teaches you a special skill, like driving
   i
5. a presentation using dance, music, acting or movement
   p

Exercise 1
1. literature
2. certificate
3. revise
4. instructor
5. performance

2 Complete the questions.
1. Do you prefer to relax and not work hard? Are you l a z y?
2. Are you shy and quiet or are you c_____?
3. Can you work well with other people? Are you good at t_____?
4. Do you know a lot about the world? How's your g_____?
5. Can you use your imagination? Are you c_____?
6. Do you have some natural skills, for example in sport or music? Are you t_____?

Exercise 2
2. confident
3. teamwork
4. general knowledge
5. creative
6. talented

3 In pairs, ask and answer questions from Exercise 2.

GRAMMAR

4 Complete the text with the correct form of the verbs in brackets.

The latest news in education…

A: Lunchbox thieves?
Recently, strange things ¹have happened (happen) in the UK. At some schools, teachers ² _____ (take) food items out of pupils' lunch boxes! Are teachers hungry? No, they ³ _____ (put) unhealthy snacks in the bin! Pupils and their parents ⁴ _____ (feel) shocked.

B: Police to get pupils out of bed!
Another UK school says it is going to ⁵ _____ (send) ex-police officers to get pupils out of bed! Apparently the officers are going to ⁶ _____ (take) lazy students to school by car. This way, pupils won't ⁷ _____ (miss) any lessons, so they will ⁸ _____ (do) better in their exams, which ⁹ _____ (start) in three months.

C: Parents must behave!
Last week we ¹⁰ _____ (read) an interesting report about a head teacher who was angry with parents who ¹¹ _____ (not come) to any parent-teacher evenings. What was his idea? He ¹² _____ (want) lazy parents to pay a fine. However, other people ¹³ _____ (not like) his plan, so he was very unpopular!

Exercise 4
2. have taken
3. are putting
4. are feeling
5. send
6. take
7. miss
8. do
9. start/are starting
10. read
11. didn't come
12. wanted
13. didn't like

5 Make questions from the prompts. In pairs, answer them.
1. what / teachers / do / with unhealthy snacks?
2. pupils and parents / feel / happy about this?
3. why / one school / send police officers to get students / out of bed?
4. this / help / students?
5. who / become / famous / last week?
6. he / popular?

Exercise 5
1. What are teachers doing with unhealthy snacks?
2. Are pupils and parents feeling happy about this?
3. Why did one school send police officers to get students out of bed?
4. Did this help students?
5. Who became famous last week?
6. Was he popular?

SPEAKING

6 In pairs, role play the situation. Imagine you are an exchange student in the UK. Choose a character from page 144 and introduce yourselves. Add two more questions and extra information of your own.

Angelina? That's a nice name. Where are you from?
France. I live in Paris.
Have you ever been to the UK before?

DICTATION

7 🔊 3.33 Listen, then listen again and write down what you hear.

SELF-ASSESSMENT Think about this unit. What did you learn? What do you need help with?

WORKBOOK p. 110

Exercise 7
The King's School in the UK has a long history as it's about 1500 years old! Pupils need to be creative and hard-working. Also, you must take a written exam if you want to study here.

215

CULTURE

Can school be fun?

Another way to learn: A day in the life of a student at an alternative school

Adam

'I go to a Steiner school. It's very different to the traditional schools that my friends go to. First of all, our learning is far more creative and interactive. We don't sit in class and memorise facts; we get up and do practical stuff, which I think is really alternative.

For example, today we had a Biology lesson. As we were learning all about the body, the teacher asked us to make clay models and draw pictures of different body parts. It was much more fun than just reading information in a book. Also, we did this in a group, so we learnt from each other. Then we took it in turns to give presentations about a subject of our choice. I gave a talk about modern-day allergies. I researched this topic because I think it's really fascinating.

Anyway, it's great that we have the freedom to do that. And the other positive thing is that there are no tests – we just revise the material in our own time!

We also usually only have one academic subject per week. It's just two or three hours in the morning, then the rest of the day we do gardening, arts and crafts. Today we did singing and dancing – my favourites! One thing that they discourage at my school is the computer. We aren't allowed to sit in front of a screen for a long time. I don't like this, but I understand the reasons – we can do that at home.

Here the teachers are very different too – they are your friends. They don't just instruct you; they help you achieve your potential. I love that. I actually look forward to going to school!'

GLOSSARY
achieve (v) to succeed in doing something
allergy (n) a medical condition that makes you ill when you eat, touch or breathe something
clay (n) a type of material that is used to make pots
discourage (v) to try to make someone want to do something less often
in turns (phrase) one after another

Unit 9

BBC CULTURE Can school be fun?

Lead in: Topic introduction

Tell students not to open their Students' Books. Put students into groups of four. If you set the homework suggestion for the unit, ask the groups to discuss any vocabulary they found difficult and their example sentences if you also set the additional task.

If students haven't done the homework, ask them to look at the glossary on page 116. Students should find the words in the text and discuss what they mean in context, e.g. *The teachers here help you to **achieve** your academic goals.*

9.5

Two very different schools

Part 1

N = Narrator   I = Interviewer   T = Teacher   G = Girl

N: Lunchtime over at King's and the playground becomes a parade ground. King's opened as a free school in 2012 and now has 280 pupils in three year groups. Each lesson begins with a handshake for the teacher and a statement of the school's values. This brings a feeling of order and discipline to the class. This is a Leadership class. The subject today is integrity.
I: Wouldn't this time be better spent teaching the pupils Maths or English or Science?
T: It's these kinds of lessons that enable the students to do as well as they do in subjects like Maths and English and Science because it teaches them 'character'.
N: All students at King's have to do martial arts.
I: The insistence on order and character building will sound old-fashioned to some. So, is this a deliberate attempt to turn back the clock?
N: They teach Latin and Public Speaking here, but they also teach Mandarin and Computer Science. The children are encouraged to have high expectations.
G: I want to be an investment banker and to do … to go to Oxford University.
I: How old are you now?
G: I'm thirteen.
N: The government also recognises the good work at King's School and hopes other schools will follow. At King's they believe they are doing something new: preparing their students for life after full-time education.
The King's free school is very different from the Steiner school system. Here, discipline and exams are not the priority and there is a very informal atmosphere. Students don't wear a uniform and don't start academic studies until they are seven. The focus is on creative play, music, drama and dance.

9.6

Part 2

N = Narrator   K = Kara

N: Another kind of alternative school is one that focuses on special needs. In the UK there are fourteen schools which specialise in teaching dyslexic children. Our reporter, Kara – a dyslexic herself – talks about her visit to one of these schools.
K: I'm really kind of excited about seeing a school that specialises in something that I've had throughout my life.
N: Shapwick is a private school with 170 boys and girls. The classes are very small, so the teacher can focus on the needs of particular students. The first class that Kara attends is an English lesson.
Dyslexia doesn't just affect reading and spelling. It can also affect your short-term memory. Here, students learn new words by linking them to colours, shapes and stories. This makes it easier for them to remember the new words.
The students are very hard-working.
Most dyslexic schoolchildren don't get this support. Schools like Shapwick are expensive and many parents cannot afford the fees. However, some families are given money by the government.
As part of their English lesson, the children spell out words with physical movements. Here, they are using bottles of water. It helps the words to stay in their long-term memory. Kara didn't have the chance to study this way when she was a girl, but she's very happy that now others can.

Exercise 1

When students have discussed the questions in pairs, ask them for their ideas about how different school subjects could be made more fun or interesting, e.g. *You could teach Maths using shopping role plays, where students have to work out how much they have spent and how much change they should get.*

Exercise 2

Check that students understand the meanings of *traditional school*, *alternative school* and *academic subjects*. When they have completed the exercise, elicit the answers and the specific extracts from the text which show if each sentence is true or false.

Answers:
1 T (*It's very different to the traditional schools that my friends go to*)
2 F (*It was much more fun than just reading information in a book*)
3 T (*I researched this topic because I think it's really fascinating*)
4 T (*It's just two or three hours in the morning*)
5 T (*I don't like this, but I understand the reasons*)
6 F (*Here the teachers are very different*)

Exercise 3

Tell students that when they read the article a second time, they should make notes of examples of surprising things and comparisons with their school, e.g. *surprising – no tests; comparison – they do more practical things than us.* When the pairs have discussed their notes, have a class discussion about the advantages and disadvantages of this alternative school and traditional schools.

Extra activity

Put students into groups of four and tell them to role play a conversation between a student who would like to go to an alternative school, his/her parents who think a traditional education is better and the student's friend who already goes to an alternative school. The student's friend should only talk when the others ask him/her questions about the alternative school. Give the groups time to practise and then invite them to act out their conversations in front of the class.

Exercise 4 9.5

Put students into pairs to discuss whether they would prefer to go to a Steiner school or King's School, and why. When the pairs have finished, ask students to share their ideas with the class. Then ask students to imagine that they are a parent of a teenage student. Ask them which school they would prefer him/her to go to and see if their answers are the same or different.

Exercise 5 9.5

Before you play Part 1 of the video again, tell students to look at the sentences in pairs and to try to remember or guess the correct options.
When students have completed the exercise, ask them to name the different subjects mentioned in the video that students study at each school (*King's School – Leadership, Latin, Public speaking, Mandarin, Computer science; the Steiner School – creative play, music, drama and dance*). Remind students about the girl in the video from King's School who wants to be an investment banker. Ask them what they think the Steiner School students might say about the girl's views, and why.

Answers: 1 discipline 2 Leadership 3 banker 4 informal 5 seven

Exercise 6 9.6

Before you play Part 2 of the video, check that students understand the meaning of *dyslexia* and encourage students to try to complete the text using the words in the box.
When students have watched the video and checked their answers to Exercise 6, ask them to close their Students' Books. In pairs, they should discuss how the school helps dyslexic children and see how much of the detail they can remember.

Answers: 1 fourteen 2 memory 3 words 4 colours 5 English 6 movements

Exercise 7

When students have discussed the question in pairs, invite them to share their ideas with the class. Have a class discussion about different kinds of schools in the students' own town, e.g. private schools, language schools, technical colleges, etc.

Exercise 8

Put students into groups of four. Discuss with the class ideas for the content of their presentations and elicit further ideas, e.g. wearing a uniform, the relationship between students and staff, class sizes, tests. Tell the groups to work together to discuss their ideal school and to agree on which kind of school they would like it to be. They should divide up the presentation equally between them, so that each student in the group is responsible for writing about and presenting one aspect of their ideal school.

Further practice

- Workbook pages 112–113
- Resource Pack
  Resource 116: Unit 9 BBC Culture Lesson – Different schools
  Resource 117: Unit 9 Culture – Education, education

EXPLORE

1 In pairs, ask and answer the questions.
  1. Describe something you have learnt recently that was fun or interesting. Why was it a good learning experience?
  2. What makes a lesson interesting or boring for you? Give examples.

2 Read the article. Mark the sentences T (true) or F (false).
  1. ☐ Adam knows that his school is alternative.
  2. ☐ He would like to read more in class.
  3. ☐ He chose a subject he liked for his presentation.
  4. ☐ The students study academic subjects at the same time.
  5. ☐ Adam would like to spend longer on the computer.
  6. ☐ He thinks that the teachers are similar to those in traditional schools.

3 Read the article again. In pairs, ask and answer the questions.
  1. What information in the text surprises you about this alternative school?
  2. How does the 'day in the life' compare to daily life at your school? Which do you prefer? Why?

EXPLORE MORE

4 ▶ 9.5 Watch Part 1 of the video. Which school would you prefer to go to? Why?

5 ▶ 9.5 Watch again. Choose the correct option.
  1. At King's School order and *creativity* / *discipline* is important.
  2. Today's class is a *Maths* / *Leadership* class.
  3. The girl interviewed wants to be a *teacher* / *banker*.
  4. The Steiner school is more *formal* / *informal* than King's.
  5. At the Steiner school academic studies start at *six* / *seven* years old.

6 ▶ 9.6 Watch Part 2 of the video. Complete the text with the words below. There are two extra words.

> memory   movements   fourteen   words
> alternative   English   forty   colours

In the UK there are ¹_____ schools which specialise in teaching dyslexic children. Dyslexia affects reading and spelling, and your short-term ²_____. So, the students learn new ³_____ with shapes and ⁴_____. Kara attends an ⁵_____ lesson. In the class the students spell out words with physical ⁶_____.

7 What's your opinion of the different schools from the video? Discuss in pairs.

I think the school that specialises in helping dyslexic children is great.

YOU EXPLORE

8 **CULTURE PROJECT** In groups, prepare a presentation based on the question: 'What would your ideal school be like?'
  1. Use these notes to help you:
     - practical tasks / academic tasks: what's the right balance?
     - use of computers: a lot or a little?
     - how much freedom of choice?
     - discipline: important or not?
  2. Write a short script to describe your ideas. Think about images or videos to use in your presentation.
  3. Give your presentation to the class. Whose ideal school is the best? Why?

GRAMMAR TIME

Exercise 1
2 are wearing
3 are dancing
4 making
5 doesn't like
6 prefers
7 go
8 show

Exercise 1
1 to stay up
2 to buy
3 watching
4 playing
5 to stay
6 helping

Exercise 2
1 to do
2 to write
3 writing
4 learning
5 to earn
6 to pay
7 to bring
8 planting

GRAMMAR TIME

1.2 Present Simple, Present Continuous and state verbs

Present Simple
We use the Present Simple for facts, permanent situations and routines.
They sing in a band.
She doesn't use her tablet every day.

Time expressions
every day/week/month/year
once/twice/three times a month
on Mondays/weekdays/holiday
always/usually/often/sometimes/rarely/never

Present Continuous
We use the Present Continuous for actions that are happening at or around the time of speaking.
They're playing a computer game right now.
I'm recording songs this week.

Time expressions
now, at the moment, this morning/afternoon, this year, these days

State verbs
State verbs express opinions, preferences, mental states and perception.
love, like, hate, prefer, want, need, understand, think, feel, hear, see
They don't normally have a continuous form, even if they refer to the time of speaking.
I want to see your new mobile phone.

1 Complete the text with the correct form of the verbs below.

(not) like   dance   go   make   prefer
show   ~~think~~   wear

I ¹think one of the favourite pastimes for my generation is watching music videos on YouTube. My favourite is the one by Ylvis called 'What does the fox say'. Do you want to watch it? Look, there's a fancy dress party and all the people ²_____ animal costumes. They ³_____ in the forest and ⁴_____ crazy animal sounds! It's amazing, although a bit old now! My sister ⁵_____ music videos – she ⁶_____ videos about shopping where people ⁷_____ shopping for clothes or cosmetics and then ⁸_____ the viewers what's in their shopping bags … Not my kind of thing, really.

2 Write a similar text about what kinds of videos you like and describe your favourite one.

1.4 Verb + ing and verb + to-infinitive

Verbs followed by the -ing form:
avoid, can't stand, enjoy, finish, (not) mind, miss, practise, stop
I avoid using flash in my camera.
The -ing form is also used after prepositions.
I'm looking forward to seeing my grandpa.
Verbs followed by the to-infinitive:
agree, allow, ask, choose, decide, forget, hope, learn, offer, plan, try, want, would like/love
I hope to become a good photographer in the future.

Some verbs can be followed by either the to-infinitive, or the -ing form:
like, love, hate, prefer, start
I love taking photos of cats. / I love to take photos of cats.

1 Complete the sentences with the correct form of the verbs in brackets.

1 Martha's parents often allow her _____ (stay up) late at night.
2 I would love _____ (buy) a new camera.
3 My boyfriend is crazy about _____ (watch) old silent movies.
4 Why don't you practise _____ (play) this song again?
5 Please, try _____ (stay) calm.
6 Would you mind _____ (help) me with this poster?

2 Choose the correct option.

A: What are you planning ¹to do / doing at the weekend, Josh?
B: I don't know. I want ²to write / writing the French essay. Finish ³to write / writing it, in fact.
A: Doesn't sound very exciting!
B: Well, no, it doesn't. I can't stand ⁴to learn / learning French. What about you, Jessica?
A: Well, I'm trying ⁵to earn / earning some money for a new camera. My old one is broken. I can help my uncle in his garden. He is offering ⁶to pay / paying me five pounds an hour. In fact, he wants me ⁷to bring / bringing a friend too … There's enough work for two people with planting apple trees.
B: That's great! I need some cash. And I'm really good at ⁸to plant / planting!
A: Really? That's new!

GRAMMAR TIME

Exercise 1

2 saw
3 rained
4 took
5 studied
6 had

Exercise 1

1 called, was taking
2 was snowing, was shining
3 were you doing, wasn't sleeping, was watching
4 Were you playing, came, wasn't, was looking

GRAMMAR TIME

2.2 Past Simple: regular and irregular verbs

We use the **Past Simple** to talk about actions and situations that finished in the past. We often mention when these actions/situations happened.
We saw a storm **yesterday**.
We didn't see the storm.
Did you see the storm?
Some verbs in English have regular Past Simple forms.
happen–happened, move–moved, study–studied, travel–travelled
Some verbs are irregular. (See page 127 for a list of irregular verbs.)

Time expressions
yesterday
two hours/days/weeks/years ago
last week/year/night
in 2001

1 Complete the sentences with the correct form of the verbs in brackets.

1 I *visited* (visit) my aunt in August.
2 I last _____ (see) a rainbow two weeks ago.
3 It _____ (rain) a lot last summer.
4 I _____ (take) a lot of photos on holiday.
5 I _____ (study) for the Maths test last night.
6 I _____ (have) fried eggs for breakfast yesterday.

2 In pairs, make questions from the the prompts and time expressions below. Then ask and answer the questions.

> yesterday   the day before yesterday
> last Monday / Friday / Saturday   a month ago
> last year   two years ago   in 2007   in June 2010

1 What / you / have / for lunch / ?
2 What films / you / see / ?
3 Where / you / go / on holiday / ?
4 What sports / you / do / ?
5 What video games / you / play / ?
6 What mobile phone / you / have / ?

A: *What did you have for lunch the day before yesterday?*
B: *Uhm … OK, I remember. I had some spaghetti.*

3 Write ten true sentences about yourself, using the Past Simple and ten different time expressions.

2.4 Past Continuous and Past Simple

Past Continuous
We use the Past Continuous to describe an activity that was in progress in the past or to describe a scene in the past.
At seven o'clock I was talking to friends online.
It was snowing.
She was doing her homework. She wasn't playing games.
They were swimming. They weren't running.
Was she sleeping? Yes, she was. No, she wasn't.

Past Continuous and Past Simple
We use the Past Continuous and Past Simple to talk about an activity that was in progress when something else happened.
I was walking in the forest **when** I suddenly saw a bear.
Anne called me **while** I was doing the Maths homework.

1 Complete the sentences with the Past Simple or the Past Continuous form of the verbs in brackets.

1 When you _____ (call), I _____ (take) a shower.
2 The weather was perfect last Christmas: it _____ (snow) and the sun _____ (shine).
3 A: What _____ (you / do) at ten o'clock last Wednesday?
   B: I'm not sure … I _____ (not sleep). I think I _____ (watch) a film on television.
4 A: _____ (you / play) games on your mobile when the teacher _____ (come) into the classroom?
   B: No, I _____ ! I _____ (look) for some information about Asia on the internet.

2 Complete the text with the correct forms of the words below.

> appear   break   fall   come   hear   ~~hike~~
> run   shout   try

Last winter I ¹*was hiking* in the mountains with my friend Jake when we ² _____ a strange sound. We were quite scared. There was lots of snow on the top of the mountain and it ³ _____ down on us really quickly. It was an avalanche! 'Run,' Jake ⁴ _____ . We ⁵ _____ when we both ⁶ _____ down the slope and my friend ⁷ _____ his leg! I ⁸ _____ to call my dad from my mobile phone when a helicopter ⁹ _____ in the sky and we were saved!

Exercise 2

2 heard
3 was coming
4 shouted
5 were running
6 fell
7 broke
8 was trying
9 appeared

Exercise 2

Possible answers:
2 What films did you see last year?
3 Where did you go on holiday two years ago?
4 What sports did you do in 2007?
5 What video games did you play last Monday?
6 What mobile phone did you have a month ago?

221

GRAMMAR TIME

Exercise 1
1 has just arrived
2 has already washed
3 Have the kids had lunch yet, haven't
4 Have you done the shopping yet, have just returned
5 have never eaten
6 haven't finished

GRAMMAR TIME

3.2 Present Perfect with *ever, never, just, already* and *yet*

The Present Perfect form is *have/has* and the past participle. For regular verbs, the past participle is the same as the Past Simple form. Many past participles are irregular (see page 127).

We use the Present Perfect to talk about:
- life experience up to now with *ever* (in questions) and *never* (in negatives).
  Have you **ever** eaten pizza with bananas?
  I've **never** been to this restaurant.
- actions that finished a short time ago with *just*.
  I'm not hungry. I've **just** had a sandwich.
- actions that are (or are expected to be) completed by now with *already* (in affirmative sentences) and *yet* (in negatives and questions).
  I've **already** cooked lunch.
  I **haven't** cooked lunch **yet**.
  Have you cooked lunch **yet**?

1 Complete the sentences with the correct form of the words in brackets.
1. We can eat pizza now! The delivery _____ (just / arrive).
2. Joshua _____ (already / wash) the dishes so we can relax.
3. A: _____ (the kids / have lunch / yet)?
   B: No, they _____.
4. A: _____ (you / do the shopping / yet)?
   B: Yes, I _____ (just / return) from the shops.
5. These almond biscuits are absolutely amazing! I _____ (never / eat) better ones!
6. We are still working on a cookery project for school and we _____ (not finish / yet).

2 In pairs, ask and answer questions about the things listed below. Use *ever*.

	YOU	YOUR PARTNER
try snails		
watch a horror film		
make a cake		
cook a family dinner		

Have you ever tried snails? Yes, I have.

3 You are preparing a party with your friend. Write them a note to say what you have already done and what you haven't done yet.

Hi, Mark! I've already bought some crisps and nuts, but I haven't bought any soft drinks yet …

3.4 Present Perfect with *for* and *since*; Present Perfect and Past Simple

Present Perfect with *for* and *since*
We use the Present Perfect with *for* and *since* to describe an unfinished action that started in the past and still continues.
Use *for* with:
a week / a month / a year / ages, etc.
They have owned this restaurant **for** two years.
Use *since* with:
2012 / March / last Tuesday / the day we met, etc.
I've had this dishwasher **since** February.

Present Perfect and Past Simple
Use the Past Simple in sentences with a reference to a specific time in the past.
I **went** to this pizzeria **last Sunday**.

Use the Present Perfect to talk about life experiences up to now.
I've been to this pizzeria. It's really nice.

We use the Present Perfect with times and dates when we want to say how long something has lasted (*for* how long or *since* when).
I've known my best friend for ten years.

1 Complete the sentences with *since* or *for*.
1. I've lived in this house _____ I was born.
2. I've known him _____ ten years.
3. I've had this furniture _____ two months.
4. I've haven't seen him _____ yesterday.

2 Write sentences from the prompts.
1. Maria / get / her mobile phone / for Christmas / two years ago.
2. She / win / her skiis in a skiing competition / last year.
3. She / make / her jumper herself / last winter.
4. She / find / her favourite book in a park / three weeks ago.

Maria got her mobile phone for Christmas two years ago.

3 Write how long Maria has had her favourite things, using *since* or *for*.

Maria has had her mobile phone since Christmas two years ago.

Exercise 1
1 since
2 for
3 for
4 since

Exercise 2
Have you ever watched a horror film?
Have you ever made a cake?
Have you ever cooked a family dinner?
Students' own answers

Exercise 2
2 She won her skis in a skiing competition last year.
3 She made her jumper herself last winter.
4 She found her favourite book in a park three weeks ago.

Exercise 3
2 She has had her skis for a year.
3 She has had her jumper since last winter.
4 She has had her favourite book for three weeks.

GRAMMAR TIME

Exercise 1

amusing – more amusing – the most amusing
big – bigger – the biggest
dramatic – more dramatic – the most dramatic
dry – drier – the driest
heavy – heavier – the heaviest
large – larger – the largest
sad – sadder – the saddest
strange – stranger – the strangest

4.2 Comparatives and superlatives

Comparative
To compare two people or things, we use the comparative form + *than*.
The theatre is **more interesting than** the cinema.
(not) as + adjective + as
We can also use *(not) as* + adjective + *as*.
The cinema is **not as interesting as** the theatre.
The film adaptation is **as good as** the book.

Superlative
The superlative form is used to compare one person or thing with the rest of a group. We usually use *the* with superlative adjectives.
Omen is **the scariest** horror film I've seen.

too / (not) enough
We use *too* and *(not) enough* with adjectives to say what we expect from a situation.
The screen is **too dark**. = The screen is **not bright enough**.

1. Write the comparative and superlative forms of the adjectives below. Then write six sentences using these forms.

   amusing   big   dramatic   dry   heavy
   large   sad   strange

2. Complete the text with the words below.

   the best   bigger   the biggest   cheaper
   closer   as comfortable as   comfortable enough
   more expensive   too expensive

   Well, I often go to the cinema, and here are my three favourites. Multi-Film and MacroMovie are two typical multiplex cinemas. MacroMovie is ¹_____ to the city centre, and it has ²_____ screens (probably ³_____ in the city), and it's also ⁴_____ than the other cinemas so I don't go there so often. The tickets are ⁵_____ if you ask me … The seats in Multi-Film cinema are ⁶_____ in Macromovie, but the tickets are ⁷_____. I often choose Chaplin cinema. Maybe the chairs aren't ⁸_____, but I think the quality of sound is ⁹_____ of all the cinemas.

3. In pairs, discuss three cinemas you know. Use Exercise 2 to help you.

   A: OK, I think … is the cheapest.
   B: Yes, and it's also the closest to the city centre.

4. Write a paragraph comparing two actresses or two TV programmes.

4.4 Quantifiers: *some, any, much, many, (a) few, (a) little, a lot of, lots of*

Countable and uncountable nouns
We use quantifiers with nouns to talk about quantity. Countable nouns refer to things we can count, e.g. a bracelet, three bracelets. Uncountable nouns refer to things we cannot count, e.g. substances and liquids (rice, milk), things that are being described together (furniture, jewellery) and abstract ideas (love, peace).

a lot / lots of, much and many
Use *a lot / lots of* with all nouns in affirmative sentences.
I've got **a lot / lots** of furniture/T-shirts.
Use *much* with uncountable nouns and *many* with countable nouns in negatives and questions.
How much furniture have you got? **How many** T-shirts have you got?
I haven't got **much** furniture. I haven't got **many** T-shirts.

some and any
Some and *any* are used with both countable and uncountable nouns. We use *some* in affirmative sentences and *any* in negatives and questions.
I've got **some** furniture/T-shirts.
Have you got **any** furniture/T-shirts?
I haven't got **any** furniture/T-shirts.

a few, few + countable nouns
a little, little + uncountable nouns
I've got **a few** T-shirts. (= some T-shirts)
I've got **few** T-shirts. (= not many T-shirts)
I've got **a little** furniture. (= some furniture)
I've got **little** furniture. (= not much furniture)

1. Read the texts. Choose the correct answers.

   I only wear sports clothes, so in my wardrobe there aren't ¹_____ smart dresses. I've got ²_____ T-shirts and ³_____ hoodies. I haven't got ⁴_____ jewellery, only ⁵_____ bracelets. *Marika*

   I like smart clothes, so in my wardobe there're ⁶_____ suits and ⁷_____ white shirts. I haven't got ⁸_____ trainers. I hate sports shoes! *Rob*

1	a	any	b	some	c much
2	a	lots of	b	a lot	c much
3	a	a little	b	a few	c much
4	a	much	b	many	c any
5	a	a little	b	little	c a few
6	a	a few	b	few	c any
7	a	some	b	any	c much
8	a	much	b	few	c any

2. Write a paragraph about the clothes and accessories you have got. Use the correct quantifiers.

Exercise 1

1 a
2 a
3 b
4 a
5 c
6 a
7 a
8 c

Exercise 2

1 closer
2 bigger
3 the biggest
4 more expensive
5 too expensive
6 as comfortable as
7 cheaper
8 comfortable enough
9 the best

Grammar Time 121

223

GRAMMAR TIME

Exercise 1
2 I'm having
3 start
4 isn't going to finish
5 are coming
6 I'll make

Exercise 1
1 'll/will go, snows
2 'll/will show, comes
3 will lose, don't change
4 isn't, will arrive
5 won't start, is
6 'll/will take up, gets

GRAMMAR TIME

5.2 Talking about the future

Use **will/won't** to talk about predictions or decisions made at the moment of speaking.
I don't think he'll win the competition.
Wait, I'll help you.
Use **be going to** to talk about intentions and plans, or to make predictions based on things we know now.
I'm going to take up kayaking.
Look at the sky: it's going to rain.
We use the **Present Continuous** to talk about fixed arrangements.
We're having a competition next month.
We use the **Present Simple** to talk about timetables and schedules.
My basketball training starts in October.

1 Circle the correct option.
1 *I'm going to buy* / *I'll buy* a new tennis racket, so I'm looking for some offers on eBay.
2 No, I'm sorry. I can't visit you on Tuesday evening. *I'm having* / *I'll have* guests.
3 In our school, all extra-curricular classes *are going to start* / *start* in October.
4 Look at Susan! She looks really pale. She *isn't going to finish* / *doesn't finish* the race.
5 Bob, I've arranged an interview with *Newsweek*. They *are coming* / *are going to come* tomorrow at 6.30.
6 A I'm starving.
  B *I'm going to make* / *I'll make* you a sandwich.

2 Complete the questions with the words below.

having going (x2) meeting will (x2)

1 What do think the weather will be like tomorrow?
2 Are you _____ to get a summer job during the holidays?
3 Are you _____ any extra-curricular classes tomorrow?
4 Are you _____ your friends tonight?
5 Do you think people _____ read books in the future?
6 Are you _____ to organise a birthday party?

5.4 First Conditional + *if*/*unless*

Use the **First Conditional** (If + Present Simple, will) to talk about things that will (or won't) happen in the future under certain conditions.
If you like gymnastics, you'll love slacklining.
You'll love slacklining if you like gymnastics.
Will you try slacklining if you have a chance?
if not/*unless*
If the condition is negative, use *if not* or *unless*.
You won't be good at slacklining **if** you don't practise.
You won't be good at slacklining **unless** you practise.
time clauses with *when*
Notice the difference between a First Conditional sentence and a time clause with *when*.
I'll tell Jack about the competition if he comes. (Jack may or may not come.)
I'll tell Jack about the competition when he comes. (Jack will come and then I will tell him.)

1 Complete the sentences with the correct form of the verbs in brackets.
1 We _____ (go) skiing if it _____ (snow).
2 I _____ (show) her some skateboarding tricks when she _____ (come) round.
3 Your team _____ (lose) the volleyball match if they _____ (not change) a few players.
4 If the train _____ (not be) late, the footballers _____ (arrive) at Brighton at 5 p.m.
5 The training _____ (not start) if the coach _____ (be) ill.
6 I _____ (take up) jogging when the weather _____ (get) better.

2 Choose the correct answers. In pairs, ask and answer the questions.
1 Will you do your English homework _____ home?
  a if you return
  b when you return
  c when you'll return
2 Will you buy a new tennis racket _____ some money for Christmas?
  a if you get
  b when you'll get
  c if you'll get
3 Will you go cycling at the weekend _____ nice?
  a when the weather will be
  b if the weather is
  c when the weather is

Exercise 2
2 going
3 having
4 meeting
5 will
6 going

Exercise 2
1 b
2 a
3 b

Grammar Time

GRAMMAR TIME

GRAMMAR TIME

6.2 Modal verbs for obligation, prohibition and advice

Obligation and prohibition
To express obligation, use *must* and *have to*. *Must* is used when the speaker feels something is necessary. *Have to* is used for external rules and obligations.
I must go now. I don't want to be late.
We have to wear uniforms.

To express lack of obligation, we use *don't have to*.
She doesn't have to work in July.

Mustn't expresses prohibition.
You mustn't smoke during the flight.

Advice
Use *should/shouldn't* and *ought to* to give advice.
Ought to is more formal than *should*.
You should/shouldn't take the train.
You ought to pack your luggage now.

Must, *should* and *ought to* are modal verbs. They have the same form in all persons singular and plural. Questions are formed with inversion.
She must/should/ought to leave now.
Must/Should she leave now?
Ought she to leave now?

Questions and negatives with *have to* are formed with auxiliaries.
She has to go now.
She doesn't have to work hard.
Does she have to pack now?

1 Complete the second sentence so that it means the same as the first sentence. Use the verbs in brackets.

1 Wearing suits and white shirts is obligatory in Joanna's office.
Joanna _____ in the office. (has)
2 Is it a good idea for us to check out before breakfast?
_____ before breakfast? (should)
3 Don't take your passport. It's not necessary.
You _____ passport. (have)
4 You should buy new sunglasses.
You _____. (ought)
5 Smoking is forbidden at the airport.
You _____ at the airport. (mustn't)
6 Is it necessary for Sue to take a sleeping bag?
_____ a sleeping bag? (does)

6.4 Modal verbs for speculation

We use a modal verb + infinitive to speculate about the present.

We use *must* + infinitive when we strongly believe that something is true.
She must feel exhausted after the trip. (= I'm sure she feels exhausted.)

We use *might*, *may* or *could* + infinitive when we think something is possibly true.
It might/may/could be cold at night in the mountains. (= It's probably cold.)

We use *can't* + infinitive if we believe something is not true.
This rucksack can't weigh more than 20 kilos. It's so small! (= I'm sure it doesn't weigh more than 20 kilos.)

1 Complete the dialogues with the words below.

1

might   can't   must

A: Look at him! He ¹_____ be exhausted!
B: Oh, yes! He ²_____ be an experienced cyclist! Look at his rucksack! It's weird!
A: Yeah. He ³_____ be an artist or something.

2

can't   must   could

A: The water ⁴_____ be freezing! Look, nobody's swimming.
B: No, it ⁵_____ be freezing, not with this sunny weather. The water is always quite warm here.
A: I'm not going in, anyway. It ⁶_____ be muddy or full of seaweed ... Brr ...

2 Complete the text with one word in each gap.

Hi Mark,
I'm writing about the cruise. I've analysed all the pros and cons and I finally think it ¹m_____ not be the best idea because a cruise in the Mediterranean ²m_____ cost a fortune! Looking at the sea ³c_____ be a bit boring. Also you usually get to the harbour in the evening. It ⁴c_____ be frustrating because it's too late to go sightseeing.
Let's go sailing instead. I think it's more exciting and it ⁵m_____ be cheaper too!
Let me know what you think.
Martha

Exercise 1

1 must
2 can't
3 might
4 must
5 can't
6 could

Exercise 2

1 might/may
2 must
3 could
4 could
5 must/might/may

Exercise 1

1 has to wear suits and white shirts
2 Should we check out
3 don't have to take your
4 ought to buy new sunglasses
5 mustn't smoke
6 Does Sue need/have to take

225

GRAMMAR TIME

Exercise 1
2 wouldn't feel so unhappy if his stepmother didn't laugh at him.
3 would your family do if your aunt didn't help you?
4 would you do if you didn't get on well with your mum?
5 I were you, I wouldn't quarrel with your grandma all the time.

Exercise 1
2 who
3 which
4 who
5 where

GRAMMAR TIME

7.2 Second Conditional

We use the **Second Conditional** (*If* + Past Simple, *would* + infinitive) to talk about imaginary situations in the present and future.
If I had a brother, I'd share my room with him.
(= I haven't got a brother, so I don't share my room.)
If I had some money, I would buy my sister a new mobile phone.
I would buy my sister a new mobile phone if I had some money.
Notice the difference between First and Second Conditionals:
I'd be very happy if my grandma visited me. (= it's not very probable)
I'll be very happy if my grandma visits me. (= it's probable)
In the first and third person singular, the form of the verb *to be* after *if* is *was* or *were*.
If I were/was taller, I'd become a model

1 Order the words to make Second Conditional sentences.

1 behave / if / how / you / were / me / would / you / ?
How *would you behave if you were me?*
2 if / laugh / feel / at him / Chris / wouldn't / so unhappy / his stepmother / didn't
Chris _____
3 if / your aunt / would / your family / do / didn't / help / you / what / ?
What _____
4 get on well / would / do / if / with your mum / what / you / didn't / you / ?
What _____
5 I / were/ with your grandma / you / I / quarrel / wouldn't / all the time / if
If _____

2 Complete the Second Conditional sentences with the correct form of the verbs in brackets.

A good friend:
1 *would help* (help) me if I *were* (be) in trouble.
2 _____ (give) me some money if I _____ (not have) any.
3 _____ (buy) me some medicine if I _____ (be) ill.
4 _____ (not be) angry with me if I _____ (do) something wrong.
5 _____ (not complain) if I _____ (not be) in a good mood.

7.4 Defining and non-defining relative clauses

We use relative clauses to give information about people, things and places. We use *who* to refer to people, *which* to refer to things and *where* to refer to places.

We use defining relative clauses to give essential information about people, things and places.
I've just seen a man who lives on my street. (this piece of information is essential to identify the man)

Non-defining relative clauses are used to give additional information.
I've just seen Frank Jones, who lives in my street. (information not essential to identify who I'm talking about)

In defining relative clauses *who* and *which* can be replaced with *that*:
This is the woman that asked about you.

In non-defining relative clauses we use commas.
This is Maria Kennel, who is going to work with us.

1 Complete the questions with *who*, *which* or *where*.

1 That's the hospital *where* I was born.
2 What's the name of the teacher _____ taught you in Year 1?
3 What's the title of the film _____ you went to see at the cinema?
4 What's the name of the person _____ taught you to sail?
5 What is the address of the kindergarten _____ the picnic is going to take place?

2 Combine the sentences using relative clauses with *who*, *which* or *where*. Add commas where necessary. In which sentences could you use *that*?

1 During my brother's wedding, I met an elderly lady. She used to know my great-grandmother.
2 She told me a lot of things. I had no idea about them.
3 My great-grandmother lived in a village near Edinburgh. Edinburgh is the capital of Scotland.
4 The lady told me about a house. My great-grandmother lived there.
5 She had Shetland ponies. She often rode them.

 Grammar Time

Exercise 2
2 would give, didn't have
3 would buy, was
4 wouldn't be, did
5 wouldn't complain, wasn't

Exercise 2
1 During my brother's wedding, I met an elderly lady who used to know my great-grandmother.
2 She told me a lot of things which/that I had no idea about.
3 My great-grandmother lived in a village near Edinburgh, which is the capital of Scotland.
4 The lady told me about a house where my great-grandmother lived.
5 She had Shetland ponies which/that she often rode.

GRAMMAR TIME

Exercise 1
1 was damaged last night
2 aren't used just for fun
3 wasn't seen in Hyde Park on Sunday
4 the robbers chased by the police
5 fingerprints found on food as well
6 was stolen

Exercise 1
2 had your bike repaired
3 have your photos printed
4 have your hair dyed
5 have a tattoo done
6 have their houses cleaned

GRAMMAR TIME

8.2 Present and Past Simple Passive

We use the passive when we think *what* happens is more important than *who* does it, or when we don't know who does it.

To say who performed an action, use *by*.
The book was published by Puffin.
Who was the book published by?

We form the passive with the correct form of the verb *to be* and the past participle.

Present Simple Passive
I am often punished at school for my naughty behaviour.
The performance is based on Agatha Christie's novel.
The tickets for the performance aren't sold online.
Are shoplifters always caught by the police?

Past Simple Passive
The witness was interviewed yesterday.
The criminals were arrested on Monday.
He wasn't found guilty.
Who were the robbers punished by?

1 Complete the second sentence so that it means the same as the first sentence.

1 Someone damaged the school gate last night.
The school gate _____ .
2 Nobody uses CCTV cameras just for fun.
CCTV cameras _____ .
3 Nobody saw the suspect in Hyde Park on Sunday.
The suspect _____ .
4 Did the police chase the robbers?
Were _____ ?
5 Do people find fingerprints on food as well?
Are _____ ?
6 Someone stole my aunt's bag.
My aunt's bag _____ .

2 Complete the text with the words below.

is based   wasn't completed   were published
was published   is sold   ~~were written~~   wasn't written

The Millenium is a series of best-selling Swedish crime novels. They ¹*were written* by Stieg Larsson, who created two fantastic characters, the rebellious hacker Lisbeth Salander and the curious journalist Mikael Blomkvist. Because of Larsson's sudden death in 2004, the series ² _____ . Only three books of the series ³ _____ out of ten planned. The first book, *The Girl with the Dragon Tattoo* ⁴ _____ in 2005, after Larsson's death. The series ⁵ _____ in over fifty countries. In 2015, a new book in the series appeared. It ⁶ _____ by Larsson but by David Lagercrantz, a Swedish author and crime journalist. The book ⁷ _____ on Larsson's characters and ideas in his novels.

8.4 have/get something done

We use *have/get something done* to talk about things that we don't do ourselves and that somebody else (usually a professional) does them for us.
I made my costume. (= I made it myself.)
I had my costume made. (= Somebody else made it for me.)
Get is more informal and is used more often in spoken English.

1 Complete the questions with the correct form of the words in brackets.

1 How often do you *have your hair cut*? (have / your hair / cut)
2 Have you ever _____ ? (have / your bike / repair)
3 Do you sometimes _____ (have / your photos / print) or do you only keep them in your computer?
4 Would you ever _____ (have / your hair / dye) blue or green?
5 Are you going to _____ (have / a tattoo / do) in the future?
6 Do you think people should _____ (have / their houses / clean) or should they clean them themselves?

2 Complete the text with the words below.

my hair cut   some photos taken
my dress made   my nails painted
them repaired   it styled

Hi Jessie,
How are you? How are the preparations going for the end-of-year party? I've already had ¹_____ . I'm really lucky as my aunt works in a small clothing company and I got a discount. The dress is red and it's got little red roses at the front. I'm going to wear my red high-heels. They are the same colour as the dress, and I had ²_____ last week. Anyway, I don't want to have ³_____ although it's a bit long now … My mum says it brings bad luck before the exams! I'm only going to have ⁴_____ before the party. And I'm not going to have ⁵_____ . I'll paint them myself. By the way, remember we're having ⁶_____ on Monday for the album. Do you know what we should wear then?
Best,
Martha

Exercise 2
2 wasn't completed
3 were published
4 was published
5 is sold
6 wasn't written
7 is based

Exercise 2
1 my dress made
2 them repaired
3 my hair cut
4 it styled
5 my nails painted
6 some photos taken

GRAMMAR TIME

Exercise 1
2 How many tests did you take?
3 What were you doing at 5 p.m. yesterday?
4 Are you going to take a gap year?
5 Have you ever cheated in a test?

Exercise 1
2 was still sleeping
3 am going
4 starts
5 have never copied

GRAMMAR TIME

9.2 Word order in questions

To form **object questions**, move the verb or an auxiliary before the subject of the sentence.

- With the Present Simple or Past Simple of the verb *to be*, swap the verb and the subject.
  He was talented. → Was he talented?

- With verb forms composed of an auxiliary verb and the main verb, e.g. *have got*, Present and Past Continuous, Present Perfect, *be going to*, Future Simple, modal verbs, we move the auxiliary verb before the subject of the sentence.
  They have failed the test. → Have they failed the test? What have they failed?
  She will succeed next time. → Will she succeed next time? When will she succeed?
  She studies abroad. → Does she study abroad? Where does she study?
  They passed the test → Did they pass the test? What did they pass?

To form **subject questions**, use *who* or *what*, with the same word order as in the affirmative sentence. Don't use inversion or auxiliary verbs to form subject questions.
Cristina often helps Sue in science. → Who often helps Sue in science?
PE makes me tired. → What makes you tired?

1 Order the words to make questions.

1 do / most useful / what subjects / you / find / ?
   What subjects do you find most useful?
2 you / how many / take / tests / did / ?
3 doing / at 5 p.m. / yesterday / what / you / were / ?
4 you / a gap year / going / to take / are / ?
5 cheated / in a test / you / have / ever / ?

2 Write one subject question and one object question, using the words in brackets.

1 My dad has bought me a new English dictionary. (Who …? What …?)
   Who has bought you a new English dictionary?
   What has your dad bought you?
2 Jessica is going to take a French exam tomorrow. (Who …? When …?)
3 Mark wants to study in Belgium. (Who …? Where …?)
4 The accident happened in the science lab. (What …? Where …?)
5 A giant spider bit the French teacher. (What …? Who …?)
6 The teachers were absent because of the strike. (Who …? Why …?)

9.4 Mixed tenses

Talking about the present
Use the Present Simple for facts and routines. Use the Present Continuous for actions happening at or around the moment of speaking.

Talking about the past
Use the **Past Simple** for finished actions in the past. Use the **Past Continuous** for actions that were in progress at some time in the past, or when another action took place.

Talking about the present and the past
The **Present Perfect** is used to talk about events that finished in the past (without saying when), or to talk about past events when their effects are visible in the present or continue up to the present.

Talking about the future
Will is used to talk about predictions and decisions taken at the moment of speaking. **Be going to** is used for general plans and predictions based on evidence in the present. The **Present Continuous** is used to talk about arrangements and the **Present Simple** for timetables and schedules.

1 Complete the sentences with the correct form of the verbs in brackets.

1 I *am sunbathing* (sunbathe) in Ibiza at the moment. (Present Continuous)
2 At 7 a.m. today I _____ (still / sleep). (Past Continuous)
3 I _____ (go) to the dentist this afternoon. (Present Continuous)
4 My karate training _____ (start) in November. (Present Simple)
5 I _____ (never / copy) an essay from the internet. (Present Perfect)

2 Choose the correct option.

I ¹(remember) / 'm remembering my first day at this school very well. It ²rained / was raining when I ³entered / was entering the building. I ⁴didn't know / haven't known anybody. In the classroom I instantly ⁵noticed / was noticing a nice girl and I quickly ⁶sat / was sitting next to her. Now Sylvia and I ⁷are / have been friends for three years! In three months I ⁸am going to finish / have finished this school. I ⁹'ve already chosen / already choose a secondary school. I hope my results ¹⁰will be / were good enough to get in to the school!

Exercise 2
2 was raining
3 entered
4 didn't know
5 noticed
6 sat
7 have been
8 going to finish
9 've already chosen
10 will be

Exercise 2
2 Who is going to take a French exam tomorrow? When is Jessica going to take her French exam?
3 Who wants to study in Belgium? Where does Mark want to study?
4 What happened in the science lab? Where did the accident happen?
5 What bit the French teacher? Who was bitten by the giant spider?
6 Who was absent because of the strike? Why were the teachers absent?

IRREGULAR VERBS LIST

INFINITIVE	PAST SIMPLE	PAST PARTICIPLE
be [biː]	was/were [wɒz/wɜː]	been [biːn]
become [bɪˈkʌm]	became [bɪˈkeɪm]	become [bɪˈkʌm]
begin [bɪˈgɪn]	began [bɪˈgæn]	begun [bɪˈgʌn]
break [breɪk]	broke [brəʊk]	broken [ˈbrəʊkən]
bring [brɪŋ]	brought [brɔːt]	brought [brɔːt]
build [bɪld]	built [bɪlt]	built [bɪlt]
burn [bɜːn]	burned [bɜːnd]/ burnt [bɜːnt]	burned [bɜːnd]/ burnt [bɜːnt]
buy [baɪ]	bought [bɔːt]	bought [bɔːt]
can [kæn]	could [kʊd]	been able to [biːn ˈeɪbl tə]
catch [kætʃ]	caught [kɔːt]	caught [kɔːt]
choose [tʃuːz]	chose [tʃəʊz]	chosen [tʃəʊzn]
come [kʌm]	came [keɪm]	come [kʌm]
cost [kɒst]	cost [kɒst]	cost [kɒst]
cut [kʌt]	cut [kʌt]	cut [kʌt]
do [duː]	did [dɪd]	done [dʌn]
draw [drɔː]	drew [druː]	drawn [drɔːn]
dream [driːm]	dreamed [driːmd]/ dreamt [dremt]	dreamed [driːmd]/ dreamt [dremt]
drink [drɪŋk]	drank [dræŋk]	drunk [drʌŋk]
drive [draɪv]	drove [drəʊv]	driven [drɪvn]
eat [iːt]	ate [et]	eaten [iːtn]
fall [fɔːl]	fell [fel]	fallen [fɔːln]
feed [fiːd]	fed [fed]	fed [fed]
feel [fiːl]	felt [felt]	felt [felt]
fight [faɪt]	fought [fɔːt]	fought [fɔːt]
find [faɪnd]	found [faʊnd]	found [faʊnd]
fly [flaɪ]	flew [fluː]	flown [fləʊn]
forget [fəˈget]	forgot [fəˈgɒt]	forgotten [fəˈgɒtn]
forgive [fəˈgɪv]	forgave [fəˈgeɪv]	forgiven [fəˈgɪvn]
get [get]	got [gɒt]	got [gɒt]
give [gɪv]	gave [geɪv]	given [gɪvn]
go [gəʊ]	went [went]	gone [gɒn]
grow [grəʊ]	grew [gruː]	grown [grəʊn]
hang [hæŋ]	hung [hʌŋ]	hung [hʌŋ]
have [hæv]	had [hæd]	had [hæd]
hear [hɪə]	heard [hɜːd]	heard [hɜːd]
hide [haɪd]	hid [hɪd]	hidden [hɪdn]
hit [hɪt]	hit [hɪt]	hit [hɪt]
hold [həʊld]	held [held]	held [held]
hurt [hɜːt]	hurt [hɜːt]	hurt [hɜːt]
keep [kiːp]	kept [kept]	kept [kept]

INFINITIVE	PAST SIMPLE	PAST PARTICIPLE
know [nəʊ]	knew [njuː]	known [nəʊn]
learn [lɜːn]	learned [lɜːnd]/ learnt [lɜːnt]	learned [lɜːnd]/ learnt [lɜːnt]
leave [liːv]	left [left]	left [left]
lend [lend]	lent [lent]	lent [lent]
let [let]	let [let]	let [let]
lie [laɪ]	lay [leɪ]	lain [leɪn]
lose [luːz]	lost [lɒst]	lost [lɒst]
make [meɪk]	made [meɪd]	made [meɪd]
meet [miːt]	met [met]	met [met]
pay [peɪ]	paid [peɪd]	paid [peɪd]
put [pʊt]	put [pʊt]	put [pʊt]
read [riːd]	read [red]	read [red]
ride [raɪd]	rode [rəʊd]	ridden [rɪdn]
ring [rɪŋ]	rang [ræŋ]	rung [rʌŋ]
run [rʌn]	ran [ræn]	run [rʌn]
say [seɪ]	said [sed]	said [sed]
see [siː]	saw [sɔː]	seen [siːn]
sell [sel]	sold [səʊld]	sold [səʊld]
send [send]	sent [sent]	sent [sent]
set [set]	set [set]	set [set]
shine [ʃaɪn]	shone [ʃɒn]	shone [ʃɒn]
show [ʃəʊ]	showed [ʃəʊd]	shown [ʃəʊn]
sing [sɪŋ]	sang [sæŋ]	sung [sʌŋ]
sit [sɪt]	sat [sæt]	sat [sæt]
sleep [sliːp]	slept [slept]	slept [slept]
speak [spiːk]	spoke [spəʊk]	spoken [ˈspəʊkən]
spell [spend]	spelt [spelt]/ spelled [speld]	spelt [spelt]/ spelled [speld]
spend [spend]	spent [spent]	spent [spent]
stand [stænd]	stood [stʊd]	stood [stʊd]
steal [stiːl]	stole [stəʊl]	stolen [ˈstəʊlən]
sweep [swiːp]	swept [swept]	swept [swept]
swim [swɪm]	swam [swæm]	swum [swʌm]
take [teɪk]	took [tʊk]	taken [ˈteɪkən]
teach [tiːtʃ]	taught [tɔːt]	taught [tɔːt]
tell [tel]	told [təʊld]	told [təʊld]
think [θɪŋk]	thought [θɔːt]	thought [θɔːt]
understand [ˌʌndəˈstænd]	understood [ˌʌndəˈstʊd]	understood [ˌʌndəˈstʊd]
wake [weɪk]	woke [wəʊk]	woken [ˈwəʊkən]
wear [weə]	wore [wɔː]	worn [wɔːn]
win [wɪn]	won [wʌn]	won [wʌn]
write [raɪt]	wrote [rəʊt]	written [rɪtn]

Irregular verbs list

CULTURE 1 — Explore India

Extra activity
Before students open their Students' Books, tell them that they are going to be reading about India. Put students into groups of four and explain that they are going to write a short paragraph about India for someone who has, somehow, never heard of this country. They can write about anything to do with India, as long as the information is true.
When they have finished, invite each group to read out their paragraph to the class.

CULTURE 1 — Explore India

Exercise 1
more than 1.2 billion

1 Read about India. How many people live in India?

2 Read about India again. Answer the questions.
 1 Which is the largest city in India?
 2 Which two languages are the most important in India?
 3 Why is 1947 an important date in India's history?
 4 Which two religions do most Indians practise?
 5 What can you find in most Indian food?

3 In pairs, answer the questions.
 1 Do people speak different languages in your country?
 2 Which religions are important in your country?
 3 What food is popular in your country?

And YOU

4 Write a short paragraph about your country. Use your answers to Exercise 3 and the India examples to help you.

Exercise 2
1 New Delhi
2 Standard Hindi and English
3 1947 is when India became independent.
4 Hinduism and Islam
5 spices

India

India is the second largest country in Asia and the largest in South Asia. More than 1.2 billion people live in India and it has the second largest population in the world. Its capital and largest city is New Delhi. Other big cities are Mumbai, Kolkata and Bangalore.

Languages
India has many different cultures and people speak over 1,600 languages and dialects there. The official language of India is Standard Hindi, but English is also very important in business and education. The reason for this is that India was part of the British Empire. It became independent in 1947. Other important languages are Bengali, Telugu, Marathi, Tamil, Urdu, Gujarati and Punjabi.

Religion
In India, religion is very important. India is the home of two major world religions: Hinduism and Buddhism. Nearly 80% of the population of India practise Hinduism, but today only 0.8% of the population practise Buddhism. Another important religion is Islam – about 14% of Indians are Muslims. In fact, India has the second largest population of Muslims in the world after Indonesia.

Food
Indian food varies from place to place and different cultures have different cuisines. Indians eat a lot of rice and most Indians use spices in their food. The most important spices are pepper, chilli pepper, black mustard seed, cumin, turmeric, ginger and coriander.

128 Culture

Extra activity
After students have completed Exercise 4, divide the class into up to nine groups. Give each group an area of India to research online: Punjab, Jammu and Kashmir, Uttar Pradesh, Goa, Rajasthan, West Bengal, Kerala, Assam, Tamil Nadu. The groups should prepare a presentation that includes information about where the area is on a map of India, a description of its geographical features and famous places, and gives some examples of the local cuisine.
When the groups are ready, invite them to present their area of India to the class.

CULTURE 2 — Explore New Zealand

Extra activity

Before students open their Students' Books, tell them that they are going to be reading about New Zealand. Put students into groups of four and explain that they are going to write a short paragraph about New Zealand for someone who has, somehow, never heard of the country. They can write about anything to do with New Zealand, as long as the information is true.

When they have finished, invite each group to read out their paragraph to the class.

CULTURE 2 — Explore New Zealand

Exercise 1

It is in the south-western Pacific Ocean.

1 Read about New Zealand. Where is it?

2 Read about New Zealand again. Answer the questions.
1 Where did the Maoris come from?
2 Who was the first European to sail to New Zealand?
3 Who made the first map of New Zealand?
4 Why did European and North American ships come to New Zealand?
5 In which century did New Zealand become part of the British Empire?

3 In pairs, answer the questions.
1 Where is your country?
2 Were there famous explorers in your country in the past?
3 What are some important dates in your country's history? Why are they important?

4 Write a short paragraph about the history of your country. Use your answers to Exercise 3 and the New Zealand examples to help you.

Exercise 2

1 Polynesia
2 Abel Tasman
3 James Cook
4 to hunt for whales and to trade with the Maoris
5 the nineteenth century (1840)

New Zealand

New Zealand is a country in the south-western Pacific Ocean. It has two large islands, the North Island and the South Island, and its capital is Wellington.

The first people in New Zealand came from Polynesia in boats about a thousand years ago. We don't know exactly when they came. They developed their own culture and today we call them Maoris.

For a long time the Maoris were the only people in the country. Then, in 1642, the Dutch explorer, Abel Tasman, arrived with two ships. Unfortunately, there was a fight between the Europeans and the Maoris and many people died. Tasman left and Europeans did not come again for many years.

In 1769, the British explorer, James Cook, sailed to New Zealand and made the first maps of its coastline. After that, many European and North American ships arrived. They wanted to hunt for whales in the Pacific and trade with the Maoris.

In the nineteenth century, many British people came to live in New Zealand and they bought land from the Maoris. In 1840, the British government signed an agreement with the Maoris, the Treaty of Waitangi, and New Zealand became part of the British Empire. In 1893, New Zealand became the first country in the world to give women the right to vote.

Today New Zealand is a quiet country famous for kiwi birds, spectacular landscapes and the filming location of *The Lord of the Rings*.

Culture

Extra activity

After students have completed Exercise 4, divide the class into groups of three. Explain that they should do online research to select and find out about a Maori legend.

When the groups are ready, invite them to present their legend to the class, telling the story of their legend and saying why the legend is important for the Maori people.

EXAM TIME 1

3.34 (See page 250.)

Exercise 1

1 C
2 B
3 B
4 A
5 C
6 B
7 A

EXAM TIME 1 — Listening

1 3.34 There are seven questions in this part. For each question, choose the correct answer A, B or C.

Tip: Remember you will hear each recording twice, so you have time to check your answers.

Example: Which film do they want to see?

1 What does the girl want to buy for her mum's birthday?

 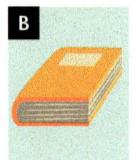 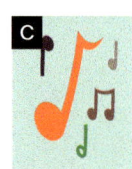

2 What is the view from the girl's window?

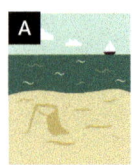  

3 What did the boy do at the weekend?

4 What was the weather like yesterday?

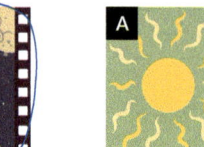  

5 What did the boy make for dinner?

6 Where is the boy's phone?

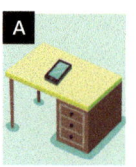 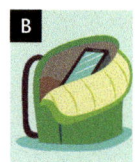 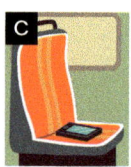

7 What is the boy's sister's job?

Exam time 1

EXAM TIME 1

🔊 **3.35** and **3.36** (See page 250.)

Exercise 2
1 (next) Thursday
2 Robot Life
3 France
4 Maria
5 8.30 a.m.
6 sandwiches and drinks

Exercise 3
1 B
2 A
3 B
4 A
5 B
6 B

EXAM TIME 1 — Listening

2 🔊 **3.35** You will hear a teacher talking about a school trip to a science exhibition. Complete the gaps with the missing information.

VISIT TO SCIENCE EXHIBITION

Day of trip: 1 _____
Name of exhibition: 2 _____
Exhibition is also going to: 3 _____
You can have a conversation with a robot called: 4 _____
The trip will begin at: 5 _____
Students should take: 6 _____

3 🔊 **3.36** You will hear a conversation between a girl, Kelly, and a boy, Dan, about a TV documentary called *All Change!* Decide if each sentence is correct or incorrect. If correct, choose the letter A for YES. If incorrect, choose the letter B for NO.

		YES	NO
1	Dan enjoyed the documentary last night.	A	B
2	Kelly agrees with Dan about the number of environmental documentaries on television.	A	B
3	Kelly and Dan both go skiing regularly.	A	B
4	One of Dan's friends was once near an avalanche.	A	B
5	Kelly and Dan agree about the importance of documentaries like these.	A	B
6	Dan is persuaded to watch the next documentary in the series.	A	B

EXAM TIME 1 — Speaking

1 Students A and B, choose TWO questions to ask your partner.
   1 Tell us about your English teacher.
   2 What's your favourite season? Why?
   3 What do you do in your free time?
   4 What's your favourite meal?

2 Work in pairs. Look at the picture and do the task together.

Tip: Talk about all the pictures first before you decide which is best.

A friend from another country is coming to stay with you. Talk together about the activities you could do with him on his first Saturday afternoon, and then decide which is best.

Exam time 1

233

EXAM TIME 1   Speaking

3 Work in pairs. Take turns to tell your partner about a photograph. Your photographs will be of people eating meals.

Tip: Describe everything you can see in the photograph: the people, their clothes, the place and the things you can see there.

Student A

It's your turn first. Look at the photograph and tell Student B what you can see in it.

Student B

Tell Student A what you can see in the photograph.

4 Work in pairs. Talk to each other about the sort of meals you like to have and where you like to eat them.

Tip: This should be a conversation, so remember to ask your partner questions to give them a chance to say something.

Exam time 1

EXAM TIME 2

🔊 **3.37** (See page 251.)

Exercise 1
1 C
2 C
3 C
4 A
5 B
6 B
7 A

EXAM TIME 2 — Listening

1 🔊 **3.37** There are seven questions in this part. For each question, choose the correct answer A, B or C.

Tip: Remember to listen to the whole conversation before you choose your answer, because the correct answer is sometimes at the end.

Example: Which film do they want to see?

4 What time will the boy go to the theatre?

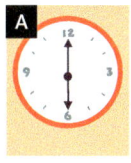 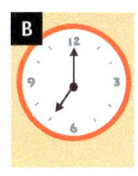 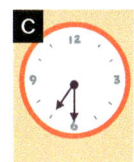

1 What holiday do the boy and girl want to go on?

5 What is the girl definitely going to take camping?

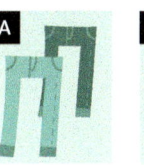  

2 What did the girl watch last night?

6 What was the boy doing yesterday afternoon?

  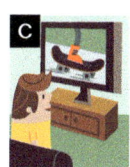

3 What did the boy do first at the Leisure Centre?

  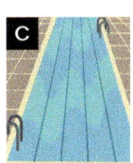

7 What does the girl want to get in town?

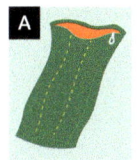  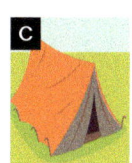

Exam time 2 133

235

EXAM TIME 2

3.38 and 3.39 (See pages 251 and 252.)

Exercise 2
1. b
2. b
3. b
4. c
5. b
6. b

Exercise 3
1. 9 and 10
2. south
3. Free Voice
4. street dance
5. Young Dancers
6. festivals.com

EXAM TIME 2 — Listening

2 🔊 **3.38** You will hear part of an interview with a girl called Suzy who has just got a role in a major film. For each question, choose the correct answer a, b or c.

Tip: Before you hear the recording, use the time you have to read the questions, so that you know what sort of information you are going to listen for.

1. How is Suzy feeling at the moment?
   a. She is worried that it may be too hard.
   b. She is excited about starting work.
   c. She is surprised that she got the part.
2. Suzy won't be swimming much in the film because
   a. she can't swim.
   b. she hasn't got a good style.
   c. her character doesn't swim much.
3. What sort of film has she been in before?
   a. a comedy
   b. a historical film
   c. an educational film
4. Why didn't Suzy go to drama school?
   a. She got the part in the film.
   b. She wasn't accepted by a drama school.
   c. She was advised to do it later.
5. How does Suzy think she'll change because of the film?
   a. She'll become more confident.
   b. She'll be a better actress.
   c. She'll learn more about jobs in film-making.
6. When this filming ends, Suzy
   a. will start another film.
   b. would like to do some travelling.
   c. is going to drama school.

3 🔊 **3.39** You will hear some information about an open-air music concert. Complete the gaps with the missing information.

Tip: You may hear several pieces of information that sound like the right answer, for example different dates, but only one of them is correct. Listen carefully before you make a choice.

MUSIC IN THE PARK

Dates of festival: ¹_____ August

Parking: ²_____ entrance

Singers: ³_____

Dance competition categories: hip hop, salsa and ⁴_____

Dancers will appear on TV show:
⁵_____

Book here for cheapest tickets:
⁶_____

EXAM TIME 2 Speaking

Tip: Remember to try to extend your answers to some of the questions, with reasons and examples.

1 Students A and B answer the questions below.
1. What's your name?
2. What's your surname? How do you spell that?
3. Where do you come from?
4. Do you study English at school? Do you like it?

2 Students A and B, choose TWO questions to ask your partner.
1. How often do you go out with friends?
2. Tell me something about your favourite band or singer.
3. Do you enjoy watching or doing sport?
4. What did you do on your last holiday?

3 Work in pairs. Look at the picture and do the task together.

Tip: Make sure you each get an opportunity to talk. Try not to talk all the time or let your partner do all the talking.

Two teenagers from your country want to go on holiday together for a week in the summer. Talk together about the different types of holiday they could go on, and then decide which holiday is best.

EXAM TIME 3

🔊 **3.40** (See page 252.)

Exercise 1
1 C
2 A
3 C
4 B
5 A
6 C
7 C

EXAM TIME 3 — Listening

1 🔊 **3.40** There are seven questions in this part. For each question, choose the correct answer A, B or C.

Tip: Before you listen, look at the pictures and think about which words you might hear.

Example: Which film do they want to see?

4 Where did the accident happen?

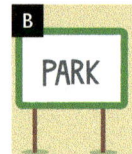 

1 When will the boy and girl's granddad go to a restaurant?

5 What is the new after-school club?

2 What did the girl take with her on her walk?

6 What time is the girls' swimming race?

  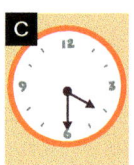

3 Where will the new students be this afternoon?

7 Which subject did both the boy and the girl fail?

EXAM TIME 3

🔊 **3.41** and **3.42** (See pages 252 and 253.)

Exercise 2
1 a
2 b
3 b
4 c
5 b
6 c

Exercise 3
1 three weeks
2 Professor Green
3 detailed guide
4 East End
5 1861
6 maps

EXAM TIME 3 — Listening

2 🔊 **3.41** You will hear a girl called Debby talk about her trip to France. For each question, choose the correct answer a, b or c.

Tip: Sometimes it helps to read just the questions and not the options before you listen for the first time. Try to answer the question and then check if your answer is one of the options.

1 Where did Debby stay while she was in France?
   a a short distance from Paris
   b in the centre of the town
   c near a theme park
2 How did Debby feel about her French language skills?
   a She wishes she could speak as quickly as the French.
   b She was surprised at how much she could understand.
   c She thinks she doesn't speak well because of limited vocabulary.
3 What does Debby say about French food?
   a She enjoys it because it's unusual.
   b She could only eat some things her host mother cooked.
   c She would like to have tried more fish dishes.
4 Why didn't they go to an art exhibition?
   a It was outside and the weather was bad.
   b She'd seen the exhibition in London.
   c It wasn't open.
5 Debby is next going to see her French friend again
   a in two weeks' time.
   b this autumn.
   c next year.
6 In the future, Debby wants to
   a become a teacher.
   b become a writer.
   c use French in her job.

3 🔊 **3.42** You will hear some information about a crime museum. Complete the gaps with the missing information.

Tip: It's important to spell easy basic words correctly when you fill in missing information, so check your spelling at the end.

CRIME MUSEUM

The museum has been open for
1 _____ .

The person who finished the work on the museum's collection was
2 _____ .

Visitors can get written information about the exhibits from a ³ _____ .
Ned and John Carson killed people from London's ⁴ _____ .
A policeman caught them in
5 _____ .
The gang of thieves that carried out a robbery left some ⁶ _____ , which are in one of the museum rooms.

EXAM TIME 3

EXAM TIME 3 — Speaking

1 Work in pairs. Take turns to tell your partner about a photograph. Your photographs will be of students learning.

Tip: Don't worry if you can't remember a specific word. Try to explain it in another way.

Student A

It's your turn first. Look at the photograph and tell Student B what you can see in it.

Student B

Tell Student A what you can see in the photograph.

2 Work in pairs. Talk to each other about the things you learned at your first school and the things you study now.

Tip: Use linking words to contrast things in the past and things now, such as *but*, *whereas* and *however*.

CLIL 1 ART — 3D printer sculpture

Extra activity

Before students open their Students' Books, have a class discussion about sculptures. Ask students if there are any sculptures in their town. If there are, discuss which sculptures they like or dislike, giving reasons why. Also talk about famous sculptures around the world, such as the Little Mermaid in Copenhagen or the Statue of Liberty in New York, and any others that students have seen.

Exercise 2

1 stone, metal, wood, ice
2 They make a cast of their sculpture and fill it with hot metal.
3 machine parts, furniture, shoes, accessories, some clothes
4 The artist makes a digital model on the computer.
5 an additive process, because it adds different layers of different shapes
6 small models of themselves

ART — 3D printer sculpture

Art from technology

When people think about sculpture, they usually think about statues made of materials like stone, metal, wood or even ice! Sculptors use special tools to make these with their hands. Sometimes they make casts of their sculptures. They fill the casts with hot metal to make bronze sculptures.

Today there is a new and interesting type of sculpture. Technology is progressing very fast and is changing many parts of our lives – even art! 3D printers are becoming very important for manufacturing, making things like machine parts and furniture, and also in fashion, making shoes, accessories, and even clothes. Now artists are also using them to create sculptures.

First the artist makes a digital model on the computer. Then the 3D printer prints it out. They print layers of material to build up the object. This is called an 'additive process' because it adds different layers of different shapes. They can make very fine pieces like tiny flowers and insects, and big, colourful, modern pieces – from life-size statues of people to huge dinosaurs! They print big statues in sections. To make bronze sculptures, they make casts from the printed objects.

It's even possible to have 3D printed selfies! We can have small statues of ourselves on our wedding cake or we can have small models of our whole family on our desk. Nearly everything is possible with 3D printing today.

1 Do you have a favourite sculpture? What do you know about it? Tell the class.

2 Read the article. Answer the questions.
 1 What materials do sculptors often use?
 2 How do they make bronze sculptures?
 3 What sort of things do 3D printers usually create?
 4 What is the first step in 3D printer sculpture?
 5 What is the next step called? Why?
 6 What can some people put on their wedding cakes?

3 What new information did you learn from the text? What was the most interesting part? Discuss in pairs.

4 Read the text about 3D printing and art. Do you think this is a good idea? Why? / Why not? Discuss in pairs.

One artist, Cosmo Wenman, wants to digitally scan famous sculptures from museums all over the world and put the files online. His idea is that everyone can print out their own copies on a 3D printer. He wants these sculptures to belong to everyone.

5 Look at the photos. Which of these sculptures would you like to create with a 3D printer? Discuss in pairs.

6 **PROJECT** Use the internet to find out about an artist who uses 3D printing. Make notes about the things below.
- his/her nationality and experience
- the types of sculpture he/she makes
- any other interesting information

7 **PROJECT** Write a paragraph about the artist. Add pictures.

CLIL 139

Extra activity

Ask students if they can think of any problems that could occur in the future if everyone had their own 3D printer. Put students into groups of three to do some online research to find out how 3D printers may change the world in the future. When they have finished, discuss what the groups found out and ask them to discuss whether they think 3D printers are a good thing or a bad thing.

CLIL 2 SCIENCE — Cooking

> **Extra activity**
>
> Before students open their Students' Books, ask them to think of a meal they have eaten which looked better than it tasted. Put students into groups of four to discuss their ideas, then invite each group to tell the class about the most interesting meal they discussed.

SCIENCE — Cooking

Cooking and science

Heston Blumenthal is an English chef. He is important because he has made people think about the science of cooking. Heston uses complicated scientific techniques all the time in his cooking and some equipment that he uses in his kitchen is from a science laboratory!

Science is part of all cooking. Every time we cook something, there is a chemical change. A chemical change means that we create a new substance. The process is irreversible – the ingredient cannot change back. To do this, we need energy – in cooking that means a high temperature. When we use heat in cookery, we change both the taste and the texture of the ingredients.

Here are some examples of chemical changes that happen when we cook. A cake looks and tastes very different before and after cooking. With the heat of the oven, it rises. This is because the baking powder ($NaHCO_3$) in the mixture changes at a high temperature. It produces carbon dioxide (CO_2) and the cake grows. But there was no CO_2 in the cake before! Another example is when we toast bread. The carbohydrates in the bread break to form carbon (C). This makes the bread brown and hard – a change in texture and colour. Proteins in meat and eggs change too. The protein molecules take the energy from the heat and change shape. The meat gets harder and the meat becomes brown. Clear egg whites become solid and white.

Chefs like Heston Blumenthal use their knowledge about chemical changes in food to create new tastes and textures. Heston's famous bacon-and-egg ice cream is made using liquid nitrogen!

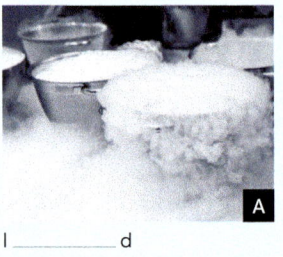  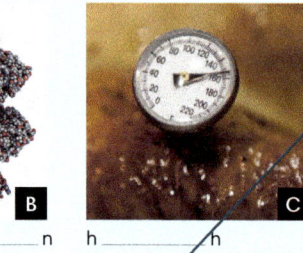 

A l_____ d n_____ n
B p_____ n m_____ s
C h_____ h t_____ e
D a s_____ e l_____ y

1 Why do you think some people say cooking is an art and others say it's a science? Discuss in pairs.

2 Read the article quickly and find words to complete the captions for photos A–D.

3 Read the article again. Answer the questions.
 1 Who is Heston Blumenthal and why is he important?
 2 What does 'a chemical change' mean?
 3 What happens to make a cake rise?
 4 What happens when bread becomes toast?
 5 What happens when we cook meat and eggs?
 6 Which of Blumenthal's dishes is made using liquid nitrogen?

4 What new information did you learn from the text? What was the most interesting part? Discuss in pairs.

5 Think of a raw ingredient which changes when cooked. Then, in pairs, take turns to describe the ingredient before and after cooking. Can your partner guess what you are describing?
 A: *Before cooking they're small, round, white and hard. After cooking at a high temperature they're light, brown and break easily.*
 B: *Potatoes which become crisps!*

6 **PROJECT** Use the internet to research another chemical change that happens to food during cooking. Make notes about the things below.
 • what happens and why
 • examples of meals where this happens
 • any other interesting information

7 **PROJECT** Prepare a short presentation. Write a paragraph about the chemical change. Add pictures and diagrams.

140 CLIL

> **Exercise 2**
>
> A liquid nitrogen
> B protein molecules
> C high temperature
> D a science laboratory

> **Exercise 3**
>
> 1 He is a chef. He has made people think about the science of cooking.
> 2 It means that we create a new substance.
> 3 The heat makes baking powder produce carbon dioxide.
> 4 The carbohydrates break to form carbon which makes the bread brown and hard.
> 5 The protein molecules take energy from the heat and change shape. Meat gets harder and becomes brown. Clear egg whites become solid and white.
> 6 bacon-and-egg ice cream

> **Extra activity**
>
> Have a class discussion about whether or not we need to know the science behind cooking. Ask students what difference they think it could make if one person understands the scientific reason for why their cake rises and another person just follows a recipe without thinking about why they are adding baking powder.

CLIL 3 DRAMA — Zigger Zagger

> **Extra activity**
>
> Before students open their Students' Books, put them into groups of three to discuss hooliganism at football matches. Ask students if it is a problem in their country and, if so, to give examples of clubs which have a large hooligan element. Tell them also to discuss why other sports don't seem to have this problem. Invite groups to share their ideas with the class.

DRAMA — Zigger Zagger

Zigger Zagger

There are many plays and films about football but Peter Terson's *Zigger Zagger* (1967) is one of the best. It was also probably the first play to show football hooliganism – fighting between supporters from different clubs. In the 1960s, football hooliganism was causing a lot of problems and in *Zigger Zagger*, Terson tried to show why this was happening. He also wanted to show how difficult life was for young people at that time.

Zigger Zagger is about a boy called Harry who is from a poor family. When he leaves school, he doesn't know what to do with his life. Harry is passionate about football and supports his local team, City End. Zigger Zagger is the name of the dangerous, angry leader of the City End fans. He offers Harry excitement at the match and after it. His world is full of singing, shouting and fighting. Les is a relative of Harry's who wants Harry to get a good job, a wife and a house. At first, Harry follows Zigger Zagger but then realises that his life is crazy and wrong.

If you see this play, you'll never forget it. The setting is a football ground and on the stage the supporters are in rows like in a stadium. They face the audience all through the play. The main characters act on the stage in front of them, and the supporters sing and shout and wave scarves between the scenes. Peter Terson wrote the play for the National Youth Theatre and the first performance in London had a cast of almost ninety young people – most of them were acting the parts of football fans. It's loud and scary but a very exciting and important play.

> **Exercise 3**
>
> 1 Peter Terson
> 2 1967
> 3 Football hooliganism
> 4 Harry, Zigger Zagger, Les
> 5 A football ground
> 6 National Youth Theatre
> 7 almost 90

1 Describe the photo. How do football club supporters show their support for their team in your country?

2 Have you ever seen a play or film with a story about sport? If so, did you enjoy it? Why? / Why not?

3 Read the article about *Zigger Zagger*, a play about sport. Complete the fact file.

ZIGGER ZAGGER
Writer: 1 _____
Written in (year): 2 _____
Topic: 3 _____
Main characters: 4 _____
Setting: 5 _____
Theatre that first performed it: 6 _____
Number of people in the first cast: 7 _____

4 Would you like to see this play? Why? / Why not?

5 Look at two film posters about sport. In pairs, discuss your ideas about what the film may be about and then compare your ideas with the class. Think about the following:
- main character or characters
- the supporting characters
- the challenge the characters face
- the ending

6 **PROJECT** Use the internet to research another play about sport. Make notes about the things below.
- the writer
- the story
- the cast
- why the play is important or interesting
- any other interesting information

7 **PROJECT** Write a paragraph about the play. Add pictures.

> **Extra activity**
>
> Put students into groups of three. Ask students for any sports-related ideas which might make an interesting play or film (e.g. a small team taking on a famous, professional team and managing to beat them).
> Explain that the groups should role play pitching an idea for a sports-related film to producers, and that they will only get finance if they can convince the producers. When they are ready, invite each group to pitch their idea to the class. When all the groups have given their pitches, have a class vote for the best idea.

CLIL 4 GEOGRAPHY — International Date Line

Extra activity

Before students open their Students' Books, tell them that a tour company has a special offer where they can spend New Year's Eve in New Zealand, then take a four-hour flight to the Cook Islands, drive to their hotel, and then get ready for New Year's Eve celebrations once more. Ask students for their ideas about how this could be possible (*New Year's Eve in New Zealand is one of the first countries **after** the International Date Line, whereas the Cook Islands are **before** it*).

GEOGRAPHY — International Date Line

Imaginary lines around the Earth

Tonga and Samoa are two islands in the South Pacific. They are 557 miles apart. If you flew from Tonga to Samoa, the journey would take you two hours, but you would arrive twenty-two hours before you left! It might be 5 November when you leave Tonga and 4 November when you arrive in Samoa. Why? Because you would cross the International Date Line (IDL). This can be confusing for travellers and cause problems with hotel bookings!

The IDL – an imaginary line, not a real one – goes from north to south. There are two other important imaginary lines across the Earth: the Equator, which divides the world into the northern and southern hemispheres, and the Prime Meridian (which goes through London), dividing the world into the western and eastern hemispheres. The IDL is on the opposite side of the world to the Prime Meridian. The world is always turning and as we travel around the world (east or west), our days become shorter or longer. The IDL tells all the countries in the world where the beginning of one day and the end of another come together.

The IDL starts at the North Pole and goes down to the South Pole and crosses through the Pacific Ocean. But it isn't a straight line – it has several zigzags in it! This is so that it is the same date in one country. For example, the line zigzags east to go through the Bering Straits so that Alaska and Russia are on different sides. The country of Kiribati used to be on the eastern side but it decided to change to the western side. It wanted to be the first country in the world to celebrate the new millennium in 2000!

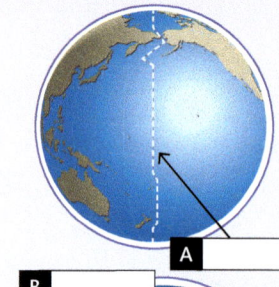
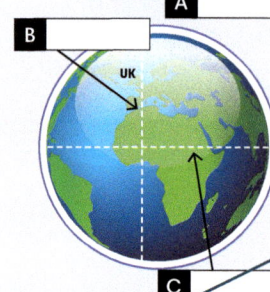

Exercise 1

A International Date Line
B Prime Meridian
C Equator

1 Read the article quickly. Label the lines A–C on the maps.

2 Read the article again. Mark the sentences T (true) or F (false).
1 ☐ It takes twenty-two hours to fly from Tonga to Samoa.
2 ☐ The IDL is on the other side of the world from the Prime Meridian.
3 ☐ The International Date Line goes in a straight line from north to south.
4 ☐ It is the same time and day in Russia and Alaska.
5 ☐ Kiribati is on the eastern side of the IDL.

Exercise 2

1 F (It takes two hours.)
2 T
3 F (It has several zigzags in it.)
4 F (Alaska and Russia are on different sides of the IDL.)
5 F (It used to be on the eastern side but decided to change to the western side.)

3 What new information did you learn from the text? What was the most interesting part? Discuss in pairs.

4 Read about how the problem of losing a day was first discovered. In pairs, take turns to make, ask and answer the questions.
1 who / Ferdinand Magellan?
2 why / he / famous?
3 what / the crew / discover?
4 what / the year?
5 what / happen / seventeenth century?
6 what / happen / 1884?

History of the IDL

In 1519 the explorer Ferdinand Magellan was the first person to sail round the world. During the journey, the crew kept careful records. When they got home, they discovered that they had lost a complete day. The date they had was a day behind the people in their country. This was the beginning of the idea of an international date line and in the seventeenth century it started to appear on maps. It became official in 1884, after an international meridian conference. However, there is still no law that says the IDL exists.

5 **PROJECT** Use the internet to find out about one of the other imaginary lines around the Earth. Make notes about the things below.
- where it goes
- its purpose and when it was named
- any other interesting information

6 **PROJECT** Prepare a short presentation. Write a paragraph about the imaginary line you have chosen and add a map with labels. Share your presentation with the class.

Exercise 4

1 Who was Ferdinand Magellan? He was an explorer.
2 Why is/was he famous? He was the first person to sail round the world.
3 What did the crew discover? They discovered that they had lost a complete day.
4 What was the year? 1519
5 What happened in the seventeenth century? The IDL started to appear on maps.
6 What happened in 1884? The IDL became official.

Extra activity

Before students look at Exercise 4, put them into groups of four. Tell the groups to discuss any famous explorers they know. They should give the explorers' names, their nationalities and where in the world they travelled to. When they are ready, invite groups to share their ideas with the class.

CLIL 5 SCIENCE — Forensics

Extra activity
Before students open their Students' Books, put them into groups of three. Write the following words on the board: *evidence*, *microscope*, *autopsy*, *post-mortem*, *saliva*. Explain that these words relate to the topic of the lesson. Tell the groups to discuss or find out the meaning of the words in a dictionary, and to discuss their ideas about what the topic of the lesson will be. When they are ready, invite groups to share their ideas with the class.

SCIENCE — Forensics

Forensics

The crime scene
When there is a crime, the police often use forensic scientists to help them find the criminal. At nearly every crime scene there is some evidence that scientists can check. This might be blood, hair, fingerprints or other very small things that they can analyse. The forensic scientist uses special equipment in a police laboratory to carry out experiments. They use a powerful microscope (an electron microscope) to check both the evidence and samples from suspects. Forensic scientists also study dead bodies to find out how and w[hen] they died. This is called an autopsy or post-mortem. All this information helps the police.

Fingerprints
Everyone has different fingerprints. These are the lines and circles on the tips of our fingers. When we touch something, we leave a pr[int]. Scientists can use special powder to copy these prints. These are compared to records of fingerprints to find out who left them.

Blood spatter
Blood is very important to forensic scientists. The way that it falls gives lots of information. For example, if it's on a wall (blood spatter) [it] can show where a killer was standing and how fast the blood was travelling. Sometimes it even shows the shape of the killer!

DNA
DNA is like a genetic fingerprint. Everyone's DNA is different (apart from identical twins). So if a criminal leaves DNA at a crime scene, [a] forensic scientist can use it. DNA can be found in many things such as blood, hair, teeth, bone and saliva (from inside our mouths). W[e] leave our DNA everywhere – on clothes and cups, in hairbrushes and on toothbrushes.

Exercise 2
- **A** fingerprint
- **B** DNA
- **C** blood splatter
- **D** electron microscope
- **E** crime scene

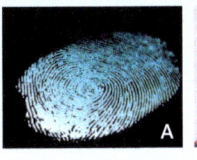 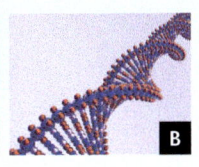   

A f _____   B D _____   C b _____ / s _____   D e _____ / m _____   E c _____ / s _____

1. What do you think a forensic scientist does? Discuss in pairs.
2. Read the article quickly and find words to complete the captions for photos A–E.
3. Read the article again. Answer the questions.
   1. What is a forensic scientist?
   2. Where does a forensic scientist work?
   3. What can they find out?
   4. What are fingerprints and how does a forensic scientist check them?
   5. What can blood spatter show?
   6. What is DNA and where is it found?
4. Do you think it is a good idea for the police to keep samples of everyone's DNA to help solve crimes? Why? / Why not?
5. In pairs, choose and read one of the texts, A or B. Tell your partne[r] the information in your text and how it helps forensic scientists.

A Hair
Our hair falls out all the time and a criminal often leaves hair at a crime scene. Scientists can analyse hair and find out if the colour is natural and if it is an animal or human hair. They can also get an idea of the age, race and gender of the person. There are fourteen things a hair can tell the scientist! If the hair ha[s] a root, it can also give DNA.

B Shoes
Shoes can leave prints. These can tell scientists about a criminal's size, the way he/she walks and the type of shoe that he/she wore. Shoes also leave dirt[.] Scientists can sometimes learn where the person lives or works, if he/she has pets, where he/she walks and even which field or path he/she has walked on.

6. **PROJECT** Find out how the police solved a famous crime using forensics. Make notes about the crime and the evidence.
7. **PROJECT** Prepare a short presentation. Write a paragraph abou[t] the crime and the forensic work involved. Add pictures.

CLIL 143

Exercise 3
1. A scientist who carries out experiments on evidence from a crime scene to try to identify the criminal.
2. in a (police) laboratory
3. who blood, fingerprints and other evidence belonged to and how and when people died
4. The lines and circles on the tips of our fingers. Scientists use special powder to copy them and then compare them with records of fingerprints to find out who left them.
5. Where the killer was standing, how fast the blood was travelling, sometimes even the shape of the killer.
6. It is like a genetic fingerprint. It is found in things such as blood, hair, teeth, bone and saliva.

Background notes
Juan Vucetich made the first identification of a criminal fingerprint in Argentina in 1892. He identified the murderer Francisca Rojas after he matched a bloody print on a door post with her thumb print, proving her identity as the murderer. The first mention of fingerprints was in a Sherlock Holmes novel, *The Sign of Four*, published two years earlier in 1890. Holmes also identified criminals through typewritten messages, matching them to a typewriter, footprints and handwriting, all of which subsequently became useful forensic tools in real life.

STUDENT ACTIVITIES

STUDENT ACTIVITIES

Unit 1 Lesson 1.5 Exercise 2

ANSWER KEY
Mostly As: You're obviously busy with other things in life, and that's great. Have fun and enjoy real time with your friends!
Mostly Bs: You know it's there when you need it, but technology isn't the most important thing in your life.
Mostly Cs: You're internet crazy! You love going online and checking messages from friends. Make sure you take time to do other things, too.

Unit 3 Revision SPEAKING Exercise 7

MENU
Food
Pizza with cheese and tomato
Chicken salad
Fresh bread rolls with tuna or cheese
Ice cream — any flavour!

Drinks
Fruit juice   Smoothies
Coffee   Tea   Water

Unit 7 Lesson 7.1 Exercise 7

ANSWER KEY
Mostly As: You don't like big crowds and are probably happy on your own. You know how to be a good friend to a few special people.
Mostly Bs: You love having lots of friends. You give your opinion honestly, and you don't mind if other people agree. You are happiest when you're busy and in a crowd.
Mostly Cs: You know how to get a balance. You can have fun when you want, but you're not afraid to do things on your own.

Unit 8 Revision SPEAKING Exercise 7

A: Your parents want you to stay with your cousins for the summer. You don't want to.

B: Your teacher says you must study more for your exams, but you want to do more sport.

Unit 9 Revision SPEAKING Exercise 5

Personal details: Selma, 14
From: Mexico
Been to the UK before?
No, this is the first time.
Interests: football, art, food
While in the UK, would like to …
go to Madame Tussauds and to a football match!

Personal details: Angelina, 15
From: France
Been to the UK before?
Yes, three times.
Interests: photography, old films, acting
While in the UK, would like to …
see some musicals at the theatre; improve my accent

Personal details: Tomek, 16
From: Poland
Been to the UK before?
Yes, once.
Interests: nature and animals, handball
While in the UK, would like to …
go to London Zoo, and eat fish and chips!

Personal details: Selim, 15
From: Turkey
Been to the UK before?
No, this is the first time.
Interests: football, history, architecture
While in the UK, would like to …
visit Stonehenge and go to a football match

Audio scripts — Students' Book audio scripts

1.09 Unit 0, 0.3, Exercise 8

S = Skye   D = Dan

S: Hi, Dan. Are you OK?
D: No, I'm a bit worried. I've got so much homework for Monday.
S: What do you mean? We haven't got school on Monday. It's a holiday, so come on … Relax! … It's party time!
D: Oh, that's brilliant. I feel much better.
S: Good. In fact, there is a party on Saturday. Can you come?
D: Sure. But I don't know many people …
S: Don't worry. You can meet some of my friends. They're really nice.
D: Thanks, Skye.

1.12 Unit 0, 0.4, Exercise 6

A = Alisha   T = Tommo

A: I'm glad Dan's at our school.
T: Me too. He's cool, but he was very shy on his first day.
A: That's true, but it was difficult for him. He lived with his brother in America last year.
T: Do you know he speaks Spanish?
A: Yes, I think his grandparents are Mexican. I'd love to speak Spanish.
T: At least you speak Hindi. I only speak English … and a bit of very bad French!

1.13 Unit 0, 0.5, Exercise 2

A = Alisha   T = Tommo   S = Skye   D = Dan

A: Hi, guys. Is the café open? Oh yes. The sign on the door says 'open'.
T: That's good. I love their homemade lemonade.
S: Me too.
T: What's Dan doing? Is he coming?
S: I think so. Er … I can phone him. Hang on. Hi, Dan? It's me. Do you know where the café is? We're all here.
D: Yes, I'm nearly there. Are you waiting outside?
S: Yes, I'm looking out for you …
D: Oh, I can see you now. Hi, everyone! This looks great!
T: Glad you like it. It's our favourite place!
S: Well, it's the *only* place to hang out in Woodley Bridge.

1.26 Unit 1, 1.5, Exercise 6

G = Gemma   RP = Radio presenter

G: Well, I think we're the same as most other families. We love our screens and all enjoy using our smartphones at home. We've all got one. On a schoolday, I use the alarm on my phone, so the minute I wake up I see my phone and er … I check my messages. Then I get up. My phone goes everywhere with me because I listen to music on it.
RP: And what about your mum?
G: Mum prefers her tablet. She often reads the news on it. She's also training for a race and she uses the app on her phone to show her how fast she runs.
RP: Your brother's older. Does he still use his phone or tablet a lot?
G: Yeh, definitely. He loves looking at funny video clips. He often sits with his earphones in and laughs. Mum gets a bit angry when she asks him something and he doesn't answer.
RP: So, do you think you talk less at home because of the technology?
G: No, not at all. We never text at mealtimes. But in the evening we like watching funny videos … and we often share photos. It's a big part of our daily life and I think it's something that we all enjoy.

1.36 Unit 2, 2.2, Exercise 8

R = Roberto   M = Marianna

R: First up on tonight's programme, Marianna Fernandez tells us more about a very strange storm. Marianna?
M: Well, last year I met a scientist who studied storms. His name was Professor Mendes. He was very interested in Catatumbo lightning, which happens over Lake Maracaibo in Venezuela. Two weeks ago, I visited Professor Mendes to see the lightning for myself. I arrived on a dark night and we watched the clouds, but we didn't see a storm. Luckily, I stayed there for five days and I saw storms on three different nights. In fact, storm clouds gather there most nights and there are about one million lightning strikes a year! Also, until recently, people thought that Catatumbo storms were different from other storms because they didn't hear thunder. I didn't hear any thunder myself. However, the storms happen over the middle of the lake, so they're far away. Professor Mendes explained that you can only hear thunder if you are near a storm. This is also the reason why the lightning looks pinkish-orange, because it is so far away. I took some awesome photos. Of course, you can't see them on the radio, but yesterday I put some photos up on our website for listeners to enjoy.

1.40 Unit 2, 2.5, Exercise 3

M = Max   A = Abigail

M: Are these your photos from *Go Wild*?
A: Yes, it was amazing. That's the sunset on the second day, Tuesday. We made a fire and told scary stories when it was dark!
M: Cool. Did you really sleep outside?
A: No. We learnt how to make a shelter when we got there on Monday, but it was cold at night so we slept in tents in the end. A girl in my tent liked listening to the wildlife in the forest, but I didn't hear a thing. I slept so well.
M: Ugh, it looks freezing.
A: Yes, but at least it wasn't raining. On Thursday night, there weren't any clouds and we watched the stars. It was awesome.
M: And were there lots of spiders?
A: No, I think it was too cold for them. Honestly, Max, it was so good to do something different every day. On Wednesday we walked up a path into the mountain to look for wild animals. Then we ate near a waterfall.
M: Did you see any bears?
A: No, don't be stupid …, but we found a cave where hundreds of bats were living.
M: Ah, now that sounds fun. I like bats.
A: It was. But the best day was the last day. We discovered unusual plants in the forest that you can use for medicine.
M: Great … Er, have you got something for a headache?

2.02 Unit 4, 4.1, Exercise 3

1 It's winter, and the birds are beginning to fly away to a warmer place.
2 Please, don't leave me, Beth. I can't live without you!
3 Who is it? Say something. I know you're behind the door.
4 Once upon a time, a young prince was born in a beautiful castle.
5 We must travel into the future. It's the only way to save this world.
6 Quick! Jump in the car. We have to catch them!

247

2.10 Unit 4, 4.5, Exercise 2

RP = Radio presenter   S = Santiago

RP: Hello, and in this series we're hearing about festivals that are special to you and your friends. In the studio today we've got Santiago.
S: Hi!
RP: Now, Santiago is sixteen and his parents come from Brazil. He was born in the United States and goes to school here. He speaks English at school and Portuguese at home, and he's here to tell us about his favourite festival.
Hi, Santiago. Welcome to the show …

2.17 Unit 5, 5.1, Exercise 3

1 K = Katia   C = Coach

K: Wow, this board is very high … OK!
C: Well done, Katia. You entered the water perfectly! Excellent.

2 C = Commentator

C: So, there are four pairs of you in the lake now. Just wait for the starting whistle …
And they're off! Max and Heather are in the lead …

3 S = Spectators

S1: Wow, this is an exciting game! They're both very strong teams.
S2: What's the score? Can you see the scoreboard?
S1: Yes, it's 20–22 at the moment. Oh no, the blue team have got the ball … but the red goalkeeper has stopped it! Well done!

4 S = Spectators

S1: Look at the green team go! They're moving very fast on the ice.
S2: Oh, and they've scored again!

5 P = Players

P1: Come on, Alexia!
P2: I'm trying! This game isn't easy!
P1: You're right. The ball moves so fast! I keep missing the table. Oops!

6 C = Coach

C: Wow! That move was so difficult. Good try, Leo.

2.28 Unit 5, 5.5, Exercise 3

B = Ben   A = Avril

B: Avril, did you hear about that footballer from Norway?
A: Martin Ødegaard? Yes, he must be really excited. He's going to train with one of the best football teams in the world.
B: He's only our age but he'll have to leave his country and live in Spain. I think that's a bit scary.
A: But he's going to train with some great footballers.
B: I know, but he'll have to learn another language. I don't think he speaks much Spanish.
A: That'll be easy and he'll learn quickly because he'll be with Spanish people all day.
B: That's true. What will he do in his free time?
A: I don't think he'll have much free time because he'll be so busy. Footballers practise most days of the week.
B: Yes, I suppose you're right. But … he'll miss his family when he goes abroad.
A: Ah, but he won't be without his family. His dad is a football coach and he'll coach Real Madrid now. He's coached his son since he was very small.
B: That's cool!
A: And don't forget the money he'll have when he's with Madrid. Footballers always get lots of money.
B: If he scores lots of goals, he'll earn lots of money.
A: Yeh, that's true. We'll have to wait and see.

2.42 Unit 6, 6.5, Exercise 2

I = Interviewer   N = Nick

I: Thanks for coming to talk to us, Nick. Now, can you explain what you do?
N: Yes, I organise holidays for teenagers who need help when they're travelling because they can't see.

2.43 Unit 6, 6.5, Exercise 3

I = Interviewer   N = Nick

I: Why did you decide to help in this organisation?
N: Well, I've always loved travelling … and once I was on holiday in South America and I met an amazing girl who couldn't see. She was on holiday with her parents and cousins and they helped her to swim in the sea. It made her very happy because she couldn't swim on her own. I decided I wanted to help people to have a good holiday.
I: And, what holidays do you offer?
N: Oh, we've got something for everybody, from city breaks and beach holidays to activity camps. On our activity camps we offer sailing, hiking and cycling. We've got special bikes with two seats. They're popular with kids who can't go cycling at home because they don't have the right bikes.
I: It must be difficult to travel to a place when you have problems with your sight.
N: It can be. We plan the journey carefully so that people feel safe. But we also want it to be exciting – the journey is as important as the holiday.
I: Is it easy to find accommodation?
N: Not always. Some hotels don't understand the difficulties our travellers have.
I: What do you mean?
N: Well, it depends but … for example, a blind person can't read a menu. Eating can be very frustrating too. Also, he or she can't read the number on their key or the door to the room. Hotels have to understand that.
I: What are the most popular holidays?
N: Both winter and summer holidays are popular, but I think our summer activity camps are the most popular because we offer sailing. Everybody loves the sun on their face and the fresh air. It's a very exciting experience.

2.44 Unit 6, 6.5, Exercise 5

Jess is sixteen years old and comes from New Zealand. She's been blind since she was born, but she's always loved adventure. Last year Jess went on a sailing holiday. During the trip, Jess decided that she wanted to do something different. With the help of the organisers she climbed the mast. It was very high, but she knew she could do it. 'It doesn't matter what disability you've got,' says Jess. 'You know you're going to have a good time and you're going to get lots of help.'

2.57 Unit 7, 7.5, Exercise 4

I've got a half-sister, Grace, who is disabled. She was born with cerebral palsy and she finds it difficult to move around and do things for herself. This means she spends most of her life in a wheelchair. Simple everyday activities, like getting dressed and getting ready for school, can take a long time. When Grace was young she hated this and often got very stressed. If she didn't want to go to school, she would shout and cry.

Then, three years ago, when she was nine, Grace got an assistance dog and she named him Snoopy. Since then, her life has changed a lot. Snoopy is a very intelligent dog who understands Grace and knows how to help with many different activities. For example, Grace hates putting her socks on, but Snoopy can get her socks from the drawer and make her laugh by tickling her feet. Then she will put her socks on quite happily. If Grace didn't have Snoopy, she would never be ready for school on time! He's her best friend, too.

2.58 Unit 7, 7.5, Exercise 6

A couple of years ago, my stepmum got a job as a puppy trainer for assistance dogs. When she and my dad got married, she brought three puppies to our house. She explained that when the dogs get older, they will help people, usually those who are disabled in some way. Mum told us that it was not like having a pet because the dogs only stay for about a year. It's very difficult to say goodbye when they go to their new owners. I found that really hard and sometimes cried. The good thing is that we often get emails telling us how much the dogs are helping their new owners.

Scooby is different. He's my dog and I trained him – with a bit of help from my stepmum. I have a condition called Asperger's, which is not exactly a disability. For me, it means that I find it hard to deal with meeting people. Scooby, who is really calm, helps me to be more confident so I can make new friends. I've got a lot better since I had Scooby. He doesn't come to school, but he's always waiting when I get home. He's definitely part of our family now!

3.11 Unit 8, 8.5, Exercise 2

RP = Radio presenter   K = Katrina

RP: Good morning, and in today's podcast we meet teenagers who are helping their communities to fight crime with the help of the internet. First up is Katrina.
K: Well, this happened a couple of months ago. My mum and I went to the shops, but we were only there for about an hour. When we got home, the front door was open …

3.12 Unit 8, 8.5, Exercise 3

K = Katrina

K: We didn't know if anybody was inside. Were they watching us, maybe? We called the police and waited until they came. Then we went in together. The kitchen window at the back of the house was open. It was very cold. I ran to my room and saw that my laptop was missing. Then we realised that Dad's new digital camera wasn't on his desk. The police started taking fingerprints and photos. They were looking for clues. Then I remembered my smartwatch – it was a birthday present from my aunt. I'd left it on the kitchen table after breakfast but it wasn't there. … That was really annoying! I showed the box to the police. After the police left the house, they searched the area behind the house. Anyway, later that day I was chatting to my friend about the burglary. She said she heard some people in the park talking about a watch. They wanted to sell it quickly on the internet. We knew we had to start looking online fast. We checked the posts of some people we knew from the park, and finally we found a comment and a photo about a watch for sale. It was my watch! I pretended I wanted to buy it so that I could get some information. Then I went to the police. They found out where the boy lived and went to his house to arrest him for burglary. I was really glad that social media helped to solve a crime. Unfortunately, we haven't got Dad's camera yet, or my laptop!

3.13 Unit 8, 8.5, Exercise 6

RP = Radio presenter

RP: Thanks, Katrina. Now, on Sky radio we'd like to help you find your dad's camera and your laptop. If you're listening this morning, perhaps you could call us if you hear anything about it. The items were stolen on October the second, sometime between three and five o'clock in the afternoon. The make of the digital camera is Nikon D61-0. That's D-six-one-zero. The laptop is HP Omen. If you hear about it, the number to call is 07836 198477. That's 07836, 1984 double 7. There's a reward of twenty pounds for anybody who finds it. Thanks a lot, and now it's time for the weather.

3.26 Unit 9, 9.5, Exercise 2

1
T = Teacher   E = Eva

T: Right. The test will start in two minutes, so no messing around now. I'd like you all to sit quietly. Your mobile phones should be switched off. Please put them in the box on my table. You can use the dictionaries on your tables. Eva, can you come here, please? I need some help.
E: Yes, sir.
T: Here are the papers …
E: OK.
T: Eva is going to hand out the papers to you. Oh, be careful, Eva. Don't drop them! …
E: Oops! Sorry.

2
M = Max   T = Teacher

M: Sorry I'm late, Miss. I had a dentist's appointment. What are we doing this lesson?
T: Well, Max, the rest of the class have gone on the trip to the Natural History Museum. Did you sign up on the list?
M: Yes, I did, Miss. But then, erm, I forgot all about it …
T: Well, we can't do much now. They are already on their way to the museum. I know, you could do a bit of research about the things in the museum that interest you. You need to look up their website online. I'll put the details on the board …

3
T = Teacher   I = Ivan

T: So, before you can go on summer camp, we need to have all the correct details for you. I hope your parents filled in the forms and signed them. Can you make sure you hand them to me after the lesson?
I: Sir?
T: Yes, Ivan? What's the problem? Did the dog eat your form like it ate your homework?
I: No, sir. It erm, it got wet.
T: Oh, well, who did that? Did you spill your drink on it? Or drop it in the toilet?
I: Nothing like that. Er, I left it in my trouser pocket when I put them in the washing machine.
T: OK, Ivan. I'll get you another form. But don't give it to the dog.

4
T = Teacher   M = Magda

T: Guys, please can you pay attention, please, while I'm writing on the board?
M: Sorry, Miss.
T: What were you doing anyway? Were you writing secret messages?
M: No, Miss. Anya and I were just finishing the homework – the one where we had to work in pairs. It was the last question and we had a good idea.
T: Show me your book then. Oh, OK.

3.28 Unit 9, 9.5, Exercise 5

T = Teacher   S = Student

1
T: Who's ready to hand in their essay?
S: I've just finished it.
T: Great … but you've only written one paragraph! It's too short.

2
S: Are we going to look over the test papers now?
T: Yes, we are. Did you revise for it, Hanna? You only got five out of twenty answers!

3
S1: Did the teachers see you when you were messing about?
S2: No, they didn't. Well, not at first. But they saw me fall off the chair afterwards!

4
S: Robbie, Robbie!
T: Could you all calm down, please?
S: Yes, Miss.
T: Now, what happened?
S: It's Robbie, Miss. He's fallen asleep.

3.34 Exam Time 1, Exercise 1

N = Narrator   B = Boy   G = Girl   A = Announcer   M = Mum

N: Before we start, here is an example: Which film do they want to see?
B: Do you fancy going out to the cinema later on? There are some excellent new films on this week.
G: Great! I've heard that the new horror film with Mike Lawrence is very good.
B: I heard that too. But I watched a horror film last night on TV and I'd prefer to see something else, if that's OK. The reviews say that both the romantic one and the science fiction one are great, too.
G: OK. I love science fiction, but I'm not that keen on romantic films.
B: Fine – that's a plan then.

1
G: I've got to get a present for my mum's birthday. Last year I got her a book. I can't do that again!
B: What's your dad getting her? Do you know?
G: Yes, he's getting her a new tablet.
B: Why don't you get her a colourful cover for it with her name?
G: Dad's got her one already. But you've given me an idea. I can buy some albums for her online and send them to her new tablet.
B: Problem solved!

2
G: Amy? Hi! It's Emma. We've just finished moving in and I just love the new house. We're very near the shops – which is good, although a bit noisy. But my room is at the back and I can see the garden. It's lovely. Of course, I'd like to live near the beach – like you – but Dad needs to be near his work. Come and stay soon. Call me back later!

3
G: I didn't see you at the skateboarding park last weekend.
B: No, we went to stay with my cousins in the countryside. It was OK, just a bit boring. I wanted to do some walking because it's a lovely area, but it rained. So I spent the whole weekend in front of the television. There was some skiing on, so it wasn't too bad!
G: I saw a bit of that too. OK – see you at the park next weekend then

4
A: There's some interesting weather in the UK at the moment. If you're in Scotland, you know it's raining and it's really cold, whereas in the London area you've got some fog right now, with cloudy skies later on. In Ireland, the winds are getting worse and there are a lot of trees down – dangerous for people on the roads. Today is certainly a different story from yesterday when we all enjoyed clear blue skies.

5
B: My cooking is improving! I cooked dinner for the family last night!
G: Wow! Did you cook chicken and mushroom soup like we did in cookery class on Monday?
B: No! That takes too long. I wanted to do chicken salad, but my sister doesn't eat meat, so I did noodles with cheese.
G: Delicious! But next time you must do some chocolate cupcakes for dessert. Yours were yummy in class!

6
B: Mum! I can't find my smartphone and I'm late for school.
M: Have you looked in your bag? Maybe you put it in there last night.
B: I don't think so. I didn't leave it on the train because I used it last night. It was definitely on my desk because I phoned Eliza about homework.
M: I hope you haven't lost it again.
B: Oh – you were right. Here it is. Now I remember. I put it in there before I went to bed.

7
G: Have you read this article in the magazine? It's all about your sister. There's a cool picture of her with a big plate of yummy food!
B: I'm not surprised. She's got a great job. She wanted to be a chef and she trained for a couple of years. Then she decided that it's a really hard job, so now she just takes pictures of food for restaurants and magazines. She's always liked working with food! She won 'Waitress of the year' when she was a teenager!

3.35 Exam Time 1, Exercise 2

OK, everyone. Listen carefully, please. We've now made all the arrangements for the school trip next Thursday. This is the visit to the new exhibition at the Science Museum. We were planning to go on Wednesday because Miss Mason also wanted to come, but unfortunately we couldn't book a coach for that day. So it will just be me and Mr Adams with you.

I'm sure you're all excited about going to the exhibition. It's called Robot Life, and there have been lots of advertisements on TV about it. The TV education series *Science Today* had a special programme two weeks ago about it, and it looked really interesting. As you can guess, it's all about robots! In my opinion, it's one of the best exhibitions to come to the Science Museum for a long time.

The exhibition is from the USA and it's visiting many countries in Europe, including the UK and France. It's a great opportunity to see the latest developments in robotics. There's a special waiter robot called 'Jack' and a hotel receptionist robot called 'Maria'. Jack takes orders and brings your food, but Maria can actually talk and reply to visitors' questions. Amazing!

So, arrangements for the day are as follows. Firstly, the coach leaves school at 8.30, so I would like everyone to be here by 8.15 at the latest! Ask your parents to be here at school to meet you from the coach at 5.30 in the afternoon. If the traffic is heavy, we might be a little late, but we shouldn't be later than six o'clock.

The restaurant at the museum is always very busy and the food is quite expensive, so please bring sandwiches and drinks. We can have them in the museum gardens. Remember to switch off all phones while we're in the museum. And also remember to pick up some leaflets for your science project.

3.36 Exam Time 1, Exercise 3

K = Kelly   D = Dan

K: Did you like the documentary *All Change!* last night? It was on at 9.30. I thought it was brilliant.
D: That was about climate change, wasn't it? At that time I was watching the film on Channel 4 about an avalanche in the Alps. That was good too. I'm a bit fed up of all these environmental documentaries. There are so many!
K: I know what you mean. There are a lot of them on TV these days. But actually there's a real link between the documentary and your film. Changes in the weather can cause things like avalanches in mountains.
D: Yes, it's scary. The film was quite frightening. I love skiing, but this film made me think about the dangers a lot. It was only a story, but the problems are real.
K: Oh, I forgot you like skiing. How often do you go? I haven't been for three years.
D: I usually go with my friend Mark twice a year. He saw an avalanche once. He was skiing with his family when they saw a cloud of snow in the distance. I think two people died.
K: And he still goes skiing? Really you should watch this documentary. It's on again on Friday. Or you can watch it on catch up. Next week it's about forest fires. At least that's something we don't get in this country.

D: No, we don't! To be honest, I think I'll probably give it a miss. I prefer to watch programmes that make me laugh, not make me worry too much. Climate change is an important issue, but we don't need to have scary pictures and stories all the time.

K: Well, personally, I think people need to learn more about the problems. Then maybe we can do something to stop it. And really – it's a very interesting series.

D: OK, OK. I'll have a look at the avalanche one. But forest fires are just too horrible.

3.37 Exam Time 2, Exercise 1

N = Narrator   B = Boy   G = Girl   D = Dad

N: Before we start, here is an example: Which film do they want to see?

B: Do you fancy going out to the cinema later on? There are some excellent new films on this week.

G: Great! I've heard that the new horror film with Mike Lawrence is very good.

B: I heard that too. But I watched a horror film last night on TV and I'd prefer to see something else, if that's OK. The reviews say that both the romantic one and the science fiction one are great, too.

G: OK. I love science fiction, but I'm not that keen on romantic films.

B: Fine – that's a plan then.

1

G: I went on the holiday website and looked at some places we could go next year.

B: Yes, anything – just not Mum and Dad's favourite seaside hotel *again*.

G: Exactly. We both love water sports, so why don't we go on an activity holiday? There's one advertised in Wales with loads of great sports to do on the river.

B: Cool! I was thinking of a winter holiday in the mountains, but that always depends on the snow. And they're quite expensive.

G: True. OK, so now, how are we going to persuade Mum and Dad?

2

B: You haven't seen the new TV talent show, have you?

G: I saw the first programme, but I didn't really enjoy it. I decided to watch the new cookery programme instead last night.

B: That is so boring!

G: How do you know? You didn't see it.

B: I've seen the reviews and they all said the same thing.

G: Well, I liked it. The reviews said that the wild animals documentary last week was terrible and they were wrong about that too!

3

B: Hi! My name's Paul Matthews and I'm phoning to see if you've found a silver smartphone? I was at the leisure centre from about two o'clock until five o'clock. I asked for some information about tennis lessons at the reception desk as I was leaving, so it's possible I left it on the desk there. I had a sandwich in the café after going swimming and I remember using it there to call a friend, so I'm sure I didn't leave it by the pool. If someone has found it, please phone me on 09876 876574. Thanks.

4

B: Emily, hi! I hope you get this message soon. As you know, the school play starts tonight and I'm really excited. Would you like to come? The play begins at 7.30 and it lasts about two hours. The audience can start to come in from seven o'clock to get a coffee or something and look at the programme. I've got to be there about an hour before that, to get ready. It takes ages to get into costume and do my make-up! Also I need to go through my lines again. Do come! We can meet afterwards.

5

G: Are you taking much with you on this camping trip at the weekend?

B: You know me! Just the jeans that I'm wearing and a couple of T-shirts. My phone and my music, of course.

G: Last year it rained all the time. Everything got really wet. I think I'll take two pairs of jeans this year.

B: Well, you have to carry your rucksack! I'd prefer to get wet I think.

G: Maybe you're right. But I must take my special coffee. I can't live without that in the morning.

B: Good idea!

6

G: Hey! You didn't come to the match yesterday! It was brilliant!

B: I know. I wanted to come. I got the dates wrong and I spent the whole afternoon watching sports on television!

G: I thought perhaps you had a skateboarding competition. I know there's an important one soon.

B: That's not until next weekend. How was the football?

G: Really good. Our school won easily. It was very exciting.

B: Oh, I'm angry that I got confused. The tennis was very boring!

7

G: Can you drive me into town tomorrow, Dad?

D: No problem. I've got to go to the bank. Where do you want to go?

G: I need to go to the camping shop.

D: Oh no! Is there a problem with your new tent? You've only had it a month.

G: It's fine. I just want to check out some new sleeping bags they've advertised. They're only fifty pounds! I've got that money from my birthday to spend.

D: That sounds good value. I'm going about 10.30. OK?

3.38 Exam Time 2, Exercise 2

I = Interviewer   S = Suzy

I: Suzy Davies has just got a part in the new *Shark Beach* movie. First up, I must say congratulations, Suzy. How are you feeling?

S: Thank you. I really couldn't believe it when I first heard the news. But that was three months ago! I couldn't tell anyone because it was a big secret then. That was very difficult. Of course, I know it's going to be hard work, very long days and lots of lines to learn! But I can't wait for the filming to start now.

I: It sounds quite a scary film! Do you need to be able to swim well for this role?

S: Yes! I think it will be scary! I learned to swim when I was younger and I'm OK, but not really fast. Also I splash a lot in the water. They've got another actor who will be me in the swimming scenes, thank goodness.

I: This isn't your first film role, is it?

S: No. I've known that I wanted to act since I was at primary school. We used to live in a small village and when I was six they were making a film in the area. They asked all the children in my class to be in the crowd scenes in the film. We had to dress up as children from the last century! It was amazing fun. So that was my first role.

I: Did you go to drama school?

S: I wanted to go to drama school and I chose a couple to apply for. However, my parents persuaded me to get a degree at university first. They don't think acting is a very safe career! Then while I was studying, I took part in a play. A famous director saw me and asked me to do this film.

I: Are you worried that you haven't done much training?

S: It's good to have training, but you can also learn while you do something. I think I'm going to learn a lot from doing this film. A lot of the other actors are very experienced and I know I'll learn a lot of techniques from them. But the director believes that I can do this and that gives me a lot of confidence. He's very good at his job!

I: Do you have any plans for later in the year?
S: Well, filming will take at least six months. At some point I shall do some real training. But this filming is on location in Australia, which is a place I've always wanted to go to! Afterwards it would be great to stay on and tour round for a while. Another director has asked me to think about a film he's going to make next year, so it might be difficult to fit in training before then. We'll see.
I: Well, good luck with everything, Suzy.

3.39 Exam Time 2, Exercise 3

I'm very pleased to tell you this morning that there will definitely be another 'Music in the Park' festival in August. Last year's event on the third and fourth of August was very successful and the organisers decided to repeat that success. So, put the dates ninth and tenth in your diaries and make sure you're free!

As last year, the festival will take place at the north end of King's Park. There is room here for many thousands of visitors and everyone can have a good view of the stage. Parking will once again be in the area at the south entrance to the park. However, please try to leave cars at home as there will not be a lot of space.

You've probably read on social media that Paul Bailey and Free Voice are going to sing at the festival. Unfortunately, that is not completely true. Paul Bailey wanted to come, but he will still be on tour in the USA at the time. Free Voice will be on stage on the Sunday afternoon to close the event.

A new feature of the event this year will be a dance competition. Contestants should apply to enter the competition at least a month before the date. The competition will take place on the main stage at lunchtime on both days, and the categories will be hip hop, salsa and street dance. No country or classical I'm afraid! The judges will include Jack Bennet and Mary Jake from the TV talent show *Time to Dance*. Should be fun! You'll be able to see the winners of the competition in Channel 5's documentary *Young Dancers* in September.

So, remember to get your tickets early. You can book by phone on 07640 832511 or you can get a better price by booking online at festivals.com.

See you there, guys!

3.40 Exam Time 3, Exercise 1

N = Narrator   B = Boy   G = Girl   HT = Head Teacher   A = Announcer

N: Before we start, here is an example: Which film do they want to see?
B: Do you fancy going out to the cinema later on? There are some excellent new films on this week.
G: Great! I've heard that the new horror film with Mike Lawrence is very good.
B: I heard that too. But I watched a horror film last night on TV and I'd prefer to see something else, if that's OK. The reviews say that both the romantic one and the science fiction one are great, too.
G: OK. I love science fiction, but I'm not that keen on romantic films.
B: Fine – that's a plan then.

1
G: Hi! How's Granddad?
B: He's much better. He came out of hospital this morning.
G: That's great. He can watch the Saturday football match in his own room! Are we still going out for his birthday tomorrow?
B: Gran thinks Sunday is too soon. He needs to stay at home for a few days. I'm going round there with a cake later today.
G: Good idea. I'll come too. We can take him for a meal on Monday.
B: Yes – I'll book a table. See you later.

2
B: Did you have a good walk with the dogs this afternoon?
G: We walked for miles. I'm very tired.

B: And the sun was shining for you!
G: Yes, it was really bright and it was so warm that I didn't need to take a jacket. That was good. I put my sun hat out to take, but I left it on the table.
B: Oh no! Did you get a headache?
G: Just a small one. Luckily I didn't forget my sunglasses.
B: It's amazing – such strong sunshine in September!

3
HT: Good morning, everyone. I wanted to tell you that we shall have some visitors in school today. These are some students who are going to start classes here next term. They will be in classes this morning and then after lunch, they will meet their future teachers and have a talk about the school here in the hall. Unfortunately, the football match against Brompton School for this afternoon is cancelled so they can't watch that. Please give them a warm welcome to the school if you see them around today.

4
A: Last night a robbery was reported at the newsagent's in the high street. Police arrived on the scene very quickly and chased a suspect in a white car through the town. Unfortunately, as it was passing the park, the white car hit a man and drove off, without stopping. The man, a Mr Downs, was taken to hospital with a broken leg. At the moment, he is doing well. If anyone saw the white car with number plate HD5 606F, please contact the police.

5
G: Have you seen the notice about the new club?
B: Yes. It's great and I'd love to go, but I already have drama club on Wednesdays.
G: That's a shame! At the moment I'm free on Wednesdays. My cookery club is on Friday.
B: Lucky you. I'd really like to learn the guitar. Mr Parks is a good teacher, too.
G: Yes, I think it's going to be fun. I must put my name down before the club gets full up.

6
G: Are you feeling worried about the swimming competition today?
B: Yes, a bit. I haven't trained much this week.
G: Don't worry. You'll win, I'm sure. I'm coming to watch you. Is your race at 4.30?
B: I think it's at five o'clock. It's the girls' race at 4.30. I must check.
G: That's OK. I'll be there at four o'clock because I want to see the whole competition. My brother's in the first race, so I can't miss that. Good luck, and remember I shall be there cheering for you!

7
B: You look very pleased. Did you do well in the exams?
G: Yes, not bad. We got our results this morning. I didn't pass Biology, but the test was very difficult. How about you? Have you got yours yet?
B: Yeah. I got mine yesterday. I didn't do that well. I failed Biology too, and Maths. You're right. The questions were really hard. How did you do in History? You're good at that.
G: I got an A! My dad's a history teacher so he'll be happy about that. I'm just not very good at science.

3.41 Exam Time 3, Exercise 2

S = Spencer   D = Debby

S: Oh, you're back! How was the school trip to France?
D: I had a great time. I was staying with my French friend, Jeanette. Nearly all of us were in Paris. Jeanette's house was a few miles outside but we went in every day by train to her school. But one of my classmates stayed near a theme park and went there every evening! I was so jealous!
S: How was your French?

D: Before I went I was very worried about understanding everything. The French people speak so quickly! I mean, when I speak, I'm OK because I can use the words that I know! But when other people speak to you, they use all sorts of vocabulary and you need to guess a lot of things. But I actually understood quite a lot. I was pleased.

S: And what was the food like?

D: I know you like unusual food, don't you? I'm not the same. I'm afraid I'm not very adventurous. Jeanette's mum is a good cook, but I couldn't eat everything she cooked. I'm not very keen on fish and we had it nearly every day!

S: Paris has got loads of great galleries and museums. Did you go to many?

D: We didn't have a lot of time at the weekends because our families took us on trips to different places. But I went to the Rodin Museum – he was a great sculptor and you can see a lot of his statues in a lovely garden. Luckily, it wasn't raining. We wanted to see a special art exhibition by Monet, but it closed the day before we went. I think it's coming to London soon though.

S: So, when do you think you'll go back for another visit?

D: Well, first, my friend Jeanette will come over to stay with us for two weeks in October. That's only a few months away. And then my parents are planning a trip to France with me in the spring. I'm hoping we can visit Jeanette then and see more of Paris, because I love that city.

S: Are you still thinking about becoming a French teacher?

D: I love French and I think I speak it a lot better now. But I'm not sure I could help other people learn it. I've started teaching my younger brother and I'm not very patient with him! I think I'd prefer to do some translating – books, reports or even films!

3.42 Exam Time 3, Exercise 3

Hello and welcome to the Crime Museum. As you know we only opened three weeks ago on the first of October, but we've had two thousand visitors since then! Everyone wants to see the exhibits from some of the most horrible crimes in the twentieth century!

The police have wanted to open an exhibition for a long time, but we have to thank Professor Green from London University for finally putting this collection together. He continued work that was started by his colleague Janet Potter, who unfortunately died last year.

There are three main rooms with exhibits and you can get a detailed guide from the information table on my left. It is in five languages, so visitors from other countries can read about the exhibits too. Our own museum expert, Miranda, will be in Room 2 to answer any queries you have. And books will be on sale in the museum gift shop at the end of your visit.

When you enter the first room, you'll find exhibits from two of the last century's nastiest murderers. These were brothers John and Ned Carson, who killed people in the East End of London, where they lived in 1856. They were arrested five years later, in 1861, by policeman Ray Briars, who spent years trying to track them down.

In the second room, there are exhibits from several big thefts. You probably remember the film about the 1967 robbery where thieves stole five million pounds' worth of diamonds? Well, we don't have the diamonds, but we do have the maps that were used by the gang and audio of interviews with the suspects.

But I'm not going to tell you a lot more. Go round the museum and see for yourselves. I'm sure you'll get some big surprises!

Audio scripts — Workbook audio scripts

02 Unit 1, Lesson 5, Exercise 4

P = Presenter   I = Isla

P: Hello, and welcome to our show. Today we're asking the question: Could you live without technology? With me in the studio are Isla, Ben and Sara. You're doing an experiment at the moment, aren't you?
I: Yes. We're switching off all our technology for a month to see what life is like without it.
P: Wow! That sounds really difficult!

03 Unit 1, Lesson 5, Exercise 5

P = Presenter   I = Isla   B = Ben   S = Sara

P: So, how's it going this month without technology? Isla?
I: I'm finding it really difficult. I usually text my friends and chat with them a lot, but of course, now I can't do that. It's OK during the day, but the evenings are a bit boring. And the worst thing is trying to do homework. I can't go online to find information and that's terrible! Books are OK, but it's much slower without the internet.
P: What about you, Ben?
B: Well, I'm really into music and, of course, I can't download any songs at the moment. But I'm finding other ways to listen.
P: Yeah?
B: Yeah, I'm listening to the radio more, which is cool, and I'm also looking through my mum and dad's old collection of CDs. Some of their music's not bad, actually!
P: And Sara, what are you finding difficult?
S: Well, I usually watch TV shows online because I'm often busy when they're actually on TV. But now if I miss a programme when it's on, I can't watch it. That's annoying!
P: And are there any good things? Isla?
I: Yeah. Usually I upload all my photos, but I can't do that now, so I'm going into town and printing them. So now I have photos I can show to my friends and put on my walls – that's cool!

06 Unit 2, Lesson 5, Exercise 4

C = Chloe   A = Alex

C: Hi, Alex. How was your holiday?
A: Hi, Chloe. Well, it wasn't really a holiday. I was really tired when I got home. But I learnt a lot – and I'm a lot fitter now!
C: Really? So what did you learn?
A: Oh, lots of skills for keeping yourself alive if you get lost in the wild. We spent five days in a forest and had to find our way back to the camp.
C: Scary! Did you see any wild animals?
A: No, we didn't see any, but we heard some at night.
C: Wow!

07 Unit 2, Lesson 5, Exercise 5

C = Chloe   A = Alex

C: So, what did you do on this survival course?
A: Well, we learned how to find food. That was cool! We found lots of fruit to eat and I caught a fish, too. So we weren't hungry!
C: Cool. And did you make a shelter?
A: Yeah. I was worried that we might be cold at night, but in fact, our shelter was quite warm. And it kept the rain out.
C: That's good. I'm not happy if I don't have somewhere comfortable to sleep! Did you make a fire?
A: Well, Dan, one of our teachers, says it's usually quite easy to make a fire. He tried to make one, but it was raining and all the wood was too wet, so we couldn't make it burn. Maybe next time.
C: What about finding water?
A: That's what my mum was most worried about. We took some water with us, but we also learned how to find water in the forest and how to make it safe to drink.
C: Did you boil it to make it safe?
A: No, we used special tablets that you put in the water to clean it.
C: And did you have a map to help you find your way?
A: Yes, we did, but they also taught us how to use the sun to find our way.
C: What about at night? Did you use the stars to find your way?
A: No. Usually they teach you how to do that, and there were no clouds, but we were all too tired, so we just slept at night!

09 Unit 3, Lesson 5, Exercise 3

So, I've just finished making my cake, and here it is. My friends want to eat it, but they can't because I've made it for a competition at my school. I started making cakes when I was ten, and I love making cakes in unusual shapes. I wanted to make a cake in the shape of a boat, but that didn't work out. It was too difficult and I couldn't make it stand up. So in the end I've made one in the shape of a giant phone. I think it's really cool. I chose chocolate flavour for the cake because that's my favourite, and there's a vanilla cream filling in the middle. On the outside, there's red coloured icing over the main part of the cake, and I've used sweets for the buttons on the phone. The best bit is that I've used icing to write a message on the screen. It says: *See you later for tea and cake!*

10 Unit 3, Lesson 5, Exercises 4 and 5

Right, before you all go off to your classes, I just need to remind you about our cake competition. This competition takes place on Saturday the twenty-ninth of June – that's the same day as the School Fair. If you're taking part, you need to bring your cake to the school cookery room. All the cakes need to be there by ten o'clock in the morning. The judges can then have plenty of time to look at all the cakes and, of course, they'll taste them all before they make their decision. Mrs Addison will announce the winner at two o'clock.

There are three different categories in the competition: cupcakes – I'm sure you all know what they are; then there are family cakes – those are larger cakes that you can share – and finally, there are novelty cakes – that's cakes in unusual and interesting shapes. I think last year we had a plane and a football field, and the winner was a cake in the shape of an elephant, which was amazing!

If you'd like to enter the competition, it's two pounds per cake to take part, and you need to fill in your entry form by next week. The winner will receive a cookery book and twenty-five pounds. You can get entry forms from Mrs Cussons or you can download them from the school website. Good luck, everyone, and happy cake making! Remember, someone's going to win that prize!

12 Unit 4, Lesson 5, Exercise 3

Right, now if you're looking for something to do next weekend, why not go to the Leeds Drama Festival? It takes place in Hyde Park from the fifteenth to the eighteenth of July and there are loads of exciting things to do. There are workshops every morning – not only drama workshops, but also different kinds of dance. In the afternoon, you can watch live shows or just relax and chat with other festival-goers. If you want to have a go at acting yourself, there are plenty of performances you can take part in, including the Festival Show on the last night on the big open-air stage. OK, on with some more music now, and …

13 Unit 4, Lesson 5, Exercises 4 and 5

M = Max J = Jess

M: I didn't know you were interested in drama. What made you go to the festival?
J: Well, my friend Rosie is always inviting me to go to drama workshops with her. She didn't go to this festival, but we've got this new drama teacher at school. We did some acting with him and I loved it. That's why I decided to go to the festival and do a workshop.
M: So, what did they teach you?
J: Well, they taught us how to mime. I learned how to show different feelings, like anger or happiness. They said it's better to hide your real feelings and just focus on acting. You don't have to show the emotions very strongly, but you need to make sure your face and your body show the same emotion.
M: Well, I guess you were good at it because you had a big part in the final show.
J: That wasn't planned. There was a really talented girl, and the plan was for her to play the main character. But she fell at lunchtime and hurt her foot. She had to go to hospital, so the teacher asked me to do it.
M: And did the show go well?
J: Hmm, quite well. The costumes looked great and the make-up artists did a great job! The music was brilliant – not too loud. And everyone remembered what they had to do. The only thing that went wrong was the stage lights – one of the switches broke, so we had to do part of the show in the dark!
M: And what was your favourite part of the day?
J: Oh, I enjoyed all of it. The show was brilliant, but it was a bit scary being up on stage. The dancing was amazing – they taught us some really good dance moves. And I made lots of new friends – I think that was probably the best bit.

15 Unit 5, Lesson 5, Exercise 3

… and news is just coming in about Anita Redway, one of the country's best young tennis players. She's won a lot of matches this year, but she's decided to give up playing competitively. It seems she's got fed up with all the training she has to do. In fact, what she really loves is coaching younger kids, so that's what she wants to do in the future. It's certainly true that you have to train very hard to be a professional player. As well as tennis, Anita also swims three times a week to build up her strength, she runs every morning for fitness and she does yoga twice a week to help keep her flexible. That's quite tough! Being a professional can be difficult for the whole family too. I know that Anita's dad goes to watch her play whenever he can get time off work and her mum is there at every match. Sometimes her younger brother comes along too, so the whole family's there watching. Well, we'll definitely miss seeing her on the tennis court. She's a very popular player, and easy to recognise, with her red headband. Other players wear headbands, of course, or wristbands or baseball caps, but not red like Anita's. So, good luck to Anita with her future career! And now …

16 Unit 5, Lesson 5, Exercise 4

A = Angela P = Paul

A: Have you heard the news about Anita Redway? It's such a pity she's giving up playing – I wasn't expecting it at all. I hope she changes her mind. She could be a big star in the future!
P: Yes, but I think she'll be happier if she does something she loves doing. I mean, there's no point in doing all that training every day if you don't enjoy it.
A: Yes, maybe.
P: She says she wants to spend more time doing other things – take up some new hobbies. At the moment she doesn't have time for anything else because she spends all her time on her tennis.
A: Yes, that's true. But she'll never become rich if she works as a coach.
P: She might, if she's popular. I think she'll be a great coach. She seems such a nice person – kids will love her.
A: Yeah, she's lovely – I'm sure young players will enjoy working with her.
P: And she says she wants to coach the stars of the future. You never know – maybe she'll end up coaching world champions one day – that will be really satisfying for her!
A: That's true.

18 Unit 6, Lesson 5, Exercise 2

I = Interviewer E = Ellie

I: Thanks for coming onto the show, Ellie. Tell us about your experiences of working holidays.
E: Well, I love them! I always choose working holidays rather than just sitting around on a beach. I think I've been to eight – no, nine different countries now. I wouldn't go on holiday any other way.

19 Unit 6, Lesson 5, Exercises 3 and 4

I = Interviewer E = Ellie

I: Why did you first choose a working holiday?
E: When I finished school, I wanted to go to South America, but I didn't have enough money. Then a friend told me about Woofing – that's working on organic farms. I looked online and it looked amazing. I spent two months in Peru working on a vegetable farm. I loved it!
I: Do you see a lot of the country where you're working?
E: Yes, you get days off, so you can go on excursions or weekend trips. And I always save a bit of money so I can go travelling at the end of the job.
I: What's your favourite kind of working holiday?
E: Well, working on farms is OK, but I prefer activity camps. I've done summer camps in America – they're great – but my real passion is skiing. So I enjoy the winter ski seasons the most.
I: Do you have to be sporty to work at activity camps?
E: It helps if you're sporty. I teach tennis and horse-riding in the summer and, of course, skiing in the winter. But you don't have to be sporty. You can do other jobs, like cooking or working at a reception desk.
I: It can't be easy working with young children.
E: Yes, it can be tiring. That's one of the disadvantages of activity camps. Also, the kids don't always behave well – that's annoying. And you don't earn much money – you get your food for free and a place to sleep, but then just a bit of pocket money, really.
I: But you must enjoy it because you keep going back.
E: Yes. Working holidays are a great way to travel. You see some amazing places, it's a great way to keep fit, and probably the best thing is that you meet other young people from all over the world. I guess it could be difficult as you get older because it's hard work – but luckily, I'm still young!

21 Unit 7, Lesson 5, Exercise 2

We started a buddy system here last year. Autism is quite a common condition, so it affects quite a lot of students. It isn't a physical or mental disability, but students with autism find it difficult to relate to other students, so they sometimes find it difficult to form relationships and make friends. We noticed that our students with autism were fine during lessons, when the teacher was there, and before and after school they had support from their families. But it was between lessons – at lunch time, for example, that they sometimes found it difficult to join in. 'Buddy' is an informal word for a friend, but buddies don't necessarily become best friends with the students they work with. Their role isn't to tell them what to do or how they should behave. It's just to be there to help when they're needed. The scheme has done very well. Our students with autism definitely don't have as many problems at break times now and actually, the buddies have also got a lot out of it – we didn't expect that, so it was an extra benefit.

22 Unit 7, Lesson 5, Exercise 3

I first started being a buddy to Matt when I got back to school after the summer holidays. I didn't really know Matt before that, although he's in my class, because he was very quiet and he didn't really fit in with me and my friends.

I didn't know much about autism before I knew Matt, but he explained that he gets quite stressed if he's surrounded by people the whole time. He's OK chatting to people in small groups, but if there's a big activity going on, like a game of football, he finds it difficult to get involved.

I think Matt felt worried that he wouldn't be able to make friends because people would think he was strange. I've helped him get over that, I think, and he's now much more relaxed about talking to different people and making friends. He even joins in with the football sometimes. If he gets a bit better, I think he'll get into the school team!

I've got a lot out of the whole experience of being a buddy. Before, I was only into football and computer games, and I thought that anyone who didn't do those things was just boring. Matt's shown me that we don't all have to be the same – it's fine to just be who you are.

25 Unit 8, Lesson 5, Exercise 2

1   P = Presenter

P: Thieves broke into a jeweller's shop in the town centre last night. The crime happened at about half past eleven and the criminals stole a diamond necklace and some earrings worth over fifty thousand pounds. Luckily, they couldn't get into the safe, so they didn't get away with any money, and they also didn't find two valuable diamond rings that were in a drawer under the counter.

2   S = Sophie   D = Dan

S: Hi, Dan. How are things?
D: Not very good. There's been a burglary at our house.
S: Oh no! When did it happen?
D: Yesterday afternoon.
S: That's awful. Were you at home?
D: No, but my dad was. He was really tired after a business trip, so he was asleep in bed. He didn't hear a thing! I was playing computer games earlier in the day, but then I went out to play football, and that's when it happened.
S: What did they take?
D: My laptop and my mum's tablet – it's a real pain!

3   P = Police officer

P: Hello, I'm PC Emma Robinson and I'm investigating some vandalism at the school last night. You probably know there have been problems in the past with vandalism – broken windows and paint sprayed on the walls, things like that. Well, this time it was the head teacher's car, which was outside the school. Someone cut the tyres, so he couldn't drive home. Did you see anyone near the school last night?

4   W = Will   L = Lucy

W: Come on, Lucy. Our train leaves soon.
L: I can't find my purse or my phone. They were definitely in my bag this morning. I think someone's stolen them.
W: Well, there are a lot of pickpockets about.
L: I know and that's why I never keep money in my back pocket – it's too easy to steal it from there.
W: Yeah. Look, there's your phone.
L: Oh! Thanks, Will. But my purse is definitely missing, so someone's taken it. I think I'll have to go to the police.

5   P = Police officer   S = Shop assistant

P: So, can you tell me what happened?
S: Yes. The shop was quite empty. There were only about four or five people in here. There was a teenage boy, about fifteen years old. He bought a game and left. Then there was a man – he was about fifty, I guess. He wanted to know about computer games for his children. I was talking to him when I saw the woman. She was about twenty-five, with long hair. She just took the game and walked out! I was still serving the man, so I couldn't run after her.

26 Unit 8, Lesson 5, Exercise 3

M = Man   L = Sergeant Linfied

M: So, Sergeant Linfield, can you give us your report?
L: Yes, Sir. We received a call at around 2.30 from Mr and Mrs Jones, of Bridge Street. They wanted to report a burglary at their house. I know the area well, so I went straight to the house. Mr and Mrs Jones were quite upset, so I interviewed them about what had happened. It seems they'd come home and found the door open and some things missing. Some other officers arrived then, and they took fingerprints and looked for clues inside the house. Mrs Jones went out into the back garden to get a bit of fresh air, and that's when she found a mobile phone, under a bush. I examined the phone and saw that it had a phone number on it labelled 'Home'. I called the number and spoke to a woman, and I asked her where she lived. I then went round to the house and found the burglar. The phone was his, and the woman I'd spoken to was his mum! I arrested the burglar, of course, and found Mr and Mrs Jones's things in his bedroom.
M: Good work, Sergeant!

27 Unit 8, Lesson 5, Exercise 4

The police are asking for information about a robbery that took place last week at the post office on Park Street. The crime took place on the fifteenth of June, at about half past three in the afternoon. This was a serious robbery, and thirty thousand pounds in cash was stolen, along with some other items. The police are looking for three suspects, who were seen near the crime scene that afternoon. They are also interested in information about a dark green car that the suspects were seen driving off in. If you have any information about this crime, please call the police on 0141 557 6231. I'll repeat that number for you: it's 0141 557 6231.

29 Unit 9, Lesson 5, Exercise 2

1   G = Girl   B = Boy

G: Oh it was so embarrassing today!
B: Why?
G: Well, I was in my Geography lesson. We were watching a film about volcanoes, so the lights were out. I was really tired. I think I was hungry because I hadn't had any lunch. I didn't even have time to eat a sandwich because I had to finish my Maths homework. Anyway, I didn't understand the film. We were meant to go on the internet before the class to learn a bit about volcanoes, but I didn't have time. And the next thing I remember is Mr Appleby telling me to wake up! I'd fallen asleep at my desk! In future, I'm going to make sure I always have something to eat before class!

2   G = Girl   B = Boy

G: Hi, Paul. I thought you wanted some help with your Maths homework yesterday. Why didn't you text me?
B: Well, I tried. I wrote you a text quietly in class yesterday afternoon saying, 'Can you give me the answers to the Maths homework?' But unfortunately, before I'd sent it, someone texted me, so my phone made a noise. And, of course, Mr Smith, the teacher, heard it!

G: Oh dear!
B: Yes, it was 'Oh dear'! He asked me to bring my phone out to show him and there was the text I'd written to you. Of course, he wasn't very pleased, and then he called my mum and told her, and she was really angry with me! I've got extra Maths for two weeks now!

3 T = Teacher   G = Girl

T: Right, quiet everyone. Today we're talking about …
G: Hello, Miss. Sorry I'm late.
T: OK, Emma. What happened this morning? Did you oversleep again and miss the bus?
G: No, Miss. I had to go to the doctor's. Remember, I broke my arm last term. Then I had to go back home again after that because I forgot to put my glasses in my bag. But I've got them now.
T: OK, Emma. Sit down and take out your notebook.

4 W = Woman   B = Boy

W: Hi, George. How did your graduation ceremony go?
B: Well, good and bad, really. It was good because, of course, I'm really pleased that I've finished and passed all my exams. But it was a bit embarrassing.
W: Why?
B: Well, you have to wear a special hat and gown. The gown's quite long and the hat isn't very comfortable. I was really nervous that my hat would fall off when I went up onto the stage. I was thinking about that so much that I tripped over my gown and fell flat on my face! It was really embarrassing! But at least I remembered to collect my certificate. Some people forget to do that, and just walk off the stage without it!

5 T = Teacher   G = Girl

T: Right. Is everyone ready? Lucy? What are you doing?
G: Er, I'm just looking for my French book and my pencil case. I'm sure I put them both in my school bag last night, but now I can't find them.
T: Well, I'm sure you can borrow a pen from someone else.
G: Yes, I know, but … Oh. Here's my pencil case, right at the bottom of my bag.
T: OK. Well, let's get started. Put your bag down now. You can share books with Karen.

30   Unit 9, Lesson 5, Exercise 3

1 T = Teacher   B = Boy

T: Have you all finished the first exercise?
B: Not quite, Sir. It's difficult.
T: OK, I'll give you a few more minutes.

2 G = Girl   B = Boy

G: Did you manage to answer all the questions in the test?
B: No, I didn't. I couldn't do the last two.
G: No, I couldn't either. It was really hard!

3 B = Boy   G = Girl

B: Could you lend me a pen, please?
G: Of course. I've got one in my bag. Here you are.
B: Thanks.

4 G = Girl   B = Boy

G: How long did you spend on your Maths homework?
B: About an hour. I didn't really understand it.
G: Yeah, I know what you mean. I think we need to ask the teacher to go over it again.

NL notes and answer key

Extra Practice

Unit 1

Vocabulary

Exercise 1
1 reading
2 downloads
3 online
4 chatting
5 text

Exercise 2
1 c 2 d 3 e 4 b 5 a 6 i 7 h 8 k 9 g

Exercise 3
1 On weekdays / On Mondays/Tuesdays/Wednesdays/Thursdays/Fridays
2 once / twice / three times / four times / five times
3 seconds
4 mealtime(s) / lunchtime / dinnertime / noon / midday
5 midnight
6 weekend

Exercise 4
Students' answers will vary. Accept all reasonable answers even if they have minor grammatical errors; the focus of the exercise is vocabulary.
Sample answers:
1 I use earphones to listen to music when I am on the bus.
2 I use a tablet to find information on the internet and to watch music videos.
3 I use a cable to connect my devices to each other or to the electricity.
4 I use a speaker to play music at parties.
5 I use a selfie stick to take selfies/photos with my phone.

Grammar

Exercise 5
Students' choice of time expression or frequency adverb will vary. Accept all reasonable answers.
Sample answers:
1 I am washing my jeans <u>at the moment</u>.
2 It doesn't <u>usually</u> rain here <u>in the summer</u>.
3 Do you <u>always</u> eat healthily?
4 They are visiting their granny <u>this week</u>.
5 Is Aggie doing the washing up <u>now</u>?
6 I always take the dog for a walk <u>in the morning</u>.

Exercise 6
The focus is on the correct use of -ing or the infinitive after a verb. Students can use any suitable tense for the main verb.
1 Do you / Would you mind turning down the music, please?
2 We decided / have decided to leave early.
3 We look / are looking forward to seeing you next week.
4 They miss / missed going to the beach every day.
5 I try / tried / have tired / am trying / am going to try not to go to bed late on weekdays.
6 Does she enjoy / Is she enjoying / Did she enjoy / Has she enjoyed looking after young kids?

Exercise 7
1 ✓
2 He stopped wearing this jacket because it's too small.
3 ✓
4 He goes out with his friends every Saturday. / He's going out with his friends this Saturday / tonight / this evening.
5 I understand what you mean but I don't agree.
6 ✓
7 I'd love to come to your party.

Exercise 8
Students' answers will vary. Accept all meaningful and grammatically correct answers.
Sample questions
1 Q: Where are you going?
2 Q: What do you usually have for breakfast?
3 Q: Does your dad drive to work?
4 Q: Are you doing anything right now?
5 Q: When does the shop open?
6 Q: Where to you live?

Unit 2

Vocabulary

Exercise 1
1 rain 2 icy 3 sun 4 snowy
5 stormy 6 cloudy

Exercise 2
1 fire 2 totally 3 leaves 4 outside
5 sunset 6 sky

Exercise 3
Students' answers will vary. Accept all reasonable answers. You can decide whether students should give their explanations in English or in Dutch. If they use English, do not penalise them if they make grammatical or syntactical errors as long as their ideas are reasonable.
1 waterfall: It is not a natural disaster.
2 wildlife: It refers to animals. A cave and a lake are natural features; a path is a manmade feature.
3 very: We use it with regular adjectives. We use all the other words with strong adjectives.
4 earthquake: A storm, a flood and rain involve water.
5 cow: It is a farm animal. Bats, tigers and bears are wild animals. / bat: It can fly. Cows, tigers and bears can't.
6 wind: We use the other words to talk about temperature.

Exercise 4
Students' answers may vary. Accept all reasonable answers. The focus is on vocabulary, so you may choose to ignore or gently correct any grammatical errors without focusing on them.
Sample answers:
1 There is a flood when water covers land which is usually dry. A tsunami is a big wave that comes after an earthquake or when an underwater volcano erupts. A tsunami hits areas near the coast.
2 Fog is like a cloud but it is close to the ground. A cloud is thicker than fog and it is in the sky.
3 A hurricane is more dangerous.
4 a) Water boils at 100°C. b) It freezes at 0°C.

Grammar

Exercise 5
1 Henry was watching TV in his room. After the earthquake, he texted his friends.
2 We were making a cake. After the earthquake, we had a cup of tea.
3 Victor was working on the 12th floor. After the earthquake, he left the building.
4 The students were having a lesson. After the earthquake, they played hockey.
5 Leslie was sleeping. After the earthquake, he sat in the living room.

Exercise 6
Students answers will vary. Accept all meaningful and grammatically correct answers.
Sample answers:
1 I'm not doing anything this weekend.
2 Everybody was happy about the wedding.
3 There's nothing in the fridge.
4 There was somebody at the door.
5 He isn't going anywhere today.
6 We'd like to buy something new.

Exercise 7
Students answers will vary. Accept all meaningful and grammatically correct answers.
Sample answers:
1 It started to rain while she was walking home.
2 Dad broke a vase while he was cleaning it.
3 Somebody stole it while I wasn't looking.
4 We met on the plane while we were travelling to London.

Unit 3

Vocabulary

Exercise 1
1 delicious
2 fry
3 vanilla
4 competition
5 Chop
6 Slice

Exercise 2
The order in students' answers may vary.

Words	Category
beef, chicken	meat
bread rolls, flour	cereals (also: wheat)
chocolate, crisps	snacks
cream, yoghurt	dairy
cucumber, lettuce	vegetables / salad / vegetables and salad
fruit juice, smoothie	(healthy) drinks

Exercise 3
1 ~~bland~~ spicy
2 ~~did~~ made
3 ~~taste~~ flavour
4 ~~stale~~ fresh
5 ~~garlic~~ honey
6 ~~good~~ best

Exercise 4
Students will probably use words from this unit to answer the questions. However, accept any reasonable answer.
1 sour
2 spicy / hot
3 tasty / delicious / yummy
4 coconut
5 coffee / tea

Grammar

Exercise 5
1 a 2 b 3 a 4 a 5 a 6 b

Exercise 6
The subject of the sentence in students' answers will vary and consequently, the form of the main verb will also vary.
Sample answers:
1 My best friend has just bought new jeans.
2 I have already seen this film.
3 My mum has ridden a motorbike since she was 18 years old.
4 My brother hasn't gone to bed yet.
5 My grandfather has never watched a cooking competition.
6 I have had the same school bag for three years.

Exercise 7
The underlined parts of the answers will vary depending on the current year or day.
1 I have already made breakfast.
2 This shop has been here since <u>1920</u>.
3 I (last) saw him <u>yesterday</u>.
4 They have worked in the cake shop for <u>18</u> years.
5 She has been in hospital since (last) <u>Tuesday</u>.
6 I have just sold my old bike.
7 Did you meet Jack at Val's party?

Exercise 8
Sources:
https://www.esquire.com/entertainment/movies/a27467433/daniel-craig-james-bond-movies-stunt-injuries/
https://www.theguardian.com/film/filmblog/2008/jan/25/justoffgoldfingeravenueat
Students' own answers.
Sample dialogue excerpt:
Me: Have you ever done anything dangerous in one of your films?
Daniel Craig: Yes, I have. Many times.
Me: Give me one example of what you did.
Daniel Craig: I jumped out of a third-floor window onto a moving bus.
Me: Wow! When did you do that?
Daniel Craig: In 2008.

Unit 4

Vocabulary

Exercise 1
1 star
2 entertainment
3 summer
4 production
5 stage
6 audience

Exercise 2
Students' answers will vary. Accept all reasonable answers even if they have grammatical errors; the focus of the exercise is vocabulary.
1 An entertainer sings, dances and/or tells jokes, etc. during a performance. An actor plays a role in a film or play.
2 An episode is a TV programme that is one part of a series. A series is a number of episodes with the same main characters. It is usually on TV daily or weekly at the same time.
3 If critics like a play, film, show or concert, it gets good reviews, but it is not necessarily a hit. If a play, film, show or concert is very popular with audiences, it is a hit.
4 A performance is the act of performing. A performer is the person who performs in a play, film, show or concert.
5 A fantasy film tells an imaginary story. A documentary is about real life.

Exercise 3
1 character
2 screen
3 workshop / course
4 story
5 performance / play / film
6 fairy tale

Grammar

Exercise 4
1 a few
2 Few
3 a little
4 a few
5 little

Exercise 5
1 long enough
2 better football player than Ben / football player who/that was as good as Ben
3 warmer than Monday / not as cold as Monday
4 a better actor than Rowan
5 hard as they did yesterday

Exercise 6
1 How much cream and butter do you need?
2 The sofa was light enough so I could move it on my own. / The sofa was too heavy so I couldn't move it on my own.
3 There are lots of / a lot of films I want to see this week.
4 They played music more loudly than they did last time.
5 She stayed up too late last night and now she's tired.
6 It's a very simple game. Anyone can play it.

Exercise 7
Students' own answers.

Unit 5

Vocabulary

Exercise 1
1 Running
2 indoor
3 changing
4 scoreboard
5 trainer

Exercise 2
1 ~~coach~~ practise / train
2 ~~mascot~~ kit / shirt
3 ✓
4 ~~goal~~ race
5 ✓
6 ~~pitch~~ fan

Exercise 3
1 gave
2 set
3 done
4 have / 've got
5 go
6 score

Grammar

Exercise 4
1 'm meeting
2 'm going to be
3 'll ask
4 starts
5 'll be
6 is flying
7 leaves
8 'm going to order
9 is going to be
10 'll take

Exercise 5
1 They will go climbing unless the weather is bad.
2 When they return, they will watch the match on TV.
3 If Anna is busy, who will coach us?
4 If I don't win this race, I'll give up running.
5 When Simon wakes up, he'll be hungry.

Exercise 6
Students' answers will vary. Accept all reasonable and grammatically correct answers.
Sample answers:
1 You won't pass the test
2 if they don't hire any well-known actors
3 If you feel better
4 someone tells them
5 will she speak to you?

Exercise 7
Students' own answers.

Unit 6

Vocabulary

Exercise 1
Other combinations are possible, e.g. camping holiday, but for the exercise to work, words can only be combined in the ways shown below.
1 backpacking holiday
2 camping trip
3 activity camp
4 sleeping bag
5 city break
6 double room

Exercise 2
1 passport
2 facilities
3 torch
4 a cruise
5 in
6 view

Exercise 3
Students' answers may vary. Accept all reasonable answers.
1 trip / holiday / journey
2 explore different
3 on holiday
4 local

Exercise 4
Students' answers will vary. Accept all reasonable and grammatically correct answers.
Sample answers:
1 A: (Excuse me,) how do I get to the airport?
2 A: What time/When do we arrive in Stockholm? / What time/When does our flight get to Stockholm?
3 A: I'd like a (single) train/bus ticket to London, please.
4 A: What platform does the train leave from?

Grammar

Exercise 5
1 We'll go sightseeing as soon as we finish breakfast. / As soon as we finish breakfast, we'll go sightseeing.
2 The machine won't stop until you turn it off.
3 We'll book the hotel after we book the plane tickets. / After we book the plane tickets, we'll book the hotel.
4 While you relax by the pool, I'll do some exercise. / I'll do some exercise while you relax by the pool.
5 They'll go for a walk before they go to dinner. / Before they go to dinner, they'll go for a walk.

Exercise 6
1 shouldn't wait
2 doesn't have to get up
3 must buy
4 has to wear
5 mustn't drive
6 ought to visit

Exercise 7
Students' answers will vary. Accept all reasonable and grammatically correct answers.
Sample answers:
1 It can't be his coat because it's too big. It must be his dad's coat. His coat might be in the wash or he might have lost it.
2 She can't be at school because her car isn't here. There must be a lot of traffic and that's why she's late. She might be ill.

Unit 7

Vocabulary

Exercise 1
stepbrother, grandchild, mates, half-sister, workmates, great-grandmother, buddies, classmate, stepparent

Exercise 2
1 dealing
2 on
3 fallen
4 put
5 at

Exercise 3
1 buy
2 bring
3 arrived
4 receive
5 become

Exercise 4
1 guests / people
2 makes
3 sense
4 background
5 bridegroom / groom

Grammar

Exercise 5
1 d 2 a 3 e 4 f 5 g 6 b

Exercise 6
1 didn't come
2 would find
3 Would you look
4 lived
5 would make
6 were

Exercise 7
1 Pam's car, which is twenty years old, often breaks down.
2 People who/that fail the exam can take it again in two months' time.
3 The house next door, which is bigger than ours, has been empty for months.
4 The sandwiches which/that are on the table are for Mum's guests.
5 The restaurant where he works has just got a Michelin star.

Exercise 8
Students' own answers.

Unit 8

Vocabulary

Exercise 1
1 punishment
2 burglary
3 vandalism
4 thief
5 robber
6 robbery
7 shoplifter
8 shoplifting

Exercise 2
<u>Right side of the law</u>
lawyer
arrest a criminal
court
detective
judge
solve a crime
<u>Wrong side of the law</u>
thief
break into a building
commit a crime
rob a bank
shoplifter
vandal

Exercise 3
Students' answers may vary. Accept all reasonable answers. Do not penalise students if they make grammatical or syntactical errors as long as their ideas are reasonable.
1 suspect: We don't know if a suspect is a criminal or not.
2 prison: A court is where a trial takes place, and a witness and a judge are people at a trial. Criminals spend time in prison.
3 robber: A fine and going to prison are forms of punishment. A robber is a criminal who steals things from a place.
4 detect: It is not an action verb. (Also accept: jump: The other verbs have to do with crime.)
5 burglary: It is a crime. A shoplifter, a vandal and a thief are criminals.

Exercise 4
Students' answers may vary. Accept variations as long as the meaning is accurate.
1 a witness
2 fingerprints, footprints, clues
3 jail
4 He escapes.
5 It moves towards you.
6 a reward

Grammar

Exercise 5
1 We had the new TV delivered
2 stolen
3 I got this dress made
4 pushed
5 did her hair
6 wrote
7 are cleaned
8 I am having my car washed

Exercise 6
1 This photo was taken last Monday.
2 Your order is usually delivered the next day.
3 This car was used in the robbery.
4 Most of the stolen objects are never found.
5 I was asked too many questions.
6 This product is only sold online.
7 These trainers are made in China.
8 Their names were added to the list.

Exercise 7
1 uncomfortable
2 illogical
3 invisible
4 disappeared
5 irresponsible
6 uninteresting

Exercise 8
Students' own answers.

Unit 9

Vocabulary

Exercise 1
1 take
2 in
3 confident
4 solving
5 up
6 took

Exercise 2
1 performance
2 memorise
3 practical
4 creative
5 teamwork
6 gifted

Exercise 3
1 revise
2 hard-working
3 make a mistake
4 intelligent
5 Biology

Grammar

Exercise 4
1 f 2 d 3 a 4 e 5 g 6 b

Exercise 5
1 Are these notes
2 taught you
3 is Hans planning
4 fell
5 did they meet
6 were they going

Exercise 6
1 have are having / at the moment on (Tuesdays)/at (11)
2 lives has lived
3 listening listened
4 snows is snowing / is going to snow
5 is never leaving never leaves / has never left
6 drove 'll drive

Exercise 7
Students' own answers.

Step it up

Unit 1

Vocabulary

Exercise 1
A Nouns
tech support
software
account
user ID
password
link
B Verbs/Phrasal verbs
freeze / be frozen
update
hack
log into
enter
click
create

Exercise 2
click on a link
create a link
create a password
create an account
create software
create a user ID
enter a password
enter a user ID
freeze an account
hack into an account
hack into software
log into an account
log into tech support
update a link
update a password
update software
update tech support
update a user ID

Exercise 3
Students' own answers.

Grammar

Exercise 4
1 **look:** state = to have a particular appearance; active = to turn your eyes towards something so that you can see it
   smell: state = to have a particular smell; active = to put your nose near something and breathe in air
2 **feel:** state = to give someone a particular physical feeling; active = to experience a particular feeling (e.g. 'I'm not feeling well') / to touch something to find out more about it

When we use a verb as a state verb, we cannot use the Present Continuous. We use the Present Simple. When we use the same verb as an active verb, we can use the Present Simple for facts, general truths, habits and routines, or the Present Continuous for actions happening now, at this period of time, or about fixed future arrangements.

Exercise 5
1 'm smelling
2 're looking
3 feels
4 smells
5 looks
6 are (you) feeling

Exercise 6
State verbs that can be used as action verbs: see, think, have
Sample answers:
I see the car but I don't see anyone in it. (I am using my eyes to perceive the car.)
We're seeing a lot of each other these days because we're working on the same project. (We are meeting each other.)
Does he know the answer?
I think this is an excellent idea! (This is my opinion.)
I'm thinking of learning Chinese. (I am considering this possibility.)
I don't want to leave the party so early.
I must go to the supermarket. We need milk and cheese.
They have a house in the country. (They own a house.)
In this photo, we're having dinner by the sea. (We are eating dinner.)

Writing

Exercise 7
1 I feel that, in my opinion, it seems to me that
2 For instance
3 such as

Exercise 8
Students' own answers.

Unit 2

Vocabulary

Exercise 1
1 Keep away from danger
2 Learn important survival skills
3 Pack an emergency kit
4 Stay calm
5 Act quickly
6 Take cover
7 Use common sense

Exercise 2
1 hurricane, tsunami
2 all types of disaster
3 earthquake
4 all types of disaster
5 avalanche
6 earthquake
7 tsunami

Exercise 3
1 first aid
2 Keep away
3 acted quickly
4 survival skills
5 common sense
6 emergency plan

Exercise 4
Students' own answers.

Grammar

Exercise 5
Students' answers may vary. Accept all reasonable and grammatically correct answers.
1 was sitting / relaxing
2 was reading
3 heard
4 saw / noticed
5 Someone / Somebody
6 was filming
7 no one / nobody
8 anything
9 swam
10 everything
11 was pulling / dragging
12 was / felt

Exercise 6
B

Exercise 7
Sample answers:
1 wearing her new coat
2 drinking tea
3 hoping to find something nice to cook

Writing

Exercise 8
1 Suddenly
2 As it turned out
3 during
4 Fortunately
Story: Students' own answers.

Unit 3

Vocabulary

Exercise 1
All the idioms have to do with food and drink.
1 E 2 F 3 B 4 G 5 A 6 D

Exercise 2
1 Nadia has a lot on her plate.
2 James is in hot water.
3 Cat wants to have her cake and eat it.
4 Romantic comedies aren't Victor's cup of tea.
5 The driving test is/will be a piece of cake for Lisa.
6 Nick went nuts.

Exercise 3
The list of idioms below is by no means exhaustive. Accept all suitable answers.
cheese
to be a big cheese = to be an important and powerful person
to be cheesed off = to be annoyed with someone or something
to be cheesy = to be cheap and not of good quality
to be like chalk and cheese = (of two people) to be very different from each other
egg
to be a good/bad egg = to be a good/bad person
you can't make an omelette without breaking eggs = you can't do something good or important without causing some problems
to walk on eggshells = to be very careful how you behave so as not to upset someone
to have egg on your face = to look stupid because you have done something embarrassing
you can't boil an egg = you can't cook even the simplest food
to put all your eggs in one basket = to have only one plan or course of action so that you have nothing else to depend on if something goes wrong
butter
to be your bread and butter = to be your main source of money
to have butterfingers = to drop things you are carrying or trying to catch very often
to know which side your bread is buttered on = to know who to be nice to so that you keep the advantages you have
bean
to spill the beans = to tell something that you or someone else wanted to keep secret
to be full of beans = to be full of energy and ready to do things
to not have a bean = to have no money
potato
to be small potatoes = to be unimportant
to be a couch potato = to spend a lot of time sitting and watching TV
to drop someone like a hot potato = to stop working/hanging out, etc. with someone because you suddenly stop liking them or when you think they can cause problems for you

Grammar

Exercise 4
Past Simple: the day after, the day before, the other day
Also: in (2012 / December), on (Wednesday), at (six o'clock), last (February / year / summer, etc.), (two minutes / hours / days / weeks /months / years, etc.) ago
Present Perfect: lately, recently, so far, until now, up to now
Also: already, ever, never, yet, for (two minutes / hours / days, etc.), since (12 o'clock / yesterday / June, etc.), just
Time expressions with a similar meaning: up to now, so far, until now, yet
recently, lately

Exercise 5
Students' answers will vary. Accept all reasonable and grammatically correct answers.
Sample answers:
1 My great grandfather planted
2 Have you changed
3 We haven't found
4 The groom broke his leg
5 I opened a new packet of
6 They haven't had

Exercise 6
These are likely answers, but accept all alternatives as long as they are used correctly.
1 all my life
2 in/last (September) / (two months) ago
3 so far / up to now / until now / yet
4 The other day / A few days ago
5 recently / lately
6 the day before / the day after / on
7 a long time ago
8 never

Unit 4

Vocabulary

Exercise 1
1 cinema
2 snack bar
3 play
4 café
5 theatre
6 film
7 series

Exercise 2
Students' answers may vary. Accept all reasonable answers.
1 good on
2 flop
3 queue
4 collect our/the tickets
5 a gig
6 interval
7 feel like going

Grammar

Exercise 3
1 2
2 1
3 4
4 1 (and) 3
5 4

Exercise 4
1 have similar / similar sounding surnames
2 slightly / a year younger than the character he plays
3 ten times as big as / ten times bigger than my house
4 different from / not the same as the one I booked online

Exercise 5
1 far
2 too
3 much
4 similar
5 later
6 same
7 from
8 than

Writing

Exercise 6
Students can use the review in exercise 5 as a model, but point out that this is only part of a review, not a complete one.

Unit 5

Vocabulary

Exercise 1
1 keep fit
2 work out
3 drop out
4 cheer on
5 cool down
6 warm up
7 take part in

Exercise 2
Students' answer will vary. Accept all reasonable answers. The focus is vocabulary, not grammar.
Sample answers:
1 Q: What do you say to cheer on your team when they're playing?
2 Q: What's the most important competition you've ever taken part in?
3 Q: Have you ever dropped out of a game?
4 Q: How do you keep fit?
5 Q: Is it important to warm up before playing a game?
6 Q: How do you cool down after exercising?

Exercise 3
Students' own answers.

Grammar

Exercise 4
1 c   2 b   3 a

Exercise 5
Students' answer will vary. Accept all reasonable and grammatically correct answers.
Sample answers:
1 … there's going to be a lot of traffic on the motorway.
 … I won't be able to go to the bank.
 … I won't have to go to work.
2 … there won't be any left.
 … we won't be able to see the play.
 … we'll have to stand in the queue at the box office.
3 … there won't be anything to eat for dinner.
 … she won't be able to finish everything before her guests arrive.
 … she'll have to ask her brother to help her.
4 … there won't be any for your friends.
 … your friends won't be able to sit next to you.
 … your friends will have to sit somewhere else.

Exercise 6
Students' answer may vary. Accept all reasonable and grammatically correct answers.
1 're having
2 's going to be
3 dropped
4 will be
5 could you (please)
6 won't be able

Writing

Exercise 7
1 Since
2 The thing is
3 However
4 it seems

Exercise 8
Students' own answers.

Unit 6

Vocabulary

Exercise 1
Students can explain what the expressions mean in Dutch or English. If they use English, do not dwell on grammatical errors as the focus is vocabulary.
1a the small bags that you carry and keep with you in the cabin when you are travelling on a plane
1b one of the bags or cases that you carry when you are travelling (*Luggage* is uncountable.)
2a to have a limited amount of money to spend
2b an airline that tries to keep its prices lower than its competitors by making you pay for things that other airlines give you for free, e.g. food and drink, pre-booked seats, no charge for luggage
3a the cheapest type of seats in a plane
3b seats in a plane that are more expensive than economy class, and which include extras like better food, lounge access, priority boarding, etc.
last-minute = happening as late as possible, before something else happens, usually with very little or no time to spare
in advance = before something happens, usually a reasonable amount of time before

Exercise 2
1 hand luggage
2 on a budget
3 luggage
4 budget airlines
5 last-minute
6 in advance
7 business class
8 pieces of luggage

Exercise 3
Students' own answers.

Grammar

Exercise 4
Students' answers will vary. Accept all appropriate and grammatically correct answers.
Sample answers:
1 shouldn't book a room at this hotel
2 might be in the living room
3 can't be Robert Pattinson
4 don't have to buy any more potatoes
5 must be Anna's mug
6 ought to leave now

Writing

Exercise 5
1 E   2 C   3 A   4 D   5 F   6 B

Exercise 6
Students' own answers.

Unit 7

Vocabulary

Exercise 1
1 B   2 D   3 A   4 C

Exercise 2
Students' explanations will vary. Accept all reasonable answers.
1 to – to be someone's husband or wife
2 with – to stop being in a relationship with someone
3 fall – to begin to love someone in a romantic way
4 get – to end a marriage
5 out – to be in a romantic relationship with someone
6 grow – to stop being close to someone
7 ups, downs – to have good and bad experiences when you are in a relationship (romantic or not)
8 touch – to stop communicating with someone
9 love – to meet the person you love more, in a romantic way, than anyone else in your life

Exercise 3
Students' own answers.

Grammar

Exercise 4
Students' answers may vary. Accept all reasonable answers.
Sample answers:
1 I'd go cycling with my friends if I didn't have a bad cold.
2 We'd meet more often if we lived closer.
3 I'd get a big dog if I lived in a house with a garden.
4 If I didn't need my bike, I'd lend it to my friend.

Exercise 5
Students' answers will vary. Accept all reasonable answers.
Sample answers:
1 I'd walk. I hate waiting in queues.
2 I'd drink some warm milk to help me relax.
3 I'd ask him/her why.
4 I'd save money and buy him/her a new one.
5 I'd take it to a police station.
6 I'd be very sad.

Exercise 6
1 , where he grew up
2 who want to take selfies with him
3 who know him well
4 where he lives
5 (which / who / whom) he calls Sausage
6 (that / which) he hates the most

Writing

Exercise 7
Students' own answers.

Unit 8

Vocabulary

Exercise 1
1 do a runner
2 hold up
3 get away with (it)
4 tip off
5 lock up
6 let off

Exercise 2
1 get away with
2 tipped off
3 holding up
4 have (never) broken
5 did a runner
6 Lock (them) up

Exercise 3
Students' own answers.

Grammar

Exercise 4
by, someone / somebody, people

Exercise 5
1 The letter was found inside an old book.
2 *Silent Witness* was directed by Alfred Hitchcock.
3 The building is protected by an alarm system.
4 The front door was damaged.
5 She was interviewed by a reporter from the *Daily News*.
6 Some crimes are never solved.

Exercise 6
2 12th / twelfth
3 was used
4 prison
5 was locked up
6 I (also accept: the first/1st)
7 was damaged
8 Second
9 was repaired
10 was opened
11 is visited
12 tourists / people

Writing

Exercise 7
Students' own answers.

Unit 9

Vocabulary

Exercise 1
1b – G
2a book – F
2b book – B
3a lesson – E
3b lesson – A
4a head – C
4b head – H

Exercise 2
1 has a good head for
2 ticks all the (right) boxes
3 is (a real) bookworm
4 to get my head round
5 should never / shouldn't judge a book by its cover
6 will teach him a lesson
7 think outside the box

Exercise 3
Students' answers will vary. Accept all suitable answers.
Sample answers:
to be a closed book = to be someone who is difficult to understand because they don't let you know what they think or how they feel
to be an open book = to be someone who is easy to know because they do not keep secrets about themselves
to read someone like a book = to be able to understand what someone thinks or feels easily
to be in someone's good books = when someone is pleased with you
to do something by the book = to do something following all the rules
to take a leaf out of someone's book = to copy what someone does because they do it well
to be the oldest trick in the book = to be a trick that does not deceive anyone because it has been used so many times before
to try every trick in the book = to do whatever you can to achieve something
to have your nose in a book = to be reading a book with a lot of interest
to hit the books = to start studying intensively
to throw the book at someone = to punish someone severely

Grammar

Exercise 4
Students' answers will vary. Accept all reasonable answers.
Sample answers:
1 Q: Who did he go out with?
2 Q: Who did you talk to?
3 Q: What did she pay with? / How did she pay for that?
4 Q: What are you thinking about?
5 Q: What is this (machine) used for? / What do they use this (machine) for?

Writing

Exercise 5
1 have
2 you
3 been
4 to
5 about
6 How
7 haven't
8 make
A 2, 3, 6
B 5, 7
C 1, 4, 8

Exercise 6
Students' own answers.

Grammar Time NL

Unit 2a Past Simple: regular and irregular verbs

Exercise 1
1 gave
2 uploaded
3 charged
4 saw
5 ate
6 forgot
7 read
8 understood
9 found
10 travelled

Exercise 2
1 I didn't ask the teacher a question.
2 We didn't sit on the sofa to watch TV.
3 My friends and I didn't chat online last night.
4 Lizzie didn't eat all her vegetables.
5 You didn't take these photos.
6 It didn't rain all night.
7 I didn't have a great time last weekend.
8 Susan didn't tell her parents the truth.

Exercise 3
1 How did you break your leg?
2 Did your teacher give you a lot of homework?
3 When did the accident take place?
4 Did the students enjoy the lesson?
5 What did your mother study at university?
6 Did the eruption destroy the village?
7 Who did he invite to the party?
8 Did you hear a strange noise last night?

Exercise 4
1 did he live
2 did the dog do
3 did you see
4 Did they watch
5 did Greg and Mike have a fight / did they have a fight
6 did the volcano erupt

Exercise 5
1 Did you hear the news about the tsunami?
2 Did they go to the beach yesterday?
3 What did I do wrong? Please tell me.
4 Where did you spend your holidays last summer?
5 Did they discover a new kind of plant?
6 Did the rain put out the fire?

Unit 2b Past Simple and Past Continuous

Exercise 1
1 While 2 When 3 while 4 when
5 When 6 While

Exercise 2
Students may give other answers, depending on their interpretation of the sentences. You could accept the alternative answers given in brackets below, with justification.
1 left; wasn't raining
2 were making; arrived

279

3 marked (was marking: two action in progress at the same time); were working
4 were you doing (did you do: two past actions, one happening after the other); happened
5 rang; was sleeping
6 were looking for; saw

Exercise 3
1 was shining
2 were singing
3 jumped
4 got
5 ran
6 could
7 was making
8 said
9 went
10 were sleeping

Unit 3 Present Perfect and Past Simple

Exercise 1
Students should tick 2, 3 and 5.

Exercise 2
1 made
2 have just finished
3 have never been
4 haven't seen
5 was
6 Has Anna ever told
7 only slept
8 has already made

Exercise 3
1 haven't seen
2 've just returned
3 did you get
4 Did you have
5 was
6 have you done
7 haven't done
8 went
9 haven't travelled
10 've already decided

Unit 4 (a) few, (a) little

Exercise 1
1 a little   2 a little   3 a few   4 Few
5 little   6 few   7 a few   8 little

Exercise 2
1 a few   2 Few   3 a little   4 little
5 a few   6 a few

Unit 5a Talking about the future

Exercise 1
1 a   2 e   3 c   4 b   5 f

Exercise 2
1 leaves
2 I'll buy
3 I'm going to study
4 I'm meeting
5 will live
6 is going to win

Exercise 3
1 starts
2 aren't going
3 is playing
4 finishes
5 does the film end
6 is driving

Exercise 4
1 are arriving
2 's going to ask
3 are meeting; Are you playing
4 'm going to look for
5 Is Sam coming; 're going to buy

Unit 5b First Conditional + if / unless

Exercise 1
1 If I get up early tomorrow, I'll go for a run.
2 We will join a gym if we have enough money.
3 Unless you help me, I won't finish the work on time.
4 Your parents will be angry unless you tell them the truth.
5 Will Joe and Katy come to my party if I invite them?
6 If you see him, will you speak to him?
7 They will miss the last bus home if they don't hurry.

Exercise 2
1 train; will the coach pick
2 won't tell; promise
3 will feel; eat; exercise
4 apologises; will forgive
5 won't go; is
6 Will they build; raise

Exercise 3
Students' own answers

Unit 7a Second Conditional

Exercise 1
1 (If you) were (me),
2 would make
3 (If my friend) told (me a secret),
4 would argue
5 (If he) didn't complain (all the time),
6 would (you) ask

Exercise 2
1 I would be upset if my friends didn't want to hang out with me.
2 If she talked about her problem, she would feel better.
3 If your parents moved to another country, would you go with them?
4 The world would be a better place if people tried to get on with one another.
5 If we had enough time, we would go for a long walk.
6 He wouldn't be bored if he had something to do.
7 Monica would cook dinner for us if we asked her.
8 Would you mind if we didn't go out tonight?

Exercise 3
1 If we didn't have a test on Monday, we would go camping.
2 If Harry didn't always study hard, he wouldn't pass his exams.
3 Mum would drive me to hockey practice if she didn't have a dentist's appointment this afternoon.
4 If there was/were some bread, I could make sandwiches.
5 Charles and Irene wouldn't hang out together if they didn't have similar interests.
6 If my parents liked animals, I would have a pet.
7 I would come shopping with you if I wasn't/weren't busy.
8 If Richard's sister didn't borrow his things without asking him, Richard/he wouldn't get angry (with her).

Unit 7b Defining and non-defining relative clauses

Exercise 1
1 where   2 which   3 who   4 where
5 who   6 who   7 which   8 who

Exercise 2
1 D
2 D
3 Australia's largest city is Sydney, which isn't the capital. ND
4 Our dog, which is very small, is scared of our neighbours' cat, Miss Muffet. ND
5 D
6 My favourite aunt, who lives in Canada, is coming to visit us this summer. ND

Exercise 3
1 Nina hasn't given me back the book which/that she borrowed from me.
2 This is the restaurant where we had dinner with my uncle.
3 Mr Quentin, who taught me Physics and Chemistry, was the best teacher I have ever had.
4 He has a large collection of classic cars which/that he keeps in a special garage.
5 I don't like hanging out with people who/that are rude.
6 Our kitchen, where we eat and do our homework, is our favourite room.

Unit 8 Present Simple Passive and Past Simple Passive

Exercise 1
1 was invited
2 are cleaned
3 was caught
4 are often used
5 was found
6 are built

Exercise 2
1 Tulips are grown in the Netherlands.
2 The password was changed by the owner of the house.
3 The crime was reported to the police.
4 The programme is shown on TV every Monday.
5 All the food is prepared by an Italian chef.
6 The crime was solved by a young detective.
7 The thieves were seen leaving the building.
8 A lot of things were stolen from this shop.
9 That picture of my grandmother was painted by a famous artist.

Unit 9 Word order in questions

Exercise 1
1 Have you been to a lot of countries?
2 Did she use her imagination to write the story?
3 Were they waiting for the bus?
4 Does David like taking photos with his new phone?
5 Will Tanya tidy her room this weekend?

Exercise 2
1 did he give
2 rang
3 stole
4 did you have
5 fell

Exercise 3
1 A: What are you going to tell them?
2 A: Who called you?
3 A: Where do jaguars live?
4 A: How much does he earn?
5 A: Why did you leave?
6 A: Who did they visit?

Writing Skills

Exercise 1
Teaching notes: Try to elicit the following:
*A **formal letter** is a letter you usually write for business or professional reasons. You write this type of letter for a specific reason and you expect a certain result. You may or may not know the person/people you are writing to.*

Exercise 2
1 B 2 C 3 A

Exercise 3
a 3 b 6 c 1 d 5 e 1 f 4
Teaching notes: You could also ask students to find a–f in letters B and C.

Exercise 4
1 The main body of your letter should be between one and three paragraphs long.
2 You have to be polite.
3 ✓
4 Do not use short forms. Write verbs in full: I am, we have got, etc.
5 ✓
6 ✓
7 Do not be chatty or make jokes.

Exercise 5
1 ✗ not polite (enough)
4 ✗ short forms
6 ✗ rude

Exercise 6
1 appreciate
2 qualified
3 expect
4 disappointed
5 enquire
6 unable

Exercise 8
Students' own answers.

Exam Time NL notes and answer key

Exam Time NL 1 Reading

Exam Strategies p45C – Preparation

As a warm-up, elicit the following strategy that students have learned in previous levels:

Do not read through the whole of the text because it will eat into the time you have to answer the questions. Read question 1 first. Then read the part of the text that it refers to. Then read question 2 and do the same.

Ask students what the difference is between open questions and multiple-choice questions (in open questions they have to write an answer in their own words, whereas in multiple-choice questions they choose one of the answer options).

Discuss which of the two they feel less confident about and ask them to give reasons for their answers. Write a list of reasons on the board. At the end of the lesson, ask students to review the list and say if any of their worries have been addressed. Keep a copy of the list and do the same after Exam Time NL 3.

Answering questions (part 1)

Open questions

Ask students if they can see any pitfalls that could lead them to give the wrong answers in question 1 and question 6.

Possible answers:

Question 1:

a) giving one or two examples instead of three

b) giving examples of real meat, e.g. grass-fed British lamb, or plant food, e.g. almonds produced in California

Question 6:

a) mentioning one type of food, e.g. animal foods, without mentioning other foods, e.g. plant foods

b) using the same words as those in question 6, e.g. 'it's fashionable to praise plant foods as the secret to personal and planetary health'.

Exercise 1

Question 1: 'fake, factory meat' / three examples
Question 6: demonise, animal foods / praise plant foods / same thing / other words

Explaining the meaning of a word or sentence

Exercise 2

Some points to make:

– To be able to answer this question, students need to understand the word or sentence. If they have unknown words, they should either try to guess the meaning or look them up in a dictionary.

– A possible pitfall is that students isolate the word or sentence from the text and try to give a 'dictionary' definition instead of saying how it is used in the text.

– The clues may be anywhere in the text, so students should also look at the paragraphs that come before and after the one that includes the sentence.

– An answer that is too long or has irrelevant information will be penalised.

Question 4:

Quote from the text: 'Whether it comes from the plant or animal kingdom is irrelevant, what really matters is how that food is produced.'

See Exam Practice Answer Key below for sample answer.

Multiple-choice questions

Exercise 3

Some points to make:

– The wrong answers often include words or information from the text as a distractor.

– If there are no clues at all about a statement, it is untrue.

– If students cannot decide between two answers, they should go with their first instinct because overthinking is likely to confuse them.

Option A

Key words: 'urge', 'not to consume'

Clues: none. There is no mention that the author advises the public not to consume these products.

Option B

Key words: 'big food companies', 'offer healthy options'

Clues: 'nuggets that contain around 40 ingredients, many of which can't be found in any domestic kitchen', 'Greggs hasn't made public the ingredient composition of its new vegan "steak" bake', 'ultra-processed food', 'manufacturers were being condemned for the health damage their products cause'

All the above clues have negative connotations about the food offered.

Option C

Key words: 'irony', 'intentions', 'Veganuary', 'effect'

Clues: 'Fast-food enterprises, formerly seen as the enemies of public health and the environment, have re-defined themselves as their saviours.' 'Just when ultra-processed food manufacturers were being condemned for the health damage their products cause, the plant-based push has given them a get-out-of-jail-free card.'

These clues support option C. The irony is that ultra-processed, most likely unhealthy foods are labelled as 'healthy' just because they are meat-free.

Option D

Key words: 'indignation', 'allowed to happen'

Clues: There are no clues to support 'indignation'. Although the author is scathing about the practices of big food companies, she never advocates that they should be stopped by law (i.e. 'not allowed').

Relationship between paragraphs

Exercise 4

Point out that even if students find the correct answer easily, they still have to make sure that the other options are not suitable. This will help them in case they have made a mistake by choosing too quickly or by misreading a statement. Ask students to say which clues led them to reject the other three options.

A: Not all methods are bad: 'Where the manure* from farm animals builds soil fertility, pesticides* and fertilisers* sprayed on intensively grown plant crops have depleted* it.'

C: The statement in paragraph 3 is 'animal foods bad, plant foods good'. The clues in paragraph 4 state the opposite: 'Indeed, free-range farm animals fertilise the soil, and the fields they graze on soak up surplus water and prevent soil erosion' etc.

D: Paragraph 3 claims that 'not all animal products are equally damaging'. The same clues as for option C, above, prove this wrong.

It explains in practical terms the point made in paragraph 3.

Exam Practice p45D – Reading

Answers: 1 'plant chicken pieces', (Mc Donald's) vegan Veggie Dippers, (Greggs) vegan 'steak' bake **2** C **3** B **4** Meat production is not harmful if it is done in a way that respects the environment. **5** D **6** paragraph 3: 'animal foods bad, plant foods good'

Exam Time NL 2 Listening

Exam Strategies p69C – Preparation

Exercise 1

Students' own answers.

If you want to elaborate on Tip 3, read out this sentence: *You need to wear specialised boots to go into this area.*

Ask students to raise their hands if they have any unknown words. The word specialised is likely to be one of them. Ask students to guess what the word means and tell you which method worked for them. They could guess from a) the context that the boots are not just ordinary boots, and b) by recognising the root word special.

Now read this out: *He had an early morning meeting at the Ministry of Health.*

Ask students to raise their hands if they know what *ministry* means. Then ask students who don't know the meaning, which Dutch word it sounds like. Elicit the word *ministerie*.

Exercise 2

Students' own answers.

Discuss with the class how the approach to answering this type of question is different from what they are used to doing. Up to now:

- students read the questions and options beforehand. They know precisely what to listen for.
- the listening is broken into short fragments. Students listen to the first fragment and answer the relevant questions during the pause.
- students read the questions that refer to the next fragment before they listen to it.

Tip 2: Ask students why it is counter-productive to write whole sentences instead of short notes. Elicit that it is counter-productive because this takes time and may prevent them from paying attention to what comes next in the listening.

Ask students to give some examples of shorthand or suggest some: + = and; ppl = people; 2nd = second; rmmbr = remember (leave out vowels); x milk = doesn't like milk.

Point out that students should use any type of abbreviation that suits them and that they are likely to remember.

Exam Practice p69D – Listening

The listening is in two parts to make it easier for students. Ask students to keep their books closed while they listen to part 1. Then ask them to open their books and cover questions 4–7 before they read and answer questions 1–3.

01 Play the audio for students

BBC interview – Part 1

Presenter: On the boat where I live, I'm often kept awake by party barges going up and down the canals late in the evenings with everyone on board singing one song – hen parties, birthdays, leaving do's … *Frozen*'s signature song has become a global empowerment anthem, and the characters in the film, sisters Ana and Elsa, one an argumentative mortal, the other a warm-hearted ice-queen, delighted 1.3 billion dollars' worth of fans in 2013. A sequel was perhaps inevitable, and we are taken, again, to the Norwegian fjords where our heroines are drawn, inexorably, towards an enchanted forest.

It's all the work, again, of writer Chris Buck and writer, director and Chief Creative Officer of Walt Disney Animation Studios, Jennifer Lee who, with *Frozen 1*, was the first woman to direct a film that earned over a billion dollars. Both movies are, in large part, about fear: recognising it, overcoming it. So, did Lee and Buck get the fear? About following up one of the biggest box office hits of recent times?

Lee: Yeah, [laughs] to do the second one?

Presenter: Yes, how to follow this up?

Lee: Yeah, you know what was so interesting, we had, erm … there was a beautiful thing, of naivety going into it. I think the naivety let us dive in and not worry about the fear, the expectations, but um –

Buck: The fear came when we … right in the middle of it …

Lee: … in the middle of it as you are really building it, and it's, it's such a hard process and we, I mean we equate it to getting lost in the woods ourselves many times. And that's what the story process is, and you don't know if you'll find the right story, you just, we knew we wanted to – I think we had faith in the team, they all wanted to come back. Ollie, Christian, Lopez. So that really anchored us.

Presenter: And the popularity of the first film is building still, as you are doing this!

Lee: That's, that's the part of the thing we didn't expect. And so, you know, we sit here, on the edge of releasing this and we've been in the story room so much, just really trying to make the – to craft the story, and the realisation of the expectations are hitting us more now, I think, than when we were making it. Because we really made sure to shut all that out and really just build it the way we built the first one and do it to be true to these themes, these characters, and not listen to all that, so I think that helped us tremendously but it doesn't make it any easier to, um …

Presenter: But did you go back to the first film and look at it and think 'What did we do so right?'

Buck: Well, not really, I mean those characters are so ingrained in us, er, those characters are so much a part of us, because we bring so much to these characters, so it's really just, sort of, trying to figure out what the next step for these characters was. It wasn't necessarily what worked in the last one, and we also didn't want to repeat ourselves. What we like to say is this one was more Act Two of a Broadway musical …

Presenter: [laughs] OK.

Buck: … where the first one was Act One and that helped us, also gave us a template for that, 'cos a lot of times in Act Twos of musicals, the songs get deeper and more emotional, a little bit richer and all that, so that's where we, we took off from it. And that gave it a nice difference between the two, it helped us.

Presenter: Is it true that you put your characters through Myers-Briggs personality tests?

Lee: [laughs] Yes, we did! We did and it was, it was, partly to shut out this like … [unclear]. Female characters get over-analysed, let's just say, they have to be perfect, there's a lot people see in them they don't want to see, and we went through that and we just said we need to go back to who they are and let's just ground ourselves, so we did a lot of work. I journaled Elsa and did some monologues as Anna and then we took these tests and what is amazing is Elsa came out as a protector, which felt right, but Anna came out as a leader and that was just such a wonderful discovery because often we think – we don't always think that the one who wears her heart on her sleeve and is, er, a little ADHD, ha ha, is a leader, but, um, so that was great and, um, but we did it to really ground ourselves in who they are really and not who the world had sort of – tug of war – decided they should be …

Presenter: You see, that's so interesting. It's like the characters are now out of your hands and they have personalities that you hadn't even fully explored or understood yourselves even though you are creating them!

Lee: You know, Elsa I wanted to get to know even more. She was, we didn't spend a lot of time with her in the first film. I looked up to her, she was a mystery, and you think you know them but you have people telling you what they see. And then you are going to manage them, so really what it was was re-grounding. And it was surprisingly easy. We did a lot of work just sort of exploring as Elsa versus Anna. Their distinctions were really clear, so at least that we felt good. We felt, yes, they're speaking to us as them versus us trying to make them what we think the world would want them to be. And that was very grounding, and we really built it from there. And particularly, realising that Anna was a fairy-tale character in the classic sense, an ordinary hero in a magical world, and Elsa was a mythic character, er, a magical person carrying the weight of the world on her shoulders with high expectations, and when we anchored them and kept them in that zone, that was very true to who they were.

02 Play the audio for students

When it has finished, ask students to read and answer questions 4–7.

BBC interview – Part 2

Presenter: The sisterhood is really more important in these films than romantic relationships. You have a power ballad in this film, don't you, where the lovely reindeer herder is really objecting to this – that he's so far down the pecking order.

I just wondered about the, the, how important – when you know you have a whole nation of children – little girls and little boys – looking to that and to the independence of these characters – these female characters – that is a big responsibility, isn't it?

Buck: There was a wonderful thing, in fact, they weren't even sisters from the first few drafts that we did, um, but the one thing we talked about early on was that we were trying to do something different than just romantic love. There are many forms, we were saying, of true love, and the one that we settled on was familial love and that gave us a difference, so in Frozen, it wasn't the kiss from the prince that saved the day, it was the true love, it's the love between the sisters. That was exciting to us and everybody embraced it, which was fantastic – it wasn't just our little thing but everyone in the studio embraced the idea of doing that – doing something a bit different. And, of course, the world embraced that too, which was terrific.

Presenter: There was no real resistance of the studio?

Buck and Lee: No, no, not at all.

Buck: No, they were totally up for it, so …

Presenter: Because it is so against the, the stereotype.

Lee: I think classic fairy tales, they're just written long, long ago and that's just sort of, the structure of how it was: the male hero saving the day, and romantic love, and all those things are part of the time they were written, and that's just … there are many other options! And I think for me too, you know, as a mother with a daughter, I think of like the huge part of growing up is facing that Hans is probably not who he seems to be – and it's not necessarily the one who's the most charming, but it's the guy who is willing to do the right thing by you and sing you the love song and introduce you to his family and not be perfect and be able to trust you and not have to be the hero every second, but that's heroic in itself. And so, for us, it was just – the men that we know in our lives are, um, much more complex than the Prince Charmings that we've seen, also.

So, Christoff for me is – not in a diminished sense – is more in a sense of showing another side that men relate to, that boys relate to as well. They fall madly in love and they want to support these women and these are the men in our lives and so, just having a character reflect that, is less of a statement of anything except to say, well, this is more authentic, I think, and wanting to go there and letting Christoff open up and say it's OK to have feelings, [laughs] you know!

Presenter: But that song he sings, it's, it's incredibly tender. [Music] And I wondered about your input with the music, how to follow *Let it Go*? [They all laugh.] How?

Buck: Yeah, it – definitely – it – *Let it Go* was lightning in a bottle, I mean it just was – it came out at a time when everybody embraced it and it's a fantastic song. Er, and we didn't try to replicate that, but one thing we did do was we tried to analyse *Let it Go* and where it was in the movie and where it was for Elsa's journey and that *Let it Go* was sort of the beginning of her journey. It's a rebellious song. And even though she is free to be who she is up there, it's a flawed one because she's trapped in her ice palace and it took Anna to sort of bring her back down. So, you know, then we go into the next film, so *Into the Unknown*, which is Elsa's first song, is sort of the next step.

So first there was this rebellious song and now there's this voice that's calling to Elsa, and now that she's accepted for her powers and who she is, er, now it's like, do you dare use those powers, and what are you going to do with those powers, and so, the voice is saying, come on, come on, come on, and she is resisting.

Lee: Act! Now's the time to act!

Buck: Now is the time to act, exactly. So she does, she acts.

Lee: Show yourself!

Buck: Yeah, and there are some consequences to that, but still!

Lee: Show yourself as a beautiful arrival, I think, and this is about change and about growing up. And the right thing I felt, we felt, to do was do what's true to the story, that's what we did the first time and we are singing them because they mean a lot to us and so I think we knew that if we tried to do comparisons we wouldn't make the songs for the wrong reasons [sic].

Presenter: The real genius of *Frozen*, the idea of *Frozen*, is that even though it breaks down a lot of the barriers of Disney as we've just discussed, what it does is the opalescence of ice. It's a glister across the screen, and just seeing in the screening that I went to – which was full of adults in the screening – it was a press screening – you could feel in the audience that you come away from the film feeling that you have seen the most Disney film that Disney ever made even though it's not doing the traditional Disney things – because of that ice and what it does – the glitter!

Buck: One of our art directors is always, we turn to her and we say: 'Is this, does this have enough sparkle?'

Lee: Yes, it's true!

Buck: And she's always, she says, 'Yes, we could use more, but this, this'll do!'

Lee: That's true!

Presenter: And that was Jennifer Lee and Chris Buck, who were surprisingly un-corporate for studio grandees. This glitteringly colourful second movie is far more convoluted than the first, though I wonder how much that bothers small children, who are happy to be lost in films.

Answers: 1 B 2 A 3 C 4 A 5 C 6 B 7 A

Exam Time NL 3 Reading

Exam Strategies p93C – Preparation

Answering questions (part 2)

Yes/No questions. Correct/incorrect questions.

Exercise 1

Point out that some statements may make a general comment, so the answer may come from more than one clue in different paragraphs. Ask students which statement in exercise 1 makes a general comment. (Answer: option 5)

Option 1, paragraph 2
Option 2, paragraph 2
Option 3, paragraph 2
Option 4, paragraph 4
Option 5, paragraphs 4 and 5

Gap questions

Exercise 2

Tell students that they need to pay particular attention to answers that look similar and note the differences between them. Ask them to look at question 2 and discuss the differences between the statements. Also point out that if there is nothing to confirm what an option states, then it is not likely to be the correct answer.

Question 2: specific information
Question 5: the author's attitude

General exam strategies

Exercise 3

Read the strategy with the class. Ask students what the difference is between the two sentences. Ask them to give some more examples of their own.

Exercise 4

Ask students to think about these two tips while they read the text and answer the questions. Discuss with the class after they have finished. Ask them if they needed to skip a question and if they think that coming back to it later helped them think more clearly about it. Tell them to underline all the words that they do not know and report how many they absolutely had to look up.

Exercise 5

Point out that they will not get a mark if they do not answer a question. On the other hand, a random guess gives them at least a chance to get a mark: with a four-option (A, B, C, D) multiple-choice question, they have a 25% chance of getting a mark, and with a correct/incorrect question, they have a 50% chance.

Exam Practice p93D – Reading

Answers: 1 1 correct (He had a European work visa, so he worked in Europe and while he was working there, he lived there too: later in the text, the author mentions being 'at home in Milan'.)
2 incorrect (He had thought about the environment: 'I realised that all my efforts to reduce my carbon footprint at home in Milan …')
3 correct ('… go home for Christmas' implies that he wanted to spend the holiday with his family.)
4 correct ('I was prepared for a long and tiring journey … and had visions of awful nights spent with my face in a sick bag')
5 correct ('… my experience on board could not have been more enjoyable. The two other passengers … were taking the sea route for the same environmental reasons and their company made time fly by.')
2 C   3 C   4 1 yes 2 no 3 yes 4 yes 5 no   5 A

Exam Time NL 4 Listening

Exam Strategies p117C – Preparation

Answering detail questions

Exercise 1

Students' own answers.

Show students how using information that is not in the listening may result in the wrong choice. After you have asked students what information they have got, ask those students who have read *Oliver Twist* to tell the class about Nancy's relationship with Oliver. Alternatively, give the information yourself. Later in the story, Nancy becomes very protective of Oliver, almost a mother figure. She is killed when she tries to protect him from being kidnapped. Someone who has this information could make a mistake with question 5 and choose option C. However, the only possible option from what we hear is B: there is no mention of Nancy's feelings towards Oliver anywhere in this listening excerpt.

Answering detail questions

Exercise 2

Discuss students' examples. Here are some possible examples.

Tip 1: Question 3, option C

This is an incorrect option that includes words from the listening as a distractor. We hear: *He [the constable] took his hands off Oliver and the boy fainted*. Here, *fainted* is a distractor because that is the word used in the listening.

The correct answer is option B, which paraphrases what happened: a witness (*'and I saw what happened'*), had seen the real criminals (*'another boy took his handkerchief. This boy did nothing'*).

Question 4, option B is another example

Tip 2: Question 5, option A. That is what the character says (*'Oh, my poor little brother Oliver!' cried Nancy, pretending to weep*). If we place it in the broader context, we understand that Nancy can't be his sister because a) she is Fagin's second choice after Bet; b) she refused at first; and c) she is only pretending to weep.

Tip 3: Question 3, option A

Mr Brounlow indeed feels sorry for Oliver. 'Don't hurt him' he says to the constable, and after Oliver faints, he takes him to his house to help him recover. However, this is not the reason why the constable lets Oliver go.

Tip 4: Question 2, option A

The words that come before and after this gap show Mr Brounlow's mild and sympathetic reaction (*'I'm afraid it is. … He has hurt himself'*), so calling the boy a 'dirty thief' is the opposite of what we expect to hear him say.

Question 4, option C is another example. It is Sikes who is angry (although we do not know why), not Fagin.

Tip 5: Question 4, option B

Even if we don't connect what Sikes saw as he came into the room (Fagin threatening to kill Dawkins, Dawkins arming himself with a knife, and Fagin throwing a cup at Dawkins' head) with joking about Fagin wanting to kill him too, we have to choose option B, since options A and C are obviously wrong.

Answering gap questions

Exercise 4

4A and 4B are angry statements.
4C shows compassion.

Exam Practice p117D – Listening

03 Play the audio for students

Ask the students to answer question 1 after listening.

Oliver Twist, Chapter Six – Oliver Among the Thieves

'Is this the boy?' they asked the old gentleman. 'Yes,' said the old gentleman, 'I am afraid it is.'

Day after day, Oliver stayed in Fagin's room, taking the marks out of handkerchiefs. Sometimes, too, he played the game with Fagin's pockets. At last he began to want fresh air. He asked Fagin to let him go out to work with Dawkins and Charley Bates.

One morning Fagin allowed him to go. The three boys left the house, walking very slowly. Oliver wondered if they were going to work at all.

They were just coming out of a narrow street into a square when suddenly Dawkins stopped. Putting his finger on his lips, he pulled his friends back.

'Quiet!' he said. 'Do you see that old man near the bookshop?'

'Perfect,' said Charley Bates.

Oliver looked at them in surprise. The two boys walked across the road and went close behind the old gentleman. Oliver followed them.

The old gentleman had white hair and gold glasses. He carried a stick under his arm. He had taken a book from a shelf in front of the shop and he stood reading it.

Oliver was shocked when he saw Dawkins put his hand into the old man's pocket and take out a handkerchief. Dawkins gave it to Charley Bates and they both ran away.

In a moment, Oliver understood the mystery of the handkerchiefs and the watches and the jewels and Fagin's games. He stood for a moment, full of fear, and then he too began to run.

04 Play the audio for students

Ask the students to answer question 2 after listening.

Oliver Twist, Chapter Six – Part 2

The old gentleman put his hand in his pocket. He did not find his handkerchief, so he turned round. When he saw Oliver running away, the thought of course that the boy had stolen his handkerchief.

'Stop, thief!' he shouted, and ran after Oliver.

Everybody in the street joined him in the chase. 'Stop, thief', they cried. Even Dawkins and Charley Bates began to shout 'Stop, thief! and run after Oliver too.

Then someone hit Oliver and he fell to the ground. A crowd collected round him. Oliver lay, covered with dust, and bleeding from the mouth. He looked wildly at all the faces that surrounded him.

'Is this the boy?' they asked the old gentleman.

'Yes,' said the old gentleman, 'I am afraid it is. He has hurt himself.'

05 Play the audio for students

Ask the students to answer question 3 after listening.

Oliver Twist, Chapter Six – Part 3

A police constable pushed through the crowd and seized Oliver by the neck.

'Get up!' he said.

'It wasn't me, sir. It was two other boys, said Oliver. 'They are here somewhere.' But Jack and Charley had disappeared.

'Oh, no, they aren't,' said the constable.

'Don't hurt him,' said the old gentleman. 'I am not really sure that this boy took the handkerchief.'

The constable pulled Oliver along the street to the police station. Oliver was too frightened to speak.

'There is something in this boy's face that interests me,' said the old gentleman to himself. 'Is he innocent? Where have I seen a face like that before?'

Suddenly, a man in an old black suit rushed into the police station. 'Stop, stop!' he cried. 'Stop a moment!'

'What is this? Who are you?' asked the constable.

'I own the bookshop,' replied the man, 'and I saw what happened. There were three boys – two others and this one. Mr Brownlow was reading, and another boy took his handkerchief. This boy did nothing. He watched and looked surprised.'

'Then the boy must go free,' said the constable. He took his hands off Oliver and the boy fainted.

'Poor boy, poor boy!' said Mr Brownlow, the old gentleman. 'Call a carriage, somebody, please. At once!'

A carriage came. Oliver was placed on one of the seats. The old gentleman got in and sat beside him. They rode away until the carriage stopped in front of a pleasant house in a quiet London street. Oliver was taken into the house and put to bed.

06 Play the audio for students

Ask the students to answer question 4 after listening.

Oliver Twist, Chapter Six – Part 4

When Dawkins and Charley Bates arrived home, Fagin was waiting for them.

'Where's Oliver?' he said with an angry look. The young thieves looked at him, but they said nothing.

'What has happened to that boy?' cried Fagin, quickly pulling Dawkins towards him. 'Speak or I will kill you!'

'A police officer took him away,' answered Dawkins. He pulled himself free and took a knife from the table. Fagin picked up a cup and threw it at Dawkins's head. It missed him and nearly hit a man who was entering the room.

'Who threw that at me?' said a deep voice. He was a strong man of about thirty-five, with dirty clothes and angry eyes. A white dog followed him into the room. Its face was scratched and torn in twenty different places.

'What are you doing to those boys, Fagin?' the man said. 'I am surprised they don't murder you.'

'Quiet, Mr Sikes,' said Fagin. 'Don't speak so loud. You seem angry today.'

'Perhaps I am,' said Bill Sikes. 'Give me a drink, Fagin. And don't put poison in it,' he added as a joke.

07 Play the audio for students

Ask the students to answer question 5 after listening.

Oliver Twist, Chapter Six – Part 5

While Sikes was drinking beer, Jack Dawkins told them about Oliver. He explained how he had been caught.

'I am afraid', said Fagin, 'that the boy may tell the constable about us. We must find him.'

But none of them wanted to go near a police station.

The door opened and Bet and Nancy came in.

'Ah!' said Fagin, 'Bet will go, won' you my dear?'

'Where?' said Bet.

'To the police station to find Oliver. He has been taken away and we must get him back.'

'No!' said Bet.

'Nancy, my dear,' said Fagin. 'What do you say?'

'No,' said Nancy.

'She will go, Fagin,' said Sikes, looking at her angrily.

So Nancy agreed to look for Oliver

08 Play the audio for students

Ask the students to answer question 6 after listening.

Oliver Twist, Chapter Six – Part 6

In clean clothes and with a little basket, she looked very sweet.

'Oh, my poor, dear little brother, Oliver!' cried Nancy, pretending to weep. 'What has happened to him? Where have they taken him? Oh, please tell me!'

'Very good! said Fagin. 'You are a fine girl, Nancy. Go and see the constable now.'

Nancy returned quickly. 'A gentleman has got him,' she said. 'Dawkins took the man's handkerchief. But the police don't know where he lives.'

'We must find him!' cried Fagin. 'Charley, you must watch that bookshop every day. I shall shut this house tonight. It isn't safe here. You know where to find me. Don't stay here, my dears, and find Oliver!'

Answers: 1 C 2 C 3 B 4 B 5 B 6 A

Pearson Education Limited
KAO TWO, KAO Pak
Hockham Way, Harlow
Essex, CM17 9SR, England
and Associated Companies throughout the world

www.pearsonELT.com/widerworldNL

© Pearson Education Limited 2020

The right of Rod Fricker and Sandy Zervas to be identified as authors of this work has been asserted by them in accordance with the Copyright, Designs and Patents Act, 1988.

All rights reserved. No part of this publication may be reproduced, stored in a retrieval system, or transmitted in any form or by any means, electronic, mechanical, photocopying, recording or otherwise without the prior written permission of the copyright holders.

First published 2020

ISBN: 978-1-292-31344-3

Set in Harmonia Sans
Printed and bound by CPI UK

Acknowledgements
The Publishers would like to thank Pamela Van Bers for her input on the Netherlands edition, as well as all the teachers and students around the world who contributed to the development of Wider World, especially the teachers on the Wider World Teacher Advisory Panel: Irina Alyapysheva, CEE; Reyna Arango, Mexico; Marisa Ariza, Spain; Alfredo Bilopolski, Argentina; Isabel Blecua, Spain; Camilo Elcio de Souza, Brazil; Ingrith del Carmen Ríos Verdugo, Mexico; Edward Duval, Belgium; Norma González, Argentina; Natividad Gracia, Spain; Claribel Guzmán, Mexico; Izabela Lipińska, Poland; Fabián Loza, Mexico; Miguel Mozo, Spain; Huỳnh Thị Ái Nguyên, Vietnam; Joacyr Oliveira, Brazil; Montse Priego, Spain; Gladys Rodriguez, Argentina; Lyudmila Slastnova, CEE; Izabela Stępniewska, Poland

Text Credits
We are grateful to the following for permission to reproduce copyright material:
Extract 3.3 from "Martha Collison: My 'car crash moment' in GBBO", The Telegraph, 25/09/2014 (Hannah Furness), copyright © Telegraph Media Group Limited, 2014; Quotes 3.3 by Martha Collison 2014. Reproduced by kind permission; Quotes 6.3 by Booker Mitchell as published in 'Why Booker Travels' by Booker Mitchell, 09-05-2013 and 'Traveler of the Year: Booker Mitchell', http://intelligenttravel.nationalgeographic.com. Reproduced with kind permission of Booker Travels; Quote 6.5 by Jess Mellish, New Zealand "JST Be Inspired: Meet Jess", 09/01/2014, Jubilee Sailing Trust, www.jst.org.uk. Reproduced with kind permission; Extract 9.3 adapted from "The Flynn effect: are we really getting smarter?", The Telegraph, 31/10/2014 (Tom Chivers), copyright © Telegraph Media Group Limited, 2014; p122 & p126 of Next Move Students' Book (Pearson Education) by Carolyn Barraclough et al ISBN 9781408293638. Article on page 45D from Veganuary is huge. But is it really as simple as animal foods bad, plant foods good?, Joanna Blythman, 22 Jan 2020, Guardian News and Media Limited; Article on page 93D from I didn't want to fly – so I took a cargo ship from Germany to Canada, Will Vibert, 7 Jan 2020, Guardian News and Media Limited.

Image Credits
123RF.com: 25, 70, 106, 129, Cathy Yeulet 113, Csak Istvan 73, duoduo 141, Oleg Dudko 139, Scott Griessel 113, Sergey Nivens 109; **Alamy Stock Photo:** Andre Babiak 61, Arcaid Images 1, Dareth Dobson 139, dpa picture alliance 80, Elroy Spelbos 85, foodfolio 44, Hemis 74, 139, Hugh Nutt 59, imageBROKER 143, Juice Images 107, Juniors Bildarchiv GmbH 10, Keith Mayhew 49, LondonView 56, Losevsky Pavel 107, Mandy Collins 27, Marmaduke St. John 65, 65, Melba Photo Agency 129, Moodboard 107, Piero Cruciatti 139, Robert Clayton 48, Rosa Irene Betancourt 6 132, The golden marshmallow / Stockimo 10, Tom Uhlman 22, Universal Images Group North America LLC / DeAgostini 142, Xinhua 24, ZUMA Press, Inc. 139; **Babar Ali:** 110; **BBC Worldwide Learning:** 10, 21, 33, 34, 46, 58, 70, 82, 94, 105, 106; **Booker Travels:** 73; **Emile Wamsteker:** 39; **Fotolia:** adrianciurea69 27, Afunbags 139, artSILENSEcom 143, audreyshot 23, blackpencil 83, 83, contrastwerkstatt 107, David Newman 140, destina 61, diy13 73, ednal 47, emiliano85 96, gpointstudio 10, 116, gradt 143, graphitte 55, Izf 12, James Threw 103, Kondor83 140, LanaPo 47, LuckyImages 77, marek 73, Miguel Garcia Saaved 96, mitrija 95, Monkey Business 132, mtzsv 62, Pakhnyushchyy 115, peresanz 97, Piotr 73, polygraphus 71, 71, pressmaster 87, sdecoret 79, SeanPavonePhoto 71, ssaronow 109, Stillfx 47, stokkete 83, theartofphoto 10, Tiramisu Studio 73, Wisky 49, wonderisland 49, wutthichaic 67; **Getty Images:** Angelo DeSantis 23, DANIEL MUNOZ / AFP 68, Denis Doyle 63, GSO Images 20, Heath Korvola 92, Lionel Dermais 138, Nuray Pictures - Footage 22, Richard Heathcote - The FA 59, Sascha Steinbach 59, Shomos Uddin 32, Wild Shutter Imaging 33, Zero Creatives 138; **Image Source Ltd:** 128, 129; **Imagestate:** John Foxx Collection 41, 106; **Jubilee Sailing Trust:** 75; **Pearson Education Ltd:** 107, 117D, Jon Barlow 4, 5, 6, 7, 8, 9, 10, 14, 16, 22, 26, 28, 34, 36, 40, 46, 50, 52, 58, 60, 64, 70, 72, 76, 82, 84, 88, 94, 98, 100, 106, 108, 112, Ken Wilson-Max 52, Naki Kouyioumtzis 37, 71, Peter Evans 139, Rob Judges 41, Studio 8 4, 5, 7, 8, 9, 12, 14, 24, 26, 36, 38, 48, 50, 60, 62, 72, 74, 84, 86, 96, 98, 108, 110, Terry Leung. Pearson Education Asia Ltd 106; **PhotoDisc:** 10, 22, 34, 46, 58, 70, 82, 94, 106, 140, Glen Allison 128, Victor Budnik. Cole Publishing Group 41; **Rex Features:** Hartswood Films 97, Imagine Entertainment 141, Warner Bros. Pictures 141; **Shutterstock.com:** 43, Alex5711 16, Alxcrs 71, Arcady 142, Aun Photographer 93C, Bauman 142, BlueOrange Studio 71, BlueSkyImage 16, 28, 40, 52, 64, 76, 88, 100, 112, Claudio Stocco 104, Curioso 128, Dar1930 35, David Crockett 106, DavidTB 21, Dragon Images 10, 17, 29, 41, 53, 65, 77, 89, 101, 113, etraveler 39, Fer Gregory 143, Foto-Ruhrgebiet 39, GrigoryL 35, Helen Bird 10, isak55 140, 143, Itana 128, Jag_cz 69D, Joe Gough 128, Kalcutta 16, Korionov 49, Laszlo Szirtesi 59, LuckyImages 141, M.Unal Ozmen 35, mamahoohooba 22, Manuel Fernandes 38, Marcie Fowler 115, Marie C Fields 106, Martin Valigursky 17, molekuul_be 140, Natalia Pushchina 129, Paulo Vilela 51, Pichugin Dmitry 129, Reny Auger 16, RTimages 106, Sean Gladwell 143, Sergey Peterman 13, 25, 37, 49, 61, 73, 85, 97, 109, Sergey Silharulidze 41, Shevtsovy 62, Shutter_M 99, skyfish 139, StockLite 15, 27, 39, 51, 63, 75, 87, 111, Studio 10ne 71, Suzanne Tucker 23, Syda Productions 70, Tupungato 129, Westend61 Premium 27, Zaikina 87; **Sozaijiten:** 41; **The Kobal Collection:** 20th Century Fox / Temple Hill Entertainment 46, Citizen Snow Film Productions 46, Illumination Entertainment / Universal Pictures 47, Marvel / Walt Disney Pictures 46, National Geographic Films 46, Paramount Pictures 46

Cover Image: *Front:* **Alamy Stock Photo:** AGF Srl

All other images © Pearson Education

Illustration Credits
Tim Bradford (Illustration Web) p. 34, 82, 83, 94, 130, 133, 136; Allesandra Chiarla (Sylvie Poggio) p. 63, 131, 135; The Boy Fitz Hammond p. 22, 58, 70, 91, 95; John Lund (Beehive) p. 15, 86, 111; Claire Rollet (Illustration Web) p. 95; Mark Ruffle (Beehive) p. 13, 23, 24, 31, 51; Maria Serrano Canovas (Plum Pudding) p. 11, 29, 53, 77, 89, 99, 101

Every effort has been made to trace the copyright holders and we apologise in advance for any unintentional omissions. We would be pleased to insert the appropriate acknowledgement in any subsequent edition of this publication.